Earth Sheltered Housing Design

Second Edition

John Carmody
Associate Director and Architect

Dr. Raymond Sterling, P.E.
Director and Associate Professor

**Underground Space Center
University of Minnesota**

790 Civil and Mineral Engineering Building
500 Pillsbury Drive S.E.
Minneapolis, Minnesota 55455

Book Design: John Carmody and Bruce Cornwall
Illustrations and Cover Design: Bruce Cornwall

VAN NOSTRAND REINHOLD COMPANY
——————————————— NEW YORK

Copyright © 1985 by the University of Minnesota
Library of Congress Catalog Card Number 84-7270
ISBN 0-442-28748-8 (cloth)
ISBN 0-442-28746-1 (paper)
All rights reserved. No part of this work covered by the copyright hereon may be reproduced or used in any form or by any means—graphic, electronic, or mechanical, including photocopying, recording, taping, or information storage and retrieval systems—without written permission of the publisher.

Printed in the United States of America
Designed by John Carmody and Bruce Cornwall

Published by Van Nostrand Reinhold Company Inc.
135 West 50th Street
New York, New York 10020

Van Nostrand Reinhold Company Limited
Molly Millars Lane
Wokingham, Berkshire RG11 2PY, England

Van Nostrand Reinhold
480 La Trobe Street
Melbourne, Victoria 3000, Australia

Macmillan of Canada
Division of Gage Publishing Limited
164 Commander Boulevard
Agincourt, Ontario M1S 3C7, Canada

16 15 14 13 12 11 10 9 8 7 6 5 4 3 2 1

Library of Congress Cataloging in Publication Data
Carmody, John.
  Earth Sheltered housing design.
  Rev. ed. of: Earth sheltered housing design/Underground Space Center, University of Minnesota. 1979.
  Bibliography: p.
  Includes index.
  1. Earth sheltered houses—Design and construction.
I. Sterling Raymond. II. University of Minnesota. Underground Space Center. III. Title.
TH4819.E27C37 1984 690'.8 84-7270
ISBN 0-442-28748-8
ISBN 0-442-28746-1 (pbk.)

Preface

Although building into or with the earth is an ancient idea, only in the mid-1970s did earth sheltered housing reemerge as an important alternative design approach for housing in the United States. Reasons for this interest include such benefits as reduced energy consumption, protection from natural and man-made disasters, increased security, noise reduction, and, in some cases, more efficient land use. In addition, earth sheltered housing is viewed as an effective means of building in harmony with nature, thus preserving the environment rather than destroying it while providing intriguing aesthetic potential.

The first edition of this book initially appeared in 1978 as a self-published research report for the Legislative Commission on Minnesota Resources by the then newly created Underground Space Center. Although the book focused on Minnesota applications and cold climate problems, the book served as a catalyst for great public interest in earth sheltered housing, further research work on a national level, and the construction of several thousand earth sheltered houses across the United States. As awareness of the advantages of earth sheltered construction increased, so did the demand for more information. Over the past five years, the staff at the Underground Space Center has produced five additional books that examine in detail certain aspects of earth sheltered or underground building design.

Since the first edition of this book was published, earth sheltered housing has become a more familiar option. During the same period, many other energy-efficient housing options have been developed as well. In 1984, during an indeterminate respite from rapidly rising energy prices, much of the initial impetus in the United States to create new energy-efficient forms of housing has subsided. A period of narrow advocacy for various energy-efficient, whole-house design concepts is giving way to a broader consideration of passive solar design, superinsulation, and earth sheltering as concepts in a palette of design techniques from which to construct energy-efficient buildings appropriate to their climate, site conditions and local market forces.

Interest in earth sheltered housing has increased considerably in many countries around the world where such techniques may, in fact, have a greater relative impact than in the United States. Non-residential applications also continue to grow steadily both in the United States and internationally. The multiple ramifications of earth sheltering and its potential application to building needs around the world will require a sophisticated understanding of the optimum design configurations and details for different types of buildings, different site conditions, and different climates.

The state-of-the-art is still evolving as information on energy performance, construction techniques, and costs continues to increase and improve. This second edition of *Earth Sheltered Housing Design* reflects current trends and provides as much up-to-date information as possible. Like the original edition, it is broad-based and comprehensive, with chapters on the history of earth sheltered design, site and building design, energy use and costs, structural design, waterproofing and insulation, public policy issues, and eighteen case studies.

Acknowledgments

The purpose of this book is to synthesize and present a wide range of information related to earth sheltered housing design. The contributions of many researchers, designers, and builders in this field have made this effort possible. A few people in particular have provided information and assisted in the development of key portions of the book. Dr. George Meixel, Jr., Louis Goldberg, and Lester Shen of the Underground Space Center staff contributed to and reviewed the chapter on energy use. Parametric studies on insulation placement are the work of Dr. Meixel and Lester Shen, while the discussion of monitoring and analyzing energy use in earth sheltered housing is based on work done by Louis Goldberg.

Brent Anderson (Brent Anderson Associates, Minneapolis, Minnesota) served as a consultant on waterproofing systems. His assistance was invaluable in providing technical information and reviewing the waterproofing chapter. Kenneth Labs of Undercurrent Design in New Haven, Connecticut, has provided information and drawings for use in the text. In addition, his research in several areas of earth sheltered design—most notably climate analysis and regional design issues—has provided a valuable basis for portions of this book. The authors also wish to thank numerous architects, builders, and home owners who contributed written material, photographs, and drawings of their projects. Individual credit for these contributions appears where the material is used throughout the book.

This second edition of *Earth Sheltered Housing Design* is an almost entirely new book. Nearly every portion of the first edition has been rewritten and expanded and several new sections have been added. Nevertheless, this book is built on the foundation of the first edition, created several years ago. A few people who made contributions to the first edition deserve mention here. The Legislative Commission on Minnesota Resources played a role in establishing the Underground Space Center in 1977 and has provided funding for a series of research projects related to underground space use and energy conservation, including the first edition of this book. Dr. Charles Fairhurst and Dr. Thomas Bligh acted as principal investigators for the first edition of the book and have been responsible for focusing considerable public attention on the potential benefits of underground space development. The pioneering heat transfer studies in the first edition were the work of Dr. Paul Shipp; additional material on energy use and structural design was provided by Martin Lunde, Terrill Tillman, and Dr. Charles Nelson. Kenneth Labs provided material for the case studies in the first edition, and Tom Ellison made contributions in a number of areas including the chapters on site and building design.

A number of people have contributed their time and talents to the production of this book. John Carmody and Bruce Cornwall collaborated on the design and layout of the book. Most of the illustrations were drawn by Bruce Cornwall under the direction of John Carmody. Keylining, graphic work, and some additional illustrations were done by Katherine Carmody and Mark Heisterkamp. The authors wish to thank Linda Venator of Van Nostrand Reinhold Company for her valuable editorial advice and assistance; Donna Ahrens, who provided additional assistance in editing portions of the text; and Arlene Bennett and Andrea Spartz, who did the extensive typing of the book.

Contents

Chapter 1: Introduction to Earth Sheltered Housing — 7
Terminology
Historical Perspective
Recent Construction
Conclusion

Chapter 2: Site and Building Design — 21
Factors Affecting Site Selection and Design
Factors Affecting Building Design and Layout
Typical Design Approaches: The Elevational Concept
Typical Design Approaches: The Atrium Concept
Multiple-Unit Design Considerations
Design Considerations for Typical Building Details

Chapter 3: Energy Use, Insulation Placement, and Cost Considerations — 65
Energy Conservation Potential of the Below-Grade Environment
Effect of Earth Integration on Heating and Cooling
Regional Design Approaches Based on Climate
Optimizing Insulation Placement
Parametric Studies of Roof, Wall, and Floor Components
Mechanical System Design and Indoor Air Quality
Energy-Use Performance of Earth Sheltered Houses
Cost-Effectiveness of Earth Sheltered Housing

Chapter 4: Structural Design — 159
Soils
Design Loads
Materials
Analysis and Design of Structural Components

Chapter 5: Waterproofing Systems and Insulation Materials — 199
Site Selection and Surface Drainage Principles
Subsurface Drainage: Principles and Details
Waterproofing Systems: Design and Application Guidelines
Waterproofing Systems: Product Selection and Evaluation
Below-Grade Insulation Materials

Chapter 6: Public Policy Issues — 233
Building Codes
Zoning
Insurance
Financing
Perceptions of Financing Earth Sheltered Homes

Chapter 7: Case Studies — 263
Solaria, New Jersey
Woods/Gundlach Residence, Pennsylvania
Winston House, New Hampshire
Private Residence, Massachusetts
Ecology Houses, Massachusetts
Schwartz Residence, Wisconsin
Clark-Nelson House, Wisconsin
Ellison Residence, Minnesota
Student Housing, Minnesota
Park Ranger Residence, Washington
Mercy Residence, Washington
Sundown House, California
Lovins Research Center/Bioshelter/House, Colorado
Patterson Residence, Arizona
Banen Residence, Arizona
Bordie Residence, Texas
Dune Houses, Florida

References — 325

Bibliography on Earth Contact Heat Transfer — 330

Information Sources — 345

Index — 347

Facade of a house dug into a cliff in the Loire Valley, France.
Drawing by Bruce Cornwall.

Chapter 1

Introduction to Earth Sheltered Housing

At the most basic level, a house shelters its occupants from the climate. Throughout history, dwellings have also provided protection from enemies and predators as well as some degree of privacy. But the housing of a culture, past or present, reflects more than simply meeting physical needs with available materials and technology. Since the design and construction of houses are based on social as well as physical needs housing also represents the values and attitudes of a society.

In recent decades housing in the United States has reflected the technological capability of our society as well as the attitude that materials, land, water, and energy resources were available in almost unlimited supply. The majority of American housing built since World War II is unquestionably clean, spacious, and of a standard consistently higher than in most other societies, past or present. The true cost and total effect of sprawling urbanization and suburban development, however, have begun to emerge only in the last decade or so.

Energy, water, and land resources are clearly not unlimited. Evidence of stress on natural systems in the form of water and air pollution surrounds us. Much natural vegetation and topsoil has been destroyed as communities have been developed. Likewise, man-made systems that supply fuel and water and remove wastes from cities are also stressed, resulting in high costs to extend and maintain them. Moreover, many find large portions of our urban and suburban environments unpleasant and unattractive places to live. Certainly housing development is not solely responsible for many of these effects; it is, however, a large and integral part of the built environment.

In recent years a number of positive trends have emerged in response to the problems mentioned above. More multiunit development and increased construction activity within existing cities conserve land and utilize existing utility and transportation systems more efficiently. A greater awareness of energy-efficient techniques in housing design has developed and a number of successful approaches have been applied on a relatively small scale. Although these trends are encouraging, the problems are enormous, and much housing construction still ignores them. The plateau reached in energy prices in the early 1980s has made energy conservation a lower priority despite the fact that traditional fossil fuels are not available in unlimited supply, and the possibility that political instability in oil-producing countries could quickly thrust us into another crisis.

Many alternative types of housing have emerged in the last decade that reflect the evolution toward a different set of values in our society and perhaps new forms of residential architecture. Among these is a design approach most commonly referred to as earth sheltered housing. Building with the earth or into the earth has deep roots in many cultures. The reemergence of earth sheltered housing in the United States and in other parts of the modern world has occurred for many diverse and interrelated reasons. It is usually built not simply to achieve one objective—to conserve energy, for example. Instead, earth sheltered housing design addresses a number of resource conservation, aesthetic, and other practical concerns. Because earth sheltered housing applied appropriately has the potential to solve a wide range of problems while intriguing and inspiring designers and home owners, it appears to be a significant option for housing design in the future. In the remainder of this chapter, the reasons for and

1-1: Solaria, an earth-covered house in Vincentown, New Jersey; Malcolm Wells, architect; photograph by Robert Homan.

methods of building earth sheltered buildings throughout history up to the present day are discussed.

Terminology

Before embarking on a discussion of the historical background and rationale for earth sheltered housing, it is worthwhile to review what constitutes earth sheltered construction. As used in this book, earth sheltered construction denotes the use of the earth in a building design to improve the energy, aesthetic, or isolation characteristics of the building. There have been several specific definitions proposed for earth sheltered construction (i.e., buildings with roofs and walls 50 percent covered with earth at least 1 foot thick), but in this book the definition of earth sheltering as a general concept is preferred.

Other general terms that are used to denote earth sheltered buildings or this architectural approach are:

- geotecture
- geomorphic architecture
- underground buildings
- earth-integrated buildings
- earth-protected construction
- earth-contact construction (sometimes used to refer to earth-bermed buildings only—see below)
- earth-coupled buildings (heat transfer aspects primarily)

Terms that are more specific to the type of construction or degree of earth contact are:

- earth-covered buildings—with earth on the roof
- earth-bermed buildings—earth against the building walls only

To aid in the description of different design approaches to underground construction, Kenneth Labs developed a taxonomy of underground space [Labs, 1976]. These classifications, shown in figure 1-2 are based on two important characteristics of underground space—the general type of opening to the surface and the relationship to grade. The windowless underground chamber has no access to the surface and is considered unacceptable for housing. The elevational approach, in which one wall is exposed and the rest are covered with earth, is the most common form of earth sheltered housing.

An atrium or courtyard scheme has many historical precedents and is also a viable form of earth sheltered housing today. The penetrational type is most similar to conventional housing in that openings occur in two or more exterior walls. These simplified general forms are useful for classification purposes but actual designs usually employ more complex combinations of forms.

The second aspect that Labs uses in his classification system is the relationship to grade. A completely below-grade structure is referred to as *subgrade,* while a building that extends above existing grade with earth placed around it is *bermed.* These distinctions are usually clear on a flat site, but on sloping sites a building can appear to be subgrade on some sides and bermed on others.

A further classification of earth sheltered houses addresses the issue of whether the roof is covered with a thin layer of earth. Although openings to the outside and relationship to grade may not be significantly affected by the roof treatment, it is an important distinction in terms of appearance, cost, method of construction and energy use. Most often, the terms *earth covered* and *earth bermed* are used to make this distinction.

A final means of categorizing underground or earth sheltered construction is based on the general method of construction. In the vast majority of cases, earth sheltered buildings are placed into soil near the surface that is not self-supporting. The structure of the building must support the weight of the earth pressing against the walls or resting on the roof. This is most commonly referred to as cut-and-cover construction. In contrast, many historical underground structures are carved out of rock or self-supporting soil, requiring no additional structure. Referred to as mined space, this type of construction is typically limited to self-supporting soil or soft rock conditions or to places where it is profitable or necessary to extract harder rock formations. Where mined space is deep below

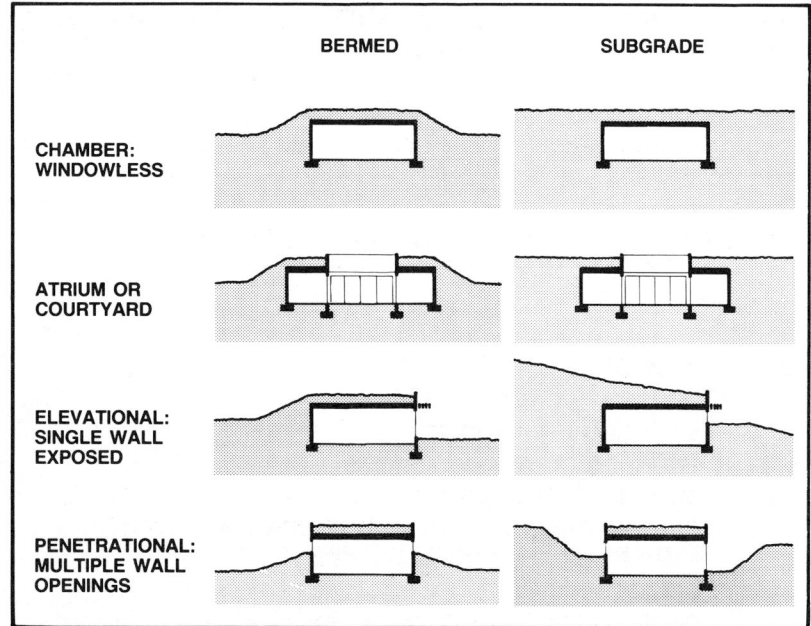

1-2: Classification of Earth Sheltered Structures
Source: Kenneth Labs, 1976 (see references).

ground and has few openings to the outside, it is more suitable for commercial or industrial uses rather than for housing. An example of this is the extensive development of offices, manufacturing and warehouse space in portions of over 200 million square feet of limestone mines near Kansas City, Missouri. Occasionally, a unique site will lend itself to mined construction for housing, as demonstrated by a recently completed house in the West Indies designed by architect John Barnard (fig. 1-3).

Historical Perspective

To say that earth sheltered construction has existed since the dawn of history is a cliche and yet a valid reflection of the natural protection and enduring applicability provided by the ground in meeting the shelter needs of man. Protection from predators and the climate, together with the lack of building materials, were strong reasons for cavemen to seek shelter in natural openings in the rock. These same advantages coupled with varying priorities and the special concerns or opportunities of a particular time or place are the common thread through the many centuries of recorded troglodyte living.

In 4000 B.C. villagers at the recently unearthed Banpo site in China lived in semiunderground pit dwellings with an A-frame roof supporting a thin layer of soil and vegetation. In later centuries cave dwelling became a widely adopted practice in the arid regions of eastern central China, where a deep loess soil provided ideal conditions for self-supporting excavations in soil (fig. 1-4). Marco Polo, in his

1-3 (above): A recently constructed house in the West Indies carved out of rock; John Barnard, architect.

1-4 (below): Underground courtyard houses in China mined out of the soft loess soil.

1-5: Underground atrium dwellings built by the Romans at Bulla Regia in northern Tunisia; photograph by Richard Kennedy.

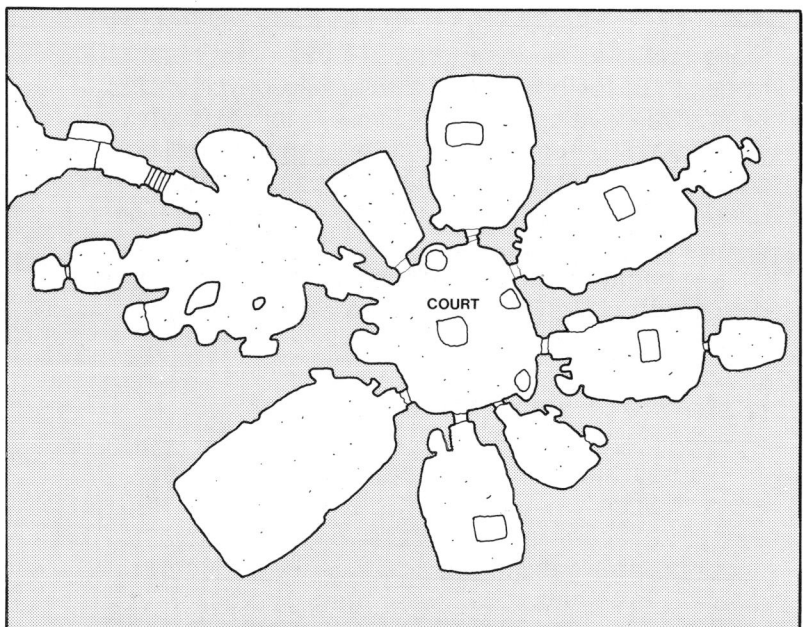

1-6: Plan of Underground Dwelling—Matmata, Tunisia

1-7: Section of Underground Dwelling—Matmata, Tunisia

travels to China in the thirteenth century A.D. noted the existence of several tribes who lived in excavated homes. Courtyard houses were used on flat sites, and terraced housing on sloping sites. The thermal advantages of the earth's temperature moderation in a continental climate with cold winters and hot summers, together with the ability to provide shelter with only a pick and shovel, have led to the construction of millions of these cave dwellings through to the present day. In many locations farming continues on the surface above the below grade houses. Most recent estimates from China indicate that approximately 20 million people live in cave dwellings in China today.

Between the second and fifth century A.D. the

Romans had an active agricultural and economic base in present-day northern Tunisia. Athough they were not accustomed to underground construction of dwellings and apparently did not use this form of construction elsewhere in their empire, they adapted to the extremely hot, arid conditions at Bulla Regia (near present day Jendouba) and constructed below-ground atrium dwellings (fig. 1-5). These were similar to typical Roman atrium dwellings except in their relation to grade. In more recent times in Tunisia, the Berbers have lived in several types of troglodyte settlements—courtyard housing in the flat desert regions (Matmata) and hillside styles in the mountains (Duiret, Ghomrassen). Figures 1-6 and 1-7 show a plan and section view of the deep courtyard housing at Matmata. Courtyards are typically 30 feet deep providing significant isolation from winds and hot temperatures on the surface.

In Turkey, the Cappadocia region and the spectacular Goreme valley are the sites of large cave dwelling settlements. Religious persecution in the ninth century A.D. forced Byzantine Christians to flee to this area where the soft rock and strange wind-eroded formations allowed the construction of elaborate underground communities, churches and homes (fig. 1-8).

Other examples of earth-integrated vernacular architecture in the Mediterranean region exist in the Gaudix region of Spain (fig. 1-9), in Sicily, and on the Isle of Santorini (Thira), Greece. An extensive troglogyte community in the Loire Valley region in central France grew partly as a by-product of of another construction activity—the building of the great French *chateaux*. The soft stone was cut and air-dried to harden into a suitable building stone for

1-8 (above): Underground village carved out of soft rock in the Cappadocia region of Turkey.

1-9 (below): Underground dwellings in the Gaudix region of Spain; photograph by Richard Kennedy.

the *chateaux*. The caverns left from the excavation were occupied by the stone masons and later by others who perceived their advantages. At its peak in the eighteenth century, there were hundreds of thousands of cave dwellings in France. As shown in figure 1-10, many of these houses are occupied today.

North America has had its own history of earth sheltered construction. The Anasazi Indian culture of the southwest United States has been held up as a model of passive housing design with southern orientations, large thermal mass walls to even diurnal temperatures swings, and small windows to prevent solar overheating. Many of the Indian buildings in this region were also set into the ground or excavated into a cliff site. Mesa Verde, shown in figure 1-11, is a well-preserved example of a cliff site settlement; the ceremonial *kiva* extensively used by Indian communities was also usually excavated below grade.

The sod houses and dugouts of the North American prairie constructed by European settlers were a response to the severe extremes of climate and the lack of building materials. Differing opinions exist as to their comfort and desirability, but they served an important function of shelter in an inhospitable environment.

On the other side of the world, the discovery of opals in the desert regions of central Australia beginning in 1915 led to below-grade living to escape the oppressive heat. White Cliffs, in New South Wales, and Coober Pedy, in South Australia, have sturdy rock formations that allow houses to be mined into the rock (fig. 1-12). Other sites in

1-10 (above): Facade of a house dug into the hillside in the Loire Valley region of central France; photograph by E. Revault.

1-11 (below): Indian cliff dwellings in Mesa Verde National Park, Colorado.

Australia have used makeshift earth-covered dwellings (Andamooka, South Australia) or excavated caves in riverbank soil (Burra, New South Wales) to provide shelter. Some special benefits have accrued to house construction in Coober Pedy, where the discovery of opals during house excavation can pay for the house. Special problems have also occurred as at the copper mining community of Burra, however, where the majority of the riverbank underground homes were washed away during heavy river flooding in 1851.

Recent Construction

Examples of earth-integrated design in the twentieth century can be found in the work of Frank Lloyd Wright in the 1930s and 1940s. In some cases earth berms were utilized as a means of integrating buildings with their sites and creating a low profile image. An earth-bermed, passive solar house shown in figure 1-13 was designed by Wright and built in 1943.

In the United States, several pertinent developments related to earth sheltered housing have occurred since World War II. The first two have provided somewhat negative connotations to subsequent earth sheltered designs: basement houses and nuclear fallout shelters. Basement houses became numerous in the United States as the demand for affordable housing outstripped its production after the war. Many house builders constructed the basement first and occupied it, intending to finish the remainder of the house in a short period of time. Inevitably, many houses were

1-12 (above): Entrance to a dwelling mined in the rock at Coober Pedy, Australia; photograph by Ray Sterling.
1-13 (below): Second Jacobs House in Middleton, Wisconsin built in 1943; Frank Lloyd Wright, architect.

1-14: Interior view of the Geier Residence, Cincinnati, Ohio; Philip Johnson, architect; photograph by Ezra Stoller, ESTO.

not finished quickly and the resulting unsightliness prompted many communities to enact "basement" ordinances to prevent the construction of this type of unfinished structure. A later effect of these ordinances has been an institutional impediment to the construction of well-designed, complete earth sheltered homes (see chapter 6).

The most common nuclear fallout shelters for residences were backyard shelters constructed specifically for this purpose during the height of the "cold war" in the late 1950s and early 1960s. A number of whole house designs, however, were based around this concept. The most notable of these was the house Jay Swayze built for the 1960 World's Fair in Seattle. Over one million people toured the house, which was in fact a wood-frame house built freestanding within an underground concrete bunker. Programmed lighting and painted scenes on the walls outside the house windows exemplified the attempt to provide a completely artificial environment below ground. This basic design was replicated in several areas of the United States but in the middle to late 1960s, the environmental movement and the anti-war sentiments in the United States created a public backlash against nuclear shelter programs.

Ecological and environmental concern did have a very positive impact on other types of earth sheltered construction, however. In 1965 Philip Johnson, most noted for his glass house and his gleaming steel and glass skyscrapers, designed an earth-covered house on the edge of a man-made lake in Ohio (fig. 1-14) and subsequently a small earth-covered museum on his own property.

Malcolm Wells in 1971 proposed several wilderness principles for building construction and expressed a philosophy of "building without destroying the earth." Wells noted that untouched wilderness land has several beneficial effects on the environment and in fact is essential to man's survival on the planet. These effects include creating pure air and water, storing rainwater, creating rich soil, producing its own food, using and storing solar energy, consuming its own wastes, providing human and wildlife habitat, moderating the climate, and creating a beautiful environment. According to Wells, modern architectural practices of destroying these natural systems in exchange for lifeless, synthetic, hard surface environments are unacceptable; he thus advocates earth sheltered architecture. In his book, *Gentle Architecture* [Wells, 1981], Wells states:

> *Green plants turn sunlight into food and fuel. They take inedible earth minerals and water and carbon dioxide, and, holding them up to the sun, give us food and fuel and oxygen in return.*

Green plants are all that keep soil from washing away.

Now take a look at what we do. Everything we build fails. It doesn't collapse or explode or melt, but it kills all the land it touches, from the mine to the site.

Few construction practices today are based on a reverence for life, but the next architecture of America will have to be. Its central rule will be this: improve the land when you build or don't build there. Then we'll be forced to revive the most devastated sites first. Slums. Worn-out farmland. Strip mines. Old parking lots. They're the kinds of places on and in which to build, and the results can be glorious—a whole new architecture in which you won't be quite sure where the land ends and the buildings begin....

Malcolm Wells' first drawing of an underground house, shown in figure 1-15, is so evocative of the intrigue of a house integrated with nature that the design has remained one of his most popular despite having never been built. Wells' first underground office reclaimed a section of wasted ground near a highway in New Jersey, and his first earth-covered house, Solaria, illustrated the natural integration possible with earth sheltered design (see fig. 1-1 and chapter 7).

This concern for the environment represents a new phase in the historical development of earth sheltered buildings. Instead of being used for basic climatic shelter and refuge from enemies or built only in places where other building materials were not available, underground construction was beginning to be seen as a technique to mitigate against the pressures of a rapidly developing world on our natural systems. In other words, it offered the potential to retain more of a site on a natural condition and to allow the building to blend inobtrusively with its surroundings.

Other early exponents of this approach were

1-15: Underground House Designed by Malcolm Wells
Source: *Underground Designs* by Malcolm Wells (see references).

David Scott, who began teaching classes on earth sheltered design in the 1960s, architects Don Metz and William Morgan, who were among the first to experiment successfully with earth-integrated housing design in the early 1970s, John Barnard, who developed his "Ecology House" in 1973, and James Scalise, who examined applications in hot, arid climates in the book *Earth Integrated Architecture* [Scalise, et al., 1975]. Design work of all these architects appears in chapter 7.

After 1973 and the first "energy crisis," the emphasis shifted dramatically from environmental preservation in general to energy conservation as a particularly crucial attribute of earth sheltered housing. Widespread development of the idea came in the mid-1970s both from research and its dissemination (including the first edition of this book) and from grass roots development by builders, many of whom had no contact with others developing similar ideas.

Between 1976 and 1980, the number of earth sheltered houses in use grew from a handful to several thousand, and widespread publicity, resulting from energy concerns and encouraged by the historical irony of a return to the cave, made the concept at least somewhat familiar to a large proportion of the American population. Unlike many energy conservation techniques, earth sheltered design offered advantages in both heating and cooling seasons. In addition, the massive structures were ideally suited for combining the benefits of solar energy and below grade placement. Between 1980 and 1983 the economic downturn and high interest rates slowed American housing construction drastically, although passive solar and earth sheltered construction were not affected as significantly as home building in general.

Although energy conservation appears to have been the major motivation for constructing earth sheltered houses in recent years, a number of other practical considerations have been equally important to some owners and designers. A more durable structure requiring little maintenance attracts some. Protection from natural disasters such as tornadoes and hail has been the cause of much interest in the south central United States where such occurances are almost common. Protection from fire, intruders, and nuclear attack are also rationales for building below grade. In fact, concern over nuclear war and fear of crime in recent years has made increased security and protection key advantages of earth sheltered houses to many people including those associated with survivalist movements.

In the last decade, interest in modern earth sheltered applications has become more visible in many countries other than the United States— sometimes in places where earth sheltered and passive design principles were in the process of being abandoned in favor of regionally unsuitable but "modern" housing. An important factor in this interest is the pressure of sheltering a growing population without diminishing necessary agricultural land. Flat land is the easiest to develop for buildings but is often the most valuable agricultural land as well. Earth-integrated housing set into hillsides combined with policies to preserve flat land for agriculture can help resolve this conflict.

As an example of this trend, research studies in China are underway to try to improve on the traditional cave dwelling in terms of ventilation and humidity control and to develop planned communities of hillside cave dwellings that maximize the land-saving and environmental benefits of this type of construction. South Korea is another country where serious research efforts are being undertaken. Eighty percent of South Korean land is hillside, which places tremendous constraints on the available flat land [Kim, 1983].

In Japan, where high population densities and limited land result in similar problems, small prefabricated plastic shell structures have been developed that can be placed into hillsides or set on flat land and covered with earth. Originally developed to house telephone equipment, these units are now used as playhouses, vacation cabins, or extra rooms. This type of construction system could easily be applied to larger-scale hillside development.

In Europe the value of terraced housing on steep hillsides has been recognized as a means of preserving limited agricultural land as well as fitting development into the natural landscape in an aesthetically compatible manner. One development in southern France includes 47 units set into a hillside with a slope of 50 percent (see figure 2-58 in chapter 2). Each unit has a view extending over the grass-covered roof of the unit below. A feeling of spaciousness is created with a relatively high density on land that is virtually useless for any other purpose.

Although pressures of population and shortage of agricultural land are not as acute in the United States, interest in multiunit developments of earth sheltered housing has also grown in America. Many of the aesthetic and ecological benefits of earth sheltered construction are best exemplified in a well-planned multiunit development; at the same time, the economics of scale can reduce costs. A proposed hillside development at Vail, Colorado, similar to the French development described above, is illustrated in figure 1-16.

Conclusion

Historically, earth sheltered buildings have offered the best and sometimes only form of shelter in different regions of the world. In more recent times, earth sheltered housing has reemerged as a means of simultaneously addressing several current problems and also as a unique form of architectural expression. In the last decade earth sheltered housing has been built because it represents protection, security, low maintenance, quiet isolation, or efficient land use. On certain sites earth sheltered design may be the only way to build on a steep hillside, to maintain quiet near a noisy freeway, or to blend inobtrusively with the surroundings. To some people, earth sheltered housing is simply an energy conservation device, but for most there are several interrelated reasons for building such a structure.

Beyond this list of individual reasons for designing and building earth sheltered structures, these buildings have come to represent a broader vision of a future in which man made architecture and the natural landscape are merged. This integration is not just visual and aesthetic, but also ecological—land, water, and energy resources are

1-16: Proposed Multiple-Unit Earth Sheltered Housing
Architerra Corporation, developers; Dennis Blair, architect; Charles Woods and Dennis Blair, designers.

conserved rather than destroyed. Although there are misconceptions and some negative psychological associations related to earth sheltered housing, it has been demonstrated that with proper design the benefits can be realized with no sacrifice of light, view, and other amenities.

So far the impact of earth sheltered buildings is limited in the present American housing market. Some early designs are more costly than typical tract housing, and much of the housing industry resists innovation. On the other hand, more efficient design and construction techniques are emerging to address some of these problems. With the broad range of benefits and diverse possibilities presented by this design approach, it seems likely that earth sheltered housing will continue to evolve as a viable future form of housing in the United States and elsewhere in the world.

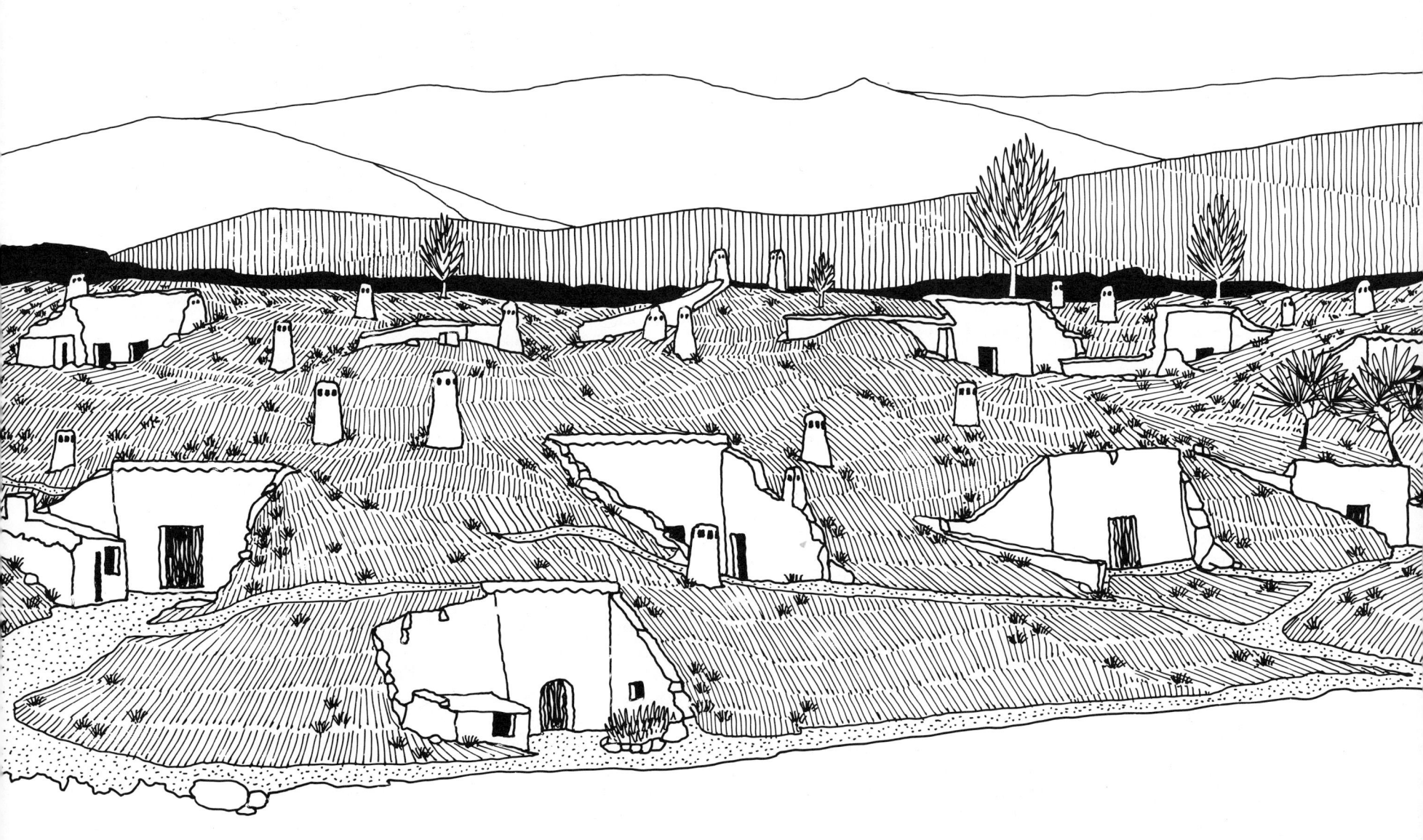

Underground dwellings in the Gaudix region of Spain.
Drawing by Bruce Cornwall.

Chapter 2

Site and
Building Design

Introduction

The decision to build an earth sheltered house can be based on many factors. General issues such as appropriateness to the local climate as well as relative costs and benefits may provide the impetus to consider the concept further. In many cases interest arises over a single practical issue such as energy conservation or tornado protection. Occasionally, a unique site or a personal attraction to the aesthetic possibilities may be the major motivation for pursuing an earth sheltered design. Assuming a decision has been made to design and build an earth sheltered house, for any combination of reasons, a wide range of design considerations emerges. The purpose of this chapter is to organize and discuss the major factors that affect the design of an earth sheltered house.

This chapter is organized into six major sections beginning with factors affecting site selection and design, followed by factors affecting building form and layout. From these more general considerations, typical design approaches for earth sheltered houses emerge. Two of the most common, the elevational and atrium concepts, are analyzed in the third and fourth sections of this chapter. Examples of these approaches are shown, and their application to various site conditions as well as many variations in their design are discussed. In the fifth section, design considerations for multiple-unit developments of earth sheltered housing are presented. Finally, there is a brief discussion of considerations in devising construction details.

The many interrelated factors that affect site and building design range from broad issues of overall form and orientation to details of walls, windows, and plant materials. Although there is a general order to the design process, which is reflected somewhat in the first four sections of this chapter, most design decisions are influenced by several factors at once, and the same issues overlap into many stages of design. This chapter is intended to focus on a general examination of site and building design considerations for earth sheltered houses that typically incorporate a variety of energy-efficient strategies. Most of the critical details and technical information that represent later stages of the design process appear in following chapters.

2-1: Geier Residence, Cincinnati, Ohio; Philip Johnson, architect; photograph by Ezra Stoller, ESTO.

Factors Affecting
Site Selection and Design

Selection and planning of a site for an earth sheltered house is usually the first and often one of the most important aspects of the entire design process. For conventional above-grade housing, site selection and planning are often routine matters because standard designs for such houses are well known and important energy-saving considerations are often ignored. With any well-designed energy-efficient house, however, it is important to understand clearly the impact of basic site considerations such as proper orientation with respect to sun and wind as well as the location of vegetation on the site. In order to select and plan a site for an earth sheltered house, it is also important to understand various site considerations that are particularly relevant for this unique type of housing. These include the topography, soil and groundwater conditions, and the surrounding site context. This section of the chapter attempts to identify these basic site considerations for an earth sheltered home and briefly explains the impact of each. Site planning considerations that are common to all types of housing, such as views, access, and privacy, are not discussed herein, however; they are presented in the later sections of this chapter that address specific design approaches.

Site Location and Context

Like most general building types, earth sheltered houses can be designed in a wide variety of styles. These design approaches can either blend into or contrast with the natural or man-made surroundings. What distinguishes earth sheltered housing from more conventional building approaches is the ability to integrate the building more completely with the natural landscape. Moreover, a completely earth-covered house can seldom be designed to appear identical to its more conventional counterpart, although it may be compatible. In selecting a site and developing a design for an earth sheltered house, the opportunities and limitations of the surroundings must be carefully considered. Not only is it desirable to use earth sheltered design to enhance both building and site, but it is also important to avoid inappropriate settings and design solutions.

In the early years of experimentation and development of earth sheltered houses in the United States, the majority of dwellings were located on large lots often in rural locations. In these cases surrounding buildings and neighborhoods presented no problem. The goal of design was usually to integrate the building form with the natural features of the site, as shown in figure 2-1.

In an urban or suburban setting, the size of the building lot and the proximity of structures on adjacent lots present some problematic design considerations for earth sheltered housing. Three issues in particular arise if an earth sheltered structure is to be placed on a small site within a development of conventional above-grade houses. First, partially recessed earth sheltered designs on flat sites require more manipulation of the landforms on the site and the creation of earth berms around the house. In addition, berms must be designed so that surface runoff does not drain onto neighboring properties (fig. 2-2). The additional area required to

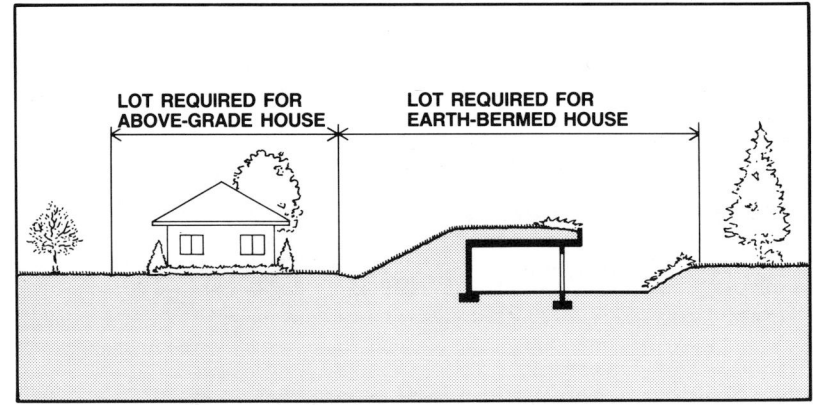

2-2: Lot Size Requirements

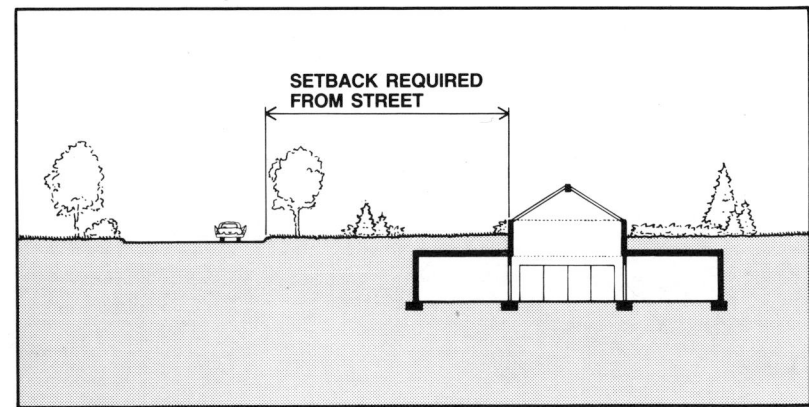

2-3: Setback Restrictions

2-4: Relationship to Adjacent Structures

achieve this type of design may necessitate a slightly larger site than normal.

The second issue concerns setback ordinances in a conventional development. A setback is the minimum distance a building must be located from the property line, street or other structure. A clear understanding of setback limitations may be critical to some earth sheltered designs. For example, arranging spaces around a courtyard is likely to use more area than building a conventional rectangular house does, so that extending portions of a subsurface structure beyond existing setbacks becomes necessary (fig. 2-3). A variance or redefinition of zoning ordinances may be required in such cases. This and other legal and zoning considerations are discussed in chapter 6.

A final consideration is the location and size of structures on adjacent property, which may interfere with views, block sunlight, or create an unpleasant feeling of being looked down upon in an earth sheltered house (fig. 2-4). In addition, the different character or lack of above-grade mass may simply seem inappropriate in an existing neighborhood. Under many circumstances these problems can often be resolved effectively by the designer.

It is important to note that these issues only arise when earth sheltered housing is used on smaller lots in existing developments. New developments that include only earth sheltered housing can be designed at fairly high densities without encountering the problems of scale and setbacks mentioned here. In addition, multiple-unit developments represent the best opportunities to realize many of the land-use and environmental advantages attributed to earth sheltered buildings. These issues are briefly discussed in a later section of this chapter.

Soil, Bedrock, and Groundwater Conditions

Since earth sheltered housing usually requires a heavier structure and may be placed more deeply into the earth than a conventional house, consideration of soil type and groundwater conditions are particularly important to site selection. Determination of the soil type is important primarily for proper structural design of footings and walls. Certain types of soils are unsuitable because of their poor bearing capacity or because they shrink or expand under changing moisture conditions. If the soil layer is relatively thin and bedrock is near the surface, excavation in rock is likely to be difficult and costly, possibly making the site unfeasible for a below-grade structure. Groundwater conditions affect waterproofing as well as structural design; a high water table may require more costly structural and waterproofing techniques, thus making a site unsuitable.

Because of the serious and potentially costly consequences of unsuitable soil or a high water table, the soil type and groundwater conditions of a potential site should be determined before any great effort or capital is expended on either the site or the design for the house. This presents a problem for someone who wants to build an earth sheltered house and is trying to find the right piece of land. If he or she has a site investigation done before the land is purchased, that investment may be lost if the site proves unsuitable. If no site investigation is done before the site is purchased, the site may prove later to be either unsuitable or very costly site to build upon. As a compromise, the builder should initially find out as much as possible about local soil and groundwater conditions without actually having a physical site investigation carried out. Such general information will be more easy to obtain in more densely populated areas, from such sources as city engineers or city offices, owners of neighboring properties, local soil exploration or soil testing firms, local consulting engineers, and local realtors.

With this preliminary information in hand, a more enlightened judgment can be made as to whether the site appears suitable (or at least that the apparent limitations are acceptable). If the results of the preliminary investigation are satisfactory, a detailed site investigation should be done before the land is finally purchased. This investigation may reveal some unforeseen soil or groundwater problems that would make rejection of the site the best alternative. The main drawback to a site investigation at this stage is the possibility that the sale may fall through even though the potential buyer has already made a substantial investment. The cost of the investigation can, however, be divided between the two parties in a number of ways: the buyer and seller split the cost; the buyer pays if the results indicate favorable conditions; or the seller pays if the results indicate unfavorable conditions.

Generally, if the site is suitable from the other planning aspects, most types of soil will not greatly affect the design of the house. The groundwater and drainage characteristics of the site can more significantly affect the design. More detailed information on the effect of soil types and groundwater conditions on the design are presented in chapter 4.

Relation to the Sun

One major facet of site planning is the actual location and orientation of the structure. Although a house is referred to as earth sheltered, it is not completely covered by earth: window and door openings are required and are desirable for a number of reasons. The grouping of these openings and the direction they face determines the orientation of the structure on the site. For orientation of energy-efficient housing, one of the major considerations is the sun. In winter the sun can provide heat, while in the summer it is important to minimize heat gain from the sun to reduce energy consumed for cooling. In addition, solar orientation affects the amount of daylight that enters the house. Daylighting enhances the livability of a house and can reduce energy used for artificial lighting.

Maximizing solar exposure in the winter and minimizing it in the summer are not mutually exclusive goals. Because of the tilt of the earth and its rotation around the sun, the position of the sun in the sky varies throughout the year when viewed from a specific location. Various techniques exist to reduce solar heat gain in summer while still collecting a significant amount of it in winter. These include the use of moveable overhangs and shutters, and of vegetation to shade the house in summer.

Various techniques or systems exist for capturing, storing, and using radiant energy from the sun for space heating in a house. Most of them involve orienting windows or collector panels toward the south. For vertical windows, glass oriented between 25 degrees east of south and 25 degrees west of south collects the maximum amount of solar energy. Windows facing further to the east or west receive a significantly reduced amount of solar energy. The path of the sun for latitudes in the north, central, and southern United States are shown in figures 2-5, 2-6 and 2-7.

To summarize, the best orientation of an earth sheltered house for the winter heating season faces all of the window openings south with the remaining sides earth covered. Where this is unfeasible because of site or program constraints, other techniques (described in the design approaches section) can be used. For the summer cooling season, the main concern is to shield the house from the lower-angle rays of the sun on the east and west walls while using overhangs and other techniques to shade south-facing windows. In climates where the hot summer is the predominant

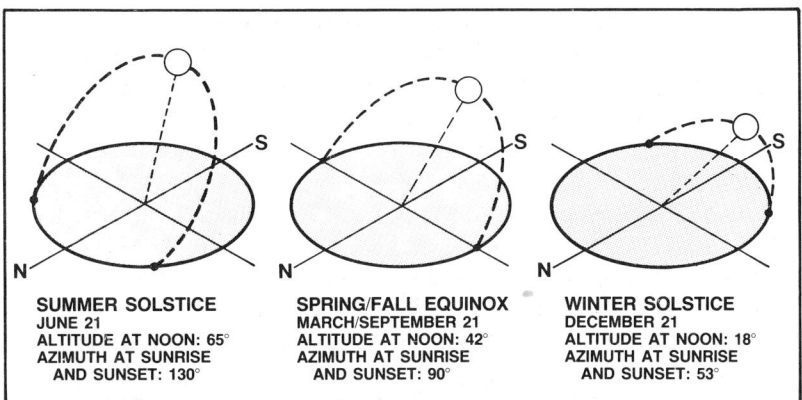

2-5: Sun Path Diagram—48° North Latitude (Duluth)

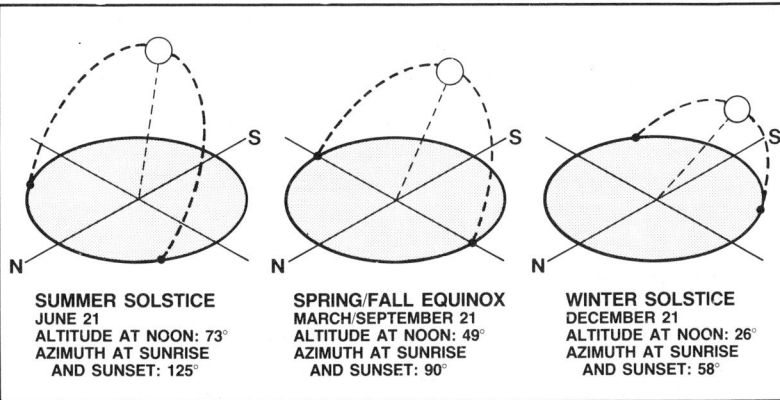

2-6: Sun Path Diagram—40° North Latitude (Kansas City)

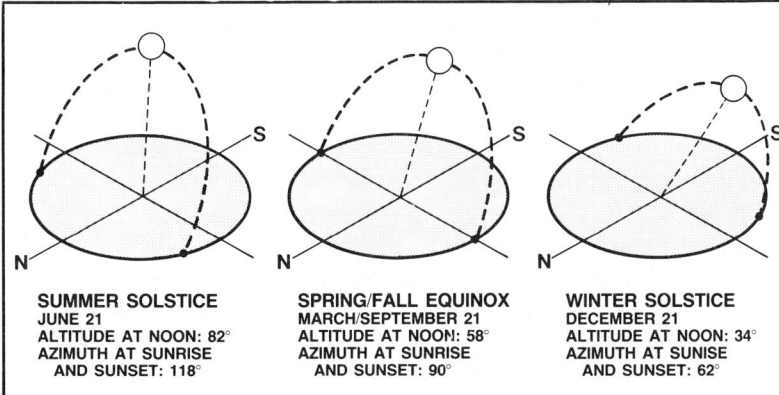

2-7: Sun Path Diagram—32° North Latitude (Phoenix)

concern and winters are mild, facing all windows north is an ideal orientation. In terms of site selection, the key issues are determining the path of the sun on the site and assuring that it is available and blocked as little as possible during the winter. Sometimes the location of the house on the site is primarily determined by the best solar access. Solar access is interrelated with the topography, location of buildings on neighboring property, and the location of vegetation.

Relation to the Wind

The direction from which the wind blows toward an earth sheltered structure is a serious energy consideration. Since direct exposure to cold winter winds increases heat loss because of infiltration, it is desirable to protect a building as much as possible from this exposure. For example, in Minneapolis the prevailing winter winds are primarily from the northwest (although this is also influenced by local site conditions). Minimizing window and door openings on the north and west side of a house in this location will enhance its energy performance.

Earth sheltered construction offers a very unique opportunity to shield the structure fully from prevailing winter winds and use the earth to divert the wind over the structure (fig. 2-8). The sudden drop on the south edge of the house can, however, create some wind turbulence, resulting in large amounts of snow accumulation in this area. It is advisable to maintain a barrier to the north of the structure to divert or drift the snow before it can be deposited at the south edge of the house (fig. 2-9). An earth sheltered design that includes a central courtyard may be substantially protected from prevailing winds, but minor wind turbulence may also occur in the atrium (fig. 2-10). The behavior of this wind turbulence depends on many specific details of a design, such as the size of the courtyards, the

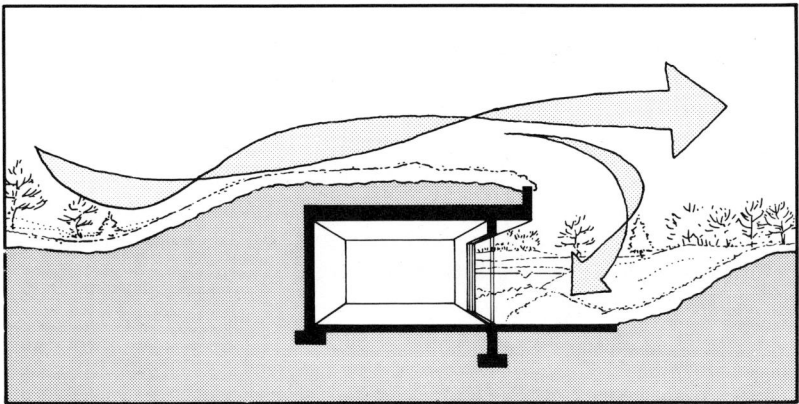
2-8: Earth Berms Divert Wind over Structure

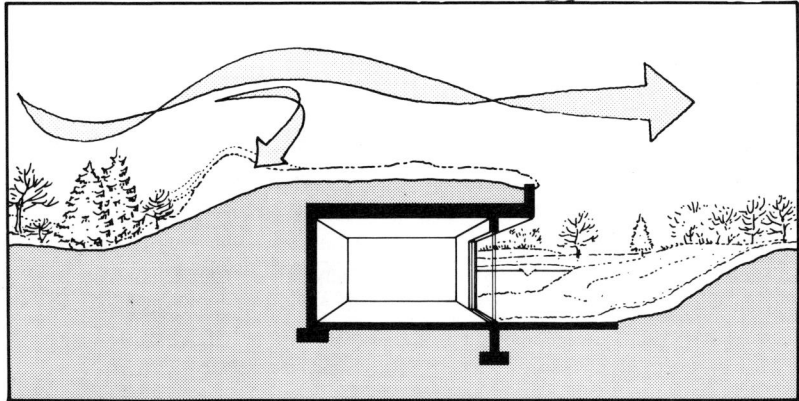
2-9: Barrier Controls Snow Accumulation

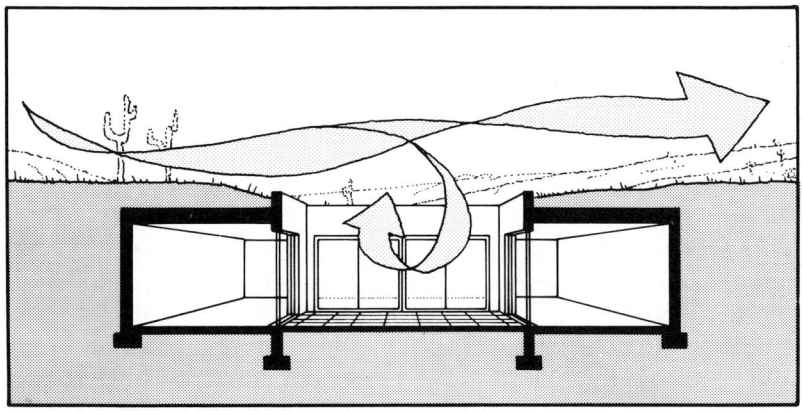
2-10: Effect of Wind in Atrium Design

edge details, and the use of landscaping.

In the summer it is desirable to take advantage of prevailing breezes to provide natural ventilation. Prevailing summer breezes vary from site to site depending on local conditions, trees, water bodies, and topography. Unfortunately, the orientation of an earth sheltered structure with all window openings to the south will not create a well-ventilated house. Natural ventilation may not be as necessary in an earth sheltered house if the interior is naturally cooler because of contact with the earth. In addition, natural ventilation during humid weather may cause excessive humidity within the house and possible condensation. For regions and time periods when natural ventilation is beneficial, certain techniques described later in this chapter, can be used to enhance natural ventilation. Energy-efficient site design for either summer or winter requires an analysis of the general wind patterns for the climate area and the unique wind patterns on the site.

Topography

The topography of a building site can affect the design in a number of ways. Changes in terrain directly affect the wind patterns and local air temperatures around a building and certainly have a great impact on patterns of water runoff. Topography is also one of the main determinants of the aesthetic character of a site. In considering basic building design options, the most important topographic criteria for an earth sheltered design is whether a site is flat or sloped and the degree and orientation of any slope. Very steep sites with slopes over 30 percent are often considered undesirable or even unbuildable for conventional housing. Such sites can, however, offer unique opportunities for earth sheltered housing.

On a predominantly flat site, a fully or partially recessed design, usually limited to one level below grade, can be implemented. These variations, illustrated in chapter 1, are sometimes referred to as subgrade and bermed designs. A sloping site offers the opportunity to set an earth covered space into the hillside. South-facing slopes, which maximize solar exposure and offer natural protection from winter winds, are more desirable in cool and temperate climates (fig. 2-11). North-facing slopes are less desirable in climates where winter weather predominates but, with appropriate design, can be used. Hilltops, where maximum exposure to cold winds occur, are also undesirable building locations in cold climates, as are valley floors where cool air settles.

In hot, humid climates where winter heating is less important, hilltops, which provide the most access to breezes, are the best locations to build. In hot, arid climates where hot, dry winds are undesirable, valley floors with cooler temperatures are the best sites (fig. 2-12).

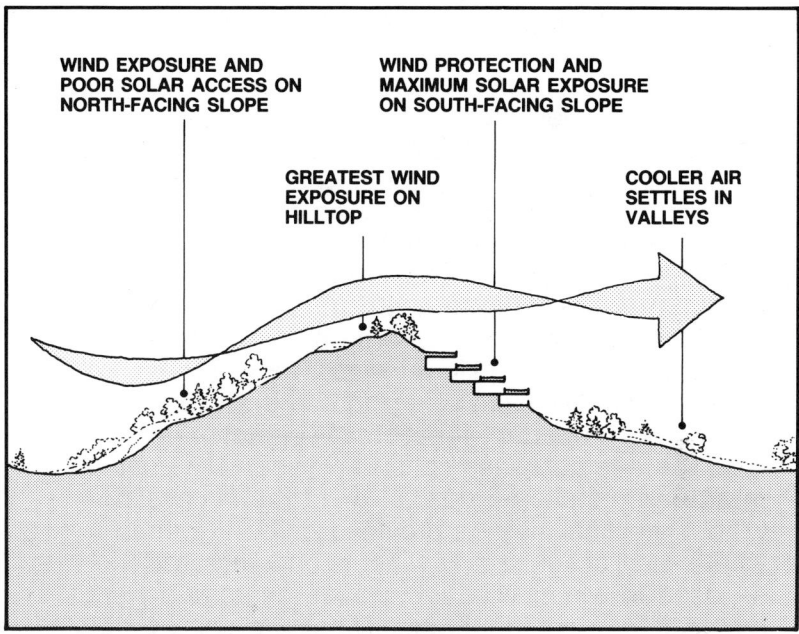

2-11: Effect of Topography in Winter

Vegetation

Trees and shrubs on a building site have a variety of functions, ranging from symbolic and aesthetic use to erosion and noise control. Included in these functions is the use of existing and newly planted vegetation to conserve energy in a building. Trees, shrubs, and groundcover can affect the amount of sunlight striking a building, as well as the wind patterns and temperatures around a structure.

Although the exact level of energy savings is difficult to predict, some uses of vegetation are known to have a significant impact on energy performance. Trees in an earth sheltered design can be effectively used to shade windows on the south side of the house in the summer when direct solar radiation is undesirable. Deciduous trees drop their leaves in autumn and allow the solar radiation to reach the southerly windows in the winter when it is

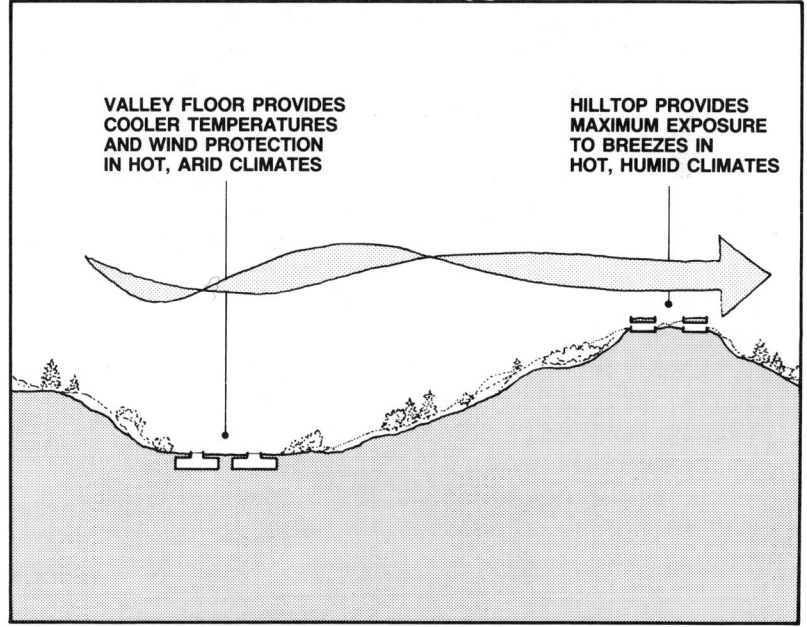

2-12: Effect of Topography in Summer

most needed (figs. 2-13 and 2-14). Groupings of trees that are too densely spaced or that include conifers can be detrimental to solar heating because they reduce solar access in winter.

Ground cover materials can be used to enhance or diminish solar radiation both in and around buildings. Grass-covered surfaces are not as reflective or as massive as lighter, harder concrete surfaces. In summer cooler grass surfaces around a building are desirable to assist in reducing heat gain. In winter, however, light-colored paved surfaces can be used to reflect sunlight inside. Snow can also increase the reflection of sunlight into a space.

Another important function of vegetation in reducing energy consumption involves wind control. In an earth sheltered design, all of the necessary wind protection may be provided by earth berms where they occur. If any window openings are exposed to winter winds, however, evergreen plant materials can contribute significantly to energy savings. A study was conducted in South Dakota in which two identical houses were compared—one with rows of trees on three sides and the other with no windbreaks. The house with the windbreaks required 40 percent less fuel for heating [Hastings, Crenshaw, 1977].

Other studies have defined the most effective size and placement of windbreaks. Solid barriers such as walls reduce winds almost completely within a short distance from the barrier (one to two times the barrier height), but the wind quickly resumes at full speed beyond that. More porous barriers such as those comprised of trees and shrubs are more effective in diminishing winds over a longer distance. A barrier with lower porosity (about 25 percent) reduces wind speeds up to 90 percent within a zone four times the height (4H) of the barrier and reduces wind speeds by 40 percent in a zone four to twenty times the (4H to 20H) barrier height (fig. 2-15). A barrier with higher porosity (about 50 percent) has increased effectiveness in the 5H to 20H zone (a

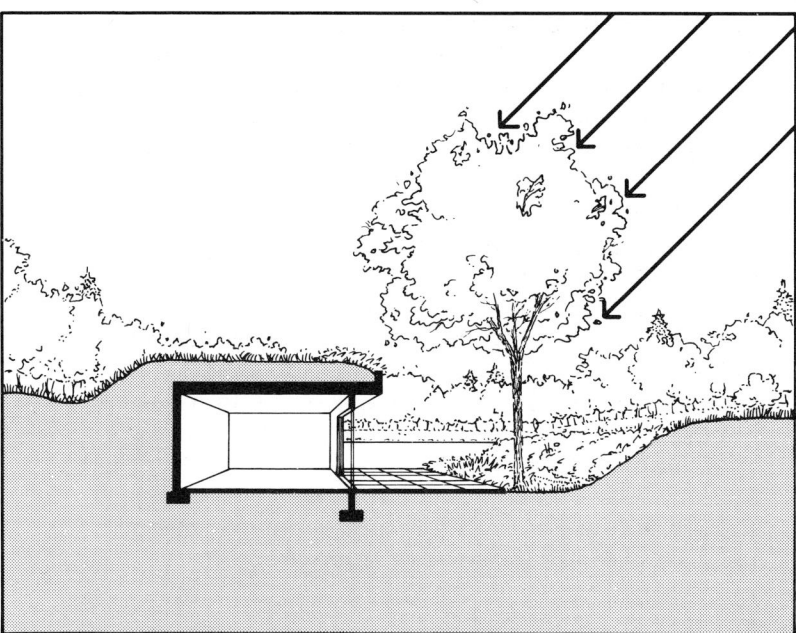
2-13: Deciduous Trees Provide Shade in Summer

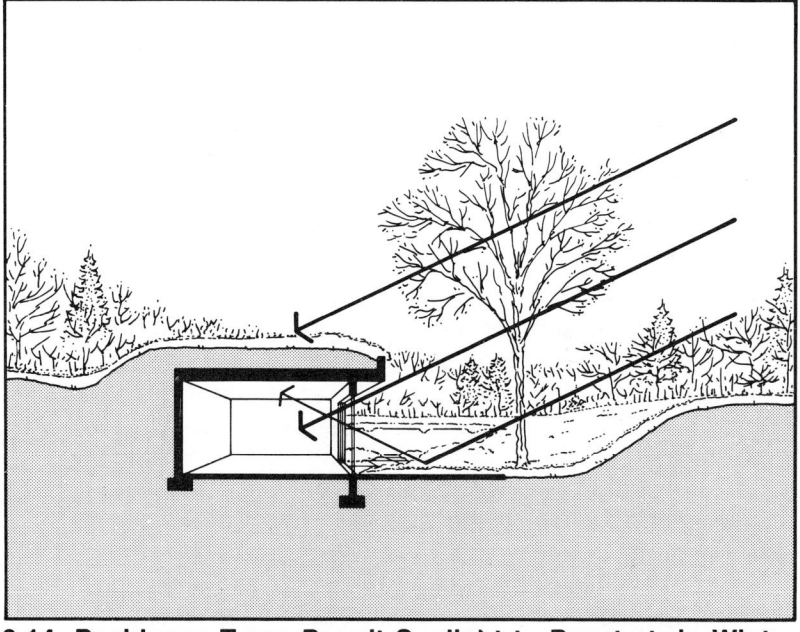
2-14: Deciduous Trees Permit Sunlight to Penetrate in Winter

reduction of 70 percent) but is less effective in the closer zone. For a windbreak to reach its maximum effectiveness, it should be eleven to twelve times as long as it is high [Watson, Labs, 1980].

Trees and shrubs can also be used to direct or channel winds on a site to promote breezes and maximize natural ventilation in summer (fig. 2-16). For this purpose, as well as for wind protection in winter and shading from the summer sun, the use of vegetation should be regarded as one of a group of energy-saving techniques that include earth berms, fences, walls, and other man-made forms. All of these elements must be integrated with the building openings to achieve the desired effects. In evaluating a site, it is useful to examine the potential uses of the existing vegetation and attempt to develop a building and landscaping plan that takes advantage of these opportunities.

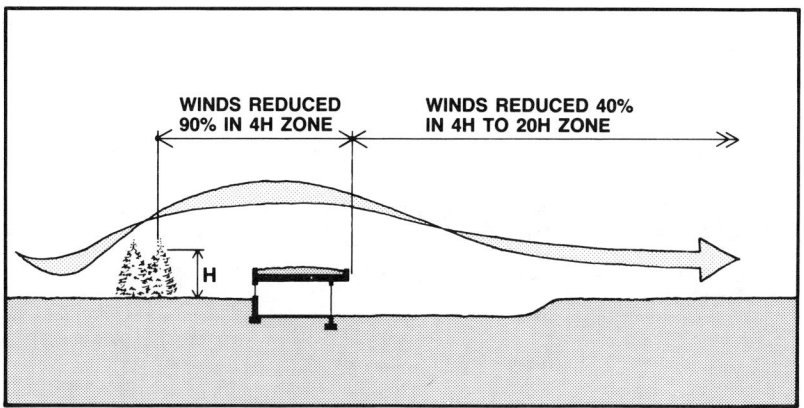

2-15: Effect of a Windbreak with 25 Percent Porosity

2-16: Vegetation Directs and Channels Summer Breezes

Factors Affecting Building Form and Layout

The form and layout of any structure is developed from a broad range of criteria. These design determinants include everything from very general and subjective concepts to specific and technical details. This section does not present a complete review of all the determinants relevant to housing design. Instead, the items discussed herein represent design considerations that are unique to earth sheltered housing or have particular significance with respect to energy-efficient design. Included in this section are four key areas that directly influence the overall form and layout of an earth sheltered house: energy conservation, the building program, the structural system, and critical building code provisions. A more detailed discussion of many of these considerations appears in chapters 3 through 6.

Energy Conservation

One of the major reasons for designing and building earth sheltered housing is the potential energy savings for space heating and cooling. Details concerning earth cover, insulation placement, and projected energy savings are presented in chapter 3. Energy conservation is also discussed here, however, since it is a major determinant of the building form. Energy conservation directly affects the

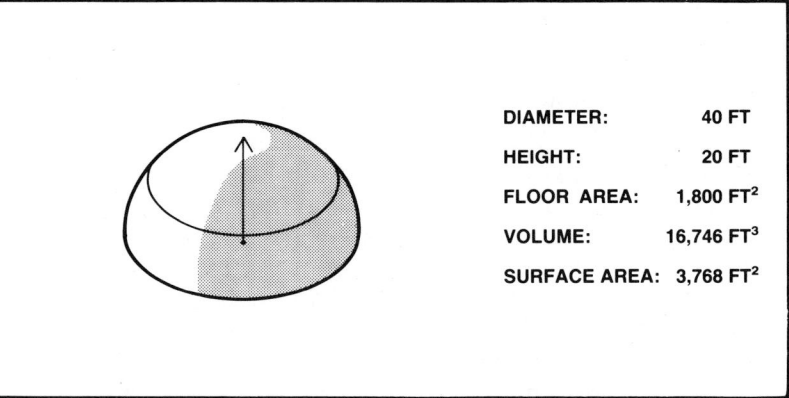

2-17: Hemisphere Enclosing Two Levels

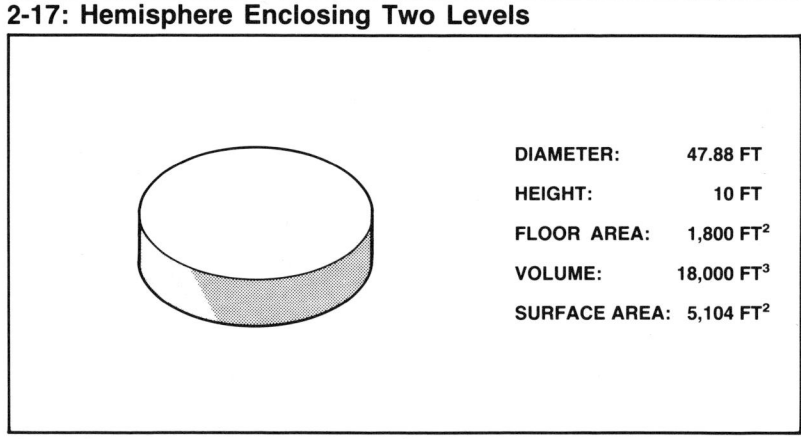

2-18: One-Level Circular Plan

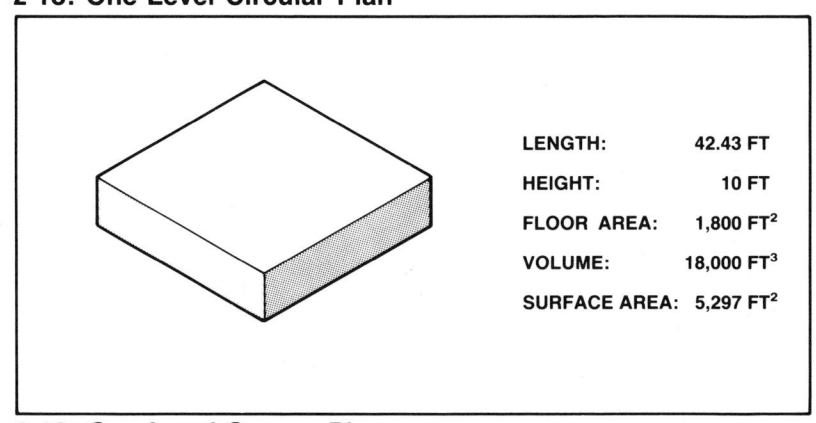

2-19: One-Level Square Plan

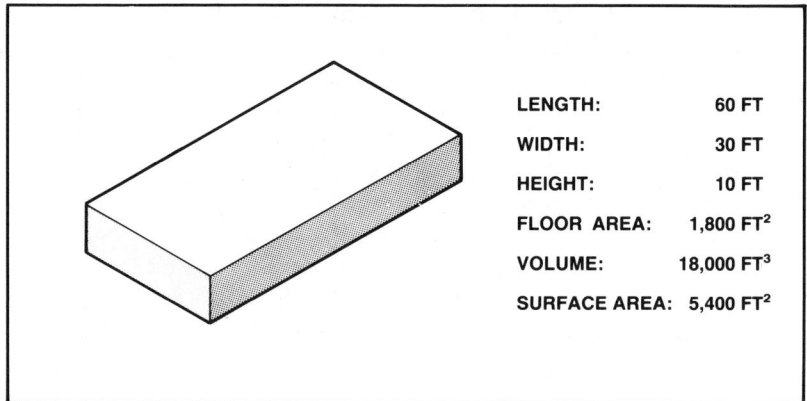

2-20: One-Level Rectangular Plan

LENGTH:	60 FT
WIDTH:	30 FT
HEIGHT:	10 FT
FLOOR AREA:	1,800 FT^2
VOLUME:	18,000 FT^3
SURFACE AREA:	5,400 FT^2

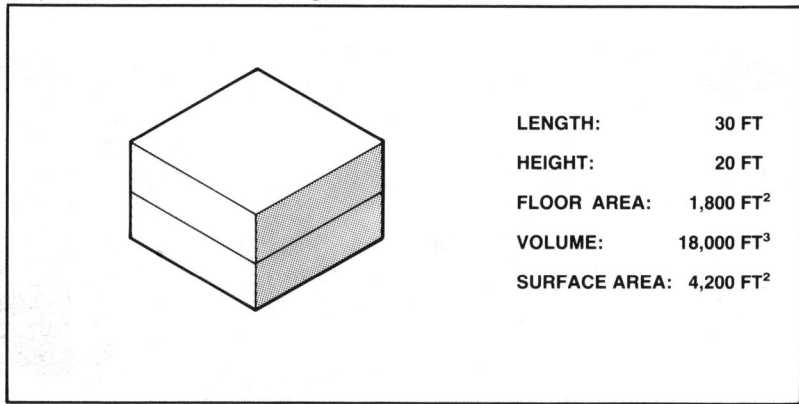

2-21: Two-Level Square Plan

LENGTH:	30 FT
HEIGHT:	20 FT
FLOOR AREA:	1,800 FT^2
VOLUME:	18,000 FT^3
SURFACE AREA:	4,200 FT^2

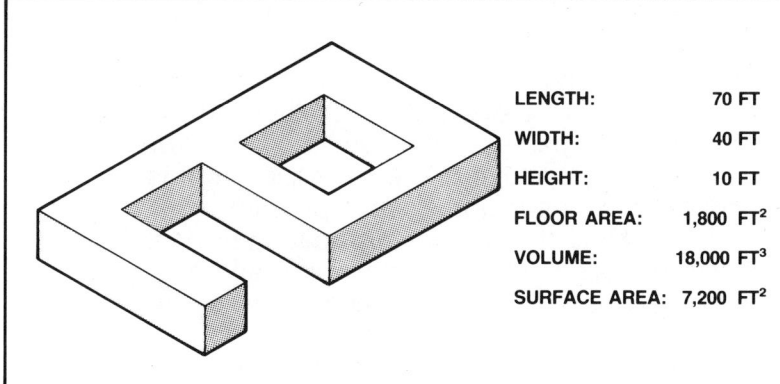

2-22: One-Level Extended Plan

LENGTH:	70 FT
WIDTH:	40 FT
HEIGHT:	10 FT
FLOOR AREA:	1,800 FT^2
VOLUME:	18,000 FT^3
SURFACE AREA:	7,200 FT^2

overall configuration of an earth sheltered house in many ways. These include the efficiency of the building geometry, the degree of earth contact around the structure, and the extent to which solar systems are part of the design.

The heat loss and thus the energy use of any building in a cool or temperate climate is a function of the area of the surface through which the heat can escape. A building with a larger surface area will experience greater heat loss in winter than one with a smaller surface area, assuming all other variables are equal. Buildings with the same floor area can have quite different surface areas depending on the configuration of the plan, as shown in the adjacent illustrations. The most compact shape, that is the shape that encloses the greatest volume with the least surface area, is a sphere. Figure 2-17 shows a hemisphere that contains 1800 square feet on two levels. Although this dome shape parallels actual earth sheltered and above-grade structures, there are some difficulties comparing it to other shapes since ceiling heights vary and some spaces may not be used as efficiently as in a rectilinear plan.

Assuming a one-level structure with a flat roof, the plan shape that encloses the most space with the least wall area is a circle (fig. 2-18). Since a circle is often impractical to construct, a square or rectangle represent relatively compact plan shapes for building design (figs. 2-19 and 2-20). When one-level and two-level designs with equal floor areas are compared, the two-level design has far less exterior surface area (fig. 2-21).

The more extended and less compact a design becomes, the greater the surface area exposed to heat loss (fig. 2-22). This principle also holds true for earth sheltered housing. It must be stressed, however, that this is not necessarily a detriment in the summer. Since the surrounding earth is cooler than the house in the summer, the flow of heat into the earth is a source of cooling. In this case a house with a greater wall area will benefit more from this cooling effect. Thus, in a cold climate such as Minnesota, more emphasis is likely to be placed on minimizing heat loss in the winter and, therefore, developing as compact a floor plan as possible. In a warmer climate such as Arizona, extending the building form to increase contact with the earth would be more desirable from an energy standpoint.

A second way in which energy conservation affects the overall design of an earth sheltered house is related to the earth mass surrounding the structure. As will be shown in the energy use chapter, earth placed against the walls and on the roof of a structure has specific energy-saving attributes. Therefore, the maximization of earth cover is one determinant of the design. If contact with the earth were the only energy-conserving strategy available, then a deep, totally enclosed underground chamber would represent the ideal design. Naturally, home owners would find this type of building unacceptable, and it would violate building codes. Window openings, courtyards, skylights, and other techniques are required to create a livable environment and provide access.

The amount, orientation and grouping of window openings in an earth sheltered house can have a major effect on its energy efficiency and whether the benefits of being in contact with the earth can be realized. For example, openings grouped on one side of a house will create a more continuous earth mass surrounding the other sides. In contrast, numerous openings penetrating earth berms on all sides of a structure reduce the effectiveness of being in a below-grade environment.

The building geometry and use of earth cover must be integrated into the family of the interrelated strategies available to conserve energy, such as providing solar heat in winter and natural ventilation in summer. These and other energy-related concerns further affect the shape and layout of the building. Since earth sheltered houses are well suited to the inclusion of passive solar systems in cool and temperate climates, the shape of the building is often heavily influenced by the desire for significant solar exposure to major living spaces. The result is that the ideal form for an earth sheltered/solar house in most parts of the United States is a rectangle elongated on the east/west axis similar to the plan in figure 2-20. In hot, arid climates, courtyard plans are likely to be the most suitable, and in hot, humid areas, plans with extensive openings and opportunities for ventilation are advisable.

Building Program

A building program establishes the needs and desires of the users of a building and then reflects these in the spaces to be designed and built. This means simply that the type and number of rooms, their size, and the relationship between the spaces must be determined before proceeding with the design. Since most families have similar basic needs, such as eating, cooking, sleeping, and recreation, the programs for most single-family dwellings are basically the same, although unique variations are occasionally developed. This similarity in home programs is reinforced by financial restrictions and the desire for conformity so that any home appeals to a broad market. Naturally, an earth sheltered home is subject to the same program determinants and market forces as an above-grade home and must be designed to include the typical functions and space requirements a home owner would expect in above-grade construction. It is important not to subjugate basic program requirements to the physical limitations of earth sheltered design. Thermal, structural, and aesthetic considerations should be balanced with the functional requirements. Although an earth sheltered house is similar to a conventional one in terms of functional requirements, a few issues are worth mentioning.

One effect of building a home either partially or completely recessed into the ground is that the large unprogrammed basement area found in many above-grade houses in the northern half of the United States will probably be costly or impractical to duplicate. The basement is considered to be relatively inexpensive space in above grade construction in colder climates since foundation walls and footings are required to be relatively deep to avoid frost heave. In an earth sheltered design, the walls are likely to go below the frost line, so the opportunity for inexpensive extra space is not present. Basements do serve several important functions in a conventional house, including use as laundry rooms, mechanical space, storage areas, workshop areas, and recreational or multipurpose space. These functions must be recognized as needs and be included in the program for an earth sheltered home. It is unlikely that they will require the extensive leftover space that they often occupy in a typical basement. It is possible that a more efficient living arrangement and use of space may result by combining these basement functions into the rest of the house, although potential problems such as mechanical room noise must be resolved.

Another program consideration that arises with earth sheltered housing is the potential use of unheated aboveground spaces for certain functions during certain times of the year. Since spaces such as a garage or a storage area do not have the same heating and cooling requirements as habitable space, it may prove to be more convenient or less costly to locate them aboveground adjacent to the earth-covered portion of the house. Other spaces that have seasonal uses, such as a porch, may also be located above grade to enhance their use. Although certain functions can easily be located above grade without reducing energy efficiency, creating small above-grade structures adjacent to a mostly below-grade house should be done with the greatest care. Such a building may dominate the overall image of the project, making it appear to be mainly a small outbuilding rather than a house designed in harmony with its site.

Structural Systems

In any building the structural system plays an important role in the overall design. This is particularly true with earth sheltered housing because the loads resulting from earth on the roof are substantial. The structural systems that can be used to support these loads can be divided into two groups: the more conventional flat roof systems and

2-23: Earth-covered house in New Hampshire; Don Metz, architect; photograph by Robert Perron.

2-24: Clark-Nelson House, River Falls, Wisconsin; Michael McGuire, architect.

a variety of more unconventional systems using vault and dome shapes.

Conventional roof systems include precast concrete planks and poured-in-place concrete slabs, as well as wood or steel post-and-beam systems. All of these systems result in flat or sloping roofs, and generally rectangular plan shapes, although more free-form plan shapes are possible with flat roofs. Typically, regularly spaced bearing walls with limited openings are a strong organizing force in the floor plan. The thickness of earth cover on flat roofs is generally limited to about two feet, as the structural costs that result from exceeding this depth are considerable. This cost factor limits some potential energy benefits to be derived from deeper placement of a building into the earth. Most earth sheltered buildings constructed today utilize a flat roof structure including the house shown in figure 2-23.

The necessity of supporting heavier-than-normal roof loads in earth sheltered housing may result in the use of more unconventional structural systems. These include concrete, steel, or even wood barrel-vault shapes and domes. These systems can support the heavier loads in a much more efficient manner than flat roof structures, although they can limit the alternatives for room layouts considerably. In addition, greater amounts of earth can be considered (4 to 6 feet), which can enhance energy performance because the entire structure is further from the surface. More than the conventional systems, these structures dictate the overall shape and form of the house and the spaces that must be placed within these shapes. Also, systems depending on arch or vault action for structural support cannot be arbitrarily penetrated for window openings or the structural system may be weakened. For example, if a large barrel-vault shape is used as the basic structure, window openings are primarily limited to the two ends and the spaces must be laid out with regard to the curved roof. Possible alternative design approaches may include a shell shape large enough for two floor levels or several smaller shapes linked together to create more openings. A house using steel culvert sections is shown in figure 2-24 and other vault and dome structures appear in chapter 4 and 7.

These types of systems can result in very attractive designs that contain some very unique spaces and maximize the effect of the earth mass. It must be recognized, however, that most unconventional systems will present a different set of limitations on the design and ultimate configuration of a house. Although most earth sheltered dwellings are and continue to be constructed with flat roofs, shell structures are emerging as a reasonable and efficient design approach.

Building Codes

The implications of building codes for earth sheltered housing and recommendations for future policy are discussed in chapter 6. It is, however, important to mention briefly one of the most profound issues concerning building codes and earth sheltered housing design. For residential construction almost all of the national building codes state that all bedrooms must have an operating window to provide light, ventilation, and a means of escape [UBC, NBC, BOCA, SBC]. Other habitable rooms must have a minimum glazing area for light, but mechanical ventilation can be substituted for an operable window. Rooms used for such functions as storage and utility are excluded, and bathrooms are excluded provided mechanical ventilation is present.

In typical above-grade construction, these provisions can be met without significantly affecting the design. Unlike a typical house, however, many earth sheltered designs tend to minimize and concentrate window openings in order to maximize energy efficiency. If this code requirement is strictly adhered to, it becomes one of the most significant design determinants since it may force unusual plan arrangements so that windows can be grouped together. There is no question that an earth sheltered home without adequate light, ventilation, safety standards, and a good relationship to the outdoors is totally unacceptable. Modification of this particular window requirement, however, allowing for other techniques of bringing light and air into spaces would have a very liberating impact. Generally, the design considerations and designs presented in this and other chapters of this book will be done within the constraints of present building codes.

Typical Design Approaches: The Elevational Concept

Earth sheltered or underground building designs can be classified in a number of ways. As discussed in chapter 1, one of the most common systems is to identify below-grade structures according to the types of openings they employ: chamber, elevational, atrium and penetrational [Labs, 1976].

The windowless chamber is obviously not a valid design approach for housing. The two most clearly identifiable approaches employed are the elevational concept (where all windows are on a single exposed side of the house) and the atrium design (where all windows face a central courtyard). The penetrational type of structure (where multiple openings occur on more than one side of the house) is also a valid design approach but most often is a variation of the elevational or atrium concepts. For this reason only the elevational and atrium concepts and their variations are discussed here in detail, the elevational approach in this section and the atrium approach in the next. It should be recognized that most houses do not perfectly fit these categories, but these classifications are useful as a means of discussing design issues.

In the cool and temperate climates experienced by the majority of the United States, the most common and usually most suitable earth sheltered designs are based on the elevational concept. The Hadley House in Burnsville, Minnesota, is an example of an elevational house set into a south-facing hillside (figs. 2-25 and 2-26). This particular house has earth berms on three sides and a conventional well-insulated roof as shown in figure 2-27; however, the plan arrangement would be similar for a house with an earth-covered roof (fig. 2-28).

Bedrooms and living spaces, located on the south side, have numerous windows to comply with building codes, while bathrooms, mechanical and storage rooms are located on the north wall. The kitchen and dining spaces on the north wall are open to the living area to benefit from the window areas. One problem with elevational houses is that internal circulation can be awkward or inefficient simply because the plan is elongated. Entering in

2-25: *Hadley House, Burnsville, Minnesota; Tom Ellison, architect.*

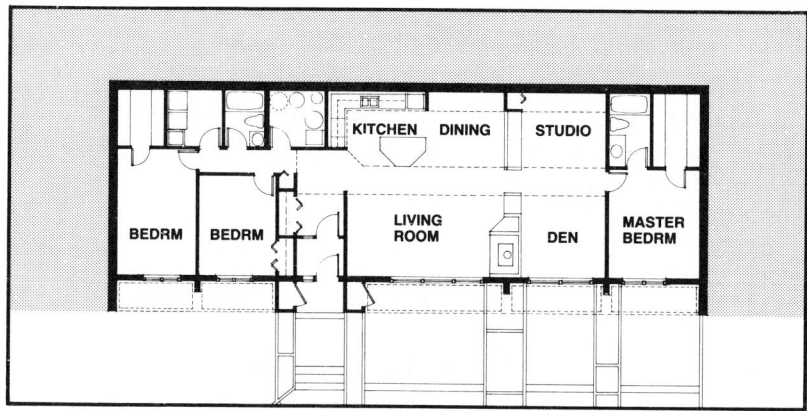
2-26: Plan of Hadley House, Burnsville, Minnesota

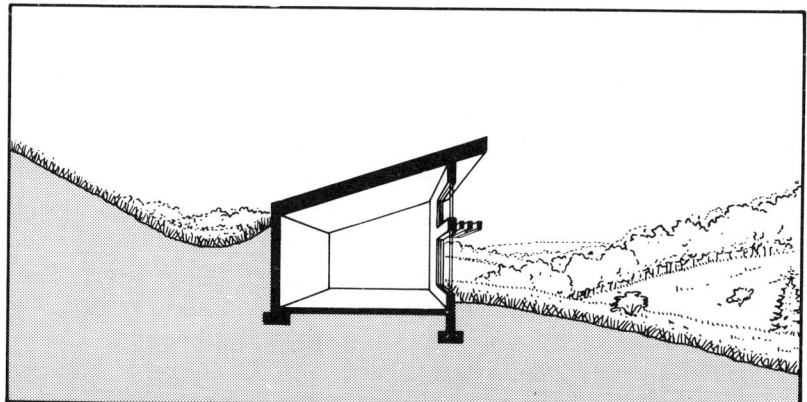
2-27: Earth-Bermed House on South-Facing Slope

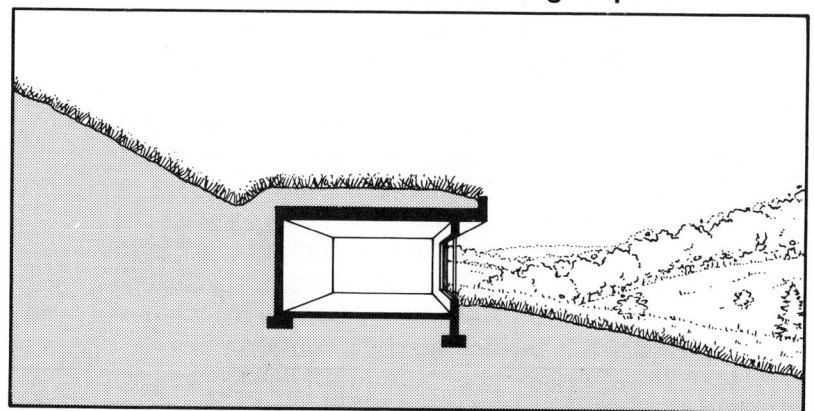
2-28: Earth-Covered House on South-Facing Slope

the center as shown in figure 2-26 helps to diminish this problem. This particular elevational house is entered from the south, and the garage is a detached above-grade structure on the south side of the dwelling.

South-Facing Slopes

With all windows oriented to the south in an elevational design, maximum exposure to solar energy is achieved. The earth berms on the other three sides provide protection from winter winds. Typically the house is elongated in the east/west direction so that all major habitable spaces are lined up along the south facade and have exterior windows. For a one-level elevational house, the ideal site is a south-facing slope, enabling the house to fit into the natural contours of the land and permitting clear exterior views to the south. Viewed from the south, such a house can have a relatively conventional appearance if so desired and can be entered at grade.

The disadvantages of an elevational design can include poor cross-ventilation and no daylight in the northern portions of the house. In addition, an elongated building can have a rather stark appearance from the exterior unless the materials, landscaping, and architectural details are carefully designed.

Surface and subsurface drainage must be properly designed for any earth sheltered house to prevent water problems. Figures 2-27 and 2-28 show an earth-covered elevational house on a south-facing slope. Water runoff from the slope must be diverted around the structure by creating a swale, and a subsurface drainage system is necessary as well (see chapter 5). To some extent the creation of a swale prevents the house form from completely fitting into the natural site contours.

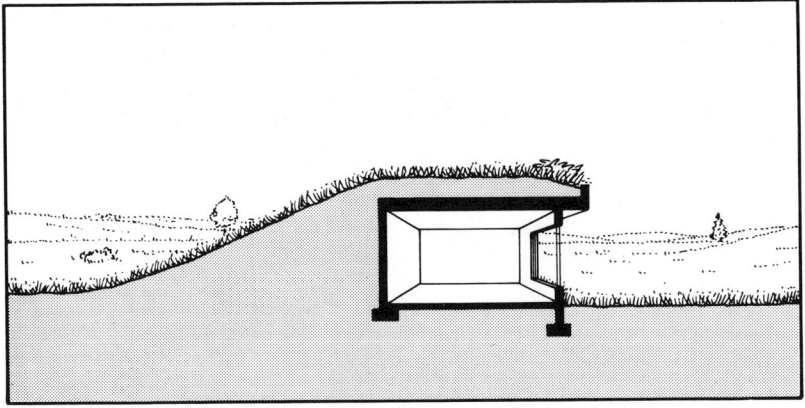

2-29: House at Existing Grade on Flat Site

2-30: Partially Recessed House on Flat Site

2-31: Fully Recessed House on Flat Site

Flat Sites

Although elevational designs seem ideally suited to sloping sites, they can also be placed on flat sites. On a flat site, the degree to which the house is recessed below grade has an impact on its exterior form, views from the windows, ease of access, drainage, and the minimum lot size required. One approach on a flat site is to place the building floor level at grade and place earth berms around the structure (fig. 2-29). The advantages of this approach are that the house can be entered at grade, there is clear exterior view, and drainage is no problem. The image of such a house is that of a definite mass on the site, not an unobtrusive below-grade approach. The character could vary from native plantings on the berms to terraces with retaining walls that create a more defined edge. Disadvantages are the needs for additional fill and a larger minimum lot size than that for a conventional house or a more recessed earth sheltered design.

Generally, a better alternative on a flat site is a semirecessed design (fig. 2-30). By placing the floor a half-level below grade, the cut and fill is balanced and the smaller berms blend into the flat site more easily. The minimum lot size would probably be slightly smaller than for the previous example. Although a sunken courtyard is created, exterior views beyond the courtyard are preserved while access and drainage should present no great problems.

Another approach on a flat site is to place the elevational structure completely below existing grade (fig. 2-31). This approach minimizes the lot size required and allows a very unobtrusive exterior image to be created. Moreover, open space on the surface can extend right over the structure. Exterior views are restricted to a sunken courtyard; however, a more enclosed, private outdoor area may be considered an advantage on some sites. Disadvantages to this approach are that access is less direct and excavated earth may have to be hauled from the site. In addition, more drainage and groundwater problems may be encountered with a deeper floor level.

On a flat site, it is also possible to combine some of the advantages of the previous cases by designing a two-level structure. Such an alternative provides a visible above grade form with a clear exterior view from the upper level while the lower level maintains a view into a sunken courtyard.

North-Facing Slopes

In cool and temperate climates, sloping sites not oriented toward the south are regarded as less desirable than south-facing hillsides for earth sheltered houses. In fact, such sites can be quite acceptable if they are carefully designed to overcome some of their inherent drawbacks. The least desirable slope is north-facing, since the slope is exposed to winter winds and access to sunlight is diminished. By placing an elevational design into a north-facing slope, with all windows facing north, energy use for space heating would be significantly greater than that for an identical south-facing house. To offset these disadvantages, windows on the north should be limited, windbreaks on the north should be used to provide protection, and south-facing skylights should be included to provide solar heat gain (fig. 2-32). To capture any significant solar heat gain in this manner, the slope angle must be less than the sun angles in winter and the hillside must be clear of vegetation and buildings north of the house.

Another approach for a north-facing slope is to create a sunken courtyard on the south side of the house (fig. 2-33). All of the glazing faces south, and the courtyard can be designed to permit low-angled winter sun to reach the house. With a sloping roof as shown in the illustration, the structure can

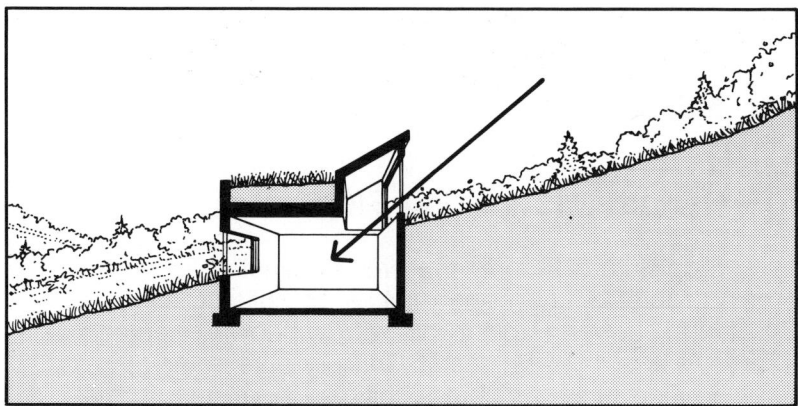

2-32: House with Skylight on North-Facing Slope

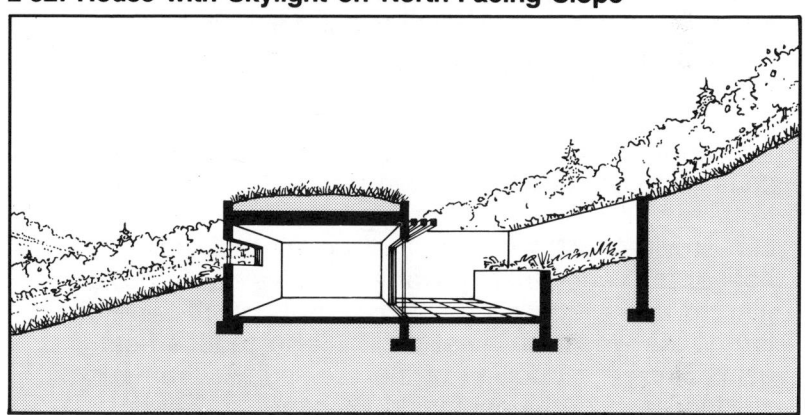

2-33: House with Sunken Courtyard on North-Facing Slope

successfully fit into the natural contours of the land, and the house is protected from winter winds by the earth. Drainage from such a sloping roof would be ideal; however, the runoff coming from the slope above the house must be handled properly. A terraced design as shown can absorb much of the runoff, and subsurface drainpipes can carry excess water to an outfall further downhill.

In a hot climate where summer cooling is the major energy concern and winter heating is less important, an elevational house with north-facing windows on a north-facing slope may represent an ideal design. Not only is heat gain through the windows eliminated, but the ground temperatures are cooler on a north slope, thus enhancing cooling by earth contact.

East- and West-Facing Slopes

Slopes that face to the east or west present their own problems and opportunities as building sites. Setting a house into the hill with windows oriented directly east or west results in very little solar gain for heating in winter, but significant heat gain in the summer, thus increasing the cooling requirements. Much like the previous illustrations for north-facing slopes, it is desirable to orient windows toward the south as much as possible in cool climates while minimizing or shading those windows facing east or west in all climates. A sunken courtyard on the south side of the building can permit some windows to face south, and south-facing clerestory windows can provide solar gain to other portions of the house. In predominantly warm climates north-facing glazing and a sunken courtyard on the north side of the house would be most desirable to reduce heat gain. Since the position of the sun is low when it is striking east- and west-facing windows, a wall or dense hedge close to the building provides the best shading. For earth sheltered houses on east- and west-facing slopes, the hill can provide some protection from winter winds. If the predominant winds strike the exposed sides of the house however, windbreaks will be necessary for protection.

Steep Slopes

Among potential sites for elevational earth sheltered houses, relatively steep slopes from 30 to 50 percent provide some unique design opportunities but also have some disadvantages to be overcome.

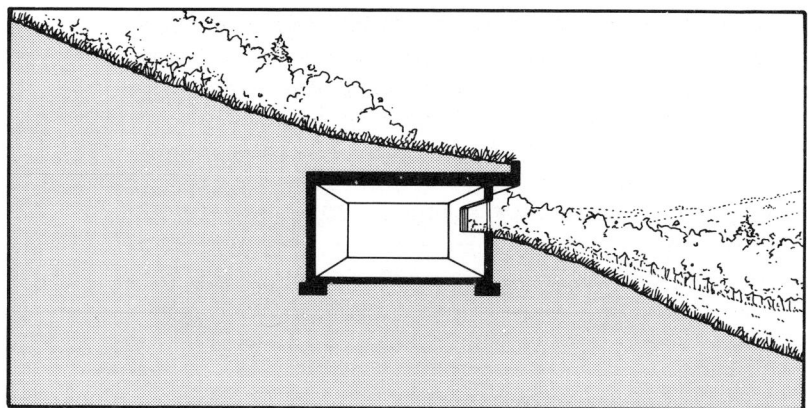

2-34: One-Level House on Steep Slope

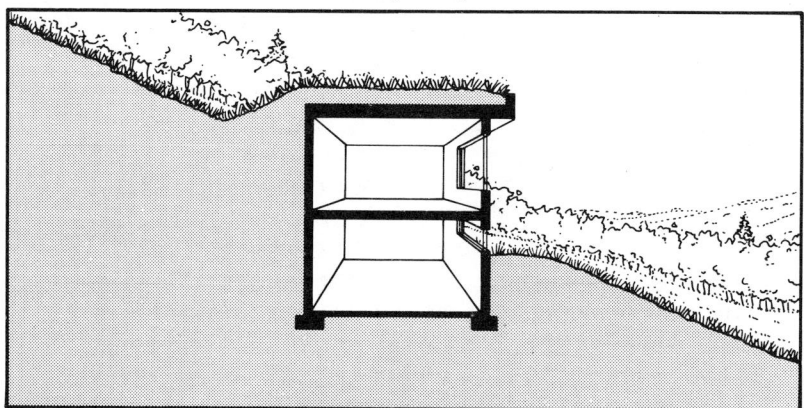

2-35: Two-Level House on Steep Slope

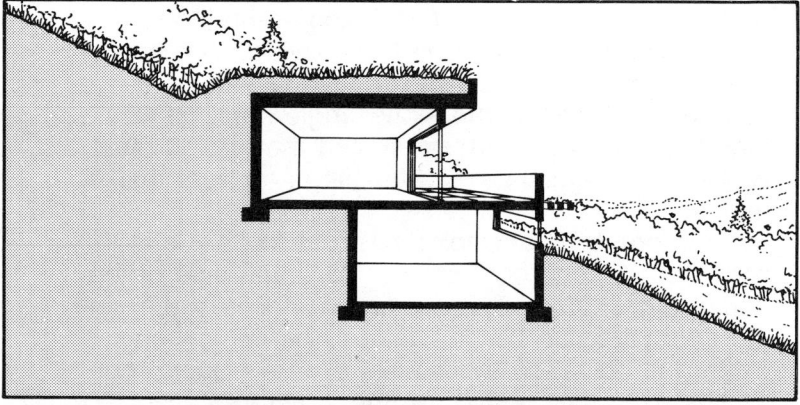

2-36: Two-Level Stepped Structure on Steep Slope

Such steep sites are often considered unbuildable for conventional housing but can be well suited to an earth sheltered house, sometimes resulting in the ability to use marginal, less expensive sites. Assuming a relatively steep (50 percent) south-facing slope, a one-level elevational design may not fit the slope easily without placing a substantial amount of earth on the roof (fig. 2-34). This approach can result in good integration with the landforms and increased thermal benefits from the deeper placement of the structure. On the other hand, structural loads on the roof and rear wall would be substantial, therefore increasing cost. Water runoff from the hillside would flow over the structure rather than being diverted around it. While this type of drainage can be handled by providing outlets along the roof edge, it is generally considered undesirable to run large amounts of water over, rather than away from, an earth-covered roof.

A two-story elevational design will generally fit into a steep slope better than a one-story design (fig. 2-35). Although structural loads on the lower portion of a two-story wall are significant, the earth load on the roof is less than that in the previous one-level design. A two-story design enables the creation of a drainage swale on the north side of the house to divert water, although the house form interrupts the natural slope of the hillside.

Another variation on the two-story approach for a steep site is a stepped-back structure (fig. 2-36). Such a building form appears to fit the character of a sloping site better than a flat two-story facade, and structural loads on the walls are reduced. In the two-story designs, a conventional roof could be used in place of an earth-covered roof. Removing earth from the roof in this or any other design affects the appearance, structure, energy use, and cost of the building. Some of these issues are discussed in greater detail in later chapters.

Natural Light and Ventilation

A typical elevational design with all windows located on one side of the house, while offering many advantages, creates potential difficulties in providing natural light and cross-ventilation throughout the house. Windows on a single wall can provide light and some solar heat for a typical room 14 to 16 feet deep; however, spaces beyond this do not benefit from the windows. Likewise, with all openings on a single wall, there is no outlet to permit natural ventilation.

A relatively simple means of providing more light to the north side of the house is to slope the roof, resulting in a higher south wall with more glazing (fig. 2-37). A taller south window wall will require larger shading devices (overhangs, trellises, or awnings) to reduce summer heat gain. The scale of the shading devices can be reduced by placing two of them on the wall as shown in the illustration. Although some air flow may be induced by opening higher windows, this approach is unlikely to be effective in providing good ventilation.

A common solution for providing natural light is to place a skylight over the rear or north area of the house. A flat skylight is not considered desirable

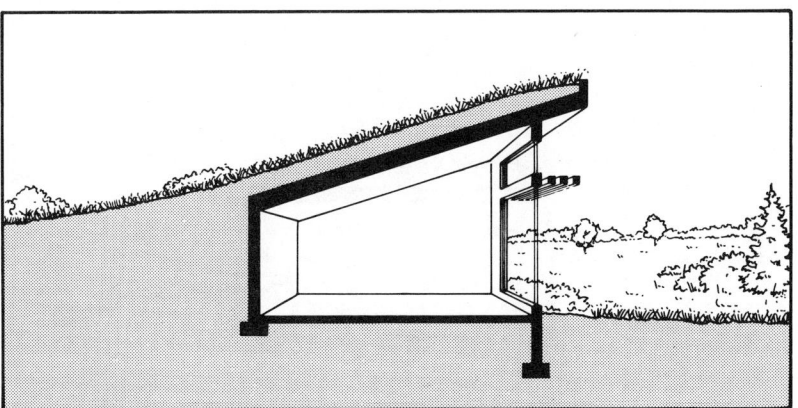

2-37: Sloped Roof Provides Increased Natural Light

from an energy standpoint, since excess solar gain is permitted in summer while winter solar gain is minimized. Vertical glazing as shown in figure 2-38 is better if designed for the appropriate sun angles. Insulating covers or shades over such skylights are advisable since the warm air will rise to this area at night, and heat loss will increase. If skylight or clerestory windows are openable, ventilation results from the stack effect of warm air rising. To provide adequate ventilation in some cases, either a wind-driven ventilator or a ventilating fan in the skylight structure may be necessary.

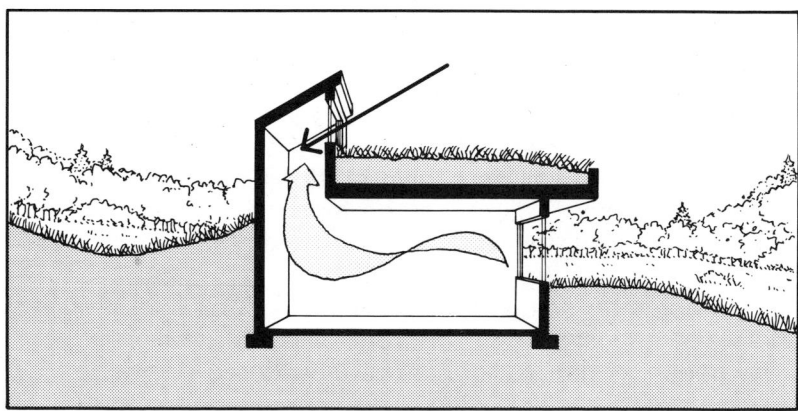

2-38: Operating Skylight Provides Natural Light and Ventilation

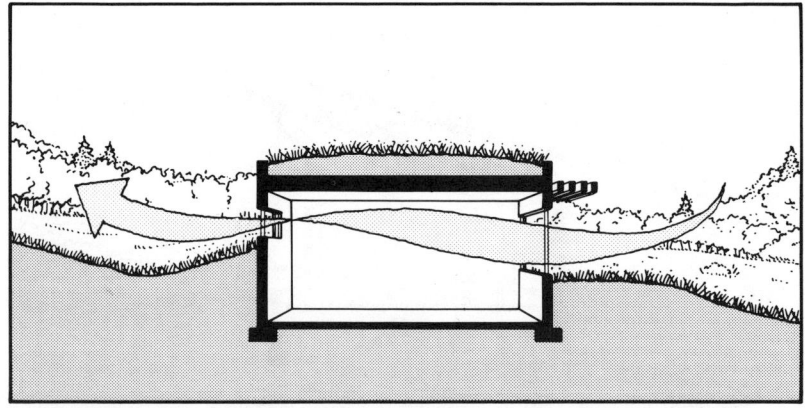

2-39: Windows on North Side Provide Light and Ventilation

Another means of providing natural light to the north side of an elevational design is to reduce the earth berm to permit periodic or continuous vertical windows in the north wall (fig. 2-39). Since no solar heat gain is possible, window sizes should be limited. Light from north-facing windows does not have the glare problems that can occur with south-facing glass, and cross-ventilation can be easily achieved. Openings on the north side create a visible edge on that side of the house resulting in an image different from a completely subsurface design. One disadvantage is that the north-facing windows are exposed to winter winds, making the use of windbreaks a desirable strategy. Vegetation should be placed far enough from the house to prevent interference with summer ventilation.

Entry and Garage Location

One very important concern with earth sheltered design is the means of entry to the house. The entry is often a focal point for building designs, but it has a particular significance in earth sheltered structures because some people have negative reactions to going underground. A properly designed entry can alleviate these misconceptions. An entry should be obvious to a visitor from the outside and, once entered, should be light and spacious and not require an excessive number of steps to arrive at the main living level.

The entry to a house is usually related to vehicular access and the garage. In an earth sheltered design, the garage could be made part of the earth-covered structure, or it could be placed above grade, perhaps connected to the entry. An earth sheltered garage may blend well into the overall design, but its construction cost may be higher than for a typical garage. Both entry and garage location affect the image and privacy of a house.

For an elevational design in colder climates, placing the entrance in the exposed south facade is usually the simplest approach. Entrance can occur at grade, and the appearance is very conventional (fig. 2-40). The entrance to the Hadley House shown at the beginning of this section (fig. 2-25) is in the center of the south wall; the detached garage is located further downhill to the south. If an attached garage is desired, it is often placed at the east or west end of the house, forming a part of the earth-covered structure (fig. 2-41). One problem with this central southern entrance is the conflict that may result between the public nature of an entry area and the private nature of outdoor spaces adjacent to the windows. Careful landscaping and locating the entry near one end of the south wall may alleviate this to some extent. Another approach is to create a link between garage and house that divides the south yard into a public entry and private side (fig. 2-42).

Placing the main entrance on the east or west end of an elevational house is another solution (fig. 2-43). This approach is demonstrated in the Winston House in Lyme, New Hampshire (see chapter 7). The entry area on the end of the house is separated from the private outdoor spaces to the south. Entering a house from the end can extend the internal circulation of the house somewhat. Exposing the ends of the house reduces earth cover, but the berm along the north wall is maintained for wind protection.

On some sites the entrance to an elevational house must be placed on the north side (fig. 2-44). An entrance on the north side of an earth sheltered house can create an image very distinct from the fully exposed south elevation (see Solaria in chapter 7). Another alternative is to place an above-grade garage on the north side linked to the house by an entry structure (fig. 2-45). An entrance on the north side clearly separates the public entry area and private outdoor areas of the house. On the other

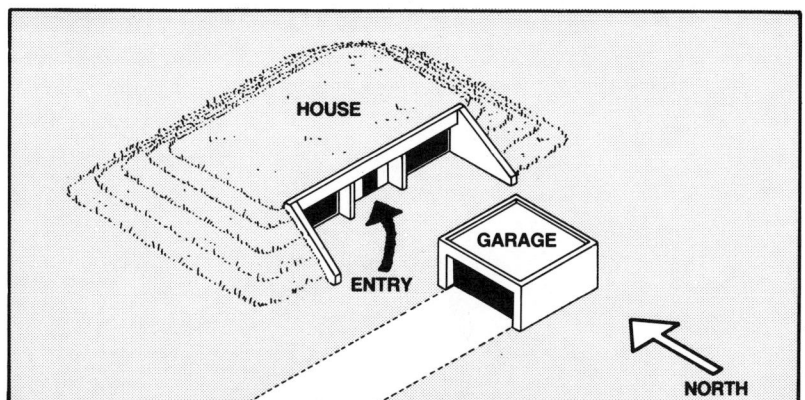

2-40: Entry and Detached Garage on South Side

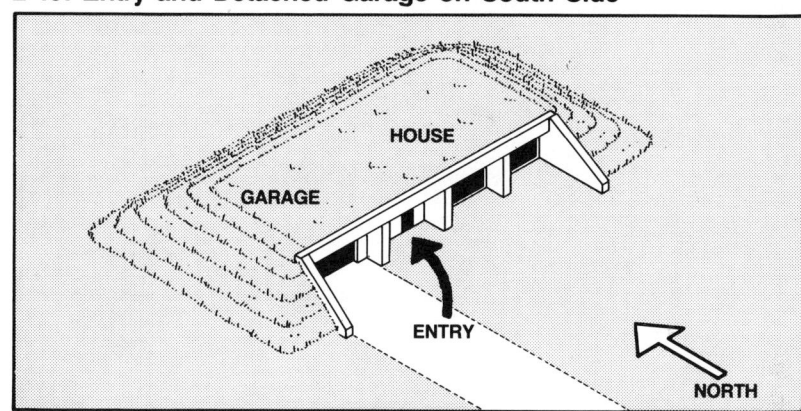

2-41: Entry on South Side with Attached Garage

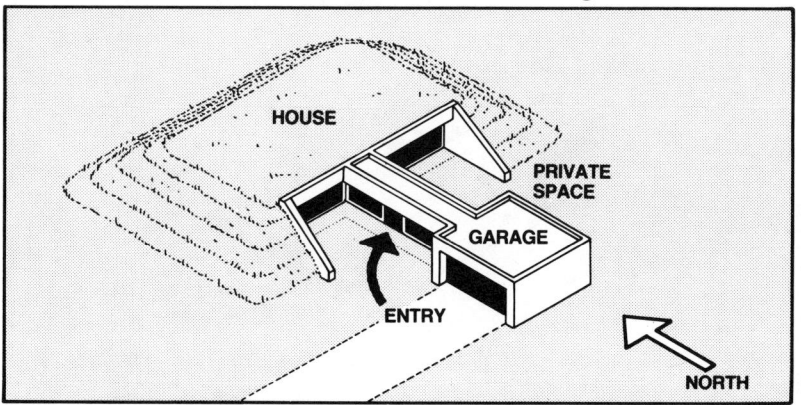

2-42: Garage Linked to House on South Side

45

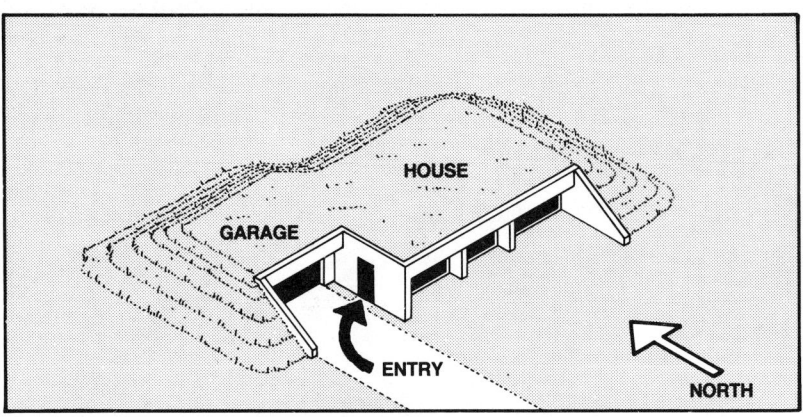
2-43: Entry on West Side with Attached Garage

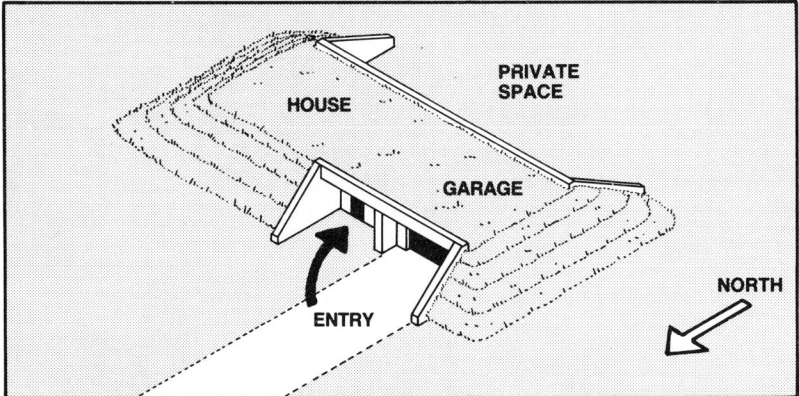
2-44: Entry on North Side with Attached Garage

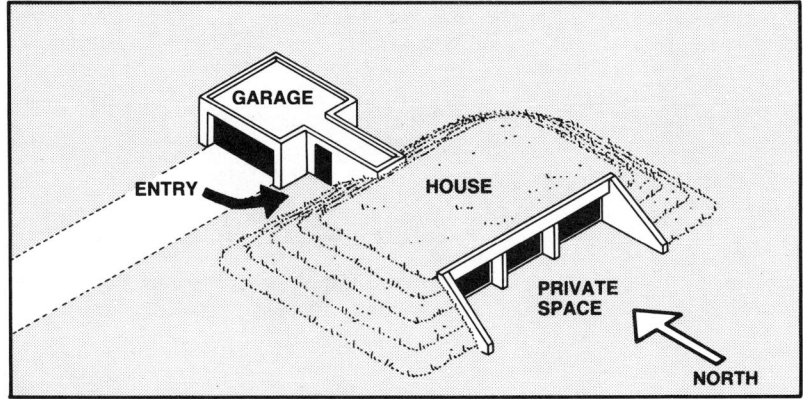
2-45: Garage Linked to House on North Side

hand, the wind protection effectiveness of the earth berm on the north side of the house may be reduced.

In all of the preceding examples window and entrance orientation is discussed in reference to cooler climates where winter heating concerns predominate. In warmer climates the layout problems of entrance, garage, and outdoor space would be similar for an elevational design but orientation toward sun and winds would differ.

Typical Design Approaches: The Atrium Concept

Based on traditional forms of housing throughout the world, the atrium concept is a major alternative design approach for earth sheltered housing. One of the earliest examples of a completely underground house in the United States is the Ecology House built in 1973 (see figs. 2-46, 2-47, and chapter 7). Placed completely below grade on a flat site, all major living spaces in the small house surround a central outdoor courtyard. Sliding glass doors separate the interior spaces from the courtyard, providing light, view, and access. The house is entered by descending a stairway from ground level to the atrium level. The exterior image of the house is extremely unobtrusive—except for the courtyard railings and solar collectors above grade, it barely interrupts the natural landscape. The atrium represents a very private outdoor space with a carefully controlled exterior view from the interior of the house. Such an approach may be ideal on sites with no good exterior views, in dense developments, and on sites adjacent to noisy or otherwise negative land uses.

An earth sheltered house designed around a central atrium can be an appropriate solution in many climate regions, although there are energy-related trade offs compared to an elevational approach. Clearly a completely below-grade design such as the Ecology House is significantly protected from winter winds and maximizes the benefits of

2-46: Ecology House, Massachusetts; John Barnard, architect.

earth contact for both the heating and cooling seasons. These are advantages in the cool and temperate climates of most of the United States. On the other hand, it is more difficult to maximize passive solar energy gain through the windows of an atrium design than through the south facade of an elevational design. To take advantage of solar energy as much as possible, the atrium should be elongated in the east-west direction, and the north-south dimension of the courtyard should be wide enough to permit low-angled winter sun to reach the north wall of the atrium during the middle of the day. In addition, south-facing windows in the atrium should be maximized while east-, west-, and north-facing windows should be minimized if winter heating is a concern.

In colder climates one approach to enhancing

passive solar collection in an atrium design is to place a glass or clear plastic cover over the atrium (fig. 2-48). With this approach some additional heat is provided in winter, and the courtyard may be usable during a longer period of the year. In addition, wind turbulence in the atrium is eliminated, and snow and falling leaves do not have to be removed. A glass-covered atrium should be carefully considered, however, since the cost may be relatively high, the additional solar heat gained may not be that significant, and there will be a tendency to overheat in the summer. If a cover is desired, ventilation and perhaps shading for summer may be essential. Another problem is that once an atrium is covered, it is no longer regarded as outdoor space and the surrounding rooms may not be in compliance with building code requirements for exterior windows (see chapter 6).

In warmer climates where capturing solar radiation is of less concern, the atrium concept can be an excellent approach. In hot, arid climates, atriums are protected from hot, dry winds during the day, and cool air settles in the courtyard at night. In hot, humid climates, ventilation is often one of the best passive cooling strategies. A simple atrium design is not ideal for natural ventilation but can be acceptable if additional outlets and openings are created in the roof and exterior walls of the structure.

The atrium plan was developed for warm climates, and the courtyard itself was used for circulation. Some earth sheltered houses have been developed along these lines in warmer parts of the United States, such as the Bordie residence in Austin, Texas, shown in figure 2-49 and chapter 7. In most of the United States, however, access to all spaces in the house without going outside the building is necessary. One simple alternative is to cover the atrium and create an interior courtyard surrounded by the living spaces. In this case, as previously discussed, the spaces do not open

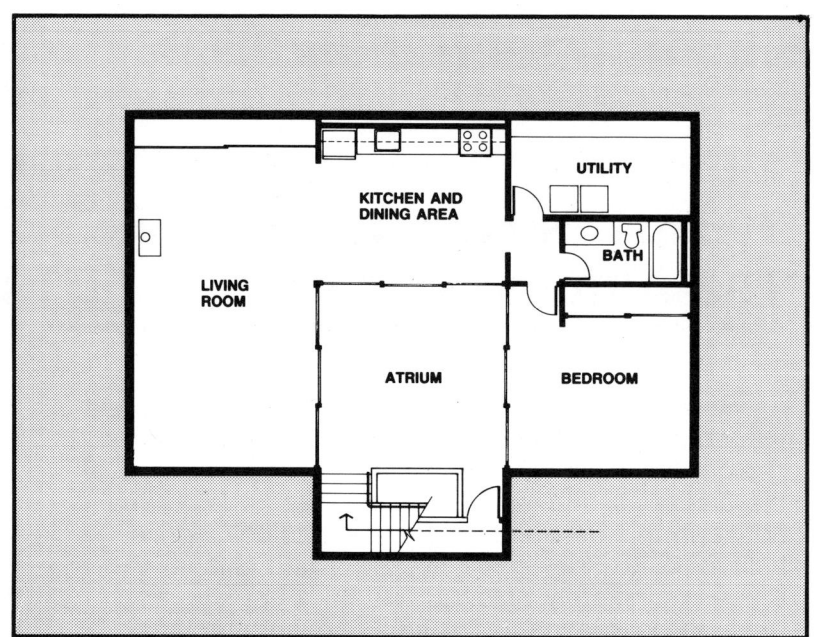

2-47: Plan of Ecology House, Osterville, Massachusetts

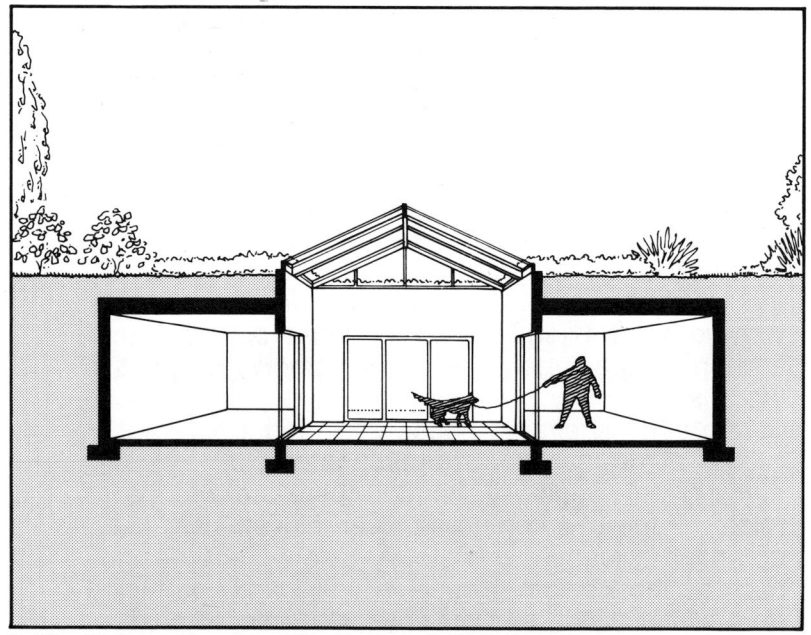

2-48: Atrium House with Covered Courtyard

directly to the outdoors and so may require a code variance. Internal circulation to spaces around a courtyard can be provided around the perimeter of the plan so that all spaces have a clear view to the courtyard, but this results in circulation corridors that are too long and inconvenient to be justified in a residence. The other alternative is circulation around the court itself, which reduces the corridor to an acceptable length. The circulation must now, however, pass between the spaces and the courtyard. It is acceptable to pass through open spaces such as a living, dining, or even kitchen area in this manner, but private spaces such as bedrooms cannot be used as corridors nor can they be cut off from windows without violating present building codes.

This problem of internal circulation in an atrium type of plan basically results from size and building code requirements for windows. A limited-size single atrium is a valid plan, as shown in the one-bedroom house in figure 2-47, where circulation only occurs through the dining area. With a larger program, the simple atrium idea must be modified in order to provide a compact, efficient plan with adequate window openings to all the required spaces. Some alternatives are the use of two or more atriums, additional window openings through the earth berms, or a two-level design. Some of these approaches are illustrated later in this section. Another alternative is a modification of present building codes so that an outside window is not required in a bedroom as long as adequate ventilation, light, and means of escape are provided.

Flat Sites

A typical simple atrium design with all windows facing an interior courtyard is well suited to a flat site. If the house is fully recessed below existing grade as demonstrated by the Ecology House, the mass and extent of the building are not obvious (fig. 2-50). The existing surface extends over the house, making the rooftop part of the outdoor space. This can result in more efficient land use in some cases. Since no land is devoted to earth berms, the lot size can be minimized, and it may be possible to build below grade space beyond the normal setback limitations if approved by local officials. Access to a structure a full level below grade by descending a staircase is not as direct or convenient as entering at grade. Another drawback is that unless excavated material can be placed elsewhere on the site, it may have to be hauled away. Drainage and groundwater may present problems on some sites for a fully recessed atrium design. Care should be taken not to drain any surface water into the atrium, and the atrium must be provided with drainage to a sump if an outfall is not available.

Another approach on a flat site is a

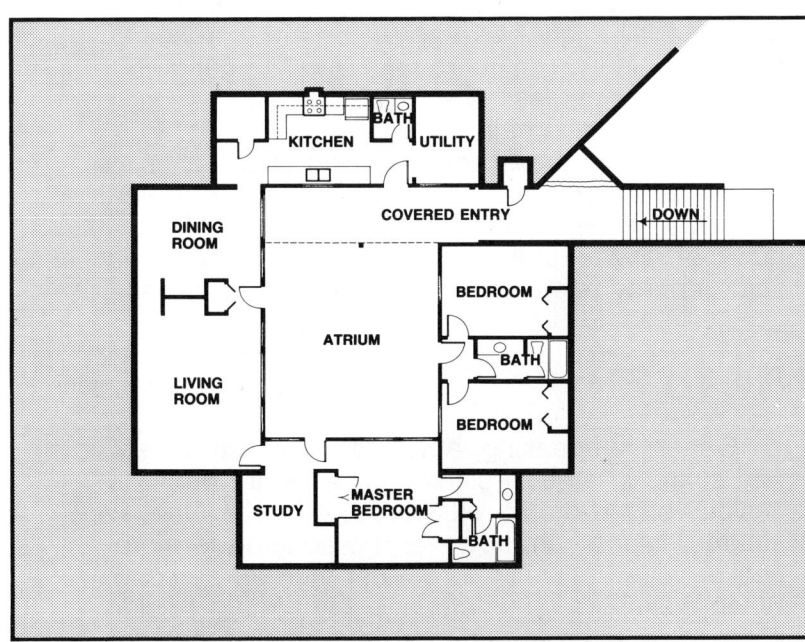

2-49: Plan of Bordie Residence, Austin, Texas

2-50: Fully Recessed Atrium House on Flat Site

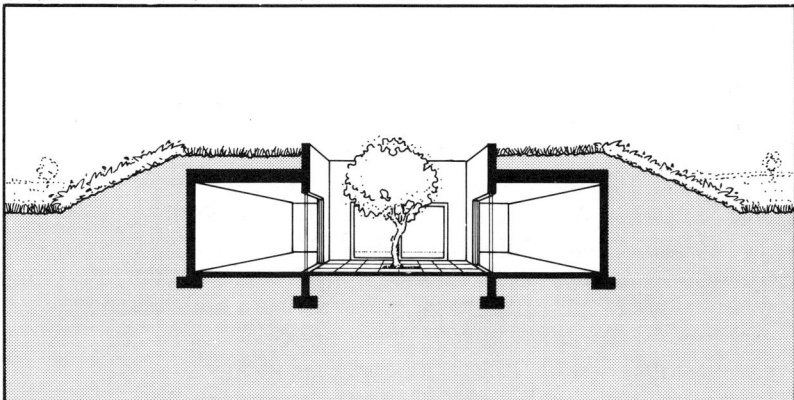

2-51: Partially Recessed Atrium House on Flat Site

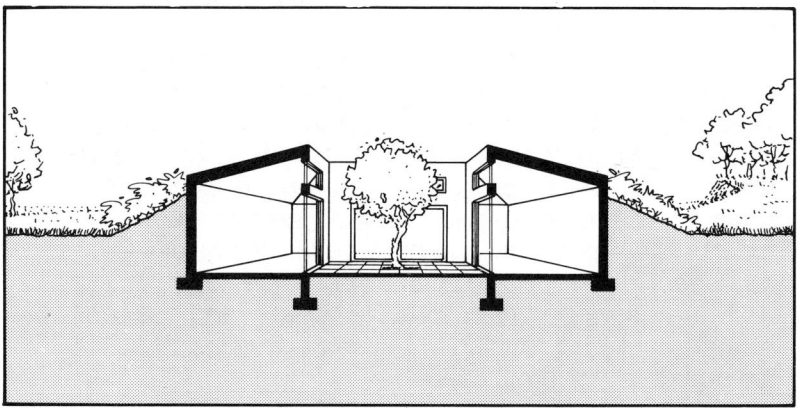

2-52: Earth-Bermed Atrium House with Conventional Roof

semirecessed design where the floor is a half-level below grade and the structure is surrounded by earth berms (fig. 2-51). The main advantages to this approach are that cut and fill can be balanced more easily, and surface runoff will drain away from the courtyard and the building. By not placing the floor level as deep, groundwater is less likely to present problems. Access to a shallower structure by using a few stairs or a ramp is simplified as well. An entrance can occur through an exterior penetration in the berm as it does in the Bordie Residence. The presence of berms rising from the surface change the character of the house and may require a larger lot size. The original flat surface no longer extends over the structure, making the lot less useful for certain purposes. Well-landscaped berms, however, may be preferable in creating a barrier to outsiders and a definite, but natural, image.

It is also possible to place an atrium design on existing grade with large earth berms around it. Although entry and drainage may be improved, additional fill might be required, and the larger berms would occupy more land area. In general, this approach seems less desirable than the semirecessed alternative.

With any of these atrium design approaches, a conventional roof could be used instead of an earth-covered one (fig. 2-52). Costs could be reduced however, the natural image, usable roof space, and some energy related benefits would be sacrificed.

Sloping Sites

Generally speaking, atrium designs are not as well suited to steeply sloping sites as are house designs based on the elevational concept. One-level atrium designs can, however, be adapted to more gentle slopes (usually no greater than 20 percent). When building a basic atrium design into a hillside, it is natural to create an open atrium as shown in figure 2-53. By opening the courtyard on one side, the enclosed feeling is maintained but more extended views to the exterior are possible. Surface runoff from the hillside should not be directed to the courtyard. A swale on the uphill side of the house can be used to divert water around the structure as shown.

On a sloping site, it is also natural to expose the exterior wall of the house on the downhill side much like an elevational design (fig. 2-54). On a south-facing slope, solar energy can be collected through both the exposed window wall and the courtyard windows. By exposing a portion of the exterior wall, some of the circulation problems inherent in atrium designs can be resolved. Generally, this approach results in a house with many of the same image, access, and exterior view characteristics as a typical elevational design.

Entry and Garage Location

As in the elevational designs discussed in the previous section, the entry and garage location for an atrium design influence the image, privacy, and use of outdoor space on the site. One major difference between the two design concepts is that an atrium house already includes a major private outdoor space within the building perimeter. In its simplest form, such as the Ecology House (fig. 2-46), the atrium is the only opening to the surface and must serve as the entrance. Descending a flight of stairs to enter may tend to reinforce negative images of going underground. In addition, the privacy of the courtyard is reduced because outsiders must enter the house through this space. If a garage is required, it would most likely be a detached above-grade structure on a flat site.

On a relatively small flat site, some of the drawbacks mentioned above could be alleviated with an above-grade entry and garage structure directly

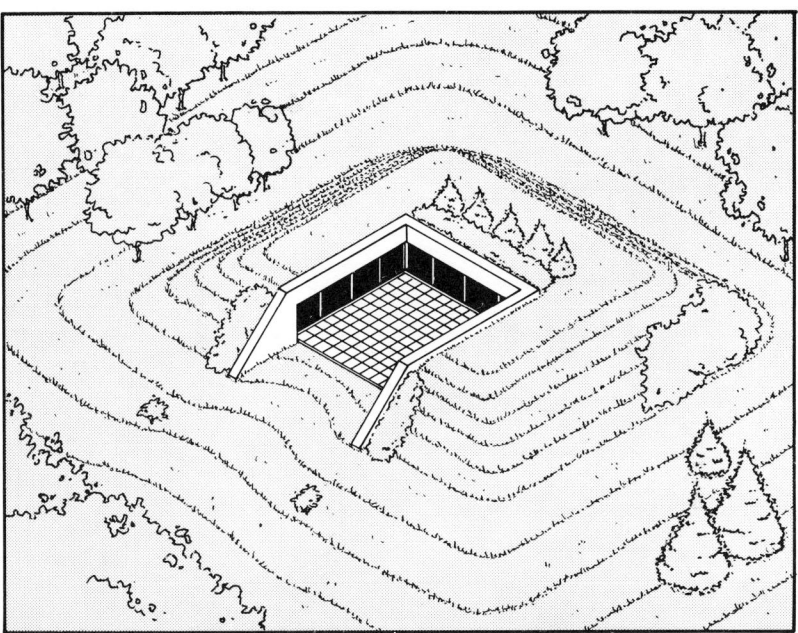

2-53: Atrium House with Open-Ended Courtyard

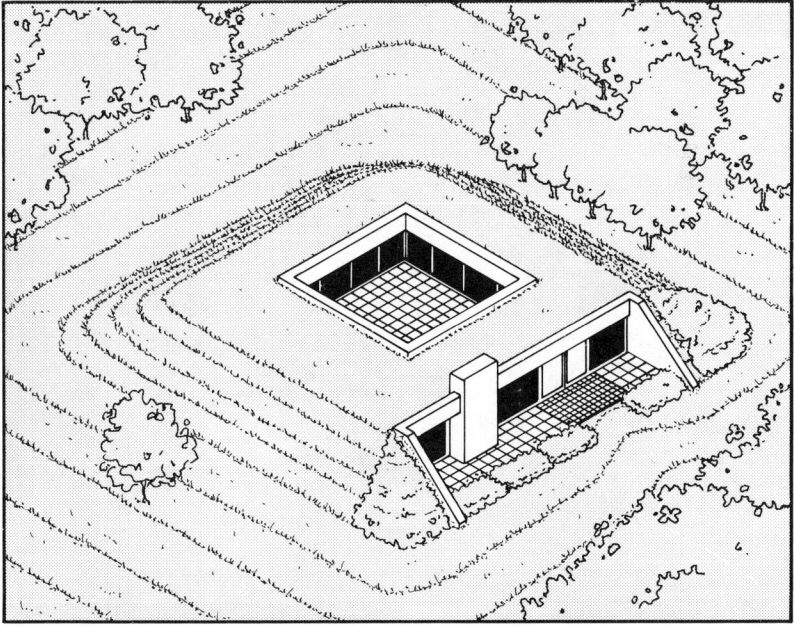

2-54: Atrium House with One Exposed Elevation

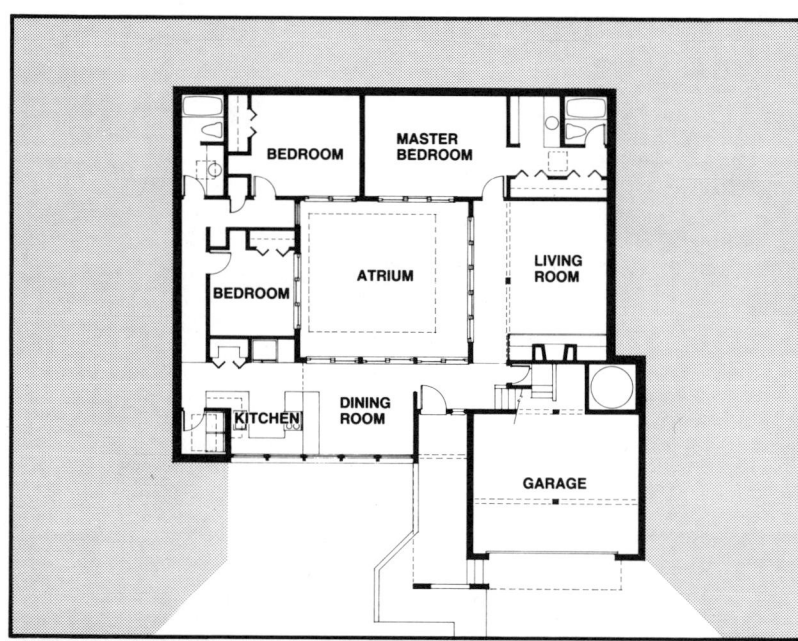

2-55: Plan of Clark House, Portland, Oregon

over part of the house. Placing this mass on the north side of the atrium would not interfere with sunlight reaching the courtyard. The above-grade structure would divide the site into public and private sides, and a conventional image and entry would be presented on the street side. Of course, the unobtrusive qualities of the completely below grade design would be compromised by resolving the access problem in this manner.

A range of options exist to provide a relatively conventional entry to atrium designs located on sloping sites or bermed structures on flat sites. Openings can be created in the earth berms surrounding a structure to provide access from the outside. For example, in the Bordie residence (fig. 2-49), one is led on a walkway through an opening in the berm to the interior courtyard. Entering the private courtyard in this manner is similar to entering a conventional house and there are few stairs to descend diminishing any negative associations with going underground. In a similar approach, an open-ended atrium could be entered directly from the outside (fig. 2-53). A design incorporating two courtyards could use one as public entry space and the other as a more private outdoor space.

One of the simplest options is to expose a portion of the exterior wall to provide an entrance. The Clark house in Portland, Oregon, uses this strategy effectively on a hilly site (figs. 2-55 and 2-56). In this case the house has a conventional relationship to the street, and the garage is integrated into the earth-covered design. This house also serves as an excellent example of a well-organized plan for a larger atrium house.

2-56: Clark House, Portland, Oregon; Norm Clark, architect.

Multiple-Unit Design Considerations

Much of the interest in individual earth sheltered houses as an alternative to conventional dwellings has led to a growing interest in multiple-unit developments utilizing these structures. In fact, some of the benefits of earth sheltered housing can be realized more completely with multiple-unit developments while some additional advantages are also created. Complete integration of buildings with the landscape can occur on a neighborhood scale with positive aesthetic effects. This also resolves the problem of earth sheltered buildings sometimes being incompatible in appearance with conventional houses. In addition, the environmental benefits attributed to increasing vegetation while reducing hard surfaces (one characteristic of an underground building) are more completely achieved when applied consistently to a large development area. Creation of earth berms and surface drainage patterns can require large lots for single earth sheltered houses. In a multiple-unit development, drainage systems and landforms can be coordinated more effectively, thus using land more efficiently. Also, opportunities exist to develop a wide range of energy conservation strategies at the neighborhood scale in addition to the energy efficiency of individual dwelling units.

In this context multiple-unit development refers to projects encompassing series of detached units on individual sites as well as attached multiple-unit buildings. Attached units generally have the

2-57: Seward Town Houses, Minneapolis, Minnesota; Michael Dunn, Close Associates, architect.

additional advantages of reducing construction costs and increased energy efficiency because of the common walls between units. Also, densities can be increased, resulting in more efficient land use as well as more potential for flexibility and variety in design.

Suitable Applications

Although earth sheltered design approaches are appropriate in a wide variety of situations, multiple-unit developments of earth sheltered housing are particularly suitable under certain conditions. The first is a site adjacent to other land uses that are particularly noisy or visually undesirable, such as a

2-58: Architerra Housing System, Valbonne, France; Henri Vidal, Yves Bayard, Architerra, Inc., architects.

freeway or a manufacturing facility. Such land is generally unacceptable for housing and is left underutilized with reduced value. A properly designed earth-integrated project can buffer housing units from the undesirable noise and views, resulting in more efficient land use. An example of this type of development is the Seward town house project in Minneapolis, Minnesota (fig. 2-57). The twelve-unit project is isolated from the freeway to the north by a large earth berm and earth cover on the roof.

Earth sheltering also allows project development on relatively steep slopes (30 to 50 percent). Often slopes greater than 20 percent are considered unbuildable for conventional housing development. Assuming access can be provided and the soil is suitable, earth sheltered units set into a steep hillside can be built at relatively high densities. In areas where preserving flat areas for agriculture is a goal, using hillsides for housing construction is an asset. In Europe, large multiple-unit developments have been built on steep slopes using a reinforced earth retaining system (see fig. 2-58).

Site Planning Considerations

In order to use a development site efficiently, earth sheltered and solar housing units are likely to require different lot sizes, shapes, and setbacks than are typically associated with conventional housing. This can create significant obstacles to development unless a Planned Unit Development (PUD) approach is employed. Although subject to the approval of local officials, such an approach provides an established method to alter conventional zoning standards within a total development, resulting in greater design flexibility.

Generally, site planning for earth sheltered and solar housing units is more complex than for conventional housing. Requirements must still be met for efficient roads and utilities, a desirable image, and maximum densities while providing community amenities. But, in addition, houses must be spaced so that sunlight is not blocked, and earth berms and drainage must be designed so land can be used efficiently. Unlike conventional housing, densities and layouts of earth sheltered units may change dramatically with changes in the slope and orientation of the land. In the remainder of this section, both elevational and atrium units are shown in multiple-unit configurations as a means of raising a few key design issues. The illustrations and information in this section have been selected from *Earth Sheltered Community Design: Energy-Efficient Residential Development* [Sterling, et al., 1981].

Multiple-Unit Elevational Designs

A prototypical elevational design on an individual lot could simply be repeated on a series of lots as shown in figure 2-59. In this case 80-foot by 25-foot units on one level with attached garages are entered from the north or south side depending on their relationship to the street. The major window openings in each unit face directly south, and the lots are elongated in the east-west direction, reflecting the shape of the houses. Disadvantages of this arrangement are that individual earth berms around each house occupy a large land area, and there is no overall design of the landforms—only a series of separate berms. Extending berms across lot lines would result in a more unified appearance, and the space between houses could be reduced. On sloping sites where berms are not created, this is less of a concern.

Land can be used more efficiently and construction simplified if the earth sheltered units are attached. Essentially the same prototypical units as in the previous example are shown in two attached four-unit clusters in figure 2-60. Landforms and drainage are further simplified compared to the detached units shown in figure 2-59. Although land-use efficiency is improved, this arrangement does not approach the densities possible with more conventional town house developments commonly built with two- or three-level units.

Both of the site plans for elevational units (figs. 2-59 and 2-60) reflect the lot sizes required on a flat site. One of the most important aspects of utilizing elevational units is that the density changes significantly with changes in topography. Figures 2-61 through 2-64 illustrate elevational units on several different slope conditions; the maximum densities are summarized in figure 2-67. On the flat site in figure 2-61, detached units could be built at a density of 2.4 units per acre, while the maximum density for attached elevational units would be 3.7

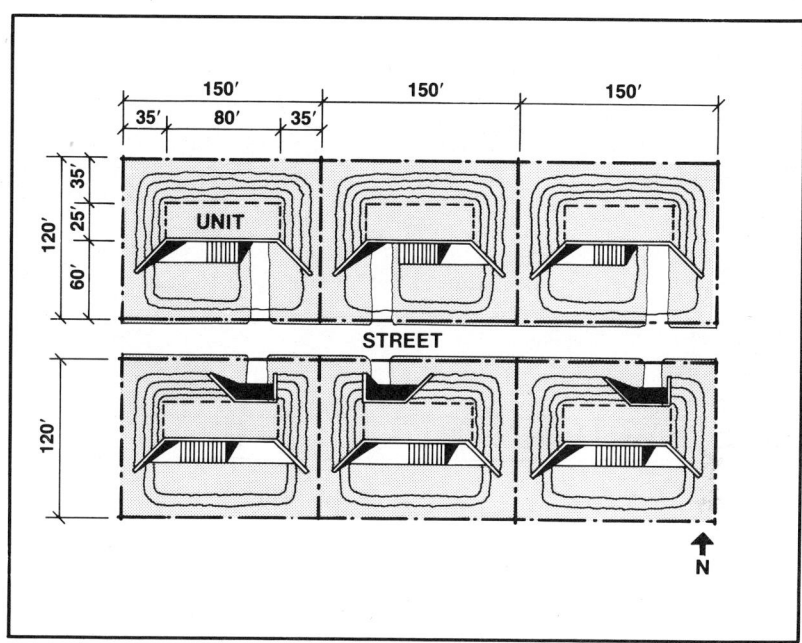

2-59: Detached Elevational Units on Flat Site

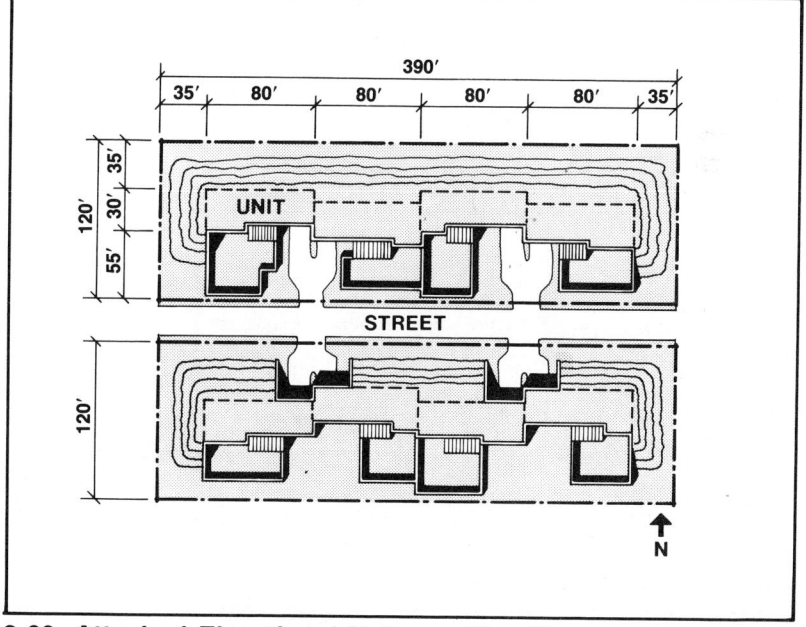

2-60: Attached Elevational Units on Flat Site

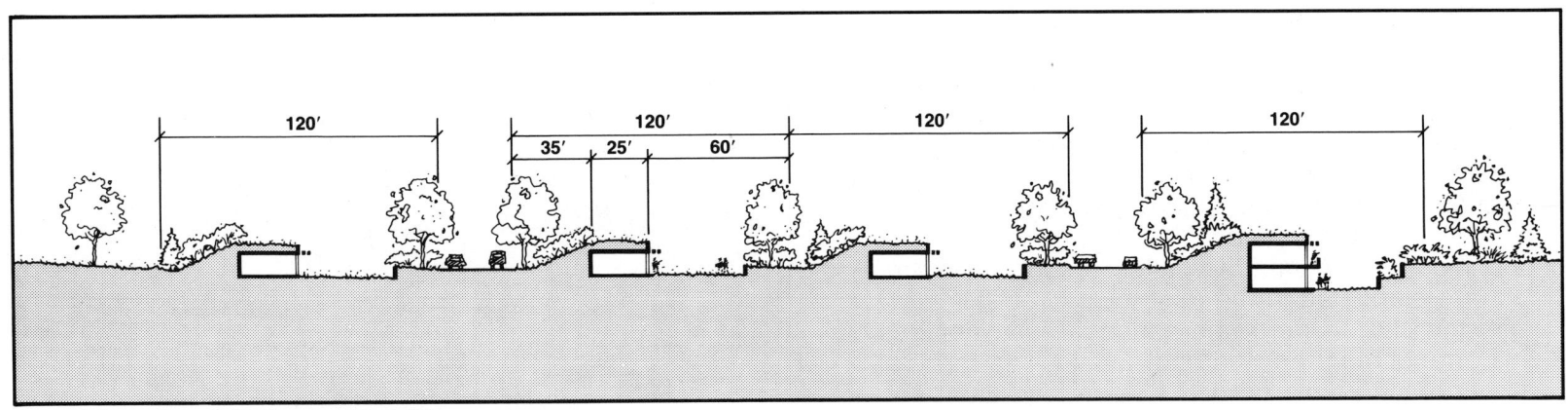

2-61: Elevational Units on Flat Site

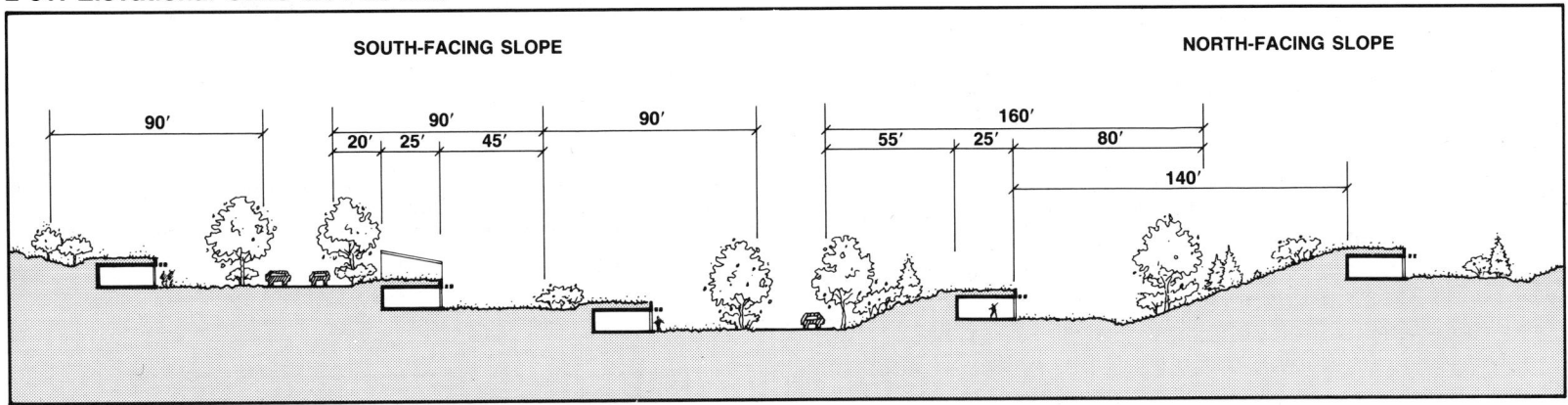

2-62: Elevational Units on Site with 10 Percent Slope

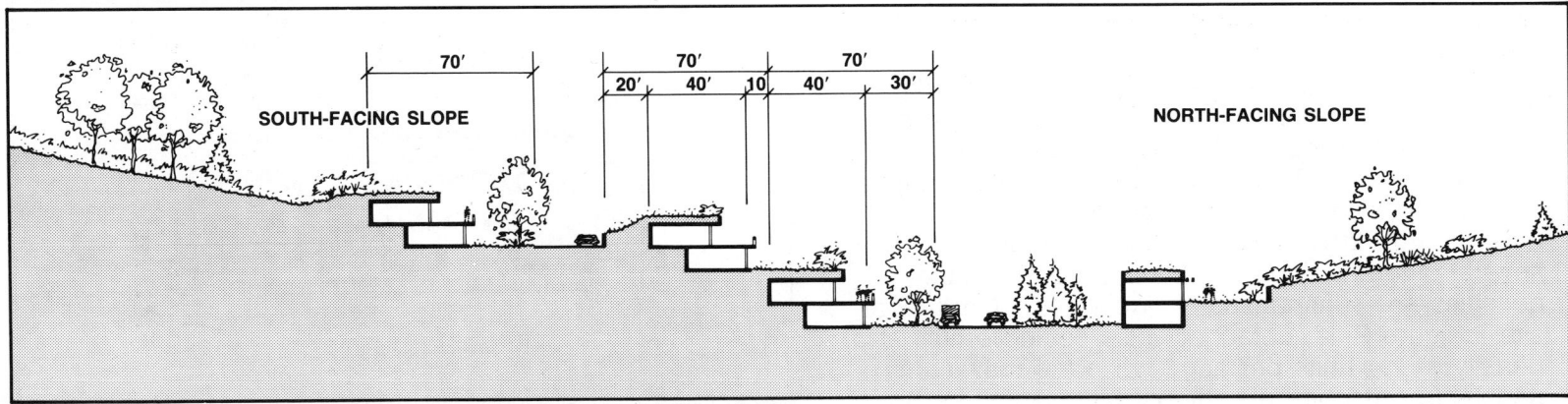

2-63: Elevational Units on Site with 20 Percent Slope

units per acre. These figures are based on the prototypical unit described previously and do not include land for streets or common areas. These relatively low densities are attributable to land required for earth berms and spacing of units for maximum solar access.

Densities can be increased by building on a 10 percent south-facing slope, but are decreased if the slope faces north. As shown in figure 2-62, the closer spacing on the south-facing slope results in densities approximately 50 percent greater than on the flat site. On the north-facing slope, however, the maximum densities are 30 to 40 percent less than for the flat site because of the greater spacing required to provide solar access.

On a 20 percent south-facing slope, maximum densities can be increased significantly to 6.9 units per acre for detached elevational units and 9.5 units per acre for attached units (fig. 2-63). On a 20 percent slope, a two-level unit is preferable to enable the buildings to fit into the form of the land. The two-level unit further helps to increase land-use efficiency.

A 20 percent slope appears to be nearly the greatest slope for a large-scale development of units with attached garages and vehicular access to each unit, unless extensive retaining walls are built. If garage structures or parking areas are separated from the units, it becomes possible to develop attached rows of units at higher densities on hillsides with slopes up to 50 percent (fig. 2-64). Densities of 30 units per acre appear possible if access and soil conditions are appropriate. The extent of this type of development is limited by the means of reaching units in the middle of the slope. Unless elevators on sloping tracks are used, people would not find it acceptable to ascend or descend more than three levels from a parking area.

Multiple-Unit Atrium Designs

A prototypical atrium design can be applied to a series of individual lots much like the elevational design in the previous section. Arranged around a single courtyard in each unit, six atrium houses with attached garages are shown in figure 2-65. In this case the units are only partially recessed on a flat site; earth berms surround the building perimeter except for the one opening providing an entrance. Relatively large lots are required for this type of development, and use of landforms and site drainage are not coordinated overall.

A much more appealing approach from an aesthetic viewpoint is illustrated in figure 2-66. Attached units are clustered around a parking area, resulting in a coordinated landscape design with more varied and interesting spaces. Attaching the units also permits the land to be used more efficiently, enabling densities to be increased. Part of

2-64: Elevational Units on Site with 50 Percent Slope

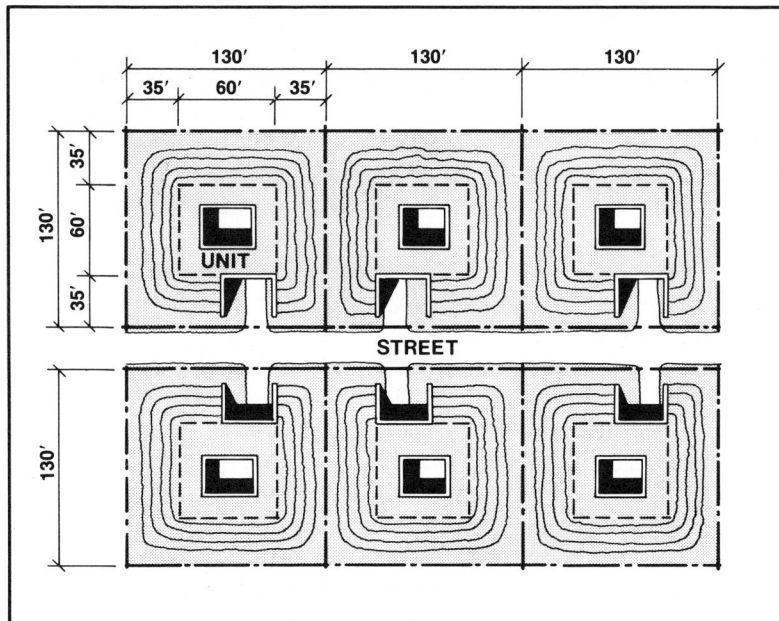

2-65: Detached Atrium Units on Flat Site

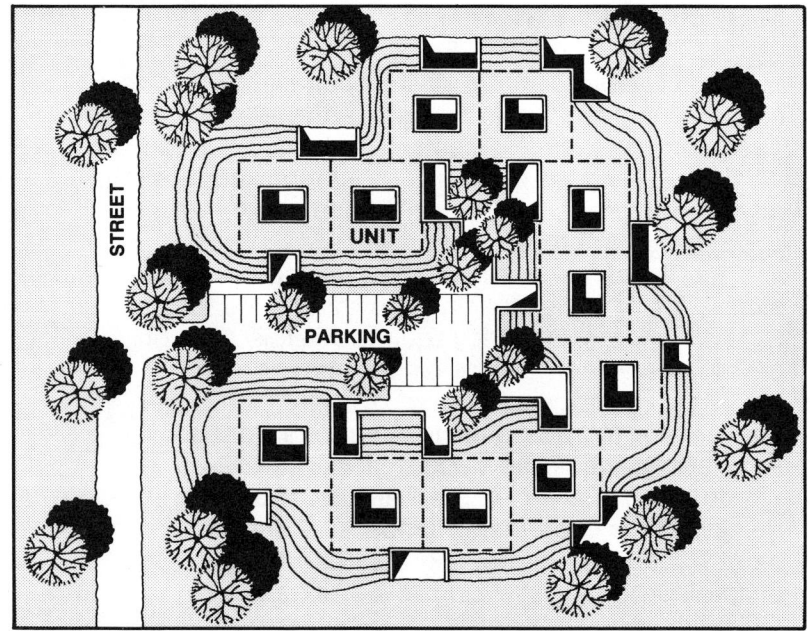

2-66: Attached Atrium Units on Flat Site

the flexibility and efficiency of this plan is attributable to eliminating an attached garage for each unit.

Generally, atrium designs offer opportunities on flat or gently sloping sites. They are particularly suitable in situations where private outdoor spaces are desirable and isolation from surrounding noise and views is sought. Solar orientation is not a dominant factor in arranging layouts for atrium designs. Gentle slopes (up to 20 percent) oriented in any direction are acceptable sites, but opportunities for higher densities on steep slopes are associated only with elevational designs, not with the atrium approach.

Density Comparisons

Densities for earth sheltered elevational designs under various conditions are summarized in figure 2-67. Compared to conventional housing, the maximum densities estimated for elevational designs utilizing solar energy are generally lower on flat and gently sloping sites but increase dramatically on slopes of 20 to 50 percent. The maximum densities on flat land (four to five units per acre) are not so low as to deter development, but it simply is not possible to increase densities beyond this amount without reducing availability of sunlight to each unit. Densities of ten to thirty units per acre for attached units on steeper slopes are relatively high; moreover, conventional housing often cannot be built on such land at all.

Maximum densities tend to be lower for multiple-unit atrium designs simply because they occupy a larger area. By enclosing the outdoor courtyard within the building perimeter, the layout becomes much less compact than for an elevational or a conventional house.

In comparing densities of conventional and earth sheltered housing, three important points should not be overlooked. Often, the earth-covered rooftops represent usable outdoor space, resulting in larger available yard spaces and possibly more efficient use of land. Also, the feeling of density is less likely to be apparent with partially or fully underground buildings covered by natural landscaping and earth. Finally, all of the density figures discussed in this section are based on generalized housing types of an assumed size and configuration at 40° north latitude; actual designs, site conditions, and the resulting densities may vary considerably from these examples.

Topography	Density (Units/Acre)		
	Detached Units with Garages	Attached 4-unit Clusters with Garages	Attached Units on Hillsides without Garages
10% Slope North-facing	1.5	2.6	—
Flat	2.4	3.7	—
10% Slope South-facing	3.7	5.2	10
20% Slope South-facing	6.9	9.5	15
30% Slope South-facing	—	—	20
50% Slope South-facing	—	—	30

2-67: Densities of Earth Sheltered Housing Units

Source: Earth Sheltered Community Design (Sterling, et al., 1981).

Notes on figure 2-67:

- Density is not gross density—roads, parking and common areas are not included.

- Detached units including garages are 80 feet by 25 feet (2,000 square feet). Land area required includes driveways, berms, and swales so that drainage is contained on each lot.

- Attached units in 4-unit clusters including garages are 80 feet by 25 feet on slopes of 10 percent or less. Attached units in 4-unit clusters including garages are 40 feet by 25 feet on two levels on slopes of 20 percent. In both cases the total unit area with garages is 2,000 square feet. Land area for the four-unit clusters includes driveways and earth berms surrounding the units.

- Attached units on hillsides without garages are 60 feet by 25 feet. Since there is no direct vehicular access or individual garages, actual densities of hillside units will vary depending on the parking arrangements.

- Spacing units for reasonable solar access is based on supplying 90 percent of available solar radiation at 40° north latitude. The same spacing is adequate to supply 85 percent of available solar radiation at 48° north latitude. For more southerly latitudes, closer spacing and higher densities are possible.

Design Considerations for Typical Building Details

For the most part, this chapter has focused on the general factors affecting the form and layout of earth sheltered buildings. While these issues are paramount in the design process, it is often the details of design and construction that make a building energy efficient, attractive, and free from water leakage or structural problems. Many of the key concerns regarding earth sheltered housing design are discussed in detail in chapters 3 through 6. These include insulation placement and materials, drainage, and waterproofing techniques, as well as structural systems and materials. While it is essential to examine each of these areas independently, in a real building design, all of these sometimes conflicting concerns must be integrated into actual construction details. A truly successful design requires the resolution of structural, waterproofing, thermal, landscaping, cost, and aesthetic concerns simultaneously.

In order to develop effective construction details, it is necessary to understand all of the technical issues and problems and then attempt to resolve them. There is no standard or ideal way to design most details—design will depend on the climate, the availability of materials and skilled workers locally, relative costs, and the objectives or priorities of the designer. It is important to remember that, unlike conventional buildings, earth sheltered structures represent a relatively new and emerging technology. In the building industry, the use of new products and details tends to evolve over a period of years, not overnight. Any specific construction details shown throughout this book should not be construed as the final resolution of a particular set of problems.

It is beyond the scope of this book to address all of the construction detail problems inherent in earth sheltered building design. Many of the critical details are illustrated and discussed in other publications, including the *Earth Sheltered Residential Design Manual* [Sterling, et al., 1982]. As a means of illustrating the complexity of construction detail problems, some key details are illustrated and discussed here.

Earth-Covered Roof Edge

One of the most complex and important detail areas in an earth sheltered house is the edge of the earth-covered roof over an exposed wall. One approach is to use a parapet wall that serves to retain the earth on the roof; however, parapets are noted for creating a number of problems unless properly designed. A concrete overhang and parapet structure can increase heat loss considerably if there is no break or separation between the concrete inside the house and that extending outside. In figure 2-68, the concrete parapet is encased in insulation to reduce the heat loss. Another problem is that water tends to collect along the edges of the roof as it freezes, lateral pressure is placed on the retaining wall that might lead to structural cracks and waterproofing failures. To reduce this possibility, the retaining wall must be designed to resist these forces, and the area must be properly drained by using a gravel layer on a sloping surface, assisted by drainpipes, as shown in figure 2-68. Of course, the waterproofing material should be selected to withstand movement and should be designed without seams in this area if possible. In addition, the drainage must be planned in coordination with the landscaping: drying out the roof completely could kill the plant materials. The proper soil must be used to retain an appropriate amount of moisture for the plants selected [Sterling, et al., 1982].

Even if all these concerns are resolved satisfactorily as illustrated in figure 2-68, the appearance of a relatively large parapet wall may not be desirable. If a guardrail is placed above it for safety reasons, it can be the dominant element in the house design while preventing any view of the rooftop plant materials from below. This concern over aesthetics can be resolved to some extent by reducing the parapet wall to a short wooden curb (fig. 2-69). Not only is the scale reduced, but rooftop plant materials are more visible and may hang over the roof edge more easily. Figure 2-69 also illustrates another approach to reducing heat loss through a concrete overhang: rigid insulation is placed between precast concrete plank, providing a thermal break between inside and outside.

Numerous other approaches to detailing the edge of an earth-covered roof have been suggested and successfully built. For example, a wooden roof and overhang structure significantly reduces the heat loss problems inherent with a concrete structure. In fact, overhangs can be eliminated entirely and replaced by freestanding wooden trellises that provide shade and architectural interest. In a similar manner, thermal, structural, and drainage problems associated with parapets can be eliminated entirely if parapets are not used at all. This concept has been suggested by Malcolm Wells, one of the earliest advocates and leading designers of underground structures [Wells, 1977]. Wells has had success in tapering the earth down to the roof edge and covering it with 6 to 12 inches of mulch (see chapter 7). Concern has been expressed over erosion with this detail; however, according to Wells, native plants thrive in this thick layer of mulch, and the plants retain the earth and prevent erosion. This approach provides the best opportunity for making rooftop plants visible from below, creating opportunities to blend the building with the natural landscape more completely.

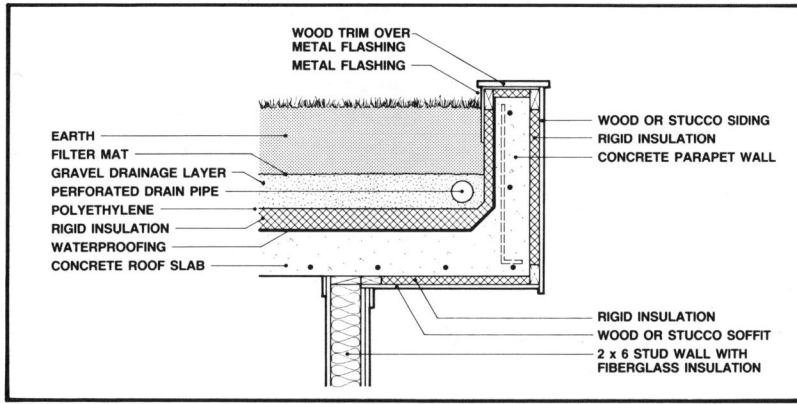

2-68: Earth-Covered Roof Edge Detail

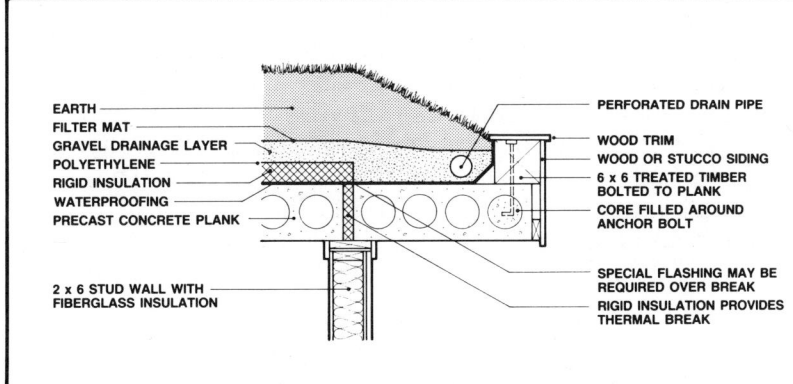

2-69: Earth-Covered Roof Edge Detail

Earth-Bermed Walls

Earth-covered roofs are not the only details deserving special design attention or involving complex interrelationships. Even a simple bermed wall on a house with a conventional roof has unique structural, thermal, waterproofing, and aesthetic

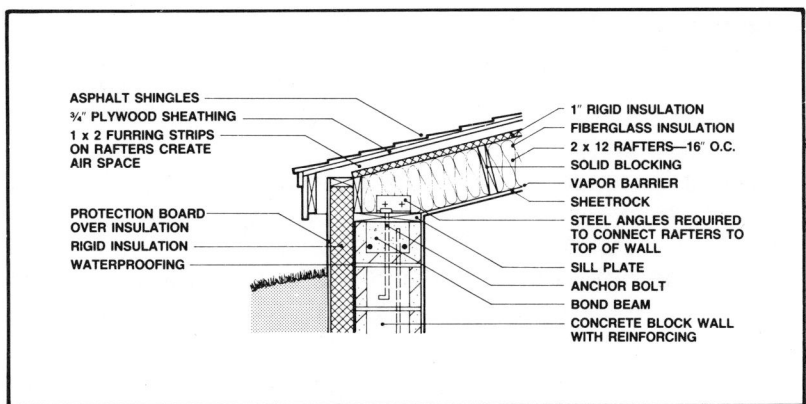

2-70: Earth-Bermed Wall Detail

concerns that must be coordinated. A bermed concrete block wall should be insulated in a cold or temperate climate, with waterproofing applied over the entire surface. As shown in figure 2-70, one approach is to apply rigid insulation to the outside of the wall. The insulation should extend above grade so that no small uninsulated paths for heat loss result. In this case openings along the roof edge permit air to ventilate the space above the roof insulation, reducing condensation and moisture problems. Another approach is to insulate on the inside of the walls: this may have some cost advantages, but the concrete block can no longer be used for thermal storage mass.

Although many basement walls are not reinforced structurally, it is important to examine the structural requirements of a bermed wall. Often the berms are deeper than a typical basement situation, and the lateral forces are unopposed (see chapter 4). The ability of the wall to resist the earth loads may depend not only on reinforcing the block, but on creating a strong connection to the roof. The roof, in turn, should act as a solid diaphrapm to distribute the loads put on it by the walls. In figure 2-70, the reinforced block wall is anchored to a sill plate that is connected to each rafter by steel angles. The two-by-twelve rafters forming the roof are connected by ¾-inch plywood sheathing and soid blocking at 4 feet on center to create an effective diaphragm from the roof structure.

A bermed wall such as this should also be examined from aesthetic and safety viewpoints. If earth begins 1 to 2 feet below the rooftop, the appearance will depend on planting materials on the berm as well as roof and siding materials. It may be desirable to extend an overhang over the berm to create a different visual effect as well as to drain water from the roof to a point further away from the building wall. It is also possible for children to gain access to the roof of a bermed house. It may be desirable to create a barrier at the roof edge or away from the house using building elements, fences, or landscaping materials.

Many other details of a earth sheltered house present concerns similar to the two discussed here—earth-covered roof edges and earth-bermed walls. The most complex problems seem to arise whenever there is a transition between an earth-covered surface and an exposed surface or between the interior and exterior of the house. Typical problem areas include skylights and other penetrations in earth-covered roofs, retaining walls extending from the structure, and foundation walls or partially bermed walls. It is important to emphasize that technical problems should not be resolved to the detriment of the appearance or the functioning of a house. The ultimate acceptability and market value of an earth sheltered house may be strongly linked to the successful use of materials and to integration of the house form with the natural landscape. This overall image is strongly linked to the manner in which construction detail problems are resolved.

Underground village in northern China.
Drawing by Mark Heisterkamp.

Chapter 3

Energy Use,
Insulation Placement,
and
Cost Considerations

Introduction

Reduced energy use for heating and cooling is one major reason often given for building earth sheltered houses. In addition, designing an energy-efficient building is desirable regardless of the motivation for placing the building underground.

The moderate temperatures found in the earth offer opportunities for saving energy in both the heating and cooling seasons in most regions of the world. Simply placing a house partially or completely underground, however, does not automatically save energy nor does it take into account the broader context of using and conserving energy in buildings. The assets of earth integration must be understood so they can be more fully exploited in design and potential drawbacks can be diminished.

Energy-efficient buildings result from the integration of virtually all phases of the design process—site planning, building form and orientation, building envelope design, mechanical system design, and construction details. Moreover, earth integration is seldom used as the single strategy for saving energy but is combined with other complementary approaches. It should also be recognized that understanding the complexities of energy-efficient design and providing accurate and useful information to designers is an evolutionary process.

This chapter consists of eight major sections that are intended to represent the broad range of energy-related issues in earth sheltered design and provide current design information and guidelines. In the first section, the energy conservation potential of the below-grade environment is discussed in an introductory manner. This is followed by a general explanation of the effect of earth integration on heating and cooling. In order to design earth sheltered buildings in response to climate, regional design approaches are discussed in the third section. Optimizing insulation placement is next, followed by parametric studies of roof, wall, and floor components. Energy-related issues such as ventilation, indoor air pollution, and mechanical system design are discussed in the sixth section. In spite of the availability of sophisticated computer simulations, the energy-use performance of earth sheltered houses is best verified by examining actual houses. A selection of energy performance data is presented in the seventh section, together with caveats on the variability and accuracy of such data. Finally, cost information on earth sheltered houses and their cost-effectiveness with respect to energy use is discussed in the last section.

Energy Conservation Potential of the Below-Grade Environment

Characteristics of the Earth

The reason earth sheltered or underground buildings provide unique opportunities for energy conservation is simply that the basic characteristics of the below-grade environment are different than the above-grade climate. Beneath the surface, it is often warmer in winter and cooler in summer than it is above grade. This effect does not occur because the earth is a major source of heat. Relatively little available heat in the ground is geothermal energy conducted to the surface from the higher temperatures deep inside the earth. Nor can the moderate ground climate found in most places be attributed to the insulating value of soil. The R-value of earth is quite low compared to typical insulating materials. At an R-value of 0.16 hr-sq ft-°F/Btu-in for average soil conditions, over 30 inches of soil would be needed to equal the R-value of one inch of polystyrene insulation. It should be noted that the R-value of soil can vary considerably, depending primarily on its moisture content; however, it never can be categorized as a good insulating material.

The characteristics of the ground that create a more moderate environment are its high specific heat capacity and large mass. Often heat must travel along a relatively long path from an underground building to the surface. In a conventional building, heat is lost through a thin exterior skin and that heat is immediately dissipated into the air. Heat lost to the surrounding earth, however, dissipates more gradually into the ground, although a large portion of this heat is eventually transmitted to the surface in near-surface underground buildings. In some cases the heat lost to the soil is not completely lost but is stored and can flow back to the building at a later time if the building interior temperature drops appreciably.

In a similar manner, heat or cold from the surface climate penetrates the ground slowly. The actual heat transfer at the surface is the result of a complex interaction of factors including the air temperature, solar radiation into the earth, nighttime radiation of heat from the earth, and warming and cooling by air movement across the surface, as well

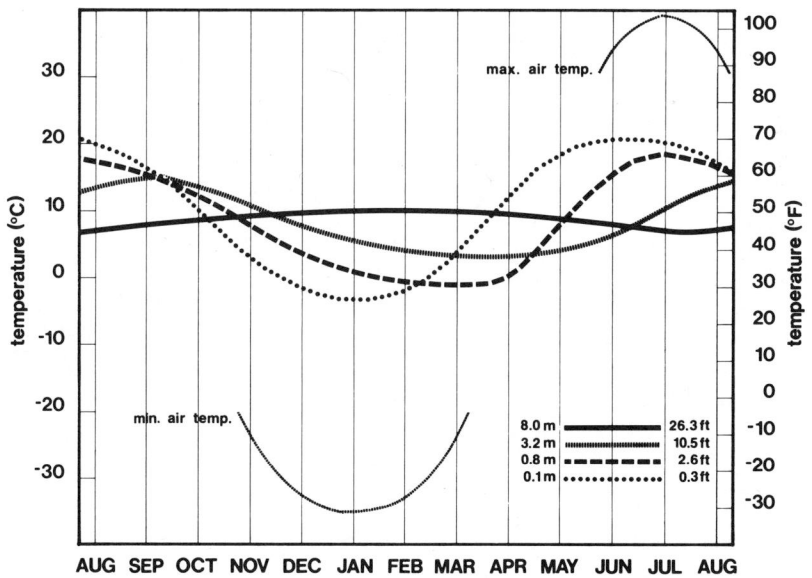

3-1: Annual Temperature Fluctuations—Minneapolis
Source: R. K. Maxwell, 1964 (see references).

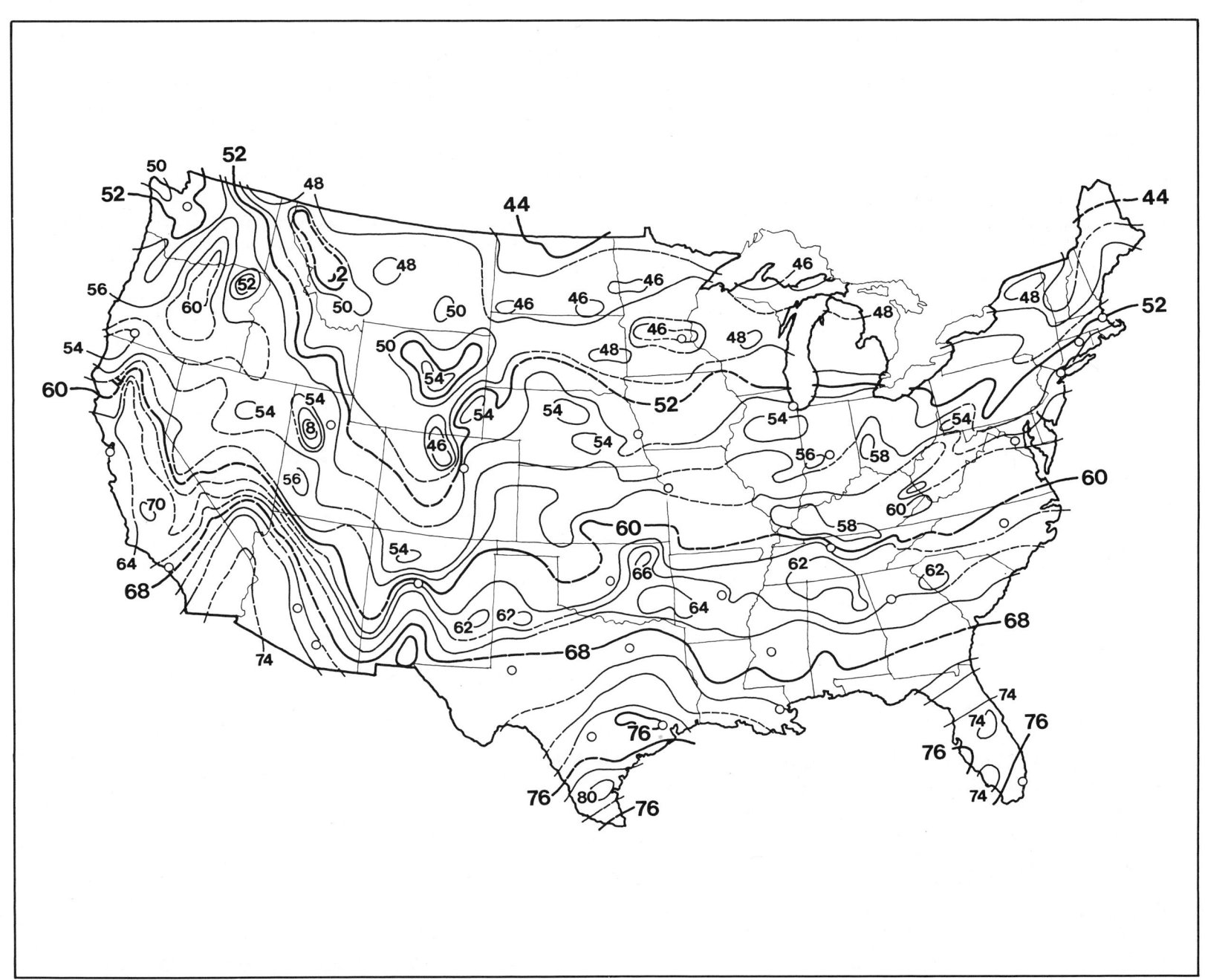

3-2: Deep Ground Temperatures in the United States

Source: Kenneth Labs, 1981 (see references).

as the cooling effect of evaporation from plants and soil. The importance of the surface condition in energy conservation is demonstrated in later sections of this chapter.

Ultimately, the effect produced by the earth is to dampen surface temperature fluctuations, creating a more moderate environment of greater thermal stability. Temperature variation decreases with depth until a virtually constant temperature is reached 25 to 30 feet below the surface. At a depth of 10 feet, the ground temperature usually fluctuates no more than 10°F above or below the annual average ground temperature. In addition, the delay or time lag between temperature variations above and below grade also increases with depth. Both of these effects are apparent from the ground temperature profiles shown in figure 3-1 for the Minneapolis-St. Paul area.

Similar effects but different ground temperature ranges occur in other climates. For example, the map in figure 3-2 indicates the approximate deep ground temperatures in the United States, which roughly correspond to annual average air temperatures. It is apparent from figure 3-2 that the ground climate varies considerably in the United States, although it does not reach the extremes encountered on the surface. Data on undisturbed ground conditions gives an indication of potential benefits for earth contact, but the ground climate is altered once a building is placed in it, and the ground climate is different at different depths at different times of the year. Although actual data on ground temperatures is not extensive, some recent research has better defined the below-grade climate in order to assess the suitability of earth sheltered buildings [Labs, 1981a].

Placing a building underground can have other energy-related benefits that are attributable mainly to its isolation from the surface, e.g. minimal air leakage. The full range of energy-related benefits and drawbacks are discussed in the next section.

Coupling the Building to the Earth

The opportunities for energy conservation offered by the moderate thermal environment of the earth can be exploited in a variety of ways. In most cases the building is passively linked to the earth by placing it in direct contact with the soil. In theory, placing a building completely underground at a depth of 25 to 30 feet would fully exploit the constant ground temperature at that depth (fig. 3-3). Obviously, such an approach is not considered feasible for housing, since windowless housing is unacceptable and the structural loads required at that depth can not be supported economically. In addition, this approach does not permit the use of some other energy-conserving strategies, such as passive solar heating, which can complement earth sheltering.

A more effective approach is to place the building near the surface in the form of an earth-covered or earth-bermed house (figs. 3-4 and 3-5). There can be a wide range of difference in these near surface houses—in some cases 3 to 7 feet of earth is placed on the roof to set the building floor 10 or 15 feet below grade, whereas bermed houses may be only set 3 to 7 feet into the earth. The

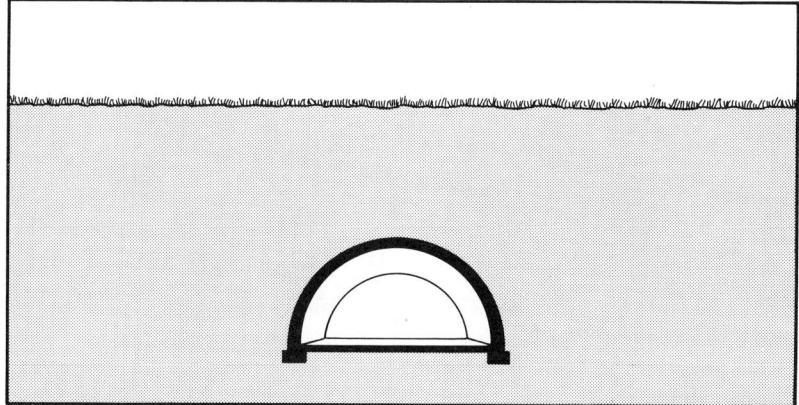

3-3: Deep Underground Building

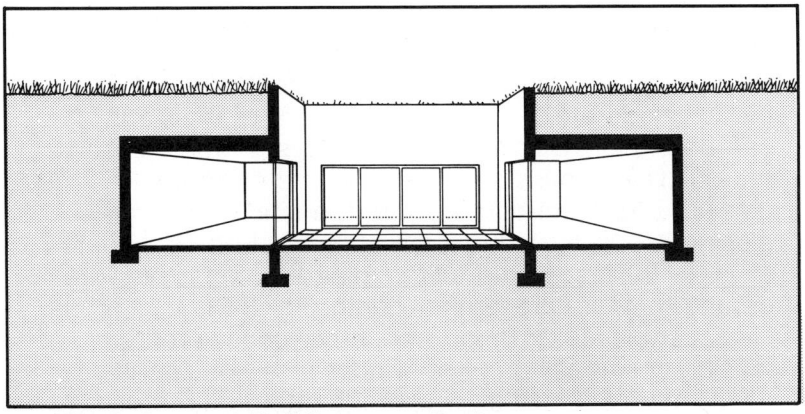

3-4: Earth-Covered Building near Surface

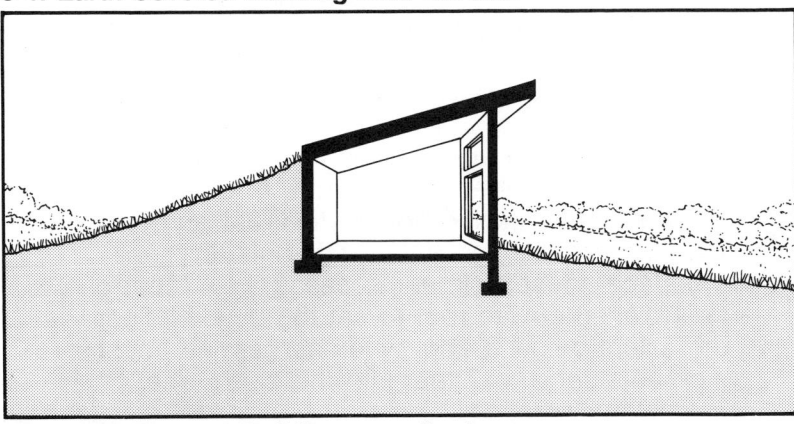

3-5: Earth-Bermed Building near Surface

3-6: Use of Ground Temperature Modification Techniques

ground temperatures near the surface, however, may not always dramatically reduce heating and cooling loads. A variety of techniques to modify the ground temperatures surrounding the building have been suggested in order to improve energy-related benefits in both summer and winter (see fig. 3-6 and the next section). Ground temperature modification techniques represent one important future direction in optimizing energy savings in earth sheltered structures.

In contrast with passively coupling a building to the earth, the moderate environment of the ground can be used as a heat sink or source for ventilation or as part of the mechanical system. Tubes placed in the earth have been used as a means of warming or cooling outside air before it enters the house (fig. 3-7). Earth/air tubes can also be used in a closed loop configuration that recirculates interior air. The cost-effectiveness of earth tubes has been questioned in many climates because of the expense of the tube system versus the energy benefit it can provide over a full heating or cooling season. In addition, concerns have been raised over the quality of the air delivered through a moist air tube which may promote fungal growth and allow the entry of radon gas from the soil. The performance of such systems is sensitive to a number of variables, including ground temperature and moisture content, as well as the depth, length, and diameter of the tube.

Another approach used to exploit the moderate ground temperatures in an indirect way is the ground-coupled heat pump, in which the earth rather than the outside air serves as a heat source or sink for the heat pump. A similar system uses the constant temperature of deep groundwater drawn from a well as the heat source or sink (fig. 3-8). It is also possible to use earth-cooled water in a heat-exchange device without first connecting to a heat pump.

Figures 3-7 and 3-8 show earth sheltered

buildings using earth tubes and ground-coupled heat pumps in combination with passive coupling of the building to the earth. Of course, the use of moderate ground temperatures in these more indirect ways is not restricted to underground buildings. Since these techniques are simply improvements in the efficiency of the mechanical system, they are not addressed in detail in this chapter (see *References* for additional information). The primary focus of this book is on the near surface structures that are passively coupled to the earth.

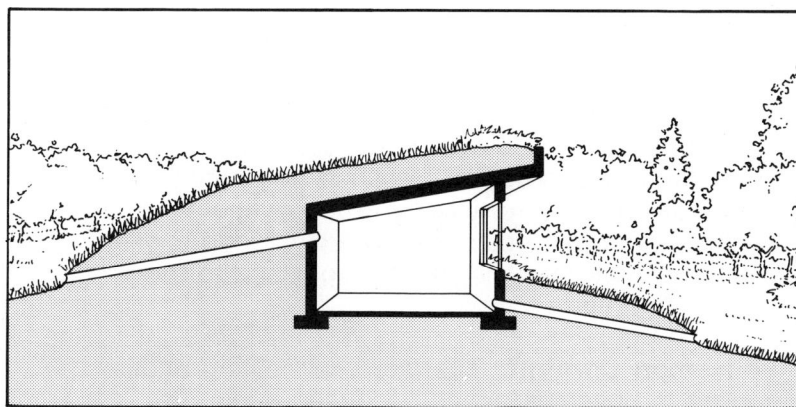

3-7: Use of Earth/Air Tubes

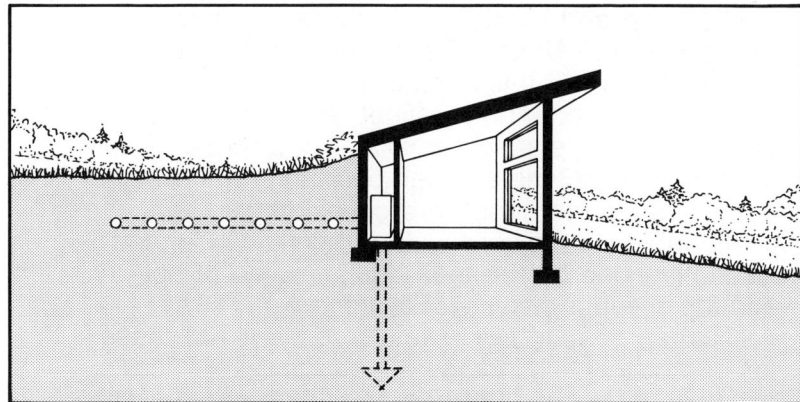

3-8: Use of Ground-Coupled Heat Pump

Effect of Earth Integration on Heating and Cooling

This section more fully explains the heating and cooling season effects of earth integration in a conceptual way for typical earth sheltered housing near the surface. To place earth integration into the appropriate context, energy-use patterns in conventional housing are discussed and the most common conservation strategies presented. The positive and negative effects attributed to earth sheltered houses are then discussed, along with the anticipated impact of some key design variations on energy use. Before examining house characteristics and conservation strategies, some basic concepts related to energy use should be reviewed.

Means of Heat Transfer: Heat can be transferred by three means: conduction, convection, and radiation. When heat is transferred by conduction, it flows from warmer objects or spaces to colder ones directly through the intervening materials. The rate at which this heat is transmitted depends on the conductive properties of the materials that the heat passes through. Through solids, heat is transferred from warm to cold areas primarily by conduction, whereas convection is the primary heat transfer mechanism through liquids and gases since they are free to move within the space containing them. One effect of convection is that warmer fluids, being less dense, will rise above colder ones as evidenced by warm air escaping through a chimney. Convection can set up complex patterns of air movement that can influence the manner heat is distributed, stored, or lost in a space.

The third means of heat transfer is radiation, the transmission of heat from warm to cold bodies through space by wave motion. Heat transfer by radiation occurs independent of the temperature of the medium it travels through, as evidenced by the warmth from the sun or a fire on a cold day. Net radiative heat transfer occurs between any two optically-coupled objects with different temperatures and can have complex and important effects in determining heat loss, heat gain, and thermal comfort in a space.

In addition to the three basic means of heat transfer, a fourth physical process can influence energy use and human comfort in buildings. When a liquid changes into a gas by evaporation, heat is absorbed in the process. Because air temperatures will be lowered in the vicinity of the evaporation, a cooling effect can occur. Conversely, when a gas condenses into a liquid, heat is released to the surrounding air.

Human Comfort: The need for heating and cooling in buildings arises because people are comfortable only in a relatively narrow range of temperature and humidity conditions. In most locations in the United States, the outdoor conditions are usually not in this comfort range. The comfort zone is most commonly defined as between 68°F and 80°F, with relative humidity in the range of 20 to 80 percent. Generally, temperatures in the higher end of the comfort zone are considered more comfortable with lower levels of humidity. Comfort is also influenced by the individuals degree of activity and the amount or type of clothing worn.

Human comfort is not totally restricted to these temperature and humidity ranges, however. For example, air movement has an impact on comfort.

Air moving across the skin permits the body's evaporative cooling system to work more effectively and can make temperatures above the normal comfort zone acceptable. Air temperatures above the comfort zone may also be acceptable if the body is losing heat by radiation to cooler surfaces, such as a wall in contact with the earth. The magnitude of this effect can be determined by calculating the mean radiant temperature (MRT) of a space which is a weighted average of the temperature of all building surfaces interacting with the occupant.

In a similar manner, air temperatures lower than the normal comfort zone can be acceptable if the body is receiving heat by radiation from a warmer object such as the sun, a fire, or room surfaces warmed by these heat sources. Thus, passive means of climate control such as solar heating, natural ventilation, and earth-contact cooling should be evaluated not only in terms of their ability to create conditions defined by the normal comfort zone. Instead, they must be considered as a means of enlarging the comfort zone so that requirements for other means of heating and cooling are reduced.

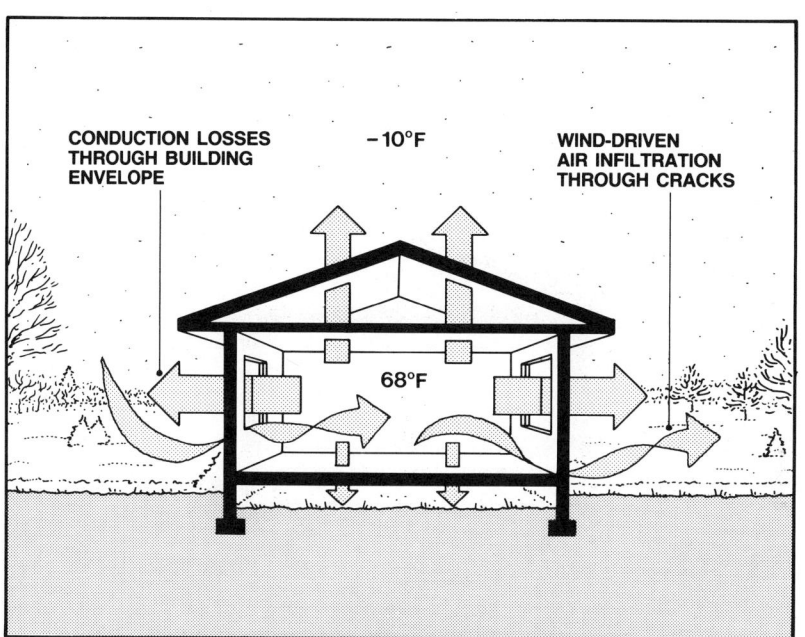

3-9: Heat Loss through Infiltration and Conduction

Winter Heating Season

In most of the United States, outdoor temperatures are usually below normal comfort conditions during a significant period of the year (three to seven months). To provide adequate comfort in conventional houses during winter, heat is usually supplied by burning fuel (gas, oil, or wood) or by using electricity. This heat, which is then distributed in the house and lost through the building envelope, must be resupplied at a rate equal to the loss. In typical housing, major sources of heat loss are infiltration (air leakage) through cracks in the envelope and conduction through the building roof, walls, windows and floor (fig. 3-9). Losses caused by infiltration increase as wind speed and exposure to the wind increase. Thus, the amount of infiltration depends on wind direction on a specific site and the orientation of openings in the building. Both infiltration and conduction losses increase as the temperature difference between inside and outside increases. Internal heat is generated by people, lights, appliances, and activities such as cooking. In addition, sunlight provides heat wherever it penetrates the windows. In the majority of houses, however, the size and orientation of the windows are not designed to maximize this solar gain. In typical non-energy-efficient housing, internal and solar heat gains provide only a small percentage of the total heat required. Not only are the overall heat losses relatively large, but the solar heat gained is not retained for use when it is most needed.

In determining winter heat losses in conventional housing, it is common to focus on infiltration and

3-10: Heat Loss Reduced with Insulation and Sealing Cracks

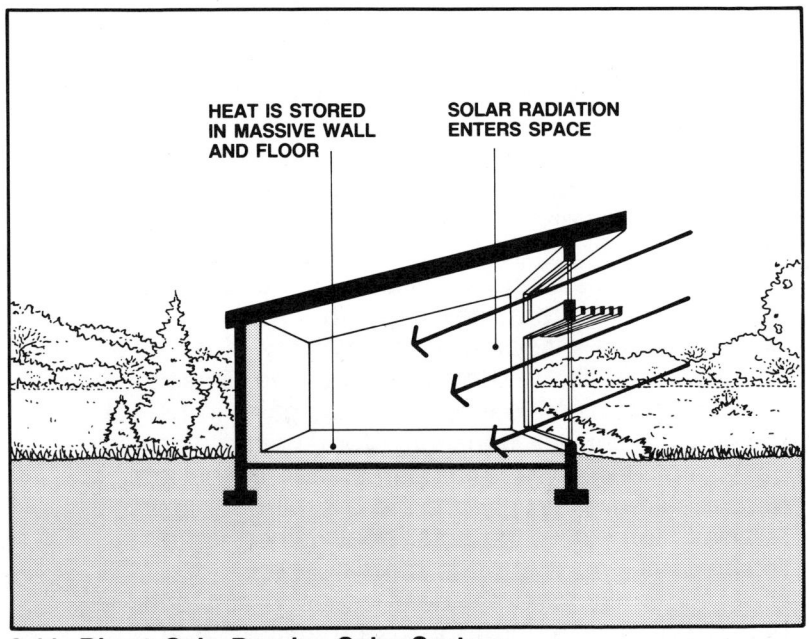
3-11: Direct Gain Passive Solar System

conduction. It should be recognized that in reality heat is distributed, absorbed, and lost through a complex interaction of conduction, convection, and radiation in a house. It should also be recognized that the building envelope is not the only factor in ultimately determining the heating energy use—the mechanical system and life-style of the occupants have equally significant impacts. The efficiency of the manner in which fuel is burned and heat distributed to the spaces in a house can vary widely. For example, heat is lost through duct pipes running in cold basements or crawl spaces, and it may be delivered below a window where heat is lost immediately to the exterior. Likewise, heating energy use will be influenced by the number of occupants and their habits of opening windows and doors or setting thermostats. Although mechanical systems and occupant life-style have been demonstrated to be major factors in winter energy use, the focus of the remaining discussion is restricted mainly to the building envelope.

Conservation Strategies for Winter

The ultimate goal of energy conservation with regard to winter heating is to reduce the amount of fuel required for the heating system. Two basic approaches can be used to accomplish this: isolation of the house from the environment to reduce heat losses and interaction with the environment to receive and retain any available heat, particularly that provided by the sun. In conventional above-grade houses, the first approach is achieved by increasing thermal resistance in the envelope and sealing cracks as well as possible to limit infiltration (fig. 3-10). Vegetation, fences, or other barriers can be used to reduce wind exposure. In addition, windows are reduced in area, are double- or triple-glazed, and are covered with insulating shades or shutters at night. This approach applied in a very thorough and complete way is exemplified by the *superinsulated* house concept. Drawbacks to this approach may be limited window area, poor indoor air quality without proper ventilation, and meticulous construction practices, which are required to seal the house completely from air leaks.

A variety of techniques are available to collect and retain the available energy from the sun. Active solar systems, which require auxiliary energy to operate, employ collector panels that heat fluids, which are then circulated for distribution to the space or stored for later use. Except for their appearance, active systems have little direct impact on the building envelope. Passive systems are usually characterized by no moving parts and the use of components of the building envelope to collect and store heat. Areas of glass serving as collectors are often enlarged and oriented toward the south for maximum winter exposure while mass is provided in the roof walls or floor to store the heat. Increased mass in a house has advantages in terms of reducing the peak load and stabilizing interior temperatures. Mass also absorbs heat from intermittent sources other than the sun, such as people, lights, appliances, and fireplaces.

In figure 3-11 a direct gain passive system is illustrated in which solar heat penetrates the windows and is stored in a concrete or masonry floor and wall. In an indirect gain passive system, a thermal storage wall is placed directly behind the glass to absorb heat and transmit it to the interior space on a delayed basis as shown in figure 3-12 where it is utilized in an earth-bermed house. Another passive approach utilizes a thermal storage roof that usually contains water for the thermal storage mass. Solar heat can also be passively collected in a sunspace and then transmitted either directly through a massive wall into the house or by natural or mechanical distribution of the air. In figure 3-13 an earth-covered house utilizing a sunspace for passive solar collection is shown. Drawbacks in solar

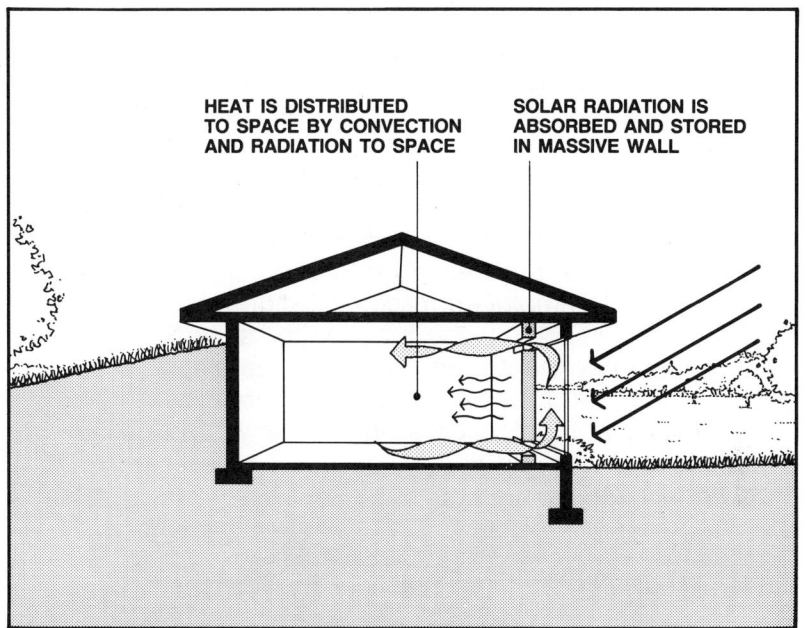

3-12: Indirect Gain Passive Solar System

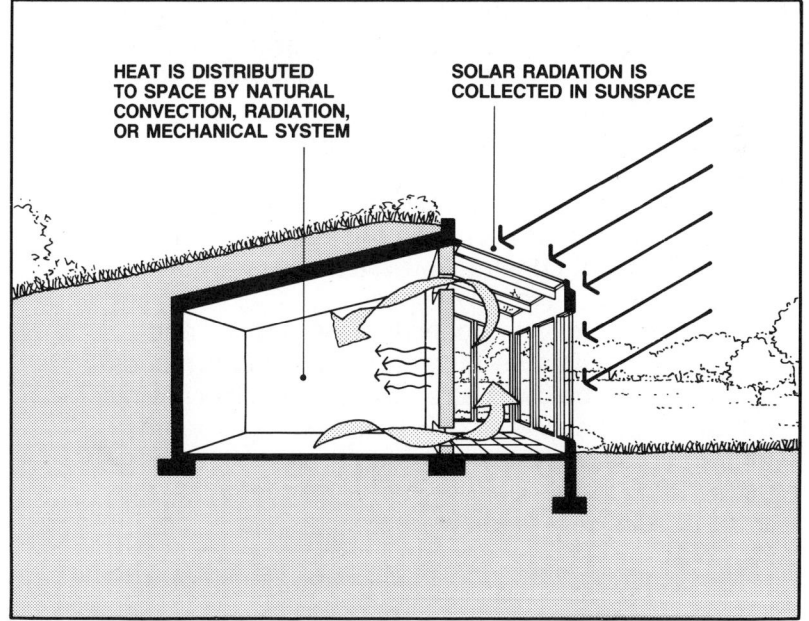

3-13: Passive Solar System Utilizing Sunspace

design may include high nighttime heat losses through glass (unless the glass area is insulated at night), overheating or underheating if mass and glass areas are not carefully designed, and extra costs associated with mass and other materials not intrinsic to conventional above-grade construction.

Although the two basic conservation approaches pertaining to the envelope, reducing losses and promoting gains, are described separately here, they are commonly employed in combination along with increased efficiency in the mechanical system and changes in occupant life-style. For example, thermostats can be set at lower temperatures (particularly at night), doors and windows can be kept closed, and curtains or thermal shades can be drawn at night.

Effect of Earth Integration in Winter

Earth integration applies to the first basic conservation approach, isolation of the building from the above-grade environment. An earth sheltered building can have very limited air infiltration and, if oriented properly, the effects of wind on infiltration and conductive heat loss (by removing the outside air film on a wall) can be diminished considerably (fig. 3-14). Achieving an extremely tight building can be easier with below-grade construction in the sense that meticulous construction practices are not required to seal the envelope.

A major difference between the above- and below-grade climates in winter is the more moderate temperatures below grade. Even in a severe winter climate with below-zero air temperatures, ground temperatures increase with depth and will seldom be below 32°F in the United States (except Alaska), even at relatively shallow depths of 3 to 4 feet (fig. 3-15). Thus, conduction losses are reduced because the temperature differential between the inside and outside of the envelope is smaller than in

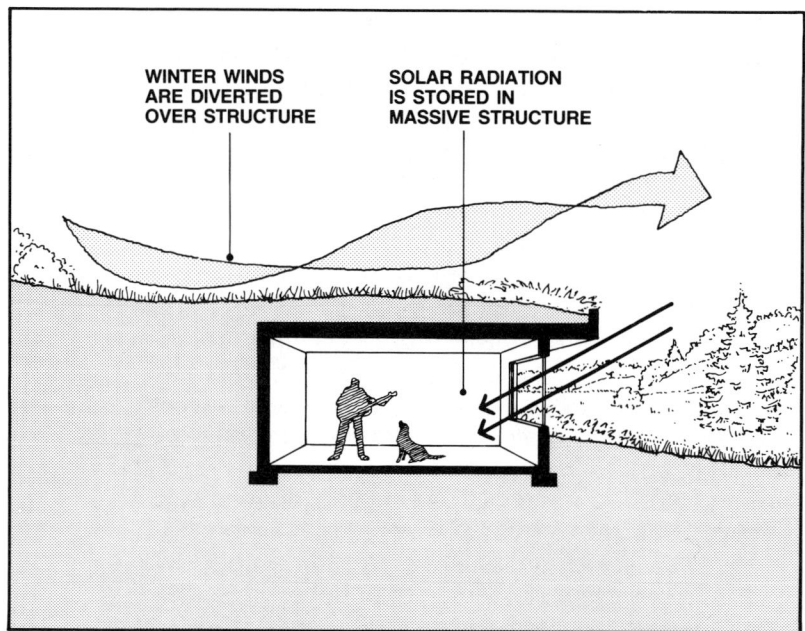

3-14: Earth Sheltered Building in Winter Condition

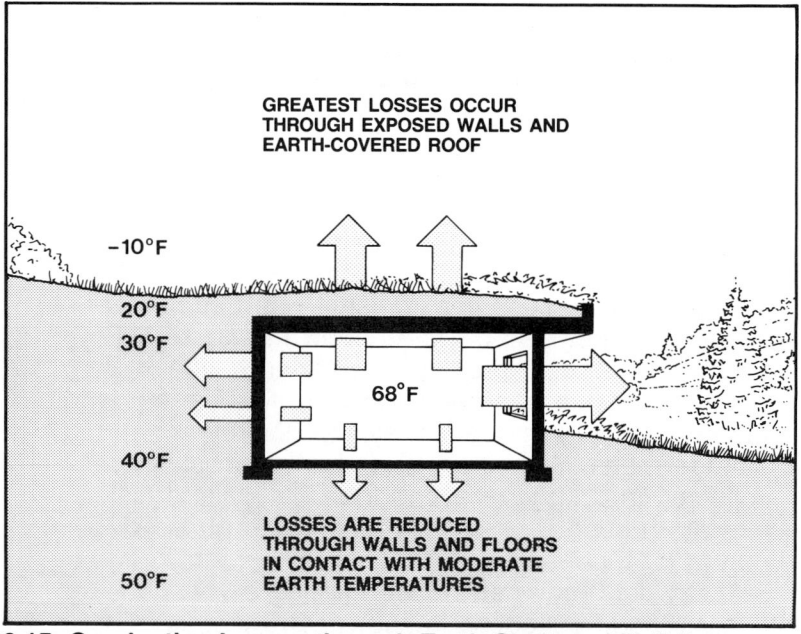

3-15: Conduction Losses through Earth Sheltered Building

above-grade conditions. This effect is enhanced because heat lost to the ground is retained in the earth to some extent, resulting in higher ground temperatures adjacent to the building than are found in undisturbed soil. Because the impact of surface temperature fluctuations on ground temperatures is delayed, the earth temperatures will be higher in the fall and early winter than they will be in late winter and spring.

In addition to isolating the building from the environment by reducing infiltration and conduction, an earth sheltered building can provide potential benefits in collecting and retaining solar energy. Because it is partially exposed, any of the basic solar design concepts can be employed in an earth sheltered house as well as in an above-grade house. Indeed, most earth-integrated buildings contain much larger amounts of concrete and masonry than are found in conventional house construction, making them ideally suited for passive solar design. A direct gain system is illustrated in figure 3-14.

Because of the more moderate temperatures below grade, protection from wind-induced infiltration, and the massive structure often used in earth sheltered houses, interior temperatures are very stable. Changes are slow and gradual and never reach the extreme fluctuations to which an above-grade building is exposed. Not only is this mass effective in storing solar energy, but it retains other intermittent forms of heat from internal sources for later use. This thermal stability also results in a reduction in peak loads, thus requiring a smaller and less costly mechanical system. A further benefit is that under these conditions the capacity of the mechanical system can be reduced which is likely to result in more efficient operation and additional energy savings. In some cases financial savings can be had by using electricity during off-peak periods where electric rates are lower and the heat can be stored for use when rates are higher. Another advantage of thermal stability is that interior temperatures will drop slowly during emergencies when power or fuel supplies are interrupted.

An earth-covered roof with a relatively shallow depth of 1 to 2 feet of soil does not provide the same degree of temperature moderation found in deeper ground adjacent to the wall and floor, but even a few inches of soil can dampen daily temperature fluctuations and provide some related energy savings. To demonstrate some of these effects in winter, a computer simulation of heat loss through two roof sections is presented in figure 3-17. As shown in figure 3-16 roof A is a lower mass structure with 4.6 inches of polystyrene insulation placed over an 8-inch-thick precast concrete plank. Roof B consists of 18 inches of earth placed over 4 inches of polystyrene insulation and an 8-inch-thick precast concrete plank.

Under steady-state conditions, both roofs have identical heat losses since the R-value for each roof is 24.68 hr-sq ft-°F/Btu. Actual temperatures, however, vary in random intervals and the high mass roof structure provided by earth cover damps out or appreciably reduces these temperature fluctuations. For example, a typical January day was selected in which the outside air temperature varied from an early morning low of 5°F to an afternoon high of 15°F. On the fifteenth day of the month, a passing cold front was assumed to cause a drop of 10°F for all daily temperatures. Temperatures then remained in this range of -5 to 5°F for five days when they returned once again to normal on the twentieth day of the month. The heat loss response of the two roof structures to these conditions is shown in figure 3-17. The daily heat loss per unit area is plotted in the graph, hence, the shaded areas beneath each line represent the total heat loss for each respective roof type. Due to its low thermal mass, roof A responds immediately to the change outside and within two days reaches a new maximum heat loss which is maintained for the

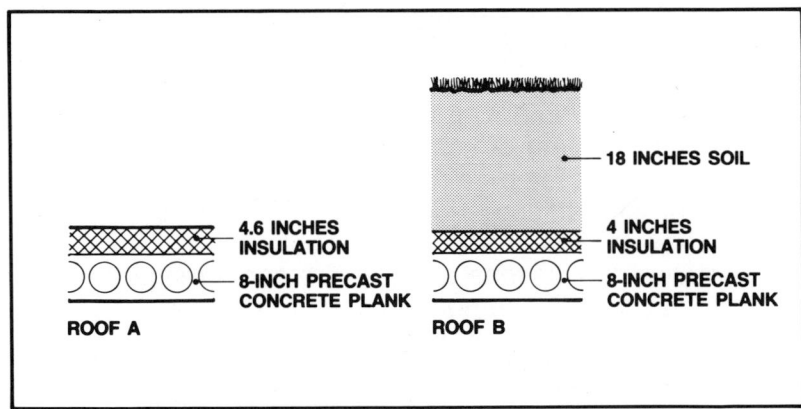

3-16: Two Roof Sections

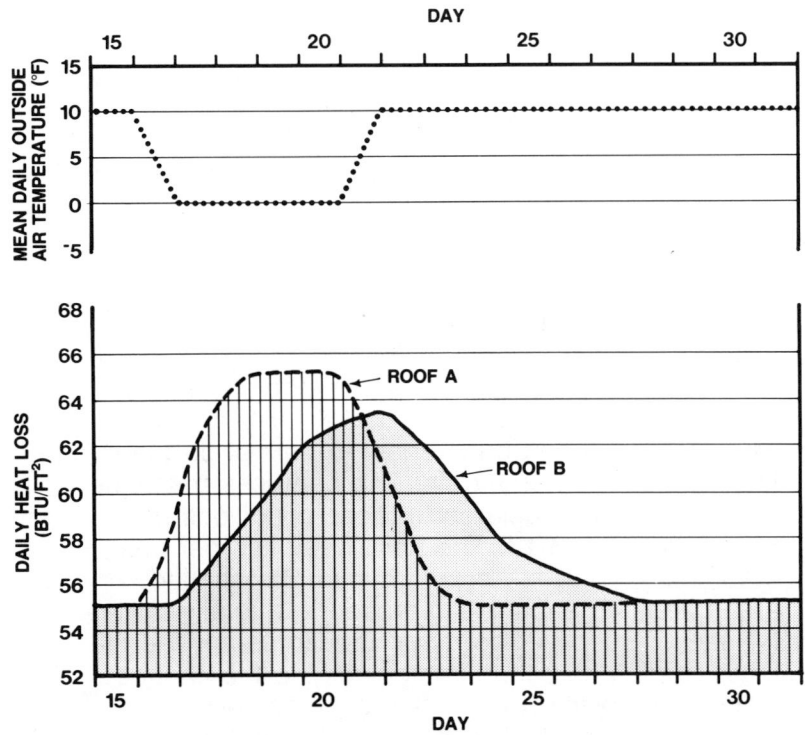

3-17: Comparison of Energy Transfer through Roof Sections

remaining three days. When the temperature returns to normal, roof A responds at once and after two days has returned to its normal January operating level. Roof B, however, requires a full day before the ceiling begins to indicate that more severe conditions now exist outside and once it does begin to respond, does so much more slowly than roof A. After five days, when outside temperatures return to normal, the heat loss of roof B is still gradually rising having attained only 77 percent of the increase of roof A. Roof B requires another full day before responding to the return of normal weather conditions.

As shown by figure 3-17, despite the much longer total response time, roof B required 8 percent less total energy than roof A to cope with the severe period. At the same time, roof B exhibited a peak increase in load which was only 85 percent of that of roof A. Furthermore, roof A's low thermal mass required almost twice as much additional energy (196 percent) during the five day period in which outside air temperatures were most severe, thereby placing the majority of its demand during the period when the outside to inside air temperature differential was at its greatest and required the most energy input from the furnace to bring ventilation air up to room temperature. While this latter consideration does not affect the net energy balance for the structure, it does increase the peak energy demand which must be supplied by the heating system since the building must provide additional energy during a cold wave to warm incoming fresh air independently of the performance of the roof. Thus, it is demonstrated that while two structures may be thermally equivalent under steady-state conditions, short term transient fluctuations will cause the high mass structure to exhibit greater stability during operation as well as demonstrate a potential for net energy savings over the low mass structure. A related advantage of placing earth on the roof of the house is that the below-grade walls and floor are 2 to 4 feet further from the surface than they would be in a bermed design. By setting the entire building more deeply into the earth, greater benefit can be derived from moderate earth temperatures.

Earth sheltered buildings share some of the potential drawbacks associated with other winter conservation approaches. Limited infiltration may mean poor indoor air quality unless proper ventilation is provided. In addition, a massive structure responds slowly to temperature changes. While this is an advantage in many respects, controlling internal temperatures to take advantage of thermostat setbacks or other conservation strategies may be more complex.

Variables Affecting Winter Performance

The degree to which an earth sheltered design actually achieves energy efficiency in a particular climate is subject to a number of variables. As discussed in a previous section, ground temperatures vary with climate throughout the United States. In the coldest part of the winter, they are invariably more moderate than the surface air temperatures. On the other hand, winter ground temperatures at any depth are still below the comfort zone in the northern two-thirds of the United States. Thus, optimal design for energy efficiency requires insulation placement on some or all below-grade areas of the building. Similar to an above-grade building, the thickness and location of insulation on a below-grade structure has an important influence on energy consumption.

Certain insulation configurations result in more heat storage in the soil, resulting in higher winter ground temperatures. In a design concept suggested by John Hait, insulation and waterproofing are extended about 20 feet horizontally beyond the structure (fig. 3-18). This "insulation/watershed umbrella" is intended to raise the ground temperature around the house to the comfort level year around by storing all excess solar and other heat from the house. By keeping the ground dry in this area, conductivity in the soil is reduced which diminishes the rate of heat flow. The incorporation of earth/air tubes to provide ventilation and to adjust ground temperatures in the storage zone is another facet of this concept [Hait, 1983]. Although ground temperature modification concepts appear to be important future directions for earth sheltered research and construction, very few houses have actually tested these ideas.

The depth of an earth sheltered building affects the extent to which benefits from moderate ground temperatures can be exploited. For economic reasons, it is unlikely that more than 2 to 3 feet of earth would be placed on a roof under normal circumstances limiting one-level designs to a floor depth of about 12 feet below grade and two-level

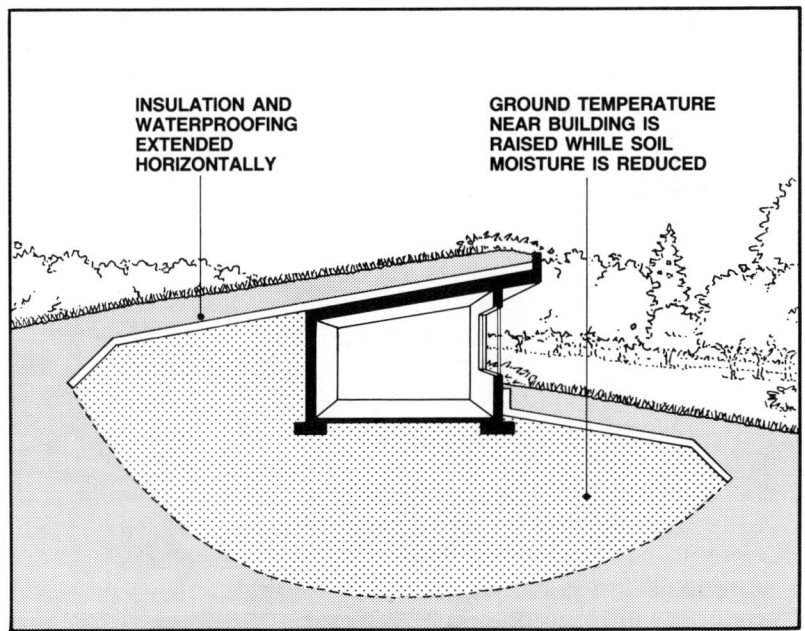

3-18: Ground Temperatures Modified with Insulation

designs to about 20 feet below grade. One common approach in earth sheltered design is a bermed design with no earth on the roof, resulting in a floor depth of no more than 7 feet below grade for a single-story house (fig. 3-19). Although a bermed design is not as deep as an earth-covered design, if properly insulated, it should still provide substantial earth-contact benefits. Earth berms can seal against infiltration and divert winds, while a very well insulated roof can perform quite efficiently during winter.

The overall performance of an earth sheltered house in winter will also be affected by the plan layout and window openings. In the previous chapter, it was suggested that a more compact plan with a lower surface-to-volume ratio will result in less winter heat loss. The size and orientation of windows not only affects solar collection and heat loss, but also determines the extent to which the building is in contact with the earth and shielded from winds. Although a design with a single exposed facade is most common, designs employing a central atrium can have winter benefits (fig. 3-20). With an atrium design, less of the total window area is oriented to the south, but the glass in the courtyard is more protected from wind. The courtyard can be further protected by a translucent cover that can trap heat, effectively converting the atrium into a sunspace. It is usually desirable to have a removable cover, however, since the space will usually become overheated in summer. It is also not clear if the cost of a covered atrium would be justified by the resulting energy savings [Wade, 1983].

Details of construction and use of materials can also affect winter benefits obtainable from earth sheltered design. For example, one potential benefit is the use of the already existing large mass of a concrete or masonry structure for passive solar storage. If the floor, wall, or roof surfaces are covered with materials such as carpet or other

3-19: Earth-Bermed House

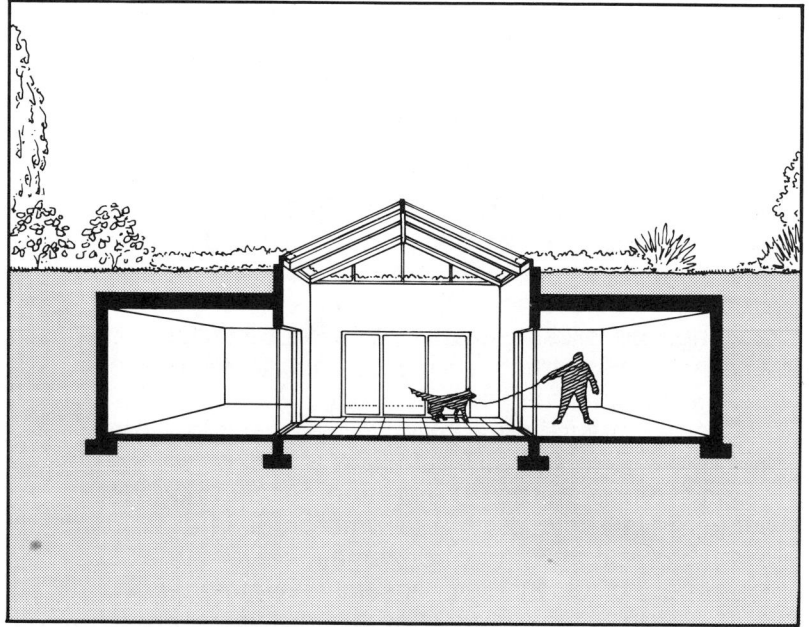

3-20: Earth Sheltered House with Glass-Covered Atrium

insulating finishes, they will be isolated from direct exposure to the heat and thus less effective as storage. Bermed houses with conventional wood-frame roofs and underground houses built with wood structural systems do not provide the same mass as a predominantly concrete shell, although mass provided in or beneath the floor slab may be adequate for solar storage if properly designed.

Summer Cooling Season

The need for summer cooling and the conditions of temperature and humidity vary considerably in the United States. In most locations daytime temperatures rise above the normal comfort zone during some period of time. This heat is conducted through the building envelope to the interior spaces; moreover, warm air enters through infiltration (fig. 3-21). Radiant heat from the sun strikes the building and penetrates windows to add heat to the space (fig. 3-22). One effect of this exposure to the sun is increased temperatures in attic spaces; this heat is in turn conducted into the building interior. In addition, internal sources—people, lights, and appliances—add heat and humidity to the interior spaces.

The problem created by temperatures above the comfort zone is compounded by the presence of humidity. Higher temperatures are more tolerable with moderate humidity. Where high external humidity does exist, water vapor enters the building through infiltration and is also transmitted through building materials. Houses that are not designed to resolve these problems efficiently offer three choices: toleration of the uncomfortable conditions, provision of some comfort with air movement, or cooling of spaces by air-conditioning, which consumes auxiliary energy. Air-conditioning effectively lowers the temperature (the sensible heat load) and extracts moisture from the air (the latent heat load). The

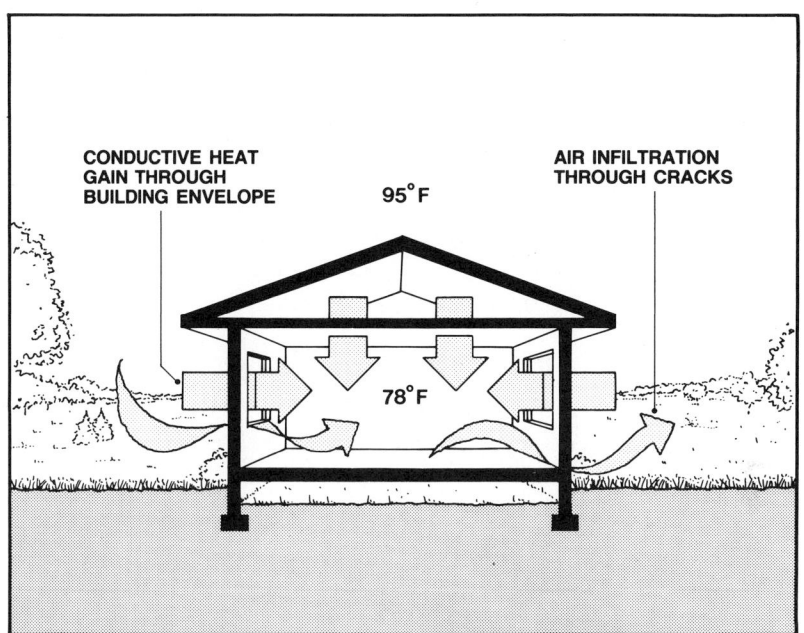

3-21: Summer Heat Gain through Conduction and Infiltration

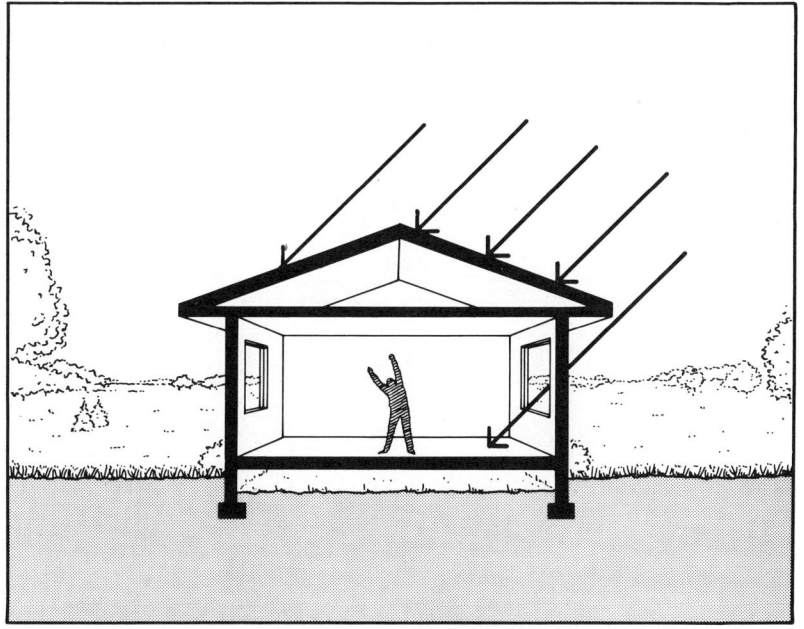

3-22: Summer Heat Gain from Solar Radiation

81

3-23: Shading and Natural Ventilation Increase Comfort

3-24: Attic Ventilation Reduces Heat Gain

amount of energy consumed by air-conditioning is related to the rate at which heat and humidity pass through the building envelope or are created within the building. When air-conditioning is not employed, comfort is commonly increased by creating air movement with fans or open windows, although many conventional houses are not designed to provide effective natural ventilation.

Similar to the heating load in winter, the energy requirements associated with summer cooling are determined by a number of factors in addition to the building envelope. If air-conditioning is used, the efficiency of the unit can vary widely. Efficiency in the distribution of the cool air varies as well, depending on duct layout and insulation. In addition, occupant behavior is important in determining energy loads and use. Not only are thermostat settings for air-conditioning an important factor, but opening windows and generating heat gains inside the house can have significant effects.

Conservation Strategies for Summer

The goal of energy conservation in summer is to reduce the need for using energy to provide mechanical cooling. All conservation stategies can be categorized into two basic approaches—isolation of the building from the heat and humidity of the environment, and interaction with beneficial aspects of the environment such as winds, evaporation, and radiation to the night sky to create more comfortable conditions. The same strategies used to isolate the building from heat loss in winter can be used to reduce heat gain in summer—increased thermal resistance of the envelope and sealing of the cracks to minimize air leakage. Minimizing window area would also contribute to reduced heat gain caused by conduction and radiation. Heat gain in summer can be reduced by shading the building from solar radiation (fig. 3-23). Landscape elements such as trees and shrubs can be used along with such building elements as overhangs, awnings, and sun screens.

Conservation strategies that attempt to use the natural environment to increase comfort are very dependent on local climate conditions. In hot, humid environments, maximizing natural ventilation is the major technique for maximizing comfort without the use of mechanical air-conditioning (fig. 3-23). This requires proper orientation with respect to breezes, lack of obstructions inside and outside the house, and correct sizing and location of window openings. Heat gain from the attic can also be reduced by natural or mechanical ventilation (fig. 3-24). Ventilation can be induced through roof openings by the stack effect alone or driven by a solar chimney. The comfort produced by air movement can also be achieved with ventilation fans that either assist natural air flow or operate independently. Ventilation is most effective when temperatures are only moderately above the comfort zone.

In regions with hot, arid climates, a clear night sky, and large temperature differences between day and night, a number of effective conservation techniques are possible. The cooling released when water evaporates can be exploited by spraying water on the roof or locating a pool or fountain in a building (fig. 3-25). A massive wall and roof structure partially isolates the building interior from the environment but also interacts with the environment by delaying the temperature cycles. Heat from the day is not felt until the cooler evening, when it is more desirable. Massive roofs can also lose heat to the clear night sky by radiation. This cooling effect has been exploited by designs using a layer of water on the roof that is covered to prevent heat gain during the day and is exposed to the sky at night for both evaporative and radiative cooling (fig. 3-25). Drawbacks of these techniques include the use of water for evaporation in an arid climate where water may quite possibly be scarce, and the additional structure and operating complexities associated with a roof-water pond system.

Depending on the climate conditions, the conservation approaches described above can be used in various combinations along with increased efficiency in the mechanical system and changes in occupant life-style. For example, windows and doors can be kept closed, shades can be drawn to reduce heat gain, thermostat settings can be raised, and air-conditioning can be used only as a last resort when other means of cooling are ineffective.

Effect of Earth Integration in Summer

An earth sheltered building can effectively reduce energy used for cooling by both isolating the house from the heat of the surface climate and actually providing a source of cooling through below-grade

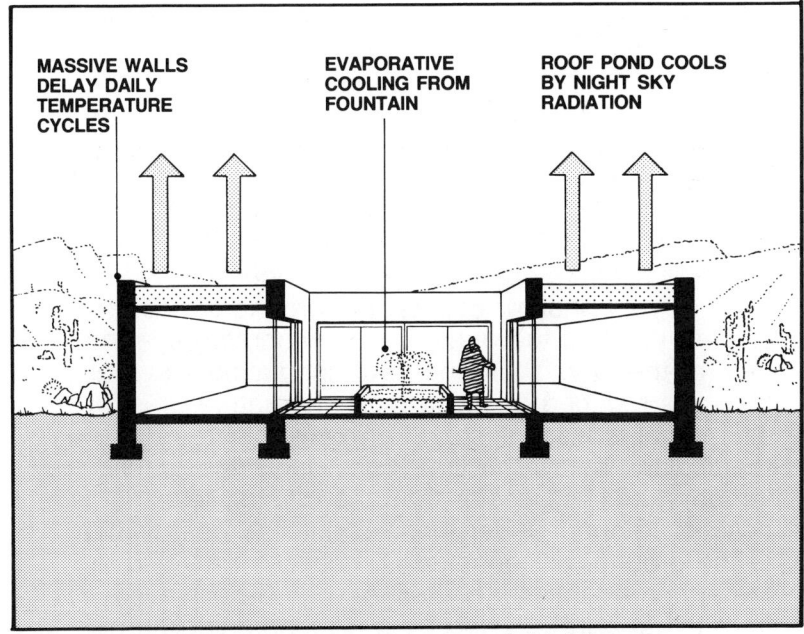

3-25: Conservation Techniques in Hot, Arid Climates

surfaces. Placing a building underground can also significantly reduce infiltration, resulting in less gain of warm, humid air, just as it results in less heat loss in winter. In addition, radiant heat from the sun striking a grass-covered surface is partially reflected and partially used in the evapotranspiration process, resulting in a relatively small amount of absorption into the earth (fig. 3-26). Seventy to ninety percent of the radiation striking well-irrigated grass can be dissipated [Labs, 1981a]. Radiant heat gain is thus effectively eliminated from earth-covered roofs and walls. It should be noted, however, that ground temperatures would be raised if the surface were bare earth or a hard surface such as blacktop.

In measurements made of the ground temperatures beneath paved and grass-covered areas it was observed that daily high temperatures during the summer can exceed 140°F on an asphalt surface even though the air temperature is no more than 90°F. In contrast, the high temperature recorded for a grass-covered surface under the same conditions are only 104°F [Kusuda, 1971]. As shown in figure 3-27, the average temperature of an asphalt surface during the summer is at least 15°F warmer than the average air temperature, while the grass-covered surface is approximately 7°F below ambient conditions.

The placing of a building below grade in a more moderate thermal environment has two implications for cooling energy use related to conduction. First, even at very shallow depths, the ground temperature seldom reaches the outdoor air temperatures in the heat of the day. Thus, the heat conducted into the house is reduced because the temperature differential is less. Second, in many climates (particularly below the first 2 or 3 feet), the ground temperatures are cooler than the comfort level desired indoors. Under these conditions heat is lost to the ground, or conversely, cooling is provided to the space by the earth. Comfort can be achieved from direct earth cooling by two means: cooling of

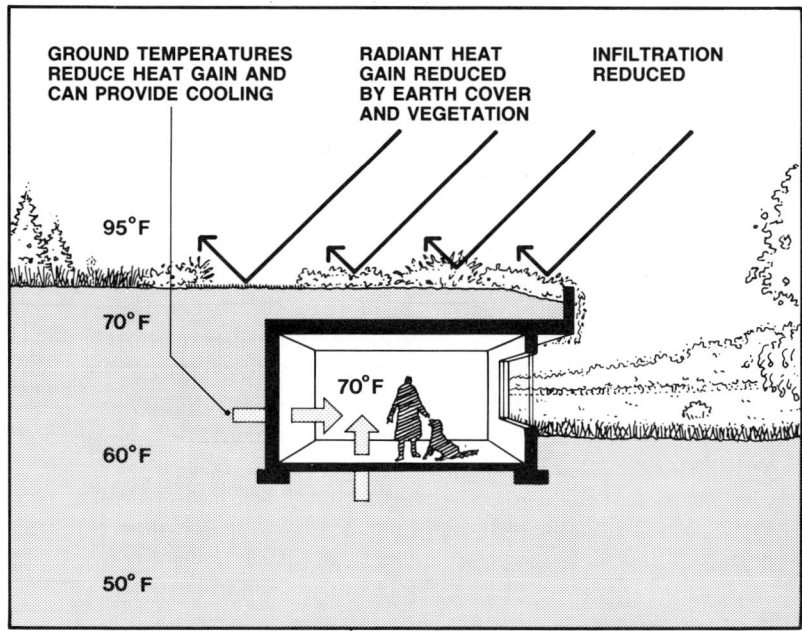

3-26: **Effect of Earth Sheltered Design in Summer**

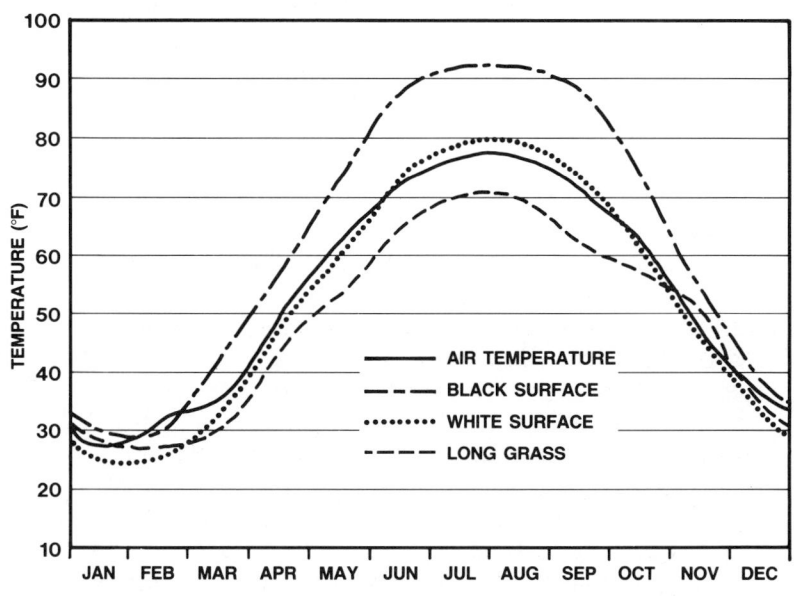

3-27: **Monthly Average Ground Surface Temperatures**

the interior air by conduction, and radiant cooling to the surfaces in contact with the earth. Adequate radiant cooling—where the body is losing heat to a cooler building surface by radiation—can create a feeling of comfort at air temperatures slightly above the normal comfort zone.

The large mass usually found in a concrete or masonry underground structure can beneficially dampen and delay daily temperature fluctuations. Just as a massive structure can retain solar heat for later use in winter, cool temperatures at night can be retained within a structure during the following day. When mechanical cooling is necessary or desired, the building structure and surrounding earth mass can retain cooler temperatures resulting in a reduction in heat gain to the structure and in peak cooling loads. Energy consumption for air-conditioning and mechanical equipment costs are reduced compared to a less massive, above-grade structure.

The potential summer cooling benefits of an earth sheltered design are not always available in every climate, and if available, their effects can be influenced by a number of factors. In some of the consistently warmest areas of the United States, ground temperatures are often too high to provide significant direct cooling. In addition, the ground will warm around a building as heat is lost from the structure. Since ground temperatures reflect surface temperatures on a delayed basis, more cooling will be provided in the early summer than in the late summer. Another potential problem related to summer cooling effectiveness below grade is condensation. Since condensation is produced by warm, humid air striking cooler surfaces, it may not be possible to combine direct earth-coupled cooling and natural ventilation in humid climates.

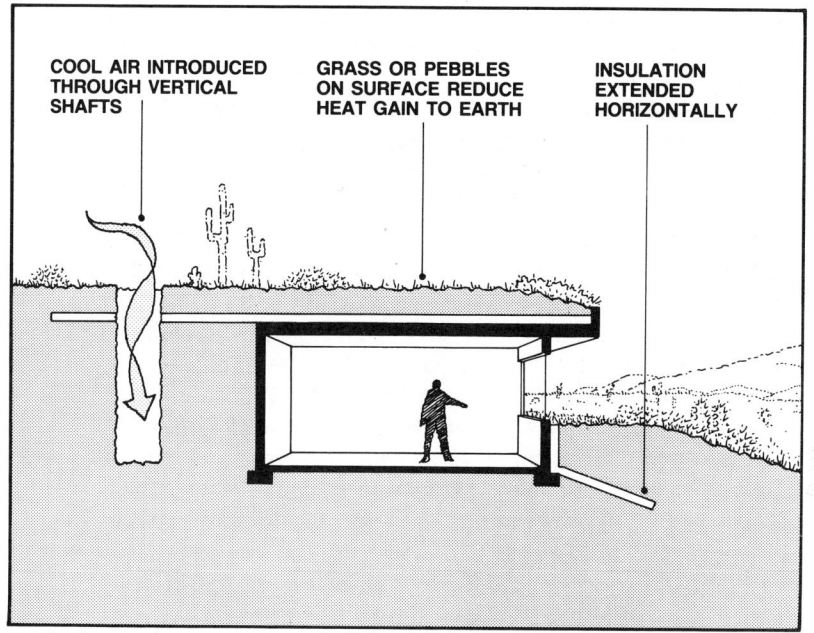

3-28: Techniques to Improve Ground-Coupled Cooling

Variables Affecting Summer Performance

Although the existing ground conditions do not always provide the cooling effects desired, several suggestions have been made to increase cooling benefits [Labs, 1981b; Givoni, 1979]. One approach devised by Baruch Givoni is to lower the deep ground temperature by introducing cooler air through a series of vertical pebble-filled shafts (fig. 3-28). By natural convection, cool winter air would settle in the air spaces between the pebbles, cooling the ground surrounding the shaft. The distance between the shafts and the building could be adjusted so the cool temperatures reach the building wall in summer. Soil thermal properties could be manipulated to inhibit or accelerate heat flow by either diminishing or increasing moisture content. Ken Labs has suggested complete shading of the ground surface around the building so that the ground temperature is affected only by air temperatures rather than by solar radiation.

Heat can be at least partially prevented from penetrating the surface to the deeper ground with the use of various surface treatments and insulation configurations. It has already been mentioned that plant materials reflect solar radiation, shade the ground, and cool through evaporation. In extremely dry climates, however, where irrigation of rooftop planting may not be possible, Givoni has suggested a layer of light-colored pebbles on the surface, which reflect solar radiation but permit cool night air to settle in the air spaces between the stones. Below-grade insulation extended horizontally can also be used to block heat penetration from the surface while containing cooler temperatures in the deeper ground (fig. 3-28).

Clearly, compromises in insulation placement must be made for optimal winter or summer performance. In addition, insulation placement can affect interior surface temperatures and thus the tendency for condensation to form. Effects of both ground cover and insulation placement on heating and cooling are discussed in a later section.

Some of the summer cooling benefits associated with underground buildings can be increased by placing the building deeper into the ground. Conversely, cooling season benefits are diminished in houses placed at relatively shallow depths. In a bermed structure, some temperature modification results from the buried walls, but ground temperatures are higher during the summer than at greater depths. A conventional roof has little of the mass and heat-gain reduction characteristics of an earth-covered roof.

Just as it is in winter, the energy performance of an earth sheltered house in summer is affected in a number of ways by the plan layout and window openings. In contrast to winter, when a compact plan is generally desirable to reduce heat loss, an extended plan that increases exterior wall area in contact with the earth can improve summer benefits. Heat gain will increase with window area; unshaded windows facing east or west should be avoided completely. More exposed surfaces for window openings also reduce the area of the envelope that can be in contact with the earth. Probably the most important concern related to the impact of plan layout and openings on summer cooling is the ability to exploit other cooling strategies, such as natural ventilation, if desired.

Regional Design Approaches Based on Climate

Previously in this chapter, the potential advantages and drawbacks of earth integration with respect to energy use have been portrayed in conditions of severe winter and summer climates and with the assumption of a favorable ground climate. While this is an appropriate means of illustrating the basic concepts, it can be misleading. The degree to which favorable conditions exist and consequently the effectiveness of earth integration in saving energy depend on the local climate.

If the climates where the greatest and least benefits from earth sheltered strategies can be identified, designers will better be able to evaluate earth integration as an alternative means of conserving heating and cooling energy. A better understanding of climatic applicabiltiy can also assist the designer in taking advantage of whatever opportunities for energy conservation exist with earth integration without inhibiting other effective climate control strategies. It is necessary, however, to reiterate that energy conservation is not necessarily the overriding consideration in the adoption of an earth sheltered design.

In evaluating the effect of earth integration in a particular climate, several basic questions must be answered:

- What are the heating and cooling requirements?
- Are the ground temperatures in winter sufficiently higher than outdoor conditions to provide benefits?
- Are the ground temperatures in summer sufficiently lower than outdoor conditions to provide benefits?
- Are summer humidity levels high enough to cause condensation problems?
- Does earth integration interfere with or complement other passive design strategies appropriate in this climate?

Although these basic questions appear simple enough to answer, analysis of above- and below-grade climate presents some complexities and problems. First, below-grade temperatures are only known in a very general sense. Second, generalization about both above- and below-grade climates must be regarded with some caution, as conditions can vary not only in different regions but even on different sites in close proximity. Finally, favorable climatic characteristics do not automatically translate into energy savings, nor do unfavorable conditions necessarily result in a wasteful design or problems such as condensation. Climatic analysis is only a starting point that can indicate potential opportunities and liabilities—the development of the individual house design will determine the extent of positive and negative effects.

In spite of these limitations of climatic analysis, recent research has produced a framework for understanding regional issues in earth sheltered design. The primary work in this field is *Regional Analysis of Ground and Above-Ground Climate* [Labs, 1981a]. Additional analysis of regional suitability was developed in *Earth Sheltered Residential Design Manual* [Sterling, et al., 1982]. In the latter publication, regional issues other than climate such as the occurrence of tornadoes and earthquakes, were considered. The purpose of this section is to clarify and summarize the design implications associated with this regional climate analysis research.

The United States can be divided into climatic regions based on a number of characteristics. Identifying a few large regions—such as north, southeast, and southwest—clearly distinguishes the major regions, but climatic conditions vary greatly within a region, and certain ambiguous areas have some characteristics of two or more regions. Dividing the country into a number of smaller climate regions produces more uniformity within a discrete region. Unfortunately, it is difficult to make clear distinctions in discussing design implications for so many regions. Not only are the differences between regions often subtle, but detailed information on below-ground climate and the effects on energy use has not yet been developed.

To provide some basic guidance on regional design implications, three general climate types are discussed here: the north, where cold winter conditions are the main concern; the southeast, where hot, humid summers predominate; and the southwest, where hot, arid conditions are the major climatic feature. Much of the following discussion is based on the work and observations of Kenneth Labs [Labs, 1981a, 1982].

Northern Regions

In the northern half of the United States, cold winter conditions are the primary concern with respect to energy conservation. Many areas also must contend with hot, sometimes humid, summer conditions, although the magnitude of the cooling load is less in this region than it is further south. Earth sheltered design is an appropriate means of reducing both winter heating and summer cooling loads. Since the need for heating predominates, designs should maximize winter wind protection with earth berming (fig. 3-29). A compact house geometry and high percentage of surfaces in contact with the earth will minimize heat loss through conduction and infiltration. Insulation is essential on below-grade roofs and walls unless ground temperature modification techniques are used. Energy-related benefits of an earth-covered roof in winter are not dramatic, making bermed structures a reasonable alternative. The large mass in concrete earth sheltered structures couples well with passive solar design.

A summer benefit in northern regions is the relatively low ground temperatures capable of providing some direct cooling. In addition, below-grade placement of the structure (particularly with an earth-covered roof) reduces heat gain. In the northeast and parts of the midwest, condensation may be a problem if earth-contact cooling is used with natural ventilation. Condensation can be reduced or eliminated by limiting the introduction of outside air or raising the temperature of interior building surfaces.

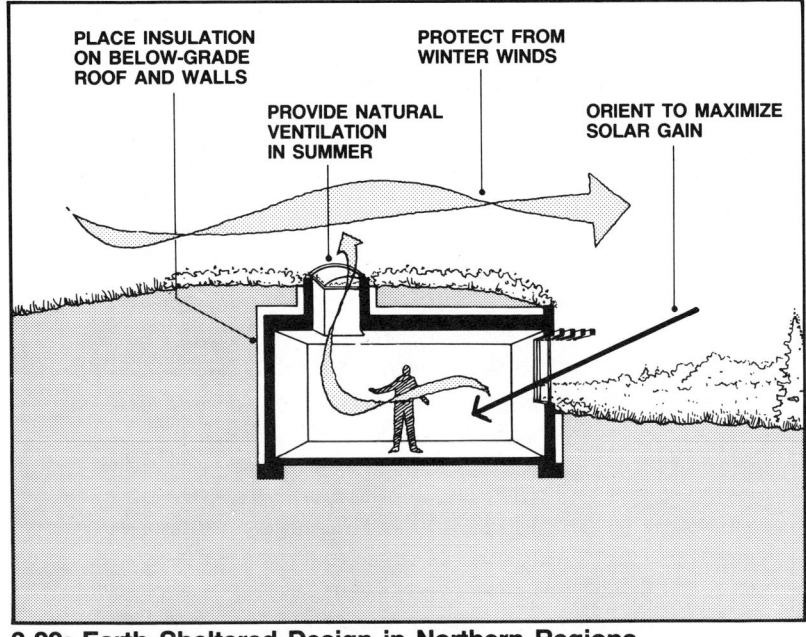

3-29: Earth Sheltered Design in Northern Regions

Southeastern Regions

The southeastern United States, particularly along the Gulf and southern Atlantic coasts, is characterized by high humidity and temperatures throughout much of the year. The large differences between day and night temperatures found in more arid regions do not exist here. The relatively small winter heating load can be easily met with solar heating and requires no extraordinary efforts to conserve energy.

In summer, the primary benefit of earth-bermed walls and earth-covered roofs in this region is the manner in which they prevent direct solar radiation from reaching the structure. Plant materials on the roof and berms play an important role in absorbing and reflecting this heat. Although below-grade designs can reduce the heat gain in a structure, ground temperatures near the surface are not low enough to provide much direct cooling. For passively cooled buildings, there is little benefit from mass in a climate with constantly high temperatures. For buildings that are mechanically cooled, however, the mass provided by an earth sheltered structure can be beneficial in storing coolth and reducing cooling loads.

In the southeast one of the best means of providing cooling is with natural and mechanical ventilation. This emphasis on ventilation in energy-efficient design for this region presents two potential problems with earth sheltered buildings: condensation from warm, humid air striking cooler wall surfaces, and the inhibition of natural ventilation in a below-grade structure.

In spite of the apparent lack of major energy-related benefits in building below-grade in this region, a number of houses have successfully used earth integration combined with other techniques to produce energy-efficient housing without major problems. One approach is to set the building only partially into the earth to maintain cross-ventilation,

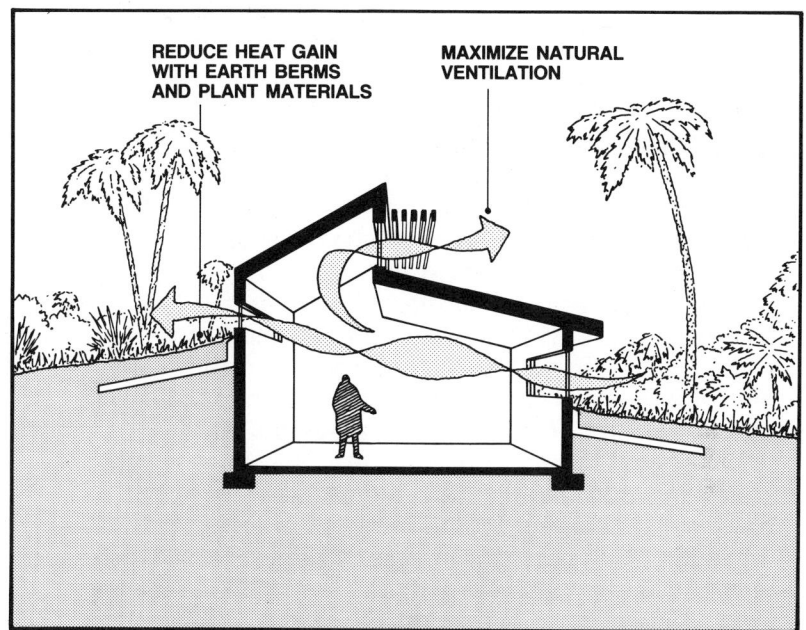

3-30: Earth Sheltered Design in Southeastern Regions

as shown in figure 3-30, and to utilize man-made shading devices combined with vegetation and earth to reduce heat gain. Mechanical ventilation, which is considerably less expensive than air-conditioning, can be effectively used in any design, including deep earth-covered buildings. A suggested technique to reduce heat gain on the below-grade walls is to extend insulation horizontally. The approach illustrated in figure 3-30 represents an attempt to combine several suitable passive cooling strategies in a hot, humid climate. If mechanical cooling is still desired or necessary, then a design with deeper placement of the building and an earth-covered roof would be appropriate to increase the mass and the isolation from the surface. Although few houses have been built in this manner for economic and practical reasons, structures set far more deeply into the ground (with 3 to 10 feet of earth on the roof) may provide the cooler ground temperatures not found closer to the surface in this region.

Southwestern Regions

The primary energy-related concern in the southwest is the hot, sometimes extremely hot, summer. In contrast to the southeastern United States, however, the climate is dry, the sky is usually clear, and large differences between day and night temperatures exist. Although the climate is predominantly arid, short periods of high humidity can exist. Similar to the southeast, the winter heating load in much of the southwest is relatively small and can usually be handled easily with passive solar heating. It is interesting to note, however, that underground placement of a structure in this climate may well virtually eliminate heat loss in winter and may even provide heat from the high ground temperatures at times.

In spite of the relatively high ground temperatures in the southwest, which can provide little direct cooling under normal circumstances, a number of cooling season benefits are associated with earth sheltered design in this arid region. Temperatures are dampened faster in dryer soil, and even though ground temperatures are high, they are cooler than the extremely high air temperatures during the day. Not only are walls removed from this heat, but a massive earth-covered roof can absorb heat during the day and radiate it back to the sky at night. Because of the arid climate, condensation is usually not a problem.

Earth sheltered design in the southwest provides unique opportunities for energy conservation because it can complement other strategies. Ground temperatures can be manipulated in several ways to produce more favorable conditions. Ventilation during the extreme heat of the day is undesirable, so complete underground placement can be achieved

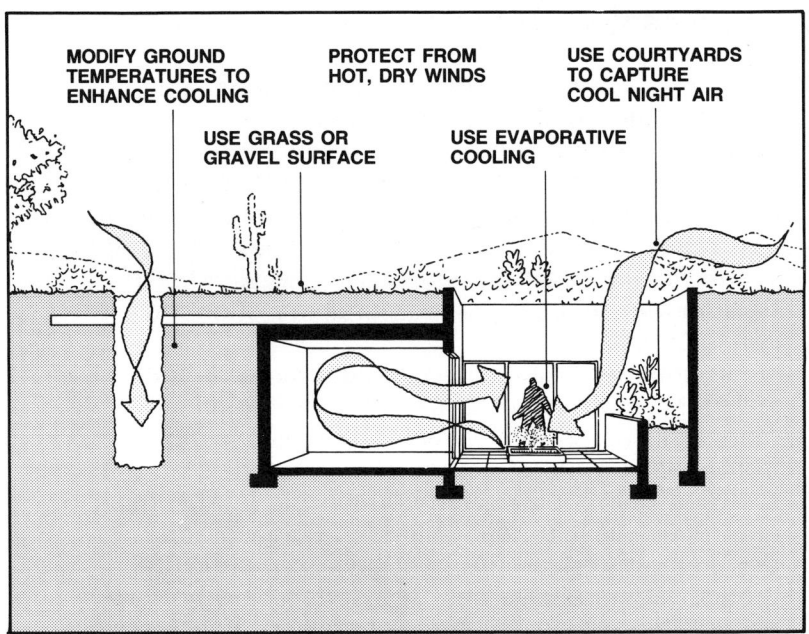

3-31: Earth Sheltered Design in Southwestern Regions

without compromise. Taking advantage of day/night temperature swings is desirable, however, and a below-grade atrium design is an ideal technique for collecting heavier cool air that settles in the courtyard and causes warmer air to rise out of the house (fig. 3-31). Evaporative cooling techniques such as a fountain in the courtyard can work effectively with an earth sheltered design. The arid climate lends itself to a number of techniques for reducing ground temperatures (discussed in the previous section). As shown in figure 3-31, these include grass- or pebble-covered ground surfaces, horizontally extended insulation, and gravel-filled trenches or shafts for collecting cool night air. If ground temperatures are reduced sufficiently to act as a heat sink and provide cooling, then it may be desirable to extend the house layout to maximize the wall area in contact with the earth.

Regional Issues in Earth Sheltered Design

Of course, many variations and combinations of these climatic conditions in the north, southeast, and southwest exist; moreover some smaller areas are quite different from any of these generalized regions. In his research Ken Labs has developed a map that attempts to identify regional issues in a more precise way than simple delineation of three large zones. As shown in figure 3-32, the nine regions overlap to some extent, indicating that clear distinctions are impossible to make. The following comments on each region are the original descriptions provided by Ken Labs [Labs, 1981a].

Zone A: Cold, cloudy winters maximize value of earth tempering as a heat-conservation measure. Cool soil and dry summers favor subgrade placement and earth cover, with little likelihood of condensation.

Zone B: Severely cold winters demand major heat conservation measures, even though more sunshine is available here than on the coast. Dry summers and cool soil favor earth covered roofs and ground coupling.

Zone C: Good winter insolation offsets need for extraordinary winter heat conservation, but summer benefit is more important here than in zone B. Earth cover is advantageous: the ground offers some cooling, condensation is unlikely, and ventilation is not a major necessity.

Zone D: Cold and often cloudy winters place a premium on heat conservation. Low summer ground temperatures offer a cooling source, but with possibilitiy of condensation. High summer humidity makes ventilation the leading conventional summer climate control strategy. An aboveground superinsulated house designed to maximize ventilation is an important competing design approach.

Zone E: Generally good winter sun and minor heating demand reduce the need for extreme heat-conservation measures. The ground offers protection from overheated air but not major cooling potential as a heat sink. The primacy of ventilation and the possibility of condensation compromise summer benefits. Quality of design will determine actual benefit realized here.

Zone F: High ground temperatures. Persistent high humidity levels largely negate value of roof mass and establish ventilation as the only important summer cooling strategy. Any design that compromises ventilation effectiveness without contributing to cooling may be considered counterproductive.

Zone G: This is a transition area between zones F and H, comments concerning which apply here in degree. The value of earth tempering increases moving westward through this zone and diminishes moving southward.

Zone H: Summer ground temperatures are high but relatively much cooler than air. Aridity favors roof mass, reduces need for ventilation, eliminates concern about condensation. Potential for integrating earth tempering with other passive design alternatives is high.

Zone I: Extraordinary means of climate control are not required because of the relatively moderate climate of this zone. Earth tempering is compatible with other strategies, with no strong argument for or against it.

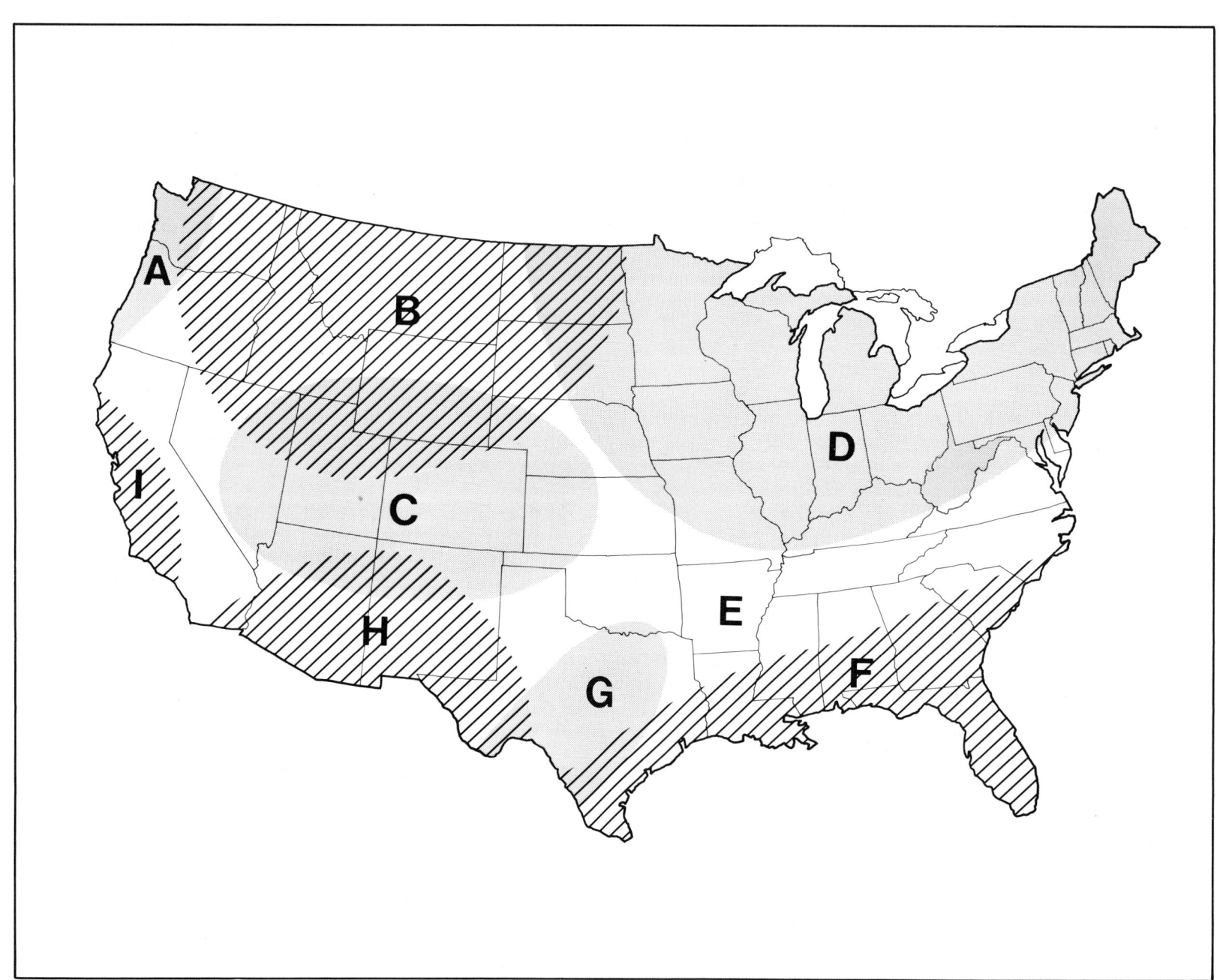

3-32: Regional Issues in Earth Sheltered Design

Source: Kenneth Labs, 1981 (see references).

Optimizing Insulation Placement

Placing earth berms around a building or setting a structure more deeply underground can be considered a relatively forgiving technology. Many of the benefits associated with earth-integrated design, such as infiltration control, moderation of outside temperatures, and reduced heat gain, will be realized to some extent almost regardless of the details of the design. On the other hand, without careful attention to critical details such as insulation placement, the house is unlikely to provide the maximum possible reduction in energy use. In order to maximize the energy savings of earth sheltered houses in a cost-effective way, calculation techniques are required that can predict energy use and help to optimize the performance in the design stage.

The design of earth sheltered houses must be carefully considered on two levels. First, heat transfer through the ground must be understood in order to determine the effects of differing amounts of insulation at different depths. Once this information is developed, the design must be approached on the second level: to achieve optimal integration of climate, earth contact, mass, insulation levels, solar systems, mechanical systems, and costs. In the relatively few years since earth sheltered housing has become a viable alternative, some progress has been made in evaluating and developing reliable calculation techniques for heat transfer below grade.

Very little effort has been directed at understanding the integration of earth contact with other systems. Rather extensive research has been done in some keys areas, however, some of which can be directly applied to earth sheltered buildings. Most notable are the many calculation techniques, computer simulations, and design guidelines developed for passive solar systems. Research on the effects of mass and optimizing passive solar systems is available in many well-known references [Balcomb, et al., 1983; Mazria, 1979]. An important direction for future research involves analyzing the effects of combining earth integration with other systems.

Although much valuable work has been done in developing methods of predicting heat transfer below grade, questions remain and simple accessible answers are elusive. Basically, the difficulty lies in the complexity of the problem. Above grade, heat flow through a relatively thin wall or roof can be easily determined from a few known variables: the thermal resistance of the wall or roof, the inside temperature, and the outside temperature. Below grade, however, the variables are less predictable, and conditions change continuously. One problem is that moisture in the soil can change its thermal resistance by significant amounts. Heat gain and heat loss at the ground surface, which help determine below grade temperatures, are affected by the surface cover. In summer, grass or light-colored rock can reflect incoming radiation, whereas bare earth or blacktop absorb it to a much greater degree. Plants, their root systems, and snow cover act as additional insulation in winter. Another problem in calculation is that heat is not lost to the earth in the same manner as it is to the outside air. Heat travels more slowly through the earth, and the ground temperatures change. Generally, the earth around a building is permanently warmer than undisturbed soil, resulting in lower heat loss in winter but higher temperatures in summer that reduce the effects of earth contact cooling. Any accurate calculation method must take into account the dynamic conditions found below grade.

Current methods of calculating energy transfer through earth-contact roofs, walls, and floors appear to fall into two categories: simple hand calculation methods and detailed computer simulations. Although the simpler methods are more accessible and could be used easily to calculate a number of alternatives, they either fail to reflect the impact of certain conditions or they are simply not considered accurate. Detailed computer simulations, on the other hand, can reflect many of the critical parameters and variables as presently understood, and some computer models have been validated against actual field conditions. The drawback to these simulations is that they are inaccessible to most designers and their complexity makes examination of a wide range of conditions time-consuming and expensive. Commonly used computer programs for determining building energy use have varying degrees of sophistication and accuracy in their approach to simulating below-grade buildings [Goldberg, 1984]. See *References and Bibliography* for further information on below-grade heat transfer calculation techniques.

Based on the available information regarding below-grade heat transfer and insulation placement, it is not possible to provide comprehsive design information for a wide range of climatic conditions and building design options. It is possible, however, to provide a good basis for making design decisions. Although designs cannot be fully optimized based on the current state of the art, major pitfalls can be avoided and sound practices can be recommended. In the remainder of this section, the basic principles of below-grade insulation placement are discussed, along with general recommendations for insulation amounts in different climates. In the following section, highlights of extensive parametric studies are presented to provide a better understanding of the many variables involved in earth sheltered design.

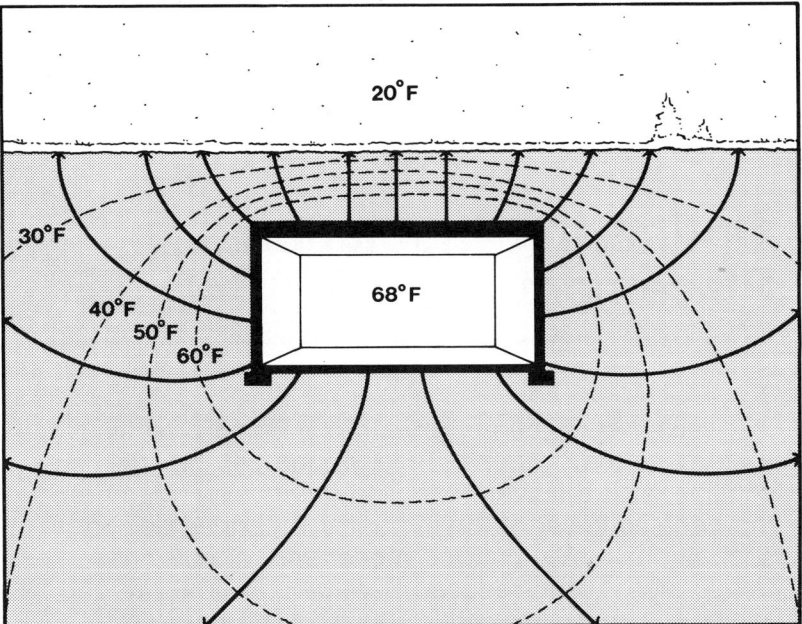
3-33: Schematic Below-Grade Heat Flow in Winter

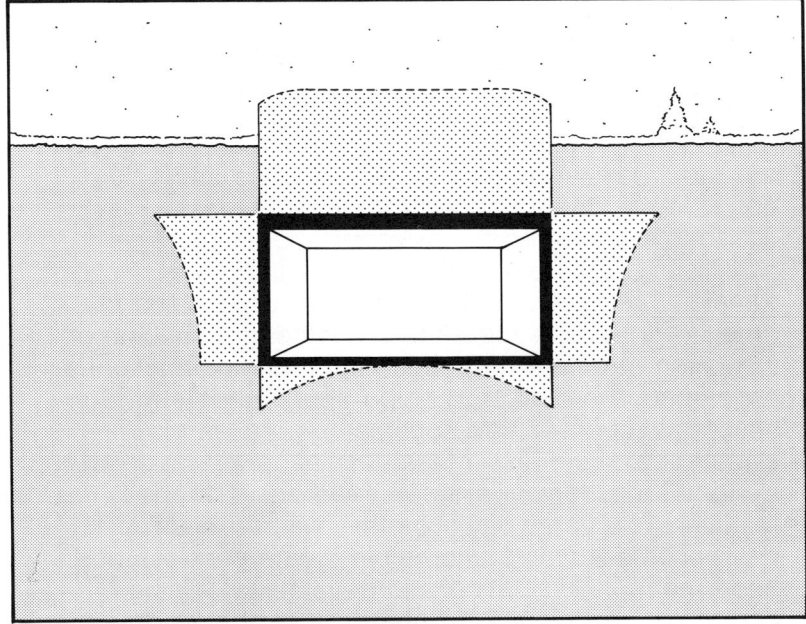
3-34: Optimal Insulation Function

The relative effects of depth, insulation amount, ground surface conditions and soil conductivity are simulated with a computer and presented.

Insulation Principles for Winter Conditions

To understand the optimal insulation patterns for winter conditions, it is useful to examine the typical patterns of heat flow through the ground. In figure 3-33, an uninsulated below-grade space is shown. Heat flows from the heated space to the colder outside air temperatures. The dashed lines represent constant temperatures, and the solid arrows indicate the heat flow. The greatest losses occur near the surface, where the path through the soil is shortest—through the roof and upper walls. Heat loss diminishes at greater depths and is at its lowest in the center of the uninsulated floor.

To minimize steady-state heat loss from a structure in an optimal way, insulation should be distributed so that the rate of heat loss through all areas of the structure is the same [Claesson and Eftring, 1979]. Thus insulation should be placed in proportion to the magnitude of loss. Setting the insulation thickness to zero at the point of minimum heat loss results in the "optimal insulation function" shown in figure 3-34. This should guide the distribution of insulation against winter heat losses but does not determine the overall quantity of insulation that is most cost-effective for each climate. Distribution of a higher or lower level of insulation is obtained by simply adding or subtracting a constant amount of insulation from the optimal insulation function. This leaves areas of the structure uninsulated when lower amounts of insulation are used.

A typical approximation of an optimal distribution against winter heat loss using conventional rigid board insulation is shown in figure 3-35. The greatest amount is on the flat roof, with the next

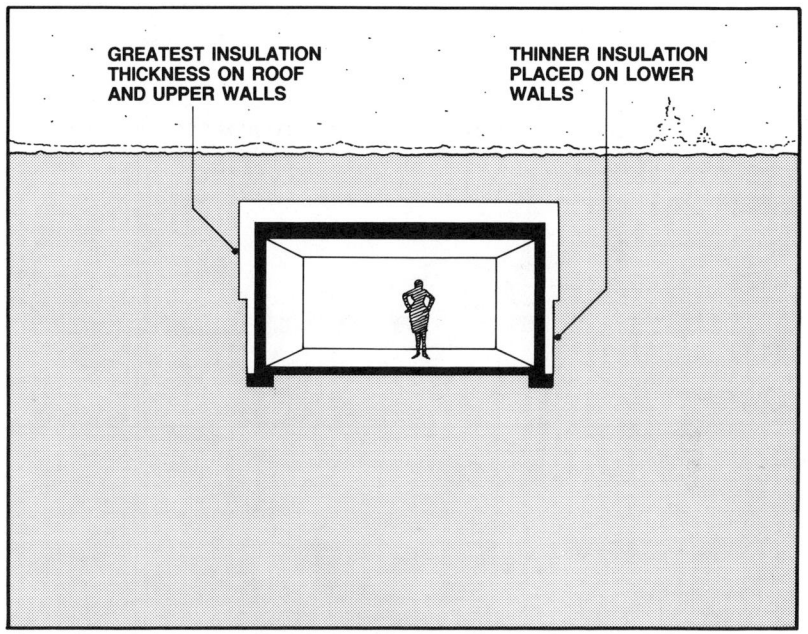

3-35: Typical Below-Grade Insulation Placement for Winter

greatest on the walls to a depth of about 6 feet. A smaller amount is placed on the lower wall and none beneath the floor. In extremely cold climates, a small amount of insulation may be placed around the perimeter of the floor, and in some cases under the entire floor.

An actual earth sheltered house is not a totally underground chamber as shown in figure 3-35, but has exposed walls and openings in roofs and walls that in effect place certain portions of the building envelope closer to the surface than is apparent in an idealized section drawing. Whenever a below-grade wall or floor is closer to the surface, excessive heat loss will occur unless insulation is placed in the path of heat flow. Figure 3-36 illustrates a common condition with an exposed wall. To prevent excessive loss, the floor slab should be insulated along the perimeter, by placing insulation either horizontally under the slab extending back at least 4 feet from the edge, or vertically as shown. Roof openings such as skylights should be insulated to the same extent that the roof is.

In figure 3-37, a typical plan of an earth sheltered house is shown. Below-grade walls near exposed walls are subject to greater heat losses than are more remote below-grade walls because they are closer to outside conditions. Insulation should be increased on the entire wall in these areas to an amount equal to the insulation thickness on the upper wall.

Insulation Principles for Summer Conditions

Although summer conditions vary considerably in different climates, two basic heat-flow phenomena affect insulation placement. As shown in figure 3-38, heat from the sun and warm outdoor temperatures penetrates the upper few feet of soil and flows into the space through the roof and upper walls. Because deeper ground temperatures are often cooler than the comfort zone, heat flows from the space to the ground through the floor and lower walls. Because it is deeper and less influenced by surface temperatures, a greater cooling effect occurs through the floor than through the walls.

One insulation pattern considered optimal for summer conditions is shown in figure 3-39. The greatest insulation is on the roof, corresponding to the greatest heat gain. A smaller amount is placed on the upper walls. No insulation is placed on the lower wall and floor to take advantage of the cooling effect of losing heat through these surfaces. The degree to which the lower wall is useful for cooling depends on climatic factors and the ground surface. These relationships will be explored in more detail in the next section.

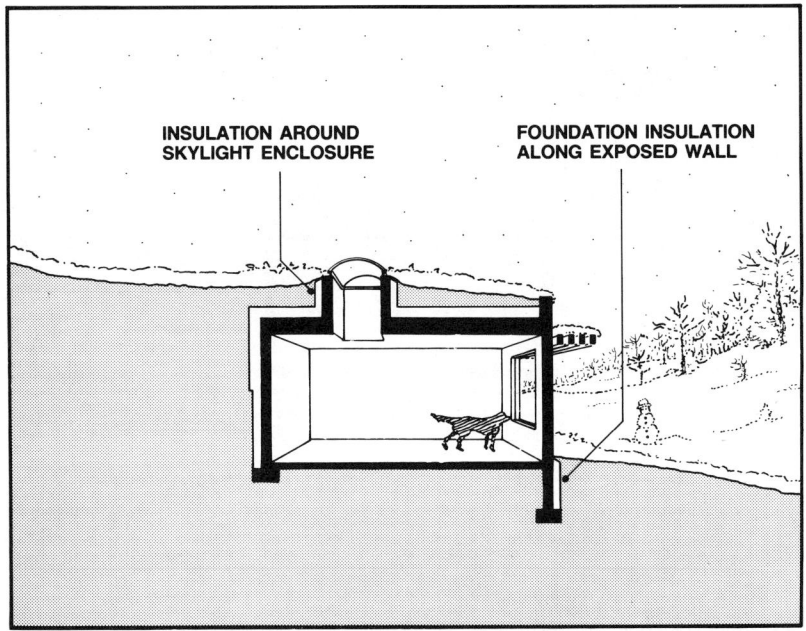

3-36: Below-Grade Insulation at Exposed Walls and Openings

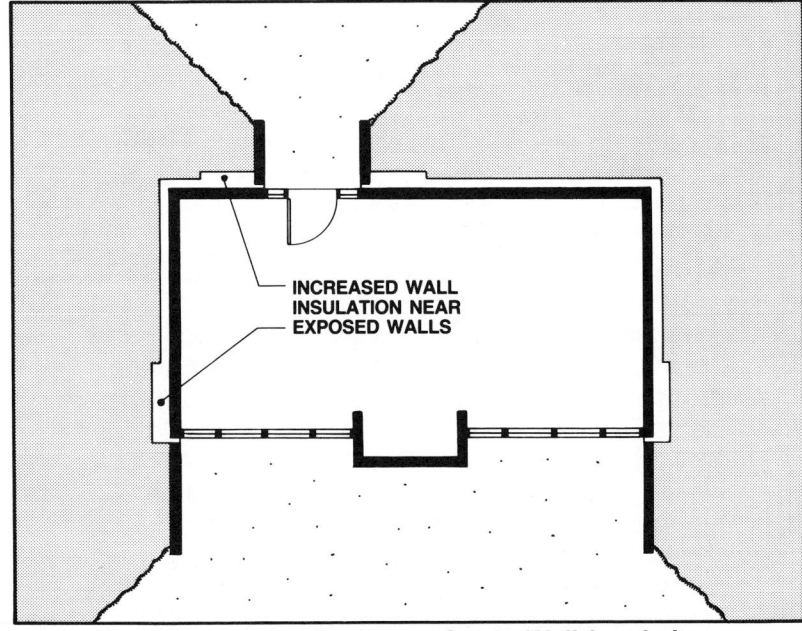

3-37: Floor Plan Indicating Below-Grade Wall Insulation

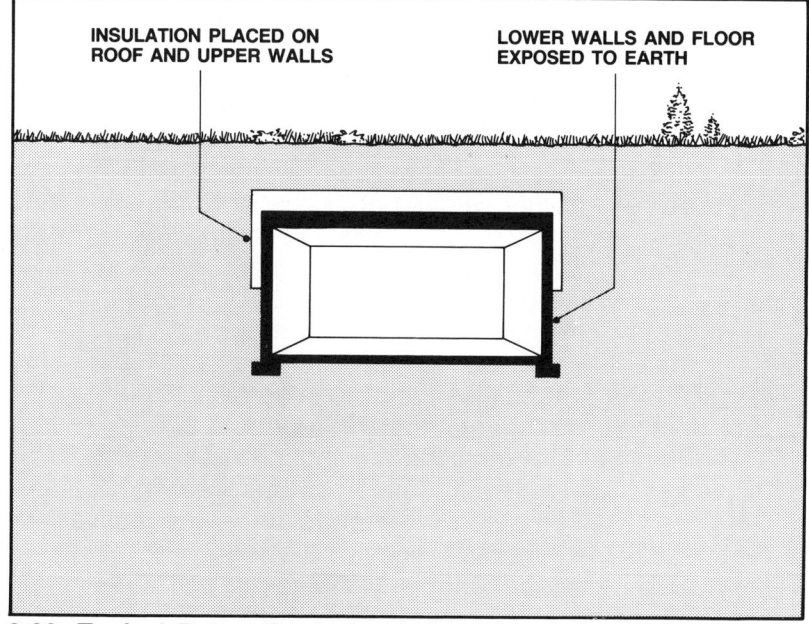

3-38: Schematic Below-Grade Heat Flow in Summer

3-39: Typical Below-Grade Insulation Placement for Summer

Alternative Insulation Configurations

In the previous illustrations of optimal insulation patterns, insulation was shown applied directly to the outside roof, wall, or floor surfaces. While this conventional approach is easy to implement, there are some potential drawbacks in achieving optimal performance. First, conventional insulation placement has no direct effect on soil and moisture conditions around the house which may not be ideal for enhancing thermal performance. A wet soil will conduct heat away from the building faster than a dry soil. This may be desirable in summer but not in winter.

The second drawback is that a single insulation configuration is usually not optimal for both winter and summer conditions in most climates causing the designer to devise compromise solutions. Conventional placement of roof insulation can usually meet winter and summer objectives with no conflict. It is often desirable, however, to insulate below-grade walls and floors to reduce heat loss in winter while leaving walls and floors exposed to the surrounding earth to enhance summer cooling. Climate and the priorities of the designer usually determine whether design for winter or summer conditions is favored. The compromise solution of insulating the upper half of below-grade walls while leaving the lower half uninsulated is somewhat effective but does not take full advantage of the potential of earth-integrated design and may increase condensation problems immediately below the insulated section.

One approach to resolving this winter/summer conflict has been suggested but the concept has only been tested on a limited basis. As shown in figure 3-40, roof insulation is extended horizontally beyond the building perimeter. The intention is to prevent heat gain from reaching deeper ground in summer while placing the entire wall in contact with the cooler ground temperatures. In winter, heat loss

97

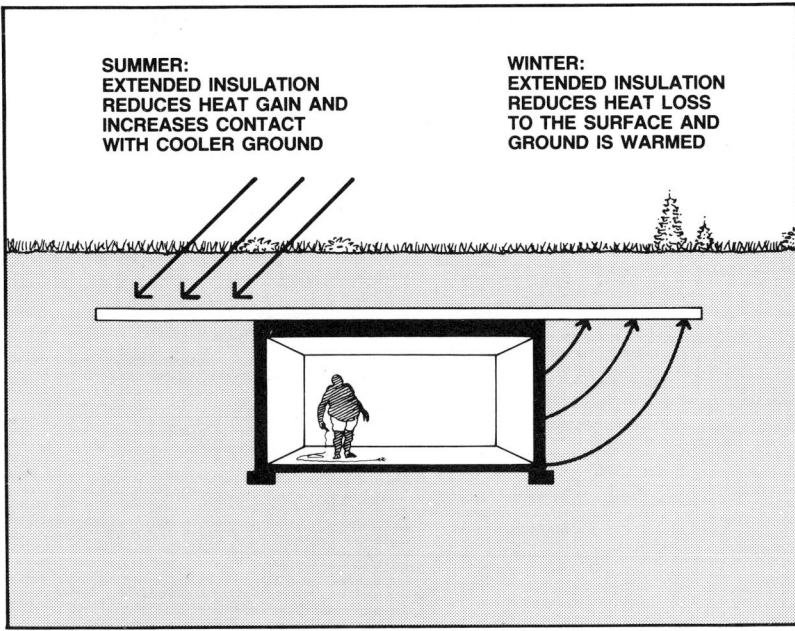

3-40: Alternative Insulation Placement

from the walls cannot flow directly to the surface without passing through the horizontal insulation. Thus, the ground adjacent to the wall is warmed further reducing heat loss. Extending the insulation a few feet beyond the structure is also a compromise solution to optimal design for summer and winter. It has been suggested, however, than extending the insulation considerably further (about 20 feet) would modify ground temperatures around the building and use the heat storage capacity of the earth more effectively [Hait, 1983]. In addition, if a waterproof membrane is extended over the insulation the earth around the building will be dry resulting in a lower thermal conductivity. Computer simulations of heat transfer with this extended insulation condition appear in the next section.

Other Insulation Considerations

Inside and Outside Placement: In most cases placing insulation outside the structural envelope of an earth sheltered building is recommended; many variables, however, can influence this decision. Factors such as cost, difficulty of construction, importance of thermal mass, and effectiveness of insulation must be considered. These issues are discussed in more detail in chapter 5.

Passive Solar Gain: The comments above concerning the low heat fluxes from the floors of earth-sheltered structures apply to the amount of heat lost when interior air temperatures are approximately 68°F and ground temperatures are in the moderate range of 50°F to 68°F. Under these conditions less than a 18°F difference will exist between interior air temperature and the deep ground temperature, and slightly less between the floor slab and the deep ground temperature. The small temperature difference and the large heat-flow path involved results in the low heat flux.

When a floor is being used for direct passive solar gain and the sun is directly warming the slab, however, it is desirable to raise the temperature of that slab significantly so that heat can be reradiated from the slab as the remainder of the building cools. The slab temperature may be raised to 80°F or higher; but now, instead of a 15 to 18°F or less temperature difference between the slab and the deep ground, the temperature difference may be more than 30°F—thus doubling or tripling the heat loss to deep ground. Insulation placed under the slab as shown in figure 3-41 will reduce this loss. The other effect of insulation in these areas is that insulation close to the underside of the floor surface will keep floor temperatures high to provide effective reradiation. Insulation deeper beneath the floor surface (perhaps beneath a gravel layer) will not provide as high a floor temperature but will provide a larger capacity of heat storage at a lower temperature.

Whether and to what level passive solar gain areas should be insulated will depend on the local climate and the expectations of how the passive solar gain is to be used in the functioning of the building. Aside from passive solar gain, insulation may be placed under all or part of the floor to reduce losses from under floor heating ducts or radiant heating systems under the slab.

Condensation: There are a number of misconceptions about the ability of insulation outside the structure to raise the surface temperature inside the structure and, hence, to reduce the sensation of cold floors and walls and eliminate the possibility of condensation. First, after the building has been in operation for a few months, the interior surface temperature will be primarily controlled by the interior air temperature adjacent to the surface, together with any radiation falling on the surface except for poorly insulated high heat loss areas of the structure. In areas remote from the surface or away from exposed portions of the building an uninsulated floor or wall will usually have a surface temperature within 2°F of a relatively stable air temperature. A small amount of insulation ouside the wall will affect surface temperatures very little; that is, surface temperatures will probably not rise by more than 1°F. A rise in the wall or floor temperature from 66°F to 67°F is unlikely to affect comfort when touching the wall. The main reason for the common perception of cold floors is that such materials as concrete or tile rapidly conduct the heat away from a hand or foot, whereas a wood flooring or carpet locally insulates the part of the body in contact with it. Thus, the sensation of warmer floors or walls is best obtained by using appropriate interior finishes rather than by exterior insulation.

Much the same argument applies to the prevention of condensation. Interior surface temperatures (except those areas exposed to solar radiation) will probably only be raised by 1°F or less by adding exterior insulation. This added insulation will only eliminate condensation problems compared to the uninsulated wall when the dewpoint lies in the 1°F range between the two potential surface temperatures. This small improvement is not enough to guarantee a greatly superior performance over the uninsulated wall. If condensation is a real problem in a particular climate, a small amount of interior insulation or a vapor-barrier stud wall will ensure that the surface on which condensation could occur will be essentially at the interior air temperature. Otherwise, provisions for occasional dehumidification can be made.

A final point about insulation and condensation: incomplete insulation of a wall can cause worse condensation problems than if the wall were not insulated at all. The insulation keeps the ground

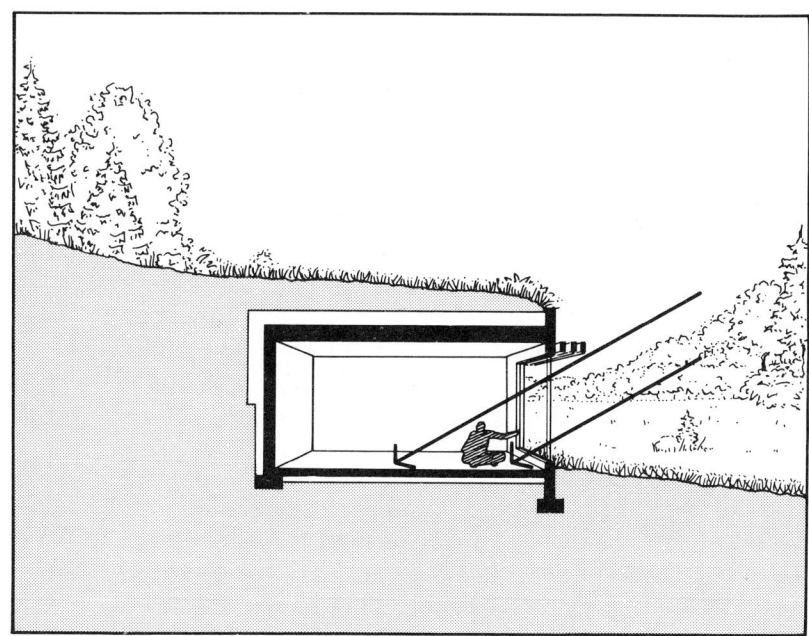

3-41: Insulation Placed under Floor Slab

temperatures outside it cool, an effect that spills around the edges of the insulation, causing the section of wall immediately adjacent to the insulation to be cooler than the insulated section and the rest of the uninsulated section [Houghton, et al., 1942]. Because of this phenomena, placing insulation only on the upper half of a wall in a humid climate is unadvisable.

Interior Surface Finishes: In many earth sheltered structures, the roof, walls, and floor are concrete and in direct contact with the surrounding earth. Interior finishes such as carpet on floors or gypsum board on furred-out strips insulate the interior space from the ground temperatures. In winter this may be desirable, but in summer it may not. Also, finishes that insulate the concrete on the inside reduce the effectiveness of the mass in storing energy and dampening temperature fluctuations. Interior finishes that do not insulate include exposed concrete and concrete block treated in a decorative manner (burnishing, coloring, exposed aggregate), ceramic tiles, and plaster applied directly to the concrete.

Thermal Breaks: Neglecting thermal breaks can cause significant heat loss in an otherwise well-insulated building envelope. A thermal break refers to the insertion of insulation in parts of the building where a high conductivity material is in contact with both the inside air and the outside conditions. Although these sections usually constitute a relatively small area, they can begin to dominate the heat loss as the overall insulation of the building is improved.

Thermal breaks can be provided by inserting small thicknesses of insulation at appropriate points within the structure or by wrapping the exposed structural element with insulation. Examples of places where thermal breaks should be considered are shown in figures 3-42 and 3-43. One approach to

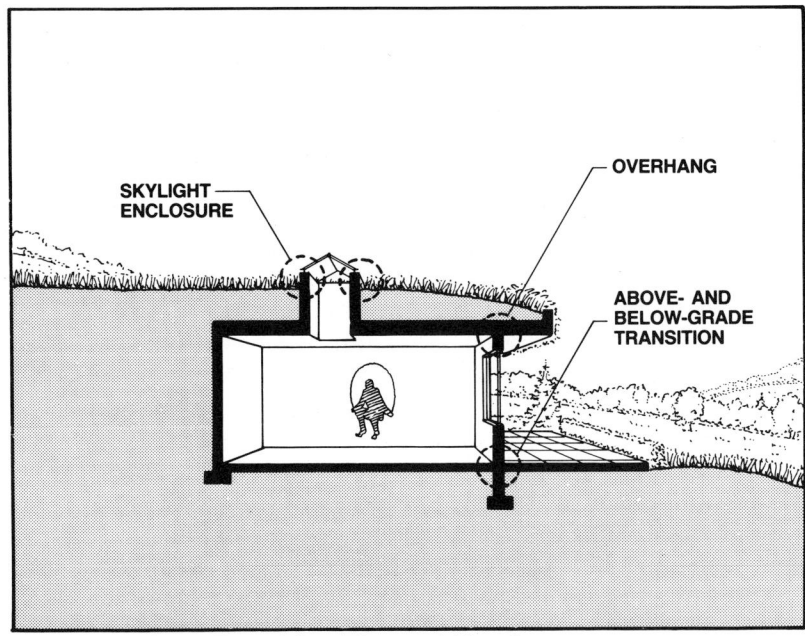

3-42: Locations Requiring Thermal Breaks

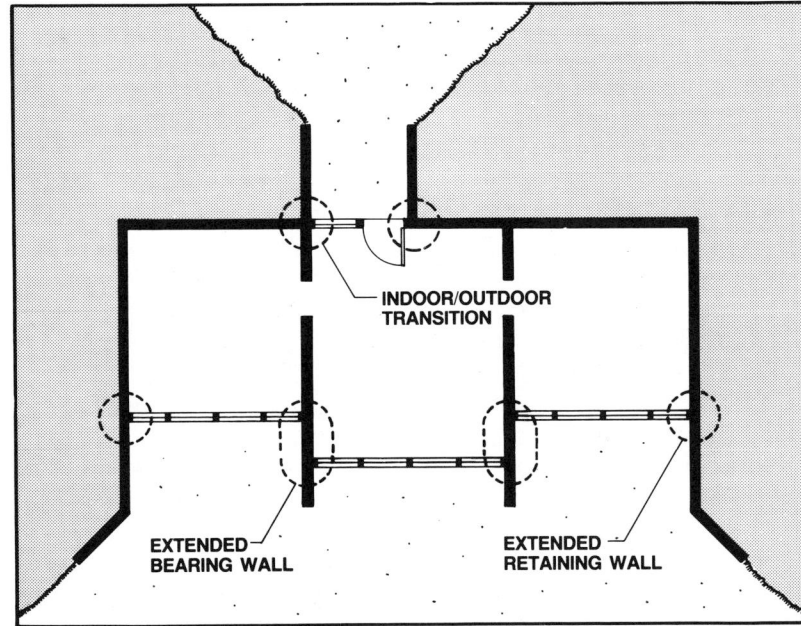

3-43: Floor Plan Indicating Thermal Break Locations

providing a thermal break in a concrete overhang is shown in figure 3-44. Construction details illustrating different approaches to providing thermal breaks are shown in *Earth Sheltered Residential Design Manual* [Sterling, et al., 1982].

Insulation Placement Recommendations

Although detailed guidelines have not been completely developed for insulation placement below grade, general ranges of suitable insulation amounts have been established and are shown in figure 3-45. These values represent engineering judgment about the relative impact of insulation on the heating and cooling loads for that climate. No detailed cost-benefit analyses have been carried out to determine more precise figures. The parametric studies in the following section serve to illustrate the relative effects of insulation placement and thickness in two climates.

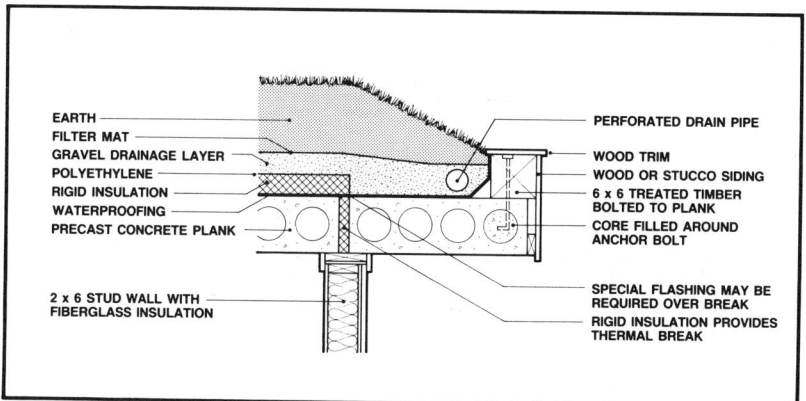

3-44: Earth-Covered Roof Edge Detail

Heating/Cooling Degree Days (Base: 65°F)	Suggested Range of Below-Grade Insulation[1]		
	Roofs and Upper Wall[2]	Lower Wall[3]	Remote Floor Areas[4]
8,000-11,000/0-500	R-20—R-40	R-5—R-20	0—R-5
5,000-8,000/500-1,500	R-20—R-30	R-5—R-10	0—R-5
2,000-5,000/1,500-2,500	R-10—R-20	0—R-5	0
over 2,000/under 2,000	R-10—R-20	0	0

3-45: Suggested Amounts of Below-Grade Insulation

Notes: This table should be used as a general guide only and has assumed an earth cover thickness in the range of 12 to 30 inches for the earth covered roof.
1. The accompanying text discusses distribution of insulation and exceptions to the norms presented in the table.
2. Earth covered roof with 12 to 30 inches of cover and walls within 8 feet of the ground surface.
3. Earth covered wall surfaces further than 8 feet from the ground surface.
4. Floor areas remote (i.e., more than 10 feet from the ground surface which are not used as a solar storage area or for heat distribution.

Parametric Studies of Roof, Wall, and Floor Components

As part of the passive cooling research sponsored by the U.S. Department of Energy, earth-contact buildings were studied. The research effort included monitoring of earth-contact structures and the development and validation of accurate computer codes to simulate below-grade heat transfer [Meixel, Bligh, 1983]. One aspect of the research was the development of a series of parametric studies of building depth and below-grade insulation placement in different climates. Highlights of the study, "Preliminary Design Guidelines for Earth Contact Buildings," are presented in this section [Carmody, Meixel, Shen, 1983].

Development of Parametric Studies

Performing parametric studies refers to doing a series of calculations in which variables are changed to demonstrate and analyze their the effects. In the case of earth sheltered buildings, parametric studies can be useful in determining the effect on energy use of a number of variables in the location, design, and operation of a structure. By examining a building at different depths with different amounts and arrangements of insulation, it is possible to see the relative impact of certain design decisions.

Unfortunately, performing relatively complete parametric studies of earth sheltered building variations requires examination of an enormous number of cases because there are so many critical variables. In addition to building depth and insulation placement, there are variations in soil conditions (especially moisture content), ground surface conditions, and the interior building conditions (e.g., indoor temperatures and whether temperature is permitted to fluctuate). To fully understand the energy-related effects of all these variables, it is desirable to examine them in a number of climates applied to a range of building configurations and orientations. Moreover, the total energy-related effects can be clarified only if other systems (such as passive solar heating) are included in the analysis.

One purpose of the passive cooling research conducted by the U.S. Department of Energy was to develop design guidelines that could assist architects, engineers, and researchers in their efforts to assess benefits and make design decisions related to earth-contact structures. The primary constraints for developing such guidelines for earth-contact structures are the wide range of interrelated variables listed above that can affect energy transfer through the building envelope, and the methods available for determining their effect.

Based on the calculation techniques available at the time of the study, it was determined that the best approach to developing preliminary design information was to apply a detailed, validated computer model to a selected range of cases in a few representative climates. Using a two-dimensional finite difference computer program to examine the energy transfer through earth contact roofs, walls, and floors, the impact of relatively subtle changes in insulation placement, degree of earth contact, and ground conditions can be assessed. The finite difference computer program is designed to simulate dynamic changes that occur in ground temperatures over a period of time after a building is placed in the ground. Most calculation techniques do not

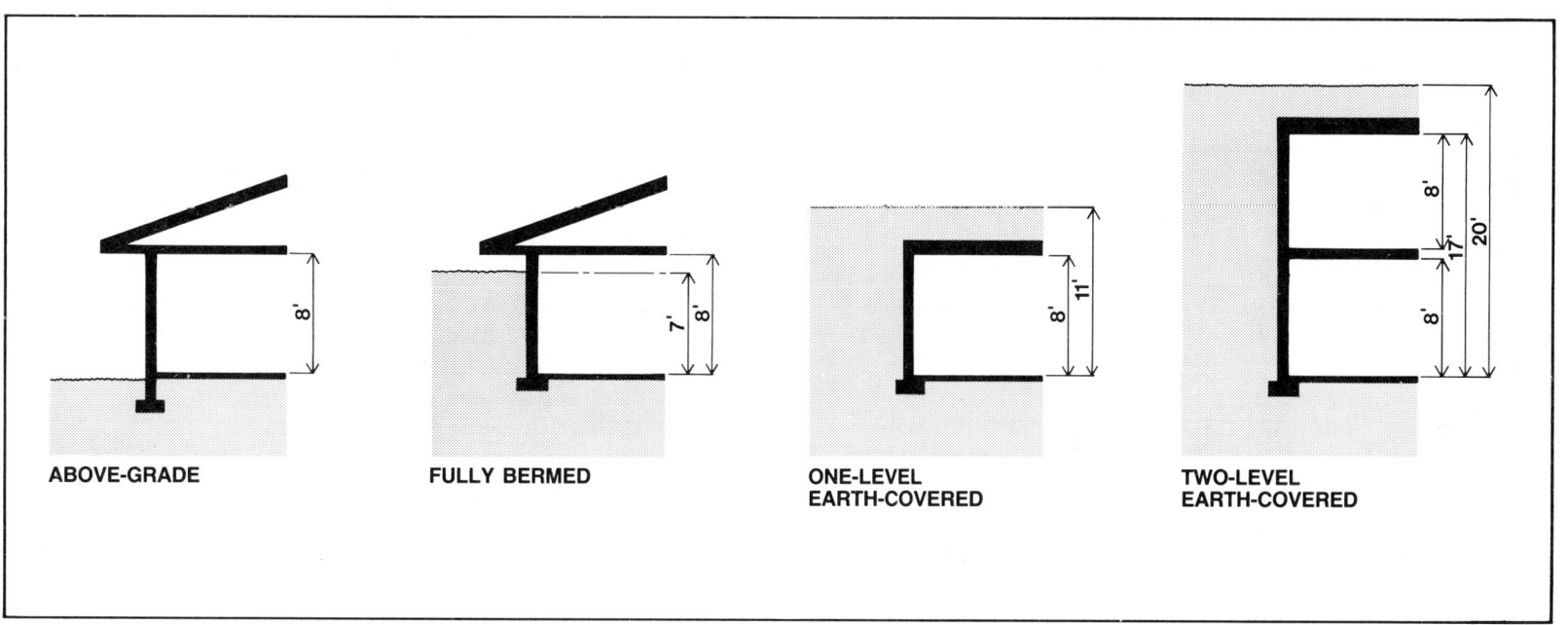

3-46: Configurations Analyzed in Parametric Studies

account for the increase in ground temperature that usually occurs gradually over a period of one to three years. The energy transfer figures indicated in the parametric studies reflect conditions after the ground temperatures have reached a relatively steady pattern. Although the parametric studies presented here are clearly not comprehensive in the range of climates and cases tested, the results can be compared with above-grade components, can be used to begin to develop design guidelines, and can indicate areas deserving future research.

Selection of Cases to Be Analyzed

The cases are based on the four prototypical configurations shown in figure 3-46 and described below.

Above-Grade: A conventional wood-truss roof system and a wood-frame wall structure placed on a concrete slab-on-grade. The wall is 8 feet high on the interior.

Fully Bermed: An 8-foot-high concrete wall bermed to a height of 7 feet. The floor of this fully bermed structure is a concrete slab and the roof is a conventional wood-truss system. Although this case is shown as a one-level bermed structure, the wall and floor conditions are equivalent to a basement in a conventional building.

103

One-Level Earth-Covered: A completely below-grade concrete structure with 2 feet of earth placed on the roof. The interior wall height of this one-story structure remains at 8 feet. This earth sheltered configuration results in a concrete wall and floor that are 4 feet deeper than in the fully bermed cases; floor level is 11 feet below the surface rather than 7 feet.

Two-Level Earth-Covered: A two-story earth sheltered structure with 2 feet of earth covering the roof. The total interior height of this concrete structure is 17 feet: two 8-foot-high spaces plus 1 foot for an intermediate floor. This configuration results in a lower floor level that is 20 feet below the surface.

Selection of Climates to Be Analyzed

Because they represent extremely diverse climates in the United States, two cities were selected for the analysis of earth-contact components. The two locations are Tucson, Arizona, a climate where cooling is the major concern although some heating is also required; and Minneapolis, Minnesota, a climate where heating is the major concern although a small amount of cooling is also required.

The computer simulation for each case provides energy transfer data on a monthly basis. For each climate the length of the heating season and cooling season is determined, and the monthly figures are combined to provide a separate energy transfer total for each season. In Tucson, the heating season is considered to be October through April and the cooling season, May through September. In Minneapolis, the heating season is September through May and the cooling season, June through August. In addition to providing separate energy transfer totals for the heating and cooling season in each case, the charts that follow include a combined energy transfer figure for the heating and cooling season.

Assumptions Concerning Energy Transfer

The major variations examined in each of these prototypical cases are different thicknesses and placement of insulation in both above- and below-grade components. Most other factors that could affect energy transfer are held constant to provide a valid comparison. One key factor in determining energy transfer through the ground is the conductivity, which depends mainly on soil type and moisture content. The following values are considered typical for the two cities and were used in all calculations (unless otherwise stated):

Tucson, Arizona: 1.3 W/m-°K
Minneapolis, Minnesota: 1.7 W/m-°K

It should be emphasized that soil moisture content is known to vary considerably depending on soil type, drainage characteristics of a site, and the time of year. The importance of thermal conductivity is demonstrated in one case for the Minneapolis climate where it is assumed to be 1.0 W/m-°K, a figure that represents a relatively dry soil.

Another factor that is held constant in all cases is the interior temperature of the space. Energy transfer through roofs, walls, and floors is calculated based on a constant interior temperature of 68°F in the heating season that is permitted to rise to 78°F during the cooling season.

The ground surface can have an impact on energy transfer, particularly in the cooling season. Grass or light-colored materials such as gravel can reduce the amount of solar radiation absorbed by the ground, whereas bare earth and asphalt paving permit a great deal of heat to be absorbed. In this analysis the ground surface in Minneapolis is considered to be grass in all cases. Grass is the most typical ground cover in this region and the energy transfer in Minneapolis is dominated more by heating than cooling, making optimization of ground cover for cooling less critical than in Tucson. The importance of cooling in Tucson and the dry climate that prevents grass from being the only typical ground cover require a different approach. For purposes of comparison, bare earth is considered to be the typical ground surface in Tucson; however, several cases are simulated using grass or light-colored gravel.

Presentation of the Energy Transfer Information

In the remainder of this section, energy transfer information for roofs, walls, and floors is presented in a number of charts illustrating various relationships and comparisons. Since earth-contact systems have important effects in both the heating and the cooling season total energy performance comparisons should reflect these combined effects. For each component in each case, energy transfer is given for the heating season, the cooling season, and the combined heating and cooling season. Energy transfer is indicated as a positive number when energy from another source is required to maintain the internal temperature (heat loss in winter or heat gain in summer). Energy transfer is indicated as a negative number when energy is being provided through the earth-contact surface to maintain internal comfort conditions or to reduce HVAC system loads (heat gain in winter or heat loss in summer). It is important to note that since heating and cooling energy are provided in different manners, often using different fuels, combined energy transfer figures do not necessarily translate directly into fuel cost differences.

The two-dimensional finite difference computer program simulates energy transfer through a 1-foot-wide section of roof, wall, and floor, as shown in figure 3-47. The one-story wall is 8 feet high, the two-story wall is 17 feet high, and the sections of roof and floor are 10 feet long. The total energy transfer through these components is divided by the area to provide an average energy transfer expressed in 10^3 Btu's per square foot. Caution is advised, however, in adapting these figures to an actual building configuration.

One reason for this caution is based on the varying nature of heat transfer below grade. Unlike above-grade components in which energy transfer through 1 square foot of roof or wall is treated basically the same as energy transfer through any other square foot of roof or wall, on a below-grade component energy transfer at different points can vary significantly, depending mostly on the distance

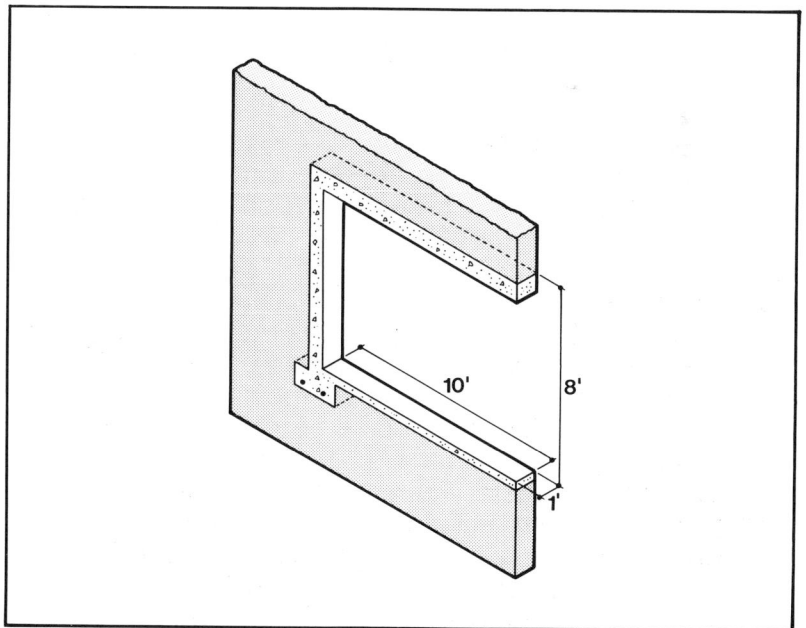

3-47: Building Section Used in Computer Simulations

from the surface. For example, the lower portion of an earth-contact wall loses less heat in winter and provides more cooling in summer than the upper portion. Likewise, the edge of a floor slab below grade will have greater heat loss in winter than the middle of the slab. Thus, the average energy transfer obtained in the simulation cannot be accurately applied to a building with different characteristics—such as wall height or floor depth—than those of the prototypical building section.

Since the two-dimensional program simulates heat transfer in a long windowless chamber, the figures do not represent actual energy transfer through below-grade wall and floor areas near openings or corners. In these situations energy transfer through the walls occurs in a three-dimensional manner, resulting in greater heat losses in winter in these areas unless additional insulation is provided. Increased summer cooling benefits are likely to occur near below-grade corners because heat flow is increased to the earth; however, less cooling will be available near openings where the conductive path to the surface is shorter.

The variations of energy transfer through the floors are mainly based on the distance from the nearest wall, but in most cases it is a three-dimensional phenomenon depending on the size and shape of the floor. The energy transfer simulated for the 10-foot-long section of floor in the parametric studies applies to the floor area adjacent to a long wall (see figure 3-47). These figures do not necessarily represent the greater losses that could occur in a corner where two walls meet or the decrease in heat loss that would occur in the center area of a large floor. On the other hand, the cooling season energy transfer figures may be more adaptable to other configurations because the main energy transfer occurs toward the deeper ground in close to a one-dimensional pattern, resulting in similar energy flows at most points on the floor.

Generally, the variation in heat transfer found in below-grade walls and floors is less of a problem with flat earth-covered roofs for which the heat flow to or from the surface is similar from most points.

Comparison of Above-Grade Roof and Wall Components

The finite-difference computer program used in the parametric studies to predict energy transfer is designed specifically to examine components in contact with the earth. In its present form it is not an appropriate tool for predicting energy transfer through above-grade components. In order to provide a comparison between earth-contact and above-grade components, another calculation method has been applied to above-grade roofs and walls. The method selected was developed by the National Association of Home Builders Research Foundation [NAHB Research Foundation, 1979]. Through the use of charts and hand calculations, both heating and cooling season loads were determined for individual building components in the two cities being analyzed. For comparative purposes energy transfer is expressed in 10^3 Btu's per square foot for above-grade roof and wall components. While this method is useful for comparative purposes in these design guidelines, its assumptions and accuracy for other analysis tasks should be examined by the user.

Limitations of Energy Transfer Information and Future Directions

The two-dimensional finite-difference model used in this analysis does not reflect three-dimensional effects in earth-contact walls and floors that would generally result in slightly greater energy transfer in both summer and winter. Also, the model is based on daily average temperatures and does not reflect hourly variations in exterior climate. In addition, the interior temperature is held constant in the model and not allowed to fluctuate. Thus, the benefits of a high-mass structure with fluctuating temperatures is not reflected in this analysis. More sophisticated three-dimensional simulation programs, which could remove some of the limitations inherent in the simulations used have recently become available. However, they have not yet been used extensively to develop design information.

Analyzing energy transfer for individual components in the parametric studies reflects the potential performance but must be put into the context of total loads and other load reduction strategies. Earth-contact structures have some inherent characteristics that are not represented in this analysis of conduction through the envelope. The first is reduced infiltration. While infiltration can be reduced considerably in properly built above-grade structures, berming and covering structures with earth—particularly on the sides toward prevailing winds—can result in very low infiltration without any extraordinary sealing techniques. Second, the concrete or masonry structures usually used in earth-contact buildings provide a great deal of mass that can be coupled with intermittent sources of energy, such as direct gain solar or wood-burning. Finally, peak loads are reduced in these more massive structures, resulting in lower costs for mechanical equipment use.

While the energy transfer information that follows provides some valuable insights, further development of parametric studies and design guidelines is required to examine the following questions:

- What are the effects on energy transfer when a three-dimensional computer model is used?

- What are the effects of varying a number of parameters including soil moisture content and ground surfaces?

- How are the relative benefits of earth-contact and above-grade components changed when interior temperatures are changed or allowed to fluctuate more widely than in the existing parametric studies?

- What are the effects of various innovative insulation configurations and ground temperature modification techniques not modeled in this study?

- How do parametric studies for more temperate climates differ from those for Minneapolis and Tucson? It can be surmised that in locations with less extreme climates, energy transfer will be reduced for all components, above-grade or below. On the other hand, earth-contact may be a very effective strategy in climates with both a moderate heating and cooling load since it can reduce energy use during both times of the year. The need for detailed information on insulation placement in these climates is important so that effective compromises can be made between summer and winter benefits.

- What are the effects of integrating earth contact components into a complete energy analysis of a structure in which all the inherent benefits of earth integration are represented (i.e. infiltration reduction, thermal mass)?

- How do different structural and finishing materials affect energy transfer?

Parametric Studies for Tucson, Arizona

Tucson, Arizona, was selected as an example of a climate where cooling is the predominant concern, although some heating is required. The Tucson climate has 1,700 heating degree days in winter and the equivalent of 1,720 full-load cooling hours in summer (based on a 78°F interior temperature). In the energy transfer data that follows, the heating season is considered to be seven months (October through April) and the cooling season, five months (May through September). In the following charts, energy transfer is shown separately for roof, wall, and floor components (figs. 3-48 through 3-51); an average energy transfer for the combined components is shown in the last chart (fig. 3-52).

Roof Component: Energy transfer through various roof components in Tucson is shown in figure 3-48. The typical conventional roof with R-19 insulation results in a moderate heat loss in winter and heat gain in summer, as shown for roof AG-1. Both of these energy requirements can be reduced to a relatively low level with increased insulation (roofs AG-2 and AG-3). The addition of earth cover can further reduce heat loss and heat gain through the roof to a virtually negligible amount depending on the ground surface treatment. An earth-covered roof with R-30 insulation and bare earth on the surface reduces heat loss in winter to a negligible amount while reducing heat gain as well, as shown for roof EC-3. On the other hand, the same roof with a grass or gravel surface reduces heat gain in summer to virtually nothing while keeping winter heat loss small (roof EC-4). The basic effect of placing small amounts (2 feet) of earth on the roof is not to provide cooling but rather to reduce heat gain. An earth-covered roof without insulation would not be advisable for either winter or summer conditions. While the effects of an earth-covered roof in this climate are not dramatic when examined alone, the earth-covered roof is part of a system that places the walls and floor at a greater depth from the surface and may be justifiable for that reason.

Wall Component: Energy transfer through various wall components in Tucson is shown in figures 3-49 and 3-50. The typical above-grade wall component in Tucson with R-11 insulation permits moderate heat loss in winter along with a much greater heat gain in summer (wall AG-1). Increased amounts of insulation to R-19 or even R-30 can almost eliminate winter heat loss and can reduce summer heat gain somewhat (walls AG-2 and AG-3). In most cases, the use of earth berms can virtually eliminate winter heat loss and summer heat gain through walls, regardless of the exact amount or placement of insulation. Among the various fully bermed walls tested there are no remarkable differences, only subtle shifts as insulation and ground cover are varied. One important exception to this is a fully bermed wall with no insulation at all (wall FB-1). Although this uninsulated wall is an improvement over the conventional walls in the cooling season and is not too much worse in the winter, a small amount of insulation can improve energy performance dramatically.

In examining the deeper walls tested in the earth-covered cases, it is remarkable to note that even a completely uninsulated wall has a very small amount of summer heat gain and actually provides heat in winter. If reduced winter heat loss or summer heat gain is the objective, increased amounts of insulation on earth sheltered walls are unnecessary. If maximizing winter heating or summer cooling energy available from earth contact walls is the objective, then more specific insulation configurations must be selected. The configuration with the best energy performance is an uninsulated wall with roof insulation extending horizontally 8 feet beyond the wall (walls EC-6 and EC-7). Energy can also be effectively provided through the uninsulated

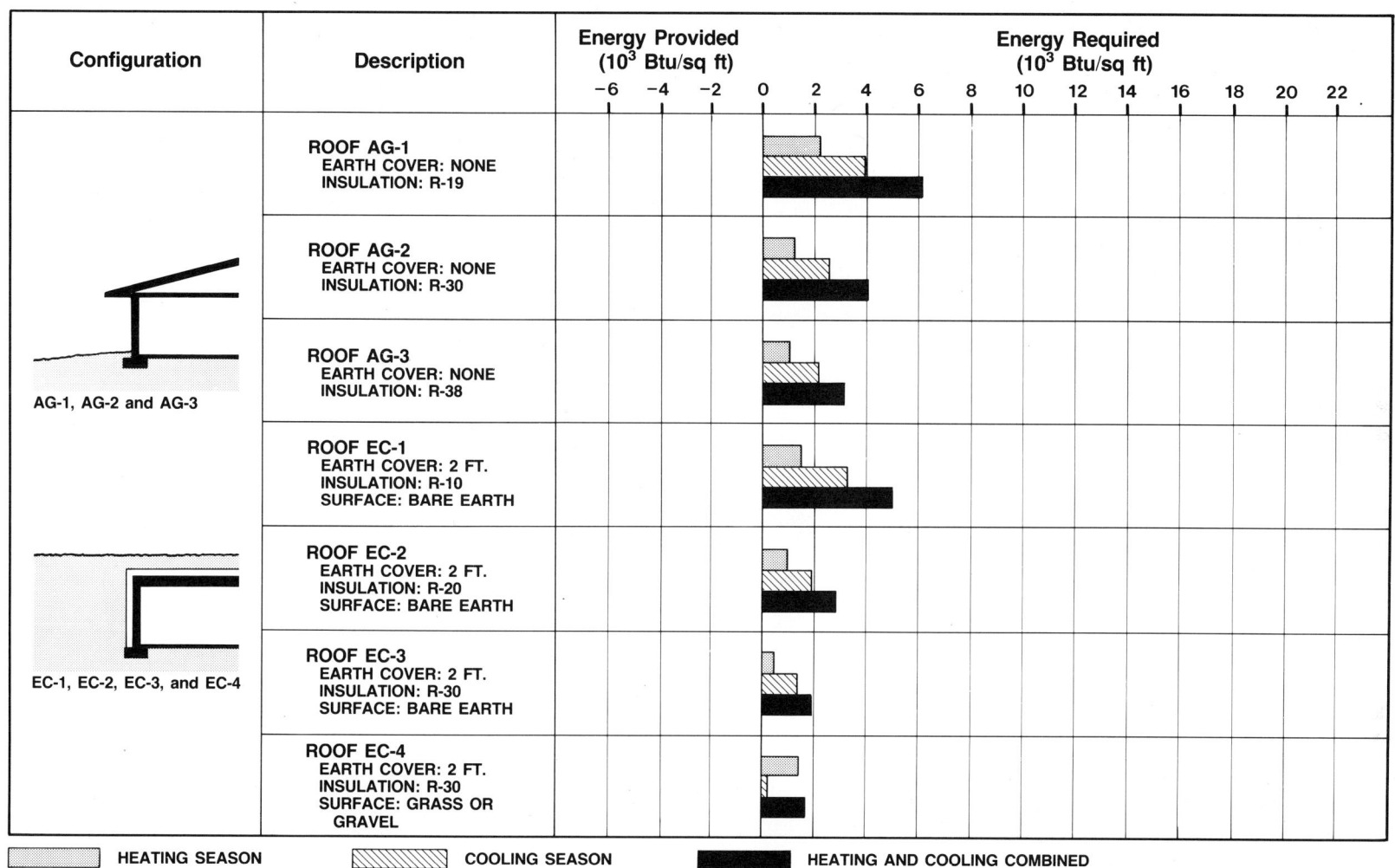

3-48: Energy Transfer through Roof Component Tucson, Arizona

Note: Thermal conductivity (K) of the soil is assumed to be 1.3 W/m-°K in all cases, AG indicates above grade, FB indicates fully bermed, and EC indicates earth covered.

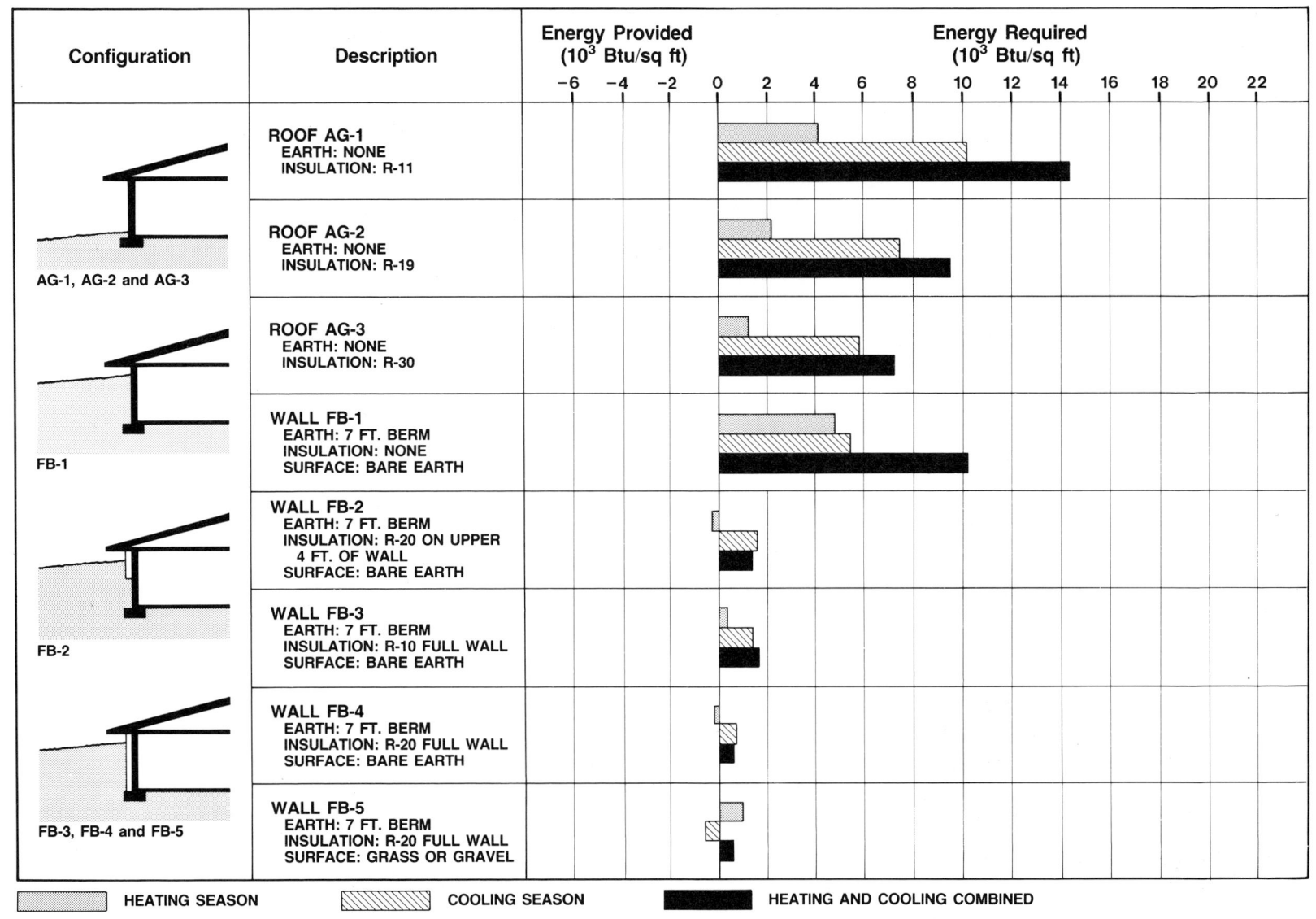

3-49: Energy Transfer through Wall Component Tucson, Arizona

Note: Thermal conductivity (K) of the soil is assumed to be 1.3 W/m-°K in all cases, AG indicates above grade, FB incidates fully bermed, and EC indicates earth covered.

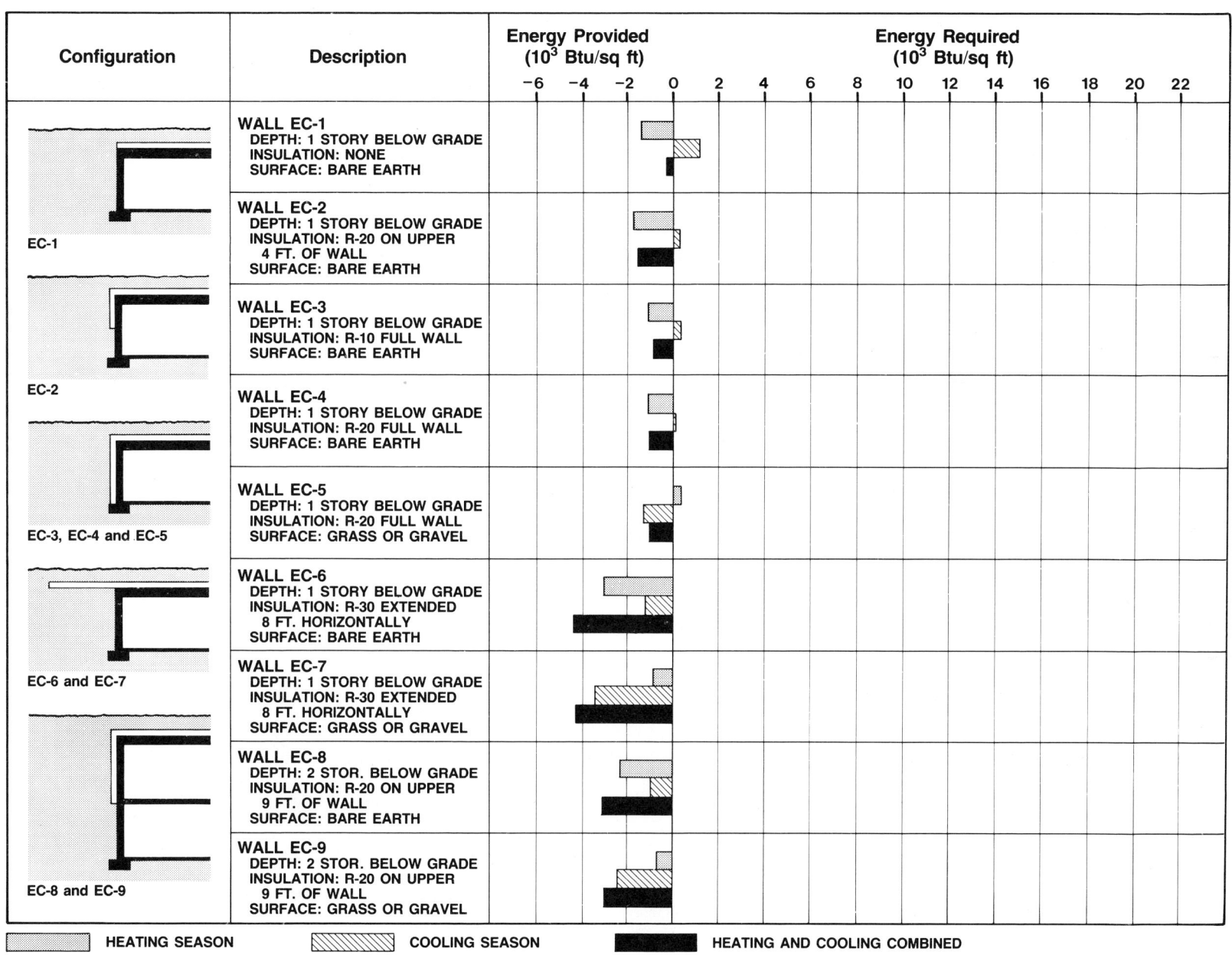

3-50: Energy Transfer through Wall Component Tucson, Arizona

Note: Thermal conductivity (K) of the soil is assumed to be 1.3 W/m-°K in all cases, AG indicates above grade, FB indicates fully bermed, and EC indicates earth covered.

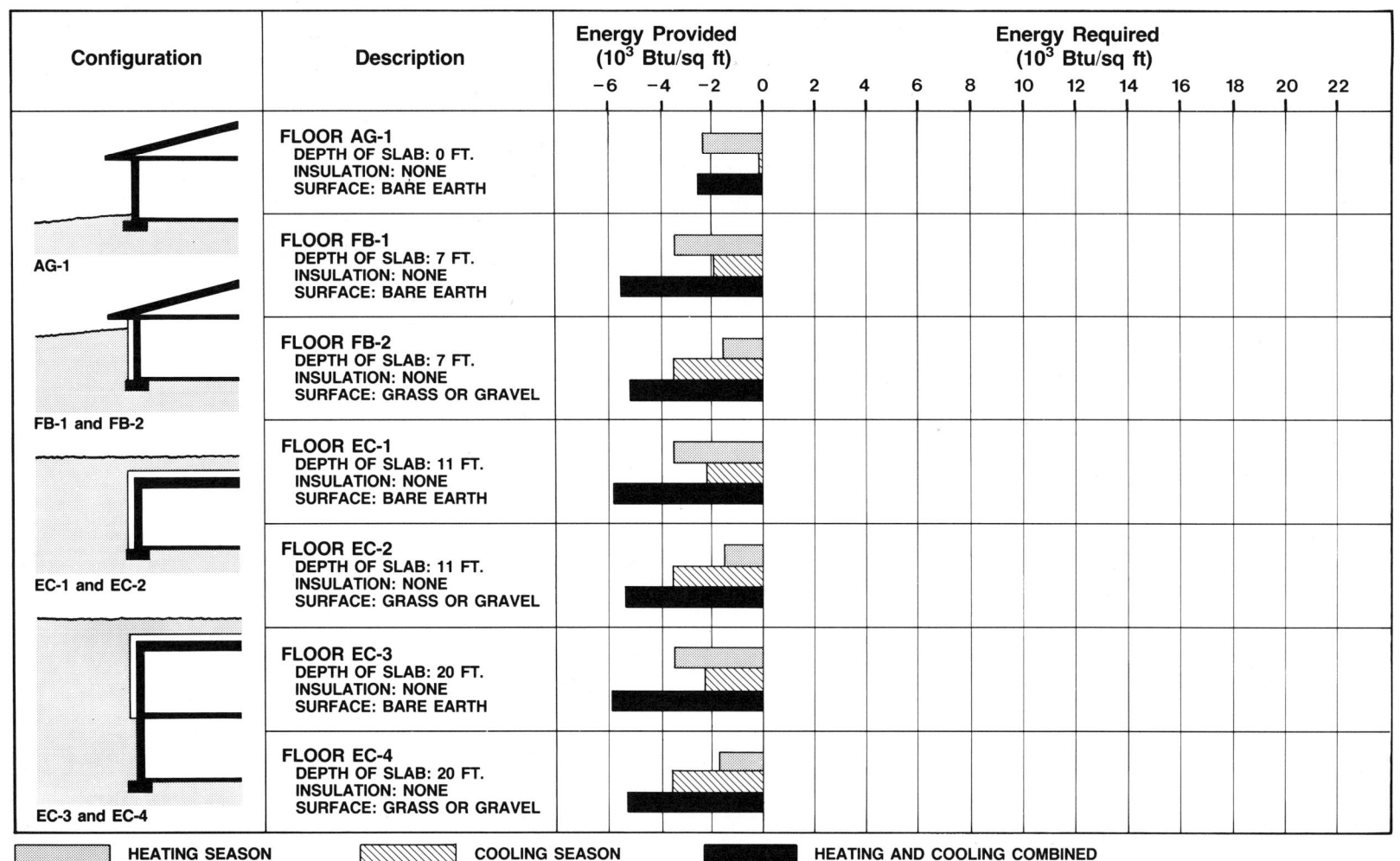

3-51: Energy Transfer through Floor Component Tucson, Arizona

Note: Thermal conductivity (K) of the soil is assumed to be 1.3 W/m-°K in all cases, AG indicates above grade, FB indicates fully bermed, and EC indicates earth covered.

lower portion of a two-story wall (walls EC-8 and EC-9). In these cases, the ground surface treatment has a significant impact on maximizing energy transfer for winter or summer conditions. Bare earth will maximize winter heat gain, as shown for walls EC-6 and EC-8; grass or gravel will maximize summer cooling, as shown for walls EC-7 and EC-9.

Floor Component: Energy transfer through various floor components in Tucson is shown in figure 3-51. A concrete slab floor in Tucson should not be regarded as a source of winter heat loss or summer heat gain even in a conventional uninsulated slab-on-grade condition. A moderate amount of heat is actually gained in the winter through a slab-on-grade if it is surrounded by bare earth (floor AG-1). In addition, no net heat gain occurs in summer. Under these circumstances insulation is unnecessary. It is possible to increase the heat gained through the floor in winter as well as to provide cooling in summer by placing the floor deeper into the ground. It appears to make little difference if the floor is 7 feet deep (as in the fully bermed cases FB-1 and FB-2), 11 feet deep (as in the one-story earth-covered cases EC-1 and EC-2), or even 20 feet deep (as in the two-story earth sheltered cases EC-3 and EC-4). Like the use of earth-contact walls in Tucson, the ground surface treatment has important effects on maximizing energy transfer for winter or summer conditions. Bare earth will maximize winter heat gain (floors FB-1, EC-1 and EC-3), whereas grass or gravel will maximize summer cooling (floors FB-2, EC-2, and EC-4).

Combined Roof, Wall, and Floor Energy Transfer: The nine cases shown in figure 3-52 do not necessarily represent the best-performing or most cost-effective configurations in the Tucson climate. They were selected to illustrate a number of interrelationships between components in terms of energy transfer only. Although the roof, wall, and floor energy transfer is combined in figure 3-52, this total should not be confused with the total load in an actual building. It is the average energy transfer per square foot for the complete building section used in the computer simulation. For all one-story cases the average is based on 8 square feet of wall and 10 square feet of roof and floor. For two-story cases the average is based on 17 square feet of wall and 10 square feet of roof and floor. The ratios of areas used in the prototypical building sections do not necessarily correspond to actual building configurations. In addition, other loads such as those from windows and doors, internal heat gains, and air infiltration are not included in this analysis.

The base case (AG-1) in figure 3-52 is an above-grade structure with R-11 insulation in the wall, R-19 insulation in the roof, and a concrete slab-on-grade floor. The surrounding ground surface is bare earth. As expected, the above-grade roof and wall components represent a heat loss in the winter and an even greater heat gain in the summer, resulting in an energy input requirement throughout the year. The slab-on-grade floor in contact with the relatively warm earth actually represents a heat gain in the winter that can offset losses elsewhere in the structure. During the cooling season, the energy transfer through the floor is negligible: ground temperatures are not low enough to provide cooling. Thus, the combined annual effects of the roof, wall, and floor in case AG-1 can be summarized as an energy input requirement, mainly in summer, because of the roof and walls. Energy is also required in winter, but this requirement is offset to a small degree by some heat provided through the floor.

The second above-grade case (AG-2) in figure 3-52 represents a change in two variables: the roof insulation is increased to R-30 and wall insulation is increased to R-19. This reduces roof and wall energy transfer in winter to a point where heating energy gained through the floor is only slightly less than heating energy lost through the other components. In the cooling season, heat gains through the roof and walls are reduced somewhat but are still significant. The combined effect of increasing roof and wall insulation is a reduction of approximately 40 percent in energy transfer.

In the third case (FB-1), the wall and floor are placed into the earth to a depth of 7 feet, which is typical for a fully bermed structure with a conventional roof or a basement wall. As in the previous cases, the ground surface is bare earth. The insulation in the conventional roof remains at R-30, resulting in the same winter heat loss and summer heat gain as for the previous case (AG-2). Insulation at a value of R-20 is placed outside the concrete wall so that the earth contact is the main variable being compared between cases AG-2 and FB-1. The wall actually gains a slight amount of heat in the winter but also gains a slight amount in the summer, resulting in a relatively small total energy requirement. While winter heat loss is less than for above-grade cases, no summer cooling is provided through the wall. The floor, on the other hand, represents a notable improvement because it is deeper than in the slab-on-grade cases. A greater amount of heat is provided through the floor in winter and some summer cooling is provided as well. The total annual effect is to almost eliminate energy transfer through the earth-contact wall component and provide both winter heating and summer cooling through the 7-foot-deep floor. The heat provided through the floor component in winter is greater than the heat lost through the roof component, resulting in a net energy gain. The cooling gained through the floor in summer is less than the heat gain through the roof, resulting in a small net energy requirement.

Changing the ground surface from bare earth to grass or gravel, as shown in case FB-2, results in no dramatic difference: energy transfer for both fully bermed cases is quite small with this amount of insulation. There is, however, a small shift in energy transfer in this case because of the lower ground temperatures created by the grass or gravel surface. In case FB-1 the net effect is to provide some heat in winter while creating a small cooling load in summer. In contrast, the net effect in case FB-2 is to provide some summer cooling while creating a small heat loss in winter.

The fifth case in figure 3-52 shows the effect of placing the entire building deeper (11 feet to the floor level). Compared to the above-grade and fully bermed cases, EC-1 represents an improvement. The net effect is that energy is provided throughout the year. This is achieved because winter heat loss and summer heat gain are reduced through the roof while winter heat gain and summer heat loss are increased through the deeper wall. The floor remains the major source of winter heat flow and summer cooling, as it is in the fully bermed case. Although it is not shown in figure 3-52, changing the ground surface to grass or gravel in case EC-1 would result in a reversal of the energy transfer in summer and winter; more cooling would be provided in summer and less heat in winter.

Like the preceding example, case EC-2 represents a building with 2 feet of earth on the roof, creating a floor level that is 11 feet below grade. The insulation in case EC-2 is configured to maximize earth contact while minimizing direct conduction paths to the surface. Thus, no insulation is placed directly against the walls; instead, the roof insulation (R-30) is extended horizontally 8 feet beyond the exterior walls. The ground surface remains bare earth.

Similar to case EC-1, the result of this configuration is that the floor does not perform much differently than in the fully bermed case (FB-1), even though it is 4 feet deeper. Cooling is still provided in summer and heat is provided in winter. The most significant change is that the wall is now performing

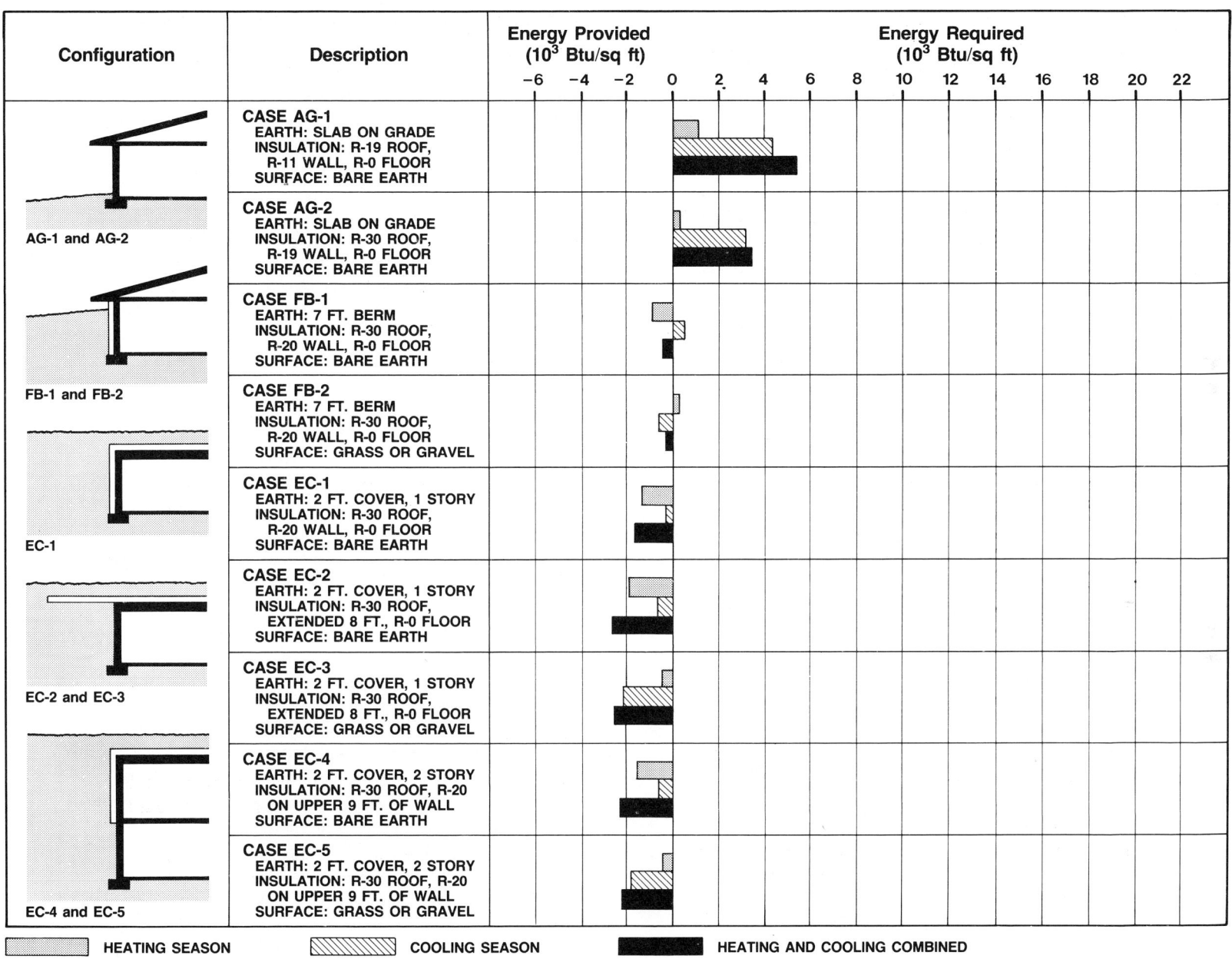

3-52: Energy Transfer through Roof, Wall and Floor Components Combined — Tucson, Arizona

Note: Thermal conductivity (K) of the soil is assumed to be 1.3 W/m-°K in all cases, AG indicates above grade, FB indicates fully bermed, and EC indicates earth covered.

as the floor is—i.e., by actually providing some heat from the earth in winter and some cooling in the summer. As with case EC-1, the winter heat loss and summer heat gain through the roof are reduced by the earth-covered design even though the R-value of the insulation is the same as in cases AG-2 and FB-1. The combined effect of these changes is to provide a significant amount of heat in winter through the earth-contact floor and wall while reducing roof heat loss to a negligible amount. In summer the combined effect is to provide a small amount of cooling through the wall and floor; more significantly, however, wall and roof heat gains are greatly reduced compared to the above-grade cases.

The only difference between cases EC-2 and EC-3 is that in the latter case, the ground surface is assumed to be gravel or grass rather than bare earth. The result is that in case EC-3, a smaller amount of heating energy is provided through the walls and floor in the winter heating season, but a more substantial amount of cooling is available. With regard to the roof component, the change in ground surface reduces heat gain through the roof to a point where it is almost negligible in the cooling season. However, heat loss through the roof in winter is increased since less solar radiation is absorbed. The net energy provided for the combined heating and cooling season is slightly less in case EC-3 than in case EC-2; however, most of it is provided for cooling rather than heating. Decisions on optimizing for heating or cooling will depend on other loads, other opportunities for passive heating and cooling, and the relative cost of auxiliary heating and cooling.

Case EC-4 in figure 3-52 is a two-story earth-sheltered building. There are 2 feet of earth on the roof and the lower floor level is 20 feet below the surface. The upper 9 feet of the wall are covered on the outside with insulation at a value of R-20 and the remainder of the wall is uninsulated in full contact with the earth. The roof insulation remains at R-30 and the ground surface is bare earth.

As expected, the roof of the two-story configuration performs the same as in the other earth-covered cases: heating gains and losses are reduced significantly. In spite of the greater depth (20 feet), the floor of the two-story structure also performs much like the floor of a one-level below-grade building. While the average energy transfer through the two-story wall in case EC-4 represents an improvement over a one-story insulated wall (EC-1), this configuration is not as effective as the one-story wall with extended insulation (EC-2). Although not shown here, a two-story wall with extended insulation would probably provide the best performance. The net effect of combining the components is that the two-story configuration (EC-4) is similar to but slightly less effective than the one-story configuration with extended insulation (EC-2).

The final case (EC-5) is identical to case EC-4 except that the ground surface is changed to grass or gravel rather than bare earth. As demonstrated in previous cases, the net result is an increase in summer cooling at the expense of providing heat in winter.

Building Configuration Considerations: Earth-covered roofs in Tucson serve mainly as a means of reducing heating and cooling loads. On the other hand, walls and floors in contact with the earth can actually provide heat in winter and cooling in summer. An earth-covered roof permits the benefits of earth-contact walls to be more fully exploited. Under these circumstances, maximizing exterior surface area in contact with earth is the recommended strategy in this climate.

While maximizing earth-contact surface area can lead to a number of design variations, one important prototypical design, exhibited in much indigenous architecture as well as in modern variations, is the atrium or courtyard type of house. This design is particularly appropriate in warmer climates such as

Tucson's. In a typical atrium design, which is usually on one level, the exterior surface area is increased compared to that of an elevational structure, and the entire perimeter wall can be placed in contact with the earth. Maximizing the earth contact in this manner is ideal for providing passive cooling in summer as well as passive heating in the winter from moderately high ground temperatures. In addition, the courtyard design reduces window area, lends itself to various shading techniques, and provides a space that can collect cool night air.

Interior Surface Considerations: The energy transfer figures indicated in the case studies are based on solid concrete walls and floors that are exposed to the interior space. Any coverings on these surfaces—furred-out walls or carpeting on the floor—would act as insulation and reduce the energy transfer. Interior finishing and design must be coordinated with any earth-contact cooling or heating strategies. For example, in some cases furred-out walls may be acceptable if most of the cooling is provided by the floor. If floors are to be relied upon for cooling, tiles may be the most energy-efficient interior finish.

Parametric Studies for Minneapolis, Minnesota

Minneapolis, Minnesota, was selected as an example of a climate where heating is the predominant concern, although a small amount of cooling is also required. The Minneapolis climate has 8,250 heating degree days in winter and the equivalent of 590 full-load cooling hours in summer (based on a 78°F interior temperature). In the energy transfer figures that follow, the heating season is considered to be nine months (September through May) and the cooling season, three months (June through August). In the following charts, energy transfer is shown separately for roof, wall, and floor components (figs. 3-53 through 3-57); an average energy transfer for the combined components is shown in the last chart (fig. 3-58).

Roof Component: Energy transfer through various roof components in Minneapolis is shown in figure 3-53. In Minneapolis a conventional roof with R-19 insulation permits a very significant heat loss in the winter as well as a relatively small amount of heat gain in the summer (roof AG-1). The winter heat loss through the roof can be effectively reduced by increasing the insulation to R-30, and R-38 is often recommended (roofs AG-2 and AG-3). The small summer heat gain is further reduced with this increase in insulation. The addition of a 2-foot-thick earth cover to the roof somewhat reduces heat loss with moderate amounts of insulation (roof EC-2), but becomes less significant with larger amounts (roof EC-3 and EC-4) when compared to conventional roofs with equivalent insulation values. In the cooling season, earth-covered roofs eliminate heat gain and provide a slight amount of cooling regardless of the amount of insulation. It is clear that, in this climate earth-covered roofs can provide only slight improvement over conventional roofs with equivalent

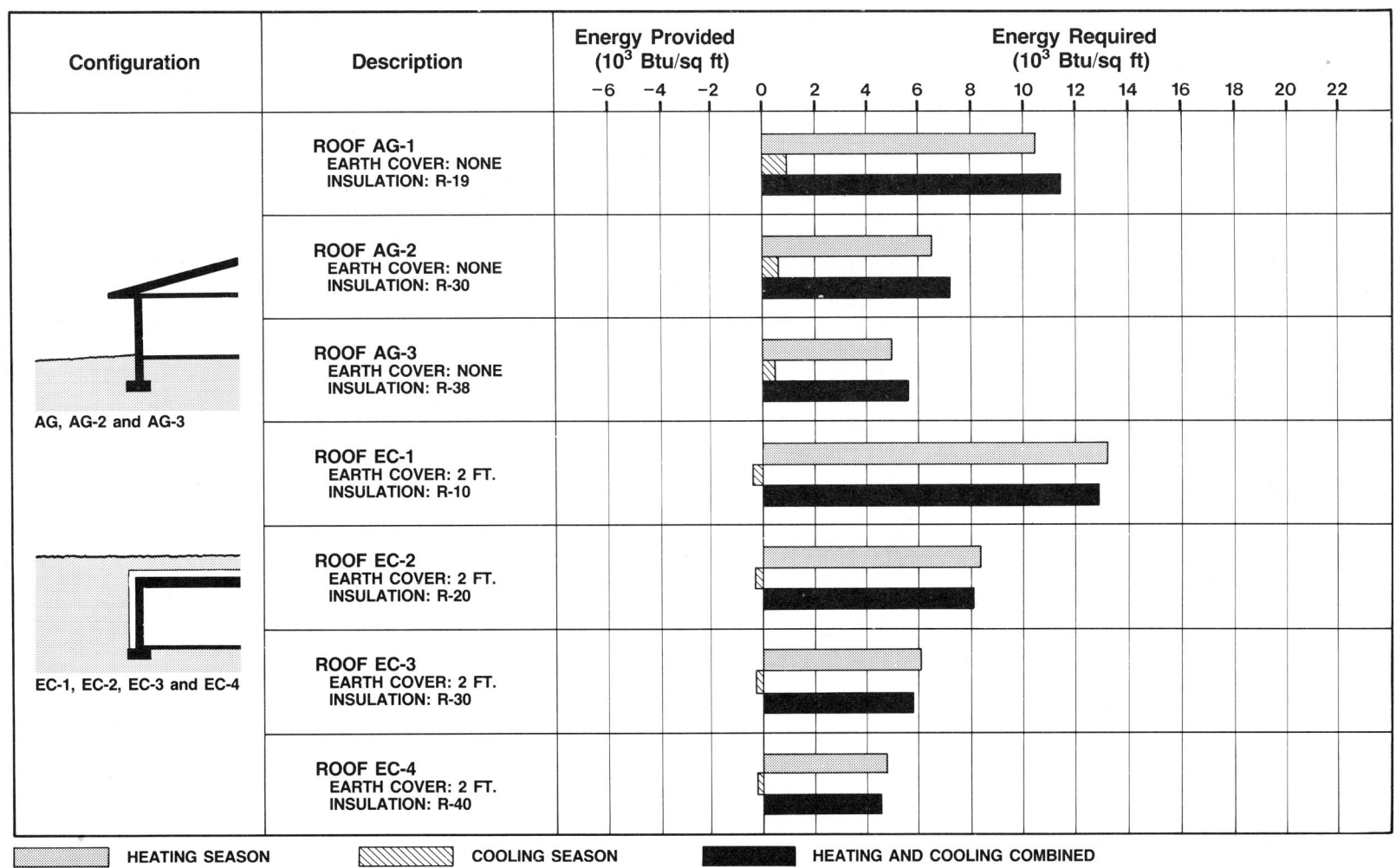

3-53: Energy Transfer through Roof Component Minneapolis, Minnesota

Note: Ground surface is assumed to be grass in all cases. Thermal conductivity (K) of the soil is assumed to be 1.7 W/m-°K in all cases except as noted. AG indicates above grade, FB indicates fully bermed, and EC indicates earth covered.

amounts of insulation. While the effects of an earth-covered roof in this climate are not dramatic when examined alone, the earth-covered roof is part of a system that places the walls and floor at a greater depth from the surface and may be justifiable for that reason.

Wall Component: Energy transfer through various wall components in Minneapolis is shown in figures 3-54 and 3-55. A conventional above-grade wall in Minneapolis with R-11 insulation permits significant heat loss in winter along with a relatively small amount of heat gain in the summer (wall AG-1). Increased amounts of insulation to R-19 or even R-30 can effectively reduce the winter heat loss and diminish the summer heat gain somewhat as well (walls AG-2 and AG-3). Placing earth against the wall to a height of 7 feet reduces winter heat loss when equivalent amounts of insulation are used above and below grade. The impact is greater with less insulation (walls FB-3 and FB-4) and less significant with more insulation (wall FB-5). A more critical difference occurs in the cooling season where the effect of berming with any amount of insulation not only eliminates heat gain, but provides a small amount of cooling. It is clearly not advisable to leave fully bermed walls uninsulated (wall FB-1) since the resulting winter heat loss is enormous compared to even a minimally insulated above-grade wall. The best alternative for fully bermed walls in this climate appears to be insulation placed over the entire wall. Insulating only the upper half of the wall, as shown for wall FB-2, results in poorer performance than covering the entire wall with an equivalent amount of insulation (wall FB-2).

When one-story walls are placed deeper to accommodate an earth-covered roof, improvements in reducing winter heat loss and providing summer cooling result, in comparison with the fully bermed walls discussed above. In the winter an earth sheltered wall appears to provide the same benefits as adding R-10 to the insulation above grade, providing the entire wall is evenly insulated. In the summer, a definite benefit that cannot be equaled by above-grade components occurs because cooling is actually provided in addition to the elimination of heat gain. A fully insulated below-grade wall provides the best performance in winter but a relatively small amount of summer cooling.

Various insulation configurations can be used to increase summer cooling. Among these are horizontally extended roof insulation with no wall insulation (wall EC-6), and insulation on the upper portion of the wall only (wall EC-2). Neither of these is recommended in this climate because the penalty in increased winter heat loss is too great and cooling is not the priority. Wall EC-7 demonstrates the importance of soil moisture and, consequently, thermal conductivity on energy use. If it is assumed that the extended insulation configuration keeps the ground dryer near the building, then heat loss is reduced significantly while cooling provided in summer is reduced somewhat. Summer cooling can be increased in a partially insulated two-story wall (EC-8) without a great penalty in winter heat loss. The best performance in terms of winter heat loss is obtained by completely insulating a two-story wall (EC-9).

Floor Component: Energy transfer through various floor components in Minneapolis is shown in figures 3-56 and 3-57. An uninsulated concrete slab-on-grade floor in Minneapolis can be responsible not only for a significant winter heat loss but also for a moderate amount of cooling in the summer (floor AG-1). Placing insulation over the foundation wall can reduce winter heat loss somewhat but does not reduce summer cooling benefits significantly (floors AG-3 and AG-4). Insulating under the entire floor slab results in an additional significant reduction in winter heat loss while still providing some cooling (floor AG-2).

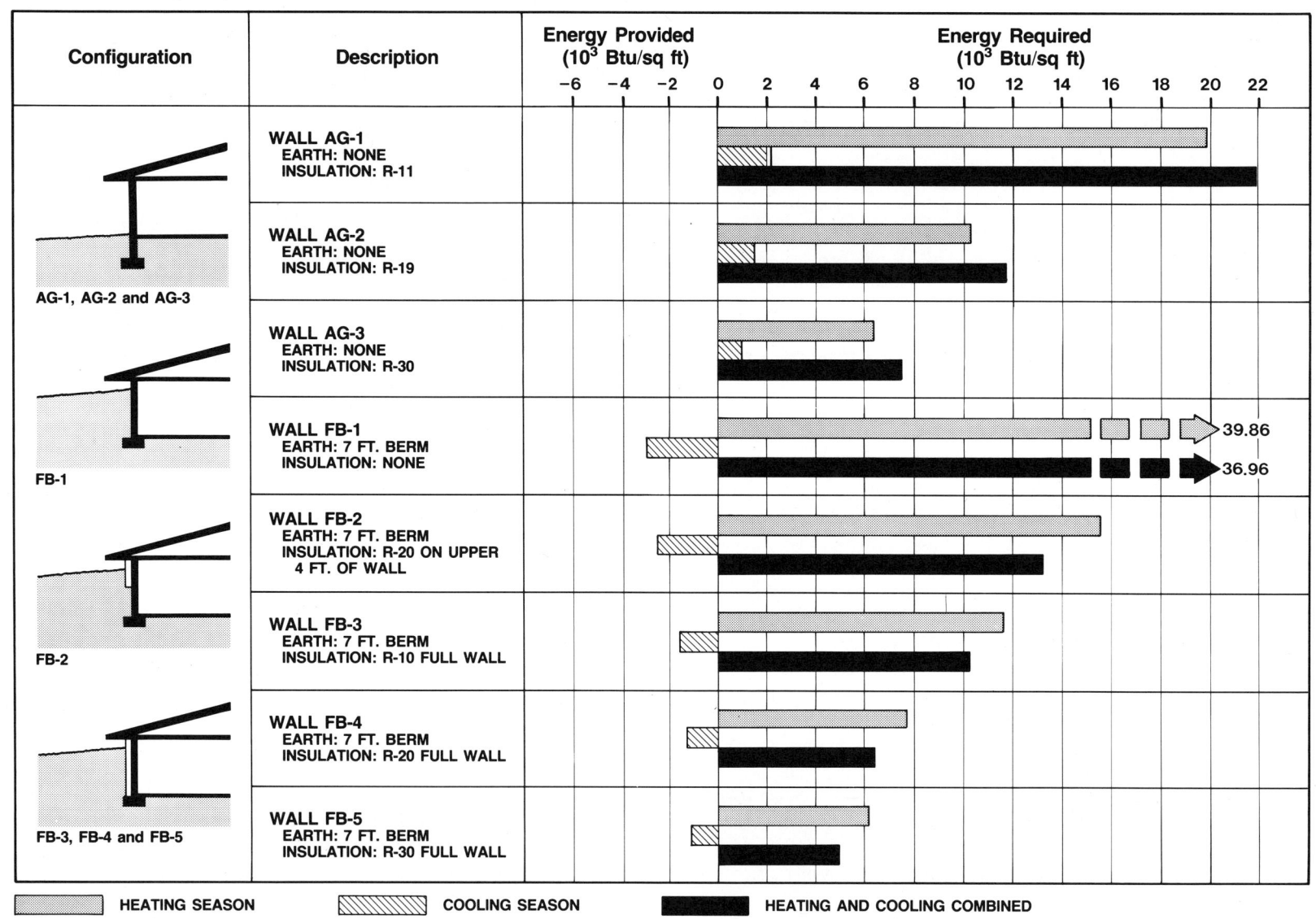

3-54: Energy Transfer through Wall Component Minneapolis, Minnesota

Note: Ground surface is assumed to be grass in all cases. Thermal conductivity (K) of the soil is assumed to be 1.7 W/m-°K in all cases except as noted. AG indicates above grade, FB indicates fully bermed, and EC indicates earth covered.

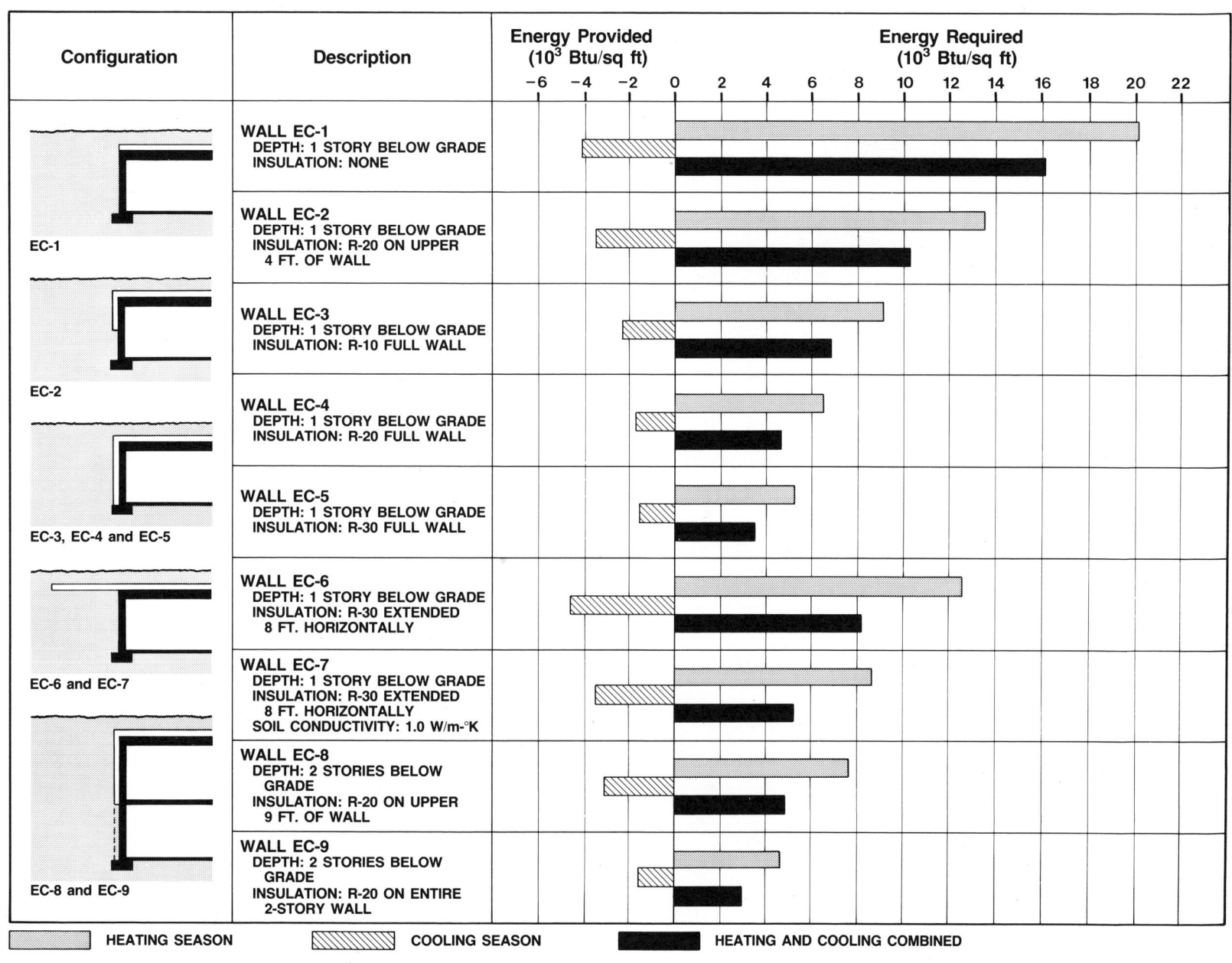

3-55: Energy Transfer through Wall Component Minneapolis, Minnesota

Note: Ground surface is assumed to be grass in all cases. Thermal conductivity (K) of the soil is assumed to be 1.7 W/m-°K in all cases except as noted. AG indicates above grade, FB indicates fully bermed, and EC indicates earth covered.

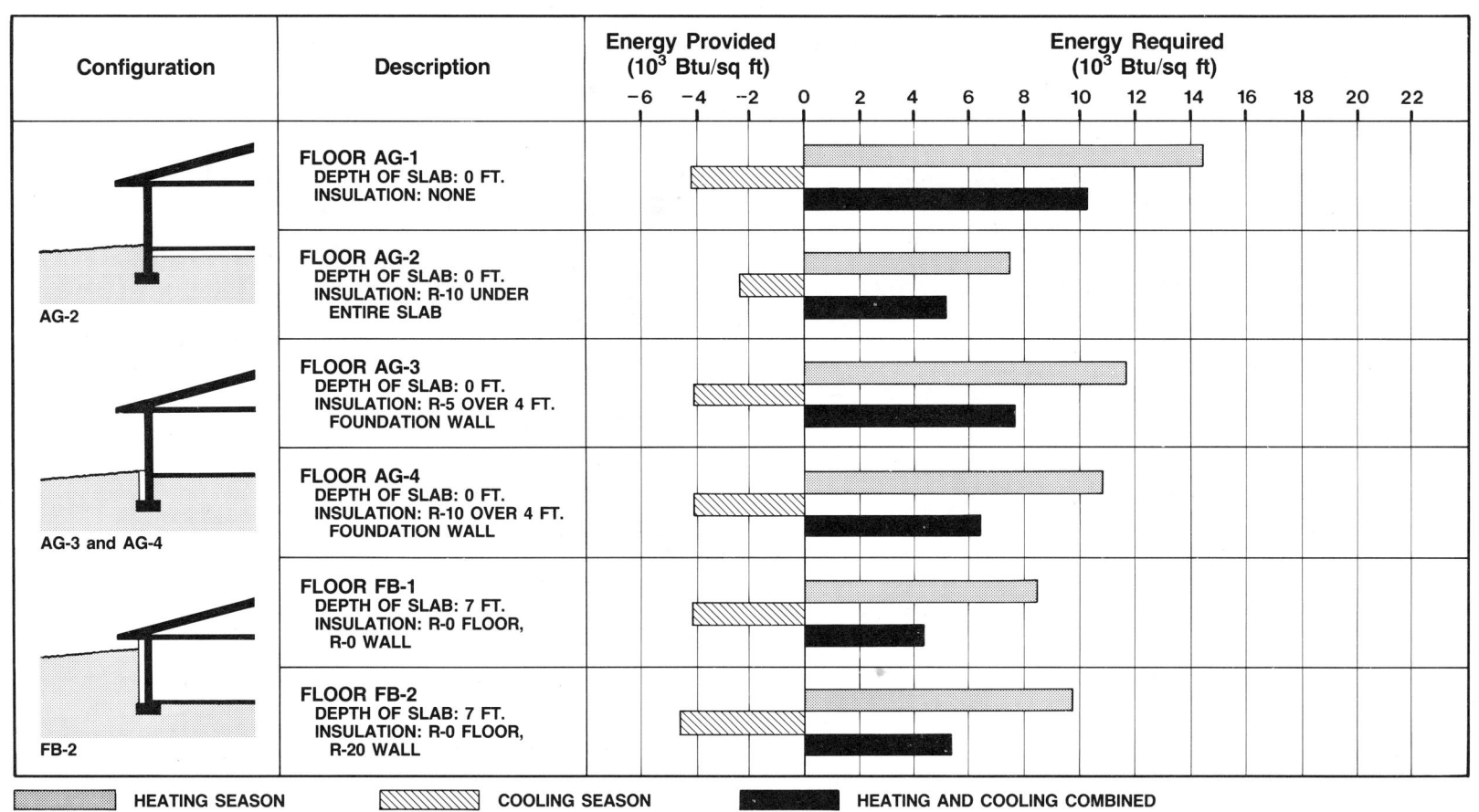

3-56: Energy Transfer through Floor Component Minneapolis, Minnesota

Note: Ground surface is assumed to be grass in all cases. Thermal conductivity (K) of the soil is assumed to be 1.7 W/m-°K in all cases except as noted. AG indicates above grade, FB indicates fully bermed, and EC indicates earth covered.

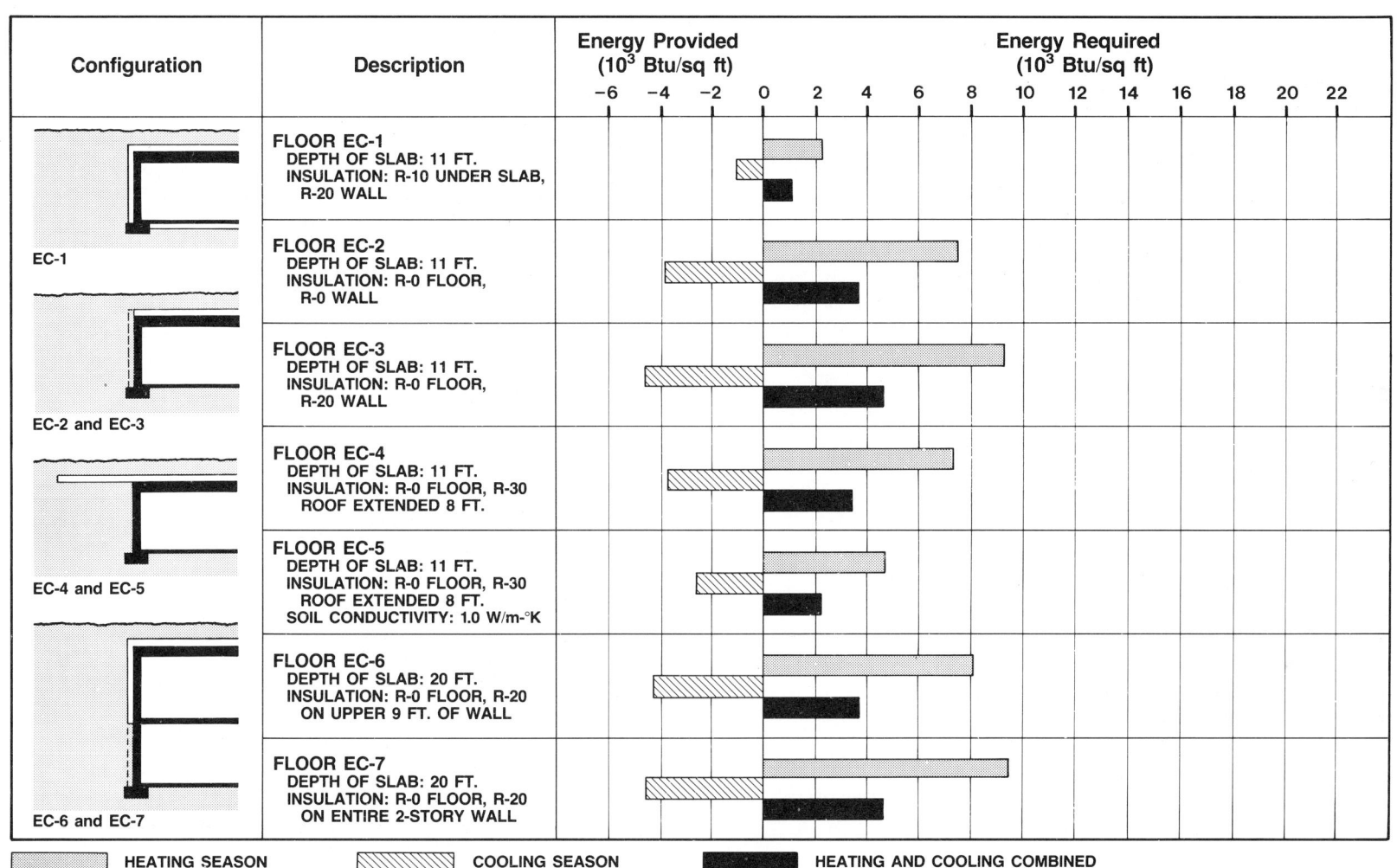

3-57: Energy Transfer through Floor Component Minneapolis, Minnesota

Note: Ground surface is assumed to be grass in all cases. Thermal conductivity (K) of the soil is assumed to be 1.7 W/m-°K in all cases except as noted. AG indicates above grade, FB indicates fully bermed, and EC indicates earth covered.

When an uninsulated floor slab is placed at a depth of 7 feet or greater, the winter heat loss is generally the same as for a completely insulated slab-on-grade, while the cooling provided is equal to an uninsulated slab-on-grade (floors FB-1 and FB-2). Except for minor variations, placing the slab deeper than 7 feet appears to have little effect in the heating or cooling season. Although the performance of an uninsulated below-grade floor is equivalent to that of a well-insulated slab-on-grade, it should not necessarily be concluded that insulation under the deeper slabs is unadvisable. The heat loss in winter is still significant and can be virtually eliminated by placing R-10 insulation under a deeper floor (EC-1). While this can significantly reduce summer cooling benefits, it may be a justifiable trade-off in this climate.

Two effects are interesting to note in these floor component simulations. First, the energy transfer through the floor varies in situations where only the below-grade wall insulation varies. For example, heat loss is greater in floor EC-3, where the below-grade wall is well-insulated, than with floor EC-2, where the wall is uninsulated. This is attributed to the colder ground temperatures around the building in the better-insulated case. Another interesting effect is the reduced energy transfer that occurs in both summer and winter when the thermal conductivity of the soil is changed (floor EC-5), in comparison with a more typical condition (floor EC-4).

Combined Roof, Wall, and Floor Energy Transfer: The nine cases shown in figure 3-58 do not necessarily represent the best-performing or most cost-effective configurations. They were selected to illustrate a number of interrelationships between components in terms of energy transfer only. Although the roof, wall, and floor energy transfer is combined in these charts, this total should not be confused with the total load in an actual building. Rather, it is the average energy transfer per square foot for the complete building section used in the computer simulation. For all one-story cases the average is based on 8 square feet of wall and 10 square feet of roof and floor. For two-story cases the average is based on 17 square feet of wall and 10 square feet of roof and floor. The ratios of areas used in the prototypical building sections do not necessarily correspond to actual building configurations. In addition, other loads, such as those from windows and doors, internal heat gains, and air infiltration, are not included in this analysis.

While the insulation values in the roofs and walls of the two above-grade cases (AG-1 and AG-2) in figure 3-58 are identical to those in Tucson, the foundation or floor insulation is increased in Minneapolis to reflect more typical protection from the severe winter. In fact, most houses in this climate are built with basements instead of slab-on-grade; this factor, however, complicates the comparative analysis. In the first case (AG-1), insulation at a value of R-5 is extended over the foundation to a depth of 4 feet while walls (R-11) and roofs (R-19) are insulated only to a minimal level. In case AG-2, which has increased roof (R-30) and wall insulation (R-19), insulation is placed under the entire floor slab at a value of R-10.

As expected, the increased roof and wall insulation and insulation under the entire floor slab in case AG-2 reduce the energy transfer significantly in winter, compared to case AG-1. The uninsulated floor slab in case AG-1 provides a moderate amount of cooling in summer that is reduced by the insulation in case AG-2. A small amount of heat gain in summer occurs through the above-grade roofs and walls; however, the net annual energy transfer for both above-grade cases is dominated by the considerable heating season requirements.

In the fully bermed case (FB-1), the wall and floor are placed 7 feet below the surface. The conventional roof is insulated to a value of R-30 and performs identically to the roof in case AG-2. The

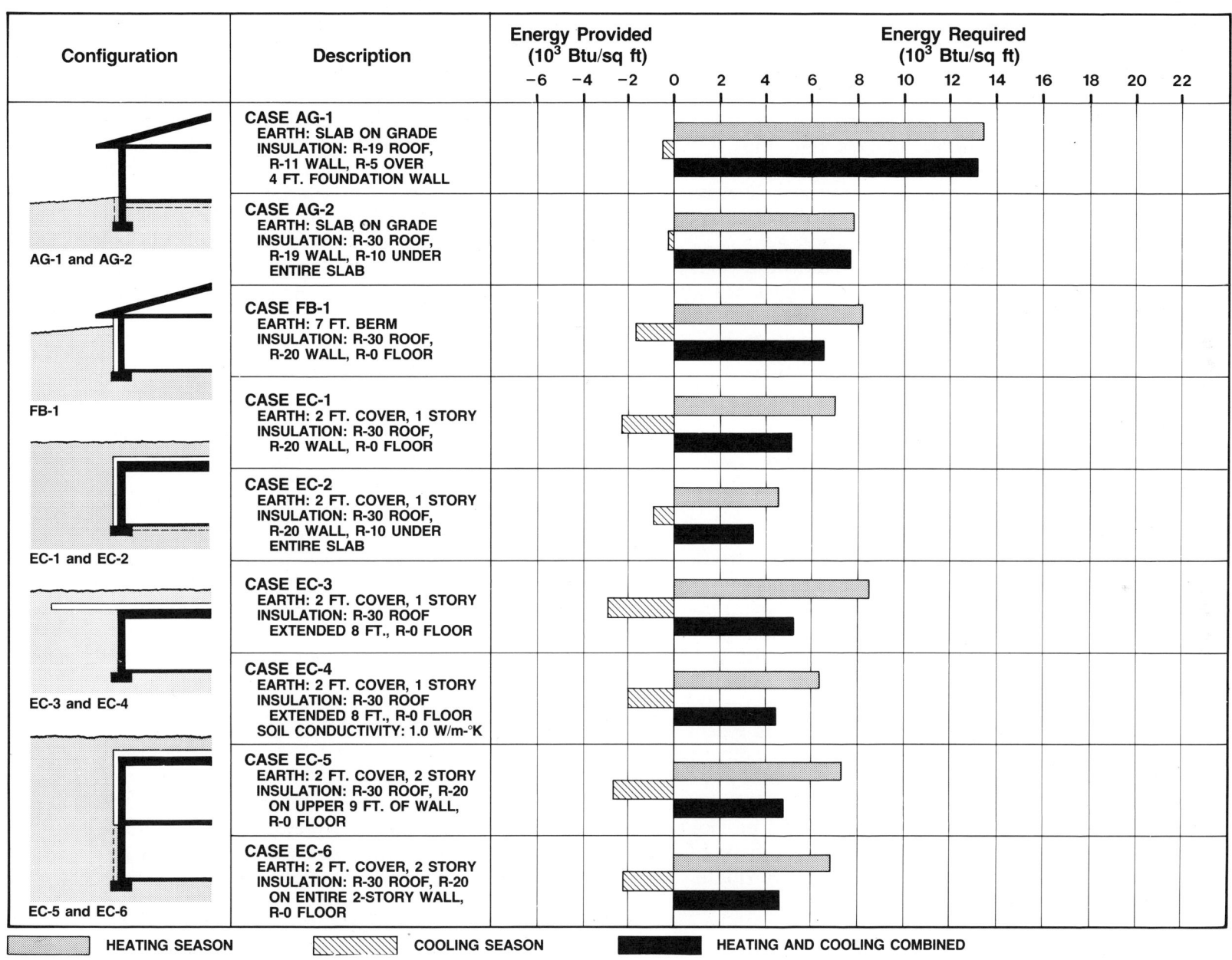

3-58: Energy Transfer through Roof, Wall and Floor Components Combined — Minneapolis, Minnesota

Note: Ground surface is assumed to be grass in all cases. Thermal conductivity (K) of the soil is assumed to be 1.7 W/m-°K in all cases except as noted. AG indicates above grade, FB indicates fully bermed, and EC indicates earth covered.

entire wall is covered on the outside by insulation at a value of R-20, but the floor is uninsulated. The wall in this case shows reduced heat loss in winter and actually provides summer cooling rather than admitting heat gain, compared to the equally well-insulated wall above grade. As expected, the uninsulated floor in case FB-1 has a greater heat loss in winter than does the insulated slab in case AG-2, but more summer cooling is provided. Although the combined effect of the three components in winter is virtually equal to the above-grade structure in case AG-2, significantly more cooling is provided in summer. Thus, the net annual energy transfer is lower than in the above-grade cases, mainly because of the improved wall performance and the provision of additional summer cooling.

The roof in case EC-1 of figure 3-58 is covered with two feet of earth, resulting in a deeper placement of both wall and floor (11 feet from surface to floor level). Insulation values remain equivalent to those in the fully bermed case (R-30 in the roof and R-20 in the wall). The earth on the roof does not significantly change the heating season performance; it does, however, eliminate summer heat gain. Compared to the previous fully bermed case, the energy transfer through the wall is reduced in winter while additional cooling is provided in summer. The energy transfer through the uninsulated floor varies little between cases FB-1 and EC-1 in either summer or winter. The combined effect in winter is a relatively small reduction in heat loss compared to cases FB-1 and AG-2, while more total cooling is provided than in any of the previous cases. The net annual energy transfer for case EC-1 represents an improvement over the above-grade and fully bermed cases with equivalent roof and wall insulation.

In case EC-2 in figure 3-58, all conditions are identical to the previous case (R-30 roof insulation and R-20 wall insulation) except that insulation at a value of R-10 is placed under the floor slab. In terms of insulation value on wall and floor components, this case is most directly comparable to the well-insulated above-grade case (AG-2). As expected, there is little change between cases EC-1 and EC-2 in the energy transfer through the roof and wall. The floor insulation, however, accounts for a significant reduction in energy transfer in the winter with a loss in summer cooling as well. Because the winter season is dominant, the net annual effect is to reduce energy transfer for the combined components to a level that is less than half that of the above-grade case with similar insulation levels (AG-2). Reducing winter energy requirements at the expense of a moderate amount of passive cooling appears desirable from this analysis. However, this trade-off should be made only in the context of analyzing the total building loads combined with other sources of passive heating or cooling.

Like the preceding examples, case EC-3 in figure 3-58 is a one-story earth-covered configuration. It differs, however, in that the R-30 roof insulation is extended 8 feet horizontally beyond the outside wall. The floor is uninsulated. The extended insulation configuration is intended to increase summer cooling while still providing adequate reduction in winter heat loss. An examination of the wall component alone indicates a relatively poor performance with extended insulation. Examining the net effect when components are combined, however, indicates that case EC-3 is not significantly worse in winter than other earth-covered cases while it provides more summer cooling than any case. This performance is attributable to the decrease in winter heat loss through the floor, which offsets greater losses through the wall.

It has been suggested that if a waterproof membrane is extended horizontally with the insulation, the ground around the building will be dry and thermal conductivity will be reduced. In case

EC-4 it is assumed that thermal conductivity of the soil is 1.0 W/m-°K rather than 1.7 W/m-°K, which is assumed for all other Minneapolis cases. The result is a 25 percent reduction in heat loss in comparison with case EC-3, which has an identical configuration. However, summer cooling is also reduced with a lower thermal conductivity. Other computer simulations not shown here indicated that the distance the insulation was extended from the structure (up to 20 feet in some cases) was far less important than the thermal conductivity of the soil in reducing energy transfer. It is inappropriate to draw conclusions about innovative insulation placement techniques based on these few simulations. Some basic assumptions about the ability of these techniques to change soil properties and ground temperatures must be verified and then included in the simulations.

Case EC-5 in figure 3-58 is a two-story earth sheltered building. There are 2 feet of earth on the roof and the lowest floor level is 20 feet below the surface. The upper 9 feet of the wall are covered on the outside with insulation at a value of R-20; the remainder of the wall is uninsulated, in full contact with the earth. The roof insulation remains at R-30. As expected, the earth-covered roof with R-30 insulation behaves identically to the previous cases. The deeper uninsulated floor represents an improvement in winter heat loss compared to uninsulated floors at lesser depths. Summer cooling through the floor remains virtually unchanged, however, because of the greater depth. The two-story wall in case EC-5 performs in a manner that is equivalent to that of the fully insulated one-story wall in case EC-1. The net effect is that the two-story configuration performs similarly to the one-story earth-covered structure. The increased heat loss due to the fact that half of the wall is uninsulated in the two-story structure, is offset by reduced heat loss at greater depths.

Building Configuration Considerations: In a climate such as that of Minneapolis, where heating is the dominant concern, earth-contact walls and floors represent small to moderate improvements in both summer and winter when compared to above-grade components with equivalent amounts of insulation. Although increased insulation in above-grade components can equal the performance below grade in winter, the same degree of summer cooling cannot be provided at the same time. Since reducing winter heat loss is more important than providing a large amount of passive cooling, the most compact geometry possible is desirable in this climate. On appropriate sites, two-story configurations are recommended to reduce exterior surface area.

The prototypical elevational type of design with a single exposed facade and earth on the remaining three sides is very appropriate to the Minneapolis climate. Either bermed on flat land or set into a hillside on one or two levels, this type of design inherently encompasses a number of conservation and passive strategies particularly suitable to colder climates. The geometry of the house is usually compact, window area is reduced, all glass faces south, the house includes substantial thermal mass to store solar gain, wind is diverted, and infiltration is reduced. These effects, combined with the improved characteristics of the earth-contact envelope, make this an appropriate energy-efficient design for housing in this climate as well as in more temperate regions.

Mechanical System Design and Indoor Air Quality

Heat Distribution Systems

Many of the considerations in the distribution of heating and cooling are the same for an earth sheltered as for a conventional house, except that the quality of the air may take on more importance and the temperature less importance for the earth sheltered house. A room that has relatively constant temperatures and low infiltration may need fresh air more often than it needs heating or cooling, or it may require that water vapor be added or removed. Although hot water heat provides quiet, economical heat that is easy to control for individual rooms, it does not deal with air quality and requires operating temperatures that may be too high to couple efficiently with some alternate energy sources, such as solar heating. Radiant heating systems can often integrate well with the mass of the structure; prestressed concrete plank cores can even be used as part of the system. Because a uniform surface temperature is achievable with these systems, the occupants can remain comfortable at relatively low air temperatures. This system cannot, however, accommodate air purification needs. Gravity systems, which are low in cost and independent in the event of power failures, may not work well with some house configurations (for example, a long, one-story elevational house).

A forced-air system works well for heating, cooling, air purification, humidification, and dehumidification; can reduce vertical stratification of air; works with low temperatures that integrate well with alternate energy systems; presents no danger of water leaks; and may provide desirable background noise in a quiet environment. In a conventional house, because the ductwork for a forced-air system often passes through conditioned space—in the walls or ceilings of rooms, the basement, or an insulated crawl space—heat lost from the duct is lost to habitable space rather than being wasted. In an earth sheltered house, it is more likely that at least some ductwork will be located below grade. It is not unusual to see detail drawings showing insulation carefully placed on both sides of the duct, below it, and even above it. This insulation arrangement is considered to be important because the air in the duct has a much higher temperature than the room air; therefore, a higher temperature differential exists between the duct air temperature and the outside temperature. The temperature differential directly affects the heat loss. Many of these insulation arrangements are labor intensive and, thus, relatively expensive. A directly insulated duct will maintain better heating distribution particularly at the ends of the duct runs where distribution air temperatures could be considerably cooler for an uninsulated duct. Factory-insulated ducts, however, may be more economical than installing insulation around the duct at the site.

Some additional study on duct placement may also be well warranted because of the different conditions that exist in passively heated earth sheltered homes. In most houses built to date, it has been customary to supply warm air below high-loss areas such as windows and to place the return air in the highest part of the house, which frequently is also located above windows. Preliminary studies have suggested that this arrangement may adequately serve only the areas near the windows [Goldberg, et al., 1984]; it leaves the north part of the house, which is usually located away from the windows, inadequately supplied with warm circulating air.

Cooling Systems

In many areas, carefully designed ventilation alone will keep an earth sheltered house comfortable. In other areas dehumidification may actually be the main concern. The designer of houses in these regions must be careful not to oversize air-conditioning units. An earth sheltered house, which realizes a substantial amount of cooling from earth contact, may need relatively little mechanical cooling but will need the same amount or possibly more dehumidification than a conventional house. In many instances a dehumidifier alone may be adequate for meeting cooling needs. In other situations a small air-conditioning unit that produces a small amount of cooling and is run much of the time may provide the best combination of cooling and dehumidification by itself. A central air-handling ventilation system incorporating a dehumidifier may be best in some cases.

Although a variety of heat sources can be combined with earth sheltering to keep inhabitants warm, electricity is by far the most common type of energy used to mechanically assist any passive cooling measure, both for conventional and earth sheltered houses. Cooling is normally distributed through the same duct system that is used for heating. The optimum placement of supply and return openings is not necessarily the same for heating and cooling; however, the compromises required to make dual use of the system are generally minor enough so that both heating and cooling can be adequately provided.

Air Purity

Every house has a substantial amount of pollutants from the occupants, their activities, and the materials within the house. Even the simple boiling of vegetables in a stone fireplace pollutes the indoor air with odors from the vegetables, steam from the boiling, carbon monoxide from the fire, and radon from the stone of the fireplace. In the past, high infiltration has diluted and dissipated the pollution before it could do any harm. Now it is possible to build a house so tight that the pollution is not dissipated, but instead will build up over a period of time if it is not dealt with properly. The many different types of pollutants come from a variety of sources [Moschandress, et al., 1978; Fuller, 1981; Lord, 1981].

Dust and particulates can be made up of smoke, soot, mists, fibers, clay, silica, organic and mineral lints, decayed biological material, and metallic fragments. While the larger particles are filtered out by the upper respiratory tract, the smaller particles may be retained in the lungs. These types of pollutants are usually considered to be a relatively insignificant health hazard. As might be expected, higher levels of particulates have been found in homes where heavy smokers reside; however, these levels rarely exceed recommended standards. Houses in which small children live also appear to have higher levels of particulates.

Microorganisms and allergens are the most epidemiologically important pollutants. This group includes viruses, bacteria, plant pollen, spores, molds, fungi, and particles to which microorganisms cling. Where tobacco is smoked, the smoke is the greatest contributor to particulate matter in the air. While these more commonly known pollutants may not be as frightening as carcinogens or some of the less familiar gases, they are a major cause of upper respiratory infection. The frequency of these infections, and the fact that they can be quite serious for those weakened by age or other health problems, make them as significant as some of the more feared but less common illnesses.

Gases from various sources are a third major group of pollutants. The principal gases are formaldehyde (CH_2O), carbon monoxide (CO), nitric oxide (NO), and nitrogen dioxide (NO_2). Formaldehyde is emitted from numerous products found in a home, including plywood, particle board, urea formaldehyde foam insulation, adhesives, and fabrics; a small amount also comes from combustion sources and cigarette smoke. Excessive formaldehyde can irritate the eyes, throat, and skin, and can cause allergies and respiratory problems. Carbon monoxide is also a product of combustion. Although it can be harmful or even fatal if concentrations are high enough, the concentrations found in monitored houses were not found to be high enough to be considered a health hazard. Nitric oxide and nitrogen dioxide levels are closely related to the amount of gas heating and cooking taking place within a space. Other gases may also be present. Because carbon dioxide (CO_2) is exhaled by occupants, its concentration level is directly related to the number and activity of people present in a given space. It is not unusual for most residences to exceed the ASHRAE standards for acceptable CO_2 levels. Small amounts of sulfur dioxide, ozone, water-soluble sulfate, and water-soluble nitrates are also found; however, in some cases concentrations were smaller inside the house than outside.

Although water vapor in the air is necessary for health and comfort and is also important in slowing the drying out of many materials within a house (for example, food, furniture), too much water vapor is undesirable. Excess water vapor can promote the growth of mold, mildew, and other microorganisms that can be detrimental to health, cause discomfort related to cold, damp conditions, or hot, humid conditions, and can cause condensation on cooler surfaces. If the house is not properly sealed, it may absorb water vapor from the soil through the building envelope. Even if the house is well sealed, water vapor is generated by the breathing and perspiration of the occupants, as well as by many of their activities, such as washing and cooking.

A final pollutant of particular concern in earth sheltered houses is radon. Radon is a very common component of our environment and was present long before human activity started to change the environment. It is a gas produced by the decay of radium 226, which in turn is a decay product of uranium 238. Because radium is a trace element in most soil and rock, it is present in many building materials, such as stone, concrete, and brick, and is also present in the soil around any building. Radon moves through the spaces between particles of soil until it escapes into the atmosphere or meets some dense barrier. It can also be transported by natural gas or water, especially water from deep wells. More radon is released when it is windy, the atmospheric pressure is low, or a shower sprays well water into the air; less is released when rain or frost make it more difficult for the radon to reach the surface. Cracks or openings in a foundation make it easier for radon to enter a house; good waterproofing and sealing techniques make it more difficult; and good drainage helps provide radon with an alternate route of escape. Radon released from masonry, plaster, and gypsum board occurs even on upper floors of conventional houses. Radon will accumulate at higher concentrations in an enclosed space. The more tightly sealed the building, the less the radon can dissipate.

Assuming that radon is present in some quantity, the first concern is understanding its potential harm. Radon has a short half-life of 3.8 days before it decays into short-lived daughter products, which emit alpha particles. These daughter products are solids. It is suspected that because of their atomic charge, the daughter products may attach themselves to dust particles that may be inhaled and retained by the lungs, thereby exposing them to alpha radiation. Radon levels in earth sheltered houses can vary widely. From studies of the radon levels in different types of housing it appears that in above-grade, energy-efficient houses and earth sheltered houses (both without special ventilation), radon levels are similar. Both are higher, however, than levels typically found in conventional houses with higher air exchange rates. The natural radon emanation from the local soil or groundwater is an important parameter in the potential indoor radon levels but the house structure and air exchange rates are major modifiers of this basic potential. For a more detailed discussion on radon exposures in earth sheltered houses the reader is referred to "Radon in Earth Sheltered Structures" in *Underground Space* [Landa, 1984].

Strategies to Reduce Pollutants

As mentioned above, there are three basic strategies for dealing with the various pollutants. Some pollutants can be controlled at their source, by preventing them from entering or being formed, whereas others can be diluted with fresh air or exhausted from the space. The third strategy is to remove the pollutant within the space. The effectiveness of each strategy depends on the type of pollutant; the importance of the strategy depends on the degree of hazard associated with the pollutant.

Controlling or eliminating the source of pollution has two components—construction and life-style modifications. The practicality of both types of control will vary from situation to situation, depending on the type and nature of the pollutant. Construction modifications include using wood-frame construction rather than masonry or concrete in order to reduce radon buildup; having the structure tightly sealed and the exterior well drained in order to prevent radon from entering; selecting electric heating and cooking devices in order to eliminate products of combustion of gas, oil, or wood; and selecting building materials and furnishings that do not contain significant amounts of formaldehyde. Life-style modifications include decisions to prohibit smoking in the house; limit use of aerosols, solvents, cleaners, paints, and varnishes within the space; limit dust-producing activities, for example, sanding wood; and cover cooking pots and limit showering times in order to reduce humidity and radon levels.

A more common and often more practical strategy is to dilute the pollutants with fresh air from the outside or to remove the polluted air. In the past, conventional houses accomplished this by infiltration through cracks in the building and around doors and windows, drafts through vents and chimneys, and air entering and leaving as people opened doors to come and go. But all of these conditions and situations waste energy. In addition, development and use of better-fitting doors and windows, weatherstripping, tighter wall construction, and air-lock entries have made it possible to reduce the energy lost from a structure—and, concomitantly, the amount of fresh air that enters it. A problem results because an energy-efficient house must still have an adequate capacity to eliminate pollutants and replace the exhausted air with fresh air. It is possible to do this in a more controlled way, rather than by ventilating the house with whatever amount of air happens to flow through the cracks in the structure. Exhaust fans over ranges and in bathrooms, as well as vents and flues for clothes dryers, furnaces, and fireplaces, remove many pollutants directly at their sources, before they can spread to the rest of the house. Such devices may, however, be too specialized in their function, too small for an entire house, or not operated frequently enough.

Determining how much fresh air is needed is a

complex issue. Some pollutants, such as formaldehyde and radon, are generated regardless of the number or activities of occupants, whereas others, such as carbon dioxide, are directly related to these factors. Still other pollutants—carbon monoxide and nitrogen dioxide—are generated in some situations but not in others. A consensus seems to be that approximately .5 air changes per hour is an appropriate minimum. It is important to note that this rate of exchange assumes a distribution and mingling of the fresh air so that most of the air is changed during a two-hour period; changing one-tenth of the air ten times over two hours is mathematically—but not functionally—equivalent. Methods of increasing the energy efficiency of this process include the use of heat exchangers and earth tempering tubes. Some type of automatic control may be necessary to achieve a specific ventilation rate, as the residents may have no way of determining when ventilation is adequate or may neglect to operate the system manually.

    The third method of enhancing air purity is to extract the pollutants from the air within the space. This can involve devices such as air filters or electronic cleaners, which remove particles, or devices to remove vapor and gas with sorbants such as activated charcoal or activated alumina.

    Elements of any or all of the strategies to purify air can be used in combination. As with energy efficiency, probably the most effective method is that which attacks the problem on all fronts, using parts of whatever strategies are appropriate. Combining air purification strategies with energy and conservation strategies adds another layer of sophistication and complexity but must be considered in terms of achieving an effective end product.

Energy-Use Performance of Earth Sheltered Houses

It is evident from the previous sections of this chapter that a considerable amount of theoretical information on the energy-conserving benefits of earth sheltered housing exists. In addition, a number of methods for calculating the energy use in below-grade structures and some clear, if general, guidelines on insulation placement are available. Even sophisticated calculation procedures, however, cannot be fully relied upon to determine the true performance of a house. The best evidence of the effectiveness of earth sheltered design in conserving energy can be found by measuring the actual energy consumption of existing houses. Unfortunately, simply recording energy use from utility bills has a number of limitations, and conclusions based on this type of data for a small sample of houses are difficult if not impossible to make. Before examining a selection of houses with monitored energy performance, the limitations and concerns related to monitored data are discussed.

Concerns over Monitored Energy Performance

Inadequate Data Base: Although a few thousand earth sheltered houses are known to exist in the United States, only a small percentage of them have accurate energy-use information that is available to the public. Where records are available, they are most commonly in the form of total fuel or electricity used, and heating and cooling energy are not clearly separated from energy for hot water heating, lighting, and appliances. In addition, interior temperature conditions are not usually recorded, so that differences in comfort level are not apparent when comparing energy use.

Influence of Occupant Behavior: The behavior of people in a house can produce a wide range of effects on heating and cooling. Probably the most dramatic effect is the thermostat setting, although patterns of window and door openings as well as the operation of shades or curtains can also have a significant impact. Moreover, the number of occupants and their activities can affect the internal heat produced. In one study some houses used three to five times as much energy for hot water, lighting, and appliances as others, resulting in lower heating loads and higher cooling loads [Goldberg, et al., 1984]. Because of the wide variation in appliance, lighting, and hot water use, subtracting assumed or average figures for these items from total utility bills to obtain heating and cooling energy use may be quite inaccurate. Thus, total meter readings do not necessarily reflect the true thermal performance of the house but instead may more strongly reflect the behavior of the occupants.

Influence of Mechanical Systems: Electricity, gas, or oil use is typically recorded at the point where it enters the building. Once inside the building, the total energy content of the fuel is not delivered to heat or cool the spaces. Losses can occur in conversion and distribution through ducts or pipes that make up the heating or cooling system. Even the exact location of registers and the thermostat will influence how much heating or cooling is demanded. Variations in the design and

3-59: Earth-covered house in north central Texas; Frank Moreland, architect.

efficiency of the mechanical system result in another element of uncertainty if total fuel use is analyzed to determine the thermal behavior of a house envelope. In newer houses with similar mechanical systems, the degree of variation is likely to be less than it is with occupant behavior.

Inability to Isolate Separate Strategies: Virtually all earth sheltered houses include a variety of energy-conserving design strategies in addition to the placement of the building fully or partially below grade. Common conservation techniques employed in earth sheltered houses include passive solar systems, increased insulation, increased mass, and natural ventilation. Recorded energy use for a house with a number of energy-conserving strategies can indicate the performance of the house as a whole but does not provide insight into the effect of individual conservation strategies such as earth berming or southerly orientation. This situation is made more complex because the individual strategies such as solar gain, thermal mass, and below-grade placement have interactive effects and really cannot be isolated from each other in determining energy benefits. Thus, in no case does the energy use for heating and cooling an earth sheltered house simply reflect the effect of an earth-integrated design.

Variation in Earth Sheltered Design: Once energy-use data for one or several earth sheltered houses are obtained, it is tempting to draw conclusions about the performance of such houses in general. It is important to recognize that the wide variation in design and detailing of this general type of housing make such conclusions questionable. Earth sheltered housing can refer to a slight degree of berming or to a completely underground chamber. Relatively minor details such as insulation placement and thickness may have a significant effect on the energy use for heating and cooling. In many cases, including a number of the examples that follow, information on accurately calculating energy use and refining the design for optimal performance was not available to the designers. In examining the performance of earth sheltered houses, particularly those built before 1980, it should be recognized that the designs are seldom as efficient as they could be if based on more current design guidelines.

Unclear Basis for Comparison: In order to evaluate energy-use data from an earth sheltered house, it must be compared to some standard use for conventional housing to determine the energy savings. One problem that arises is that houses with different climates, sizes, interior comfort conditions, numbers of occupants, and occupant behavior patterns cannot be directly compared. The first two concerns can be addressed somewhat by expressing energy use as a function of floor area and degree days in the heating and cooling season. Heating degree days are calculated by determining the difference between the average daily temperature and a base temperature, usually 65°F, and then adding the figures for all days in the heating season. Cooling degree days are calculated in a similar way for the cooling season, usually using a higher base temperature of 78°F. This results in the commonly used Thermal Integrity Factor (TIF) expressed in Btu/sq ft/heating degree day or Btu/sq ft/cooling degree day. The remaining concerns over interior conditions and occupant variables are not as easily resolved. They can be addressed by more sophisticated monitoring and analysis techniques [Goldberg, et al., 1984].

A second major problem associated with analyzing energy performance data is that there is no absolute standard of comparison. In some cases earth sheltered houses are compared to poorly insulated housing built before 1975, whereas in other cases they are compared to well-insulated housing as it is built today. Occassionally attempts are made to compare earth sheltered houses with superinsulated or solar houses. These comparisions are seldom clear since earth sheltered and other energy-efficient houses actually employ a combination of these conservation strategies. Since there is no standard of comparision, data should be examined not only in comparison to a few houses but to the wide range of energy use found in the broader context of the housing stock.

In spite of the concerns expressed here, actual energy-use figures are useful in evaluating earth sheltered design as long as the limitations are understood. In the remainder of this section, data is presented on three earth sheltered houses from different climate regions of the United States: Texas, Wisconsin, and Colorado. This is followed by a discussion of the results of a broader study of energy use in over fifty earth sheltered houses in the south-central portion of the country, the results of detailed monitoring of five houses in Minnesota, and the results from Lawrence Berkeley Laboratory's BECA-A Database on new, low-energy homes.

Earth-Covered House in Northern Texas

Architect Frank Moreland has designed several earth-covered houses in the northern Texas region. The energy consumption of one house shown in figure 3-59 was monitored from June 1980 through July 1981 [Moreland, 1981]. The 2,100-square-foot dwelling which is occupied by three people, faces slightly west of north to provide a view of a creek and fit the site topography [Ahrens, et al., 1981]. Northerly orientation to avoid solar gain is an acceptable strategy in this predominantly hot climate.

	Conventional House		Earth-Covered House (with 3 feet of earth)		
	kWh/ft²/yr	Percent of Total	kWh/ft²/yr	Percent of Total	Percent Reduction
Heating	5.99	29	1.30	13	78
Cooling	5.32	26	2.02	20	62
Total Dwelling Consumption	20.71	100	9.85	100	52

3-60: Comparison of Energy Consumption for Earth-Covered and Conventional Houses in North Central Texas

Note: The energy demand of the conventional dwelling has been adjusted to account for differences in climatic conditions between the time periods that data were collected. The total dwelling consumption includes all energy demands. Both conventional and earth-covered dwellings are all-electric.

Source; Moreland, 1981 (see references).

When the house was completed in April 1980, it had 2 inches of polystyrene insulation (R-10) and 2 feet of earth on the roof with no vegetation. In October 1980, 1 foot of topsoil was added. The summer of 1980, when the monitoring occurred, was the hottest summer on record in Texas, with sixty-five days over 100°F. It is anticipated that the cooling performance will be further improved in subsequent summers with the additional earth and vegetation.

Energy use was recorded separately for the heat pump, HVAC blower, hot water, and the base load (lights and appliances), as well as the total and peak demands. The monitored data on the house appears in figure 3-60. In order to provide a comparison, a utility company survey of similar-sized conventional dwellings 45 miles away was used. A 78 percent reduction in heating energy use and a 62 percent reduction in cooling energy use was evident in comparing the earth-covered dwelling to the conventional houses. These figures translate into a cooling season TIF of 1.73 Btu/sq ft/CDD and a heating season TIF of 1.87 Btu/sq ft/HDD for the earth-covered house.

Earth Sheltered House in Northern Wisconsin

Designed by architect David Wright, the Schwartz residence in northern Wisconsin combines earth sheltering and passive solar heating to conserve energy. Approximately half of the roof and 75 percent of the walls of the 1,035-square-foot structure are earth covered. A direct gain solar system utilizes a rockbed storage mass beneath the floor. The characteristics of the house are discussed in greater detail in the case studies that appear in chapter 7.

During the winter of 1980-81, no furnace energy was required to heat the house and one-half cord of wood was burned in the wood-burning stove. All other heating energy was supplied by solar heat and internal gains in this 8,046-heating-degree-day climate. One-half cord of wood corresponds to approximately 6.79 million Btu's which translates into a TIF of 0.8 Btu/sq ft/HDD. The daily indoor temperature swing was limited to 4°F and the average temperature varied from 68°F in winter to 76°F in summer. Cooling needs in summer were completely met by night ventilation, and interior temperatures never exceeded 80°F.

During its design the energy performance of the house was simulated using the energy analysis program CALPAS 3. The simulation indicated a total auxiliary heating requirement of 5.84 million Btu's and a total auxiliary cooling requirement of 0.098

3-61: Sun Earth House, Longmont, Colorado; Paul Shippee, Colorado Sunworks, designer.

million Btu's. These figures are remarkably close to the actual energy use in 1980-81. The simulation also indicated that the peak load in winter was 10,000 Btu's and in summer, 3,000 Btu's. As a means of comparison, the energy performance of a reference house was also calculated using the CALPAS 3 program. The reference house had similar size and insulation levels, but the window area was distributed on all four sides of the structure. The resulting energy requirements for the reference house was 69.82 million Btu's in the heating season and 8.40 million Btu's for cooling. Based on this simulation, the actual design of the house resulted in a 92 percent reduction in heating and a complete elimination of the cooling load compared to the reference house [Wright, 1981].

Sun Earth House in Central Colorado

In 1978 Paul Shippee of Colorado Sunworks designed and built an earth sheltered house that utilizes an indirect gain passive solar system (fig. 3-61). The exposed south wall of the 1,800-square-foot structure has 300 square feet of windows. Placed behind the windows are fifty-four 55-gallon black metal drums filled with water. Air heated by the drums rises into an open plenum between the ceiling and the roof. This warm air is then distributed to the rest of the house. At night the glass area is insulated using the Beadwall™ system. In summer the house is cooled with turbine ventilators in the roof. The earth-covered roof has 2 inches of polystyrene insulation and 9 inches of fiberglass. Earth-bermed walls on the north, east, and west are insulated with 4 inches of polystyrene [Ahrens, et al., 1981].

As part of the National Solar Data Network funded by the U.S. Department of Energy, the Sun Earth House performance was extensively monitored, with over seventy different conditions continuously

Space heat supplied by solar system:	35.93 million Btu
Space heat supplied by internal gains:	10.63 million Btu
Space heat supplied by fireplace:	1.56 million Btu
Total building load:	48.12 million Btu
Average building temperature:	70°F
Average ambient temperature:	35°F

3-62: Winter Performance of Sun Earth House
Source: Weston, 1979 (see references).

recorded. Energy-use data was analyzed for the 1978-79 winter (November through May) [Weston, 1979]. In this 6,200 degree day climate, the house was heated entirely by the passive solar system and internal heat gains except for the incidental use of the fireplace. Since the 1.56 million Btus supplied by the fireplace was the only auxiliary heat required, the TIF would be 0.14 Btu/sq ft/HDD. Calculations based on the monitoring produced characteristics of the winter performance shown in figure 3-62.

Of particular interest in the monitored data produced from the Sun Earth House are temperature profiles, which demonstrate the beneficial effects of mass both inside and outside the insulated envelope. In his paper "Results of Thermal Performance Analysis of Passive Solar Space Heating Systems in the National Solar Data Network," M.W. Weston compares the Sun Earth house to above-grade buildings without earth mass on the roof or a high amount of internal mass [Weston, 1979]. The following observations and conclusions were drawn from this comparison:

Appropriate use of mass in a passive system can also result in savings from an energy conservation standpoint. The use of mass on the

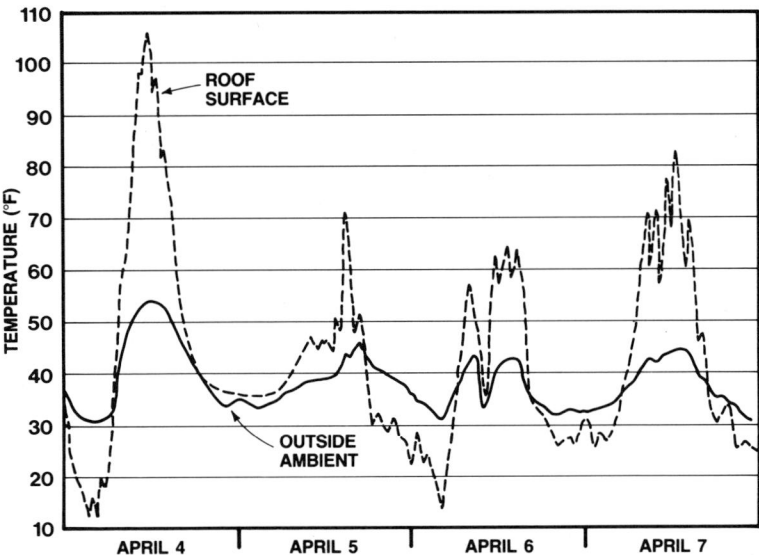

3-63: External Roof Surface Temperatures on a Typical Above-Grade Building

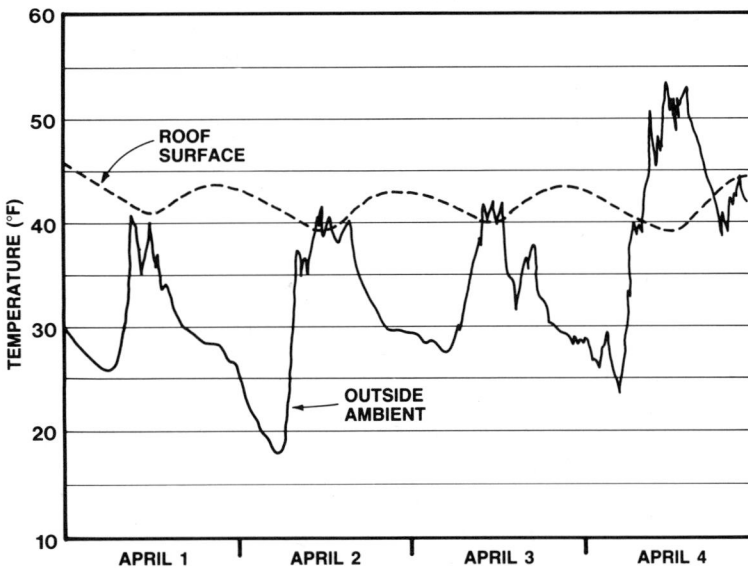

3-64: External Roof Surface Temperatures beneath One Foot of Earth on Sun Earth House

Source: Weston, 1979 (see references).

outside of the exterior surface (wall and roof) insulation provides a moderation of temperature extremes at the outside of the layer of insulation.

[Figure 3-63] presents a plot of the outside ambient temperature and the roof external temperature of a typical above-grade building for several days in April. As a result of the sunlight striking the roof, the roof temperature is generally higher than the outside air temperature during daylight hours. At night, radiative cooling of the roof surface causes the surface temperature to be significantly lower than the ambient air temperature. Consequently, if the building temperature remains reasonably constant, the effect of the exposed roof surface on the building load is a decrease in the heating load during the day when incident solar energy is available and an increase in the heating load at night when stored solar energy must be used. Additional system thermal storage mass is necessary to prevent overheating during the day when solar energy is available and to provide enough stored solar energy to satisfy the load at night when the load is higher.

In contrast to the large variations of roof surface temperature seen in [figure 3-63] the roof external surface temperature at the [Sun Earth House] shown in [figure 3-64] exhibits a minimal variation from day to night. This low variation is due to the approximately one foot of earth above the roof surface. The layer of earth provides a small amount of insulation causing the average roof surface temperature to be slightly higher than the outside air temperature. The major effect of the layer of earth, or mass, is to provide a time lag between extremes in outside air temperature and roof surface temperature. This time lag, approximately 10 hours, is sufficient to yield higher roof external surface temperatures at night than in the daytime, resulting in a higher heating load during

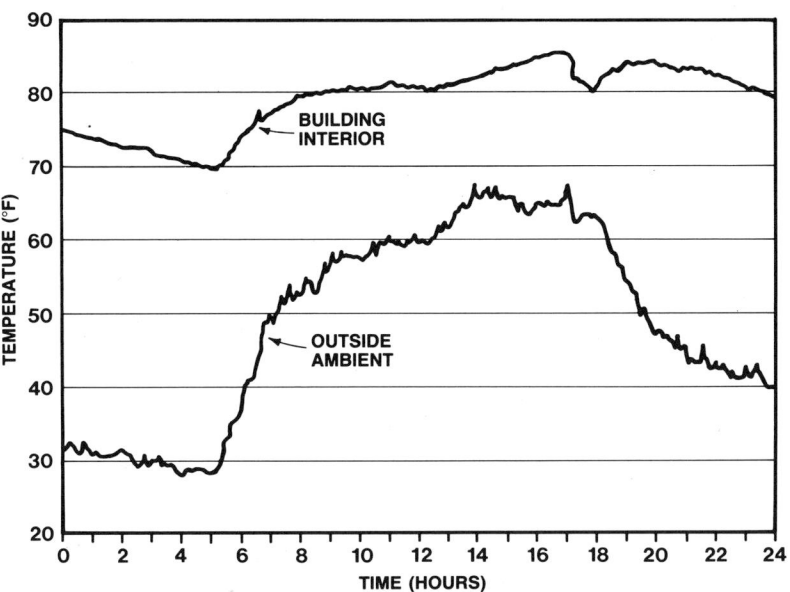

3-65: Comparison of Above-Grade Building Interior and Outside Ambient Temperatures—May 7, 1979

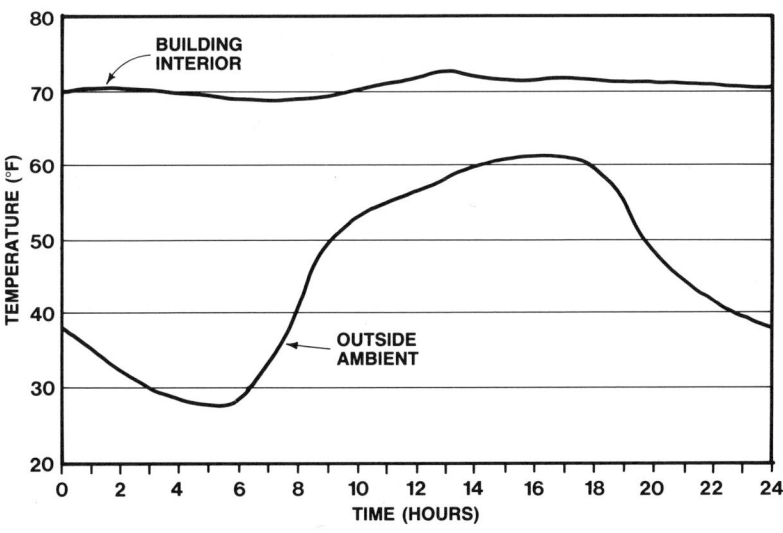

3-66: Comparison of Sun Earth House Interior and Outside Ambient Temperatures—May 8, 1979

Source: Weston, 1979 (see references).

the day when sunlight is available and a lower load at night when energy must be drawn from storage.

Mass placed inside the building envelope not only provides a medium for storing collected solar energy, but also helps to reduce the building load during periods of time when considerable variations in outside ambient temperature are encountered, such as the spring and fall months. The system response presented [in figure 3-65 for an above-grade building with little mass] shows a considerable change in building temperature from early morning to early evening. In contrast, the response presented in [figure 3-66] from a system with higher amounts of internal mass [the Sun Earth House] illustrates the beneficial effect of system mass during the transition periods of the spring and fall.

Earth Sheltered Houses in the South-Central United States

Professors Lester Boyer and Walter Grondzik and their associates at Oklahoma State University have conducted studies of energy use in earth sheltered houses in the south-central United States for several years. In one of these studies, the performance of five earth sheltered houses built before 1978 was compared to several dozen randomly selected conventional homes in the same area. The results, shown in figure 3-67, indicate dramatic reductions in the peak usage in both winter and summer and a total reduction in energy use of 40 percent [Boyer, Grondzik, 1983]. The earth sheltered and conventional houses in this study were all-electric, and the energy use figures are total meter readings including space heating, cooling, hot water heating, lights, and appliances. If the heating and cooling had been monitored separately, the energy savings for these uses alone would be in the 50 to 80 percent range.

In another study conducted by Oklahoma State University, utility bills were collected from fifty-five earth sheltered houses in an eight-state area [Grondzik, et al., 1981]. Total average energy consumption for the houses was 9.25 kWh/sq ft (31,540 Btu/sq ft). Of particular interest was the manner in which consumption varied in different areas of the eight-state region. Total average energy use for earth sheltered houses in the southern states of Texas, Oklahoma, and Arkansas (11.89 kWh/sq ft) was considerably higher than in the more central states of Kansas and Missouri (7.02 kWh/sq ft) and the northern states of Iowa, Nebraska, and Colorado (7.77 kWh/sq ft), as shown in figure 3-68. There is no obvious explanation for this except that the ages of the houses, design approaches, construction details, and the intention to save energy in the house design vary throughout the sample. In fact, some earth sheltered houses are built in this region with tornado protection, rather than energy savings as the primary goal.

Since heating and cooling energy use were not separately metered in this survey, detailed conclusions about energy use are difficult to draw. In addition, the houses were disbursed across such different climate zones that comparisons with conventional housing were difficult to make: a separate standard of comparison would be required for each house. Clearly, earth sheltered houses in this region exhibit a wide range of performances. Some designs are exceptional in dramatically reducing heating and cooling loads, while others do not perform up to expectations. The researchers attribute poor performance to improper building orientation and misuse of insulation and thermal mass. In most houses the researchers feel the performance could be enhanced considerably with proper design.

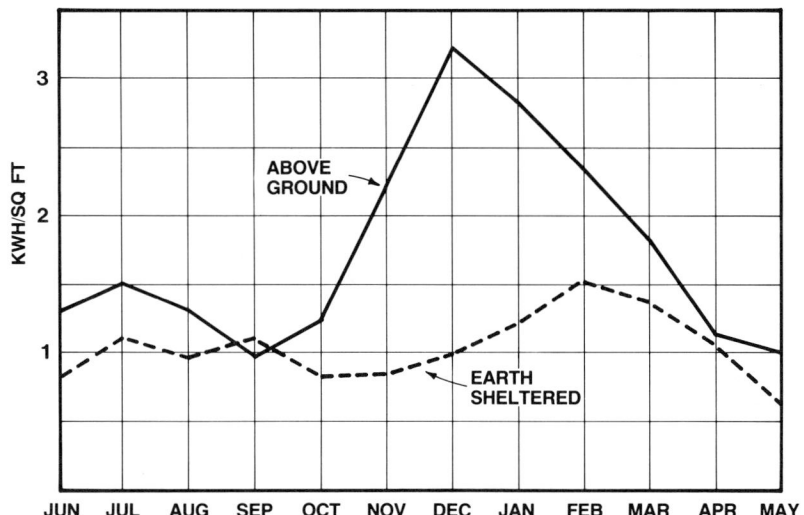

3-67: Monthly Total Energy Use in Above-Grade and Earth-Covered Houses in the Central United States

Source: Boyer, Grondzik, 1983 (see references).

State	Number of Houses in Data Base	Total Energy Use (kWh/ft^2)	Total Energy Use (Btu/ft^2)
Iowa Nebraska Colorado	8 5 2	7.77	26,500
Kansas Missouri	8 6	7.02	23,940
Oklahoma Texas Arkansas	15 2 2	11.89	40,540
Total	48	9.25	31,540

3-68: Energy Use in Earth Sheltered Houses in the South-Central United States

Note: Total use is based on electric meter readings for space heating, cooling, hot water heating, lighting, and applicances combined.

Source: Grondzik, Boyer, et al., 1981 (see references).

Earth Sheltered Houses in Minnesota

In 1977 the Minnesota state legislature appropriated $500,000 to fund a demonstration program to explore the feasibility of earth sheltered housing construction. The Minnesota Housing Finance Agency (MHFA) was assigned to oversee the program, and the Underground Space Center at the University of Minnesota was engaged to design and perform the monitoring functions of the program.

Lack of public acceptance and lack of available data on the energy performance of earth sheltered structures were identified as the two major obstacles that the demonstration program should address. These guidelines led to a program design that included, as its major components, maximum possible public exposure to earth sheltered structures and substantial energy performance monitoring. The resulting program saw the completion of seven earth sheltered projects, three houses owned by the state and located in state parks and four projects that were built and sold on a speculative basis.

The Underground Space Center has collected overall energy performance data for a period of three years (1980-83) from six houses and detailed performance data for at least one year from five houses. The presentation and analysis of this data appears in the report, "Solar/Earth-Sheltered Demonstration Project: Energy Performance Monitoring and Results" [Goldberg, et al., 1984]. Some highlights of the project are discussed below.

Description of the Monitored Houses: A total of six houses were monitored as part of the MHFA program. Five of the houses were earth sheltered

3-69: Two-level earth-covered house, Burnsville, Minnesota; Tom Ellison and John Carmody, architects.

3-70: One-level earth-covered house, Camden State Park, Minnesota; Architectual Alliance, architects.

House	Camden	Wild River	Burnsville	Seward	Willmar	Lynn Park
Type	Earth-Covered One-Story Detached	Earth-Covered Two-Story Detached	Earth-Covered Two-Story Detached	Earth-Covered Two-Story Town House	Earth-Covered Two-Story Detached	Above-Grade Two-Story Detached
Gross Floor Area (ft^2)	1,645	1,959	2,129	1,316	1,970	1,325
Gross Volume (ft^3)	15,746	19,431	21,602	12,782	20,004	14,206
Surface-to-Volume Index[1]	1.72	1.30	1.42	1.32	1.36	1.31
South-Facing Glass Area (ft^2)	262.1	333.2	289.7	87.8	205.2	434.9
Glass-to-Floor Area Ratio	.16	.19	.15	.07	.12	.35
Internal Mass Heat Capacity[2]	57,634	36,296	61,231	36,921	74,341	11,593
Rockbed Heat Capacity (Btu/°F)		3,440		1,732		25,110
Earth-Covered Roof	90% covered 18" soil	69% covered 18" soil	95% covered 18" soil	98% covered 18" soil	73% covered 18" soil	No earth
Roof Insulation	R-25 average	R-10	R-30	R-20	R-20	R-50
Roof Structure	10" precast conc. plank	Timber beam and plank	10" precast conc. plank	10" precast conc. plank	Timber beam and plank	Wood truss
Earth-Bermed Walls	66% bermed	49% bermed	40% bermed	24% bermed 50% common	55% bermed	None
Below-Grade Insulation	R-20 to 4 ft. R-10 below	R-10 to 8 ft. R-5 below	R-20 to 5 ft. R-5 below	R-15 to 8 ft	R-20 to 8 ft R-10 below	
Below-Grade Wall Structure	Reinforced conc. block	Reinforced conc. block	Reinforced conc. block	Reinforced conc. block	Reinforced concrete	
Above-Grade Insulation	R-16	R-19	R-23	R-19	R-19	R-28
Above-Grade Wall Structure	2 × 4 frame	2 × 6 frame	2 × 6 frame	2 × 6 frame	2 × 6 frame	2 × 6 frame

3-71: Characteristics of Monitored Houses in Minnesota

Source: Goldberg, et al., 1984 (see references).

[1] This index is the actual surface-to-volume ratio divided by the optimal surface-to-volume ratio for an equal volume, that of a sphere.

[2] The heat capacity of the mass within the insulated envelope of the building is expressed in Btu/°F.

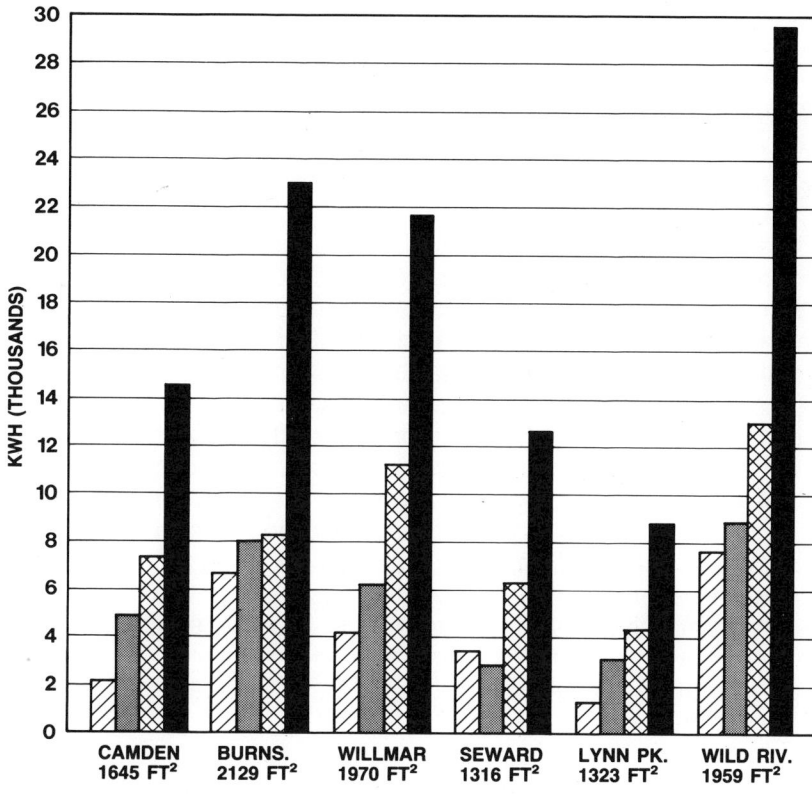

3-72: Annual Energy Consumption for Six Monitored Houses

Note: Figures are based on annual average energy use during the monitored period (1980-83). No conclusions about the relative energy performance of the houses can be drawn from these figures since the floor area, local climate, and occupant behavior vary considerably. Floor area figures given above are gross heated floor area.

Source: Goldberg, et al., 1984 (see references).

and a sixth house was an above-grade, well-insulated, solar house. The purpose of including the above-grade house was to provide a standard of comparison for the earth sheltered houses, although this extremely efficient above-grade house is not at all representative of conventional housing. Among the five earth sheltered houses are three two-story detached houses, a one-story detached house, and the center unit in a row of two-story town houses (figs. 3-69 and 3-70). All of the earth sheltered houses have earth-covered roofs and can be classified as elevational designs, as the majority of the windows are placed in the exposed south elevation. Information on these houses is presented in the book *Earth Sheltered Homes: Plans and Designs* [Ahrens, et al., 1981], and key characteristics are summarized in figure 3-71. The six monitored houses incorporate a broad spectrum of energy conservation strategies including:

- varying degrees of and approaches to passive solar space heating (six houses)
- active, forced-air solar space heating using rockbed thermal storage (two houses)
- active solar hot water heating (two houses)
- earth berming and earth covering (five houses)
- high levels of above-grade wall insulation—exceeding R-20 (four houses)
- high levels of roof insulation—exceeding R-40 (one house)

Monitoring Approach: With some minor exceptions, the space heat and all other energy use in the six houses is supplied by electricity. In the Wild River house, a wood-burning stove supplies a large portion of the space heat; a kerosene-burning heater contributed heat to the Burnsville house in the winter of 1982-83; and the Seward town house uses natural gas for cooking and hot water heating.

Three basic levels of monitoring were employed in the six houses. In the Wild River house, manual

	Cooling Season		Heating Season	
	Minimum	Maximum	Minimum	Maximum
Seward				
Upstairs south (°F)	71.0	74.3	54.7	57.7
Upstairs north (°F)	72.2	76.8	53.9	56.7
Downstairs (°F)	72.2	76.9	56.3	61.3
Relative humidity (%)	45.3	58.2	45.3	54.2
Willmar				
Upstairs south (°F)	65.9	72.0	57.6	81.0
Upstairs north (°F)	66.6	74.8	59.7	81.5
Downstairs (°F)	65.1	68.0	60.4	72.2
Relative humidity (%)	61.1	66.5	38.7	47.4
Burnsville				
Upstairs south (°F)	72.6	81.3	59.8	68.7
Upstairs north (°F)	76.3	81.8	62.8	67.9
Downstairs (°F)	70.2	75.8	60.6	67.2
Relative humidity (%)	68.2	77.1	58.5	63.9
Lynn Park				
Downstairs south (°F)	62.4	81.9	48.3	82.7
Downstairs north (°F)	62.5	79.2	48.3	72.4
Upstairs (°F)	64.9	78.2	54.4	68.4
Relative humidity (%)	38.0	69.0	54.4	97.7
Camden				
Southwest (°F)	68.0	79.2	62.2	80.5
Northwest (°F)	74.5	85.5	73.9	80.4
northeast (°F)	65.9	83.1	59.3	67.9
Relative humidity (%)	51.0	83.3	38.9	46.4

3-73: Internal Temperature and Humidity Conditions

House	Heating season mean internal temperature at which furnace heat is supplied (°F)		
	Minimum	Mode	Maximum
Seward	62.1	70.0	72.0
Willmar	58.5	68.4	70.0
Burnsville	60.4	64.6	68.2
Lynn Park	51.1	60.3	65.3
Camden	59.5	65.7	69.6

3-74: Heating System Control Characteristics
Source: Goldberg, et al., 1984 (see references).

collection of data from several meters to determine energy consumption distribution was required. An automatic data-capture system was used in the Willmar, Burnsville, and Seward houses. In addition to collecting data on consumption for major uses (furnace, water heater, lights, and appliances), measurements were taken of external temperatures, internal temperatures at several locations, internal barometric pressure, and relative humidity. The remaining two houses, Camden and Lynn Park, were instrumented with a more sophisticated system that collected all the measurements mentioned above plus data on the behavior of specific building envelope components. Envelope heat fluxes and temperature gradients, weather data, and external barometric pressure were recorded.

Continuous recording of such detailed information provides a large data base that can be used to analyze energy performance in a more comprehensive manner than simply reading electric meters. Most important, variations in energy performance caused by occupant behavior can be examined more carefully.

Results of Monitoring: The annual average energy consumption for the six houses based on monitoring from 1980 to 1983 is shown in figure 3-72. The wide range of difference in space heating as well as total energy consumption is partly attributable to differences in house size and local climate. But there are undoubtedly significant differences in the number and behavior of occupants as well. This is demonstrated partially by the remarkable differences in energy use for hot water heating, lights, and appliances.

In all of the houses except Wild River, interior temperature and relative humidity were recorded constantly. The temperature distribution and humidity ranges experienced during the heating and cooling season periods are summarized in figure 3-73. In general, all the earth sheltered houses exhibit lower temperature swings than the above-grade Lynn Park house. Conversely, the Lynn Park house has a lower minimum relative humidity during the cooling season while the relative humidities for all the houses are comparable during the heating season. Although these phenomena may be partially ascribed to differences between earth sheltered and above-grade envelopes, a more significant factor appears to be the air movement patterns that are unique to the individual houses.

To understand the differences in internal conditions maintained in the houses, it is useful to analyze the mean internal temperature at which the furnace supplies heat. In figure 3-74 the minimum and maximum internal temperatures at which heat is supplied is shown for each house. In addition, the mode temperature, which represents the temperature at which furnace energy is most frequently demanded is shown. The mode temperature gives an indication of the overall "setpoint" temperature for the entire envelope. The mode temperatures range from 60.3°F for Lynn Park to 70.0°F for the Seward town house. These temperatures are very different from the 65°F base temperature assumed in typical TIF calculations. This difference in internal conditions would tend to make Lynn Park appear artificially superior to the other houses based on a TIF comparison.

A typical calculation of the thermal integrity factor (TIF[1] in figure 3-75) for each house results in a range from 1.55 to 2.98 Btu/sq ft/HDD for the earth sheltered houses and 1.50 Btu/sq ft/HDD for the above-grade Lynn Park house. These figures compare to TIFs in the range of 8 to 12 for Minnesota houses built before 1975 and TIFs of 6 to 8 for typical housing built since 1980.

One way in which typical TIF calculations do not truly reflect the envelope behavior is that occupants contribute significantly different amounts of heat to the space indirectly by using lights, appliances, and heating water. To correct for this, the thermal integrity factor could be calculated to include all internal energy use (TIF[2] in figure 3-75). This approach, however, does not account for heated water that is drained out of the building envelope, and more important for differences in internal temperatures between houses.

To provide a more accurate picture of house

House	Average TIF[1]		Average TIF[2]		Linear Model Performance Line Slope		Mean Energy Performance Index	
	Value (Btu/ft^2/°F-day)	Ranking	Value (Btu/ft^2/°F-day)	Ranking	Value (W-h/day/K)	Ranking	Value (W-h/day/K/m^3)	Ranking
Burnsville	1.55	2	3.88	3	−1730.3	1	4.211	1
Willmar	2.31	4	3.97	4	−1996.0	2	4.461	2
Lynn Park	1.50	1	2.61	1	−2490.5	3	5.065	3
Seward	2.17	3	3.79	2	−a	—	7.009	4
Camden	2.29	4	3.89	3	−2865.7	4	7.835	5
Wild River	2.98	5	5.92	5	−b	—	−b	—

3-75: Energy Performance Summary

Source: Goldberg, et al., 1984 (see references).

Notes: a. Water heater consumption was not monitored; therefore, value can not be determined.
b. Not monitored in sufficient detail for performance data to be computed.
c. TIF[1] is based on energy consumed for space heating only.
d. TIF[2] is based on energy consumed for all uses inside the house.

envelope performance in spite of wide variations in interior conditions, other methods of measuring building envelope performance are used. The "linear model," of which there are several versions, transforms the TIF method into a graphical procedure in which, for a given time interval, the net energy lost by a building envelope is plotted against the mean external temperature occurring during the time interval. Results using the linear model on four houses are shown in figure 3-75. Because it attempts to account for the effects of occupant life style with statistical procedures, the linear model is an improvement over the TIF method.

Another alternative method, the "energy performance index model," was developed during the course of the monitoring project by Louis Goldberg of the Underground Space Center. This model uses analytical techniques to quantify the envelope performance while minimizing the effects of occupant life style. As shown in figure 3-75, both the performance index and the linear model produce a different ranking of the envelope performance of the houses than TIF method produces. The above-grade Lynn Park house is ranked in the middle of the group rather than ahead of the earth sheltered houses when the effect of the occupant variations is reduced.

General conclusions drawn from the results include the following:

- All the houses monitored have a conventional thermal integrity factor (TIF) that is less than 3, and thus all may be classed as energy efficient and superior to conventional housing.

- The conventional thermal integrity factor (TIF) is not an objective energy-efficient housing performance indicator as it produces comparative results that are arbitrarily biased by the occupant life-style.

- The above-grade, well-insulated Lynn Park house has a conventional TIF of 1.50, compared with those of the earth sheltered houses, which range from 1.55 to 2.98. Hence, during the heating season, in a Minnesota-type climate, the earth sheltered and well-insulated, passive/active solar houses monitored have a similar energy performance based on a conventional TIF comparison.

- Based on the alternative performance index model, the above-grade, well-insulated house ranked third with a mean index of 5.065 in a list of five houses with an aggregate index range of 4.081 to 7.923. All the remaining houses are earth sheltered.

- The earth sheltered houses benefited from passive cooling as a result of being below grade during the summer months. No such benefit was experienced by the above-grade house.

- The internal relative humidity conditions in the earth sheltered houses were on average equivalent to those in the above-grade house both in terms of peak values and weekly variations during the heating and cooling seasons.

- The internal temperature distributions in the earth sheltered houses were on average more uniform and exhibited lower diurnal variations than those in the above-grade house.

The results presented and the energy performance listed relate to houses designed in 1978/79 (earth sheltered houses) and 1980 (Lynn Park). Recommended insulation levels for superinsulated and earth sheltered construction have risen since that time.

Homes in the BECA-A Data Base

The Building Energy Use Compilation and Analysis Program, Part A (BECA-A) carried out by the Buildings Energy Data Group at Lawrence Berkeley Laboratory has compiled heating performance data on 319 single-family, multifamily and manufactured low-energy houses in the United States, Canada, and northern Europe. The overwhelming majority of the houses are single-family homes; all were constructed within the last decade; and the buildings use a variety of conservation strategies including superinsulation, passive and active solar, earth sheltering and double-envelope.

Table 3-76 gives a summary of the energy performance results from the current compilation [Busch and Meier, 1984]. Readers are referred to the paper cited for a full description of the procedures used in arriving at the performance indices. The conclusions of the study concerning performance of the respective building types are quoted below:

In general, the low-energy homes in our compilation are consuming significantly less energy than those built using current practice. But there is a wide range in performance, even after taking account of variations in climate. As a group, buildings with earth-shelter features appeared to perform best, that is, had the lowest k-values and balance temperatures, but the sample size is too small to be conclusive. Furthermore, cost-effectiveness could not be verified. Buildings with passive solar and superinsulated features have only slightly inferior performance. More important, the life-cycle cost analysis indicates that investment in energy saving features is cost-effective as compared to both electric and natural gas prices. Houses with active solar features performed significantly worse than the other homes; their k-values were roughly twice those of the earth-sheltered homes. The active-solar houses had a high cost of conserved energy, nearly three times that of passive and superinsulated homes, indicating that active-solar houses are relatively poor investments. Again, the small sample size means that these conclusions should be accepted cautiously.

Category	Number in Data Base[1]	K-value[2] (Watts/°C)	Balance Temperature (°C)	Cost of Conserved Energy	
				All-Electric Homes ($/GJ)	Homes Using Gas ($/GJ)
Earth Sheltered	9	116	10.2	—	—
Passive Solar	197	132	10.1	5.63	4.20
Superinsulated	196	146	15.0	5.77	3.92
Active Solar	26	244	13.9	15.93	—
All Homes	319	188	12.9	7.81	5.01

3-76: Energy Performance Results from BECA-A Data Base
Source: Busch and Meier, Lawrence Berkeley Laboratory (see references).

[1]Note that the sum of the four categories exceeds the total for the entire data base. This is because many of the buildings incorporate several conservation techniques and thus appear in more than one category.

[2]The k-value includes infiltration.

Cost-Effectiveness of Earth Sheltered Housing

In understanding and evaluating earth sheltered design as a housing option, energy use is one of many interrelated variables. Others include initial construction, financing, maintenance, and insurance costs. Typically the questions to be answered are simple: how much does earth sheltered housing cost, and if it costs more, to what degree are increased initial costs offset by decreased operating costs? Unfortunately, accurate answers to these questions are not as simple to provide. The design and construction of earth sheltered housing can vary considerably and, consequently, so can initial costs, energy use, and maintenance costs. Assumptions must be made about a number of economic variables such as financing costs, inflation, and future energy costs, and these assumptions may have a great degree of uncertainty. In this section the variables and concerns related to determining cost-effectiveness will be discussed to provide a framework for making judgments. The section is in three parts: initial construction costs, life-cycle costs, and conclusions.

Initial Construction Costs

Components Affecting Costs: It is generally agreed that an earth sheltered house with a flat, earth-covered roof will cost more than a conventional house of comparable size and quality. The primary reason for the increased costs is the additional structure required to support the weight of the earth on the roof. Also, waterproof membranes, more expensive insulation materials, and additional earthwork and landscaping can represent cost increases over conventional construction. The offsetting cost advantages of below-grade construction are reduced exterior finishing materials, reduced size of the HVAC system, reduced interior finish materials if the concrete or wood structure can be exposed on interior, and in some cases the elimination of frost footings and basement construction since the earth sheltered house is already below the frost line.

The costs associated with a flat earth-covered roof—structure, waterproofing, and some earthwork—usually outweigh the offsetting savings in other categories. If a more efficient structural system is used to support the earth or if the house employs earth-bermed walls and a conventional roof, then costs can be reduced, possibly to a point where those of the earth sheltered house are equivalent to those of conventional construction.

Actual Costs: There is some difficulty in verifying the relative costs of earth sheltered construction for a number of reasons. In addition to variations in design, there are widely varying methods of estimation and construction, and there are problems in making a fair comparison to conventional housing. Because of these factors, reported construction costs for earth sheltered housing vary as widely as costs for conventional buildings.

On the lower end of the cost scale are owner-built houses. The amount of work done by the owner-builder varies, but usually no profit and overhead for the general contractor are involved and total labor costs are reduced to some degree. In an extreme case, Mike Oehler reports building underground houses for a few hundred dollars

[Oehler, 1978], while another owner-builder, Rob Roy, has built a 900-square foot house for $8,000 ($8.88/sq ft) [Roy 1979]. In the book *The Earth Sheltered Owner-Built Home*, two residences that were built for $15 and $30 per square foot are described [Kern, Mullan, 1982]. Owner-built houses are usually reported to cost less than conventional housing built by a contractor. The lower costs for owner-built homes do not usually indicate the relative costs of earth sheltered and conventional housing in a directly comparable situation.

Although a large number of earth sheltered houses are owner-built to some extent, the majority of dwellings are built by contractors just as most conventional houses are built. There is an important distinction, however, between contractors that are familiar with and even specialize in earth sheltered housing and other contractors who have little experience with this type of structure. Usually the same building can be built for a lower cost by the experienced contractor. The unconventional nature of earth sheltered construction will often cause an unexperienced contractor to estimate higher costs because of uncertainty.

Architects and contractors with experience in earth sheltered construction generally state that their projects cost from 5 to 20 percent more than conventional construction, although more extreme cases can vary from costing 10 percent less to over 40 percent more. One of the pioneers of earth sheltered design, architect John Barnard, found that his Ecology House, built in 1973 for $27 per square foot, actually cost less than comparably sized Cape Cod cottages built for $30 to $34 per square foot at that time (see chapter 7). Malcolm Wells has stated that his underground buildings cost about 10 percent more than comparable above-grade construction [Wells, 1977]. More recently, Brent Anderson, an experienced designer and builder of earth sheltered homes in the upper midwest, indicated that custom-designed high-quality earth sheltered housing was costing $60 to $70 per square foot compared to $50 to $60 per square foot for conventional housing of similar quality. Anderson noted that earth-bermed houses without earth-covered roofs cost about the same as comparable conventional construction. Based on his experience designing earth sheltered houses in north central Texas, architect Frank Moreland supplied the following costs for a study of cost-effectiveness (described below): $52 to $60 per square foot for earth-covered houses compared to $38 to $42 for typical tract housing [Moreland, 1981]. It should be noted that the earth-covered houses used in Moreland's comparison have 3 and 7 feet of earth on the roof—substantially more than most other designs.

The Solar/Earth-Sheltered Demonstration Project conducted by the Minnesota Housing Finance Agency provided an opportunity to obtain accurate cost information on several dwellings built by contractors with no previous earth sheltered housing experience. The costs of five houses built in the 1979 and 1980 are shown in figure 3-77. The cost of the houses (from $29 to $58 per square foot) is comparable to or only slightly higher than conventional housing of similar quality [Goldberg, et al., 1984].

Two trends that appear to significantly affect costs are the use of more efficient structural systems to support earth loads and standardized components. One firm, Earth Systems, Inc. in Durango, Colorado, has developed a concrete dome system in which components are sold in a package form throughout the country (see chapter 7). Over one hundred packages have been sold, and resulting total construction costs are $27 to $35 per square foot for owner-builders and $35 to $50 per square foot for homes built by contractors [Earth Systems, 1984].

In evaluating construction costs for earth sheltered housing, it is important to recognize that except for the standardized systems described above, most individual houses represent a small, custom-designed and custom-built project. It has been suggested that multiple-unit projects of earth sheltered houses would result in lower costs due to economies of scale and because larger, commercial contractors with experience in concrete structures and waterproofing would be involved. Two projects built in Minnesota appear to indicate that costs are reduced with multiple-unit construction. A twenty-unit, earth-covered student housing project built in Collegeville, Minnesota, in 1982 cost $52 per square foot (see chapter 7). An additional $10 to $12 per square foot was spent on site work, furnishings, and fees, however, these costs are typically not included in direct construction cost comparisons. A twelve-unit, earth-covered town house project was built in Minneapolis in 1979 at a total cost of $46 per square foot (see figs. 2-57 and 3-77). These costs included $5 to $10 per square foot for solar panels and storage that could have been eliminated with no significant change in performance resulting in construction costs of around $40 per square foot.

Another means of identifying relative costs of earth sheltered and conventional housing is to apply traditional techniques of cost estimating to hypothetical building plans. Richard Behr of Texas Tech University compared conventional and earth-covered housing in this manner by soliciting bids from local contractors [Behr, 1981]. Bids of $53 per square foot were received for his earth-covered design, which compare to $37 to $42 per square foot for conventional housing in this area of Texas. Behr attributes this 43 percent increase in part to the lack of experienced contractors, little competitive bidding, and a relatively low price for conventional housing in Lubbock, Texas, compared to the national average of $45 per square foot in 1980.

In a comprehensive study conducted in 1981, Oak Ridge National Laboratory sought to provide a direct and fair comparison of earth sheltered houses to conventional houses in five different regions of the United States [Shapira, et al., 1983]. Detailed plans of earth sheltered and conventional houses were drawn and then sent to a consulting firm for cost estimates based on regional data and consultation with some contractors. Results of this process indicated earth sheltered building costs ranging from 30 to 49 percent more than conventional housing (see figure 3-78). All of the earth sheltered houses in the study were designed with flat, earth-covered roofs.

Although the Oak Ridge and other similar studies were done in a thorough, unbiased manner, there are always concerns about the ability to generalize from a particular set of drawings or bids obtained in this manner. Bid prices do not necessarily reflect costs from more experienced or specialized contractors (who are more likely to build such houses), and the situation is not necessarily

House	Total Cost ($/ft^2)	Cost not including solar system ($/ft^2)
Seward	46.23	41.23[1]
Camden	58.43	53.43[1]
Burnsville	39.96	39.96
Wild River	47.81	47.81
Willmar	28.97	28.97
Average	44.28	42.28
Average not including Willmar[2]	48.11	45.61

3-77: Cost of Five Earth Sheltered Houses in Minnesota

[1]Total costs of Seward and Camden houses include active solar systems that add $5 to $10 per square foot to the construction costs. By substracting the cost of these systems, a more accurate cost of earth sheltered construction can be determined.

[2]The Willmar house was built partially with student labor resulting in lower than typical costs. To provide a fair reflection of earth sheltered construction costs, averages were computed not including the Willmar house.

Note: All houses were built between 1979 and 1981.

Source: Goldberg, et al., 1984 (see references).

competitive. For example, four Minnesota earth sheltered houses actually built by contractors (without previous experience) in 1979 and 1980 cost from $40 to $58 per square foot, while the estimate for an earth-covered house in Minneapolis from the Oak Ridge study was $72 per square foot. Disparities in relative costs are often rooted in varying definitions of what is a reasonable design for "typical" earth sheltered housing and what represents comparable conventional housing. Some of the problems of providing a direct comparison between earth sheltered and conventional housing are discussed in the following sections.

Comparing Earth Sheltered and Conventional Buildings: Although it may seem unimportant to examine how earth sheltered and conventional buildings differ in certain aspects, the cost difference of theoretically comparable buildings is one of the key variables in assessing cost-effectiveness. Problems seem to arise in three areas of comparison:

- whether both types of houses include equivalent garages, basements, and attics that are typically not included in house area calculations.

- whether interior finishing materials must be identical to be considered equivalent when the basic structural systems and most appropriate and economical finishes are quite different.

- whether an earth sheltered design has the effect of increasing or decreasing land costs.

In conventional housing, attics and basements are not typically created as living space but are by-products of the house form and the need to place a foundation beneath the frost line (in northern climates). These "extra" spaces are useful for

Location	Conventional Houses		Earth Sheltered Houses	
	Cost ($)	Cost per ft^2	Cost ($)	Cost per ft^2
Minneapolis	72,099	48.72	107,144	72.39
Boston	79,044	53.41	112,882	76.27
Salt Lake City	62,603	42.30	81,530	55.09
Knoxville	59,313	40.08	77,514	52.37
Houston	60,597	40.94	86,337	58.36

3-78: Estimated Construction Costs from Oak Ridge Study

Note: All houses include attached double garages or carports. In Minneapolis and Boston, conventional and earth sheltered houses have basements.

Source: Shapira, et al., 1983 (see references).

storage and expansion of the living space if necessary. Attics and basements are not a natural by-product of earth sheltered design since they are not required for the same function. Comparing an earth sheltered house without this extra space to a conventional house with it (the typical method of calculating house areas) does not seem to be a fair comparison. To compensate for this, the hypothetical designs developed for the Oak Ridge cost study included basements under the earth sheltered houses in northern regions [Shapira, et al., 1983]. Unfortunately, this solves one problem but raises another—a basement beneath an already below-grade house results in greater excavation and structural costs than a conventional basement or a single-story earth sheltered house. This may account in part for the high costs found in the Oak Ridge study.

Attached garages provide a similar dilemma. On an above-grade house, an attached garage or a tuck-under garage is a relatively inexpensive addition to the structure and is typically not included in house area calculations. To provide the equivalent amenity of an attached garage for an earth sheltered house may require much more expensive construction with bermed walls and perhaps even an earth-covered roof. The earth-covered garage may have benefits such as a moderate temperature but is likely to cost more than its above-grade counterpart. Economic considerations may result in a detached above-grade garage instead. Making an equivalent comparison is difficult in any case.

Determining equivalent interior finishing materials in earth sheltered and conventional housing is also open to a number of somewhat subjective judgments. Gypsum board nailed to the structure of a conventional wood-frame house is the typical and most economical way of finishing interior surfaces. In an earth sheltered house, however, interior walls are likely to be concrete, and ceilings may also be concrete or wood timbers. To finish these surfaces in an identical manner with gypsum board requires, in effect, a second wall or roof system to be built. Using decorative concrete block and simply spraying a texture onto a concrete ceiling are the most economical finishing materials for a below-grade structure, but these methods raise questions about equivalent cost comparisons. In the case of a timber beam-and-plank roof structure, it is common to have the wood system exposed. Since richly textured exposed wood beams represent a higher-quality finished surface than conventional gypsum board, the question again becomes whether these two systems can be compared fairly.

Earth-sheltered designs on flat sites may require additional land for berming and may not easily fit onto a conventional lot. This could restrict lot choices or in some cases require the purchase of a larger lot. On the other hand, earth sheltered design is particularly suited to sloping sites and can sometimes fit into steeply sloping sites considered unbuildable for conventional housing. The ability to use "problem" sites effectively can be a cost advantage since the land cost may actually be reduced. Also, some earth-covered designs result in a larger usable yard area if the earth-covered roof is accessible. These land-cost and land-use issues should also be considered when attempting to make equivalent economic comparisons between earth sheltered and conventional housing.

Life-Cycle Costs

Determining the total costs and benefits related to a particular building over its lifetime is commonly referred to as calculating life-cycle costs. If a higher initial investment in an earth sheltered house is offset in a reasonable period of time (the payback period) by decreased energy, maintenance, and insurance costs, then the project is considered cost-effective. It is often assumed that energy-related improvements in housing should have a payback period no longer than ten years, but there is some debate over what is a reasonable payback period for a structure with a useful life span of several decades.

Actually calculating life-cycle costs depends on a number of variables in addition to the initial construction and operating costs. The cost of borrowing money (the mortgage interest rate) and the ability of the home owner to deduct interest from his income taxes are factors. In addition, assumptions must be made concerning the rate of inflation in the value of the house and the rate of inflation in energy costs. Based on a given set of assumptions, the payback period can be calculated on a straight cash basis. For example, if the payback period is seven years, the initial investment is recovered at this time and net cash savings will accumulate indefinitely into the future. Another method of analysis referred to as the Present Value Method discounts the value of benefits in the future by a certain percentage. As the discount increases, the payback will be extended because there is the implicit assumption that money in the present has more value than longer term benefits.

Impact of Life-Cycle Cost Variables: As a means of demonstrating the impact of changing the many variables in life cycle cost calculations, two hypothetical comparisons are shown in figure 3-79. In comparison A, an interest rate of 16 percent, an energy savings of $300 per year, and an energy inflation rate of 12 percent are assumed. A conventional house costing $60,000 is compared to an earth sheltered house costing X amount more initially. The graph indicates the relationship between the initial cost difference (X) and the payback period. For example, if the earth sheltered house in comparison A costs 10 percent more to build ($6,000), then the payback period is over ten years. If the earth sheltered house in comparison A costs 20 percent more to build ($12,000), then the payback period is over twenty years.

The payback periods, however, are dramatically reduced given a different set of basic assumptions. In comparison B, mortgage interest rates are 14 percent, the energy savings is $560 per year, and the energy inflation rate is 20 percent per year. Based on these assumptions, the relationship between the initial cost difference (X) and the payback period is shown by line B in figure 3-78. In comparison B if the earth sheltered house costs 10 percent more to build, there is an immediate payback; if it costs 20 percent more, the payback is about seven years. An initial cost difference of 30 percent ($18,000) results in a payback of twelve years based on these assumptions.

The comparisons in figure 3-79 reflect a straight cash method of analysis— interest costs are included but future benefits are not discounted. If they were, payback periods would be lengthened. On the other hand, potential savings in maintenance and insurance costs for earth sheltered buildings are not included in the analysis shown here. Any further reduction in operating costs would decrease payback periods. From this and other analyses, it is clear that increased initial costs for earth sheltered houses and higher mortgage rates will extend the payback period. The payback period will be diminished by higher relative savings in operating costs and a higher rate of inflation for energy.

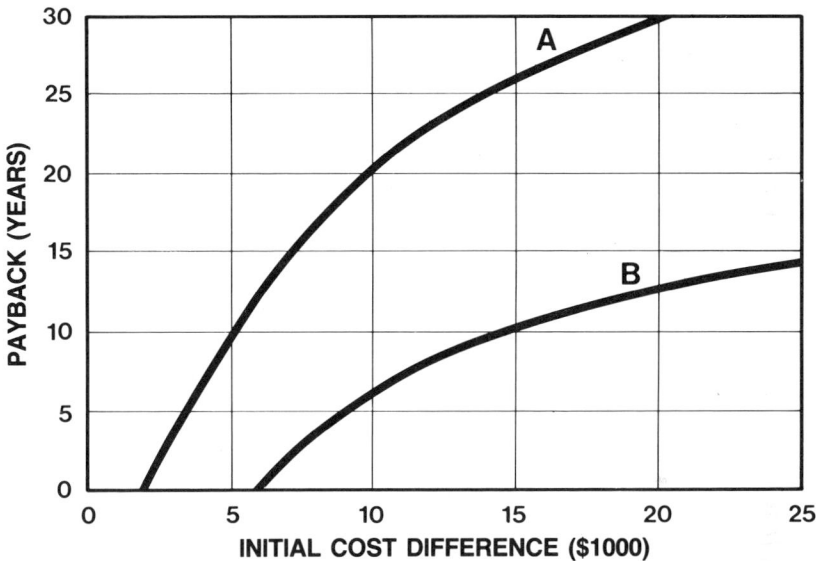

3-79: Comparison of Payback and Initial Cost Difference

Assumptions		Conventional	Earth-Sheltered
Comparison A:	initial cost	$60,000	$60,000 + x
	interest rate	16%	16%
	energy cost	$600	$300
	energy inflation	12%	12%
Comparison B:	initial cost	$60,000	$60,000 + x
	interest rate	14%	14%
	energy cost	$800	$240
	energy inflation	20%	20%
All cases:	term of loan	30 years	
	tax rate	35%	
	annual insurance cost	$500	
	insurance inflation rate	12%	

Manipulating these variables within reasonable ranges will result in payback periods from one to over thirty years. Two recent studies illustrate the disparity in conclusions that can be reached in economic analysis of earth sheltered structures.

Oak Ridge National Laboratory Study: In 1983 a study was published by Oak Ridge National Laboratory that analyzed the cost-effectiveness of earth sheltered structures [Shapira, et al., 1983]. Energy use, costs, and other economic variables were determined for conventional and earth sheltered houses in five American cities. The details of the study are too extensive to present here, but some key assumptions included:

- The initial construction costs of earth sheltered houses were 30 to 49 percent more than for comparable conventional houses based on estimates from a consulting firm.

- Mortgage rates ranged from 14 to 16 percent based on 1981 market conditions.

- Energy costs for the earth sheltered houses ranged from 64 to 88 percent less compared to conventional construction.

- The energy cost inflation rate was assumed to range from 3.9 to 10 percent until 1985, and then energy costs were assumed to increase at rates less than 1.5 percent annually and even to decrease beyond 1985 in some locations.

- Maintenance costs were not assumed to be significantly different for earth sheltered houses in comparison to conventional houses—about 15 percent less on average.

- A discount rate of 10 percent was assumed using the Present Value Analysis Method.

Using the above set of assumptions, the Oak Ridge study concluded that earth sheltered houses were not cost-effective in any location, since payback periods were not reached within thirty years. Four critical assumptions appear to lead to this negative conclusion: high construction estimates for earth sheltered houses, a high discount rate, high mortgage rates, and a low estimate of future energy cost inflation. All of the assumptions in the study have been well researched and are within the broad range of possibilities. On the other hand, actual construction costs have not proven quite so high in many locations while future energy costs could easily exceed the levels projected in this study.

Ehrenkrantz Group Study: As part of a study for the Federal Emergency Management Administration published in 1981, the Ehrenkrantz Group, a private consulting firm, undertook an economic analysis of earth sheltered housing [Moreland, 1981]. The focus of the study was on earth-covered dwellings in north-central Texas, but much of the information is applicable to other locations where similar assumptions apply. Two methods of analysis were used: the Present Value Method described above and the Internal Rate of Return, which examines the earth sheltered house as an investment. A number of cases and assumptions were tested in this analysis including two time frames—a thirty-year period and an eighty-year period. Some of the key assumptions were:

- In one series of cases, a house with 3 feet of earth cover on the roof cost $52 per square foot and was compared to a conventional house costing $38 per square foot. In another series of cases, a house with 7 feet of earth on the roof cost $60 per square foot and was compared to a conventional house costing $42 per square foot.

- A number of mortgage rate and term options were analyzed, including twenty-year mortgages at 11 percent, 8.25 percent, and 5 percent; and a ninety-year mortgage.

- Energy costs in the two earth sheltered houses were 65 and 85 percent less than for the conventional houses.

- The energy cost inflation rate was assumed to be 20 percent for five years and 11 percent for twenty-five years in the thirty-year economic analysis period. In the eighty-year period, energy costs were assumed to increase at 15 percent for fifteen years and 10 percent for sixty-five years.

- Maintenance costs for the earth sheltered cases were 0.5 percent of the building value per year; for the conventional houses, 1.5 percent.

- The discount rates in the Present Value Analysis Method were assumed to be 5 percent and 8 percent. General inflation rates were assumed to be 8 percent for the thirty-year analysis period and 5 percent for the eighty-year analysis period.

A variety of cases were analyzed based on the ranges of assumptions outlined above. The following conclusion was drawn using the Present Value Method:

These results indicate that the underground buildings—in all cases—are less costly to operate than the tract houses. The investment becomes more attractive if low interest mortgages are available for the underground buildings. The underground house with 7 ft. of earth cover produces greater savings than the house with 3 ft. of earth cover. A 5% discount rate is most favorable to the underground buildings. [Moreland, 1981].

The other analysis method employed indicated a discounted payback period and an internal rate of return for each case. Payback periods ranged from eight years to over twenty-seven years depending on the assumptions used. The authors concluded:

The underground house is an attractive investment in all the situations investigated. The house with 3 ft. of earth cover produces a slightly better return on investment than the house with 7 ft. of earth cover. An underground house with a conventional 11% mortgage at 8% discount rate will produce returns on investment of 17.84% for 3 ft. of earth cover and 16.78% for 7 ft. of earth cover in the short term. When a long term, low interest mortgage is available, the investment has a payback period of less than 10 years with returns of investment of 23.13% and 21.25% for the 3 ft. and 7 ft. of earth cover, respectively. [Moreland, 1981].

Just as with the Oak Ridge study, many assumptions can be debated in the Ehrenkrantz analysis. Similar to the Oak Ridge study, the relative costs of the earth sheltered houses are quite high because, due in this case, of the heavy earth loads of 3 to 7 feet on the roof. In contrast, some of the economic assumptions, such as relatively low mortgage interest rates and relatively high energy cost inflation rates, may not prove to be accurate.

Conclusion

Numerous cost studies and economic analyses of earth sheltered housing have been done in recent years. There is general agreement that buildings with flat earth-covered roofs cost more than conventional wood-frame construction, although the assumed increase ranges from 5 percent to 50 percent. There is less agreement on the cost-effectiveness of earth-covered structures.

Unfortunately, cost effectiveness is not as easily calculated for earth sheltered housing as it is for products with very fixed costs and predictable results. Key questions remain about the true costs and energy savings. In addition, the ability to perform an economic analysis on earth sheltered housing is clouded by concerns over making a fair comparison with conventional houses and establishing a correct set of economic assumptions. Relatively minor changes in assumptions can produce quite different conclusions.

It appears that for every general conclusion about costs and cost-effectiveness that can be drawn, a number of exceptions can be found. Virtually any hypothetical study can be challenged as to its broad scale applicability. Because of the diversity in earth sheltered design and construction, variations in the reported costs and energy savings, and the fluctuations in economic conditions, cost-effectiveness can most accurately be determined only on a case-by-case basis.

While life-cycle cost analysis techniques are useful in evaluating alternative building techniques, the limitations of such analyses should be kept in mind. Determining payback on a house design implies a value system that is not universally shared. Whether one is viewing a house in a five-year, thirty-year, or even one-hundred year time frame is an important economic, as well as philosophical, question. An even more basic question is to what extent does one choose a particular house design based on economic factors. For most people houses are chosen based on a number of criteria in a manner similar to other major purchases such as cars, furniture or clothing. In some cases a cost-benefit analysis is a major criteria, but often it is one of many interrelated variables.

In evaluating earth sheltered houses in particular, it is important to consider that such homes are seldom built solely to invest in energy conservation. Multiple benefits are usually cited by builders and occupants, including storm and tornado protection, lower maintenance, longer-life structure, noise reduction, and security. In certain cases marginal sites can be utilized, resulting in lower land costs. For some, earth sheltered houses represent a means of building in harmony with the site and its natural systems in a way that is impossible with conventional buildings. These personal, aesthetic, and environmental benefits, along with the other non-energy-related benefits mentioned above, have value that is seldom quantified in a cost-benefit analysis.

Except for a few pioneers, design and construction of earth sheltered housing in the United States has only been pursued for a few years. Research on the optimization of earth sheltered designs has been limited. As more earth sheltered housing is built, it is likely that techniques will be refined. The natural evolution of a new concept is for costs to be reduced while performance is improved. A number of possibilities exist that are likely to increase the general cost-effectiveness of earth sheltered structures in the future. These include:

- Thinner layers of earth on the roof in the range of 6 to 12 inches, as opposed to the 2 to 3 feet that is more common. In some climates many benefits can be retained with less earth cover, as long as the cover can adequately support plant materials.

- Efficient vault and dome structural systems to support earth loads at lower costs than possible with flat roof structures.

- Building component systems along with refinement of construction details to simplify construction and reduce costs.

- Earth-bermed structures without earth cover on the roof, which eliminates most or all of the initial cost increase.

- Simpler interior and exterior finishing materials that are economical and intrinsic to the heavier structural system, rather than a costly duplication of above-grade finishes.

- Multiple-unit construction, which is likely to overcome increased costs caused by uniqueness, provide economies of scale, and may reduce land costs and provide more efficient overall land use.

- Improved energy performance in both heating and cooling seasons using various techniques of ground temperature manipulation and improved mechanical system design.

Indian cliff dwellings in Mesa Verde National Park, Colorado. Drawing by Bruce Cornwall.

Chapter 4

Structural Design

Introduction

The structure of an earth sheltered house must be considered at an early stage in the planning and layout of the building. Structural design has become so commonplace and the restrictions on design so well known for conventional houses that it does not usually have to be a conscious part of the planning exercise. For the above-ground portion of a conventional house, the loadings are relatively light, and hence the load paths by which a load (such as from wind or snow) are carried to the ground are not crucial to the design. The conventional structure can be modified easily according to well-known empirical rules—for example, doubling headers and studs around windows or doubling joists where large holes are cut in the floor. For a conventional basement, the burial depths are generally less than 5 to 6 feet of earth, and for these depths of burial it has been found by wide experience that plain concrete, concrete block or treated wood foundations are, in the overwhelming majority of cases, adequate structurally. Because the burial depths (and hence the earth pressures) are low, there is little to be saved in the structure by determining the exact soil type and from that a better estimate of the actual earth pressure that will act on the wall.

In contrast to the conventional house, the earth sheltered house has large depths of burial, the earth on the roof is a very significant load (approximately 100 to 120 lbs per square foot of roof for each foot depth of earth cover), and the structural form of the house can have a great impact on the ease with which these heavy loads can be carried. In some cases, as with arch structures for instance, the structural form will dominate the entire layout of the house. In more standard methods of construction, there is a fair amount of flexibility in the design, but the needs of the structural system must be borne in mind or a price will be paid in higher than necessary structural costs. Because of the heavier loads, openings in structural members must be made with more care.

This chapter cannot instruct anyone who is not an engineer to design and size structural systems for an earth sheltered house. There are many variables in the determination of earth loads and pressures, and the design of structural members carrying such heavy loadings should not be attempted by an amateur. If standardized designs were prepared for particular elements of the structure for different earth loads on the roof and depth of burial on the walls, they would necessarily assume the worst earth loading conditions likely. For more favorable earth loading conditions that would normally occur, the structure would be overdesigned. This does not matter much for lightly loaded structures (e.g., the conventional basement), but as the earth loads and the structural strength required increase, larger and larger savings can normally be made by a careful individual structural design.

The services of a professional engineer (usually listed in the Yellow Pages of the telephone directory under "Consulting Engineers") should be employed to prepare or at least check the structural design of an earth sheltered house. In some cases it will not be necessary for the individual home owner to contact a structural engineer directly. For instance, if an architect is involved, he will arrange for any necessary assistance in this area. If precast concrete plank manufacturers are involved, they often have registered professional engineers on their staff who prepare the structural design for the parts of the structure where their planks are used. Reputable contractors will usually have an engineer to whom they can turn for the design of structures outside their normal competence. This individual design approach to earth sheltered structures may become less necessary as more such structures are built in a particular area, especially if the same firm is involved in several houses. For the design of similar elements in this case, it would be necessary to check only the site investigation information to make sure that the loading and support criteria were the same in order to determine whether the same structural design could be used.

It should not be construed here that earth sheltered housing only gives problems with the structure. There are in fact several advantages to offset the greater strength and more involved design required. Some of these advantages are:

- The structures will generally be constructed of massive and relatively permanent materials that will give the buildings a very long expected life.

- The buried structure will be subject to much smaller temeprature fluctuations than an above-ground structure. For a conventional roof, for example, the temperature of the roof surface may fluctuate in Minnesota from well below 0°F in the winter to over 140°F on a hot, sunny day in summer. For a buried roof, under the insulation recommended, the temperature fluctuation of the structure will be of the order of only 5°F to 10°F.

- Both the advantages above will contribute to a low maintenance structure.

- Concrete construction methods will give a very fire-resistant structure. Should a fire occur, the structure is likely to be little damaged unless an unusual fire hazard from stored materials exists in the house.

- Simple layouts and structural systems (which reduce costs) can be used because the attractiveness of the house from the outside may not be as dependent on an interesting (and usually expensive) exterior shape or on the use of expensive facing materials for all the walls and roof. In contrast to a conventional above-grade house, the aesthetic appeal of the design is likely to depend more on landscaping and the way the house blends with its surroundings.

This chapter will identify the major parameters affecting the structural design of an earth sheltered house so that a house can be conceptually designed without making layout decisions that will cause expensive solutions in the structural design. The cost for the structural design process will be kept to a minimum if the house has a sound layout before it is brought to the structural engineer. In this case he will only have to design the necessary structural members and provide the details and any specifications. If the house is poorly layed out when he becomes involved, several stages of redesign may be required before an acceptable compromise between structural system cost and desired layout is achieved. In keeping with this intent, most of the discussions are generally in nature with advantages and disadvantages of various systems given and special problems noted.

Soils

Classification of Soils

The type of ground in which the house excavation is made will have several implications for the design. For geotechnical engineering purposes, soils are generally classified using the soils classification chart shown in figure 4-1. Figure 4-2 illustrates the general suitability of soil types for earth sheltered housing. Strength and loading parameters of the soil are usually estimated for small structures such as a house from the soil description and the use of simple empirical measures such as a penetration test, which involves forcing a probe into the soil and measuring the force or number of blows needed to move the probe a certain distance.

Rock is classified somewhat differently than soils since the material itself is usually very strong but the overall strength of an excavation wall is dependent on the jointing of the rock. Except for certain prime locations such as a river bluff, the cost of small excavations in rock will generally make houses dug into rock an economically unattractive proposition.

Soil properties and design criteria are discussed in greater detail in the *Earth Sheltered Residential Design Manual* [Sterling, et al., 1982] and can also be found in any soil mechanics textbook.

Implications of Soil Type for Structural Components

Roof: Most soils are close enough in density that any density variations will not have a large impact on the house design. The strength of the soil will not generally be important for the roof design except in curved roofs or where the depth of soil on the roof approaches twice the span on the roof (an unlikely condition). The soil on the roof is usually treated as a permanent load equal to its total weight and the roof must carry this entire load. The susceptibility of the soil to frost heave and the ability of the soil to support vegetation are the major characteristics to ascertain. Fine-grained soils, especially silts, are the most susceptible to frost heave. For small burial depths, the roof will not require large amounts of fill, and it may be possible to bring a suitable material to the site for the roof cover if the site material is not suitable.

Walls: Larger differences in the lateral pressures on walls occur among different soil materials. Most soil materials can be used, however, and it is more important in this case because of the greater quantities required to use as much of the local site material as possible for landscaping and backfill. It is expensive to haul material away from the site and to bring in new material. Nevertheless, when considering the structural design of the walls in conjunction with the drainage and waterproofing requirements, it is customary to use a sand or gravel backfill immediately adjacent to the wall to drain groundwater to the foundation drain. The primary soil to avoid is an expansive clay. Expansive clays swell when they become wet and can exert high pressures that are too large to design against economically. Soft clays at the site can also present problems of excavation slope stability and difficult site conditions during construction.

Major Divisions			Letter Symbol	Typical Descriptions
Coarse Grained Soils More than 50% of material is larger than no. 200 sieve size	**Gravel and Gravelly Soils** More than 50% of coarse fraction retained on no. 4 sieve	**Clean Gravels** (little or no fines)	GW	Well-graded gravels, gravel-sand mixtures, little or no fines
			GP	Poorly-graded gravels, gravel-sand mixtures, little or no fines
		Gravels with Fines (appreciable amount of fines)	GM	Silty gravels, gravel-sand-silt mixtures
			GC	Clayey gravels, gravel-sand-clay mixtures
	Sand and Sandy Soils More than 50% of coarse fraction passing no. 4 sieve	**Clean Sand** (little or no fines)	SW	Well-graded sands, gravelly sands, little or no fines
			SP	Poorly-graded sands, gravelly sands, little or no fines
		Sands with Fines (appreciable amount of fines)	SM	Silty sands, sand-silt mixtures
			SC	Clayey sands, sand-clay mixtures
Fine Grained Soils More than 50% of material is smaller than no. 200 sieve size	**Silts and Clays**	Liquid limit less than 50	ML	Inorganic silts and very fine sands, rock flour, silty or clayey fine sands or clayey silts with slight plasticity
			CL	Inorganic clays of low to medium plasticity, gravelly clays, sandy clays, silty clays, lean clays
			OL	Organic silts and organic silty clays of low plasticity
	Silts and Clays	Liquid limit greater than 50	MH	Inorganic silts, micaceous or diatomaceous fine sand or silty soils
			CH	Inorganic clays of high plasticity, fat clays
			OH	Organic clays of medium to high plasticity, organic silts
Highly organic soils			PT	Peat, humus, swamp soils with high organic contents

4-1: Soil Classification Chart

Foundations: The major parameter for foundations is the permissible bearing capacity of the soil. For the walls, which carry a substantial portion of earth loads from the roof, the foundation loads will be much higher than for a conventional structure. This will make a good estimate of the bearing strength of the soil worthwhile, since general code values are necessarily quite low where no special determination is made (see Site Investigation Procedures). Soils to avoid at the foundation level are any soft or loose deposits. Special care should be taken when dealing with existing man-made fills, because very uneven bearing conditions may exist, which can cause severe structural problems. A properly compacted fill, however, should not cause problems.

Floor: The floor of the structure will not present any structural problems under normal circumstances. Extra problems will have to be dealt with when expansive clays are present or when a high water table is not drained and water pressure will act on the underside of the floor.

Suitability of Various Soils

The adjacent chart indicates the appropriateness of various types of soil for an earth sheltered house (fig. 4-2). Most soils will not fall neatly into these categories, but a more detailed discussion is not possible without detailed data from a soil investigation.

Site Investigation Procedures

In the absence of other advice from a competent architect or engineer familiar with local conditions, the following information should be sought for use in house design and in determining the suitability of a site. Soil testing firms usually carry out the physical aspects of the work and they, or a consulting engineer, can supply the necessary other information and recommendations.

1. At least one soil boring extending to a depth of approximately 10 feet—20 feet below the proposed foundation unless bedrock is encountered or knowledge of local conditions makes this depth unnecessary. Borings should be made using the standard-penetration split-spoon method in accordance with ASTM D1586.

Category	Type	Qualifiers	Suitability
Cohesionless	Gravels Sands	Very loose Loose	Good drainage but may need compaction for adequate bearing.
		Med. dense Dense Very dense	Excellent—good drainage, good bearing, low lateral pressures
	Silty Sands Clayey Sands		Will depend on whether cohesive or cohesionless elements dominate its behavior. Should generally be workable unless soft or loose conditions prevail.
Cohesive	Silts Clays	Very Soft Soft	Careful evaluation needed.
		Med. stiff Stiff Very stiff Hard	Should present no particular problems structurally. Drainage of high water requires granular backfill. Septic tank system can have problems.
		Expansive	Avoid
	Highly Organic Soils	Peat Humus Swamp soils	Would probably require extensive replacement of soil or use of special foundation techniques.

4-2: Soil Suitability

2. The types of soil should be logged as the boring proceeds. Soil samples should be taken and kept in airtight jars.

3. The depth at which groundwater appears to be encountered should be noted (this is difficult to determine exactly because drilling water or mud is normally used in the drilling process).

4. If the groundwater table is close to the footing depth on the structure, a perforated plastic pipe can be installed so that the groundwater table and any fluctuations in it can be monitored. The measurements can be made quite simply with a tape and bobber.

5. A testing firm or consulting soil engineer should comment on the suitability of the site based on their information. They should recommend design values for allowable foundation loads and lateral earth pressure.

6. To keep the subsurface investigation costs low, it will help if the potential position of the house on the site and some major parameters of the design have been considered. The location of the boring, the depth of the boring, and the depth of penetration tests for bearing values will depend on such information.

7. A percolation-test soil-boring program is usually required when a septic tank and drain field are to be used. Testing can be done at the same time as the remainder of the investigation if this will be necessary.

Design Loads

Because many structures use loads on one part of a structure to balance the loading on another portion and because many structural materials respond differently to long-term and short-term loads, structural loads are usually divided into two main categories: dead loads and live loads. Dead loads refer to any load on the structure that may be considered permanent, such as the weight of the structural components (a concrete or wood roof, steel beams, etc.), waterproofing, finish plaster, and permanent equipment. Although soil loads are normally considered dead loads because they are long-term loads, the effects of possible later partial excavation of the earth on the roof or adjacent to the walls of an earth sheltered building must be considered in design. Soil pressures are depended on to resist lateral loading of an earth sheltered structure and to balance lateral earth pressures when the opposite walls of the structure are buried. Unequal excavation or backfilling around the structure can call these assumptions into question, however. The likelihood of maintaining a permanent soil load must be considered in designing an earth sheltered building, particularly if it is a post-tensioned structure.

Live loads are transient: they are likely to change in magnitude, location, and/or point of application over the life of the building. They include snow, rain, wind, people, cars, backfilling equipment, partitions, and furniture. It is important to assess how many of these possible loadings can occur simultaneously and to design for a reasonable likelihood of such combinations of circumstances occurring. In roof or floor designs, an average live load (calculated in pounds per square foot) is usually assessed to cover almost all eventualities. Examples of typical live-loading assumptions are given under each category of loading discussed below.

Roof Loads

The most dominant roof loading condition is the presence or absence of soil on the roof. Normal soils can vary in weight from 90 pounds per cubic foot to 135 pounds per cubic foot, although it is possible to design lighter soil mixes by including a lightweight filler material. Even though a fully saturated soil may well weigh more than 135 pounds per cubic foot, if the roof is well drained, the water loading can be considered a live-load condition. The soil density most commonly assumed in design is 120 pounds per cubic foot, which equals 10 pounds per square foot of loading for each 1 inch of soil depth. Thus, a 2-foot soil depth would yield a

Component	Weight (psf)
8-inch prestressed concrete plank	55
10-inch prestressed concrete plank	65
12-inch prestressed concrete plank	80
2-inch concrete topping on plank	25
8-inch poured concrete deck	100
10-inch poured concrete deck	125
12-inch poured concrete deck	150
Wood plank and beam system	20
Conventional wood truss roof	10

4-3: Typical Roof Component Loads

loading of 240 pounds per square foot on the roof structure.

For roofs that have reasonable spans and are carrying heavy loads, the weight of the structure itself can also be important. A 12-inch prestressed concrete plank will weigh approximately 80 pounds per square foot, and a 12-inch poured concrete slab approximately 150 pounds per square foot. Figure 4-3 lists typical weights for different roof structures; figures 4-4 and 4-5 provide examples of complete roof loadings for different design configurations.

Live-load allowances for earth-covered roofs usually range from 50 pounds per square foot to 100 pounds per square foot. These figures include an allowance for snow load, any vehicular traffic expected on the roof, and rain-saturated soil. When heavy snow is typical and extensive drifting of snow on the roof can occur or when large vehicles can drive onto the roof, the design must allow for these possibilities. Although wind uplift is not a problem for earth-covered roofs, it must be considered in the design of exposed roofs. Live loads for inaccessible conventional roofs in areas where snow seldom falls may be as little as 10 pounds per square foot, which allows for occasional maintenance. Large landscaping elements, such as trees, will require special consideration of their dead weight and the transfer of wind loading to the structure.

Wall Loads

Walls in an earth sheltered structure must resist lateral earth pressures if they are placed against the earth; if they are exposed, they must resist wind loadings. The walls also act as components of the structure, transferring forces from the roof and other walls to the foundations. This section examines only the external applied loads.

Lateral soil pressures will vary considerably with type of soil and depending on whether the wall is

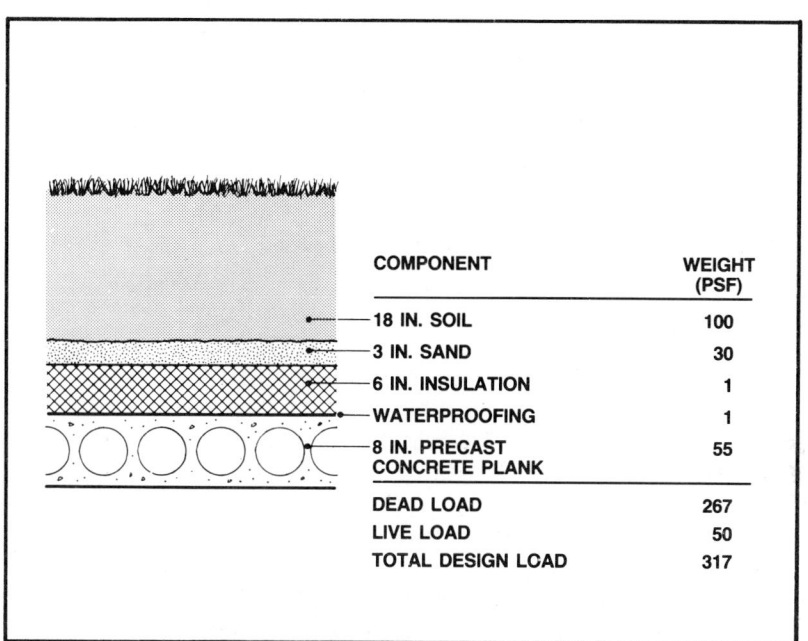

4-4: Loads on Roof Covered with 18 Inches of Earth

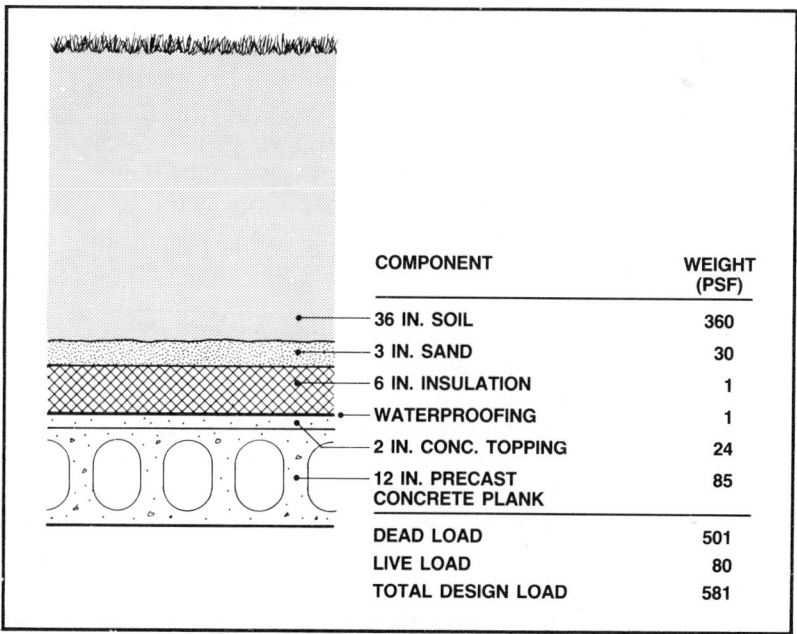

4-5: Loads on Roof Covered with 36 Inches of Earth

able to deflect away from the load (active pressure), is held rigid (at-rest pressure), or is actually forced towards the soil (passive pressure). Although the actual soil pressure conditions are greatly affected by backfilling procedures and building geometry, at-rest pressures should generally be used in the design of the earth retaining walls of a fairly rigid structure such as a concrete wall, roof, and floor system; active pressures can be used for external cantilever retaining walls. Figure 4-6 through 4-11 illustrate the differences in the magnitude of the loading caused by different building and berm arrangements. Stepped walls reduce lateral pressures against the lower wall section but also increase the surface area of the building (fig. 4-9). Berms that slope down and away from the building will also reduce lateral pressures to a degree. Figures 4-10 and 4-11 also illustrate the typical triangular loading assumption for two different soil pressures that correspond roughly to active (the lower value) and at rest pressure conditions, respectively. The deeper the structure, the more important an accurate assessment of the lateral loading becomes.

When the lateral pressure exerted by a backfill material is used in design, it is important that other soil materials that would exert a higher pressure on the wall be placed outside the zone in which they could influence the wall. A rule of thumb is to assume that this zone lies within a line drawn at 30 degrees from the vertical, extending out from the base of the wall.

Other loads that must be considered in wall design include the following:

Saturated Soil Conditions: Water pressure can add significantly to the wall loading. The pressure exerted by water increases with depth at a rate of 62.4 pounds per square foot, per foot of depth. A granular backfill, which provides good drainage in addition to lowering normal lateral pressures, is generally used for backfill whenever it is available.

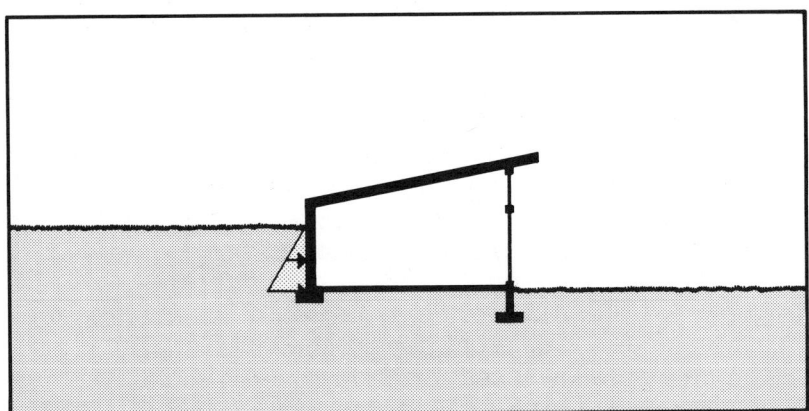

4-6: One-Story Partially Bermed Wall

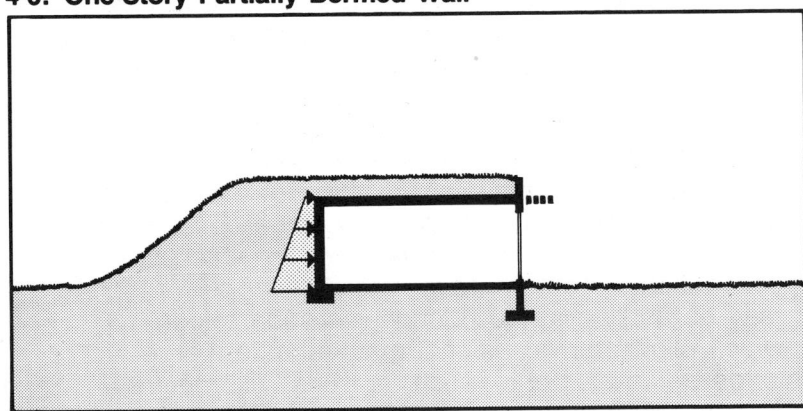

4-7: One-Story Fully Bermed Wall

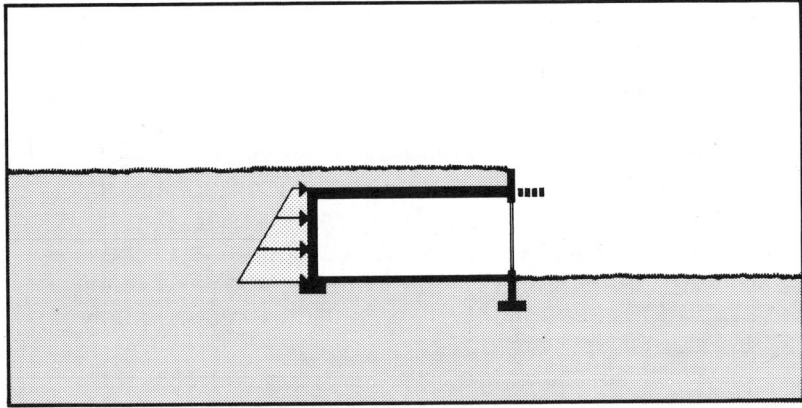

4-8: One-Story Below-Grade Wall

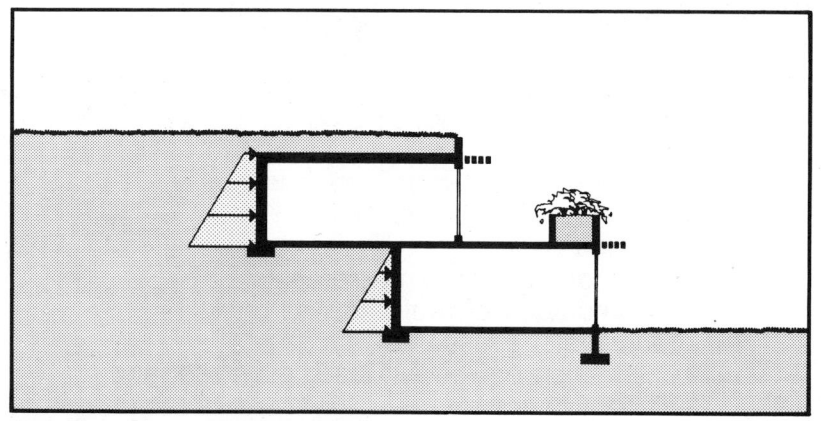

4-9: Two-Story Stepped Wall

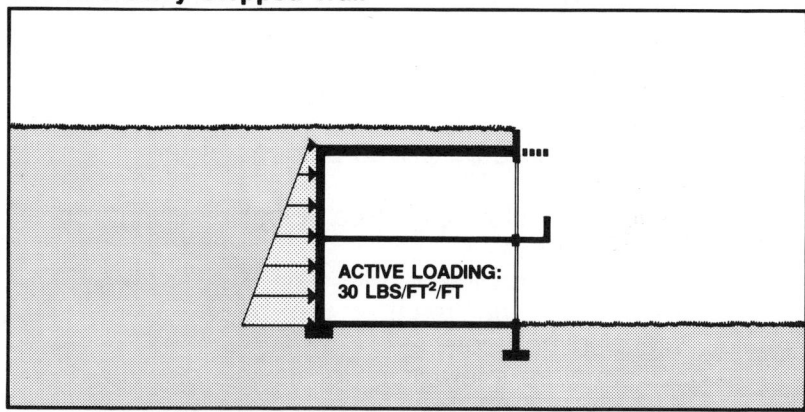

4-10: Two-Story Wall with Active Loading

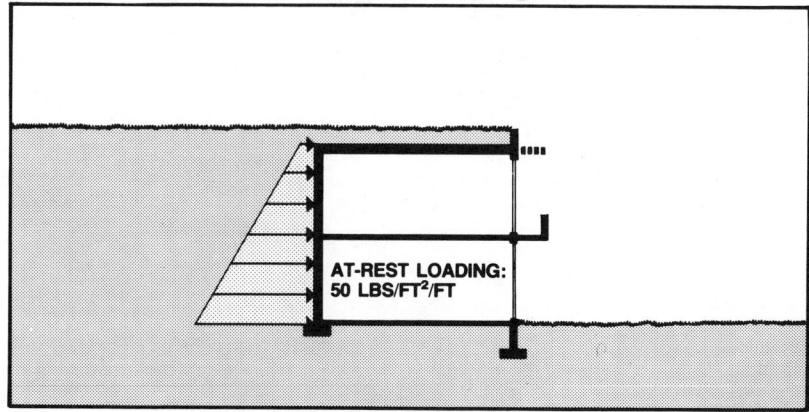

4-11: Two-Story Wall with At-Rest Loading

When gravel backfill and drainage tile are used, the wall is normally designed for unsaturated conditions.

Swelling Pressures/Frost Pressures: These pressures must be considered in design whenever soil conditions are potentially hazardous.

Surcharge Loads/Live Loads: These are heavy loads placed on the surface of the soil adjacent to a retaining wall. The vertical pressure from the load causes a corresponding increase in the horizontal pressure on the wall. If any live loads are considered in retaining wall design, they are usually treated as a surcharge load. A major live-load item will be the surcharge load from any heavy vehicle that may be driven on the surface adjacent to the top of the retaining wall. Fire-fighting equipment access should be considered in calculating these loads.

Backfilling Pressures: Overcompaction of backfill as a result of using heavy equipment can place a higher load on a retaining wall than the wall might have to withstand in the course of normal service. Backfilling procedures should be specified to avoid this problem.

Floor and Foundation Loads

Interior floor loadings are usually treated as a uniform load; design loads for different types of residential occupancy are specified in the building code. Values for a single-family residence are normally 30 pounds per square foot for sleeping areas and 40 pounds per square foot for other rooms [UBC, 1976]. Floor loadings for slabs cast directly on the ground are assumed to be carried directly by the ground below. All other floor loadings must be carried by the floor system to beams or wall supports. Exterior loads on floors and foundations can arise from groundwater pressures, swelling clay, frost-heave pressures, or earthquake forces. Distributed loads from other portions of the structure can result from providing horizontal support to the base of an exterior retaining wall, resisting shear and sliding forces from retaining walls and shear walls, or transferring the vertical load of the building to the ground through the foundations.

Curvilinear Structures

Not all structures can be neatly divided into roof, wall, and floor components. Curved structures below ground normally support a soil pressure perpendicular to the surface of the structure with a magnitude of an equivalent fluid pressure, which increases with the depth below ground. Relatively flat shell structures essentially must carry the full weight of the soil across the span. Flexible structures that have a more complete arch and smaller radius of curvature are often designed using empirical coefficients to adjust the design pressure from the pressure at the top of the arch [American Iron and Steel Institute, 1971]. Thin-shell structures, which are usually flexible, will deform relatively easily under soil loading; this phenomenon tends to equalize pressures over areas where the radius of curvature is constant.

Checklist of Loading Conditions

The following conditions should be considered in calculating the potential loading on the structure:

- self-weight of structure and finishes
- vertical soil loading on roof
- snow loads
- loads from landscaping elements
- rain saturation of roof and wall backfill
- groundwater pressures
- construction equipment loading on roof and adjacent to walls
- service vehicle access to roof and adjacent to walls
- swelling clay conditions
- frost-heave pressures
- earthquake forces
- wind loading on exposed portions of the structure
- flying projectiles (e.g., tree limbs) resulting from storms/tornadoes
- live loading on interior floor structures
- mechanical equipment on roof or on intermediate floors
- soil/structure interaction (for flexible structures such as thin shells)
- slope stability (for structures on hillsides)

Materials

The common structural materials for earth sheltered housing are concrete, masonry, steel, and wood. In this section these materials are subdivided into major categories of use; advantages and disadvantages are listed for each category. Following this section are a description of more specialized uses of structural materials and a discussion of the basic materials with reference to each structural component.

Concrete

Cast-in-Place Concrete: Reinforced and plain cast-in-place concrete are the most common materials for earth sheltered structures. It is used for floors on grade, self-supporting floors and roofs, bearing walls, retaining walls, shear walls, columns, beams, and footings. Plain, unreinforced concrete is usually restricted to noncritical structural elements such as floors on grade, exterior building walls that have less than 6 feet of earth cover, and mass concrete foundations. Concrete can also be used for curved structures in beams, columns, or thin membranes.

Advantages of concrete are its durability, fire resistance, and high compressive and shear strength, which can be tailored to the required strength for specific applications. Concrete can be placed in large or complex shapes. Well-designed concrete mixes that are carefully placed, vibrated, and reinforced can be quite watertight because the reinforcing limits the width of any shrinkage or settlement cracks. The heavy weight of concrete resists uplift and sliding pressures.

A disadvantage of concrete is that some cracking will usually occur as a result of shrinkage, temperature movement, and settlement. These cracks can allow some water seepage under pressure; hence, a waterproofing membrane is required for habitable building applications. In addition, the heavy weight of concrete increases the size of foundations required. Poured concrete is usually not a very rapid building system, and concrete curing can delay construction unless high-early-strength concretes are

4-12: The earth-covered Wheeler House in Enid, Oklahoma utilizes a concrete waffle slab roof structure; Elbert M. Wheeler, architect.

used. Cold-weather concrete work requires special provisions to prevent the fresh concrete from freezing. The residual moisture load in concrete can also cause high humidities in a building for several months after construction.

Precast Concrete: Precast concrete is used to simplify the forming process of concrete by casting the concrete at an on-site location or in a remote factory or casting yard. The uses for precast concrete are similar to those for cast-in-place concrete, except that precast concrete works best in simple or repeatable shapes.

Although many of the advantages of precast are also similar to those of cast-in-place concrete, precast offers the special advantages of rapid construction on site (because there are no cure time delays) and prefabrication of the building components. Factory precasting can use mass-production techniques that reduce costs, and factory controlled conditions can produce a high-quality concrete and finish. The concrete sections themselves are usually quite watertight, and if the components have not been produced immediately before placement, there will be less moisture load in the building following construction.

Special disadvantages of precast concrete include the need to tie the structure together carefully with well-designed joints and the difficulty of sealing these joints against water penetration. The price of precast units depends on the distance required for transporting the units. Simple, standard units must usually be used in order to obtain the lowest cost. Although specialized shapes can be produced for large projects, their production usually requires a substantial lead time.

Prestressed Concrete: Prestressed concrete was included above as a form of precast concrete because it is always used in a precast form. The advantage of prestressing is that it allows higher-strength steels to be used; hence, smaller steel areas are required. If these higher-strength steels were not prestressed, the concrete sections would deflect excessively before the steel was strained sufficiently to reach its capacity. Wires are stretched in a casting bed to tensions close to the yield point of the steel (as much as 180,000 psi). The concrete is cast around the steel. When it has hardened, the wires are cut at the ends of the section, thereby causing the steel to contract and place the concrete in compression. This compressive force in the concrete limits cracking of the sections. Factory precasting generally ensures good quality control.

4-13: In the Ecology House in Osterville, Massachusetts precast concrete roof planks are supported by concrete walls and steel beams; John Barnard, architect.

The steel in simple concrete sections is usually at the bottom of the plank or beam. When this steel contracts, the eccentric force induces a tension on the upper side of the beam, thus creating an upward curvature in the beam. The prestressing force is designed so that the beam will not be overstressed in tension at the top surface before any load is applied and so that the downward deflection of the beam when it is loaded will approximately equal the initial upward camber. Prestressed beams must be carefully handled during erection in order to avoid damaging them: lifting a prestressed beam only at its center, for example, would almost certainly cause failure of the beam. The uneven deflection of adjacent planks must also be considered in waterproofing design and the design of interior partitions that are non-load-bearing. Simply prestressed planks should only be used in simple span situations, when there are no intermediate supports.

Post-tensioned Concrete: Post-tensioned concrete is actually a variation of prestressed concrete, in which the steel is not tensioned until after the concrete has hardened. It can be used in precast or cast-in-place concrete construction. Instead of casting the reinforcing bars directly into the concrete, sleeves are used so that the bars or wires can be stressed with jacks after the concrete hardens. Conical wedges or nuts and threads are used to lock the stress into the steel after the bars have been stretched. Usually the sleeve is then grouted to protect the steel against corrosion. The advantages of the post-tensioned format are its adaptability to site-cast concrete and the possibility of carrying out the tensioning in stages so that it can balance permanent loads on the structure (this level of tensioning could cause tension failure on the upper surface if it were done with no load). The main disadvantage of post-tensioned concrete is that it requires specially trained crews on the site and is

4-14: Using the Bernold system, Shotcrete is sprayed onto perforated metal plates to form a barrel-vault structure; photo courtesy of Integrated Building Systems.

a more exacting method of construction not usually contemplated on single-family housing construction. Post-tensioning can be used for both the walls and roof of an earth sheltered structure.

Shotcrete/Gunite: Shotcrete and Gunite are both types of concrete that is pneumatically sprayed onto surfaces where it will harden to form a structural member. Shotcrete uses larger-sized aggregate, similar to normal concrete; Gunite is sprayed concrete composed of smaller, sand-sized aggregate. Because mixes of these materials can be designed so that the concrete will stick to overhead as well as vertical and horizontal surfaces, they can be used to form concrete shells when they are sprayed on a preformed reinforcing mesh. In one patented system, after an air-inflated mold is erected, urethane foam and then Gunite are sprayed on the inside of the dome surface to form a concrete exterior-insulated shell (see *Shell Structures,* below). Shotcrete and Gunite, which are commonly used in rock excavation work, are also often used for swimming pool construction and water canals. Advantages of Shotcrete and Gunite are that their application requires no conventional formwork and that they can be used to create curved surfaces easily. The disadvantages are that specialized equipment and experience are necessary for successful application and that the spraying process involves substantial waste of concrete.

Masonry

Unreinforced Masonry: Unreinforced masonry is used for exterior building walls that have significant vertical loads from earth cover. These vertical loads create compression stress to offset flexural tension caused by lateral earth pressure loads. Unreinforced masonry walls do not depend upon steel reinforcement to resist loads generally; however, a nominal amount of horizontal joint reinforcement (16 to 24 inches on center) is generally used for crack control.

Reinforced Masonry: Reinforced masonry is used where significant tension stress occurs. Tension is resisted by steel bars placed in the cores of masonry and bonded by concrete grout to the units.

Because formwork is not required and the elements are mass-produced, unit costs for masonry are relatively low as compared to cast-in-place concrete. In areas where concrete block is commonly used for basements and commercial buildings, plants are usually well distributed and trucking costs are low. Blocks can be assembled into large and relatively complex shapes. In addition, there is less residual moisture in masonry than in poured concrete.

The disadvantages are that a structure constructed of unreinforced or reinforced masonry units contains voids within the blocks that provide water transmission paths for any water leakage. Cold-weather work needs special provisions [NCMA, 1978]. Cure time for the concrete mortar is required to gain sufficient strength to withstand the subsequent applied loading.

Steel

Steel is rarely used for the primary structural envelope in an earth sheltered building. Exceptions include corrugated highway culvert sections used to form a thin-shell structure and extruded metal decking used in roof structures either as the roof element itself or as a permanent formwork/reinforcement to a concrete roof. Steel is present in most earth sheltered structures, however, as an integral structural material used in beams, bar joists, columns, concrete reinforcing, and special formwork systems.

Advantages of steel include its very high strength in both tension and compression. It can also be formed into efficient structural configurations such as I beams, tubular columns, or the curved corrugated plates that are used to construct thin-shell structures. Because individual steel sections are completely watertight, the joints between sections of exposed steel are the only areas of concern for water leakage. Construction with steel can be continued without undue difficulty in cold weather.

The primary disadvantage of steel is that it requires corrosion protection when exposed to exterior or groundwater conditions and may need protection against rapid structural weakening during a building fire. Because steel also has a high unit price, it must be used efficiently to be economical as a structural material.

Wood

Wood is the one material that is almost certain to be used in any house constructed in the United States. It is used extensively both for interior finish work and, structurally, for floors, roofs, and exterior and interior walls of earth sheltered houses. Depths of burial of wood-framed walls that must resist lateral pressure are usually restricted to one story because of the rapid increase in wall costs beyond this depth of embedment. Wood has also been fabricated into curving panels to form components of shell structures.

Advantages of timber as a structural material are its high strength/weight ratio and similar strengths in tension and compression. Its light weight reduces foundation sizes and eases construction handling. Timber framing can be constructed rapidly by standard house-building carpenter crews, and constuction is relatively unaffected by weather conditions. Finally, producing timber as a structural material requires only a low level of embodied energy.

The most obvious disadvantage of timber is that it requires chemical treatment to prevent decomposition under moist conditions or in situations where the possibility of undetected water seepage exists. There are some lingering concerns about the possible toxicity of these preservative treatments. Also, in certain areas of the country, the timber must be protected against termite attack. Nailed timber structures are more likely to distort with time than more rigidly connected materials, and timber members themselves can develop substantial deflections over the long term. An earth sheltered structure built with wood requires good drainage because its light weight does not resist sliding and uplift pressures well. High shear strength and diaphragm action in walls and floors are difficult to develop without considerable nailing and gluing of components to help the wood transfer the stress. Timber is also combustible.

4-15: Timber beams support the earth-covered roof of this one-level house in New Hampshire; Don Metz, architect; photograph by Robert Perron.

Analysis and Design of Structural Components

The variety of structural systems available for earth sheltered housing can be divided into two general categories. The first group includes the more conventional systems, for example, those that incorporate concrete walls with precast or poured concrete roof structures, as well as steel and wood post-and-beam systems. These most commonly used systems create houses that have vertical side walls and flat or sloped roofs. The second group comprises a variety of more unconventional structural systems, including concrete and steel arch and dome shapes, which offer unique potential for earth sheltered structures. Because the conventional systems are not only the most likely to be used, but also have a number of general structural characteristics in common, most of the major structural components discussed in this section pertain to the first group. A brief discussion of the more unconventional systems is included at the end of the section.

Roof

Most buildings are designed beginning with the roof because the roof span and its loading will significantly influence the sizing of the walls, columns, and foundation. The primary function of the roof is to support the vertical loads above it (soil, snow, vegetation). In flat-roof systems (which need not necessarily be completely horizontal), support is primarily accomplished by bending (see fig. 4-16). Because bending is a relatively inefficient load transfer method, sufficient vertical supports must be provided to produce an economical structural system. Intermediate supports can be provided by bearing walls, beams, and columns.

Most roof systems will be designed to span in only one direction and will use simply supported slabs or beams. An exception is a poured concrete roof design, which can span in two directions if the ratio of the sides of the slab is less than one and one-half to one. It can also be designed to transfer moments at the connection of the roof and walls. Although designing some fixity (moment capacity) at the end of the beam increases the overall carrying capacity of the roof slab, it necessitates proper connection detailing and wall design to withstand this moment transfer. Bending moments in the roof are

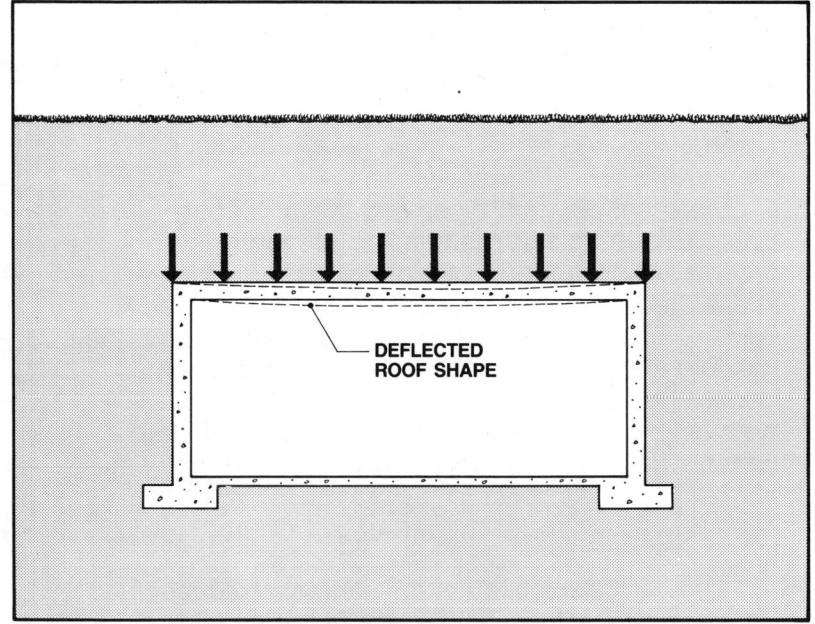

4-16: Roof Loading and Deflected Shape

proportional to the vertical load imposed as well as to the square of the length of span.

Deflection and drainage are other important criteria in roof design. The inevitable deflection of a perfectly flat roof slab will cause ponding of water on the roof, which in turn will lead to additional deflection and an increased likelihood of water drainage problems. When precast components are used, the differential deflection between individual planks that can occur can rupture the waterproofing system. A concrete topping, which will help distribute loads to even out the deflection, can be tapered to improve drainage. A minimum slope of at least 1 percent is recommended for all roof designs that do not incorporate internal drains. Tapered insulation can be used to provide a roof slope, but this reverses the sequence of waterproofing and insulation. Precast planks that have different spans should not be used adjacent to each other because they have different deflection characteristics. For a house that has an earth-covered roof, non-load-bearing interior partitions should allow for deflection of the roof structure, both immediately upon loading and as a result of long-term creep deflections.

The secondary function of the roof is usually to provide support to the walls of the structure that are retaining an earth pressure. The compressive or diaphragm forces in the roof structure that this support involves must be considered in the roof design. For reinforced cast-in-place concrete and precast concrete roofs, providing support should not have great design implications for the roof except when large openings through the roof are located close to the wall being supported. For a timber roof, it is difficult to provide sufficient diaphragm action and compressive strength perpendicular to the beams when the lateral earth loads are high. These design issues are discussed further in the section below on intermediate floors; they should not be overlooked in designing the roofs of earth-bermed structures that have conventional roofs. Figures 4-17

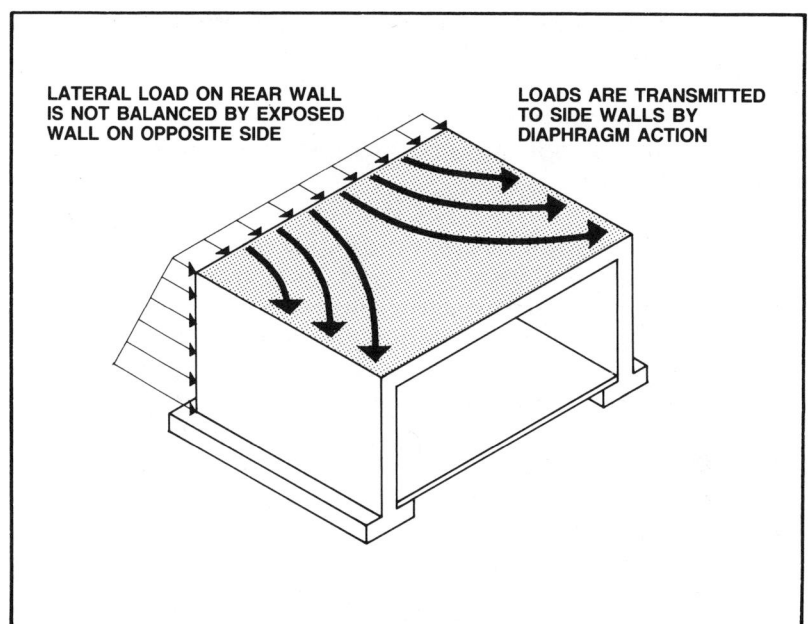

4-17: Roof Acting as a Diaphragm

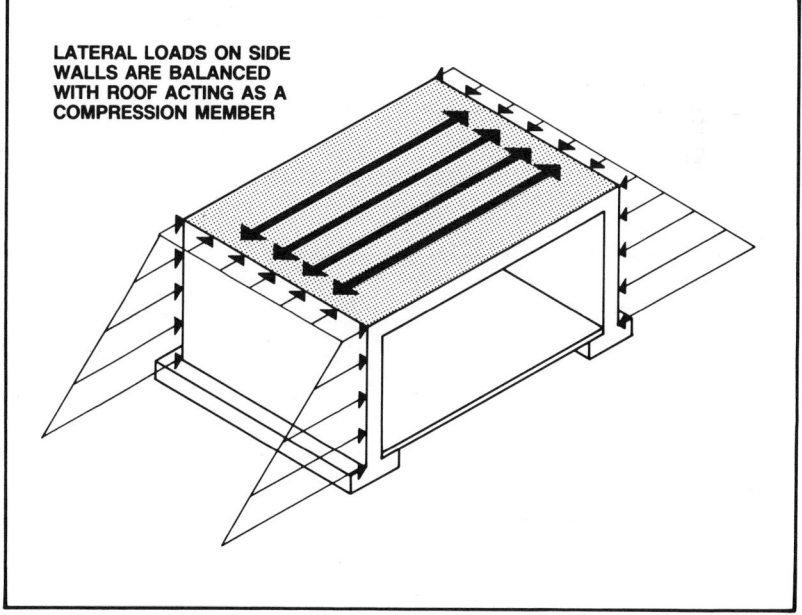

4-18: Roof Acting as a Compression Member

and 4-18 illustrate how the lateral earth pressures are distributed through the roof structure.

Characteristics of the wide variety of components for an earth-covered roof system are discussed below. Typical roof systems are shown in figures 4-19, 4-20, and 4-21.

Concrete Roof Systems: One of the most common concrete systems, used for both roofs and floors, incorporates flat slabs that have a minimal structural depth. This minimal slab depth reduces the total height of the structure and, hence, lateral earth pressures for an earth-covered structure. Flat slabs are not efficient for long spans; spans should typically be less than 20 to 25 feet for earth-covered roofs. Flat slabs can easily be designed to span in one or in two directions.

Beam-and-slab construction uses a thinner concrete slab than does the flat-slab system. Because of the depth of the beams, however, this type of system requires a greater depth within the structure in order to support the roof. Either integral or separate beams can be used to support the slab.

Waffle slabs are similar to flat slabs except that they replace the structurally ineffective positions of flat slabs with voids that are open on the underside of the slab. Although this type of slab reduces both the amount of concrete required and the self-weight of the roof structure, the formwork costs are higher. Waffle slabs are usually used for two-way roof spans. They are generally considered to have a positive effect on the interior appearance of the structure.

Post-tensioned slabs have been discussed above under *Materials.* Less steel reinforcement is used and smaller stuctural depths are usually possible with this type of slab than with conventional reinforced slabs. Although the steel can also be

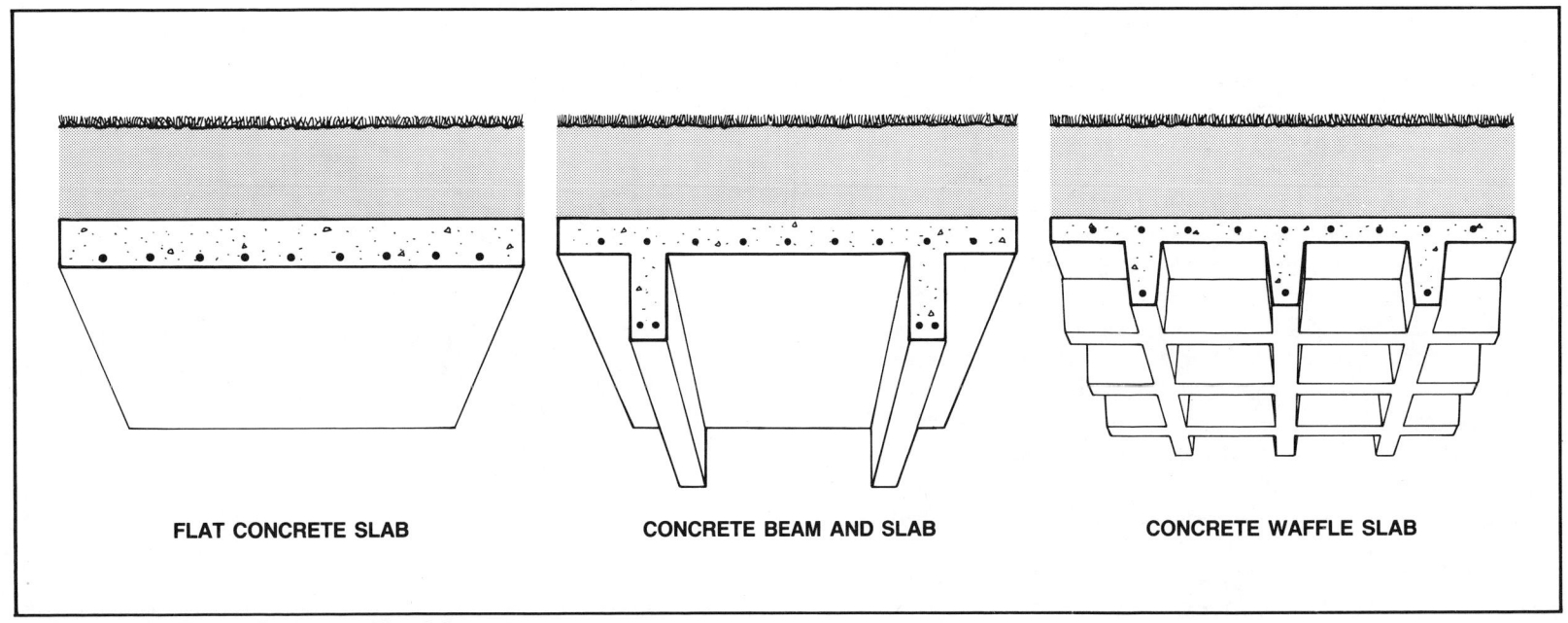

4-19: Cast-in-Place Concrete Roof Systems

more widely spaced in the slab, it must be of higher strength. Construction involving post-tensioned slabs requires skilled crews.

Prestressed concrete planks were also discussed under *Materials.* They are readily available in well-populated areas. Planks usually come in standard widths of 2 feet; 3 feet, 4 inches; 4 feet; and 8 feet. Because the plank supplier will not necessarily be known until after construction bids are received, it is wise to design the structure to fit a standard 2-foot module. Engineering for the roof system is usually supplied by the plank manufacturers. Economical spans are generally in the 15- to 25-foot range, although occasionally planks can be used in spans of more than 30 feet, with low levels of earth cover. A concrete topping is normally used over the plank to provide additional strength and a smooth surface for waterproofing. To enhance the bond between the plank and the topping, the top surface of the plank can often be specified as "rough." Hollow cores of the plank are sometimes used for utilities and air handling.

Single-T or double-T beams are similar in many respects to precast planks except that they are optimized for long, lightly loaded spans and have great structural depth. It is possible, however, to use the depth of these beams for building services.

Timber Roof Systems: Heavy timber beams and wood decking can provide a decorative interior appearance if exposed to the interior and need not be treated with preservative if there are no concealed areas in which moisture could collect. Bentonite waterproofing should not be installed next to nontreated decking because it is moist when activated. Rough sawing of lumber maintains a larger structural cross section for the beams. Less expensive green lumber can be used if the drying

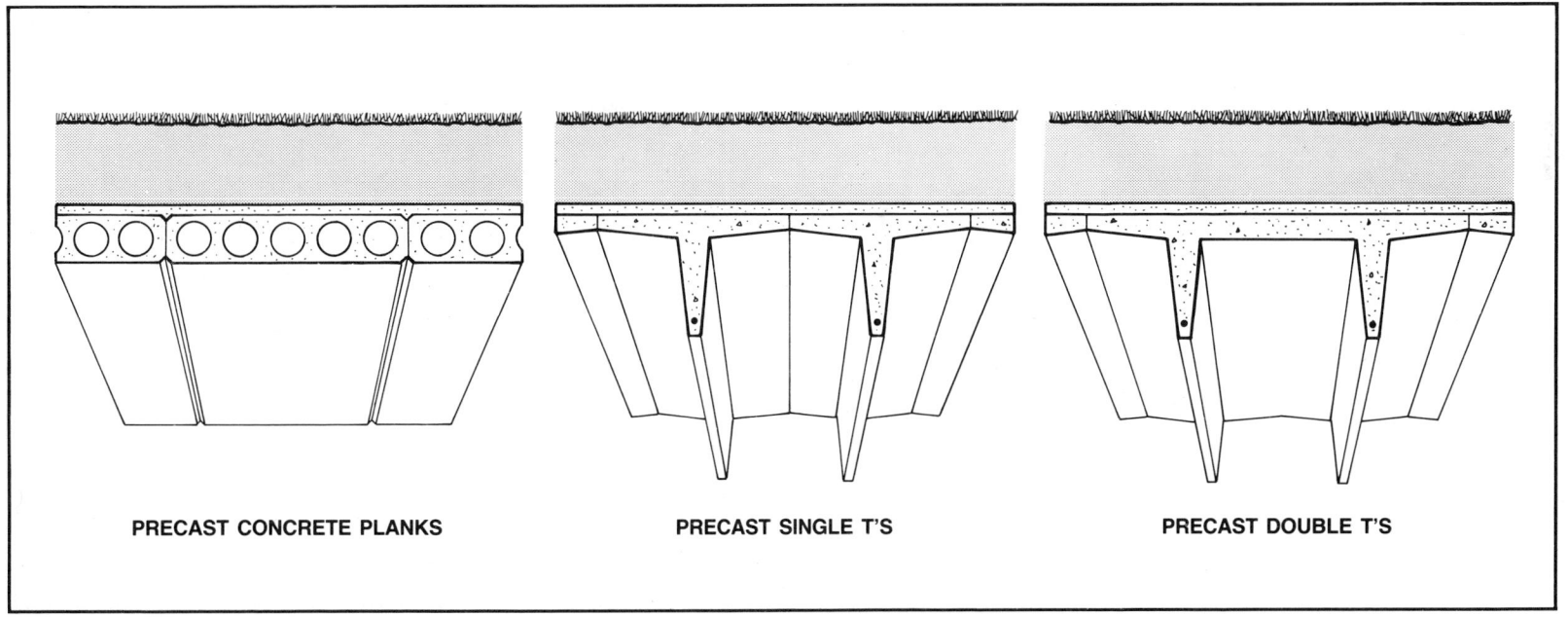

4-20: Precast Concrete Roof Systems

shrinkage movement and deflection of the wood is anticipated and allowed for in the design.

Thinner wood decking or plywood with deep, closely spaced wood joists is an alternative to the heavy timber beams but is less suitable for an exposed interior finish. Glue-laminated beams or microlaminated lumber can also be used with wood decking for an earth-covered roof. Glue-laminated beams are usually manufactured for specific projects that require ¾- to 1½-inch thick laminations. Microlaminated lumber uses thinner laminations (approximately 1/10 to 1/8 inches thick) and is purchased more as standard lumber is. It is available in standard sizes from 2½ to 24 inches deep and up to 80 feet long. The primary advantage of laminated beams is that the quality of lumber can be varied in the laminations, so that the best quality is provided only where needed. In addition, because individual flaws in the wood do not affect the strength of more than one lamination, allowable stresses are higher for laminated beams than for sawn lumber. The lamination process provides warp-free lumber that is easy to use.

Manufactured configurations of lumber, such as box beams and I beams, are also available. Here again, the intent is to use the lumber more efficiently for structural purposes. The cost of fabrication suggests, however, that these configurations should be used primarily for larger structural sections, where significant savings of material can be realized. These configurations are usually not as suitable as timber beams or glue-laminated beams for an exposed interior finish.

Wood decking with steel joists is an alternative to an all-wood system. It should be used with a false ceiling for living spaces; however, services can be run through the ceiling area if open web joists are used.

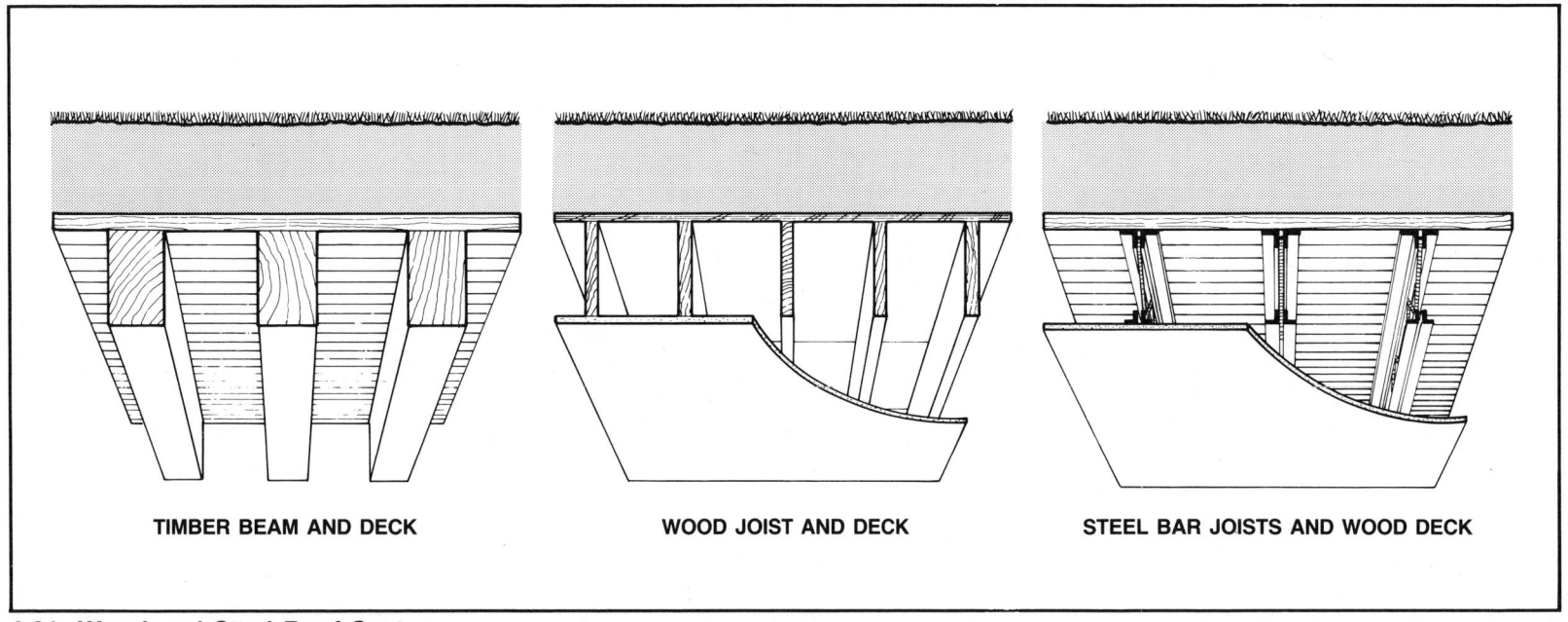

TIMBER BEAM AND DECK **WOOD JOIST AND DECK** **STEEL BAR JOISTS AND WOOD DECK**

4-21: Wood and Steel Roof Systems

Exterior Building Walls That Retain Earth

Unlike the roof, which is loaded from above, external building walls that retain earth are essentially slabs loaded from the side. Support for the wall is provided either by the roof and floor slabs or by designing the wall to be self-supporting, as is a typical exterior retaining wall. Where two walls retaining earth are on opposite sides of the building, the balancing reactions between the walls induce only low compressive stresses in the roof and floor system (fig. 4-22). These stresses will not present problems in most roof and floor designs. Where the earth pressures are not balanced on either side of the house, the unbalanced reactions require the roof to be designed as a diaphragm to transfer the load to the end walls (fig. 4-23). This transfer of load in the plane of the floor can usually be accomodated without problems in a concrete roof structure. A timber roof structure cannot provide as substantial a diaphragm action although for one-story designs with a small amount of earth cover sufficient shear strength should be available. One approach to resisting earth pressures on walls without relying on the roof to transfer loads is a cantilever wall design (fig. 4-24). A cantilever design must be designed for larger wall moments and requires a larger footing to transfer these moments to the soil. It is an expensive solution where floors, roof, and other walls are available to provide a balancing reaction.

Loading pressures are assumed to be triangular in form (see discussions under *Loads*). During the design process, it is necessary to decide on the end-restraint conditions of the wall at the roof, at intermediate floors, and at the foundations. In design practice it is normally assumed that the connection of the wall at the foundation and the roof will not transfer a bending moment, that is, a pinned condition, except when cast-in-place concrete is to be used. The condition at an intermediate floor will depend on whether or not the wall system is

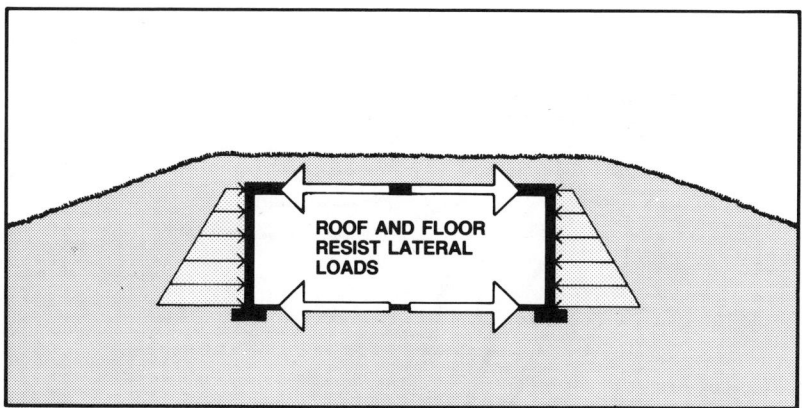

4-22: Balancing Below-Grade Wall Loads

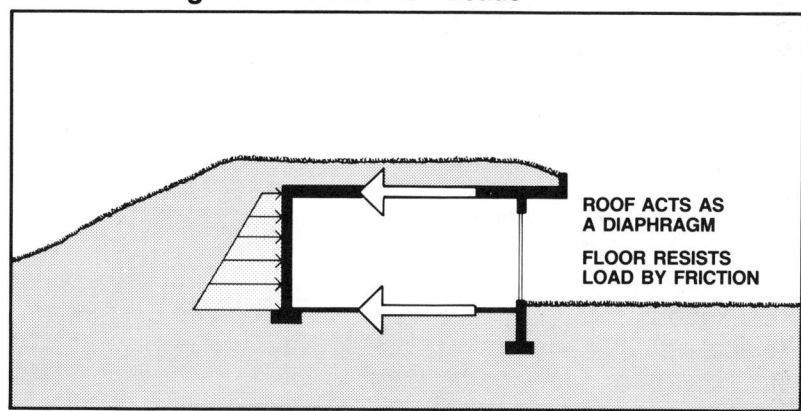

4-23: Balancing Below-Grade Wall Loads

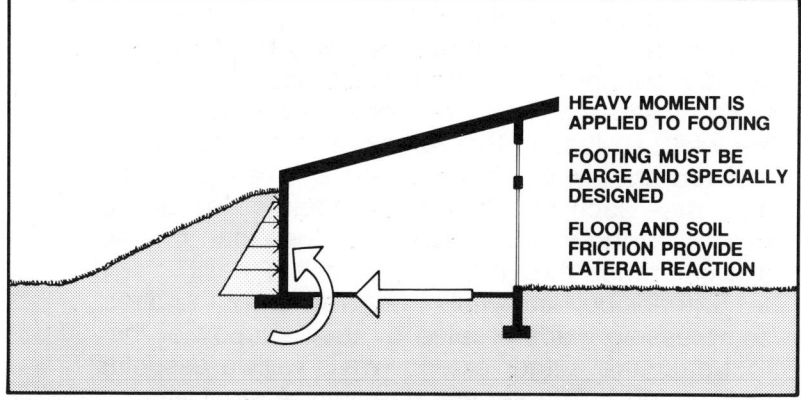

4-24: Below-Grade Wall Designed as a Cantilever

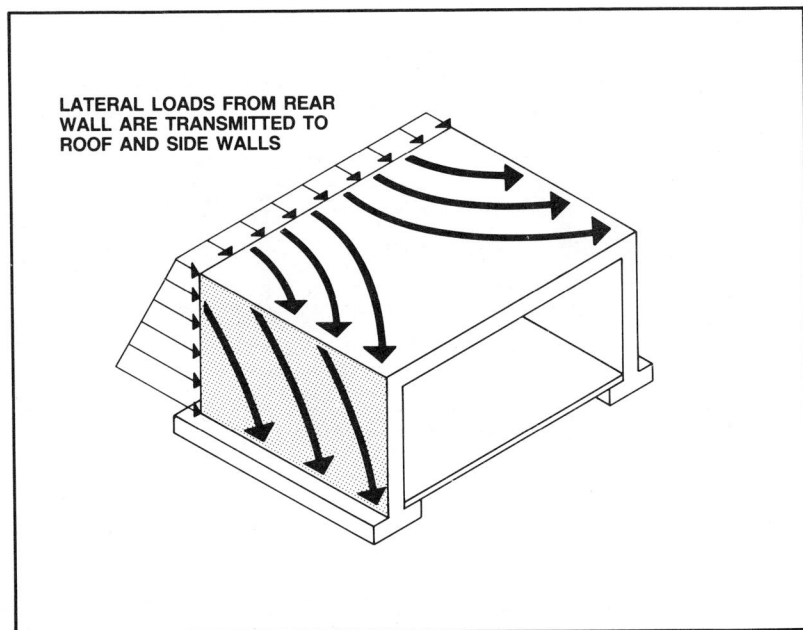

4-25: Exterior Shear Wall Action

building walls will be required to act as a shear wall or diaphragm to a lesser or greater extent, as shown in figure 4-25.

In determining wall heights and burial depths for earth sheltered structures, it should be remembered that the maximum moment in a fully buried wall increases as the cube of the wall height. Therefore, in order to achieve low structural costs, the height of walls adjacent to the earth should be kept to a minimum. Also, when floors or roofs are designed as supports to the wall, they must be installed prior to backfilling the wall.

The major wall systems of concrete, concrete block, and pressure-treated wood have been discussed under *Materials*. Additional design information on these systems is presented below. A number of less common systems that can be and have been used for earth sheltered structures are also briefly described. Typical wall systems are shown in figures 4-26 and 4-27.

continuous through that section. In reinforced cast-in-place wall systems, partial or full fixity at the foundation or roof can be used to lower the maximum moments in the wall; however, this is only possible if the connections, roof slab, and foundation are designed appropriately.

Retaining walls that are part of a building are usually designed as vertical strips spanning from roof to floor. Although horizontal or two-way spanning of the wall can lessen the vertical moments to be resisted, they will only be effective if vertical wall supports—such as pilasters or shear walls—provide support to the wall at intervals of less than one-and-one-half times the vertical span of the wall.

Exterior building walls may also carry the direct compression loads created by their support of the roof structure. Other exterior walls will be essentially nonbearing in the vertical direction. Almost all

Unreinforced Block Walls: Lateral earth pressures on unreinforced block walls are stabilized by vertical compression stress or tensile strength of the wall or a combination of vertical load and tension strength. The tensile strength of masonry in the vertical direction is limited. According to model building codes on basement construction, without an offsetting compression load, 12-inch basement walls should not be backfilled more than 7 feet. Lateral earth pressures may span horizontally in running bond walls, in which case the tensile strength is twice that of the vertical direction. In the horizontal span, however, there is no vertical load to offset flexural tension.

Reinforced Block Walls: The reinforcing in the block wall provides the tensile resistance in bending. After the reinforcing bars have been placed in the cores of the wall, the cores containing reinforcing are grouted solid. Design parameters for this type of wall are the size and spacing of the reinforcing bars and the compressive strength of the concrete blocks. Reinforced concrete block can be used for both one- and two-story earth retaining walls provided that the intermediate floor can provide sufficient reaction.

Requirements for minimum reinforcement, reinforcement spacing and allowable ratios of unsupported height or length to the thickness of the wall may be found in the American Concrete Institute publication A.C.I. 531.

Surface Bonding of Concrete Block: In this system, after concrete blocks have been dry-stacked to form the wall, a thin fiber-reinforced coating is applied to both sides of the wall in order to provide the necessary tensile strength to resist bending moments. The coating, which is also resistant to water penetration, is intended to function as the waterproofing. Although dry-stacking the blocks without worrying about concrete bedding or reinforcing steel permits very rapid erection of the wall, the absence of mortar bedding makes it difficult to keep the wall level and perfectly flat unless the blocks are manufactured with a high degree of dimensional accuracy.

It is imperative that the wall be designed to resist lateral loads, such as from earth pressure; in many instances, reinforcing steel may be necessary in addition to the flexural strength provided by the glass fibers. Cracking of the fiber-reinforced coating caused by wall movements not accounted for in design is a concern. Design criteria is furnished by surface bonding material manufacturers.

Rammed Earth and Adobe: These techniques involve using earth as the primary wall construction material. Wall strength is achieved by compacting the soil by force (rammed earth) or by puddling the

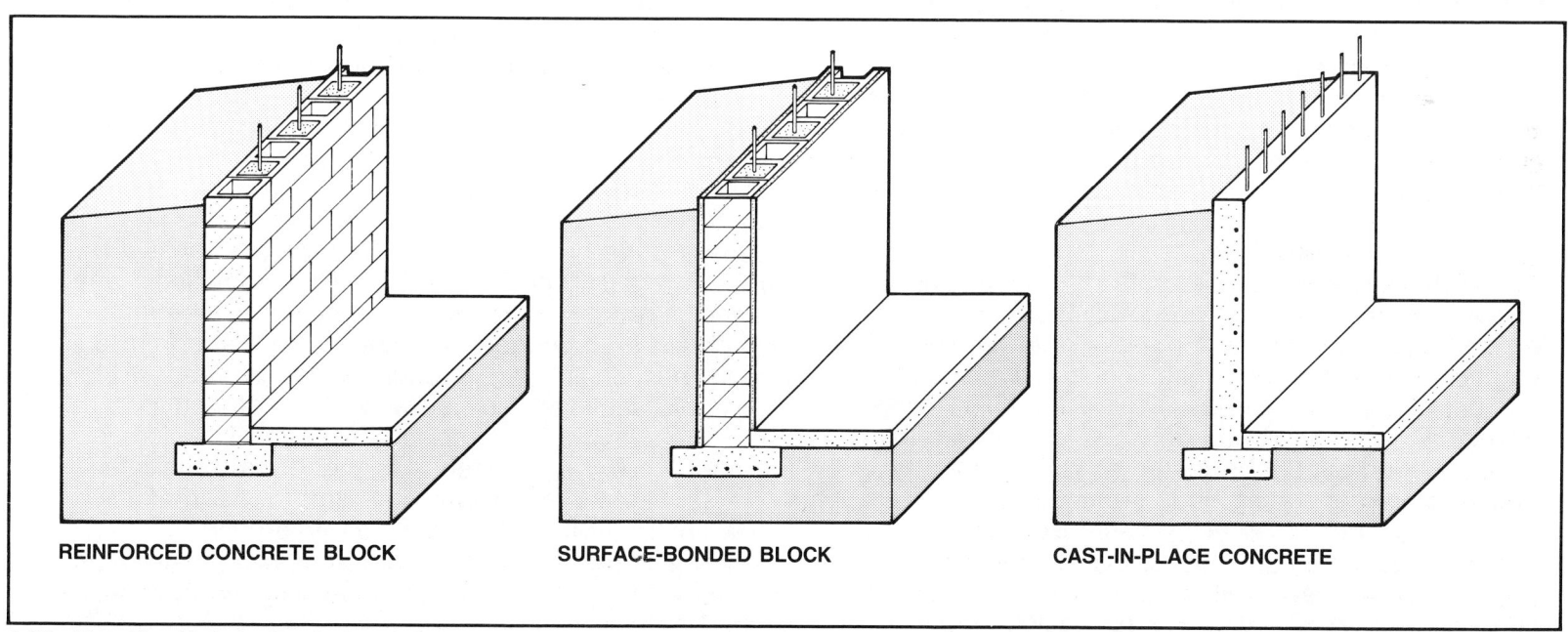

4-26: Exterior Below-Grade Wall Systems

soil with an organic reinforcing such as straw (adobe). It is relatively easy to build thick walls at low material cost with these systems, and when hardened, both have good resistance to occasional rain. Although the techniques were developed in hot, arid regions where the earth walls will remain predominantly dry, it may be possible to adapt them to wetter regions if proper water protection is provided. Overall, the solutions that these techniques offer are low in cost in terms of materials but are also labor intensive. Although structures using these systems may provide savings to the owner-builder, they will probably be substantially more expensive than conventional systems if they are constructed commercially in areas typified by high labor costs.

Plain Cast-in-Place Concrete: Use of plain concrete basement walls should be limited to less than a full-story embedment. The minimum thickness for such a wall is usually 8 inches. Concrete that is intended to be watertight should have a maximum water/cement ratio of 0.48. A stronger and more waterproof concrete is obtained when a low water/cement ratio is used and adequate vibration of the concrete occurs during placement. When sulphates are present in the ground in high concentrations, sulphate-resisting cements should be used.

When pipes are embedded in concrete (as for radiant heating), the temperature of the contents should not exceed 150°F and pressures should not exceed 200 psi. Aluminum pipes should not be embedded in concrete. Pipes should not exceed 4 percent of the stress area of a structural slab unless special analysis has been done. Pipes that are to be embedded should be tested at 150 psi for four hours before concreting. This test requirement does not apply to drainpipes or to pipes used for pressures of less than 1 psi above atmospheric pressure. The shear wall capacity of a poured concrete wall usually presents no design problems.

Reinforced Cast-in-Place Concrete: Reinforced concrete can be used for both one- and two-story construction, as the reinforcement can be easily varied to suit the varying stress conditions within the wall. Eight-inch-thick walls should be sufficient for most house construction unless the intermediate floor cannot provide the necessary reaction. Costs associated with reinforced concrete walls rise very slowly with increasing depths of embedment in the soil because only the cost of the reinforcing steel increases significantly. The minimum concrete cover for reinforcement exposed to earth or weather is 2 inches for bars that have a ¾-inch or larger diameter and 1½ inches for bars that have a diameter of ⅝ inch or less. The minimum concrete cover for reinforcement when concrete is cast directly against the earth is 3 inches.

Precast Concrete: Precast concrete planks can be used for one- and two-story construction. The cost of the planks rises very little with increasing wall height: although the material costs rise, bigger units are handled, thus reducing the handling costs per square foot of wall. Precast units usually have good quality control and an excellent finish. In many cases it is possible to spray-texture walls and ceilings directly and thus save on finishing costs.

Structural design involving precast planks is usually done by the supplier. The supplier should be PCI (Precast Concrete Institute) Plant Certified, have a registered civil or structural engineer on the staff, or obtain the stamped approval of the plans from a registered engineer. Generally, the more precast concrete sections used on a job from one supplier, the cheaper the cost per square foot of installed plank. If the travel distance to the job is significant, erection teams are usually charged to the job for a full day, even though installation time may be a matter of only two or three hours. Hence, installation of additional planks may increase only the material and transport costs.

Normal plank widths vary from 2 to 8 feet. The narrower planks are not usually recommended for wall construction because of the higher costs involved in erecting and tying together the larger number of elements required for a wall system. Precast wall panels (as opposed to planks) are also available; they are generally designed for one-story embedment. Precast concrete shear walls are designed using a shear friction approach, which should present few problems unless the shear wall is very short.

Integral Forming and Insulation Techniques: For several available products, hollow blocks of insulation serve as the concrete formwork. The insulation in the concrete remains in place to provide the insulation for the structure. Most of these systems provide for horizontal and vertical steel in the wall, although both the thickness of the concrete section and positioning of reinforcing bars are quite limited. When the limited strength of readily available sections is adequate for the wall under design, this technique can be a fast and inexpensive way to construct an underground wall. For passive solar houses, this system has the disadvantage of providing insulation inside the mass of the concrete in the wall, thereby limiting the ability of the mass to diffuse heat. Other mass within the structure may be able to compensate for this situation, however.

Tilt-up Walls: This technique reduces the formwork required for wall construction and simplifies the placement of the wet concrete for the wall. The wall is cast in a horizontal position on the ground adjacent to its final position; a bond breaker is used to separate the wall from the ground surface. When the slab has hardened, it is tilted into position by a crane and held in an upright position until supporting walls and the roof are installed. No formwork is needed for the major surfaces of the wall, however, and the concrete is easy to place and finish. This technique does require lifting equipment on-site, and the walls must be designed to resist the handling stresses. The system is not as easy to use on a confined site as on an open site, and the construction cycle will probably take longer than the cycle for a conventional poured system because of the curing time required before tilting. As with any precast system, the connection details must tie the structure together to form a coherent unit.

Trenched Walls: This technique can be used in certain soil conditions where trenches for vertical walls will stand for a considerable period of time [Behr, et at., 1980]. In this system, narrow, vertical-sided trenches are excavated with a backhoe at the locations where the walls will be placed. A reinforcing cage is then lowered into each trench, and the concrete is poured to create the walls, using the earth sides of the trenches as formwork. The roof can be poured at the same time as a slab on grade. When the concrete has hardened, the earth is dug out from underneath the slab between the walls. This digging out is done in a careful pattern so that strips of the floor can be poured to brace the walls against the side earth pressures. This type of structure has an unusual foundation arrangement: the vertical loads are carried by wing slabs at the roof level because it is not possible to pour conventional footings using this technique. The trenched wall system is similar to slurry wall design except that the bentonite slurry is not required to support the trench walls. Slurry techniques are usually too cumbersome to use on a single-family residence.

Reinforced Earth: Reinforced earth is a patented retaining system using steel straps laid horizontally in a vertical grid pattern in a prepared backfill. The straps act as tension reinforcement in the fill, thus forming a stable gravity earth wall to resist pressures in the earth behind the backfill. The wall itself becomes merely a facing to hold the earth between the straps in place. Water protection is provided primarily by using a free-draining material for the backfill, as the attachment of the straps to the wall makes external waterproofing difficult to apply. Because corrosion of the straps is probably the most serious concern with this system, the straps must be galvanized. The reinforced earth technique has been used on a number of large-scale earth sheltered housing developments built on steep slopes in Europe.

Pressure-Treated Wood: Widely available lumber sizes can be used for one-story wood foundation walls. For earth burial deeper than one story, member sizes increase rapidly. Although wood can appear to be economical in first costs for conventional basement embedment depths, it quickly becomes uneconomical for embedment deeper than one story.

Shear wall action can be a problem when the reactions from the floors are considerable. Design nail spacing decreases rapidly as higher shear loads are carried. Again, wood walls will normally be strong enough for one-story structures that have a small amount of earth cover.

Because of potential problems with connection details, wood walls are most practical when used with a wood roof system. When cuts in the pressure-treated lumber are made on site, a concentrated preservative solution should be painted on the cut end. Creosote and pentachlorophenol preservatives are not permitted for wood foundations of dwellings. CCA and ACA treatments are the only waterborne preservatives permitted for this use.

Pressure-treated wood suppliers recommend that a dampproofing and drainage system be used with the wood foundation. Stainless steel nails or staples

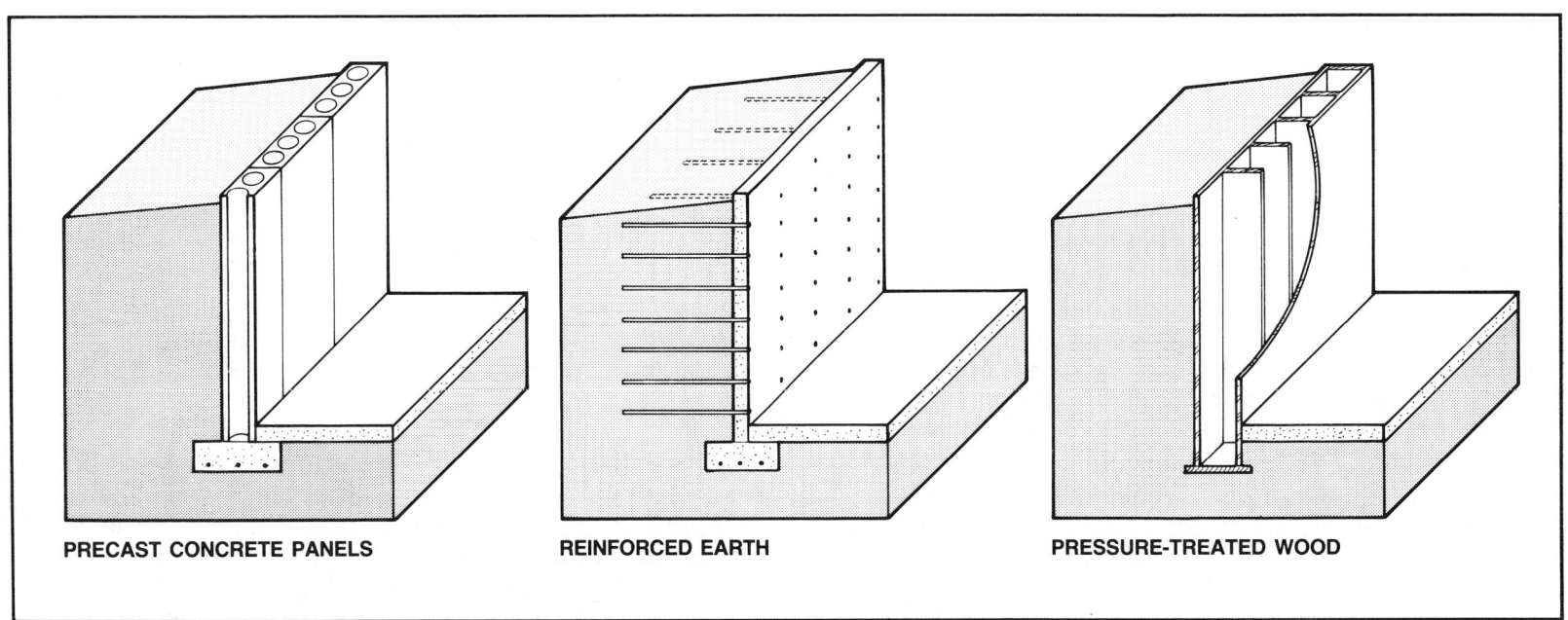

PRECAST CONCRETE PANELS   **REINFORCED EARTH**   **PRESSURE-TREATED WOOD**

4-27: Exterior Below-Grade Wall Systems

are recommended except under very dry conditions, when hot-dip-galvanized nails are a possible alternative.

Exposed Exterior Walls

These walls may carry a vertical load from the roof, as shown in figure 4-29, or they may be required only to provide protection against wind and inclement weather as shown in figure 4-28. Because window openings in an earth sheltered house will tend to be massed on any exposed wall, that wall will not have the same kind of continuous load-bearing capability as other exterior walls. When the wall does support vertical loads, steel or reinforced concrete beams will usually be required above any openings. Even when the wall does not continuously support vertical loads (fig. 4-28), columns may have to be incorporated into the wall to support cross beams. The question of whether these walls should be designed to carry substantial loads must be considered in conjunction with the roof design and the extent of the proposed openings in the wall. If the exposed wall is nonbearing, it may have to be designed with a gap at the top of the wall that is sealed with a compressible sealant to allow for deflection of the roof structure. As for interior walls, the effect on fire rating of using combustible materials should be checked with an insurance company.

Load-Bearing Interior Walls

Interior walls in an earth sheltered house may be required to resist vertical loads from the roof in compression and transfer lateral earth pressures from the outside walls to the floor and footings by acting as shear walls (fig. 4-28). The direct compression loads on an interior bearing wall can

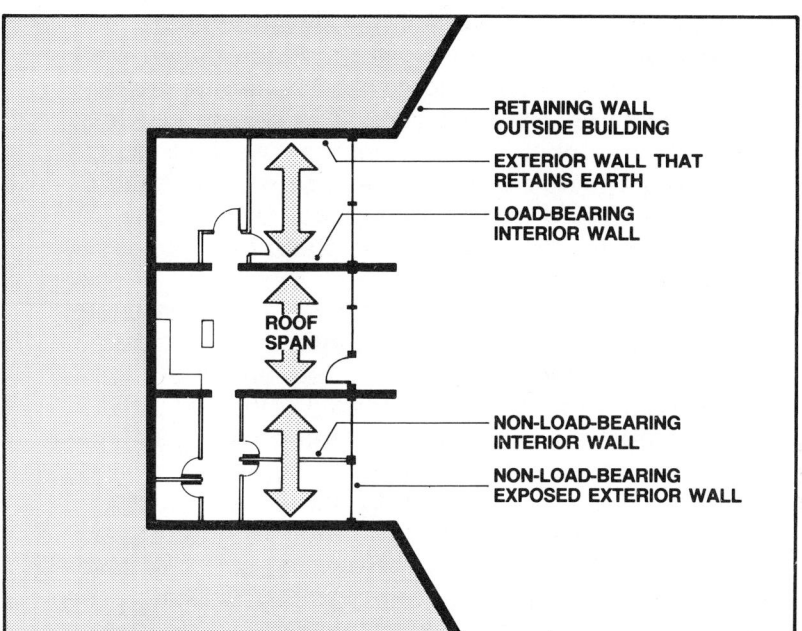

4-28: Floor Plan of House with Interior Bearing Walls

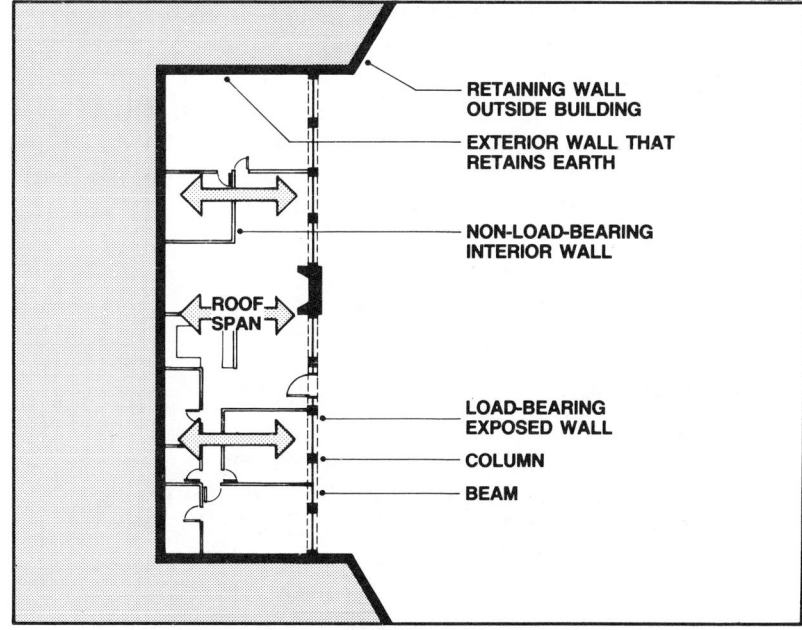

4-29: Floor Plan of House without Interior Bearing Walls

187

be substantial, often twice those on an exterior bearing wall. But, because interior load-bearing walls are not subject to bending forces caused by lateral earth pressures, they are simpler to design and less costly than exterior walls retaining earth. If shear wall design proves to be critical, the most common solution is to add another shear wall between the existing shear walls, perhaps in place of a nonstructural partition.

Materials for interior walls are basically the same as those for exterior walls—predominantly concrete or masonry. A wood-frame wall may be used if the loads are not too great. Because the interior walls carry no lateral loads, concrete and masonry interior walls have far less need for reinforcement. Similarly, reinforcement is generally not required for concrete and masonry walls to resist the direct compressive loads on load-bearing walls. Resisting shear stresses should be no problem for reinforced or unreinforced cast-in-place concrete walls. There should be few problems in providing masonry walls with adequate resistance to shear unless such a wall is very short (less than 10 feet) or the total width of openings in the wall is large. Precast concrete shear walls are designed using a shear friction approach that should present few problems unless the shear wall is very short. Shear wall action can be a problem in wood structures, however, when the reactions from the floors are considerable. Nail spacing must be decreased considerably so that wood walls can carry higher shear loads.

Non-Load-Bearing Interior Walls

Interior walls that are non-load-bearing pose no special restrictions on design (figs. 4-28 and 4-29). Non-load-bearing walls should not be constructed tight against the earth-covered roof slabs because the deflection of the slab can damage the partition finishes. Wood studs are normally acceptable for

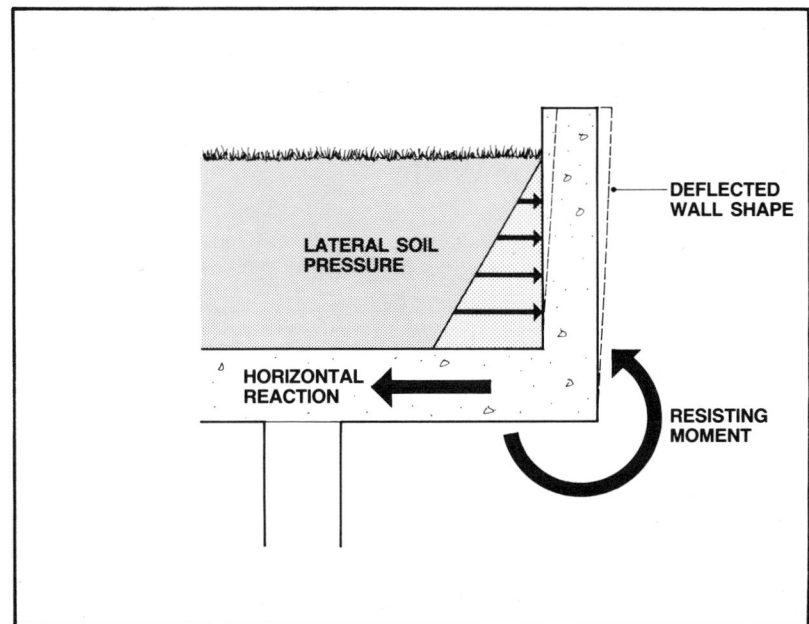

4-30: Parapet Loading

non-load-bearing walls, unless insurance provisions require that steel studs be used to obtain the fireproof rating given to the rest of a concrete structure. Interior walls should be designed to allow the maximum number of building services to be placed within the non-load-bearing partitions because it is easier to run services within such partitions.

Parapet Walls

Parapet walls are sometimes used at the exposed edges of earth-covered roofs. A parapet acts as a small retaining wall for the typically small thickness of earth cover on the roof (fig. 4-30). In urban or suburban areas, parapets also usually serve as the base for guardrail systems installed to provide structural safety. The main concerns in designing parapets are to provide structural continuity with the remainder of the structure and to resist soil pressure, repeated freeze/thaw action, and any guardrail forces. Parapets cast integrally with the roof slab will induce torsional stresses that should be considered in their design. Typical materials for parapets are concrete, masonry, or wood. Concrete and masonry are usually reinforced to resist deterioration from freeze/thaw action and any external applied forces, such as those from a guardrail.

Retaining Walls Outside Building

Exterior retaining walls are usually designed to be self-supporting: they do not derive support from other elements of the building in the same fashion as do building walls supporting earth loads. The types of stresses to be designed for in exterior retaining walls depend to a great extent on the type of retaining wall selected (discussed below). Although massive walls that depend on gravity for their resistance generate low stresses within the wall, they will be large in size and their construction will require large quantities of material. Many retaining walls are cantilever-type walls, with bending stresses that increase downward from the top of the wall to the point of embedment. The bending moment at the bottom of the wall is resisted either by a foundation or by an additional depth of embedment for the wall itself. Bending stresses are greater for a cantilever wall than for a wall supported at both top and bottom by the building.

Although exterior retaining walls can derive some support from the building structure adjacent to the building, relying on such support can cause thermal isolation problems for the retaining wall. Because

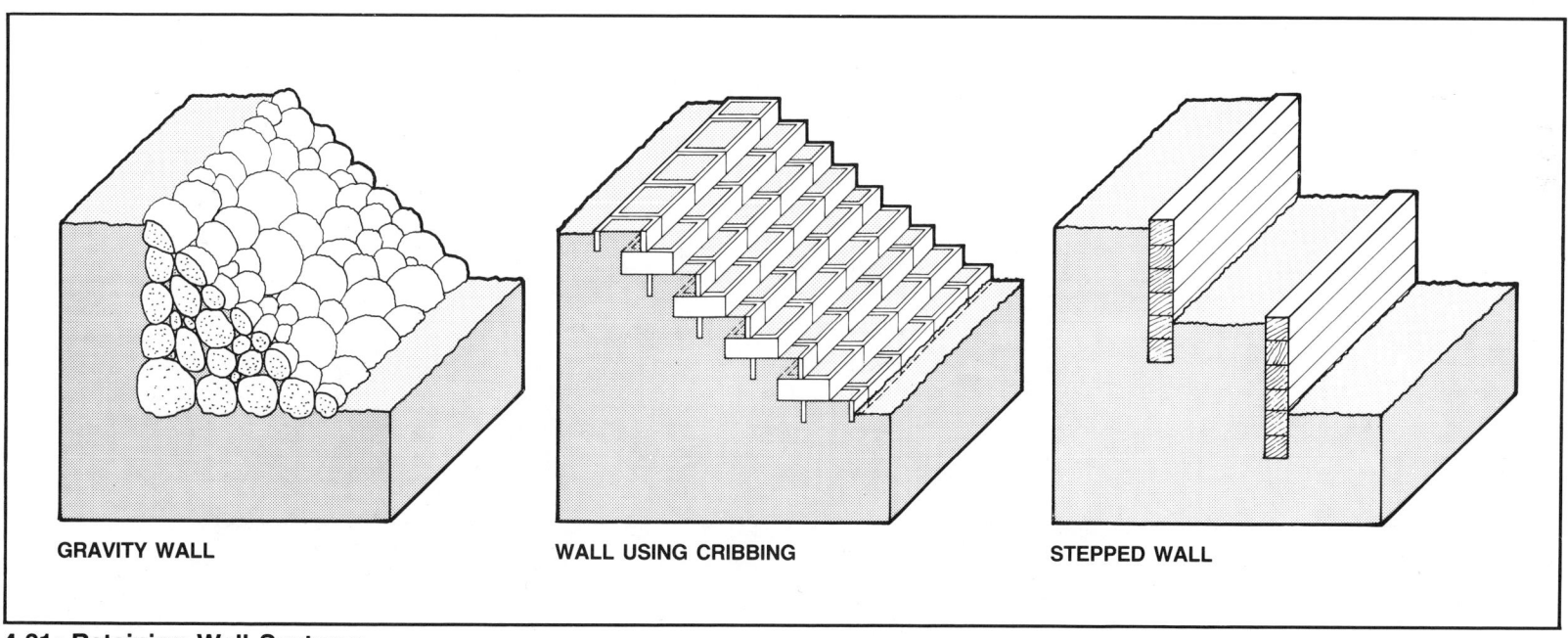

4-31: Retaining Wall Systems

retaining walls can add significantly to the cost of an earth sheltered structure, their use should be minimized through careful site design and grading.

Some common techniques for retaining earth are illustrated in figures 4-31 and 4-32 and discussed below.

Gravity Wall: The mass of wall resists overturning and sliding. Because the wall is usually designed to induce no tension within the wall, plain concrete or loose-laid stones may be used.

Cantilever Wall: Earth pressures are resisted by bending moments in the wall. The placement of the footing relative to the wall affects both the stability of the wall with regard to overturning and sliding and the amount of extra excavation required. Although any structural material capable of resisting the bending stresses may be used, it must also be capable of developing the moment resistance at its connection to the footing (with the exception of the pile retaining wall). Reinforced concrete is the most commonly used material for cantilever walls.

Tiebacks: These are tension members connected to ground anchors in the soil. Although tiebacks can be used with the exterior walls of the building, they are unlikely to be used in situations where an intermediate floor can limit the vertical wall span to 8 feet. Steel cables protected against corrosion are used for large retaining walls. Timber tiebacks can be used for residential-scale retaining walls.

Reinforced Earth: In this earth-retaining technique, reinforcing strips laid in the soil at frequent spacings resist any tensile forces that develop in the soil near the face of the wall. The soil transfers the load to the reinforcement in shear,

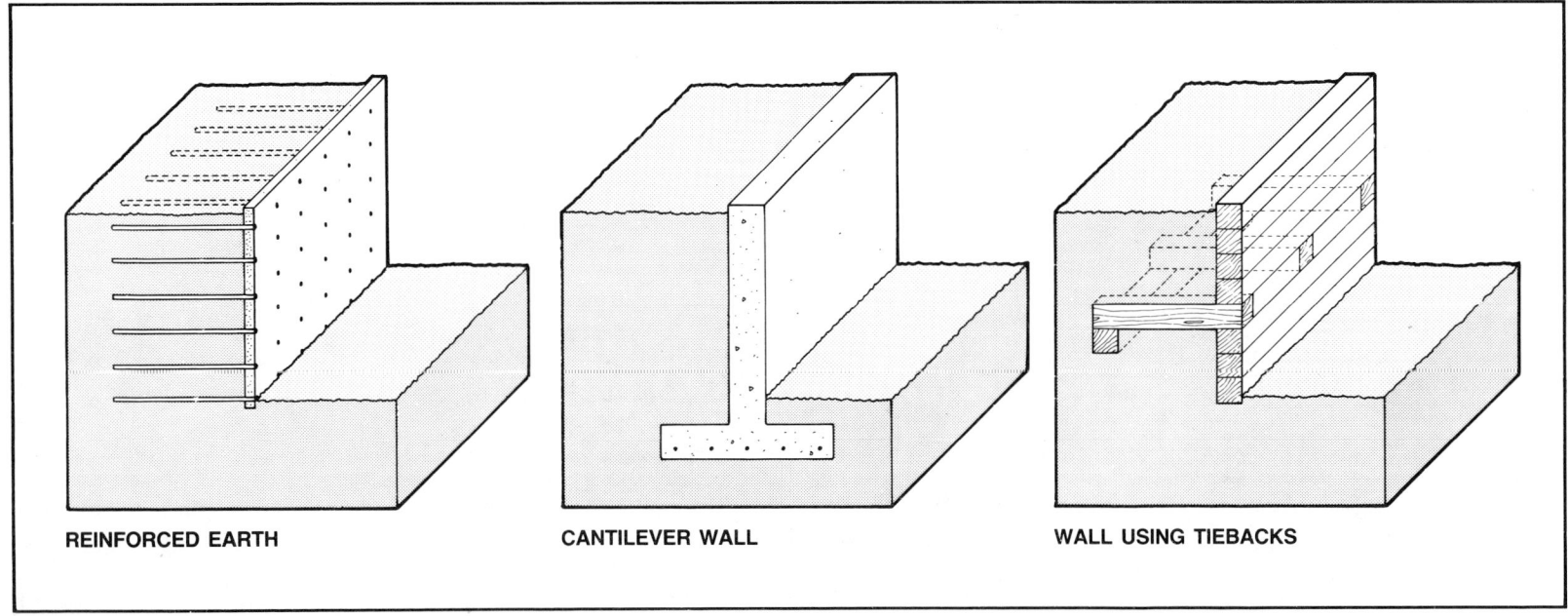

REINFORCED EARTH   CANTILEVER WALL   WALL USING TIEBACKS

4-32: Retaining Wall Systems

and the reinforcement will be in tension. The nonstructural facing provides resistance to erosion. Reinforced earth is most effective for high retaining walls where great shear stresses can be transferred to the strips because of the vertical pressure. The strips are galvanized steel, and the backfill is closely specified to provide drainage and minimize corrosion.

Cribbing: Cribbing involves containing the earth to form a steep but stable embankment. Concrete shapes, railroad ties, wire mesh baskets, and rubber tires, for example, can be used for cribbing. Cribbed retaining walls usually have a slightly backward slope when their height is substantial. Stepping the cribbing provides an excellent opportunity for landscape planting that can soften the appearance of the wall.

Stepped Retaining Walls: The basic types of retaining wall described above can also be used in smaller segments in a stepped retaining wall. Although the change in grade cannot be as abrupt, maximum bending moments in a cantilever wall decrease with the cube of the wall height. Often lower-quality structural material can be used for each segment of the wall than would be needed for a single wall. To take full advantage of this technique, the angle of a line through the footings of the individual walls must not be greater than the stable slope angle for the soil.

Some techniques for reducing wall costs are:

- wrapping the earth around the front of the retaining wall to reduce unsupported wall heights
- stepping the retaining wall horizontally to stiffen the structure and reduce the foundation reaction
- curving the retaining wall to induce membrane stresses rather than bending stresses
- using tiebacks (described above)

- using rock or boulder slopes when available and appropriate to the design
- exposing small portions of side walls to lower necessary retaining wall heights

Intermediate Floors

Intermediate floors include the upper-level floor of a two-story design as well as any lower floor that is designed as a suspended floor system. A suspended ground-floor system may be used either to isolate the floor from movement—as when a house is built in soils that contain swelling clays—or in an underfloor plenum system that distributes air and routes other building services beneath the suspended floor. Intermediate floors must support the floor loadings in bending and transfer any necessary forces in diaphragm action (see figs. 4-33 and 4-34).

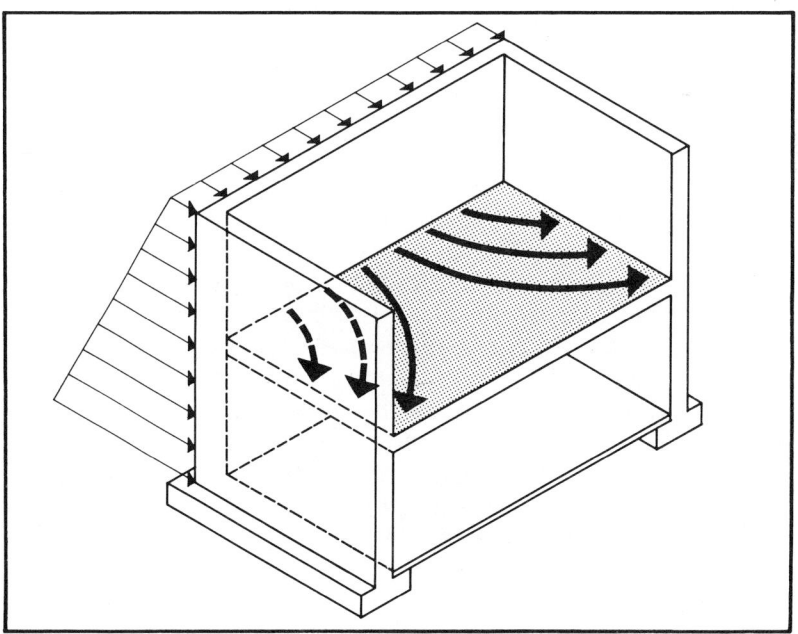

4-33: Intermediate Floor Diaphragm Action

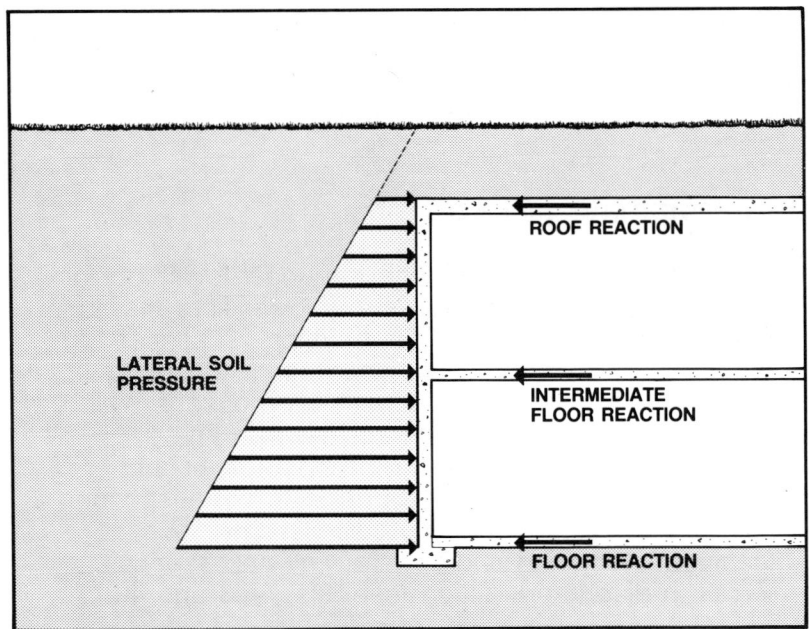

4-34: Reactions to Two-Story Wall Loading

Slab-on-Grade Floor

This is generally the simplest floor system because the concrete slab is poured directly on the ground. Required building services are placed in trenches beneath the level of the floor. If any fill is required beneath the floor slab, fill that has a low Plasticity Index should be used, compacted in 6-to 8-inch lifts to fill 95 percent of Standard Proctor Density

Unless underfloor pressures are expected from sources such as groundwater or swelling clays, the floor is poured at a nominal thickness of 3½ to 4 inches. The floor is usually lightly reinforced with a reinforcing mesh. The manner in which a slab-on-grade floor and the building foundations share the lateral forces from the building walls and transfer them to the soil is not easy to analyze. Normally, the slab will have adequate strength to provide diaphragm action (fig. 4-33); however, a sliding analysis should be carried out for light one-story construction or for two-story construction.

Slabs subjected to underfloor water pressures must be much thicker; the floor will transfer loads to walls and interior supports in much the same way that the roof does. When the design water pressures are substantial, a more continuous construction is substituted for the conventional footing-and-slab construction.

Compared to the roof and lower floor slab, the intermediate floor in a two-level design must provide a greater horizontal reaction to a wall supporting earth pressures unless this requirement is specifically eliminated by designing the wall to span two stories from floor to roof. Therefore, the floor design should avoid large openings in the floor adjacent to an exterior building wall that is resisting an earth load. Floor sections adjacent to the wall should be wide enough to enable them to support the wall as a beam on its side. Because the wall reactions on the intermediate floor are so great, typical wood floor construction is not suitable when the floor must act as a diaphragm unless frequent shear walls are used to limit the shear buildup.

Footings

Foundation design is a relatively simple matter to deal with after the soils engineer has determined an allowable bearing pressure. The load-per-foot length of wall is divided by the allowable bearing pressure to determine the necessary width of the foundation. On medium-to-poor bearing soils, the foundations of walls carrying earth loads from the roof will be substantially larger than the foundations of conventional houses. When some wall loads are heavier than others, it is not wise to design all the foundations to be equally wide, as this not only wastes materials, but may cause uneven settlement problems. Although footings and floor slabs can be combined into a raft foundation for the house, this is usually done only if special soil problems or underfloor water pressures exist.

In a conventional footing, the load from the wall is distributed over a larger soil area based on a 45-degree spread (fig. 4-35). When the base of the footing extends beyond a 45-degree spread from the edges of the wall (fig. 4-36), the footing must be reinforced to spread the load from the wall across the entire width of the footing. Although the actual pressures on the underside of the footing are seldom uniform, they are assumed to be so in design unless the footing has a moment transferred to it from the wall. Footings are usually made of concrete. In a wood foundation system, the footings may be a combination of pressure-treated wood and gravel. The wood bearing-plate and gravel foundation is not recommended for walls carrying roof earth loads; a concrete footing could be substituted.

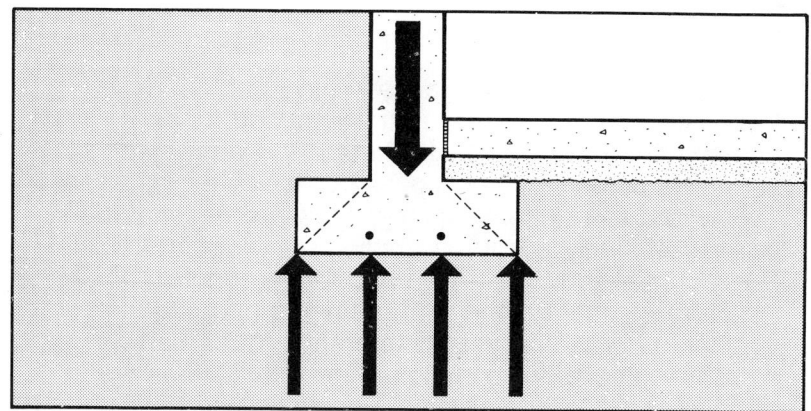

4-35: Conventional Footing

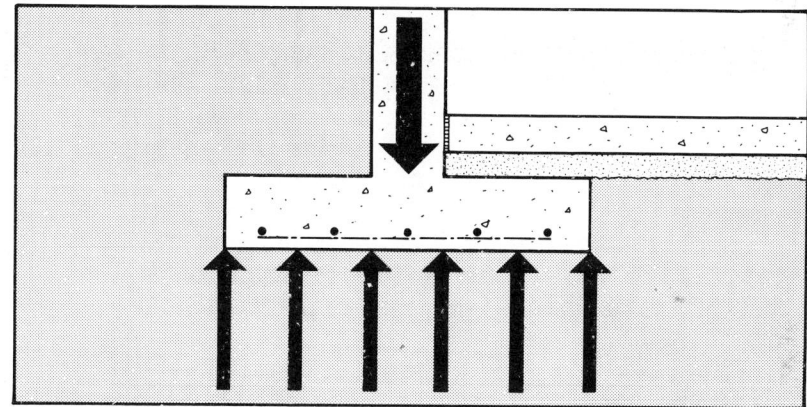

4-36: Spread Footing

Shell Structures

A shell structure is relatively thin in comparison to its clear span and resists the imposed loads primarily in compression. In nature, the equivalent of such a structure is the eggshell, which is extremely strong under a uniform applied pressure but may be broken relatively easily by applying large point loads. Curved shell forms can be used for the entire structure or only for the roof elements carrying high vertical loads. Moreover, simple shell forms can be combined into more complex ones with various types of openings possible. Typical variations used in barrel-vault and dome shapes are shown in figures 4-37 and 4-38. An example of an earth-covered barrel-vault structure is shown in figure 4-39.

Shell structures are well suited to earth loadings for house-sized structures because the magnitude of the loading is less important than the uniformity of loading obtained. The use of exposed shell structures is hampered by the need to design for eccentric loadings and the stresses induced by temperature fluctuations. Both of these conditions are less problematic when the shell is placed underground.

The materials used for earth-covered shell structures are usually concrete and steel although wood arch forms have also been used. Concrete shells may be poured, placed, Shotcreted, Gunited, or made from ferro-cement—a high-strength concrete of fine aggregate that is troweled over a thin reinforcing mesh. Steel shells are usually restricted to corrugated steel-plate culvert sections such as those used for highway drainage structures.

The major advantage of shell structures is that the heavy earth loads are carried more efficiently by the structure, thus allowing thinner sections—and, hence, considerably less structural material—to be used than are required for a rectangular wall-and-roof system. Disadvantages are related to the marketability and desirability of curved interior

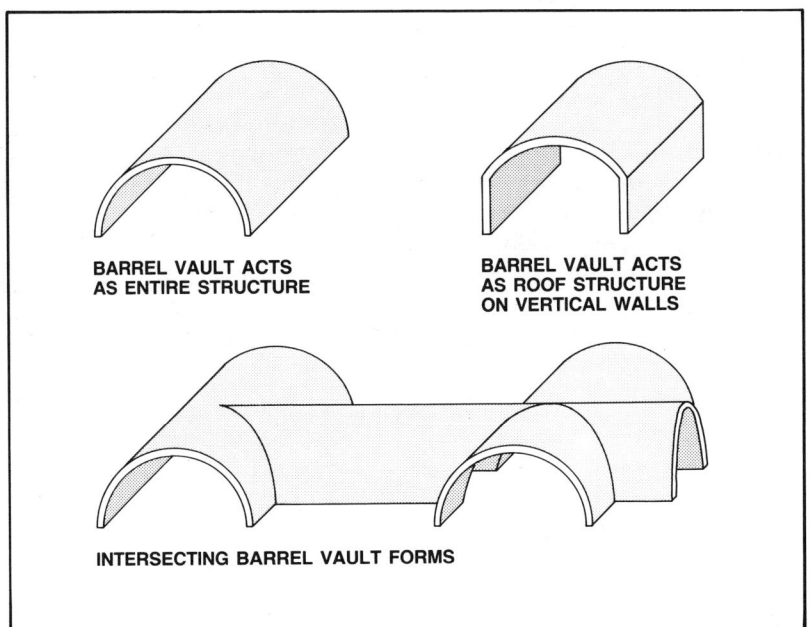

4-37: Barrel Vault Variations

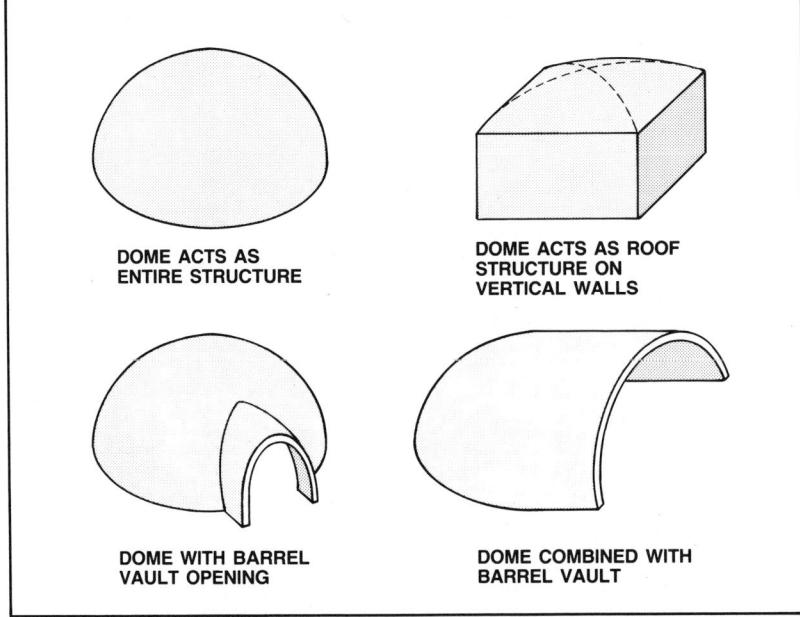

4-38: Dome Variations

boundary, the additional design time usually required for structural analysis and detailing, and the greater labor cost of erecting and forming the curved structural shape. Openings through shell structures, which interfere with the continuity of the load transfer and can thus defeat the advantage of this type of structure, should be minimized and carefully designed. In addition, the support points for shells must be capable of resisting both the horizontal and vertical components of the force within the shell structure. For relatively flat shells, which are subject to great horizontal forces, structural ties or special foundations will be required.

Not all of these disadvantages apply to all shell systems or in all locations; for example, in areas where labor is cheap and structural materials expensive, a shell structure should make considerable sense. Using repeatable forming systems for shell construction will greatly reduce both design costs and labor costs per structure. Several systems are available for constructing shells without designing and forming the system as a one-time-only job. Applications of several types of shell systems are briefly discussed below.

Corrugated Steel Plate Culvert Sections: Curved corrugated steel-plate culvert sections are available in spans of up to 40 feet. The structure is erected by bolting sections of the curved corrugated plate together to form the arch. Generally, these structures can easily withstand several feet of earth cover; in fact, they may not be stable if sufficient earth cover is not provided. Thin-wall structures such as these are most effective when uniform pressures are exerted on the arch. Because interruptions in the continuous profile generally introduce local bending stresses, they should be avoided if possible. Design criteria for steel culverts can be found in the American Association of State Highway and Transportation Officials' (AASHTO) book, *Standard Specification for Bridges*. The following three major

4-39: A wood panel system forms the barrel-vault structure in this two-level, earth-covered house; design and construction by Integrated Building Systems, Grand Haven, Michigan.

concerns should be addressed when these structures are used for a dwelling:

- The plate arches are usually used for drainage and for highway structures, where the structure can easily be inspected from the inside and can be relatively easily replaced if problems occur. Because a poor structural performance will have much greater consequences for a dwelling, design safety factors for a house should reflect greater concern for providing a stable, safe structure.
- Corrosion is always a problem with steel structures underground. Again, when such a

structure is intended for use as a residence, greater attention should be paid to ensuring a long-life structure than is necessary in designing for the normal uses of the plate arches.
- Even and careful backfilling is important in working with these flexible structures.

Barrel-Vault Structures: Poured concrete shell stuctures are easily constructed using barrel-vault reusable forms. The cost of the formwork decreases with the number of reuses of the specially constructed forms; however, more than one form may be required to allow rapid construction. A more recent application of a patented system shown in figure 4-40 is the use of curved, perforated steel plates (originally developed for tunneling) as a base for the application of Shotcrete, in order to form a rigid barrel-vault [Langley, 1980].

Arch structures can also be developed using wood as the structural medium. An example of a prefabricated wood panel arch structure is shown in figure 4-39.

Modular Concrete Shells: In these systems reusable formwork is provided to construct shell modules. A variety of house plans can be achieved by using different numbers and arrangements of the modules. One system uses formwork modules that are square in plan with vertical side walls and a dome roof. An example of an earth-covered house using this system is shown in figure 4-41. Another

4-40: Earth is placed on the roof of this house utilizing a Bernold structural system; two intersecting barrel vaults are formed with Shotcrete sprayed over perforated steel plates; photo courtesy of Integrated Building Systems.

4-41: A modular concrete dome roof structure is utilized in this earth-covered house in Independence, Missouri; design and construction by Terra-Dome Corporation; photograph by Holiday Productions.

system uses segments of full domes or arches to create a variety of building shapes (see Patterson Residence in chapter 7). This technique introduces a flexibility into the use of shell structures that is typically not possible with repeatable whole-shell forming methods.

Air-Formed Concrete Domes: In this patented system, a flexible membrane is anchored to the ground on the site and then inflated [Techmar Constructions Inc., 1981]. The profile of the shell to be created is controlled by the shaping and seaming of the flexible membrane. An air-lock door is included in the membrane so that the dome can be entered after it is inflated. Then, using spray equipment and applicator protection from the toxic chemicals, a layer of urethane foam is built up on the inside of the membrane. Although this layer will insulate the final shell, it serves primarily to stiffen the membrane so that the Shotcrete can be applied to the inside of the foam after the foam has hardened (see fig. 4-42). Shells that have spans greater than 100 feet can be constructed using this system.

Earth-Formed Concrete Shells: When the soil conditions are suitable and the excavating and labor costs are reasonable, the ground surface can be shaped to act as the bed on which the concrete shell is poured. When the concrete has gained sufficient strength, the earth beneath the shell is excavated, leaving a clear-span structure. Structures that have very large spans—clear spans greater than 300 feet—have been constructed using this technique, as have small, house-scale structures such as those constructed by architect Paolo Soleri. In figure 4-43 construction of an earth-formed concrete shell is illustrated in which a trenched wall forming system is used.

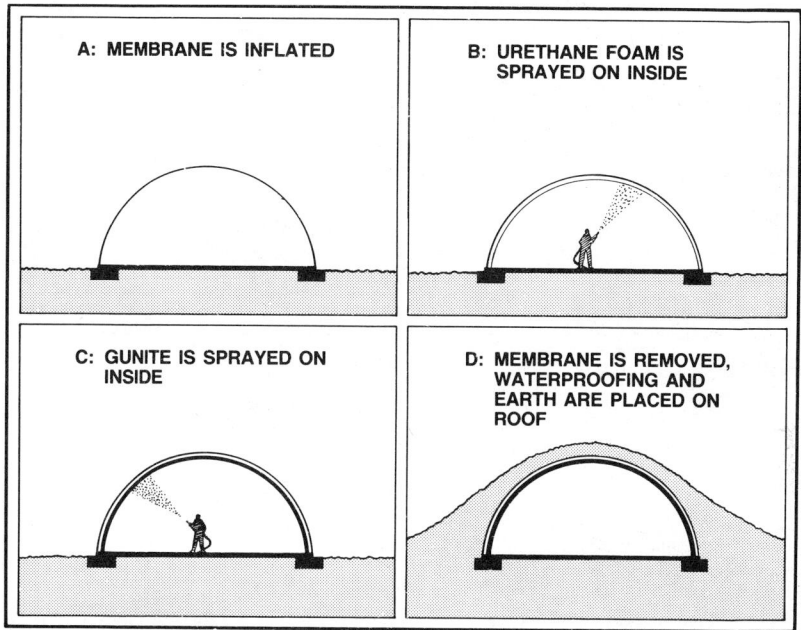

4-42: Air-Formed Concrete Dome

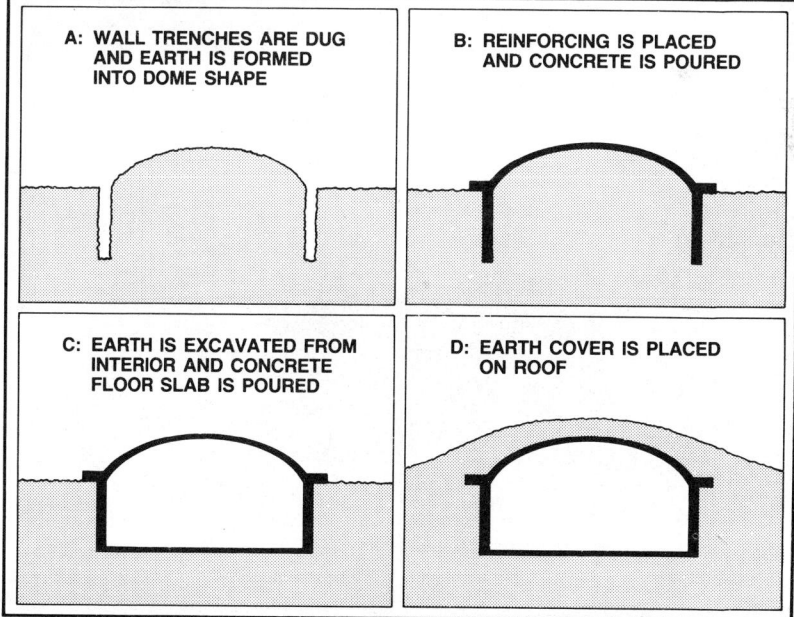

4-43: Earth-Formed Concrete Shell Structure

Underground village in northern China.
Drawing by Mark Heisterkamp.

Chapter 5

Waterproofing Systems
and
Insulation Materials

Introduction to Waterproofing, Moisture, and Insulation Problems

Of the many technical problems and details related to earth sheltered house construction, none are of greater concern than waterproofing and insulation. The initial image of living in underground space is often associated with typical basements which are not built to handle damp or wet soil conditions. In addition, improper selection and placement of insulating materials below grade can impair energy performance considerably. The characteristics and costs of the numerous waterproofing and insulation products on the market make effective comparisons difficult. The purpose of this chapter is to identify problems and solutions related to waterproofing and insulation products.

Water and Moisture from the Earth

The soil adjacent to an earth sheltered house can become saturated with water from a number of sources and transmit moisture and water to the inside of the building. The sources of moisture outside the building include surface runoff from rain and snow, the below-grade water table, and broken water and sewer pipes.

Water that builds up in the soil will leak into the house through cracks and joints in the structure. In wet soil, moisture will penetrate through concrete and masonry surfaces by capillary action. In addition, water vapor will be transmitted from the exterior to the interior of the structure under certain conditions of differential temperature and relative humidity between the building and the soil. To prevent these water and moisture problems originating from outside the building, a system employing three major components is recommended (fig. 5-1). These are:

- site selection to avoid water problems combined with surface drainage to divert water away from the building.
- subsurface drainage around the structure to collect and drain away water.
- waterproof membrane or coating to seal the structure from water leakage and vapor transmission.

Moisture Produced within the Building

Not all moisture problems in earth sheltered houses are attributable to wet soil conditions outside the building. High humidity and condensation can result from internal sources of moisture, causing uncomfortable conditions, mold, and damage to building materials and insulation. Moisture is added to the air from cooking, washing, people, and concrete curing after construction. Unlike less energy-efficient houses, the limited natural air exchange causes moisture from these sources to accumulate in an earth sheltered house. In the summer, ventilation may allow warm, humid outside air to enter the house, introducing more moisture. Because the walls and floor of an earth sheltered house are usually cooler than the air, condensation on these surfaces is a potential problem when interior relative humidities are high. Most solutions to these internal moisture problems are not directly affected by the waterproofing system chosen.

Instead, adjustments such as the following have been suggested:

- Recirculate inside air with ceiling fans to distribute the heavy, moist air that normally settles near the floor evenly.
- Provide dry, fresh air through an air-to-air heat exchanger in winter.
- Provide exhaust fans in kitchen and bathroom areas to reduce moisture at the source.
- Use mechanical dehumidification temporarily during the period after construction when concrete is curing (note: dehumidifiers will add heat to the building; if cooling is also desired, a small air conditioning unit can be used).
- Limit natural ventilation during warm, humid conditions.
- Place insulation beneath the floor and outside walls to avoid cool surfaces where condensation can form (this recommendation may conflict with thermal objectives).

Another problem results from water vapor that flows through the building walls to the ground outside. Moisture may be trapped within the wall, damaging some types of insulation and even the waterproof membrane itself by breaking its adhesion to the structure. A vapor barrier should be placed on the inside (warm side) of any insulation subject to moisture damage. This mainly applies to fiberglass insulation placed inside of the structural wall; vapor barriers are of less concern for insulation outside the wall. Most waterproofing products are relatively impermeable so water vapor moving outward is likely to be trapped beneath the membrane. By far the greatest problems result from excessive moisture caused by the concrete curing. After curing, vapor transmission outward is unlikely to be significant. To avoid these problems, a waterproofing product with some vapor permeability can be selected, or waterproofing can be applied after the concrete has cured.

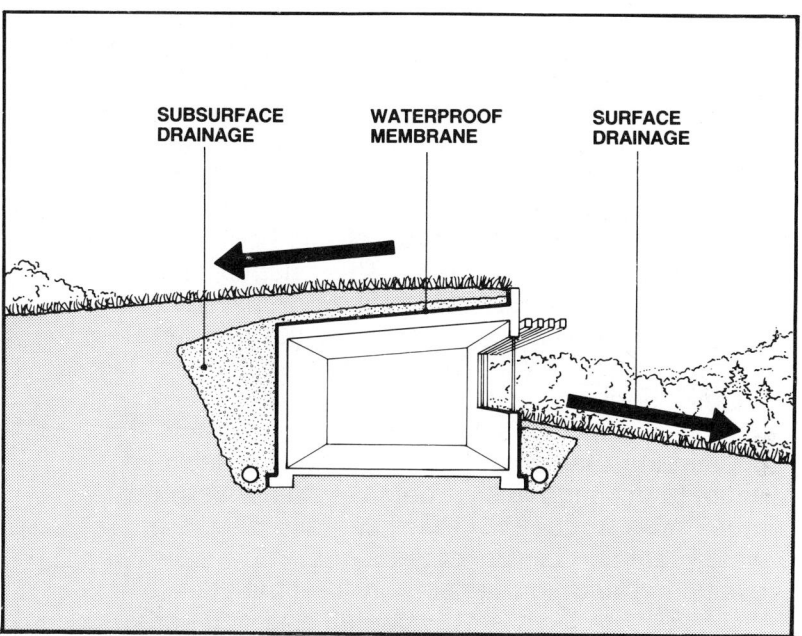

5-1: Three Major Components of Waterproofing System

Insulation Problems

There are three major concerns related to below grade insulation: where to place it, what amount to use, and what type to use. In chapter 3 the location and amount of insulation on the structure is discussed as it pertains to energy use. In this chapter the type of insulation and its placement inside or outside the structural shell are discussed in relation to durability and moisture problems. Selecting insulation below grade is strongly related to the waterproofing approach. In many cases problems result because the chosen insulation is not appropriate for the moisture conditions to which it is exposed, resulting in poor thermal performance. Also vapor barriers must be properly installed to protect insulation from moisture originating within the house.

This chapter focuses on two areas: proper design and selection of a below-grade waterproofing system to eliminate problems with moisture originating outside the structure, and selection of appropriate insulation materials for use below grade. Basic information on waterproofing and insulation products has been collected in many other publications, as well as in the original edition of this book [Anderson, 1983; Sterling, et al., 1982]. This chapter is intended as a refinement and simplification of this material. Basic principles are reviewed and specific detailed guidelines are given. The next two sections of the chapter deal with the first two lines of defense against water: site selection/surface drainage and subsurface drainage. The following two sections address the third line of defense: the waterproof membrane or coating. Principles and details of waterproofing are presented along with product evaluation and comparison. In the final section, insulation products are evaluated and compared for use below grade.

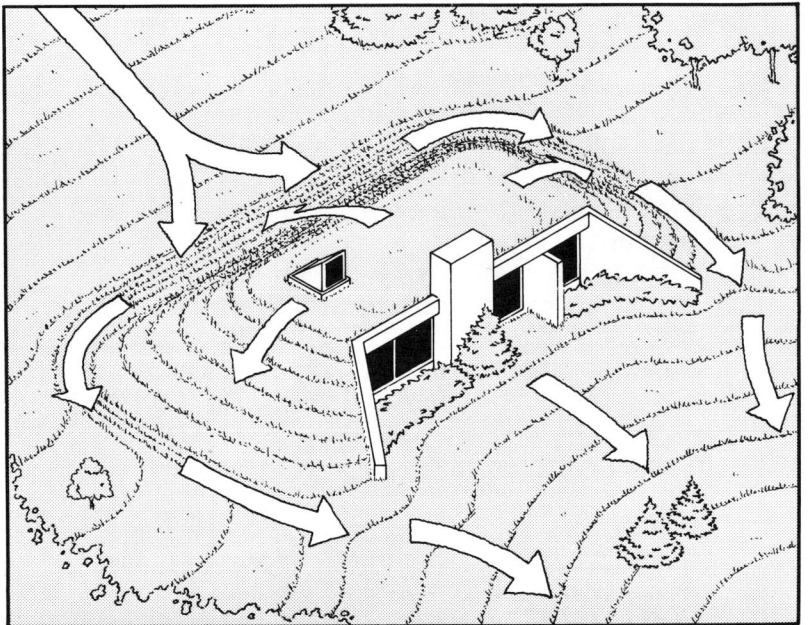

5-2: Surface Drainage on Sloping Site

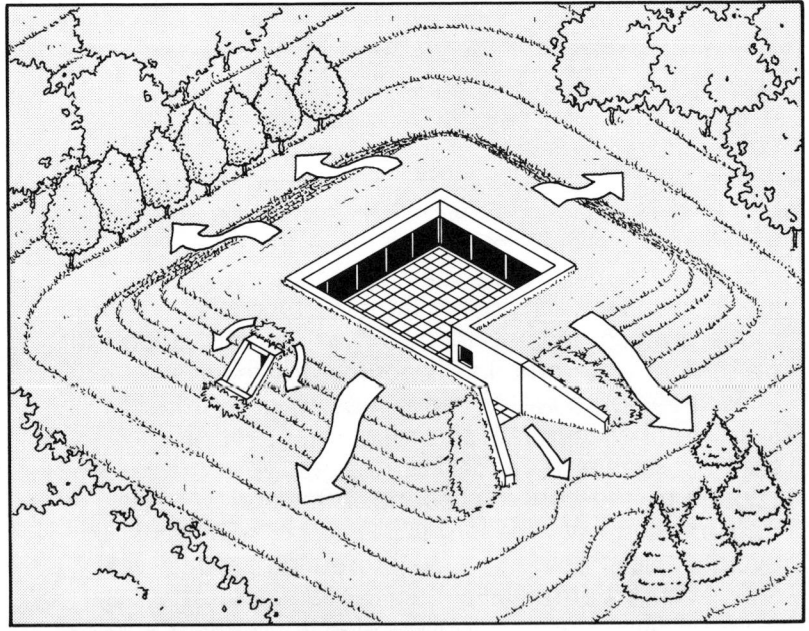

5-3: Surface Drainage on Flat Site

Site Selection and Surface Drainage Principles

Many potential water problems in an earth sheltered house can be avoided by selecting a site carefully and utilizing appropriate surface drainage principles. Directing surface runoff away from the immediate vicinity of the structure is the first line of defense against waterproofing problems and is recommended in all cases. On an unusual site where surface drainage cannot be properly designed, however, it is still possible to handle water problems with a more extensive subsurface drainage system and a good waterproofing system.

Site Selection

Conditions to Avoid: In selecting a site for a house, low-lying areas, gullies, and floodplains should be avoided. It is not advisable to build on a site with a high water table. Standing water on the site is a good indication of the water table level. The floor of the house should be at least 3 feet above the annual high water mark.

Conditions to Seek: Sites with more varied topography provide more opportunities to select a building site that is on higher ground and naturally less vulnerable to water. On the best sites, the floor level of the house can be located above the lowest land. This permits foundation drains at floor level to emerge at an outfall downhill from the structure.

Surface Drainage

Basic Principles: As much as possible, the land surface surrounding an earth sheltered house should slope away from the structure to prevent water from being directed toward it. In addition, there should be no flat areas where water can accumulate on or near the building. The surface of a flat earth-covered roof should have a slope of 1 to 5 percent.

Sloping Site: On a sloping site, it is common to build an earth sheltered house into a hillside from which surface runoff is actually directed toward the house. The land surface should be formed into a drainage swale, or a trench should be provided that collects and diverts surface runoff around the structure (fig. 5-2).

Flat Site: A completely underground structure on a flat site provides little opportunity to remove water effectively with surface drainage. By raising the structure so that it is only partially recessed into the ground, the surrounding earth berms provide excellent drainage and the floor level is not as low (fig. 5-3). Subsurface drainage will still be required for any sunken courtyards, however. Directing large amounts of runoff onto neighboring properties should be avoided.

Subsurface Drainage: Principles and Details

A subsurface drainage system is the second major line of defense against water problems and is essential in all earth sheltered houses. Surface runoff that is not diverted away from the structure can be collected and carried away from the building through a subsurface system. This helps to reduce the frequency and duration of water conditions that actually test the waterproof membrane.

Generally, a good subsurface drainage system removes most, if not all water, from the vicinity of the building. This may make waterproofing on underground walls seem unnecessary; the capacity of a good drainage system can, however, be exceeded in unusually wet conditions. Drainage should not be considered as a substitute for a membrane except possibly in extremely dry climates with virtually no water problems or when a drainage mat is combined with a free draining backfill and foundation drain system. Even under these conditions only walls which do not receive the water drainage from a roof area should be considered for the elimination of waterproofing. In addition, good drainage without a capillary break does not ensure that moisture cannot enter the walls via capillary draw and in the form of water vapor. In very wet conditions or on sites where the water table is high, subsurface drainage can be used to draw the water table down to a certain level, making the site more usable.

A subsurface drainage system consists of three basic components to collect and direct water: porous soil types such as sand and gravel (or a substitute drainage mat), drainpipes, and a collection area with a pump if water cannot be drained to an outfall. The specific design of the system depends on several factors, including the location of the house on the site, the presence of a high water table, soil type, and the building configuration. Usually the subsurface drainage system is placed immediately adjacent to the building roof, walls, and floor. Unconventional techniques of diverting subsurface water away from the structure have been suggested however, in which large membranes extend beyond the house as shown in figure 5-4 [Hait, 1983]. Although this concept is somewhat experimental, it has advantages in reducing the need for a membrane on the structure itself and the soil around the structure is dry, maintaining a lower thermal conductivity. In the remainder of this section, design of conventional subsurface drainage systems is discussed for the site in general, as well as for earth-covered roofs, earth-bermed walls, and floor slabs.

Subsurface Drainage on Site

Interception of Runoff: In addition to providing a subsurface drainage system adjacent to a structure, it may be necessary or desirable to utilize subsurface drainage techniques on the site at a distance from the building. As shown in figure 5-5, a drainpipe in a gravel-filled trench can be placed at the base of a hill to intercept surface runoff and divert it away from the house. Although this function can usually be performed by a simple drainage swale, such a system can be used in place of a swale where space is limited. Subsurface drainage may be required in addition to a swale in areas of high rainfall or poorly draining soil.

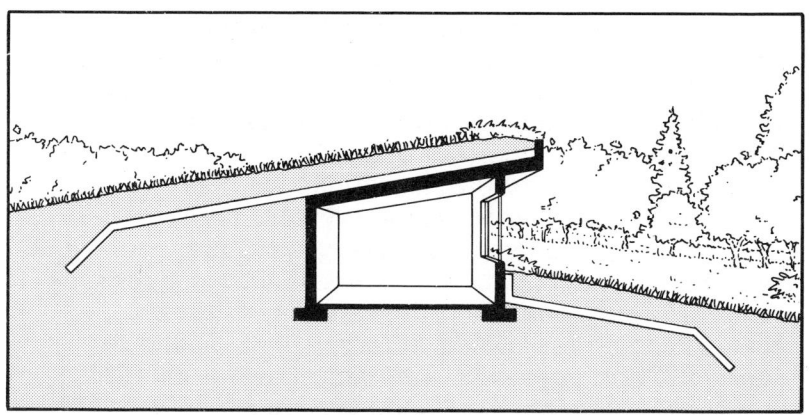

5-4: Subsurface Membranes Divert Water Away from Structure

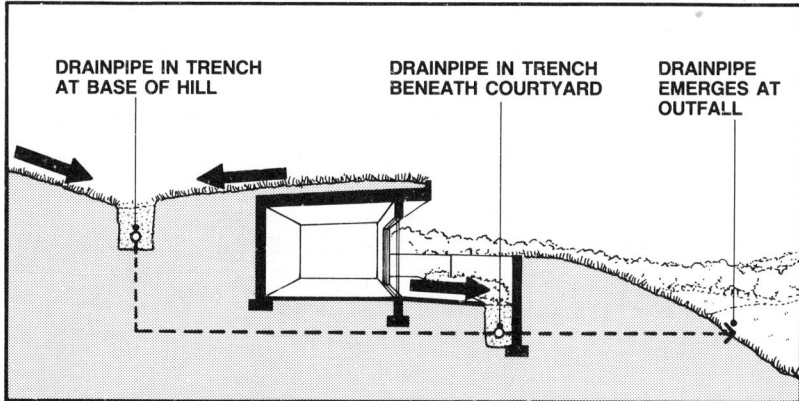

5-5: Subsurface Drainpipes Intercept Runoff

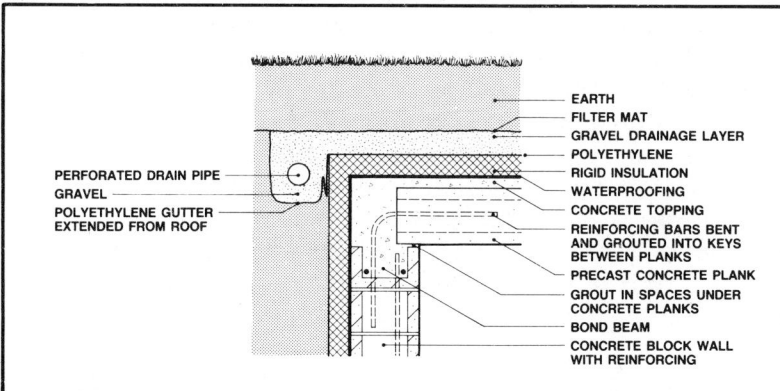

5-6: Earth-Covered Roof Detail

Collection in Low Areas: In some cases the existing site conditions or the design of the house will result in runoff being directed to low areas near the structure. Without sufficiently rapid drainage, water levels can rise and create problems. For example, in a sunken courtyard adjacent to an earth sheltered house, it is important to direct water away from the house and into a subsurface drainage system (see fig. 5-5). Drainpipes can carry water to an outfall or to a sump area.

Drainage Design for Earth-Covered Roofs

Deck Design: To provide adequate drainage, the concrete or wood roof deck itself should be sloped at least 1/10 of an inch per foot. For a typical house with an exposed south facade and earth covering the remaining walls, it is most common to slope the deck downward to the north or downward to the east and west with a ridge at the center. Where a flat precast concrete deck is used, a sloped concrete topping poured over the planks is recommended. As much as possible, the deck should slope away from any parapet walls, penetrations, or skylights in the roof. For large structures where the distance water must travel on the roof exceeds 40 feet, the deck may be sloped toward one or more interior drains.

Components of Rooftop Drainage System: The recommended practice is to apply the waterproof membrane directly to the sloping deck, cover it with insulation or protection board, and place a layer of 6 mil polyethylene over that. Sloping the deck alone is not considered adequate for providing good drainage on earth-covered roof deck; thus, 4 to 6 inches of sand or gravel placed over the polyethylene is recommended to create a drainage layer. This should be covered by a filter mat that prevents fine soil particles from interfering with drainage. Earth is then placed over the filter mat (fig. 5-6). The

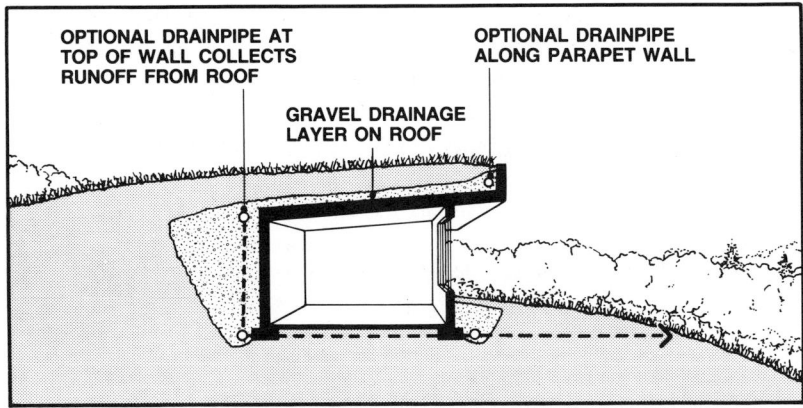

5-7: Location of Drainpipes at Roof Edges

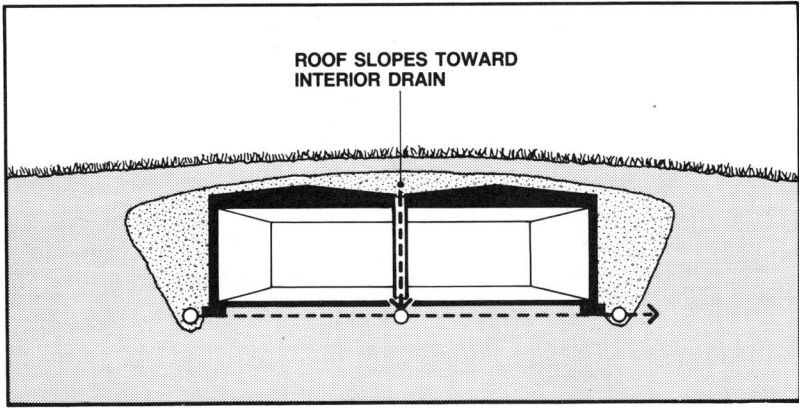

5-8: Interior Roof Drains

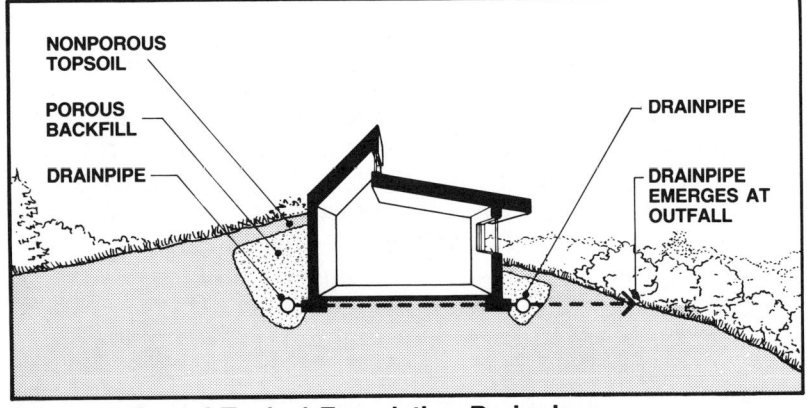

5-9: Location of Typical Foundation Drainpipes

thickness of earth can range from a few inches to several feet depending on a number of factors. In many cases a clay base is placed beneath a layer of topsoil. The relatively nonporous clay controls water migration to the roof deck and holds moisture for the plant materials, while the topsoil nourishes plant growth. Soil types used vary considerably depending on the landscape design, climate, and planting approach. One alternative is to use a thick layer of mulch, permitting native plants to seed themselves on the rooftop [Wells, 1977]. Whatever the landscape approach, the main drainage principles are similar: provide a drainage layer covered with a filter on a sloping roof deck.

Drainpipes at Roof Edges: If an adequate drainage layer is provided on a sloping roof deck, water will flow to the perimeter of the building and then drain down through the soil along the exterior walls. Assuming there is relatively porous soil and drainpipes along the foundation, this is generally adequate for most houses. It is possible to enhance drainage from the roof deck by placing drainpipes around the roof edge as shown in figure 5-7. A drainpipe such as the one shown in figure 5-6 will be most effective if the polyethylene from the roof deck extends to form a gutter beneath the drainpipe. A fold in the polyethylene permits some movement without tearing as the earth settles. Although such drainpipes are an improvement over simply draining the roof into the soil, they are not considered essential unless there are special concerns over high rainfall, excessive runoff directed at the roof, or poorly draining soil. Because these drainpipes are placed on fill that is often not compacted very well, settlement causes them to be less effective. Good compaction of the backfill is essential when they are used.

Drainpipes along Parapet Walls: Drainpipes are sometimes placed on the inside of the parapet walls that retain the earth on the roof, as shown in figure 5-7. A water buildup in this area is undesirable, but in most cases a sloping roof deck with a drainage layer should be adequate. An additional drainpipe along the parapet is only necessary when water must travel over 40 feet or when the roof has no slope. When such drainpipes are used, they should be placed directly on top of the waterproof membrane, not at a higher level.

Interior Roof Drains: Rather than directing water to the perimeter of the structure, it is possible to place drains in the center of the roof deck. Vertical drainpipes are usually placed within walls of the house and are connected to a subsurface drainage system beneath the floor (fig. 5-8). Drains are typically spaced 16 to 30 feet apart to correspond with the wall structure below. The deck should be sloped so that water runs toward the drains. Interior drains represent a penetration of the waterproof membrane and must be carefully sealed to prevent leakage. Generally, interior drains are recommended only for situations where simpler systems are not adequate. For example, in larger structures where water must flow over 40 feet on the roof deck to reach the perimeter with less than $\frac{1}{10}$ inch per foot slope, an interior drain system would be desirable. Interior drains are also useful on completely confined roof decks where it is not possible to drain to the perimeter of the structure.

Drainage Design for Earth-Bermed Walls

Drainpipes at Foundation: To provide good drainage along an underground wall, 4-inch-diameter perforated drainpipes placed at the base of the wall are always recommended (fig. 5-9). As shown in figure 5-10, the drainpipe should be located at least 4 inches below floor level and wrapped in filter fabric with gravel placed around it.

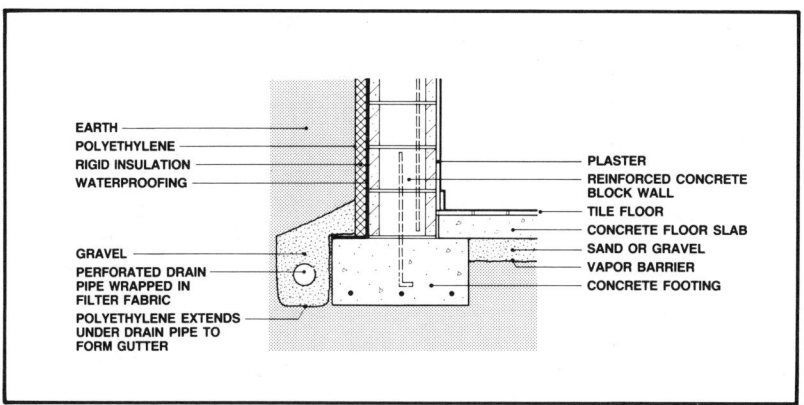

5-10: Foundation Detail

Soils Used for Backfill: For the subsurface drainage system to function most effectively in the vicinity of an earth-bermed wall, a very porous backfill material such as sand or gravel is most desirable. If the existing soil on site is porous, it can be used. Otherwise, sand or gravel may have to be brought to the site. In cases where this is not possible, a drainage mat system (discussed below) may be advisable. Generally, the porous backfill should be covered with a relatively nonporous material such as clay or a topsoil (fig. 5-9). If this is not done, surface runoff will be directed down toward the wall through the porous material.

Drainage Mat Systems: A number of manufacturers make drainage mats of various types that are placed directly against an underground wall. The mats are designed so that an air gap is created, providing an open path for water to drain down along the wall. In addition to enhancing drainage, the air gap prevents capillary draw through the wall from saturated soil. Drainage mats appear to be useful under two conditions. When no porous backfill is available, a drainage mat provides a path for water to reach the foundation drains. In this case the mat should be used with a waterproof membrane so that the structure is protected if drainage does not occur fast enough and water fills the gap. Since the soil is nonporous and can be saturated, structural loads against the wall will be higher with this approach.

In some instances drainage mats can be used instead of a complete waterproof membrane on the wall while performing the added function of insulating the wall. Materials which can be used in this dual purpose approach are high density rigid fiberglass boards, expanded polystyrene boards, and rigid fiber boards. This approach has been used successfully in Sweden and Canada, and has undergone some testing in the United States. As shown in figure 5-11, however, the surrounding area must be well drained with no potential for saturation. Usually a dampproof coating is placed on the wall before the insulation. In some cases a thick coat of asphalt or other waterproofing covers the lower portion of the wall in case there is temporary water buildup.

Drainage Design for Floor Slabs

Drainage Materials Beneath the Floor: In most cases floors of earth sheltered houses will be built well above the water table, and foundation drainpipes will handle all of the surface runoff and temporary subsurface water surrounding the structure. Only in unusually wet conditions will a positive water pressure occur beneath the floor slab. To prevent vapor transfer and capillary rise, however, a 6-mil polyethylene sheet should be placed beneath the slab. A 4- to 6-inch layer of sand or gravel placed between the slab and the vapor barrier is recommended to facilitate pouring and curing of the concrete (fig. 5-10). If water rises to a level near the floor, it may penetrate the seams of the vapor barrier and be trapped in the sand layer between the concrete and polyethylene. To prevent this in cases where the water table is near the floor level, an additional layer of gravel beneath the vapor barrier may be advisable.

Drainpipes Beneath the Floor: Although building on a site where the floor is at or below the water table is not recommended, occasionally it is necessary. In such cases a network of drainpipes set into the gravel layer beneath the floor slab can effectively draw down the water table by removing excess water rapidly when it occurs (fig. 5-12). When this approach is not adequate, the structure

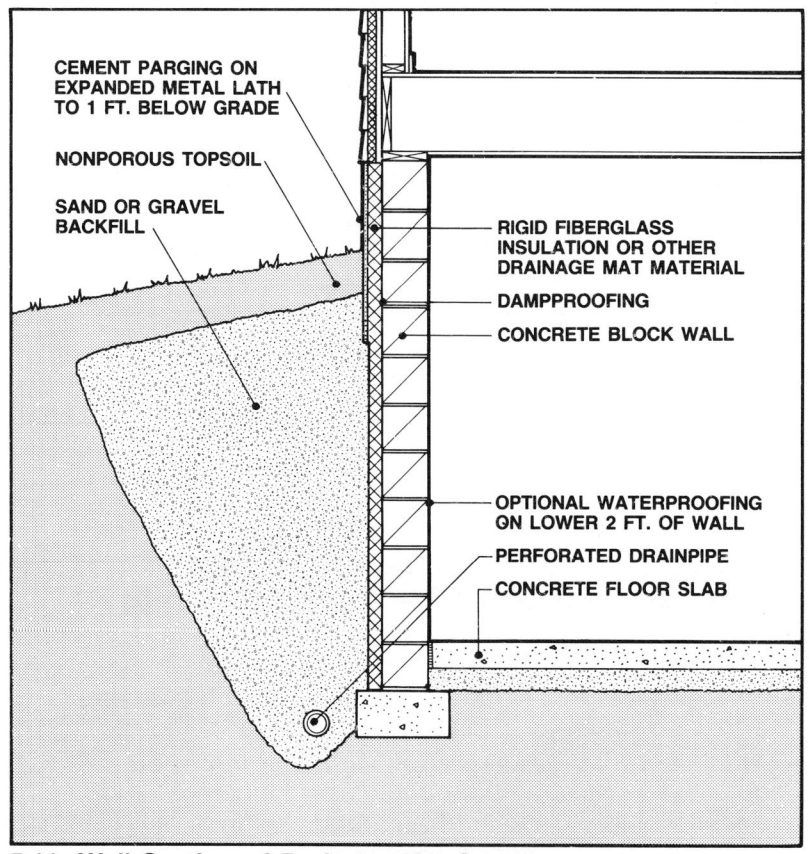

5-11: Wall Section of Drainage Mat System

must be completely waterproofed and structurally designed to resist the upward water pressure with no subsurface drainage. Usually structures requiring such measures are constructed for special purposes; such designs would seldom be economical for housing.

Drainage System Details

Slope and Outlet: All drainpipes, whether located at the roof, walls, foundation, or under the floor, should be part of an interconnected system that leads to an outlet for the water. The pipes should be sloped ⅛ inch per foot and preferably lead to an outfall. An outfall is most desirable because it depends only on gravity to function, although it does require a site with quite varied topography. The exposed pipe at an outfall should be covered with a rodent screen and designed so that water cannot back up in the pipe and freeze. If an outfall is not available, drainpipes must lead to a storm sewer or a sump area from which water can be periodically pumped out. This would be necessary for drainage from a house with a sunken courtyard on a flat site as shown in figure 5-13. Normally drainage water cannot be drained directly into a sanitary sewer.

Drainpipe Materials and Filter Fabrics: The most common material for subsurface drainage systems is 4-inch-diameter perforated plastic pipe. The pipe is installed with the holes on the bottom side. Wrapping the pipe in filter fabric is recommended to prevent soil particles from entering and eventually clogging the pipe. A more sophisticated product is a prefabricated sleeve for the perforated drainpipe. The sleeve is manufactured from a filter fabric (material often referred to as a geotextile) and can be an integral part of a drainage mat system.

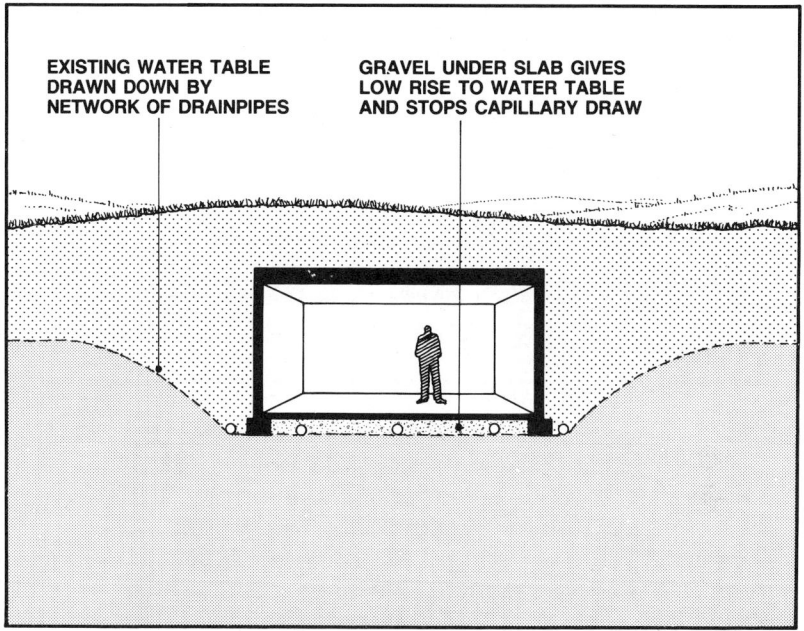

5-12: Subsurface Drainage for Structure Below Water Table

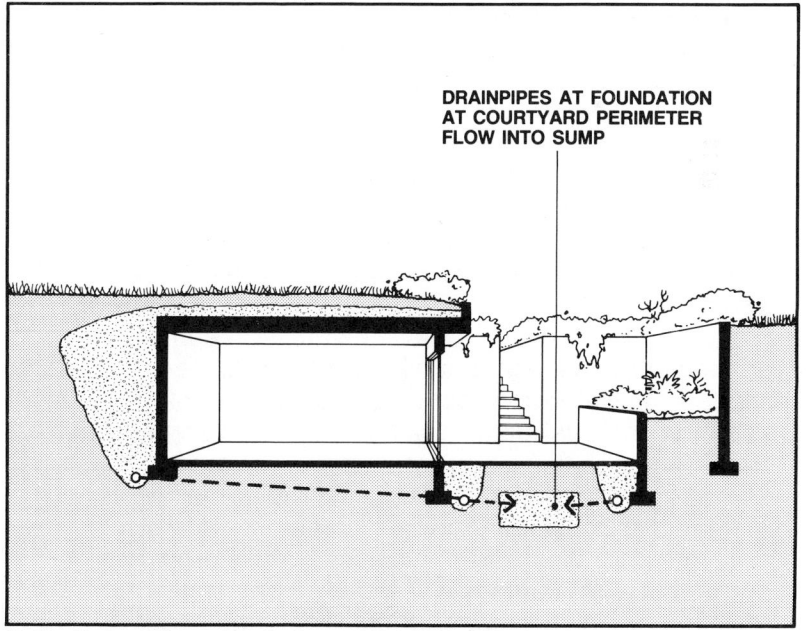

5-13: Subsurface Drainage on a Flat Site

Waterproofing Systems: Design and Application Guidelines

A waterproofing system can be defined as a membrane, protective barrier, or coating applied to a building as a means of preventing water from penetrating and entering the structure. Waterproofing materials also usually limit the passage of water vapor, although their vapor transmission characteristics may vary considerably. The waterproofing system is the third and final line of defense against water in the earth originating from rain, snow melt, or the underground water table.

A waterproofing system is almost always necessary below grade. The exterior structural shells of earth sheltered buildings are usually wood, masonry, or concrete. In a few cases the shell may be metal panels assembled into a vault structure. Wood and masonry surfaces have numerous joints and have no inherent water resistance. A system of metal panels is likely to have extensive seams and connecting bolts penetrating the structure, resulting in a need for waterproofing. Concrete, the most common material underground, can be waterproof by itself under certain conditions. A wall or roof composed of precast concrete panels is unlikely to resist water, however, since it contains joints similar to a masonry wall. Poured concrete with proper mix proportions, reinforcement, and placement has good resistance to water penetration. Post-tensioned concrete can be more effective because of the reduced cracking that occurs in the concrete. There will always be movement in concrete that result in cracks where water can penetrate, making waterproofing essential.

Below-grade structures are subject to a number of forces that may result in movement of the structure producing cracking or enlargement of existing joints. In most parts of the country, pressures result from continual freezing and thawing cycles. Differential settling of structures is also common because of variations in soils and loading conditions. In addition, building materials expand and contract with temperature, and normal concretes undergo shrinkage as they cure. Finally, structural deformation in an underground building can occur as the earth is placed against the walls and on the roof during construction.

When external forces cause movement of the building, cracks and enlarged joints will generally occur at the weak points of the structure. In a concrete building, cold joints represent likely places for cracks to occur. Another place subject to movement is the connection between a roof and a wall, especially if different construction materials are used. Cracking caused by pressure from freezing and thawing is common on parapet walls at roof edges, as well as on penetrations through the structure such as skylights and pipes. A roof drain, a chimney, or any other interuption in the basic structure or waterproofing system represent places where leaks caused both by movement, as well as by the difficulty of perfectly sealing these areas, can occur. All of these places of particular vulnerability to leakage require special attention in the design and application of a waterproofing system.

A wide range of products and systems are suitable for waterproofing underground structures. Failures often do not result from the shortcomings of a product but because the product is chosen for an inappropriate condition, is improperly applied or protected, or the basic construction details are incorrectly devised.

Waterproofing systems should be clearly distinguished from dampproofing products that are commonly applied to conventional basements. Dampproof coatings are intended to prevent some degree of vapor transmission and moisture from passing through the wall but do not effectively seal the building from free water present in the soil. The ineffectiveness of these products is one reason why underground spaces evoke negative images of dampness. Specific characteristics of dampproofing and waterproofing products are discussed in the following section. This section addresses general guidelines in the design and application of all products.

Location of Waterproofing and Critical Details

Type of Substrate: Under the right conditions, it is possible to successfully apply waterproofing to most substrates or structural materials—concrete, wood, masonry, or metal. In cases where wood is used below grade and waterproofed, only preservative- and pressure-treated wood is recommended for all locations concealed from the interior. Treatment should be according to American Wood Preservers Bureau Standard AWPB-FDN. Plywood should be bonded with exterior glue and caulked at the joints. Masonry walls can be rough and uneven, sometimes requiring a layer of concrete to provide a smooth surface. For similar reasons, a concrete topping is recommended over precast planks.

When concrete forms the substrate, proper mix design and placement can contribute to a structure that is more watertight. Too much water in the mixture can result in voids as the concrete cures as well as in greater shrinkage and cracking. This increased permeability can be avoided by keeping water/cement ratios below 0.55 by weight. In addition, aggregate must be properly sized to ensure workability. Air entrainment during placement is recommended to create a more durable, cohesive, and workable concrete that will be more watertight.

Placement of Waterproofing: On an underground building, the waterproofing should be applied to the outside of the building structure, not the inside. Not only is the wall kept dry, but the waterproofing is held against the wall, roof, or floor by the pressure of the earth and water. Waterproofing should be applied directly on the substrate, with insulation or protection board then placed over the waterproofing as shown in figure 5-14. Placement of waterproofing over insulation or insulation between two layers of waterproofing is not recommended. A layer of polyethylene placed over the insulation that covers the waterproofing will allow the earth to slide over the surface during backfilling and settlement without damaging the waterproofing. Water passing from the earth through the polyethylene layer must be free to drain from the insulation, however.

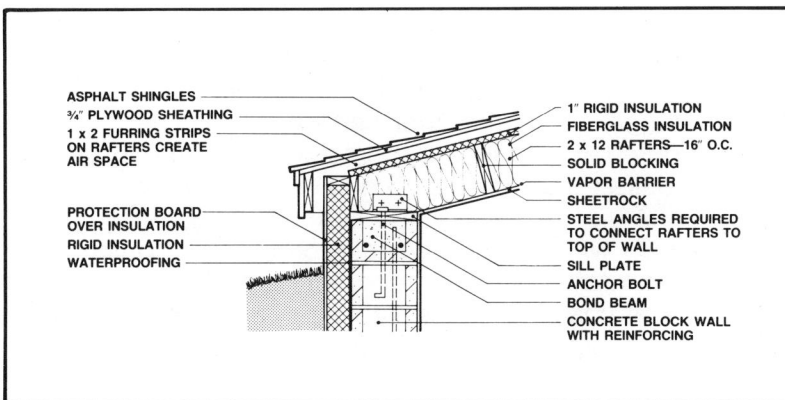

5-14: Earth-Bermed Wall Detail

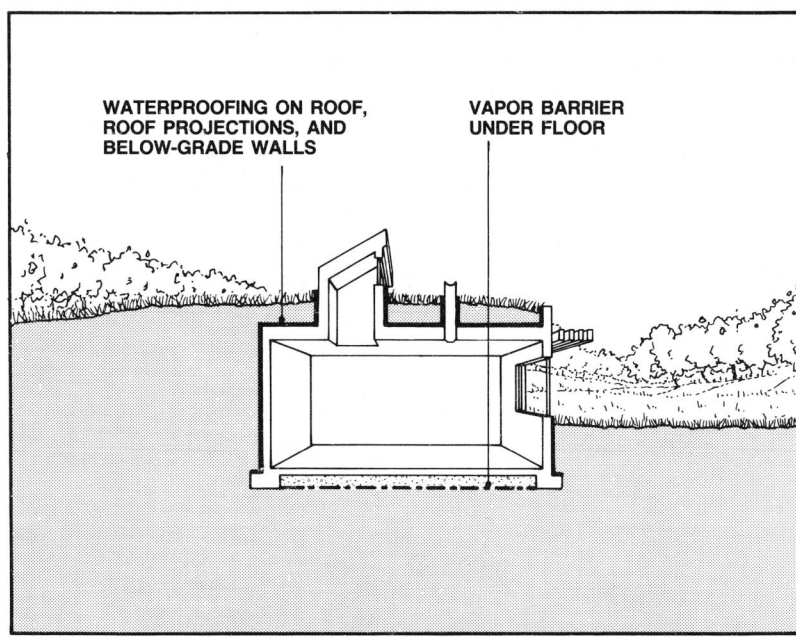

5-15: Location of Waterproofing in Typical Conditions

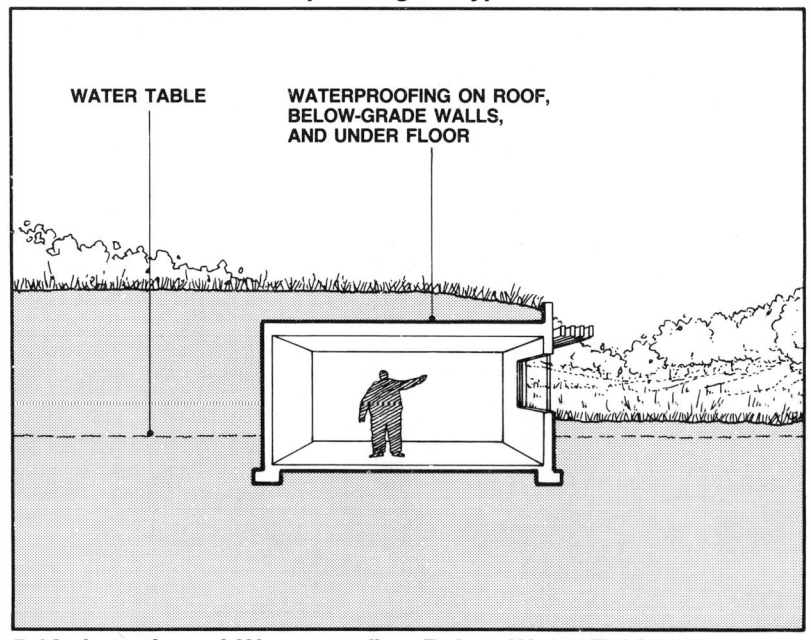

5-16: Location of Waterproofing Below Water Table

Earth-Covered Roof Application: A complete waterproofing system is always recommended on an earth-covered roof. The roof should be sloped at least 1 inch in 10 feet either toward the outside edges of the structure or toward an interior drain system. Waterproofing should also be applied to all parapet walls, skylight support walls, pipes, vents, or other protrusions as shown in figure 5-15.

Earth-Bermed Wall Application: Waterproofing is recommended on below-grade walls. The waterproofing on the wall should extend below the floor level to cover the top of the footing. Only in unusual circumstances is it possible to consider not using a waterproofing system on the walls. An example would be a building surrounded by extremely porous soil in an area with very low rainfall. A drainage mat with partial waterproofing is a promising alternative to a complete waterproof membrane or coating.

Under-Floor Application: Under normal conditions in which soil is adequately drained and the water table is several feet below the floor, waterproofing is not necessary under the floor of a structure. A layer of sand or gravel and a polyethylene vapor barrier are recommended, as shown in figure 5-15. If the floor of a structure is built at or below the existing water table, two approaches are possible; the water table can be lowered by extensive drainage (described in the previous section) or the floor can be completely waterproofed. The second approach, shown in figure 5-16, requires that the membrane be completely continuous and that walls and floor are structurally designed to withstand hydrostatic pressure. Building in the water table is never recommended since it is difficult and costly; it consequently is an unlikely choice for a housing structure in any case.

Building Geometry: Generally the building geometry should be simplified and projections, pipes, and vents should be consolidated as much as possible in order to simplify the waterproofing. Corners, bends, and joints usually require seams and represent the weak points or problem areas for many waterproofing systems. Sharp corners and bends tend to place stress on membranes. Either rounding corners or placing a cant in them as shown in figure 5-17 will reduce the stress at these points. The difficulty of sealing at corners and other unusual shapes can vary considerably depending on the waterproofing system chosen.

Flashing: Where a below-grade wall extends above grade, the waterproofing should also extend above grade for at least 4 to 6 inches. Flashing should then cover the waterproofing (as well as any insulation or protection board) and extend below grade at least 4 to 6 inches (see fig. 5-17). All flashing should be sealed and caulked. Particular types of flashing and specific details depend on the waterproofing product chosen and the appearance desired.

Thermal Breaks and Expansion Joints: In below-grade concrete structures, interior and exterior portions of the building must often be separated thermally. In figure 5-18, insulation separates a concrete overhang from the concrete slab roof on the interior. This thermal break represents a potential weak point in the waterproofing because it is not attached to the substrate and movement is likely to occur. Often metal flashing is recommended to bridge the insulation and support the waterproofing. For some products additional reinforcement is recommended along the break. A similar approach would be used for an expansion joint; most houses, however, are small enough not to require expansion joints.

Waterstops: Waterstops placed in the joints of concrete structures are considered unnecessary if a high quality waterproofing system is used. Conventional rubber waterstops were developed to provide some degree of protection at the joints for concrete structures without waterproofing. A drawback of rubber waterstops, however, is that water travels along them and may emerge in the building at a place remote from the source of the leak. Chemical waterstops can be used to prevent lateral water movement along a construction joint and may be appropriate if there is particular concern over leakage at construction joints.

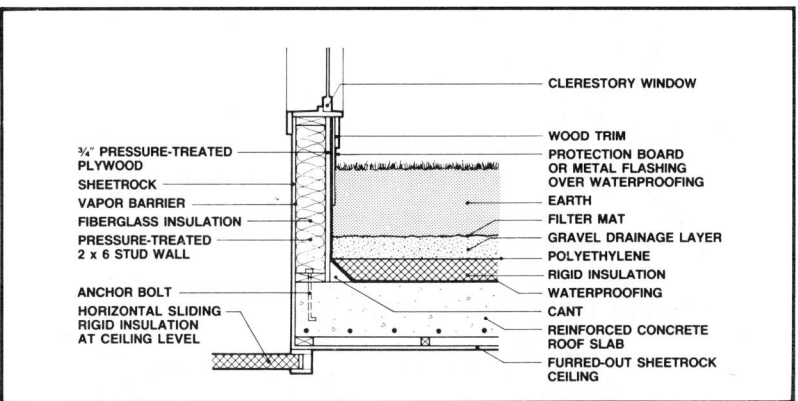

5-17: Clerestory Window Detail on Earth-Covered Roof

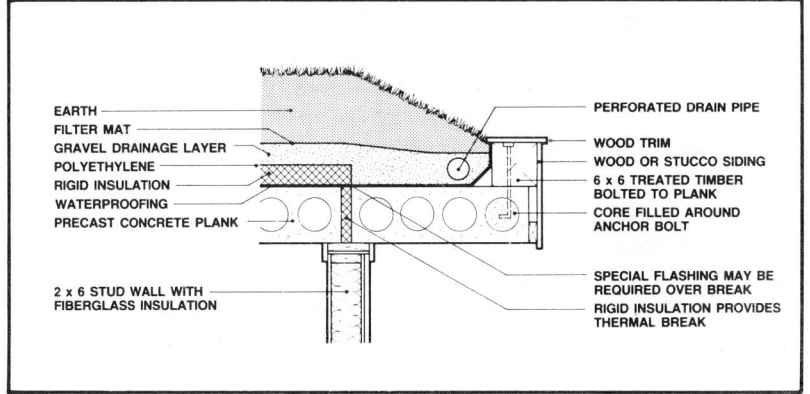

5-18: Earth-Covered Roof Edge Detail

Guidelines for Waterproofing Application

Qualifications of the Applicator: Most high-quality waterproofing products cannot be effectively applied by home owners or inexperienced contractors. Membranes often require great precision and care in sealing seams, while coatings must be applied to exact thicknesses usually with specialized equipment. Whenever possible, waterproofing products should be applied by professionals that have considerable experience with the selected product.

Surface Preparation: Concrete and masonry surfaces are usually somewhat rough and may be covered with form release agents or other substances. For most waterproofing products, a smooth, clean, dry surface is required. This surface preparation is mandatory for almost all materials except for some bentonite-based products, which cannot be punctured and can effectively coat an uneven surface.

Relation to Concrete Curing: As concrete cures it releases moisture to the air. If a waterproofing product is bonded to the concrete while curing is still in progress, moisture beneath the membrane or coating may destroy the adhesion to the wall. For these types of products, it is essential to wait until the concrete is fully cured before applying the waterproofing. Other products, however, may be applied at any time if they allow the moisture to pass through without harming the waterproofing system.

Weather Conditions: Most waterproofing products must be applied only under specific temperature and humidity conditions. Liquid-applied systems require proper conditions for curing while sheet membranes require certain conditions for bonding to the substrate. If applied in excessive heat, membranes may expand considerably and then contract in cooler conditions, creating stress in the membrane.

Chemical Compatibility: Some waterproofing and adhesive products contain relatively volatile chemicals. This is a concern for applicators, who should be properly protected. In addition, adverse chemical interactions may occur between adjacent components of a waterproofing/insulation system. For example, adhesives used to bond the waterproofing may harm the insulation or the substrate. Products should be chosen that are chemically compatible or tested on the site before application.

Flood Testing: After waterproofing is complete on horizontal surfaces, flood testing is recommended before backfilling. Since the waterproofing on earth-covered roofs is inaccessible after backfilling, flood testing provides an opportunity to find and repair any small leaks or flaws in the system. Bentonite-based products cannot be flood-tested since they expand when wet and only waterproof effectively when held in place by soil pressure.

Backfilling after Application: For some waterproofing products, backfilling should occur as soon as possible after application. These include rubberized asphalt covered by polyethylene, which degrades in sunlight, and bentonite, which must be under earth pressure before it can be wet. Other products, however, such as many liquid-applied coatings, must cure in the air for a period of time before backfilling. To avoid damage to the waterproofing during backfilling, it should be covered by insulation or protection boards. Backfilling should be done very carefully and only with small lightweight equipment on earth-covered roofs. Backfill should be compacted to reduce future settling, which can place stress on insulation and waterproofing materials.

Waterproofing Systems: Product Selection and Evaluation

Selection of a specific waterproofing material for an earth sheltered house can be a complex and even bewildering experience. Not only do numerous products exist, all with different characteristics, but each building and job location presents its own set of unique requirements. A product that is appropriate for all below grade applications regardless of location and building design simply does not exist. On the other hand, there are a number of waterproofing products that have performed very successfully below grade when applied under the right conditions.

In evaluating various waterproofing products, it is apparent that each system has certain strengths and weaknesses. In many cases the weaknesses can be overcome by proper application or by combining materials to form a composite system. For example, a disadvantage of sheet membranes is that water can travel beneath a loose-laid sheet, requiring great cost and effort to locate and repair the source of a leak. If the material is bonded to the substrate however, this potential problem is solved. Many coatings are excellent on large, flat surfaces but are considered weakest near joints and at transition areas where flashing is required. Sheet membranes can be placed over these critical areas to form a composite system that has the inherent advantages of two or more products without the weaknesses.

5-19: A synthetic rubber membrane is laid over a precast concrete roof deck. Insulation and earth are then placed over the waterproof membrane.

In this section of the chapter, guidelines or criteria for product selection are briefly discussed. Then several generic categories of waterproofing materials are described and evaluated in general terms based on most of the criteria. Two criteria for product selection—guarantees and availability of materials and applicators—are so specific to individual products and locations that they are not included in the evaluation. This approach is not necessarily intended to reveal the best products, because each situation presents different requirements. It should, however, provide a framework for builders and design professionals to judge and select products.

Guidelines for Product Selection

Durability and Stability: The most fundamental characteristic of any waterproofing material is its ability to resist water penetration without deteriorating in a below-grade enviroment. Since replacement of products below grade is extremely costly if not impossible, materials should last the life of the structure. This means that waterproofing materials and their adhesive or bonding agents must be compatible with soils and other materials used in construction.

Ability to Withstand Movement and Cracking: Because concrete will usually crack and below grade structures will normally experience slight displacements, waterproofing materials must be able to withstand these movement conditions without failing. For many products the ability to stretch and bridge cracks is sufficient. Other products rely on an ability to expand and reseal cracks in the presence of moisture.

Ability to Minimize Leaks and Facilitate Repair: A leak can occur in any below-grade waterproofing system regardless of its quality. It is important to be able to locate the source of the leak and repair it without extensive and costly excavation. Waterproofing systems should not permit water from a leak to travel freely behind the membrane and emerge elsewhere in the structure. Such water migration makes identification of the source of the leak extremely difficult. To avoid this, materials should be fully bonded to the substrate or at least bonded in a gridlike pattern that enables leaks to be localized.

Versatility of Application: The versatility of a waterproofing product can be examined in a number of ways. Whether a product is equally suited to horizontal as well as vertical surfaces is one consideration. The product's applicability to complicated or curving geometrical shapes in addition to flat surfaces is also a concern. Some products may be applied directly to rough, uneven surfaces, saving surface preparation time and making such materials suitable for surfaces that cannot be made smooth and flat very easily.

Ease of Application: Generally it is advantageous to select a waterproofing product that is relatively easy to apply, resists damage, and is not overly sensitive to surface and weather conditions. Materials with these characteristics will require less application time, have less chance of error during application, result in better quality control, and probably cost less for a system of similar quality.

Cost: Although waterproofing is no place to cut costs in an earth sheltered house, relative costs among good products are a criteria for product selection. The cost of a waterproofing product should be evaluated in relation to the longevity of the material.

Availability of Materials and Applicators: Many waterproofing products must be applied by contractors with specialized equipment. Selecting a product that requires an applicator who is not in the local area may introduce additional costs.

Guarantees: The warranty or guarantee accompanying any waterproofing system is the final criteria for product selection. A one- to five-year warranty is common with most manufacturers. Warranties often cover only defects in the product itself. The cost of excavating, backfilling, and repairing interior damage is not included in a limited warranty. Many problems are not caused by product defects but by errors in application. The liability of the applicator can vary considerably.

Dampproofing Materials

Commonly used on basements and foundations, this group of products does not completely waterproof a structure. The term dampproofing indicates that the materials are intended to seal out dampness and moisture but not really protect from water below grade. The most commonly used dampproofing products are asphalt and pitch coatings. Acrylic latex and epoxy coatings can also be considered as dampproofing materials. Covering a concrete or masonry wall with a relatively thin but dense coat of cement is another dampproofing technique known as pargeting. In many cases dampproofing treatments are covered with polyethylene, which acts as an additional vapor barrier. Polyethylene (discussed in a later section) is a water-resistant membrane but does not keep the structure watertight because it is vulnerable to puncture and its seams are very difficult to seal. Characteristics of dampproofing materials are shown in the adjacent chart for comparison purposes.

Another approach to reducing water problems in concrete walls involves the use of various additives and admixtures in the concrete mixture. Although some of these products can produce a concrete wall that is more water resistant, there is usually little ability to bridge or reseal significant cracks in the concrete structure. Because these additives are regarded as insufficient waterproofing, their characteristics are not discussed in detail here.

Durability and Stability Underground	Some asphalt-based coatings tend to emulsify in the presence of groundwater and lose their effectiveness over a long period of time. Other asphalt, pitch, acrylic latex, epoxy, and cement coatings are stable underground.
Ability to Withstand Movement and Cracking of the Structure	The relatively thin coatings of asphalt, pitch, acrylic latex, epoxy, and cement have little ability to bridge cracks and respond to movement in the structure. Polyethylene can bridge cracks but seams cannot be adequately sealed.
Ability to Minimize Leaks and Facilitate Repair	None of the common dampproofing products have the ability to reseal any breaks in the coating. Tar and pitch used below grade lack the flexibility and resealing capabilities they have when used on above-grade roofs because they are not exposed to enough heat to facilitate resealing.
Versatility of Application	Coatings can be applied to a variety of surfaces and shapes, but this attribute is irrelevant because the products are considered to be ineffective for waterproofing both vertical and horizontal surfaces below grade.
Ease of Application	Most of the coatings are brushed, troweled, or sprayed on and can be applied by relatively unskilled labor.
Cost[1] ($ per sq ft)		asphalt coating	asphalt with polyethylene
	material	.10-.15	.11-.16
	labor	.03-.05	.04-.09
	overhead/profit	.10-.15	.15-.20
	bid price	.23-.35	.30-.45
Comments	These relatively inexpensive, easy-to-apply coatings are an inadequate means of protecting an underground building from water problems. Dampproofing products should be clearly distinguished from waterproofing products, which use some of the same basic materials in more effective ways.

[1] Cost information is based on 1983 data from *Underground Waterproofing* [Anderson, 1983].

5-20: Characteristics of Dampproofing Materials

Cementitious Materials

Most cementitious waterproofing materials consist of cement, fine silica sand, water, and various chemical admixtures. These materials can be brushed, sprayed, or troweled onto the inside or outside of concrete and masonry walls. Although similar to a cement parget coating in some respects, cementitious materials have certain sealing characteristics that distinguish them from basic dampproofing products. The many cementitious waterproofing products fall into three general categories. The first group includes high-strength dense surface coatings. These materials are formulated to minimize shrinkage cracks and bond extremely well to the substrate. The second category of products consists of integral surface coatings with penetrating characteristics. Most of these integral coatings react with the moisture and unhydrated cement in the wall to form crystals in the voids of the concrete. These crystals are small enough to prevent water molecules from passing through but large enough to permit air and water vapor to penetrate. A final category of cementitious products includes latex-formulated surface coatings combined with water repellents. These materials do not penetrate the concrete wall and have similar characteristics to the acrylic latex coatings discussed in the previous section on dampproofing products.

Durability and Stability Underground	Generally, cementitious materials are stable underground and resist most soil chemicals.
Ability to Withstand Movement and Cracking of the Structure	Cementitious materials have the ability to fill small, hairline cracks but cannot bridge the larger cracks of 1/16 to 1/8 inch common in many concrete structures.
Ability to Minimize Leaks and Facilitate Repair	Because the materials are not elastic and have only limited resealing capabilities (in tiny cracks), they are not very effective in minimizing leaks once a crack occurs. Repair may be simpler than with some materials, however, if applied from the inside.
Versatility of Application	Limited to concrete and masonry surfaces, these products can be applied to unusual, complex, or curving shapes if necessary. They can also be applied to both vertical and horizontal surfaces.
Ease of Application	Most of the coatings can be applied by moderately skilled labor and are not as susceptible to damage as other products. Manufacturers' recommendations usually specify application on damp, newly poured concrete at temperatures above 40°F.
Cost[1,2] **($ per sq ft)**	material .40– .80 labor .15– .20 overhead/profit .40– .55 bid price .95–1.55
Comments	The effectiveness of cementitious materials is limited by their inability to bridge larger cracks in concrete structures. They may be most appropriate for post-tensioned structures where large cracks are limited.

[1] Cost information is based on 1983 data from *Underground Waterproofing* [Anderson, 1983].
[2] Prices are for two-coat process.

5-21: Characteristics of Cementitious Materials

Built-up Membranes and Bitumen Sheets

Conventional built-up membranes consist of layers of hot-mopped asphalt or pitch alternating with felt or fabric reinforcing. These membranes are commonly used on above-grade roofs where the asphalt or pitch is heated by the sun, giving it flexibility and resealing capabilities. Built-up roofs typically require periodic maintenance and replacement. Below grade, the membrane is at a cooler temperature, making it more brittle, and it is generally less accessible for maintenance and repair. In spite of these drawbacks, built-up membranes have been used successfully below grade. Although not strongly recommended for below-grade use, their characteristics are shown in the adjacent chart for comparison purposes.

Bitumen sheets, sometimes referred to as modified bitumens, represent a category of products with many similarities to built-up membranes. Usually manufactured into 4- by 8-foot rigid sheets, these materials can be applied in a cold form with only the seams sealed in the field by a hot-mopping process. These asphalt-based sheet products can be self-adhering and may contain a reinforcing sheet of plastic or fabric embedded in the material. The surface is protected by a plastic coating or other protective layer. Most of the basic characteristics of built-up membranes apply to modified bitumen sheets. Rubberized asphalt membranes (discussed in the next section) represent a variation on the conventional asphalt built-up membrane that is specifically designed for below-grade conditions.

Durability and Stability Underground	Some asphalt-based products tend to emulsify and deteriorate below grade over a long period of time. Cooler temperatures below grade may make some asphalt and pitch formulations brittle and inflexible. Inorganic fabrics are preferable to organic fabrics for longevity underground.
Ability to Withstand Movement and Cracking of the Structure	Fabric and felt layers provide some ability to bridge cracks, however, the potential brittleness and inflexibility of the material make its ability to withstand movement questionable.
Ability to Minimize Leaks and Facilitate Repair	Below grade, asphalt and pitch will not reach the higher temperatures required for them to liquefy and reseal punctures or leaks. Also, the membrane may not be extremely well-bonded to the structure, permitting leaks to travel under the membrane.
Versatility of Application	Typical hot-mopped built-up membranes can be adapted to a variety of shapes and types of surfaces. It is more difficult, however, to apply this system to vertical walls; it is most suited to horizontal surfaces with a slight slope.
Ease of Application	Built-up membranes can be applied by relatively unskilled labor in a variety of temperature and humidity conditions. Surfaces need not be extremely smooth and clean; however, after application the membrane is soft and requires protection from damage.
Cost[1] ($ per sq ft)	material .50– .75 labor .30– .50 overhead/profit .60– .75 bid price[2] 1.40–2.00
Comments	Generally, asphalt and pitch built-up membranes are not recommended for below-grade use. Questions about long term stability and difficulty of providing maintenance underground are the main concerns.

[1] Cost information is based on 1983 data from *Underground Waterproofing* [Anderson, 1983].
[2] Prices are for modified bitumen sheets; total cost of built-up membranes should be similar.

5-22: Characteristics of Built-up Membranes

Rubberized Asphalt

Asphalt is combined with a small amount of synthetic rubber and applied to a polyethylene sheet to form rubberized asphalt membranes. A second polyethylene sheet is sometimes placed between two layers of the compound. The membrane generally comes in 3- or 4-foot-wide rolls and adheres directly to the substrate. The material is overlapped and adheres to itself to form seams. This combination of asphalt, rubber, and polyethylene is suitable for below-grade applications because it overcomes many of the deficiencies of conventional dampproof coatings and built-up membranes.

Durability and Stability Underground	The material has generally good stability and resistance to chemicals below grade. Ultraviolet rays of the sun will deteriorate polyethylene if left exposed. The tendency of asphalt to emulsify is reduced by polyethylene protection, except at the seams.
Ability to Withstand Movement and Cracking of the Structure	Polyethylene and asphalt provide tensile strength, while rubber has softness and flexibility. The material can bridge cracks up to ⅛ inch, but seams must be well sealed to resist pressure.
Ability to Minimize Leaks and Facilitate Repair	Water from a leak will not travel under the membrane if the material is fully bonded to the surface. This requires the use of a primer and great care in application.
Versatility of Application	Roll goods are best suited to simple, flat (horizontal) rectilinear surfaces, although it is possible to cover more complex shapes. Generally applicable to all materials and both vertical and horizontal surfaces as long as there is some slope.
Ease of Application	Smooth, clean, dry surfaces are required. The material must be applied at 40°F or above. Good adhesion to the surface and at the seams is critical.
Cost[1] ($ per sq ft)	material .30– .50 labor .20– .50 overhead/profit .55– .80 bid price 1.05–1.85
Comments	Generally acceptable for below-grade use but not recommended for completely flat, horizontal surfaces with standing water because of the numerous seams and potential for emulsification.

[1]Cost information is based on 1983 data from *Underground Waterproofing* [Anderson, 1983].

5-23: Characteristics of Rubberized Asphalt

5-24: Rubberized asphalt membranes are applied to a roof deck before covering with insulation and earth.

Liquid-Applied Elastomers

To provide a seamless waterproof membrane underground, various plastics, polyurethane, elastomers, rubbers, and other synthetic compounds can be applied to the structure in a liquid form. After two to three days of curing, an elastic membrane results that is completely bonded to the substrate. These liquid-applied systems may be applied by spray, trowel, roller, or brush. The most common general types are listed below:

- polymeric asphalt
- polyurethane elastomers
- polyisobutylene (PIB)
- polychloroprene (neoprene)
- chlorosulfonated polyethylene (hypalon)
- polyvinyl chloride (PVC)
- polysulfide
- styrene budianene rubber (SBR)

There are numerous variations on the chemical compositions and characteristics of these products. Polyurethanes have the longest history of use underground and are the most commonly used of the liquid-applied systems. Formulations can be made to create a certain set of characteristics—elasticity or resistance to abrasion are examples. In the adjacent chart, general characteristics of liquid-applied systems are presented. To determine specific characteristics of individual products requires contact with manufacturers, contractors, and design professionals.

Durability and Stability Underground	The basic chemical composition of these products varies, and hence, the durability and stability underground may vary. Assuming an appropriate formulation is chosen for the below-grade environment, good durability and resistance to degradation is available.
Ability to withstand Movement and Cracking of the Structure	Most liquid-applied products are elastic and can bridge cracks. Since they are fully bonded to the structure, however, the ability to absorb stress is limited to a small area over the crack. This could cause failure of the membrane over a large crack.
Ability to Minimize Leaks and Facilitate Repair	Liquid-applied systems have no ability to reseal any tears or punctures in the membrane. Locating a leak is easier than with a loose-laid membrane since liquid-applied systems are fully bonded and water cannot travel beneath them.
Versatility of Application	A liquid-applied product can be applied equally well to horizontal and vertical surfaces. It is suitable for curving and complex forms and structures with numerous penetrations. With proper formulation products can bond to any normal substrate.
Ease of Application	More than any other product, application methods and conditions are critical. Surface must be smooth and clean; concrete should be cured. Temperature and humidity should be in correct range for curing of the membrane. Precise thickness of material should be applied, with no air bubbles.
Cost[1, 2] ($ per sq ft)	material .35– .80 labor .05– .15 overhead/profit .55– .70 bid price .90–1.65
Comments	Liquid-applied systems are versatile and can be effective below grade in the proper formulation. Two-component polyurethane systems are likely to produce a durable, elastic membrane. Problems are usually related to application—great care and proper conditions are essential.

[1] Cost information is based on 1983 data from *Underground Waterproofing* [Anderson, 1983].
[2] Prices are for a polyurethane coating that is moisture cured. Other liquid-applied elastomers would be in a similar price range.

5-25: Characteristics of Liquid-Applied Systems

Bentonite: Raw Form and Panels

Bentonite (montmorillonite) is a highly plastic clay that expands from ten to twenty times its original size when saturated with water. It returns to its original volume as it dries and can repeat this cycle indefinitely. If bentonite is confined between a building surface and the soil, it will expand when wet to create an impermeable, waterproof barrier. In its raw form, it is used in well casings and to seal the bottoms of lakes and reservoirs. In this dry powdery form, however, it cannot be directly applied to a building structure in a consistent thickness. One method of applying bentonite to building surfaces is to encase the raw material in corrugated cardboard panels. The voids of the 4- by 4-foot panels are filled with bentonite, resulting in a constant thickness. As moisture and organic material in the soil come in contact with the cardboard, it deteriorates and the bentonite is left in place to act as a waterproof barrier. The characteristics indicated in the adjacent chart apply mainly to the cardboard panels, since raw bentonite by itself is inappropriate for use on buildings.

Durability and Stability Underground	Bentonite is inorganic and stable underground. Its effectiveness is diminished in soils with a high salt content. Since the cardboard panels are intended to deteriorate in the soils exposing the bentonite, problems can result in soils lacking sufficient bacteria.
Ability to Withstand Movement and Cracking of the Structure	Because bentonite can expand to many times its original volume when wet, it fills voids and cracks that occur in the structure.
Ability to Minimize Leaks and Facilitate Repair	The ability of bentonite to expand provides a unique ability to reseal punctures or holes. Leaks can occur around loose-laid cardboard panels before the cardboard has deteriorated. This can be prevented by setting panels in a gel.
Versatility of Application	Panels are suitable for flat, rectilinear surfaces but not curves, unusual geometries, or buildings with numerous penetrations. Vertical and sloping horizontal applications are appropriate; however, cardboard may not deteriorate sufficiently on earth-covered surfaces when isolated from the soil by insulation or polyethylene layers.
Ease of Application	Panels do not require extremely smooth surfaces although a cement plaster is recommended over masonry walls. They can be applied at any temperature. Panels must be handled carefully to prevent damage and must be kept dry before backfilling.
Cost[1,2] **($ per sq ft)**	material .45– .55 labor .07– .15 overhead/profit .45– .50 bid price 1.00–1.20
Comments	Raw bentonite is difficult to apply to building surfaces. Cardboard panels containing bentonite, however, can be effective when the problem of possible nondeterioration of the cardboard is addressed.

[1] Cost information is based on 1983 data from *Underground Waterproofing* [Anderson, 1983]
[2] Prices are for bentonite panels, not raw bentonite.

5-26: Characteristics of Raw Bentonite and Panels

Durability and Stability Underground	Bentonite is inorganic and stable underground. Its effectiveness is diminished in soils with a high salt content.
Ability to Withstand Movement and Cracking of the Structure	Because bentonite can expand to many times its original volume when wet, it fills voids and cracks that occur in the structure.
Ability to Minimize Leaks and Facilitate Repair	The ability of bentonite to expand provides a unique ability to reseal punctures or holes since spray- and trowel-grade products fully adhere to the substrate; leaks can be located from the interior and sometimes repaired from the interior by injecting more bentonite into the area.
Versatility of Application	Spray- and trowel-on products are suitable for vertical and horizontal surfaces as well as curving shapes and complex geometries. They are appropriate on virtually any substrate and can be applied in unusual situations unsuitable for the application of other products.
Ease of Application	Spraying or troweling of the product is relatively easy and does not require the surface preparation or precision of many liquid-applied systems. Once applied, however, the coating must be protected from water and should be backfilled immediately if possible. Reapplication is necessary if the bentonite becomes wet before backfilling.
Cost[1, 2] ($ per sq ft)	material .30– .50 labor .04– .08 overhead/profit .45– .82 bid price .80–1.40
Comments	Bentonite-based mixtures are suitable for below-grade waterproofing and have been successfully used. Particular assets are the resealing capability and ability to locate leaks. A composite system using bentonite with membrane strips at exposed edges and critical joints is recommended. Disadvantages are primarily in the difficulty of quality assurance in the product and application.

[1]Cost information is based on 1983 data from *Underground Waterproofing* [Anderson, 1983].

[2]Prices are for one-component spray; two-component spray is similar. Material costs for trowel-on mixture would be similar to spray grade; however, labor costs would be higher unless owner-applied.

5-27: Characteristics of Bentonite Mixtures

Bentonite: Trowel-on and Spray-on Mixtures

One approach to utilizing the unique expansion and waterproofing capabilities of bentonite clay is to mix it with other substances. Since raw bentonite should not be directly applied to buildings, it is necessary to combine it with materials that bind it and adhere to the substrate. In the past bentonite has been mixed with asphalt for this purpose; however, the asphalt can coat the clay particles and reduce their effectiveness in expanding and sealing when wet. Bentonite is presently available in two basic formulations. It is mixed with a binding agent that forms a gel when applied. Sometimes referred to as a one-component mixture, it can be sprayed or troweled onto building surfaces. Polyethylene is

5-28: Bentonite mixture is sprayed onto below-grade surfaces before covering with insulation and backfill.

placed over the gel to protect it and assist in the curing process. A second formulation, referred to as a two-component mixture, is sprayed on in a form that dries very quickly. The ability of bentonite to expand ten or twenty times its original volume is the key to its waterproofing effectiveness. A dense, impervious layer will only be formed if the coating is restrained by the weight of the earth; it is not effective above grade in exposed conditions. Approximately 30 pounds per square foot of pressure (about 4 to 6 inches of soil) is adequate to restrain the bentonite and prevent separation. Often the bentonite coating works best as part of a composite system that utilizes a membrane material to cover or reinforce exposed areas and critical joints [System 7, 1984].

Durability and Stability Underground	Most sheet membranes are tough, puncture resistant, and resistant to most soil chemicals. They are capable of lasting the life of the structure. PVC sheets may be susceptible to shrinkage and eventual brittleness. Resistance to ultraviolet exposure varies.
Ability to Withstand Movement and Cracking of the Structure	Sheet membranes are elastic and have great tensile strength providing excellent ability for bridging cracks. If a membrane is fully bonded to the structure and cracks occur, stresses will be greater since they cannot be widely distributed.
Ability to Minimize Leaks and Facilitate Repair	Membranes have no resealing capabilities if punctured. If they are loose-laid, water from a leak can travel under the membrane, making location of the source difficult. To prevent this, full bonding or bonding the membrane in a grid pattern is recommended.
Versatility of Application	Large, heavy sheets are best suited for flat, rectilinear horizontal surfaces. Sheets are often too heavy to apply easily to vertical walls. Curved surfaces, complex building geometries, and extensive penetrations create more seams and problems for flat, preformed sheets.
Ease of Application	Placement, bonding, and seaming of membranes requires experienced, skilled professionals. Surfaces need to be clean and relatively smooth to prevent punctures. Weather conditions for application can vary. Flood testing is recommended.
Cost[1] ($ per sq ft)	PVC sheet CPE sheet EPDM[2] Material .40– .50 .65– .70 .45– .55 Labor .12– .17 .12– .17 .07– .14 Overhead/profit .50– .60 .55– .65 .45– .55 Bid price 1.05–1.20 1.20–1.50 1.05–1.80
Comments	Membranes are generally considered high-quality, durable, and effective products below grade. Usually, they are best suited to horizontal rather than vertical surfaces. Seams must be very carefully bonded in the field; at least partial bonding to the substrate is recommended to help localize leaks.

[1] Cost information is based on 1983 data from *Underground Waterproofing* [Anderson, 1983].
[2] Other synthetic rubber membranes would be similar in cost to EPDM.

5-29: Characteristics of Sheet Membranes

Plastic and Vulcanized Sheet Membranes

Large sheet membranes made of plastic compounds or of natural or synthetic rubber represent one of the most common types of underground waterproofing. A wide range of chemical formulations, properties, sizes, and thicknesses of material fall into the sheet membrane classification. One of the most common plastic sheets is polyethylene. Although it is used as a component of some suitable waterproofing products such as rubberized asphalt, it is not a suitable material by itself because seams cannot be sealed effectively and it is usually too thin to be puncture resistant. Four plastic sheets that are potentially suitable for below grade use are listed below (although hypalon is usually not recommended for this condition):

- high-density polyethylene
- chlorinated polyethylene (CPE)
- polyvinyl choride (PVC)
- chlorosulfonated polyethylene (hypalon or CSPE)

Vulcanized membranes or synthetic rubbers that are appropriate below grade include the following:

- isobutylene isoprene (Butyl)
- ethylene propylene diene monomer (EPDM)
- polychloroprene (neoprene)
- polyisobutylene (PIB)

Sheet membranes are discussed here as a group, and their basic characteristics presented in the adjacent chart. While this is useful for general comparison to other types of products, it does not distinguish clearly between the properties of individual membranes. Manufacturers and contractors should be consulted to determine the membrane type and thickness best suited for a particular situation.

5-30: Neoprene rubber flashing material is applied to a timber curb at the edge of an earth-covered roof. The neoprene is bonded to a butyl rubber membrane that is placed over the concrete roof deck.

Below-Grade Insulation Materials

The function of any insulation material is to reduce the unwanted transfer of heat from one area to another. Although this objective appears quite simple, it becomes more complex when the insulation must perform in the harsher environment encountered below grade. Because they mainly influence energy use, the specific thickness versus location aspects of insulation with respect to the structure are discussed in chapter 3. The focus of this section is on the appropriate placement and selection of insulating materials in a below-grade application.

Placement Alternatives

There are three basic conditions of insulation placement with respect to the building structure. Insulation can be placed inside the below-grade wall or roof as shown in figure 5-31. If the structure is masonry or concrete, additional framing is required to enclose the insulation. If, however, the below-grade wall or roof is a wood structure, the insulation may be placed within cavities in the wall as it is in conventional frame construction. In either case, the insulation is inside the protective waterproofing. A second condition is insulation placed on the outside of the wall but inside the waterproofing as shown in figure 5-32. Insulation placed outside the wall and the waterproofing as shown in figure 5-33 represents the third condition. Even though the insulation may be covered by a protection board or by polyethylene, it is still exposed to soil moisture and chemicals. When insulation is placed in the soil and detached from the structure, the conditions to which the insulation is exposed are similar to the third condition (fig. 5-33).

Insulation Placement Concerns

Energy Use and Comfort: Placing insulation outside a concrete or masonry structure exposes the mass of the wall or roof to the interior air. Locating the mass inside the insulating envelope in this manner can provide such energy-related benefits as storing solar heat gain or other intermittent sources of energy and reducing peak loads in the space. Comfort can be enhanced because temperature fluctuations are modified in both summer and winter. Some of these effects can be increased by extending insulation into the soil mass beyond the structure. On the other hand, mass within the heated envelope makes the structure slow to respond to temperature changes, which can be a disadvantage under certain conditions. These effects are severely curtailed when insulation is placed inside the massive structure. In a wood-frame structure where the insulation is typically placed within the wall, placing insulation outside the wall results in relatively little increase in mass compared to the increase in mass resulting from such a change for a concrete wall.

Thermal Stress on Structure and Waterproofing: When insulation is placed on the inside of a wall or roof, the structure and waterproofing are exposed to the full range of temperatures in the adjacent soil. In some cases near the surface, the structure and waterproofing will

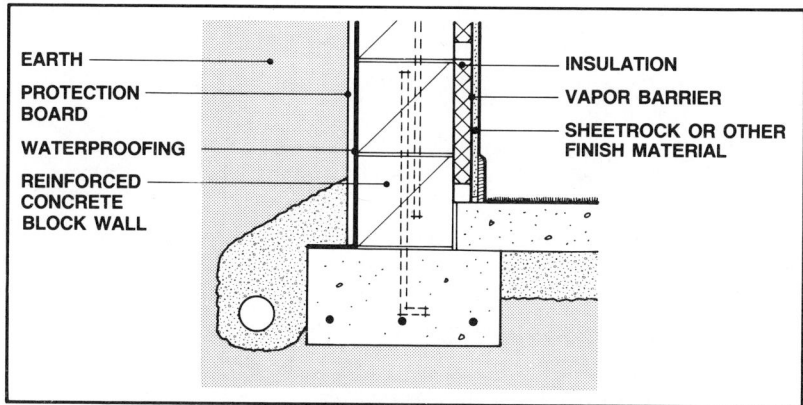

5-31: Insulation inside Structure and Waterproofing

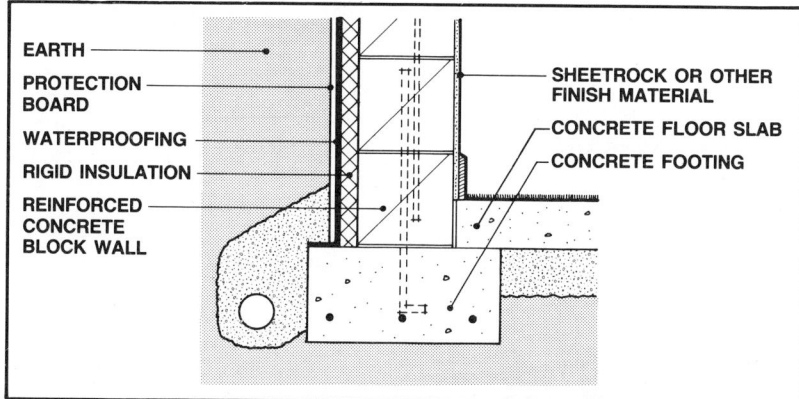

5-32: Insulation outside Structure and Inside Waterproofing

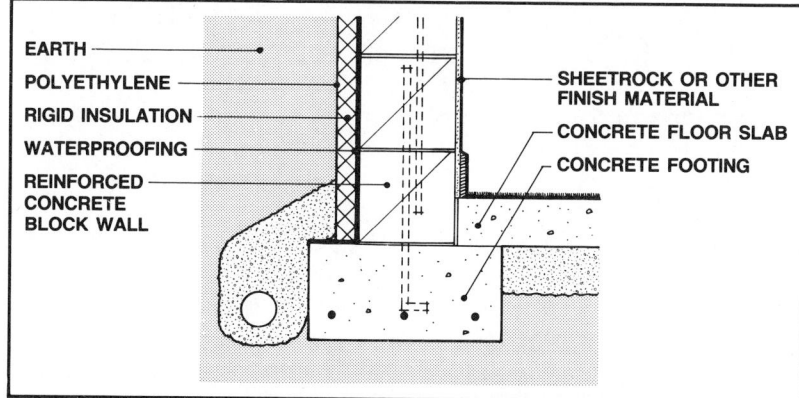

5-33: Insulation outside Structure and Waterproofing

be exposed to freeze/thaw cycles. Insulating outside the structure but inside the waterproofing protects the structure but not the waterproofing. Locating the insulation outside of both structure and waterproofing reduces the thermal stress on both components considerably.

Interior Space and Finish: When insulation is placed inside a concrete or masonry structural wall, additional framing and a covering of sheetrock or wood paneling is required. In effect, a second wall must be built and the available interior space is reduced by the thickness of the framing. This may be an acceptable sacrifice if a sheetrock or wood finish is desired in any case. If however, exposed concrete or masonry surfaces are acceptable, then outside insulation placement permits any thickness of insulation to be added with no additional framing or reduction in floor area. Exposed masonry can be made attractive with the use of burnished, rough or other decorative blocks. Plaster, paint, or both can also be directly applied to interior exposed concrete and masonry.

Insulation Placement Guidelines

Concrete and Masonry Structures: To reduce thermal stress on the structure and provide mass within the heated envelope, placement of insulation outside the wall or roof is recommended. It should be noted that this approach may be more expensive than interior placement (primarily because of the quality of insulation required), and interior placement is an acceptable alternative where it does not interfere significantly with energy performance.

Wood Structures: Since typical wood-frame walls and roofs have relatively little mass and contain cavities for insulation placement, there is little justification for placing insulation outside the wall. In contrast, placing insulation outside of a plank-and-beam timber roof structure may be the best alternative for aesthetic reasons.

Relationship to Waterproofing: When insulation is placed outside the wall, it should also be placed outside the waterproofing. Although waterproofing could be used to protect the insulation from moisture, there are disadvantages to this approach. Waterproofing membranes or coatings should be applied directly to the stable substrate of the structure, not to a softer layer of insulation subject to movement. Moreover, if a leak occurs, it can travel in the insulation layer and emerge elsewhere in the structure, making the source of the leak difficult to locate.

Drainage and Protection: Even if an insulation material can be exposed to soil and moisture, no product will perform at its best when totally saturated. When insulation is placed outside the structure and waterproofing, it should be covered by a layer of 6- to 10-mil polyethylene. The polyethylene should be open on the ends to prevent water from being trapped in the insulating layer. The structure and drainage system should be designed so that no ponding occurs on or around the insulation, where it can absorb moisture.

Product Selection Criteria

Outside Placement Criteria: The following characteristics of insulation materials are desirable for placement outside the structure.

- High compression strength to resist earth loads (at least 20 psi).
- High resistance to water and very low water absorption so that the R-value is not significantly reduced in wet conditions and insulation is not damaged by freeze/thaw cycles.
- High resistance to chemical properties of soils.
- Good dimensional and R-value stability over a long period of time.
- Tongue and groove configuration to reduce cold spots and water movement between the insulation sheets.
- Relatively low cost, readily available, and easily installed.

Inside Placement Criteria: The following characteristics of insulation materials are desirable for placement inside the structure.

- High resistance to fire and no production of poisonous fumes during fire.
- Good dimensional and R-value stability over a long period of time. Retaining R-value in moist conditions may require a vapor barrier.
- High R-value per inch of thickness to minimize interior space loss.
- Relatively low cost, readily available. and easily installed.

Product Comparison and Recommendations

Figure 5-34 shows the basic characteristics for the major types of insulation considered for below-grade use. Evaluating products based on initial R-value per inch is not considered an adequate comparison for outside placement because the R-value can change as the product ages and is exposed to moisture. Thus, the table shows initial R-value (which applies to inside placement) and R-value with time (which applies to outside placement). R-value with time can only be determined by product testing, which has not been carried out for all the available insulation products. Where data is available, R-value with time is expressed as a range, as individual test results differ

Insulation Material	Density (pcf)	Initial R-value per inch	Probable R-value per inch with time[1]	Cost per board ft. ($)	Initial R-value per $	R-value per $ with time	Recommendation for interior placement below grade	Recommendation for exterior placement exposed to soil
Low-Density Expanded Polystyrene	1.0	3.8	2.8-3.0	.12	31.7	23.3-25.0	Yes, with vapor barrier and fire resistant coating.	Only recommended on vertical walls in dryer, well-drained areas. Higher densities should be used for deeper applications to withstand higher soil pressures.
High-Density Expanded Polystyrene	1.6	4.5	No data	.23	19.6	—	Yes, with vapor barrier and fire resistant coating.	
Extruded Polystyrene	1.7-2.7	5.0-6.5	4.5-4.9	.27	18.5-24.1	16.7-18.1	Yes, with fire resistant coating.	Yes, has shown good resistance to water absorption and freeze/thaw damage.
Urethane Foam	2.0	6.2-7.2	3.0-5.2	.35[2]	17.7-20.6	8.6-14.9	Yes, with vapor barrier and fire resistant coating.	Not recommended based on moisture gain in laboratory and field tests.
Fiberglass Boards	3.2-4.5	4.5	No data	.20-.35	12.9-22.5	—	Yes, with vapor barrier and fire resistant coating.	Yes, has dual function as drainage area. Use in areas not subject to saturation.
Fiberglass Batts	—	3.2	—	.05	64.0	—	Yes, with vapor barrier and fire resistant coating.	Not applicable

5-34: Characteristics of Various Insulation Materials

1. Probable R-value per inch with time refers to situation where insulation is under adverse moisture conditions as it would be if exposed below grade. Figures in the chart for R-value per inch with time are based on testing of previously buried samples [Dechow and Epstein, 1977], controlled laboratory testing under a vapor pressure differential across the sample [Tobiasson and Ricard, 1979; Tye and Baker, 1983], and recent test data from an underground building installation [Severson, 1981].

2. Cost of urethane foam varies with R-value and type of facing.

according to the conditions of exposure.

Approximate costs are also shown in figure 5-34 for each of the insulating materials. Since cost must be evaluated in relation to the insulating value of the material, R-value per dollar can be calculated for direct comparison purposes. In figure 5-34, two R-value per dollar calculations are shown: one based on the initial R-value that applies to inside placement and the other based on R-value with time that applies to outside placement. Cost comparisons between different products and between inside and outside placement should not be based on the cost of insulation alone. Additional materials and labor related to the insulation approach must also be included. For example, fiberglass insulation installed on the inside of a masonry wall requires framing, vapor barriers, a gypsum board or wood-finished surface, and protection board over the waterproofing on the outside. Exterior insulation acts as protection board and may require none of the additional items listed above depending on the interior finishes desired. Exterior drainage/insulation layers may also offset the need for a high quality waterproofing on vertical building surfaces. Costs may also be examined in the context of the effects of a massive wall on energy use and comfort, although this is difficult to calculate (see chapter 3).

In the final two columns of figure 5-34, recommendations are given for each material used under two conditions: placement inside the structural wall and waterproofing as well as placement outside, exposed to the soil. It is clear that for inside placement, any materials are suitable if used properly. Fiberglass and low-density expanded polystyrene should be covered with a vapor barrier on the inside. Polyurethane, polystyrene, and fiberglass which can release toxic fumes when burned, must be covered with a fire-resistant material (building codes usually specify a minimum of ½-inch gypsum board).

The most reliable product for placement outside the structure and waterproofing is extruded polystyrene. Expanded polystyrene is also suitable under well drained, dryer soil conditions. Draining insulation materials such as rigid fiberglass panels or some types of expanded polystyrene board have a dual function of assisting drainage in addition to providing insulation below grade. Polyurethane and polyisocyanurate insulations are considered unsuitable when exposed because of their tendency to absorb moisture and deteriorate.

There are numerous products with widely varying characteristics that are referred to as "polystyrene." Standard classifications for polystyrene materials are shown in figure 5-35. Types I and II are the low-density materials which should be evaluated carefully for exposure to the ground because of a low compressive strength and lower resistance to water absorption. Type III is a high-density expanded polystyrene material with adequate compressive strength. Although expanded materials absorb some degree of moisture, they regain their R-value if permitted to dry. Generally, expanded polystyrene products are recommended for vertical rather than horizontal placement in well-drained, dryer areas. Type IV is extruded polystyrene typically recommended for outside placement because of its low degree of water absorption. Type V is an extruded material with very high density and compressive strength. These characteristics are unnecessary for typical below-grade construction.

Classification	Minimum Density (lbs/cu. ft.)	Minimum Thermal Resistance (R-value/inch)	Minimum Compression Strength (psi)	Minimum Flexural Strength (psi)	Maximum Water Vapor Transmission (perm-inch)	Maximum Water Absorption (% volume)
Type I	0.9	3.6	10.0	25.0	5.0	4.0
Type II	1.3	4.0	15.0	40.0	3.5	3.0
Type III	1.6	4.4	20.0	55.0	1.5	2.0
Type IV	1.6	5.0	20.0	60.0	1.1	0.3
Type V	3.0	5.0	100.0	100.0	1.1	0.3

5-35: Classification of Polystyrene Insulation Board

Notes: Information in this table is based on Federal Specification HH-1-524C.
Thermal resistance is based on 1-inch board thickness at a temperature of 75° F.

Underground dwellings on the Isle of Santorini, Greece.
Drawing by Mark Heisterkamp.

Chapter 6

Public Policy Issues

Introduction

Few houses today are built in remote areas where individual buildings will have little or no effect on the surrounding land. As houses and buildings have been built closer together while larger and larger cities are formed, many problems have arisen from unrestricted building design. These concerns have included, for example, sanitation conditions, percolation of sewage into drinking water supplies, the drastic changing of surface water runoff conditions, the danger of fire spreading from one building to those nearby and the property value impact of a tumbledown shack erected amongst more elaborate houses. Out of these problems and the need for more regulations have grown the present building codes, property laws, and zoning ordinances.

The building codes, discussed in the first section of this chapter, regulate the standards of design and construction for individual buildings, including standards for mechanical, electrical, and plumbing work as well as the building structure itself. These codes carry the force of law where they have been adopted by states or local communities. A closely allied set of building standards has been the Department of Housing and Urban Development (H.U.D.) Minimum Property Standards. These have not carried the force of law but have been the basis of acceptance for government underwritten loans on housing. At the time of writing, however, these standards are planned to be phased out at the end of 1984, with appropriate national or local building codes used in their place. The Occupational Safety and Health Administration (O.S.H.A.) also has regulations that can affect housing construction. They are concerned with the safety of the workmen during construction and do have the force of law.

Legal problems with housing pertain mostly to problems of liability to surrounding properties resulting from house construction. The legal aspects overlap into both the code and zoning areas since code or zoning laws may legislate some parts of the construction procedure to help avoid legal problems. Legal aspects of particular note for earth sheltered housing include solar rights, the effect of excavation on adjacent buildings, and the disturbance of surface water flow patterns by changes in ground surface elevations.

Zoning ordinances, discussed in the second section of the chapter, control the type, size, and setting of buildings within an area to preserve a desired neighborhood character. They can vary greatly from one locality to another, as opposed to code provisions, which are very similar even in different parts of the country.

Financial aspects include the taxation, insurance, and home-financing aspects of constructing an earth sheltered home. Tax structures have little implication for earth sheltered housing except in calculation of house size and building valuation for property taxes. The existence of thick structural walls means the net living area is smaller in relation to the gross house size (commonly used for taxation purposes) than for conventional housing. A similar concern is over how the absence of conventional basement space used for storage and services in northern climates is adjusted for in valuation. Responses to these issues in tax structures are developed locally, and they are not examined further in this chapter. Insurance and home financing are important issues for earth sheltered housing and are discussed in the last sections of the chapter.

Building Codes

Building codes provide minimum standards for life safety, health, public welfare, and the protection of property by regulating and controlling design, construction, use and quality of materials, occupancy, location, and maintenance of all buildings. A building code becomes law once it is adopted by a local community or state legislature. Several model building codes are prepared for adoption into law. The major ones are the Uniform Building Code (UBC), the Basic Building Code (BBC), the National Building Code (NBC) and the Standard Building Code (SBC). The provisions regarding housing from all of these codes have been combined into a document called the One and Two Family Dwelling Code (FDC). Although these various codes generally apply to specific regions of the country, it is virtually impossible to indicate exactly where each applies since every state or local community may choose among and amend the model codes as it sees fit. Some areas, particularly small towns and rural areas, have no code at all. Since it would be impossible to research all the local code variations, this section deals with constraints found in the major model building codes. Individual communities will have to determine the extent to which these issues apply to their particular code.

Many earth sheltered homes have been built to meet the requirements of the various codes. Most code requirements are compatible with the concept of earth sheltering, although the codes are oriented toward more conventional construction. Several areas in the codes deserve special consideration by those designing or evaluating earth shltered homes because they are major determinants of form and they deal with standards that may present problems for designers who wish to use an unfamiliar or unusual construction technique. The chief areas of concern are fire safety and egress, the effects of grade changes on safety, and provision of natural light and ventilation. A more detailed treatment of code issues appears in *Earth Sheltered Housing: Code, Zoning, and Financing Issues* [Sterling, et al., 1981].

Building code requirements for structural integrity, waterproofing, and energy use are aimed more at conventional construction and usually do not specifically address issues related to earth sheltered construction. Generally, the physical requirements of earth sheltered construction are as rigorous as the code requirements for conventional housing, if not more so; hence, if the functional requirements have been met, the legal requirements very probably have automatically been met or exceeded.

Prescriptive and Performance Standards

One aspect of building codes that is important to clarify is the difference between prescriptive and performance types of standards. The simplest code standards are the prescriptive or "deemed-to-satisfy" provisions. These are specific requirements that, if met, will automatically mean the building will perform safely and properly. An example of a prescriptive standard would be the requirement of a certain maximum area of windows and minimum thickness of insulation in all walls and roofs. This automatically will meet the general goal of providing a well insulated house. Most of the code provisions that represent potential constraints for earth sheltered housing are prescriptive ones that indicate a specific way of achieving fire egress, light, and ventilation in a residence.

A performance standard, on the other hand, states a more general goal that must be met without specifying exact methods for achieving it. In the example of providing a well-insulated house, a performance standard might indicate an acceptable overall maximum heat loss without mentioning specific insulation thicknesses or window areas. Obviously, both types of standards have their advantages and disadvantages. Prescriptive standards are simpler and easier to enforce but can inhibit innovation. Performance standards allow more freedom for design innovation but are more open to interpretation by code officials. Personal attitudes and judgments can be a factor, since the ultimate decision is based more on the building inspector's interpretation and discretion. With performance standards, the burden of proof lies more with the builder or owner, which may cause additional time, money, and hardship.

Presently codes use both prescriptive and performance standards, although prescriptive standards seem to be more prevalent. In general, performance standards are considered more favorable to earth sheltered housing than prescriptive ones. Some architects and builders are wary of general performance standards, however, since they are subject to too much latitude and may result in structural failures.

Alternate Materials and Methods

In examining the various code documents with respect to constraints on earth sheltered housing, it is clear that no major revisions are required—but merely the allowance for additional alternatives. It is important to recognize that all of the codes provide for variations from the basic codes in a section called "Alternate Materials and Methods of Construction." The specific provision from the UBC 1982 edition is quoted below:

UBC (1982)
Sec. 105

The provisions of this code are not intended to prevent the use of any material or method of construction not specifically prescribed by this code, provided any alternate has been approved and its use authorized by the building official.

The building official may approve any such alternate, provided he finds that the proposed design is satisfactory and complied with the provisions of this code and that the material, method or work offered is, for the purpose intended, at least the equivalent of that prescribed in this code in suitability, strength, effectiveness, fire resistance, durability, safety and sanitation.

The building official shall require that sufficient evidence or proof be submitted to substantiate any claims that may be made regarding its use. The details of any action granting approval of an alternate shall be recorded and entered in the files of the code enforcement agency.

All of the provisions found in the various model codes are quite similar. Some code officials have expressed the opinion that specific code changes for earth sheltered housing may not be necessary since the Alternate Methods and Materials section allows for variations. This is certainly true in many cases, and designers, builders, and owners should be aware of these provisions.

There are some problems, however, with relying on this provision to deal with all of the questionable code issues that may arise. First, this provision seems to be directed more toward the performance of specific materials and methods of construction. It seems to be best suited for questions such as the equivalent fire resistance properties of various materials or the safety of a structural design where there are fairly specific performance criteria. The issues of greatest concern for earth sheltered housing do not fall into these categories, however. That is, equivalent alternate methods of fire egress or natural light are not as easy to judge on a case-by-case basis. This puts the local code official in a difficult position, since some of these issues question fundamental standards in the code and may require the official to possess considerable information in order to make an informed decision. Thus, the Alternate Materials and Methods provision may result in varying standards of acceptability since equivalent performance is ultimately up to the discretion of the code official. In addition to the possible variance in interpretation, there is simply additional work and hardship placed on the owner or builder to prove his case.

Appeal Procedures

Another important provision of all of the model codes that can work in conjunction with the provision for Alternate Materials and Methods of Construction is the appeal process. A Board of Appeals is available for final decision on the suitability of alternate materials and methods of construction and for interpretations of the code. The structure and process varies slightly in each code. The exact provisions for each code are found in the following sections:

UBC (1982)	204
BBC	126
NBC	107
SBC	112/113
FDC (1983)	R-107

Usually the Board of Appeals represents an opportunity for acceptance of an alternative to the code when the local building official has denied the request. It is a useful mechanism when innovative, unconventional buildings are in question.

Fire Safety and Provision of Egress

One of the most fundamental goals in building codes is safety from fire and the provision of egress in case of fire. All of the codes approach this issue with a very similar prescriptive requirement for sleeping rooms in residences. The following is the provision in the 1983 One and Two Family Dwelling Code:

FDC (1983)
Sec. R-211
Every sleeping room shall have at least one operable window or exterior door approved for emergency egress or rescue. The units must be operable from the inside to a full clear opening without the use of separate tools. Where windows are provided as a means of egress or rescue they shall have a sill height of not more than 44 inches above the floor.
All egress or rescue windows from sleeping rooms must have a minimum net clear opening of 5.7 square feet. The minimum net clear opening height dimension shall be 24 inches. The minimum net clear opening width dimension shall be 20 inches.
Exception: Grade floor windows may have a minimum net clear opening of 5 square feet.

These requirements are the same in all of the codes with some important exceptions. In addition to the same window provision, the NBC allows for two doors providing separate paths of escape as an alternative. The BBC does not offer specific

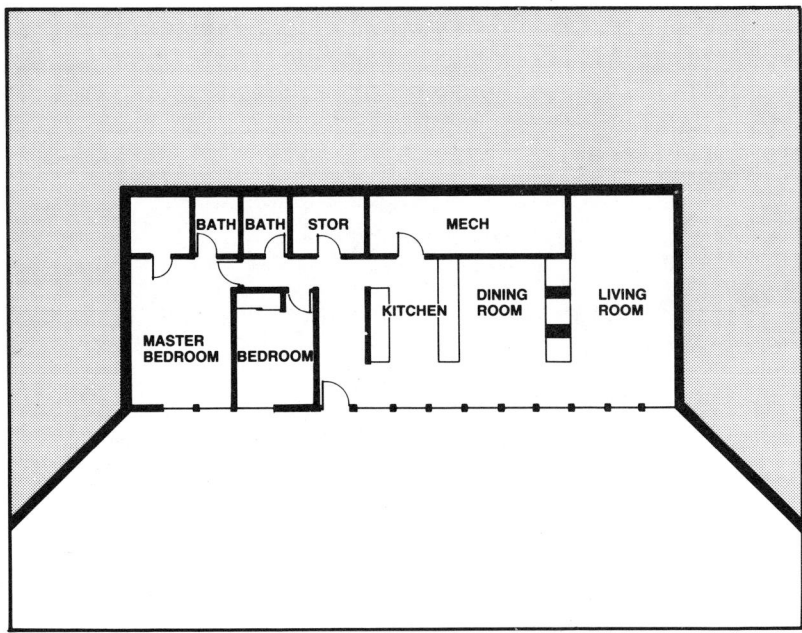

6-1: Floor Plan

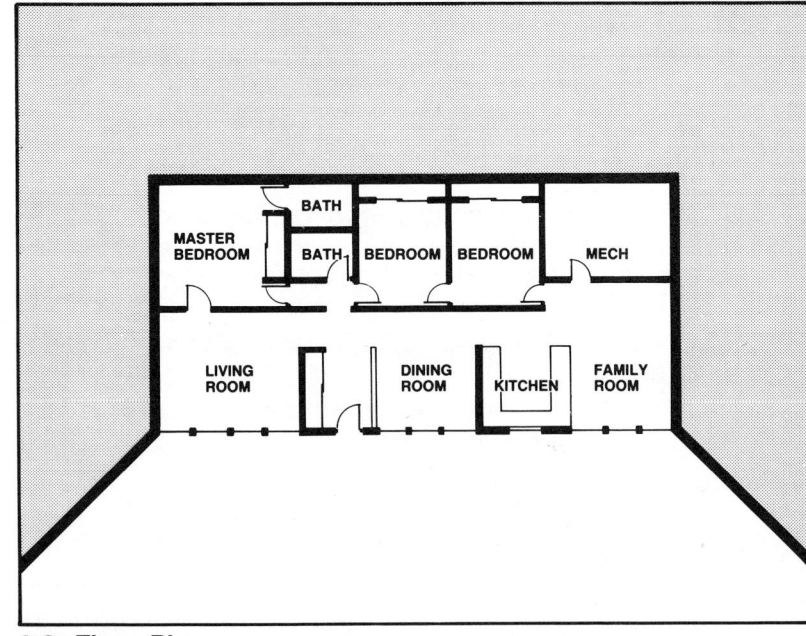

6-2: Floor Plan

alternatives but states in 600.2 that "when strict compliance with provisions of this code is not practical, the building official may accept alternate means of egress which will accomplish the same purpose." One final minor exception is that the NBC allows the egress window sill to be 48 inches off the floor instead of 44 inches.

Many earth sheltered house designs provide windows in all bedrooms that meet these egress requirements, figure 6-1 illustrates such a house. Others, however, do not meet the requirements. Usually a compact plan with window openings limited to one elevation of the house will result in greater energy efficiency and lower construction costs. To accomplish this, it is sometimes easier not to provide windows in every space. The bedrooms are strong candidates to be windowless spaces since they are often used only at night. Assuming that it is desirable to have the option of a windowless bedroom in house design, the important issue then becomes establishing adequate alternative methods of fire safety and egress.

The intent of the egress requirement is clear. If a fire should start in any part of the house other than the bedrooms, occupants should have a clear means of escape directly to the outside without going into a smoke- or fire-filled part of the house. Since the occupants may not be young and healthy, further restrictions are placed on the window size and height from the floor.

It is interesting to note that the provision of an operating window in all sleeping spaces applies to structures up to three stories high. In the case of windows above the first floor, the purpose is not direct egress but access to fresh air and a place to be visible for rescue. In sleeping rooms above the third story, as in hotels and apartment buildings, egress is provided by other means such as stairways, which are designed to be smokeproof enclosures. Obviously, there is a precedent for providing alternative methods for fire egress, even though for housing most of the codes are written in a prescriptive way that requires bedroom windows with no alternatives.

In examining the various alternatives to this code provision, one promising solution seems to be the substitution of a second means of escape in place of a window. There are several interpretations of such an alternative. The plan shown in figure 6-2 illustrates an unsatisfactory interpretation of the use of two separate means of escape from each bedroom. There are two doors from each room leading to different paths of escape, but neither path is smoke- or fire-separated from the other. Hence, a single fire could block both exits. A similarly unsatisfactory alternative would provide one door from the bedroom leading into a corridor with two paths of escape.

A more costly but safer alternative is the use of a separate corridor leading to a fire exit. This type of exit, illustrated for a similar house with windowless bedrooms in figure 6-3 should include fire rated doors from the bedrooms. This would hold the fire and smoke out of the corridor long enough to provide a safe exit. Another technique that is used in larger buildings is to ventilate the exit corridor positively so that smoke will not leak into it during escape. This type of corridor, with or without positive ventilation, definitely appears to be an adequate alternative based on similar acceptable schemes in hotels and apartments.

A variation of two paths of escape occurs in the use of glass-covered atriums and greenhouses in earth sheltered house designs. Windows that open into these types of spaces are technically not exterior windows. Figure 6-4 illustrates a home with both an atrium and a greenhouse. Note that bedroom #3 has no direct exterior access but does have two alternative escape routes, one through the house and another across the covered atrium to an exterior door. A greenhouse on the south side adjacent to bedroom #1 provides a second means

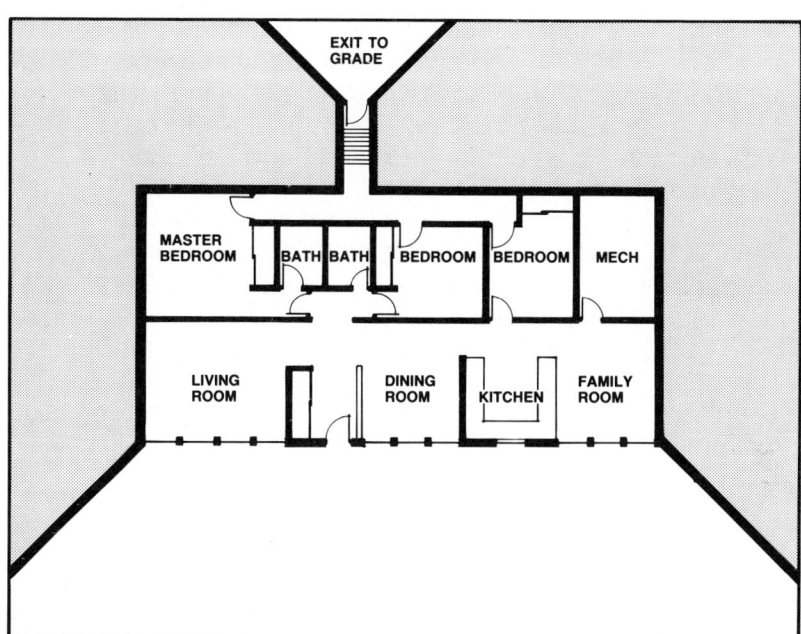

6-3: Floor Plan

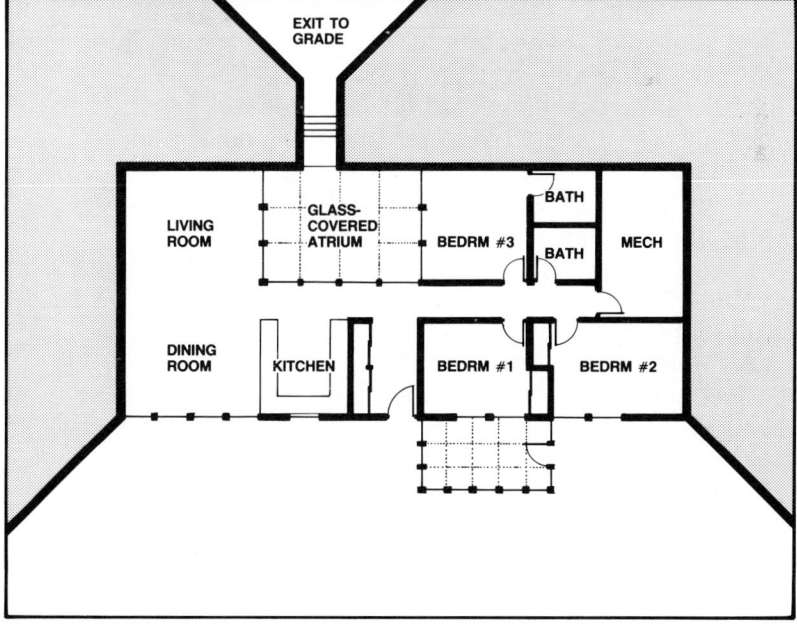

6-4: Floor Plan

of escape. Although these are varying interpretations, the concept of two separate paths of escape from bedrooms is in compliance with the NBC and HUD Minimum Property Standards, and appears to be a safe acceptable alternative to direct-egress windows provided fire and smoke separation standards between the separate paths of escape are met. Emergency escape routes are not permitted through garages or storerooms since the escape routes may become obstructed over time.

Two other solutions that have been suggested for fire safety in windowless bedrooms are the use of sprinkler systems and smoke detectors. A sprinkler system, as is used in commercial structures, could be a rather expensive addition to a single-family house. Although a certain degree of protection would be provided, sprinklers are mostly designed to protect buildings and their contents rather than people. Most present codes require smoke detectors in the bedroom area in addition to egress windows. It has been suggested that a smoke detector outside of each bedroom would provide adequate warning and protection especially in the case of a completely exposed concrete structure and lack of any combustible partitions and finishes. Nevertheless, furnishings alone provide substantial smoke and fumes to overcome occupants in case of fire, and smoke detectors are not considered a substitute for a proper escape route.

Another technique for escape from a windowless bedroom is the use of an operable skylight with a rung ladder cast into the wall below it (fig. 6-5). As with many of the other alternatives, a second means of escape is clearly provided. The main reservation expressed about this alternative is the inability of older, handicapped, or very young children to use such an escape effectively. Although an individual owner may not see this as a problem for his particular family, the code must consider that it is likely that any property will have a series of owners and therefore must assure the protection of the public in general.

A final code issue regarding egress from bedrooms is that of the maximum windowsill height of 44 inches from the floor. If a wall is substantially earth covered, it may be possible to provide a well to a window near the top of the wall, similar to a typical basement. It may be more costly and difficult, however, to provide a large, deep well to a window of the lower standard height. A similar condition might exist with a high clerestory window. The 44 inch (48 inch in some codes) height is required to ensure that most people would be able to climb out

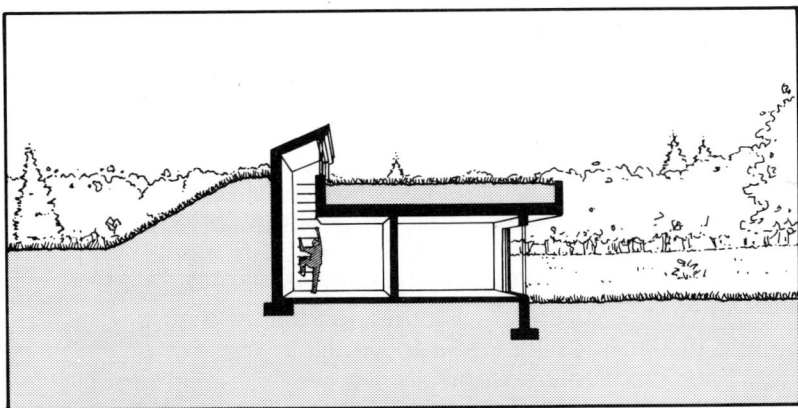

6-5: Ladder Provides Escape through Skylight

6-6: Permanent Steps Provide Access to High Window

of the window or at least be visible to rescuers. A reasonable alternative would seem to be the provision of a permanent chest/seat combination or a raised floor built adjacent to the wall under the window (fig. 6-6). Then the sill of the window could be raised to within 44 inch of the top of the seat or raised floor. Naturally, the same minimum dimensions of the window opening would apply.

A number of code officials, architects, builders, and others in the construction industry were contacted concerning these various alternatives [Sterling, et al., 1981]. Most were quite open to considering changes as long as the primary concern of equivalent safety was met. The general consensus was that two separate means of escape provided adequate and equivalent protection as compared with an egress window. This includes the use of atriums, greenhouses, and separate escape corridors as well as two indirect escape paths through the house. The use of a rung ladder and operable skylight was not acceptable to most because of the definite reservations about the difficulty of such an escape route for young children and old or handicapped people. Great reluctance was expressed over the use of smoke detectors alone to offset the loss of a window egress. Sprinker systems were an acceptable alternative to some, but very unlikely since they are so unnecessarily expensive for a house. Finally, the use of a permanent step up structure to allow for higher windowsill heights seems to be a very acceptable alternative.

It can be concluded from these reactions, as well as from research into the various codes, that reasonably safe egress can be achieved by certain alternatives other than bedroom windows. Although a flexible attitude toward alternatives was expressed, many professionals commented that whenever possible a bedroom egress window still seemed to be the most direct and best solution.

Natural Light and Ventilation

The requirements for natural light and ventilation in buildings are intended to ensure a pleasant and healthy environment. With housing in particular, most codes use a similar type of prescriptive window requirement to meet this goal. The following is the provision in the 1982 Uniform Building Code:

UBC (1982)
Sec. 1205

(a) Light and Ventilation. All guest rooms, dormitories and habitable rooms within a dwelling unit shall be provided with natural light by means of exterior glazed openings with an area not less than one tenth of the floor area of such rooms with a minimum of 10 square feet. All bathrooms, water closet compartments, laundry rooms and similar rooms shall be provided with natural ventilation by means of openable exterior openings with an area not less than one twentieth of the floor area of such rooms with a minimum of 1 square feet.

All guest rooms, dormitories and habitable rooms within a dwelling unit shall be provided with natural ventilation by means of openable exterior openings with an area of not less than one twentieth of the floor area of such rooms with a minimum of 5 square feet.

In lieu of required exterior openings for natural ventilation, a mechanical ventilating system may be provided. Such system shall be capable of providing two air changes per hour in all guest rooms, dormitories, habitable rooms and in public corridors. One fifth of the air supply shall be taken from the outside. In bathrooms, water closet compartments, laundry rooms and similar rooms a mechanical ventilation system connected directly to the outside, capable of providing five air changes per hour, shall be provided.

For the purpose of determining light and ventilation requirements, any room may be considered as a portion of an adjoining room when one half of the area of the common wall is open and unobstructed and provides an opening of not less than one tenth of the floor area of the interior room or 25 square feet, whichever is greater.

Required exterior openings for natural light and ventilation shall open directly onto a street or public alley or a yard or court located on the same lot as the building.

Exception: Required windows may open into a roofed porch where the porch:
1. *Abuts a street, yard or court; and*
2. *Has a ceiling height of not less than 7 feet; and*
3. *Has the longer side at least 65 percent open and unobstructed.*

Note: According to Sec. 409 habitable space (room) is defined as space in a structure for living, sleeping, eating or cooking. Bathrooms, toilet compartments, closets, halls, storage or utility space, and similar areas, are not considered habitable space.

The 1979 One and Two Family Dwelling Code introduced a major change by allowing the substitution of artificial lighting for natural lighting in habitable rooms. This change in the code means that the FDC no longer represents a consensus among the four major national codes.

FDC (1983)
Sec. R-204.1

All habitable rooms shall be provided with aggregate glazing area of not less than eight (8) percent of the floor area of such rooms. One-half (½) of the required area of glazing shall be openable.

Exceptions:
1. *The glazed areas need not be openable where an approved mechanical ventilation system is provided capable of producing a change of air every thirty (30) minutes and the opening is not required by Section R-211.*
2. *The glazed areas may be omitted in rooms where an approved mechanical ventilation system is provided capable of producing a change of air every thirty (30) minutes, artificial light is provided capable of producing an average illumination of six (6) foot candles over the area of the room at a height of thirty (30) inches above the floor level, and the opening is not required by Section R-211.*

All of the other codes are substantially the same in that they require at least one window in all habitable spaces, although there are minor differences in the exact size. The UBC, NBC, and SBC require the same window area equal to 10 percent of the floor area, with half of it operable. The BBC and the FDC allow a smaller area—8 percent, with half of it operable. It has been proposed [Sterling, et al., 1981] that an acceptable resolution between code requirements and design flexibility may be achieved by allowing natural light requirements for habitable rooms to be treated on an aggregate basis; that is, the total window area for all habitable rooms must exceed 8 percent of the total floor area of the habitable rooms. Individual habitable rooms could be windowless provided they met ventilation and exit requirements.

The requirement of an operable window for ventilation does not seem to present a major problem for earth sheltered housing. All of the codes except for the NBC allow mechanical ventilation as an option. If a forced-air heating or cooling system is used, this requirement represents no additional cost. Mechanical ventilation to provide an acceptable air exchange rate in tight houses is considered mandatory because of the problems of winter indoor air quality even when operable windows are present.

Several alternatives exist for providing natural light to spaces without conventional windows. Skylights are one of the most common means (fig. 6-7). Glazing on an interior wall, permitting a windowless room to "borrow" light from a room with windows, can be effective but does not technically meet the code requirement in some cases (fig. 6-8). Another code conflict in the provision of natural light may result because some earth sheltered designs include rooms with windows opening into a glass-covered atrium or greenhouse. Figure 6-9 illustrates a house that uses a glass-covered atrium in this way. Technically this would not meet the natural light requirement of a window opening directly to the outside. The quality and amount of natural light is certainly adequate, however. There is already a code exception for windows opening onto a roofed porch, which, in fact, would provide less light. It seems that amending this to include greenhouses and glass-covered atriums would be reasonable.

Prohibition of Below-Grade Space

The complete prohibition of below grade space as habitable for housing is not a common constraint in the model codes. It is, however, clearly mentioned in the National Building Code. The exact provision is quoted below.

> NBC
> Sec. 601.4a
> *Habitable rooms for residential occupancies shall have not less than 50% of their story height above grade.*

This particular requirement would directly prohibit earth sheltered housing. The intent of such a

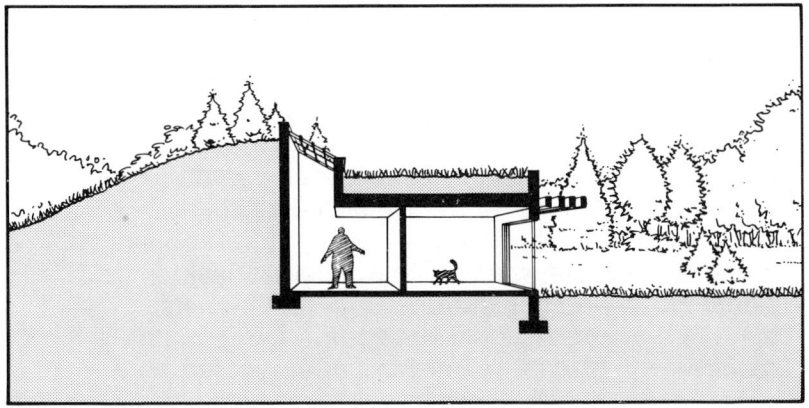
6-7: Skylight Provides Light to Interior Spaces

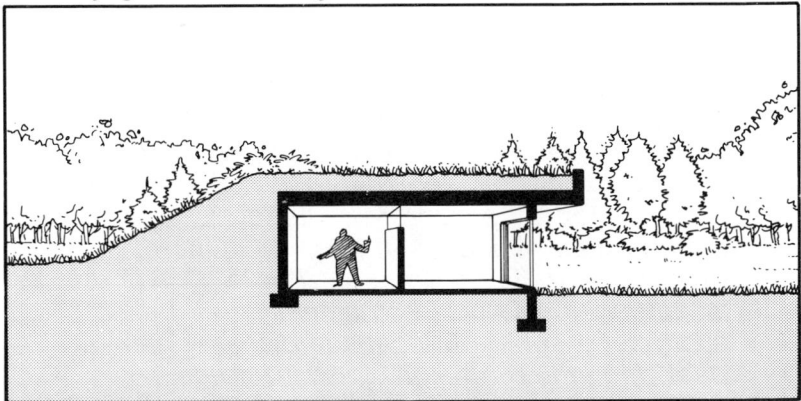
6-8: Clerestory Window between Rooms Provides Light

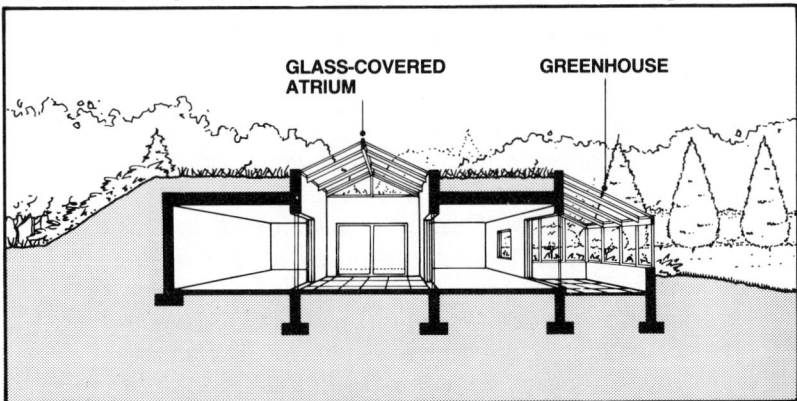
6-9: Light Provided through Atrium and Greenhouse Spaces

provision is, obviously, to prevent substandard habitable space. It has been demonstrated, however, that well-designed earth sheltered space that may be fully below grade is an acceptable living alternative, provided it meets various other code requirements for fire safety, ventilation, and lighting. This conflict could be resolved by the elimination of any code provisions that use the amount of earth cover as a criterion for defining habitable space.

Grade Changes

The use of guardrails at the edges of earth covered roofs and on retaining walls is an important issue in designing an earth sheltered house. There are really three related issues that need clarification. The first is the determination of whether or not earth-covered houses with retaining walls actually represent an unsafe condition and thus, require some protective measures. Second, the actual code provisions for guardrails must be analyzed to determine how they affect earth-covered housing. Finally, assuming that some protection is required in some cases, it is necessary to explore various alternatives to guardrails.

Typically, earth sheltered houses have a vertical drop of 10 feet or more from the edge of the roof to the ground. Often 4- to 10-foot-high retaining walls are adjacent to the structure. The earth-covered roof is usually accessible from the surrounding grade. Although these characteristics seem to represent an unsafe condition, most earth sheltered houses built so far do not provide protective guardrails. One reason for this is that the earth-covered roofs, although available for use, often are not actively used as outdoor space by the owners. The plant-covered roof is regarded more as an aesthetic element, and a guardrail would not be a pleasing addition. Another reason for so little protection from falling off of a roof is that most earth-covered houses are located in rural areas where there is little chance of someone inadvertently wandering onto the property and accidentially falling. Although it is obvious that an unsafe condition may exist in some cases, there are differing opinions as to what the code actually requires and what alternative solutions would be acceptable.

In examining the various codes, there appears to be no actual disagreement but simply a lack of clarity as to whether the guardrail requirements apply. Of all the national codes, the UBC guardrail requirement is most extensive and is quoted here:

UBC (1982)
Sec. 1711

All unenclosed floor and roof openings, open and glazed sides of landings and ramps, balconies or porches which are more than 30 inches above grade or floor below and roofs used for other than service of the building shall be protected by a guardrail. Guardrails shall be not less than 42 inches in height. Open guardrail and stair railings shall have intermediate rails or an ornamental stair pattern such that a sphere 6 inches in diameter cannot pass through. The height of stair railings on open sides may be as specified in Section 3306 (j) in lieu of providing a guardrail. Ramps shall, in addition, have handrails when required by Section 3307.

Exceptions:
1. *Guardrails need not be provided on the loading side of loading docks.*
2. *Guardrails for Group R, Division 3 and Group M, Division 1 Occupancies may be 36 inches in height.*
3. *Interior guardrails within individual dwelling units or guest rooms of Group R, Division 1 Occupancies may be 36 inches in height.*
4. *The open space between the intermediate*

rails or ornamental pattern of guardrails in areas of commercial and industrial-type occupancies which are not accessible to the public may be increased such that a 12-inch-diameter sphere cannot pass through.
5. *Guardrails on a balcony immediately in front of the first row of fixed seats and which are not at the end of an aisle may be 26 inches in height.*
6. *Guardrails need not be provided on the auditorium side of a stage or enclosed platform.*

The concern over handrail provisions for earth sheltered houses is focused mainly on the edge of an earth-covered roof and other places where large vertical drops occur, such as retaining walls. Most of the model codes do not directly address earth-covered roofs and retaining walls in their specific guardrail requirements. Only the UBC and the HUD Minimum Property Standards directly refer to the necessity of guardrails on roofs or roof decks. The FDC requires guardrails for raised floor surfaces, which could be interpreted as an earth-covered roof. The BBC, SBC, and NBC refer directly only to ramps, stairs, and balconies in their guardrail requirements. There are differing minimum standards for the height of the rails as well. Similar to the UBC, the SBC, FDC and BBC allow 36 inch rails for housing, while the NBC standards require 42 inch.

Although most of the national codes have no specific provisions for guardrails on top of retaining walls, the BBC standards deal with this directly. The exact provisions are quoted below:

BBC
Sec. 870.5
Guardrails: Retaining walls with a difference in grade level on each side of the wall in excess of four (4) feet shall be provided with a

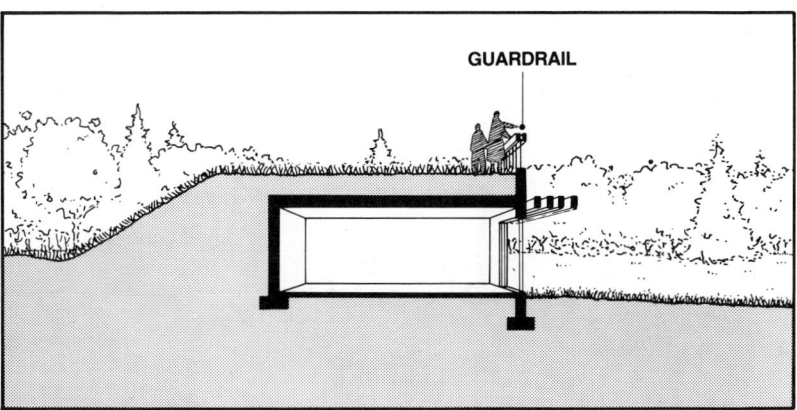
6-10: Guardrail at Roof Edge

forty-two (42) inch high guard rail or other approved protective measure.

It is interesting to note that both provisions allow alternatives to guardrails, referred to as "other approved protective measures" in BBC.

The adjacent illustration shows a typical guardrail at the roof edge (fig. 6-10). In cases where access is required or permitted to the roof, two variations can be used to create a less visible appearance than a conventional guardrail at the edge. A shorter rail of at least 18 inches could be placed 4 to 6 feet back from the edge. This would still block small children and cause any adults to stay back from the edge. A second possibility is to rely on a horizontal projection that is slightly below the roof plane catch anyone falling over the edge. An example would be the overhang shown in figure 6-11. This approach requires adequate size and structural strength for the horizontal projection. The necessity for and design of a protective measure at the edge of an accessible roof depends on the height of the vertical drop, the slope of the roof, and the proximity to adjacent property. Detailed requirements for these alternatives

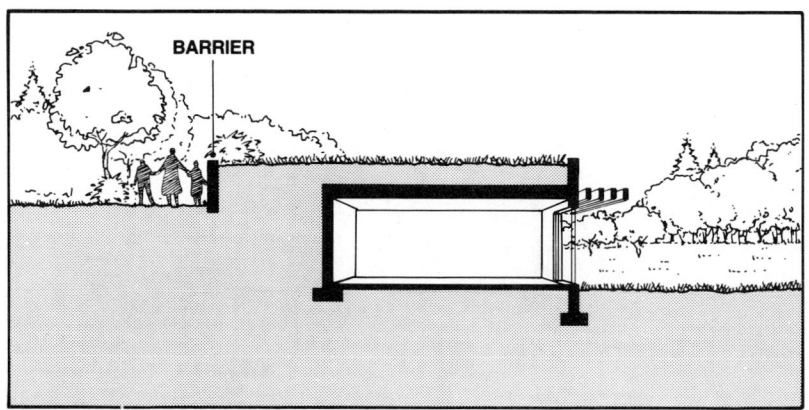

6-11: Barrier Away from Roof Edge

have been suggested in *Earth Sheltered Housing: Code, Zoning and Financing Issues* [Sterling, et al., 1981].

In cases where no access to the roof is required, an alternative solution to a guardrail at the edge of the roof is a guardrail or barrier away from the edge. An example of this in which a retaining wall provides a barrier around the structure is shown in figure 6-11. This certainly appears to be a safe solution that allows some design flexibility.

Another alternative solution that has been suggested is the use of a thick hedge as a barrier in place of a guardrail. The hedge could be located at the roof edge or away from it, thus preventing access. For such a hedge to be a truly equivalent barrier, a certain size and thickness of foliage would be required. It is questionable whether such an alternative could really be enforced and, more important, whether children would be adequately deterred.

Zoning

The general goals of zoning ordinances, like those of building codes, are to protect the health, safety, and general welfare of the community. With respect to housing, this usually means the separation of housing from more offensive industrial and commercial uses in order to preserve a quiet, healthful living environment. It also means organizing the population so that public services such as transportation, policing, fire protection, water and power supply, and waste removal can be most efficiently rendered. This is achieved through specific regulations concerning the size, height, bulk, location, and use of buildings.

Zoning ordinances are locally adopted and administered. Unlike building codes, however, there are no model national documents that communities can adopt intact to meet their needs. As a result, zoning regulations vary considerably from community to community. The most drastic differences can be found in comparing zoning for urban, suburban, and rural communities. Each community must, in effect, determine its own definition of desirable community standards. Zoning ordinances do, however, have a number of general similarities since they are all attempting to accomplish similar things.

When existing ordinances are applied to innovative housing types such as earth sheltered structures, certain conflicts and obstacles may arise. Since ordinances are tailored to regulate existing conventional housing, they may inadvertently regulate against or at least make more difficult the construction of earth sheltered houses [Swenson, 1979; Labs, 1979]. This is ironic in that many earth sheltered homes achieve some of the goals of zoning ordinances better than conventional houses can. These goals include noise reduction in residential areas as well as providing a beautiful, natural environment with maximum open space. At the root of this problem is the fact that these generally good goals are often carried out through restrictive regulations that prevent much experimentation. Clear prescriptive standards are far easier to administer than general performance standards.

Even though local zoning is not directly affected by national policy or national institutions such as the building code groups, it is useful to identify the most common zoning issues that represent constraints for earth sheltered housing. It should be noted, however, that restrictive covenants imposed on the buyer of a property by the developer as part of the deed title to the land can be far more restrictive than zoning ordinances and are usually less amenable to change. The potential earth sheltered home builder should research any covenants applying to the land before purchasing.

Local ordinances can be amended or otherwise restricted at a statewide level. This has been done in Minnesota to remove constraints to earth sheltered development. The actual legislation amends the authority for zoning provision so that no local ordinance may prohibit earth sheltered construction (Sec. 42, Minnesota Statutes 1978, section 462.357). The state of Minnesota has also prepared a guide for Minnesota communities on zoning for earth sheltered buildings that includes model language for planning goals, building type definitions, and zoning ordinances [Minnesota Department of Energy and Economic Development, 1983]. Potential constraints to earth sheltered houses typically found in zoning ordinances are discussed below.

Prohibition of Underground Spaces

Some communities have ordinances that prohibit living in basement or below-grade space. The definitions of basement and cellar in these ordinances vary. Nevertheless, they can be considered to prohibit earth sheltered housing and thus represent a serious constraint. Many of these so-called basement ordinances stem from two basic concerns. One is the obvious assumption that basement living is substandard, unhealthful living that is contrary to the intent of the local codes and zoning. Another reason for some of these basement ordinances is that they were originally intended to prevent the practice of constructing a basement and then living in it until the family could complete the upper portion of the house. This condition was prevalent after World War II, when there were problems with financing and material shortages. Certain communities acted to prevent half-built houses from remaining for years without being completed. The community's concern was to prevent unsightly as well as substandard housing, which might have lowered surrounding property values.

Well-designed earth sheltered houses do not represent a substandard or unhealthful environment. In addition, they can blend into the natural environment in an aesthetically pleasing manner. These characteristics should not lower surrounding property values. The problem with these ordinances stems from an old definition of "basement space" being inappropriately applied to a suitable, efficient new alternative in housing. Obviously, applying these regulations to prohibit earth sheltered housing violates their intent and does not serve the general welfare of the community. Two approaches could be taken in revising such ordinances. The first would be to define earth sheltered space differently than basement space and allow earth sheltered space to be an acceptable building alternative. The second approach would be to eliminate the basement ordinance and redefine habitable space based on criteria other than the average level of the surrounding grade.

Maximum Lot Coverage

Many community zoning ordinances prescribe the maximum percentage of a residential lot area that may be occupied by buildings. One intention of such ordinances is to provide a certain amount of yard or open space around buildings. This is both for the use of the residents and the general appearance of the neighborhood. Also, these ordinances serve to limit the amount of hard surface area that can create water runoff problems that overload storm sewers and are ecologically undesirable. Maximum lot coverage ordinances can be a definite constraint to earth sheltered housing if the total area occupied by the building, whether above or below grade, is included in the calculations. This occurs not because earth sheltered houses are larger than typical houses, but because they often are all on one level in order to blend into the natural contours of the land. With all spaces on one level, the maximum lot coverage may be exceeded in many cases.

An earth-covered house can be designed to satisfy the concerns of water runoff and open space expressed in these ordinances. A roof with 12 inches or more of earth, plant cover, and proper drainage can absorb rainwater effectively. The rainwater will be absorbed to the saturation point of the soil, which varies according to soil type, previous saturation level, and intensity of rainfall. Drain tiles at the perimeter of the house can handle any excessive runoff. Thus, the roof should not be considered as hard surface area in maximum lot coverage calculations. Earth covered roofs can provide usable as well as visual open space. This is done most effectively with flat roofs that are close to the level of the surrounding landscape. It must be

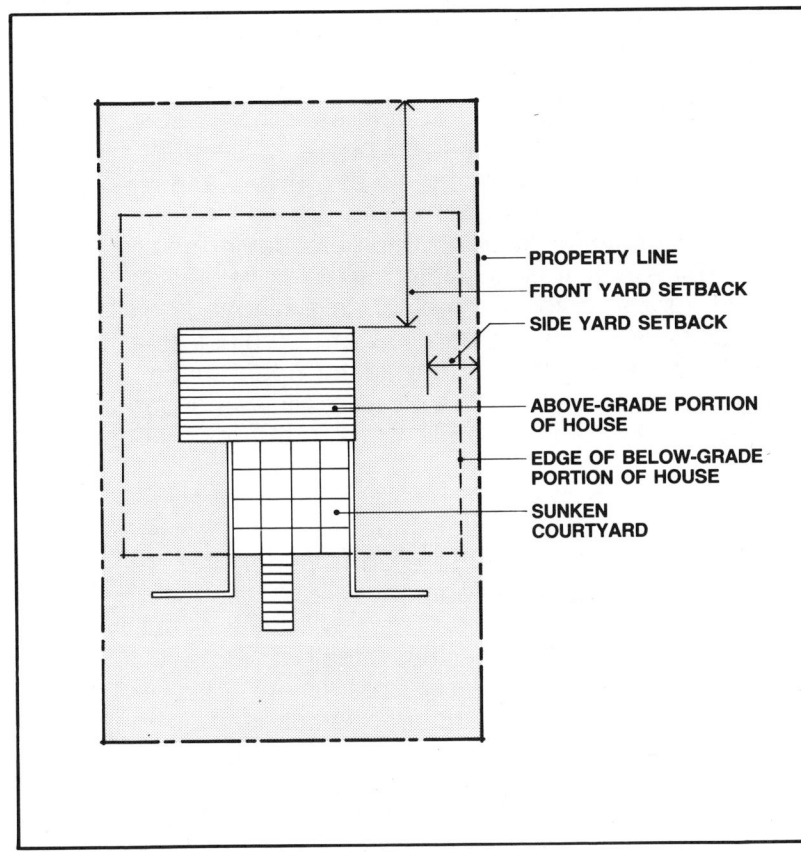

6-12: Site Plan of Atrium Design

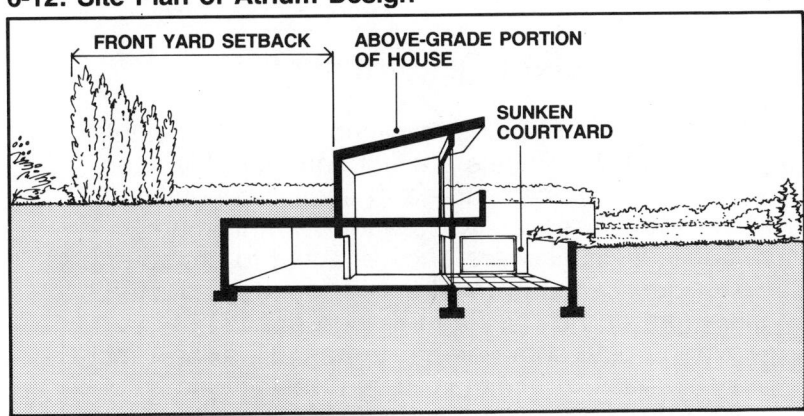

6-13: Section of Atrium Design

noted that not all earth sheltered designs will result in usable open space on the roof because of a sloping roof deck or general inaccessibility. Nevertheless, a certain natural character will be preserved. It definitely appears that reexamination and clarification of ordinances is in order so that completely below-grade, earth-covered space is not included in maximum lot coverage calculations.

Setbacks

Ordinances concerning minimum yard setbacks represent another potential obstacle to earth sheltered construction, particularly in urban and suburban areas with relatively small lot sizes. The problem arises because earth sheltered houses are often on one level and have a plan configuration that organizes the rooms into a long line or around an atrium. This results in long overall dimensions for the building that may infringe on the existing setback requirements. The adjacent drawings (figs. 6-12 and 6-13) illustrate an earth-covered house organized around an atrium in which the below-ground structure intrudes into the normal setback area. In order to examine the validity of changing setback requirements for earth sheltered houses, it is necessary to examine the purposes of such ordinances. Setback ordinances are intended:

- to maintain uniformity of appearance for neighborhood aesthetics
- to provide open space
- to provide access for fire department and utilities
- to provide proper light and ventilation to windows
- to allow room for maintenance between buildings
- to ensure stability of neighboring buildings, streets, and sidewalks during excavation

As shown in the illustration, the first purpose of maintaining a uniform appearance can be met by completely underground structures even if they do not meet the setback requirements. Similarly, the second and third concerns of providing open space and access for fire can also be met even though the setbacks are exceeded. Adequate space for utilities depends on many variables and would have to be examined for specific circumstances. It should be noted, however, that an earth-covered structure that is set only partly into the ground and is surrounded by earth berms does not have exactly the same characteristics as a completely below-grade structure. With respect to setback concerns, the berms do create a different physical form on the site, and steeply sloping berms do not clearly create open space and fire access. A possible solution to this would be to allow completely below-grade portions to exceed setbacks, while bermed structures could have a fixed setback-to-height ratio.

The last three purposes of setbacks listed above fall more into the area of building code considerations. The concern for proper light and ventilation to windows is irrelevant for a buried wall. The HUD Minimum Property Standards have allowed zero setbacks for windowless walls above grade. The concern for maintenance of a wall can be alleviated if legal access to the adjacent property is secured for maintenance. This provision has also been acceptable under HUD standards. Since reasonable precedents exist for allowing zero setbacks on windowless walls, maintaining setback limitations for buried walls for light, ventilation, and maintenance reasons seems inappropriate. Finally, there is the concern over ensuring stability of neighboring buildings, streets, and sidewalks during excavation. Excavations for earth sheltered houses must be safe and pose no threat to existing structures. Existing setbacks may, however, be in excess of required safe practice as indicated in various building code and engineering documents.

Modification of setback requirements for earth sheltered houses should focus on safe practice standards based on soil type, depth of excavation, and location of adjacent structures. Since setbacks do represent an unnecessary obstacle to earth sheltered housing in many cases, review and modification of these ordinances are desired.

When several dwelling units are being built by one developer, it is possible for the developer to apply for status for the project as a planned unit development. This status allows the project as a whole to be considered in meeting open space requirements, and the like. It also allows houses to be built with common party walls in the town house or condominium style, that is, with zero side wall setback. Since many of the advantages of earth sheltered housing become more apparent when a number of units are considered together, the status of a planned unit development will make such projects doubly attractive. There will be a flexibility in layout and use of space that usually could not be achieved under conventional restrictions. Planned unit developments are administered locally and so may not be recognized in all areas. A check should be made with the local planning office as to the availability of such status and the minimum number of units required to qualify.

Minimum Height Requirement

Although ordinances requiring minimum heights for residential buildings are not common, they can represent an obstacle to earth sheltered housing where they do occur. Apparently, old minimum height restrictions were once enacted to promote the higher-quality, safer construction found in structures taller than one story. Even though this is not relevant today, some old laws may still exist. A more likely purpose of minimum height restrictions is to ensure a uniformity of houses in a residential area.

This conformity of design is intended for aesthetic reasons, which implies the stabilization of property values. A minimum height restriction is likely to be an obstacle for a completely below-grade design; however, some earth sheltered houses include above-grade portions that may satisfy this requirement. Potential owners are advised to check into local ordinances for minimum height restrictions, since a variance might be required and could be difficult to obtain.

Minimum Floor Area

Community zoning ordinances requiring a minimum floor area for housing are quite common. Problems arise when these ordinances are applied to earth sheltered housing because they often exclude "basements" or "cellars" in their calculations. The obvious intentions of the original ordinances are to ensure a certain minimum amount of habitable space to provide a decent living environment and in some cases to protect property values by requiring larger houses to be built. It is assumed that basement space under above-grade structures is unacceptable as habitable space because of its dark, musty characteristics. Since earth sheltered space technically may fall under the definition of "basement" or "cellar" space, the minimum floor area requirements cannot be met. Obviously, well-designed earth sheltered space should be included in minimum floor area calaculations even though it is technically below grade.

Insurance

Insurance of buildings is based on ratings given to the particular type of construction, location, and occupancy, for the building under consideration. These ratings can be made by the insurance companies themselves but in over half of the states, the rate-making body is the Insurance Services Office. This office prepares ratings and furnishes data for use by the individual insurance companies; an individual company is still free to adjust the ratings or prepare their own if they so desire.

Housing insurance is typically class rated. This means essentially that it is not worth the insurance company's time to inspect each home individually for fire and other hazards. The losses from any particular house are minute in relation to the total pool of houses insured, and the insurance companies do not feel there is sufficient difference in risk between different types of houses to warrant individual treatment. There are, however, some modifiers that affect the home owner's premium, and these will be outlined below.

The class of insurance coverage desired is the first determinant of the insurance rate. There are five major classes of insurance for residential buildings:

- fire and extended coverage—protects from fire, wind storm, and hail
- theft—protects from loss by theft of goods from the property
- public liability—protects from liability to persons injured on the property
- tenants form—protects only contents
- broad form—general policy including coverage under 1, 2 and 3, and providing some additional coverages

The insurance rate for the type of coverage is then modified by the following factors, which can be grouped into the three major determinants of rate that apply to any building:

1. Type of construction: As mentioned above, houses are not graded by construction in detail. There may be a simple split between frame and masonry construction in some ratings.

2. Type of occupancy: The only major determinants here will be information as to the number of families living in the dwelling and whether the building is owner or nonowner occupied.

3. Exterior grading: This refers to the quality of public fire protection; for instance, water availability, water pressure, distance to fire station, and so forth. There are ten grades of protection, with Grade 10 having no protection and Grade 1 the best protection. The cities of Minneapolis and St. Paul, for example, are considered Grade 3.

Insurance rates are also adjusted yearly by a loss ratio, which indicates whether, for an identified class of risk, the rates have proven to be too low or too high in the past.

An analysis of the comparative insurance risks for earth sheltered and aboveground houses was prepared in 1980 by the Clarkson Insurance Group, U.K. [Muller and Taylor, 1980] and is shown in figure 6-14. This analysis of the comparative risks indicates a slightly lower risk for earth sheltered houses under both building and contents coverages

Risks	Building Coverages		Contents Coverages	
	Aboveground Massive Construction (%)	Earth Sheltered Housing (%)	Aboveground Massive Construction (%)	Earth Sheltered Housing (%)
Fire, lightning	50.0	35.0	27.5	25.0
Explosion	2.5	5.0	2.5	5.0
Riots, civil commotion	2.5	2.5	2.5	2.5
Burglary, theft	2.5	2.5	30.0	25.0
Storm, tempest	20.0	15.0	17.5	12.5
Subsidence, landslip	2.5	12.5	1.0	5.0
Earthquake	2.5	5.0	2.5	5.0
Aircraft	0.5	0.5	0.5	0.5
Impact	0.5	0.5	0.5	0.5
Total	83.5	78.5	84.5	81.0

6-14: Insurance Risks for Aboveground and Earth Sheltered Houses

Source: Muller, Taylor, 1980 (see references).

although the differences in the overall assessment of risk for each building type is minor.

The actual experience with home owners' insurance costs for earth sheltered housing, however, has been mixed. The majority of premiums has not been changed from that for conventional construction. Lower premiums have been offered by a number of companies—usually on the basis of local discretion by the insurer rather than a national rate adjustment. There have also been cases where an insurance company has refused to insure an earth sheltered home.

Financing

The importance of the availability of financing cannot be overstated for the widespread acceptance and use of earth sheltered housing. Small numbers of people will always be able to have sufficient down payments or be such sound credit risks that they will be able to receive financing. The bulk of the population, however, would need to have financing readily available and on terms similar to other forms of housing before they could realistically think of proceeding with such a project.

It appears that the problems of financing earth sheltered houses have eased somewhat from those faced by the early earth sheltered housing practitioners. The concept is more widely known and understood than it was in the 1970s, and specialist builders have accumulated a track record of performance that greatly facilitates their ability to finance new projects. Potential owners of individually designed projects (and especially owner-built projects) can still have considerable difficulty in obtaining financing.

The discussion on financing included in this chapter is a condensed version of work carried out by the Underground Space Center for the Department of Housing and Urban Development in 1980 and updated as *Earth Sheltered Housing: Code, Zoning and Financing Issues,* published by Van Nostrand Reinhold Company in 1981. More recent research on loan officers' perceptions [Hanzal-Kashi, et al., 1984] has developed a more solid statistical analysis of the importance of the various factors affecting the financing of earth sheltered houses. There are now also available consumer-oriented books developed to help potential earth sheltered home owners through the financing process [Rollwagen, 1983].

Introduction to Home Financing

For those readers who are not familiar with the system that provides the bulk of home financing, a general overview will be given here. The financing discussion will deal with new-home financing and primarily with single-family dwellings. At present, financing of earth sheltered houses will fall almost entirely into the new-home financing category because very few earth sheltered houses are yet available for resale. Single-family dwellings are more indicative of typical financing procedures and acceptance because the financing of multiple dwelling units is a far more complicated procedure and depends greatly on other aspects of the loan appraisal besides the type of structure involved.

Types of Loans: The two major types of loans necessary for new home construction are a relatively short-term construction loan for the contractor and a long-term mortgage loan for the occupant. The mortgage loan is usually the key loan approval to receive because this financing will be used to pay off the construction loan when the house is completed. There are several different typical sequences in the loan and construction process depending on the type of owner/contractor relationship.

A house contractor building on speculation will usually try to get his house preapproved for financing, assuming that the eventual buyer will be credit-worthy enough to be granted the loan. This loan approval will not only make the house easier to sell in a short time, but also will help in obtaining the construction loan, although in the case of a reputable and well-known builder, the lending institution will often be lending on the basis of his past record.

In the case of a house being constructed for a particular client, the owner will need to seek the permanent financing and the builder will arrange his own construction financing. He will normally have little trouble doing this since he has an assured sale.

In the case of an owner/builder or where the owner acts as his own general contractor, both types of financing have to be arranged by the owner. Again, it is a more practical procedure to seek the permanent financing first, especially when there is any question about whether the project would be financed (as is still the case for earth sheltered houses).

Sources of Loans: There are many possibilities for raising the money for new home construction but the vast majority (over 90%) of residential mortgage loans are provided by four types of institutions. These are:

- savings and loan associations or mutual saving banks (commonly grouped as "thrift" institutions)
- commercial banks
- life insurance companies
- mortgage companies or mortgage bankers

Mortgage Insurance

Mortgage insurance programs operated by the federal government make insurance available for mortgage loans made by private lenders. The primary purpose of the government insurance program is to shift the risk of a loss on a loan default from the private lender to the federal government. This not only pools the risk among a much larger number of loans but, more important, enables the loan to be granted with a much lower down payment than if the risk was borne completely by the private lender.

There are three main federal credit agencies:

- The Federal Housing Administration (FHA) is now part of HUD. The HUD Minimum Property Standards, which are the guidelines used by the FHA in their mortgage underwriting process for evaluating the property, are the industry standard and are used by the other government agencies as well as by the private insurers.

- The Veterans Administration (VA) administers a special insurance program established for ex-servicemen.

- The Farmer's Home Administration (FmHA) also administers a special insurance program designed for rural and farm housing needs.

There are also private mortgage insurance companies (PMIs) that fulfill much the same function as the federal agencies. They pool the risk of mortgage default and hence allow a lower down payment to be made. Typically, however, they do not insure the entire mortgage but only a portion, which is usually sufficient for the private lender to recoup his money even after sale of the property at a reduced cost. Such mortgage insurance may only, in fact, cover the top 10 to 15 percent of the loan.

Loans made without recourse to such insurance programs are termed conventional loans. As one would expect, they usually require higher down payments but are simpler to obtain because there is less additional paperwork and administration.

Secondary Mortgage Market

As with the mortgage companies that act as brokers for the large insurance companies, other large investors have sought to purchase mortgages as investments. Instead of making loans directly, they purchase mortgages from the private lending institutions and pay them a fee for handling the mortgage. This has two advantages for the primary lender: he gets new capital with which to make more loans, and he also receives a handling fee for the mortgage he has sold. These purchase arrangements for existing mortgages constitute what is called the secondary market. Primary lenders can also buy mortgages from other lending institutions in this market if they have surplus funds.

The secondary mortgage market is now strongly influenced by the federal government through three government-supported agencies. These agencies, which provide a steadying influence on the supply of mortgages to the residential market, are:

- The Government National Mortgage Association (GNMA), commonly referred to as "Ginny Mae." GNMA is a part of the Department of Housing and Urban Development and hence is federally owned. The smallest of the three groups, it was organized to provide a secondary market for the government-subsidized interest rate program (e.g., FHA, VA and FmHA loans).

- The Federal National Mortgage Association (FNMA), commonly referred to as "Fannie Mae." This is a privately owned but federally regulated stock corporation. Its principal purpose is to assist the flow of money to the primary lenders by purchasing mortgages when local capital is in short supply.

- The Federal Home Loan Mortgage Corporation (FHLMC), commonly referred to as "Freddy Mac." This is also privately owned but federally regulated and was organized to assist savings institutions in the Federal Home Loan Bank system.

The importance of the secondary market is that since primary lending institutions may wish to sell their mortgages to the secondary market, they must be careful to ensure that their mortgages will be readily purchased by these institutions. "These secondary entities perceive their basic public functions—i.e., contributing to liquidity in the mortgage market and stabilizing the flow of capital into housing production—as necessitating a conservative stance towards underwriting the risks associated with unproven housing technologies" [Regional and Urban Planning Implementation, Inc., 1976]. Hence, the primary institutions that deal with the secondary market also feel pressured into being conservative. A secondary market can also be a strong component of change, however, if a special program is created to buy certain types of mortgages. The ability to readily sell such mortgages can make them much easier to obtain at the primary level. A program similar to this was introduced to ease financing problems with mobile homes.

Parameters for Granting Loans

In order to understand why earth sheltered home buyers have problems in obtaining financing, the criteria that lenders use in deciding whether or not to grant a loan must be understood.

There are several general issues that affect the response of a lending institution to financing a project, particularly an unusual project. The four major issues are:

1. Financing Responsibility: The lending institution is responsible to its stockholders and depositors to use sound financial practices and not to put the institution's capital unnecessarily at risk by making unsound loans.

2. Ability to Sell Loans on the Secondary Market: As discussed earlier, it can be important for a primary lender to be able to sell its loans. Unusual or unsound loans will be difficult to sell.

3. Community Responsibility: Most large lending institutions feel a strong sense of responsibility to their community and its welfare. This means that a socially significant project may still have a chance of receiving a loan even though it presents a greater-than-normal risk to the lending institution.

4. Personal Values and Beliefs: The attitudes of personnel and management can also be very important. A project can be turned away at the first meeting between a client and the lending official by a bias against the type of project. The attitudes toward and values placed on the different loan criteria can vary considerably from institution to institution and from one individual to another.

The detailed parameters for granting loans include the following:

5. Credit Worthiness of Buyer: Clearly the potential borrower must have sufficient means and expectation of income for the bank to be confident of his or her ability to repay the loan.

6. Personal Standing with the Bank: Linked to credit worthiness is the banker's trust in the individual concerned. Personal friendship, position of high standing in the community, and the like, should ease problems of obtaining financing since the individual will be less likely to default on the loan even if the project runs into trouble.

7. Alternative Collateral: Even if the project under consideration is an unacceptable risk to the lending institution when considered on its own merits, the loan may still be granted if other collateral is used to secure the loan.

8. Soundness of Home: The lending institution will usually be concerned that the house for which the loan is being requested will fulfill its intended function and not develop major structural flaws or be uninhabitable. If this occurs, the owner may be tempted to "walk away" from the home and default on the loan, viewing this as the least expensive solution at the time.

9. Cost of Home: In new home construction, the cost of the home will affect the size of mortgage being sought and hence will interact with the credit worthiness of the buyer and the maximum amount that he can afford to spend for a home. The difference between the cost of the home and its appraised value (discussed below) will be a factor in determining the required down payment.

10. Appraised Value of Home: The appraised value of the house to be built is the value the house would be expected to sell for on the open market under average market conditions. This is usually determined by a professional appraiser who uses recent sales of similar houses in the area (called "comparables") to determine the resale value. The appraised value does not necessarily reflect the construction cost of the house.

11. Down Payment: The required down payment for the loan will be determined by subtracting the percentage of the appraised value of the house that the institution is willing to lend from the amount needed to construct the house. Thus, if the construction cost is $85,000, the appraised value is $75,000, and the bank is willing to loan 80% of the appraised value (i.e., $60,000), the required down payment will be the difference between $85,000 and $60,000, or $25,000. This is a $33\frac{1}{3}$% down payment on the appraised value rather than the nominal 20 percent down payment because of the reduced appraised value with respect to the construction cost. The other aspect in determining down payment is the ability of the buyer to make the payments. Rules of thumb such as 25 percent of gross income or $33\frac{1}{3}$ percent of gross income less fixed expenditures are used to determine the maximum payments allowed. The down payment must keep the actual loan amount small enough for the payments to be within the guidelines. It should be clear from the preceding discussions that an increased down payment reduces the lending institution's risk on all counts and hence will almost always make the loan easier to obtain.

12. Risk of Loss on Default: All of the above issues can be grouped into one major concern, the risk of loss on default. Lending institutions would prefer to avoid defaults on loans, but they are especially eager to ensure that should a default occur they will be able to recoup their investment through a reasonably rapid sale of the property.

13. Mortgage Insurance Programs: Since mortgage insurance programs reduce or eliminate the risk of loss on default, the qualification of the property for such an insurance program (e.g., FHA, VA, FmHA insurance) should greatly improve the chances of receiving financing. Not all financial institutions are eager to go through the additional paperwork required, however, and since they apply for the insurance on the home owner's behalf, it can prove more expedient for the reluctant lender to discourage the home owner.

14. Availability of Funds: All the loan particulars discussed above can be viewed substantially differently according to the funds the lending institution has available. If it has no money to lend, even the safest project will not get financing. More typically, funds may be restricted, thus encouraging the institution to lend on the projects involving the least effort and risk.

15. Ease of Loan Processing: The discussion of insurance programs and availability of funds both mentioned the effort involved in making a loan. Although this will not form a regular parameter for granting or not granting a loan, unusual projects that require additional effort in review or professional analysis will be less desirable than a straightforward common type of loan application unless charges are levied to cover the additional effort.

Perceptions of Financing Earth Sheltered Homes

Attitudes about the existing financing picture can vary widely from the practitioner's to the lender's viewpoint. These attitudes are also very dependent on the level of familiarity with the earth sheltered housing concept.

Building practitioners as a group strongly indicated financing as their major problem, as evidenced by their responses to questions asking about specific financial problems one could expect to encounter with an earth sheltered house, as well as in interview items requesting additional comments. Seven out of ten people said financing was the major problem they expected to encounter in building an earth sheltered house. The perception of financing difficulties among practitioners varies from despair and bitterness to an understanding of the lender's problems mixed with frustration nevertheless. The most frustration appears to occur when a lender insists on discussing the idea of financing a project based on personal preconceptions and whims, as is evidenced by the following direct quotes from letters received by the Underground Space Center.

...the loan officer with whom I spoke had little time for me after I mentioned an underground house. He continued to refer to it in terms such as "novelty" and "fad," immediately ruled out any hope of F.H.A. approval, and told me his institution has a responsibility to its members to invest money wisely.

...With all the publicity of "Energy Conservation" I felt sure that we would be able to build an energy-saving home. My husband and I hired an architectural firm to design a semi-underground home with a passive solar heating system.... When it came time for financing, we started at our bank. They approved the loan until they saw the plans. When we were turned down we went to two other lending institutions.... As a last resort, I then went through the yellow pages calling and explaining the type of home this would be: still the same answer. Their concern was "resale market and conventionality," not energy savings.... I must be misunderstanding the government's definition of "energy conservation" as I took it to be a future, as well as present effort to conserve our natural resources and utilize the other forms of natural resources, i.e. the sun, earth, wind, etc. to the fullest.... If you could feel the frustration at this point.... If you know the anger we feel...giving lip service to energy conservation and when it's time to actually get something done, you get nothing but bureaucrats saying what a nifty idea it is but "Sorry"....

A 1979 study by the firm of Donovan, Hamester and Rattien, Inc. for the Department of Energy [Donovan, et al., 1979] which is referred to later as the DHR study, also found several responses expressing bitterness and resentment and reporting loan officers laughing at the proposals submitted. Their study also raised the problem of institutions being officially receptive while having little intention of granting financing. The following quote is taken from their study and is extracted from a letter of one of the government agencies to a potential earth sheltered home buyer:

At this time underground type housing is considered experimental and acceptance by the general public is unknown. We will accept only those houses which have demonstrated continued marketability and that meet the minimum property standards. Until underground housing is less of an experimental type and is more acceptable to the general public, we will be unable to finance this type of housing.

On the other side of the financing picture, lending institutions, mortgage insurers, and secondary market entities usually see their cautious stance on financing as being both necessary and desirable. In government or government-regulated agencies, their conservatism may be mandated by law, as in the case of the Federal Home Loan Mortgage Corporation (FHLMC). This agency is restricted by law to purchasing "investment-quality" loans, which are defined as "a loan to a borrower from whom timely repayment of the debt can be expected and secured by real property which provides sufficient value to recover the lender's investment if loan default occurs." Lending institutions often feel that by taking a conservative stance, the institution is not only treating its investors' money with the care that it deserves, but it is also avoiding feeling partly responsible for a costly and unfortunate project experience when it felt the project was unsound in the first place. Paraphrasing the words of one banker, "The majority of earth sheltered projects presented for financing so far would be better off if they went no further than the drawing board." In line with this sentiment, the DHR study reported that 26 percent of those applying for financing an earth sheltered home were encouraged to drop the idea completely.

One perception that seems common in discussing financing issues with major financial institutions is that very few earth sheltered loan applications are received, and therefore there is little need to review or set up precedures to deal with this type of construction. This is in complete contrast to the experiences of the potential home owners looking for financing, who usually have to contact several institutions before gaining approval—if, in fact, approval is obtained at all. While it is clear that, in relation to the total number of loan applications, earth sheltered housing loan applications comprise a small percentage, banks ought to have a more accurate picture of the demand for the financing of this type of house than they apparently do. The problem appears exist because many loan applicants for earth shelters are turned away without ever completing a formal loan application. This was evidenced in the Minneapolis-St. Paul area by a senior bank officer who reported only one or two applications for earth sheltered home loans to his bank, when many times this number of people had contacted the Underground Space Center for financing advice, saying that they had already contacted the bank in question.

The question of turnaways also brings up the question of the potential difference in attitude between loan officers and the upper level management of a financial institution or government agencies dealing with financing. People in the higher-level positions will usually have a desire to respond to community problems and national issues. This attitude, however, may not be effectively communicated to the loan officer, whose primary responsibility is to make a safe loan that complies with the institution's guidelines.

Financing avenues that have been used successfully include:

- savings and loan institutions
- banks
- FHA insurance

- HUD Section 203B insurance
- HUD Section 233 insurance (for experimental housing)
- VA programs
- Federal Land Bank

The existence of several government programs on this list indicates that there have been projects that have met the Minimum Property Standards and the other requirements of most of the government programs. There have, in fact, already been moves to increase awareness in the financial community of earth sheltered housing as an option. The HUD Section 233 insurance listed above has been a valuable program in allowing the more rapid introduction of experimental housing (including earth sheltered houses). Loan applications under this program are reviewed by the central HUD office in Washington, DC. If approval is given, the loan is then processed by the appropriate local office under Section 203B insurance. Reporting of construction problems and operational experience is included as a part of the program in order to gain feedback on the viability of the housing concept under test. More than twenty-five earth sheltered house loans have been given approval under this program.

Currently, only unusual earth sheltered houses would be considered experimental enough to warrant placing them in the Section 233 program. The remainder would now be considered directly in the 203B program.

In 1980 HUD stressed the need to encourage new concepts in housing (specifically earth sheltered houses) in a letter from Milton J. Francis to its Regional Administrators, Area Office Managers, Service Office Supervisors, and Housing Division Directors. Key sections from this letter are included below.

...In a recent limited survey made by the Office of Single Family Housing and Mortgagee Activities, we found that whereas some Field Offices provided all help possible to those proposing earth sheltered housing, other offices evidenced a negative attitude toward such proposals. While it is true that we have little experience with this type of housing we need to encourage its use...

...Because of its newness in the marketplace, earth sheltered housing proposals present a problem in determining marketability and value. Generally speaking, a well designed, attractive and well sited proposal which provides amenities commensurate with conventionally built housing and with an approximately similar replacement cost should, pending the development of market comparable data, have an FHA estimated value at least approximating that of the conventionally built new housing.

Additionally, when considering the financial ability of the borrower to qualify for the loan, the expected significantly reduced utility and maintenance costs must be utilized in determining housing expense.

Finally, while we should be properly concerned about the integrity of the insurance funds, that concern should not be cause for the rejection of emerging new and worthy concepts of housing which offer a significant solution to our pressing energy situation and still retain the amenities the marketplace has come to expect...

Second Jacobs House in Middleton, Wisconsin built in 1943, designed by Frank Lloyd Wright. Drawing by Bruce Cornwall.

Chapter 7

Case Studies of Earth Sheltered Houses

Solaria

Vincentown, New Jersey

As one of the earliest advocates of underground architecture, Malcolm Wells has stated much of the philosophy behind earth sheltered buildings. In his books and designs, he has expressed a new direction for architecture that preserves and restores the natural landscape rather than destroys it [Wells, 1977, 1981]. With a broader focus than simply creating earth sheltered buildings to reduce energy use, Wells addresses aesthetic and ecological issues in the concept and details of his designs.

One of Wells's earlier designs, Solaria represents a serious effort to incorporate energy efficiency with the aesthetic aspect of earth sheltering. Built in 1975, it has been described as the first solar-heated, earth-covered house in New Jersey. It is not truly "subsurface" in that its sod roof cover is discontinuous with all exterior grades. The structure is earth sheltered because the roof is generously blanketed with up to 2 feet of earth and mulch. Lifting the roofline above the exterior grade on the north side allows natural lighting at the rear, aids cross ventilation, and provides entry without making a major change of grade.

Approached from the north side, elements of the house are visible—a low wall, small windows, and a chimney. The structure, however, is subordinate to the thick natural grasses on the roof, vine-covered walls, and surrounding trees and shrubs. This natural image is achieved partly because the sloped roof is more visible than a flat earth-covered roof. In addition, Wells does not use parapet walls on the roof edge, which often create a heavier man-made image. He says parapets are subject to damage from freezing and thawing, and also hide the plant growth on the roof. By covering the roof with mulch and permitting native plants to take over, a rough, natural appearance is achieved that further diminishes the presence of the house below. In contrast to the north side of the house, the tall southern facade includes floor-to-ceiling windows beneath an array of flat-plate solar collectors.

The plan for Solaria is organized similar to a typical elevational scheme—all major living areas have generous southern exposures, and almost all utility and nonliving spaces are located along the north wall, with its smaller window areas. The elongated plan actually includes three major zones—a quiet bedroom area on the west end, an open living area in the center, and a studio/work area on the east end. The sloping roof structure is on heavy timber framing, with a wood plank deck. The roof is supported primarily on timber columns set on concrete footings. The height along the south wall opens up large interior spaces with adequate room for second-level lofts.

The flat-plate solar collectors used in this house are sometimes referred to as "Thomason-type" collectors. Storage for the system is in a space beneath the living room floor. Wells reported in his book *Underground Design* that the earth-covered, solar-heated combination worked so well that, in the winter of 1977, no auxiliary heat was required to supplement the Solaria heating system [Wells, 1977].

Project Data

Project: Solaria

Location: Vincentown, New Jersey

Date of Completion: 1975

Architect: Malcolm Wells, Brewster, Massachusetts

Photographs: Robert Homan

Gross Floor Area: 2,800 square foot

Structure: Timber and wood-deck roof system supported on timber columns, reinforced concrete block walls

Earth Cover: Entire roof is covered with 12 inches of subsoil, 8 inches of mulch, and 4 inches of topsoil; about 50 percent of exterior walls are partially bermed

Insulation: Extruded polystyrene, 2 inches on roofs, walls, and under edge of floor slab

Waterproofing: ⅛-inch Butyl rubber membrane on roof, foundation coating on parged concrete block walls

Heating System: Flat-plate solar collectors with oil-fired backup furnace

Cooling System: Conventional air-conditioning with rock storage

Heating Degree Days: 4,952 (Trenton)

Cooling Degree Days: 968 (Trenton)

Energy Use: No auxiliary heating required in winter of 1977

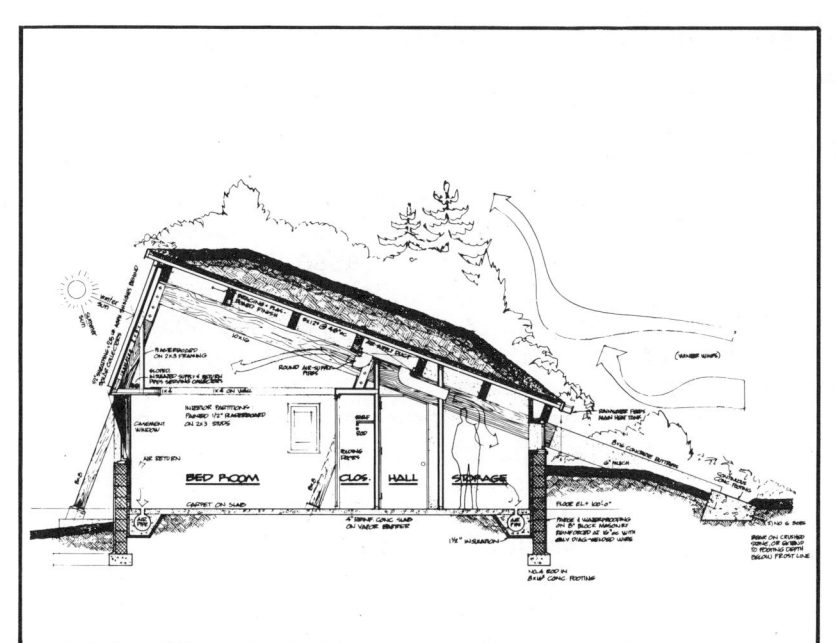

Section

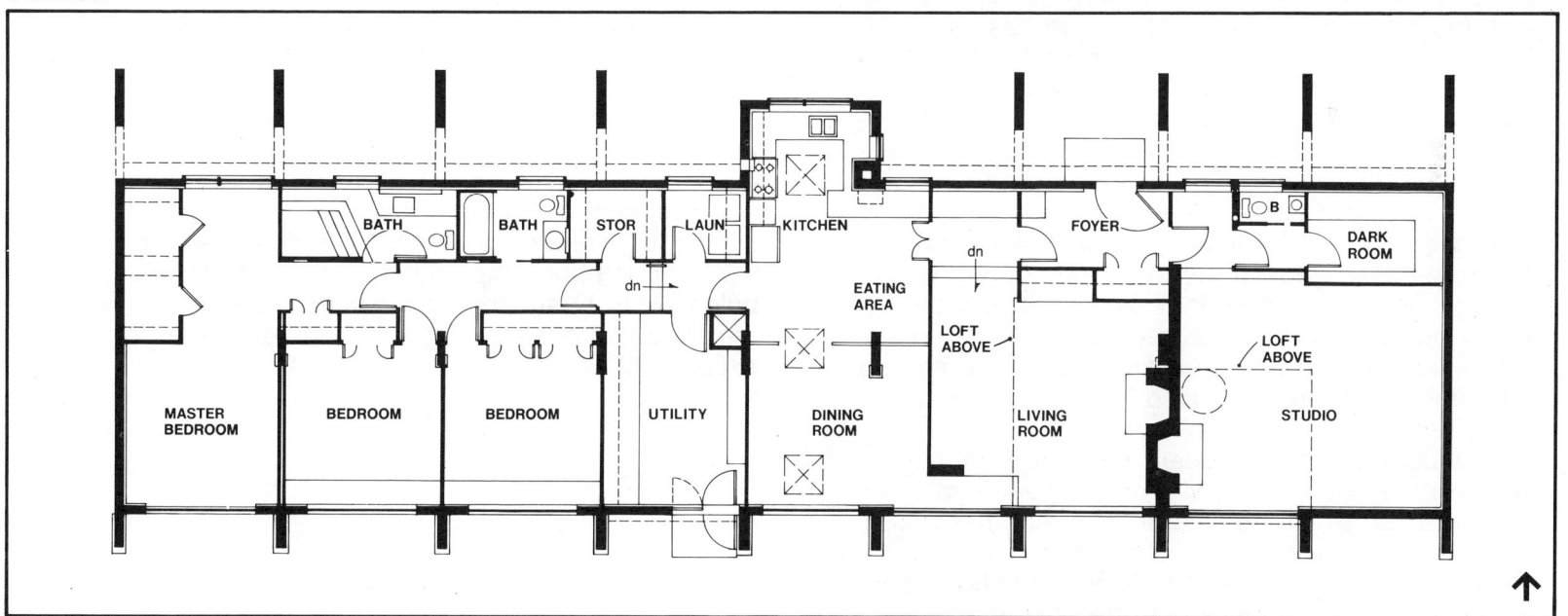

Floor Plan

Woods/Gundlach Residence

Honesdale, Pennsylvania

This relatively small and simple earth sheltered home blends beautifully into its wooded sloping site in northeastern Pennsylvania. Viewed from the north, only a slightly bermed form is evident on the landscape, as the native plant materials extend over the earth-covered roof. As one descends around the structure on the west end, the exposed south facade appears. The glass wall that serves as the entrance is actually oriented 30 degrees to the east of south.

Because of the unorthodox requirements of the owners, the building layout is unique. Essentially there are two separate but connected studio spaces in the center of the building, each with a bathroom, kitchen, and storage area adjacent to it. Both studio spaces have entrances from the outside, floor-to-ceiling glazing on the south wall, and skylights. While this arrangement fits the needs of the two owners who live and work in the house, it could easily be adapted to other needs. The two studios could serve as a living area and a bedroom area, or the structure could be divided into two separate living units.

Although the 1,100-square foot structure is a simple rectangle in plan with only a portion of one wall exposed to the outside, the building materials and details provide visual interest and rich texture. Rough-sawn 6- by 12-inch beams that support the cedar roof deck are visible on the interior and extend outside the building to support a trellis which shades the south-facing windows. Exterior structural walls are reinforced concrete, but they are mostly covered with cedar on the interior and portions of the exterior where they are exposed. Interior walls are covered in spots with plaster or tile, and the floor is dark-colored slate, which helps in absorbing and storing solar heat gain. Because the plan is only 16 feet deep, sunlight penetrates into a majority of the house from the south wall. Two operable skylights provide additional natural light and some ventilation.

Rather than construct large retaining walls on the exterior, designer Charles Woods has chosen to slope the earth along the south wall of the building from the roof down to the floor level. Massive retaining walls, which can be costly and may block light and views, are eliminated. Moreover, because of these sloping forms, the house appears to merge with the surrounding landscape. Another technique used in this design to reduce costs is the placement of only 6 inches of earth on the roof. Woods reports that grass grows adequately even though this thin layer of soil is very well drained.

One advantage of an earth sheltered house is thermal stability. In this house the owner has tested this concept by not providing any heat from the wood-burning stove and turning off the electrical heat supply for a few days in winter. Without backup heat, the interior temperature has never dropped below 60°F. In summer, even with 100°F temperatures outside, interior temperatures never exceed 75°F.

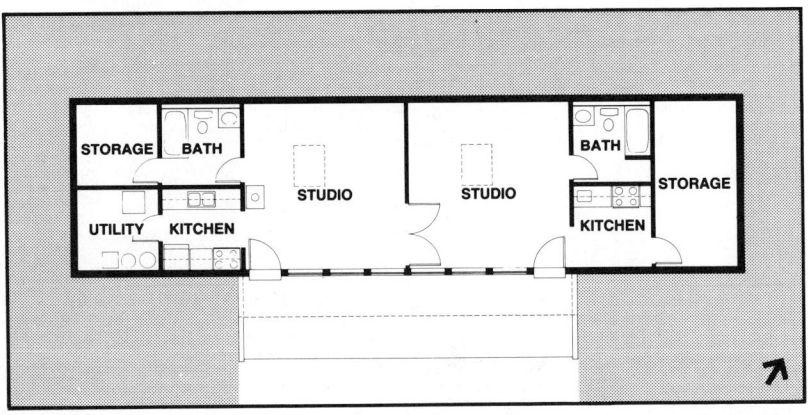
Floor Plan

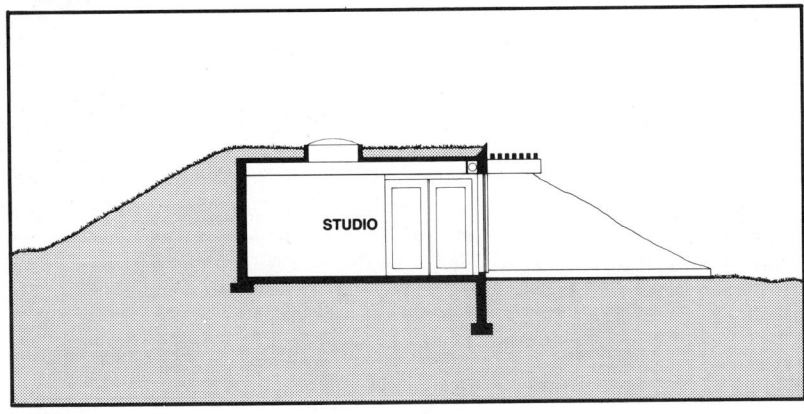
Section

Project Data

Project: Woods/Gundlach Residence

Location: Honesdale, Pennsylvania

Date of Completion: 1981

Designer: Charles Woods, Honesdale, Pennsylvania

Engineer: Herman Gundlach Engineering/Construction

Contractor: Walter Kuntz

Photographs: Julie K. Gundlach

Gross Floor Area: 1,100 square feet

Structure: Wood beam-and-plank roof, 8-inch-thick reinforced concrete walls

Earth Cover: Entire roof covered with 6 inches of soil, 70 percent of exterior walls are earth bermed

Insulation: Rigid polyisocyanurate foam (Thermax), 4 inches on roof (R-28), 2 inches on walls and footings (R-14)

Waterproofing: Butyl rubber membrane on roof, tar and felt paper (4 coats) on walls

Heating System: Electric baseboard supplemented by a wood-burning stove

Cooling System: No mechanical cooling

Heating Degree Days: 6,277 (Scranton)

Cooling Degree Days: 608 (Scranton)

Construction Cost: $65,000 to $70,000 for building, $95,000 including land and site improvements

Winston House

Lyme, New Hampshire

Although it was built in 1972 before general awareness of energy conservation or earth sheltered houses existed in the United States, the Winston House remains a classic example of good earth-integrated design. Surrounded and covered by the natural vegetation of its rural mountainside site, the house commands dynamic views extending 50 miles to the south. Designed and built on speculation by architect Don Metz, the house was sold before it was completed.

The Winston House is a clear example of an elevational-type design extended along an east-west axis with the entire north wall of the house below grade. Primary service and utility areas are located along the north wall of the house. The bedrooms and the living areas are positioned along the southern facade, with a large amount of window area to provide views and to maximize passive solar heat gain in the winter. The overhang on the south wall and the bearing walls help shade the midsummer sun.

A cast-in-place reinforced concrete wall on the north side of the house resists earth pressures. A series of concrete block bearing walls support a timber-and-wood-plank roof system overlaid by 12

inches of soil. The exposed timber ceiling adds warmth and character to the interior spaces.

Although the design of the Winston House is simple and almost prototypical for an earth sheltered dwelling, the architect has successfully solved several layout and aesthetic problems common to this type of house. When an earth sheltered house is entered from the exposed south side, there is often no separation of public entry and private outdoor space. In the Winston House, the garage is offset, and the house is entered from the east end, creating an entrance area separate from the outdoor terraces south of the house. Offsetting the garage from the south wall of the house also alleviates the overly long, flat facade of some elevational designs. By covering the garage with earth and treating it in a manner similar to the house, it becomes a well-integrated part of the design rather than a separate, unrelated structure.

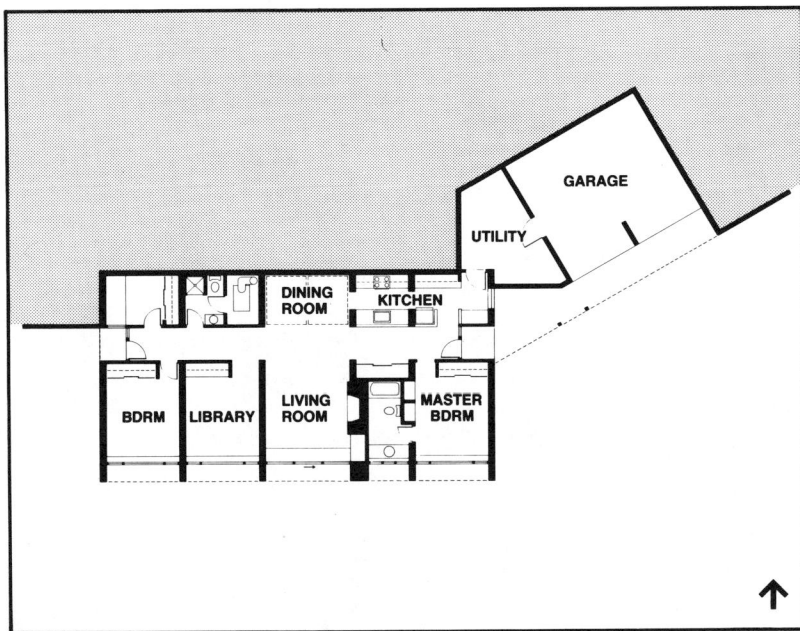

Floor Plan

Project Data

Project: Winston House

Location: Lyme, New Hampshire

Date of Completion: 1972

Architect: Don Metz, Lyme, New Hampshire

Structural Engineer: Frank Zamecnik

Photographs: Don Metz, Robert Perron

Gross Floor Area: 2,800 square feet including garage

Structure: Timber-beam-and-wood-deck roof, concrete block bearing walls, reinforced concrete retaining wall on north side

Earth Cover: Entire roof is covered with 12 inches of soil except skylights

Insulation: 1⅝-inch compressed fiberglass on roof, Zonolite in block cores of exterior walls, 1 inch urethane foam under floor perimeter

Waterproofing: 5-ply coal tar pitch built-up membrane on roof, 2-ply coal tar pitch built-up membrane on walls

Heating System: Oil-fired furnace supplies hot water to baseboard fin-tube radiators

Cooling System: No mechanical cooling

Heating Degree Days: 7,360 (Concord)

Cooling Degree Days: 349 (Concord)

Private Residence

Massachusetts

Since designing and building the Winston House in 1972 and his own earth sheltered residence in 1977, architect Don Metz has continued to design passive solar/earth-integrated houses in the northeastern United States. Shown here is a more recent example of his work: a 5,200-square-foot private residence in Massachusetts, completed in 1981. Like the Winston House, this project is a one-level earth-covered structure with most of its windows facing south for maximum solar gain in this cold climate. In contrast to the smaller Winston House, however, this residence is more complex in its layout and appearance while reflecting an evolution toward more energy-efficient earth sheltered design.

Built into a south-sloping gravel bank, the house and attached garage roofs are almost completely covered with 12 inches of earth, and the north and east walls are mostly below grade. The appearance of the house is not that of a totally unobtrusive non-building, however. Viewed from the lake at the base of the slope, the white forms and glazed south facade contrast with the landscape. Sculptural masonry chimney forms and a large sloping skylight rise from the flat roof. The garage and main entrance are visible from the mostly exposed west side. A large arch form signifies the entry and reflects other arches and rounded forms used throughout the design. Placing earth on the roof of the garage area has better integrated it with the total house design.

The plan arrangement is not typical of most smaller earth sheltered houses. Like many plans, major living spaces and the master bedroom are placed along the south facade for solar gain and view of the lake below. The interior atrium, however, brings light into the north side of the house, permitting a deeper plan with a variety of window orientations and views. One bedroom faces the interior atrium while another looks into a sunken courtyard on the east end of the house. A library has windows facing both the atrium and the entry area to the west. By extending the garage wing to the northwest, the public entry area on the west side of the house is separated from the private outdoor area to the south.

Rather than placing flat skylights overhead in the atrium area, vertical clerestory glazing is used in the "light scoop" roof form. This skylight placement increases passive solar gain while reducing heat losses, in comparison to flat skylights. Metz believes there is also less feeling of being underground when light enters horizontally through vertical glazing rather than through a skylight overhead. In addition to providing ample natural light, the high ceilings and open plan help offset the sense of being below grade. Although light and spacious, the interiors are also characterized by the dark rich textures of heavy timber ceilings, quarry tile floors, and the curving forms of the walls.

The heat loss for this large structure was calculated to be a relatively low 38,000 Btu/hour at −20°F. It is anticipated that solar energy will provide 100 percent of the required heat on sunny days, while a small amount of heat from the three wood-burning stoves may be required during cloudy periods. No mechanical cooling is required in summer. This energy performance is attributed to several factors. First, the house is well insulated, with 8 inches of polystyrene (R-40) on the roof and 3 inches (R-15) on below-grade walls extending to the footing. In addition, the earth protects the house from wind and moderates exterior ground temperatures. Finally, the massive exposed building materials (especially masonry and tile) should effectively store solar energy to help maintain interior temperatures at 70°F on sunny days.

One goal of this design was to provide a long-life, low-maintenance structure. Earth and masonry provide these characteristics, and exposed exterior surfaces are also low maintenance. The plaster-like siding material is a synthetic stucco mix (DRYVIT) that needs no painting.

Project Data

Project: Private residence

Location: Massachusetts

Date of Completion: 1981

Architect: Don Metz, Lyme, New Hampshire

Engineer: Robert Thornton, P.E.

Contractor: Tom Proe

Photographs: Robert Perron

Gross Floor Area: 5,200 square feet total including 1,700 square foot garage and storage wing

Structure: Cast-in-place reinforced concrete walls and interior columns support wide-flange steel carrying beams, 6- × 10-inch timber beams, and 2- × 6-inch wood deck roof

Earth Cover: 90 percent of roof is covered with 12 inches of soil (only skylights and light scoope are not covered); approximately 60 percent of exterior walls are covered

Insulation: Extruded polystyrene, 8 inches on roof, 3 inches on below-grade walls to footing

Waterproofing: 60-mil EPDM membrane on roof and upper 2 feet of wall; trowled-on plastic roofing cement covered with 6-mil poly on remaining below-grade walls

Heating System: Three wood stoves and electric baseboard heating

Cooling System: No mechanical cooling

Heating Degree Days: 5,621 (Boston)

Cooling Degree Days: 661 (Boston)

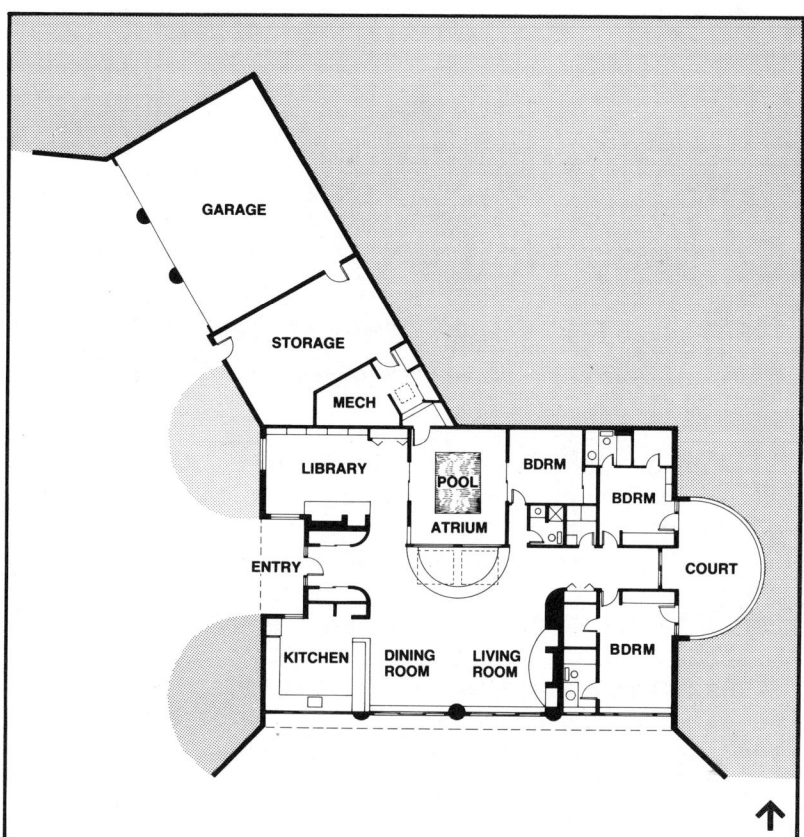

Floor Plan

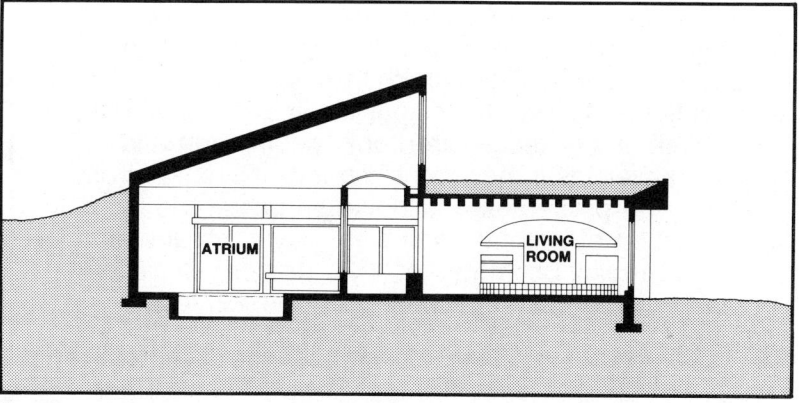

Section

Ecology Houses

Osterville and Stow, Massachusetts

Architect John Barnard built the first Ecology House for himself in 1973 as a vacation cottage and demonstration model to promote underground living. Shown here, the 1,200-square foot structure is completely below grade with all rooms facing a central outdoor atrium. The house is entered by descending a staircase into the courtyard. This single atrium arrangement works well for a relatively small house, but additional atria or other exposed walls become necessary to provide windows in larger, more complex floor plans.

Barnard's style of underground design has been the model for much of the discussion and argument made in favor of subsurface dwellings. His achievements include: a reduction of 75 percent in energy costs for heating and cooling, a reduction of about 25 percent in construction costs over conventional surface buildings, elimination of virtually all maintenance needs, fireproof construction and related lower insurance rates, superb insulation from neighboring properties and noise sources, and preservation of natural amenities—lawn, shrubs, and other greenery. Estimates of a 25 percent reduction in construction costs are based on the $27-per-square foot cost of the first Ecology House compared to $30- to $34-per-square foot costs for conventional houses in the same area during 1973.

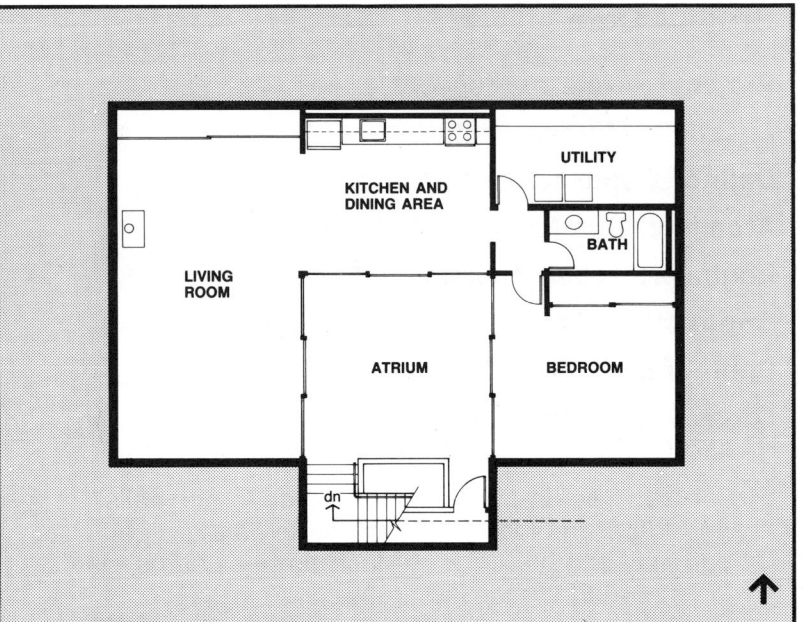
Floor Plan

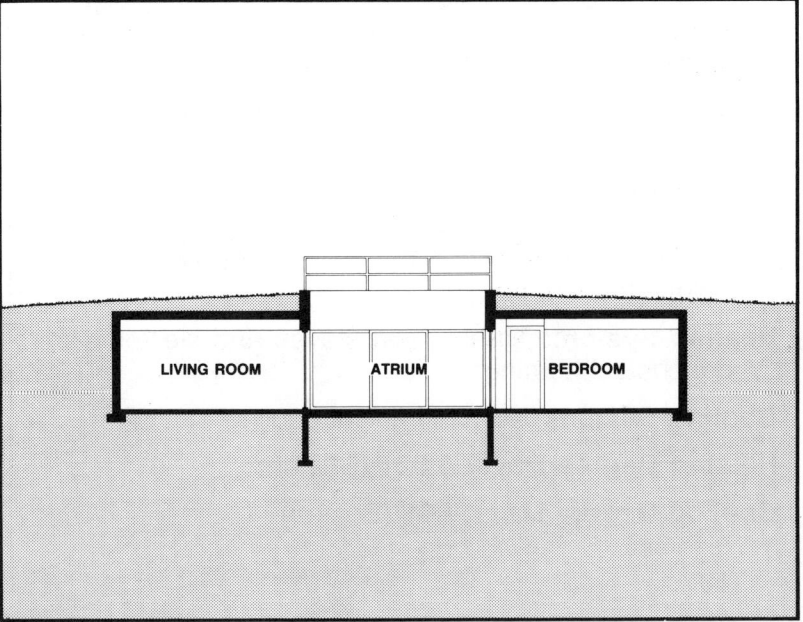
Section

Project Data

Project: Ecology House with Single Courtyard

Location: Osterville, Massachusetts

Date of Completion: 1973

Architect: John Barnard, Osterville, Massachusetts

Photographs: Jack Lane

Gross Floor Area: 1,200 square feet

Structure: Precast concrete plank roof supported on steel beams, reinforced concrete walls

Earth Cover: Entire roof covered with 10 to 16 inches of soil, 75 percent of exterior walls are below grade

Insulation: Extruded polystyrene, 2 inches on roof and below-grade walls

Waterproofing: 3-ply coal tar pitch and felt built-up membrane on roof, hot mopped pitch on walls

Heating System: Solar collector panels with backup furnace supply heat to a forced-air distribution system

Cooling System: Conventional central air-conditioning

Heating Degree Days: 5,621 (Boston)

Cooling Degree Days: 661 (Boston)

Construction Cost: $32,400 ($27 per square foot)

Tremendous publicity resulting in a great amount of interest has led Barnard to design at least four other variations on the atrium-type design (one with two courtyards), plus three standard designs for sloping lot, elevational-type plans. One variation from the standard plans is a hillside version shown here, which Barnard prepared for a family in Stow, Massachusetts. The greenhouse-like enclosure over the interior courtyard serves as a passive solar collector. Air is sun-heated in the space below and is circulated throughout the house, supplementing the regular heating and air-conditioning heat pump system. The owners of this house have fully taken advantage of the earth cover on their house by growing vegetables on the roof. In some places an exit stairway and smoke-venting system must be included in a glass-covered courtyard so that local fire codes can be met.

All of Barnard's Ecology House plans make use of simple, standard details that are easy to build and are certain to endure. Cast-in-place concrete walls, structural steel framing, and precast concrete plank roofing are common to all Ecology House designs. The simplicity with which the Ecology House components fit together is designed to enable the house to be built by relatively unskilled workers. This offers great potential for the owner-builder, and could result in additional savings in construction costs.

Project Data

Project: Ecology House with Exposed Elevation and Glass-covered Courtyard

Location: Stow, Massachusetts

Date of Completion: 1975

Architect: John Barnard, Osterville, Massachusetts

Gross Area: 2,300 square feet

Structure: Precast concrete plank roof supported on steel beams, 8-inch-thick reinforced concrete walls

Earth Cover: 90 percent of roof is covered with 15 inches of soil (except glass-covered atrium); approximately 75 percent of exterior walls are below-grade (not including interior atrium)

Insulation: Extruded polystyrene, 2 inches on roof and below-grade walls

Waterproofing: 3-ply coal tar pitch and felt on roof and walls

Heating System: Heat pump with forced-air distribution system supplemented by a wood-burning stove

Cooling System: No mechanical cooling

Heating Degree Days: 6,848 (Worcester)

Cooling Degree Days: 387 (Worcester)

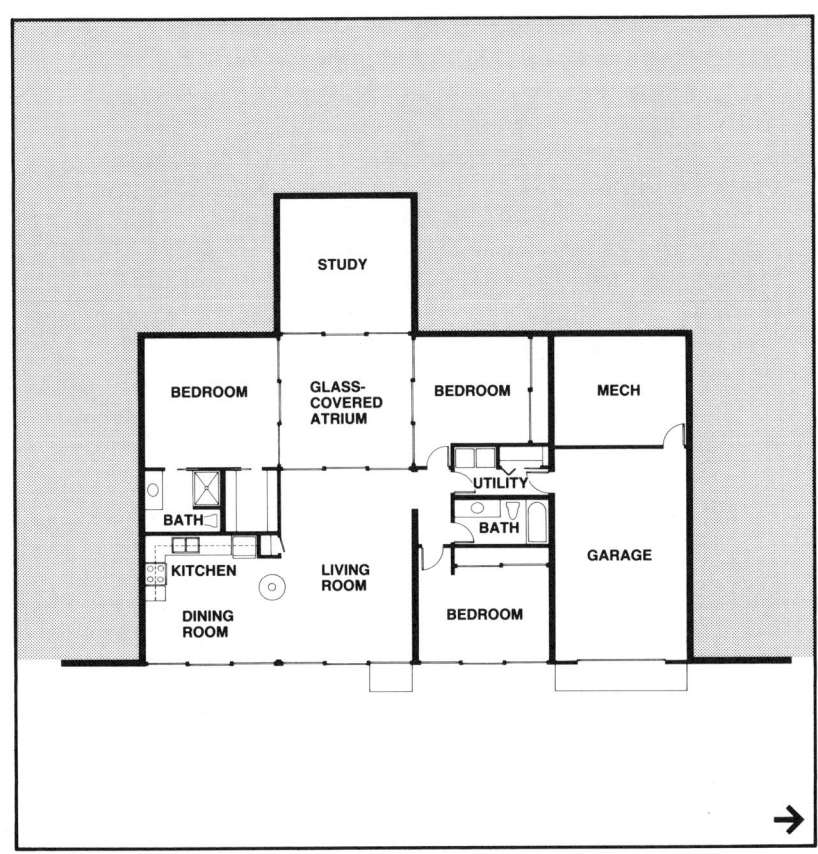
Floor Plan

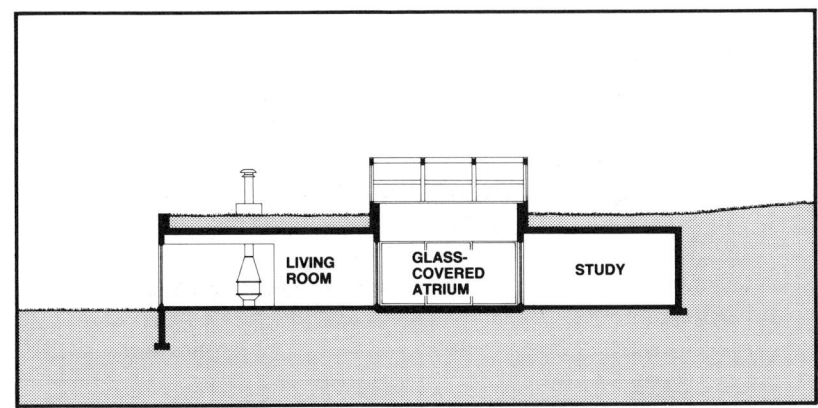
Section

281

Schwartz Residence

Marshfield, Wisconsin

Architect David Wright was asked by his clients to design a simple, highly energy-efficient house for a site in the rolling farmland of central Wisconsin. In addition, a greenhouse for growing herbs, vegetables, and flowers in the winter was desired. The house Wright designed for this cold, often cloudy climate utilizes earth integration and a number of passive solar strategies.

Set into a south-facing slope, the 1,035-square foot structure is bermed on the north, west, and east sides, while approximately half of the roof is earth covered. The exposed south facade is almost entirely glass, and the berm on the east is penetrated by the main entrance. The most remarkable feature of the house is a 24-foot-diameter fiberglass silo dome placed on the roof, which encloses the main two-story living space. These dome structures are commonly visible on the rural Wisconsin landscape. Not only are they readily available, but they are quite economical.

The fiberglass dome is placed on 12-inch-thick curved concrete walls, poured by a silo contractor. The resulting two-story space is entered from the east at the lower level. An open living, dining, and kitchen area with views to the south are located on the lower level of the dome area, while a bedroom loft is above a portion of the space. The remainder of the house, which includes the greenhouse, bathroom, and utility/storage room is a one-level structure extending to the west. A timber beam-and-plank roof structure supports the 12 to 16 inches of soil covering the roof in this section of the house.

Energy-efficient strategies are incorporated into this house at many levels of design—the site plan, the building form, and the details of insulation, solar heat gain, and interior air distribution. The house is placed to the south of a densely wooded area, which provides a windbreak. Winter winds glide around the smooth dome form and are deflected over the structure by earth berms. The spherical dome structure has a very low surface-to-volume ratio, resulting in inceased energy efficiency since a larger volume of space is enclosed by a smaller surface area exposed to the weather. Heat from a wood-burning stove at the center of the main living space rises to the top of the dome and then drops along the outside skin, providing even distribution of

heat in the space below.

The greenhouse, which also serves as additional living space, is the main solar collection area. Solar heat is absorbed and stored in the massive concrete walls and tile-covered floor. Excess heat is drawn from the sunspace by fans and directed to a rockbed beneath the floor of the domed living area. The fans automatically turn on when sensors indicate that the greenhouse is 10°F warmer than the rockbed. This heat then warms the living area by rising as radiant heat through the slab or can be mechanically drawn into the space by a fan. In the greenhouse, insulating panels made of 1.5-inch-thick polyurethane cover the glazing at night and during extremely cloudy periods.

Although the primary concern in Wisconsin is winter heating, hot, humid periods in the summer must also be addressed. Shading with overhangs and plant materials as well as direct cooling from the earth reduce the need for mechanical cooling. Typically, the owners keep the house closed on hot summer days and then ventilate it with cool night air. The massive structure can store the cooler temperatures and potential humidity problems are reduced by keeping humid air out during the warmest parts of the day.

This design has proven to remarkably effective in a cold, cloudy climate. In the winter of 1980-81, only one-half cord of wood was used to heat the house in addition to solar heating, which provides 92 percent of the total requirement. One-half cord of wood is approximately 6,560 Btu per square foot or 0.8 Btu/sq ft/HDD (based on 8,046 heating degree days). The daily indoor temperature swing is limited to 4°F while the average temperature varies from 68°F in winter to 76°F in summer. Interior temperatures never exceeded 80°F in summer, and no mechanical cooling was required [Wright, 1981].

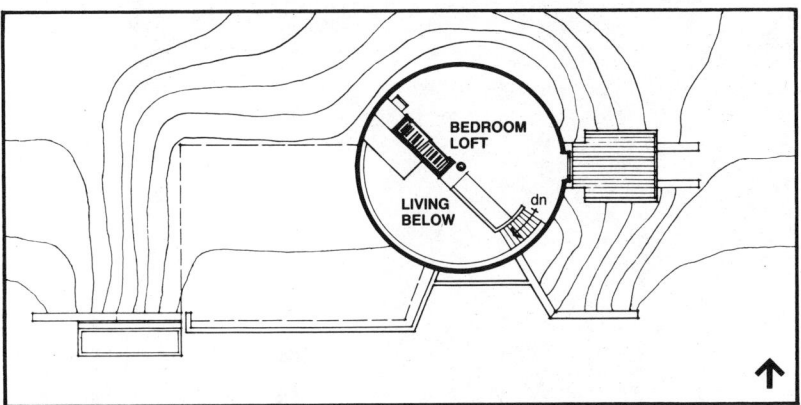
Upper Level Floor Plan

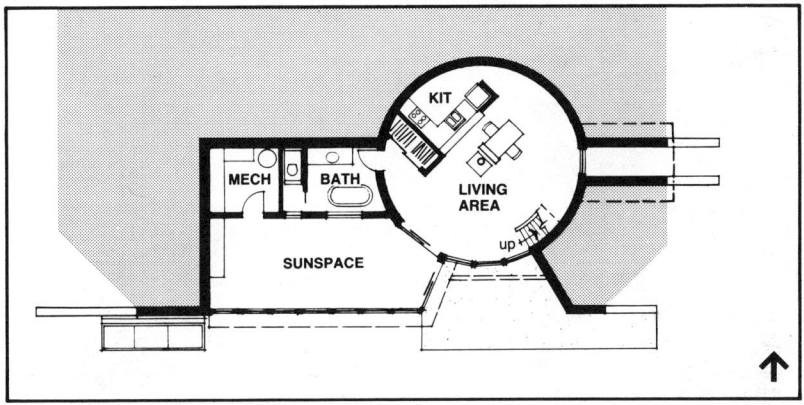
Lower Level Floor Plan

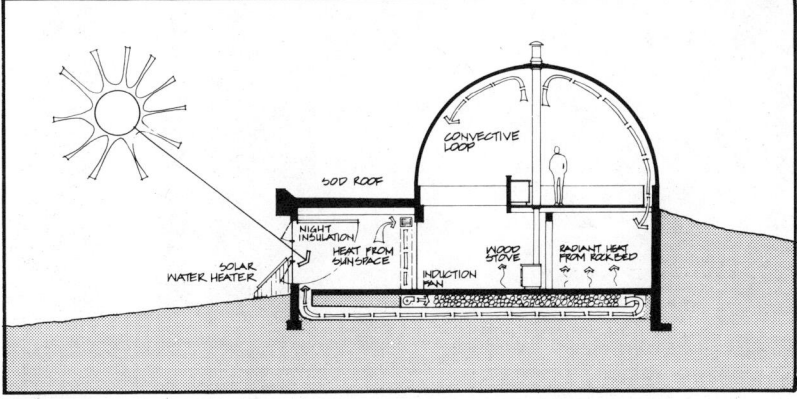
Section

Project Data

Project: Schwartz Residence

Location: Marshfield, Wisconsin

Date of Completion: 1980

Architect: David Wright Associates, AIA, Nevada City, California

Contractor: Stu Schwartz

Photographs: David Wright and Stu Schwartz

Gross Floor Area: 1,035 square feet

Structure: Timber beam-and-plank structure supporting flat earth-covered roof, fiberglass dome, reinforced concrete walls

Earth Cover: Approximately 50 percent of the roof is covered with 12 to 16 inches of soil, 75 percent of exterior wall area is bermed.

Insulation: 4-inch polyurethane foam in dome roof; 3-inch polyurethane, 1-inch polystyrene and 4-inch fiberglass on flat earth-covered roof; 2-inch polystyrene on below-grade walls; 1-inch polystyrene under floor

Waterproofing: 60-mil synthetic rubber membrane on roof

Heating System: Direct gain solar system combined with rockbed storage, wood-burning stove is used as a backup source

Cooling System: No mechanical cooling

Heating Degree Days: 8,046

Cooling Degree Days: 130

Energy Use: ½ cord of oak wood burned in winter of 1980-81 (corresponds to 6.79 million Btu's), no mechanical cooling required

Construction Cost: $60,000

Clark-Nelson House

River Falls, Wisconsin

Located in the rolling countryside of western Wisconsin, the Clark-Nelson house clearly demonstrates the potential of earth sheltered housing to be well integrated into its environment. It is set into a hillside, the arching forms complementing and blending with the surrounding shapes. By disturbing the existing shrubs and trees very little and by allowing the natural grasses and wildflowers to overtake the earth-covered roof and walls, the house itself has become reclaimed by the landscape.

Responding to the owners' interest in new building forms, architect Michael McGuire combined what he called "the advantages of a traditional sod house" with a unique use of a steel-culvert structural system. The arch form of the steel culvert was designed to support large earth loads economically, but is normally used only for drainage ditches, creeks, and road work primarily because of its severe geometric restrictions. The limited amount of material in this thin metal shell structure is in stark contrast to the heavy wood or concrete structural systems used for flat earth-covered roofs. Efficient structures such as this represent one important opportunity to reduce costs for earth-covered buildings.

By placing two culverts side by side, one for private spaces and the other for living and common spaces, and creating a link that houses the laundry and mechanical functions, McGuire has utilized the strict geometry to create dynamic and interesting spaces. The house is entered from the north end of the shorter of the two 24-foot-diameter culverts. A kitchen space in the center of this culvert and the living-dining area at the south end both receive abundant natural light from skylights overhead. The longer culvert actually contains two separate but similar private suites, each containing a bedroom area overlooking a large sitting/studio space. Again skylights provide natural light, and each suite has a wall of glass providing views and access to the outdoors. The house contains almost no rectilinear surfaces. In order to integrate the interior design with the curving, undulating surfaces of the culverts, interior walls, fireplaces, and other forms are sculptural and irregular.

One difficulty with shell structures is the unsuitability of typical flat, rigid insulation materials. In this case interior surfaces were sprayed with 2 inches of polyurethane foam, which provides insulation and gives a textured plaster appearance. Because of changes in building codes, exposed polyurethane is no longer an acceptable interior finish in most places as it gives off toxic fumes in a fire. Either a layer of fireproof material on the inside is required, or the foam could be applied to the exterior and covered with waterproofing. Built in 1972, the house was insulated to a reasonable level based on standards at that time. Today, two to three times as much insulation would be recommended in this cold climate.

Project Data

Project: Clark-Nelson House

Location: River Falls, Wisconsin

Date of Completion: 1972

Architect: Michael McGuire, Stillwater, Minnesota

Engineer: Paul Bredow and Associates

Gross Floor Area: 2,500 square feet

Structure: Steel culverts anchored to concrete floor slab and footings

Earth Cover: Entire roof is earth covered (except skylights and chimneys), minimum soil thickness is 6 inches at peak, approximately 70 percent of exterior walls are earth bermed

Insulation: 2 inches of polyurethane sprayed onto interior of structural shell

Waterproofing: Rubberized asphalt and polyethylene with asphalt

Heating System: Oil-fired furnace with forced-air distribution

Cooling System: No mechanical cooling

Heating Degree Days: 8,159 (Minneapolis)

Cooling Degree Days: 585 (Minneapolis)

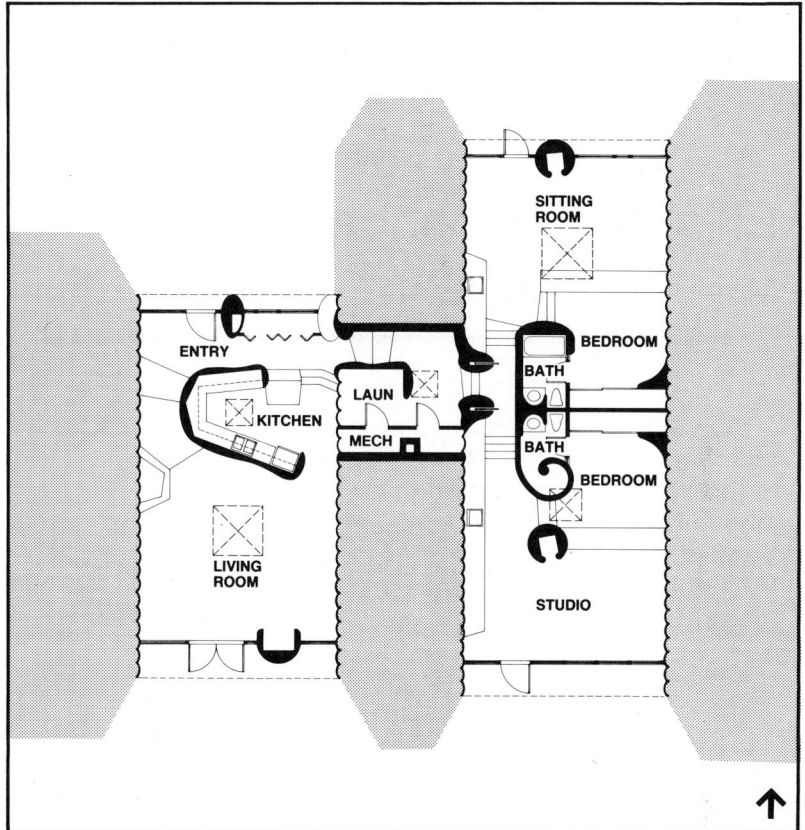

Floor Plan

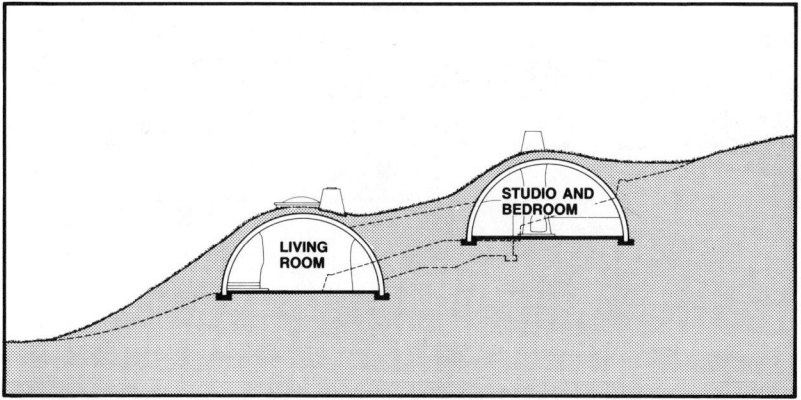

Section

Ellison Residence

Minnetonka, Minnesota

On a wooded, sloping site in suburban Minneapolis, architect Tom Ellison has designed a house for his family that demonstrates some innovative construction details and reflects current trends in energy-efficient design for northern regions. Elements of earth sheltered, passive solar, and superinsulated design approaches are combined to meet special requirements of the site and owner as well as to conserve energy in this predominantly cold climate.

By setting the house into the earth on a south-facing slope, it is protected from cold northwest winds and all windows can face south for maximum solar exposure. Ellison decided not to place a layer of earth on the roof for three reasons: structural costs would be reduced; winter heat loss would not be dramatically affected by the earth if large amounts of insulation were used; and the aesthetic benefits of an earth-covered roof were not as important on this particular site, where the house is never viewed from above and the roof is mostly flat.

Although the roof is not earth-covered, the house maintains a low profile and fits well into the natural setting. This effect of integration with the site is achieved by the earth berms that cover most of the east, west, and north walls; the emphasis on the horizontal forms of the flat roof; and the use of wood siding left natural. A triangular form enclosing a small second-story space rises above the first level but does not interfere with the predominant effect of a low-profile building.

The house is extended along an east-west axis in a typical elevational plan arrangement with all major living and bedroom spaces along the south wall. A wing containing the main entrance, the garage, workshop and storage areas extends to the north. One enters the central living area, a two-story-high space with a row of skylights overhead and floor-to-ceiling glass on the south wall. In addition to the two-story living area, which extends above the flat roof, is a study on the second level. From the study one can overlook the living space below or walk onto the roof deck.

Unlike most earth sheltered structures, which employ masonry or concrete walls, the Ellison Residence utilizes pressure-treated wood-frame walls below grade, which the designer believes to be a

less expensive structural system. Although the building mass is reduced with wood-frame walls, insulation can be increased more easily than with a concrete wall. In this case, the below-grade walls constructed with 2-by-10 studs are filled with fiberglass insulation, resulting in an R-value of 29. The wood-truss roof contains 22 inches of fiberglass (R-70) and the exposed walls contain 12 inches (R-38) of fiberglass. Double-wall construction (two 2-by-4 walls) used for the exposed south wall is a common element of superinsulated design.

In this case, and in his other energy-efficient designs, Ellison expresses the philosophy that earth sheltered, passive solar and superinsulated design approachs are to be applied appropriately and often in combination. For example, many superinsulated designs tend to minimize windows; however, on this site, large window areas providing extensive views were a priority. By using high levels of insulation and setting the building partially into the earth, any energy penalty associated with large windows is offset.

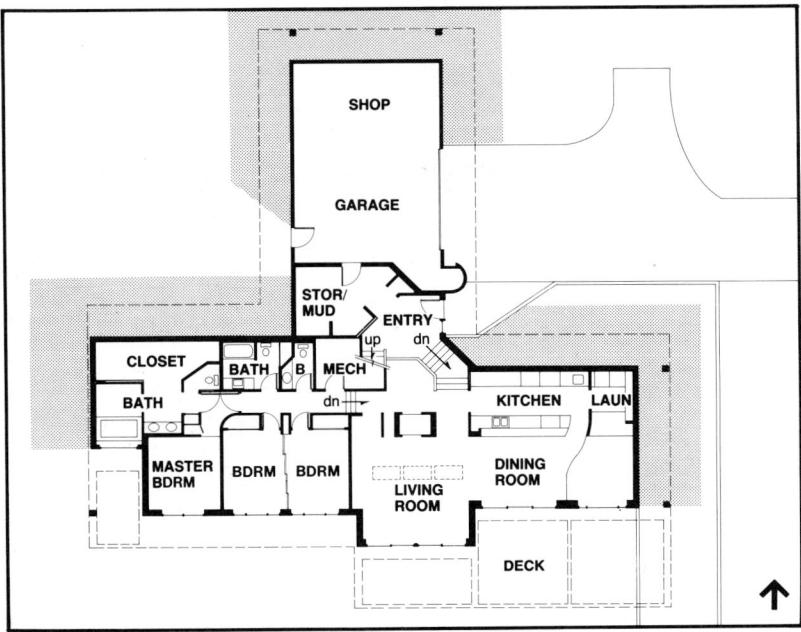
Lower Level Floor Plan

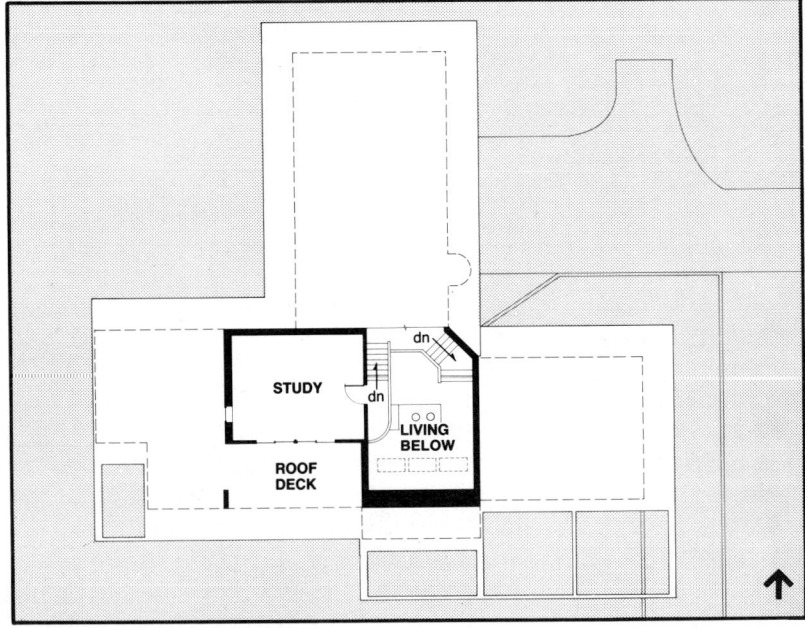
Upper Level Floor Plan

Project Data

Project: Ellison Residence

Location: Minnetonka, Minnesota

Date of Completion: 1983

Architect: Tom Ellison Architects, Inc., Minneapolis, Minnesota

Contractor: Tom Ellison

Photographs: Tom Ellison

Gross Floor Area: 2,832 square foot house plus 1,000 square foot unheated garage, shop, and storage wing

Structure: Flat wood trusses on roof; 2 x 10 pressure-treated wood-frame walls below grade; double-wall construction (two 2 x 4 stud walls) used on exposed walls

Earth Cover: No earth cover on roof; approximately 50 percent of exterior walls are bermed to a height of 7 feet

Insulation: 22 inches fiberglass on roof (R-70), 12 inches fiberglass in exposed walls (R-38), 9¼ inches fiberglass in below-grade walls (R-29)

Waterproofing: Rubberized asphalt on below-grade walls, EPDM membrane on flat exposed roof

Heating System: Gas-fired forced air; air-to-air heat exchanger for ventilaton

Cooling System: No mechanical cooling

Heating Degree Days: 8,159

Cooling Degree Days: 585

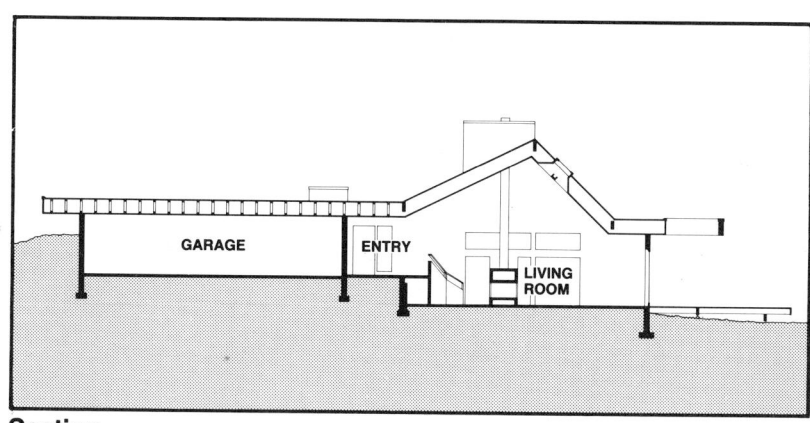
Section

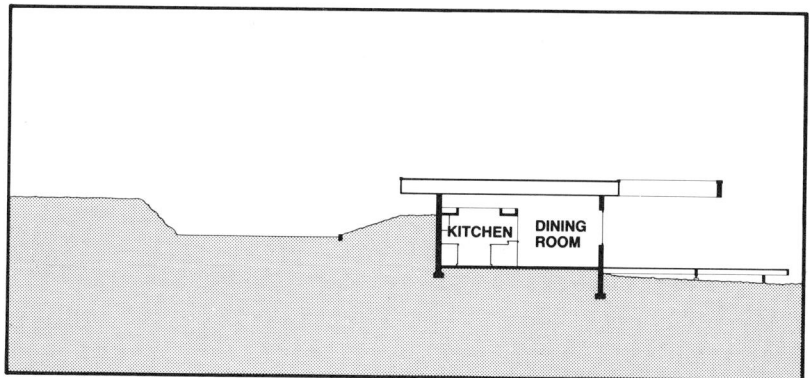
Section

Student Housing

St. John's University
Collegeville, Minnesota

The Benedictine community at St. John's University has a long tradition of conserving resources and protecting nature. When additional student housing units were needed, an earth sheltered design approach was seen as an appropriate choice—to conserve energy resources in this cold northern climate, to merge the buildings with the land, and to provide extremely low-maintenance structures. In addition, the earth sheltered design project was intended to serve both as a learning experience for the students who occupied the buildings and as a symbol of the values of the Benedictine community. The project also represents one of the few modern examples of multiple-unit earth sheltered housing.

Set into a gently sloping site, the twenty housing units are grouped into five separate buildings. All window and door openings are on the south facade of the two-story structures, providing maximum solar heat gain and views of the lake at the base of the slope. A sunken courtyard along the south wall of each building permits sunlight to reach the lower level of each unit, which is completely below grade. The upper level of each unit, which is entered on the south side via a bridge over the sunken courtyard, is mainly above grade. The south, east, and west walls are exposed, resulting in an appearance much like that of a conventional structure. The sloping earth-covered roof and bermed north wall create a wedge-shaped building form that has a low profile and merges with the existing grade. This bermed form is ideal for protecting the structures from the cold winds in this 8,868-heating-degree-day climate.

Each of the units houses four students. The lower level, which has contains two bedrooms, serves as a quieter area for individual study and rest while the upper level is an open living, dining, and kitchen area. High sloping ceilings with extensive glazing on the upper level permit sunlight to fill the space and maximize solar heat gain. The massive concrete structure is very effective in storing the solar heat and moderating temperatures. Red clay tile floors along the south wall enhance absorption of solar heat in this area while insulated drapes reduce heat loss through the windows at night.

Sixteen-inch-thick reinforced concrete block walls resist lateral earth pressures and support the intermediate floor and roof, which are made of precast concrete planks. The east and west walls, which are partially exposed above grade consist of 4-inch split-faced concrete block on the outside, 3 inches of polystyrene insulation, a 1-inch air space, and 8-inch concrete block on the inside. Although there is no insulation along the below-grade north wall, the 4-inch layer of polystyrene on the earth-covered roof extends 8 feet beyond the north edge of the structure. This unique horizontal insulation placement is intended to reduce heat loss to the surface in winter while maintaining more direct contact between the earth and the interior space. Earth temperatures outside the wall will be warmer in winter and cooler in summer with this configuration than they would be if conventional insulation placement against the wall had been used.

Energy use for the individual units was recorded during the winter of 1982-83. However, space heating was not separated from other uses of electrical energy such as hot water heating, lights, and appliances. Average total use per unit was

19,938 kWh from September 1982 through May 1983. The variation between units ranged from 15,989 kWh to 30,711 kWh, indicating the impact of occupant behavior on energy use. Since space heating and thermostat settings are not monitored separately, it is difficult to draw definite conclusions about the energy use performance of the buildings. Moreover, the students have no direct incentive to conserve energy.

Basic construction costs for the complex were $1,154,412, which is $51.89 per square foot. This moderate cost compares favorably with individual units of conventional and earth sheltered housing, indicating that some economies of scale are achieved with multiple-unit projects. Additional costs for site work, furnishings, and fees raised the total project cost to approximately $65 per square foot.

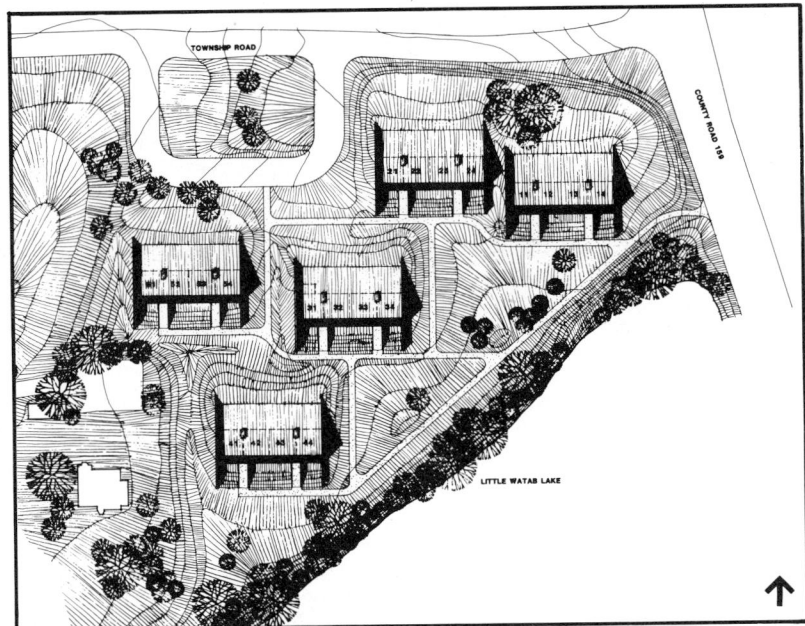

Site Plan

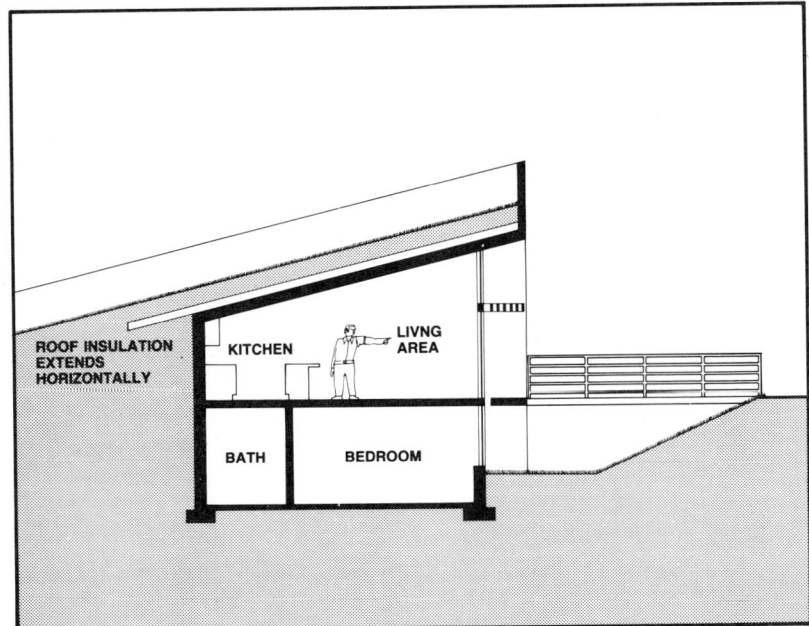

Section

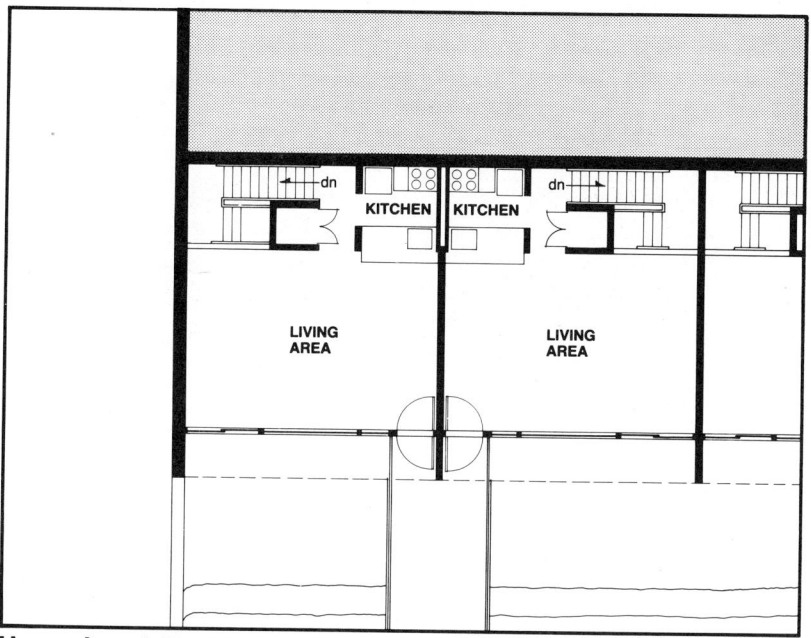
Upper Level Floor Plan

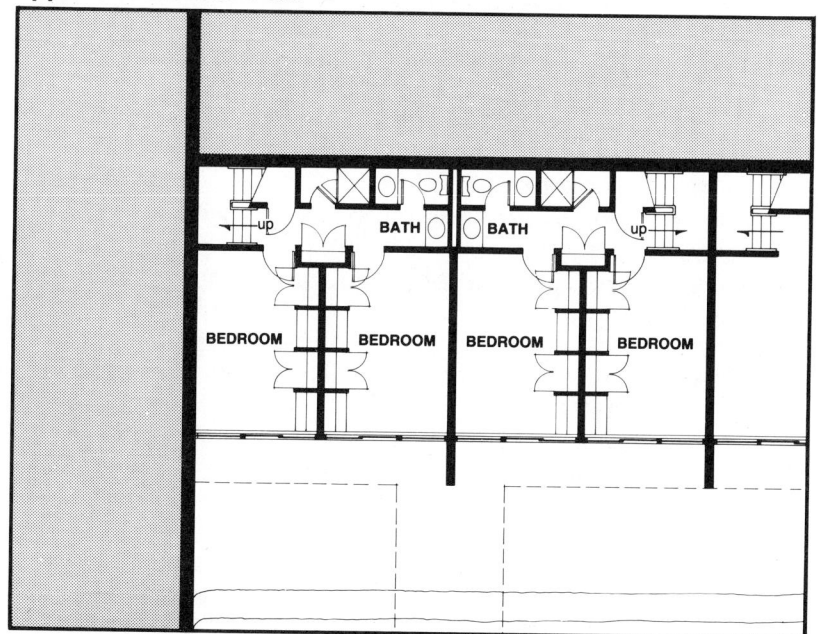
Lower Level Floor Plan

Project Data

Project: Student Housing for St. John's University

Location: Collegeville, Minnesota

Date of Completion: 1982

Architect: Hammel, Green and Abrahamson, Minneapolis, Minnesota

Engineer: Hammel, Green and Abrahamson

Contractor: Gohman Construction

Photographs: Lea Babcock and Lee Hanley (aerial)

Gross Area: 22,248 square foot total in five buildings; twenty units of 1,100 square feet per unit

Structure: 10-inch precast concrete plank roof; 8-inch precast concrete plank intermediate floor; 16-inch reinforced concrete block walls below grade

Earth Cover: Entire roof is covered with 4 inches of gravel and 16 inches of soil; 50 percent of exterior walls are covered with earth

Insulation: Extruded polystyrene, 4 inches on roof extended 8 feet beyond north wall; 3 inches inside above-grade side walls; 2 inches to a depth of 6 feet on below-grade side walls

Waterproofing: Synthetic rubber membrane on roof and below-grade walls

Heating System: Electric base board heating

Heating Degree Days: 8,868 (St. Cloud)

Cooling Degree Days: 426 (St. Cloud)

Energy Use: 19,938 kWh average total use per unit (including hot water heating and appliances) from September 1982 through May 1983

Construction Cost: $52 per square foot for construction only, $65 per square foot including additional site work, furnishings, and fees

Park Ranger Residence

Wawawai Park, Washington

In one area of southeastern Washington, the Snake River has carved out a 1,500-foot-deep canyon. Where a side canyon, the Wawawai, joins the main river canyon, a small park is located. The 49-acre park provides opportunities for camping, hiking, and fishing in this unique and powerful natural environment. In 1981 an earth sheltered structure was completed that serves as the residence for the park ranger.

Originally, a mobile home set into a cut in the hillside was planned for the park ranger residence. As evidenced by other development along the river, a brightly colored mobile home would have a very negative visual impact on the mostly treeless sweeping landforms of the canyon. An earth sheltered building concept was considered as a means of preserving the powerful natural landforms both visually and ecologically. In addition, such a structure provided a number of other advantages including energy efficiency, disaster protection, reduced maintenance, and a long-term flexible structural shell. An earth sheltered building in a public setting such as this could also serve as a demonstration project, leading the way to more sensitive future development of the canyon.

The 2,692-square foot structure is rectangular in plan, and the exterior forms are purposely simple so that the building truly is subordinate to the landscape. Exterior retaining walls continue the sloping landform of the canyon. Viewed from above, only skylights are visible, and from across the canyon, the structure appears to be a simple opening in the hillside. Future plans for landscaping will hide the house further so that it appears to be only a grove of trees.

Unlike many earth sheltered houses with a single exposed elevation, there is a private and public side to this house. The entrance and garage are located in an opening in the southeast facade, while the majority of the windows face a private outdoor space to the southwest. Set into the hillside, the northeast and northwest walls of the house are below grade, and the roof is completely earth covered. A berm at the south corner of the house separates the private and public sides and further integrates the building with the land.

The plan of the house is arranged so that bedrooms and most major living spaces have windows. Skylights provide natural light to the family

room and utility area along the below-grade northeast wall. On the interior, a shelf runs along some walls at a height of 6 feet, 8 inches, to give scale to the spaces and to enclose electrical wiring and indirect lighting fixtures. A shelf such as this is particularly useful in a concrete structure since wiring is accessible and can be adapted to future uses.

For many years, architect David Scott has viewed earth sheltered buildings as an important alternative to conventional housing for a wide range of resource and energy conservation reasons. In designing this project, he has attempted to address a broader range of short- and long-term goals than is common for an individual residence. Not only is the park ranger's house visually subordinate to the landscape, but it is designed to prevent erosion, reducing hard surfaces and absorbing runoff. This is accomplished with an earth-covered roof and the use of concrete paving blocks around the house, which permit grass to grow in them. These blocks also reduce glare and heat gain in summer. Other considerations in the design were choosing materials and techniques that were locally available, designing a house for handicapped access, and creating a structure that will last a long time with little maintenance.

In order to provide flexibility for future modifications in the house, there are no interior bearing walls. Cast-in-place concrete walls on the exterior and concrete columns support the cast-in-place flat slab roof. Similar to most earth sheltered building, polystyrene insulation is placed outside the structural shell on the earth-covered roof and below-grade walls. In this house, the insulation is also placed outside the concrete structure of the exposed

walls. It is then covered with a textured synthetic plaster material (the DRYVIT System). This approach has the advantage of enclosing all of the building mass inside the insulation and reducing the number of places where thermal breaks are required.

Project Data

Project: Park Ranger Residence

Location: Wawawai Park, Washington

Owner: Whitman County Parks and Recreation Department

Date of Completion: January 1981

Architect: David M. Scott, FAIA, Pullman, Washington

Structural Engineer: Larry Peden, P.E.

Mechanical Engineer: Thomas Gerard and Associates

Electrical Engineer: Cook and Wanless

Contractor: C and S Builders

Photographs: Herb Howard and Glen Sprouse

Gross Floor Area: 2,692 square feet, including 570-square foot garage and shop area

Structure: Cast-in-place concrete flat-slab roof, 9 inches thick; cast-in-place concrete walls

Earth Cover: 98 percent of the roof is covered with 24 to 36 inches of soil; 62 percent of the exterior walls are earth covered

Insulation: Extruded polystyrene, 3 inches on roof and below-grade walls to the footing

Waterproofing: Bentonite sprayed on walls and roof, covered with two layers of 6-mil polyethylene and one layer of Enka drain over 1 inch of sand

Floor Plan

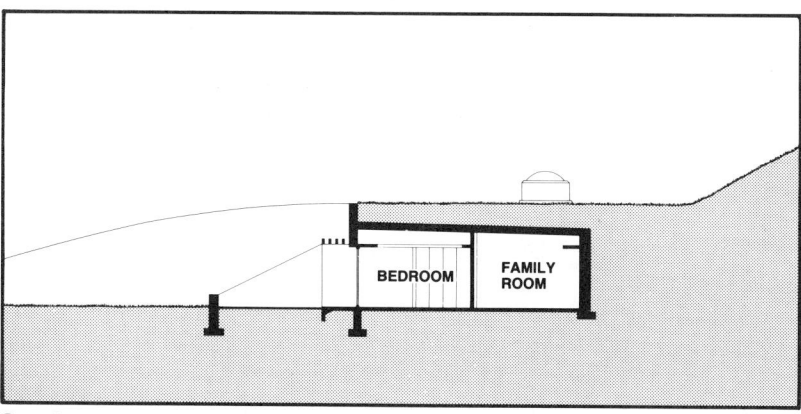
Section

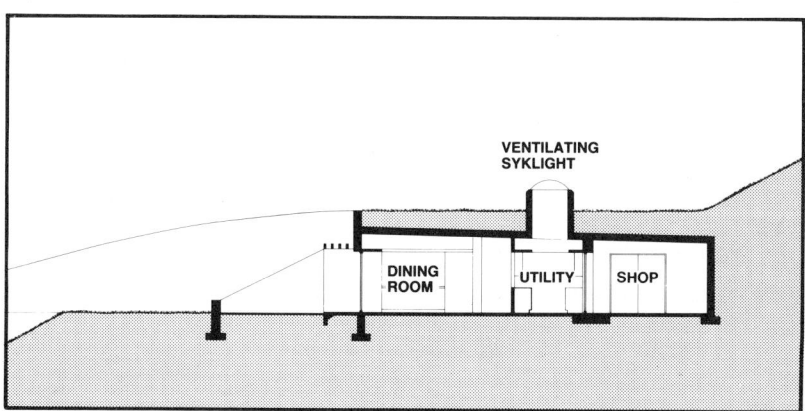
Section

Heating/Cooling System: Heat pump supplies counterflow air-handling unit, supply ducts are below the floor slab

Heating Degree Days: 5,483

Cooling Degree Days: 862 (Walla Walla)

Energy Use: Total electrical use for one year was 22,580 kilowatt-hours including heating, cooling, hot water, lighting, and appliances

Construction Cost: $95,000

Mercy Residence

Carnation, Washington

The Mercy Residence was set into a steep slope and covered with earth to lessen the impact of a building on this beautiful, thickly wooded site as well as to conserve energy. Surrounded by tall Douglas fir and cedar trees, the house overlooks a small lake at the base of the west-facing slope. The site is entered via a loop road from the east at a level higher than the house. Approaching the house, a glass-covered carport and the earth-covered roof of the house are the most visible features. The light-appearing carport structure is above the house but is visually related to it by the wood and glass materials.

Although one descends further to reach the house entrance, there is no darkness or negative associations with entering an underground building. Glass set into a wooden framework on the east entry wall of the house permits views of the open living area and the lake beyond, creating a light and transparent feeling. This open feeling is further enhanced by the high ceilings in the kitchen and living areas. A greenhouse, which also serves as an eating area, is attached to the west wall of the house. Wood-framed roll-up door sections turned on edge form the greenhouse walls. Since they can be completely opened in good weather, the greenhouse can be converted into a glass-covered porch.

Along the south wall of the living area, a narrow band of glass slopes just above the grade line, providing glimpses of the forest floor. Extending to the north in this basically elevational design are three bedrooms with views of the lake. Bathrooms, utility room, and a multipurpose corridor area are placed along the windowless east side of the bedroom wing. Because this house is mostly shaded by the forest, the benefits and drawbacks of solar gain are less of a concern in this design. There is greater freedom in window orientation than in most passive solar houses, and overheating through skylights and the greenhouse are less likely.

Heavy timber poles on the interior support glue-laminated wood beams, which in turn support a system of wood purlins and decking. Glazing is placed between the purlins to lighten the feeling of the heavy roof structure, which supports 18 inches of soil. Reinforced concrete retaining walls are exposed on the interior of the house.

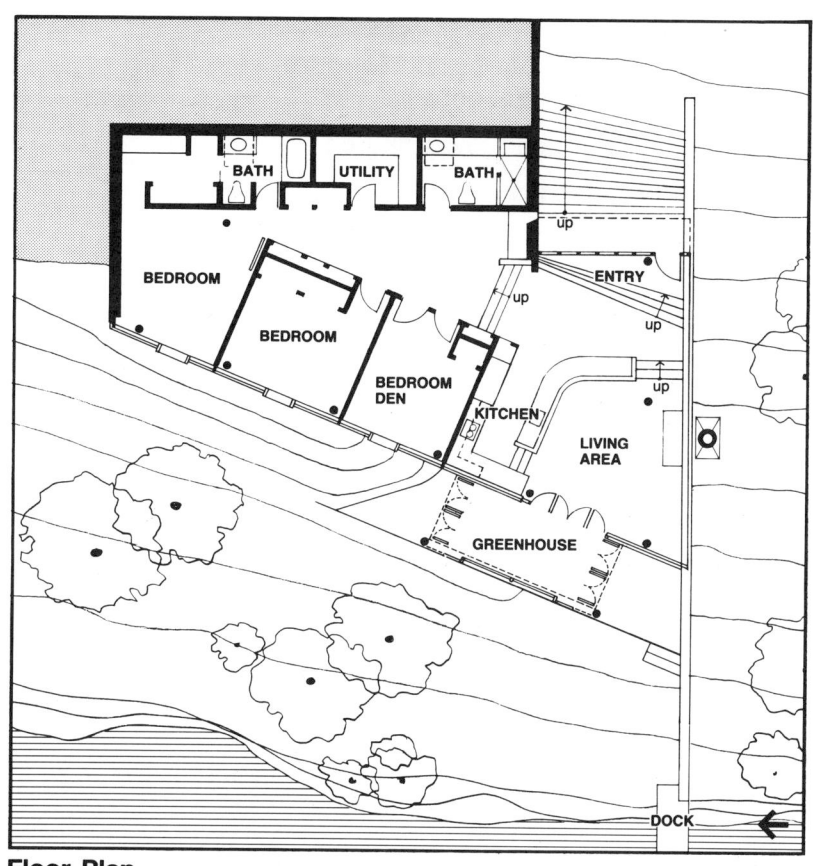
Floor Plan

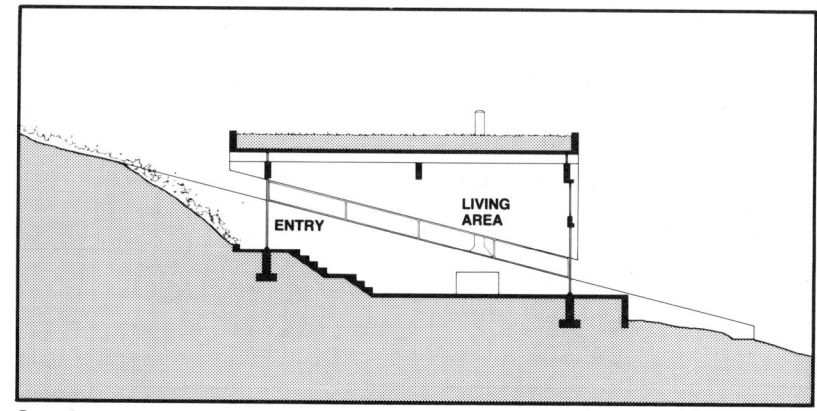
Section

Project Data

Project: Mercy Residence

Location: Carnation, Washington

Date of Completion: 1982

Architect: Miller/Hull Partnership, Seattle, Washington

Structural Engineer: Bud Guergens and Associates

Landscape Architect: Ned Gulbran

Contractor: Carlin Construction Company

Photographs: Miller/Hull

Gross Floor Area: 2,200 square feet

Structure: Timber plank-and-beam roof structure supported on wood columns, reinforced concrete walls in contact with the earth

Earth Cover: 90 percent of the roof is covered with 18 inches of soil, 60 percent of the exterior wall area is earth covered

Insulation: Extruded polystyrene, 5 inches on roof, 2 inches on below-grade walls.

Waterproofing: EPDM synthetic rubber membrane on roof, bentonite applied to below-grade walls

Heating System: Heat pump, wood-burning stove, and fireplace

Cooling System: None

Heating Degree Days: 5,185 (Seattle)

Cooling Degree Days: 129 (Seattle)

Construction Cost: $175,000

Sundown House

Sea Ranch, California

The Sundown House, designed and owned by architect David Wright, is placed partially underground both for energy efficiency and to blend unobtrusively into a remarkably beautiful natural setting along the California coast. The continuous grade of the sod roof makes the structure almost invisible from most places on the site. Native meadow vegetation has reclaimed the roof, blanketing the house in wild grasses that shade the soil from the summer sun.

Only a small form, which houses a loft for viewing the ocean, projects above the landscape. The larger masses of the house and garage/studio structures are evident as one approaches from the south. An exterior courtyard space has been created by careful placement of the garage/studio and earth berms in relation to the house and by being partially recessed. This creates a "weather-conditioned" front yard that is fully exposed to the south but sheltered from the prevailing winds.

There is no lack of sunlight inside the house, since it has been oriented to optimize penetration of winter solar radiation. The roof is pitched rather steeply to accommodate the low winter sun, which provides approximately 95 percent of the heating

required in this climate. A wood-burning stove serves as a backup source of heat. The passive solar design makes use of finish and structural materials, such as the rear concrete wall and brick flooring, to store solar heat. Thermal shades are used to reduce nighttime heat loss in winter. The shades also can be drawn on hot summer days to reduce heat gain and to set up a convection current that draws air through the house when vents are opened. Operable roof skylights admit daylight to the recesses of the interior and are hinged to vent rising hot air in the summer.

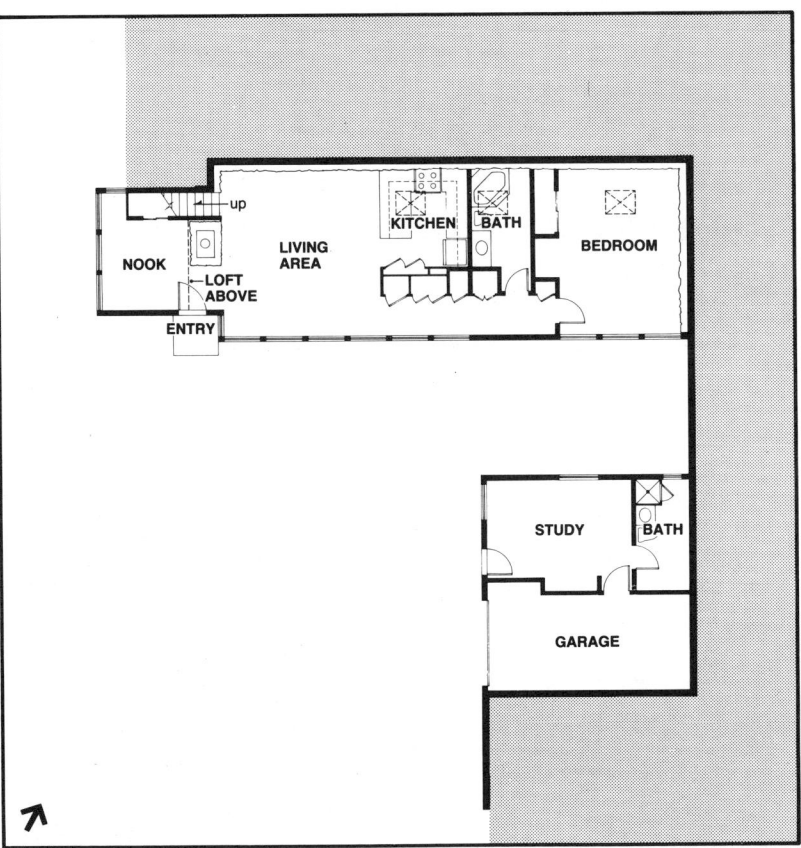

Floor Plan

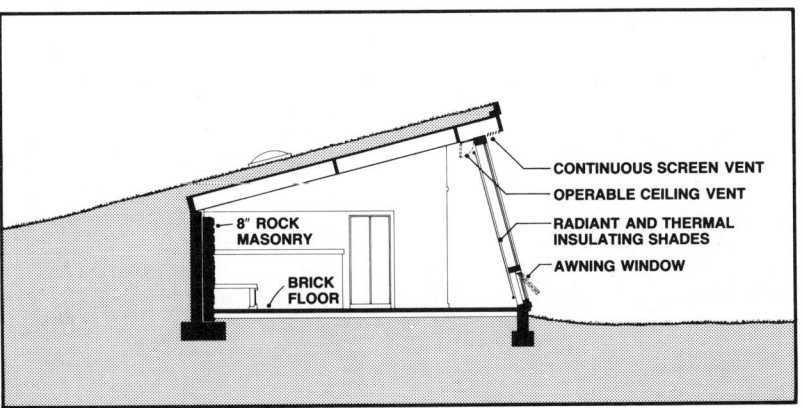

Section

Project Data

Project: Sundown House

Location: Sea Ranch, California

Date of Completion: 1976

Architect: David Wright Associates, AIA, Nevada City, California

Photographs: Darrow M. Watt

Gross Floor Area: 1,200 square foot house plus a 400-square foot garage/study

Structure: Wood rafters and plywood roof deck, reinforced concrete block walls

Earth Cover: Entire roof including garage is earth covered with 6 inches of soil except for above-grade loft structure and skylights, approximately 50 percent of exterior wall area is bermed

Insulation: Extruded polystyrene, 2 inches on roof and walls, 1 inch under floor

Waterproofing: Two 20-mil synthetic rubber membranes on roof, asphaltium on walls

Heating System: 95 percent passive solar heating with wood-burning stove providing backup heat source

Cooling System: No mechanical cooling, naturally induced ventilation

Heating Degree Days: 3,042 (San Francisco)

Cooling Degree Days: 108 (San Francisco)

Energy Use: Approximately ¾ to 1 cord of oak wood burned each winter

Construction Cost: $90,000

Lovins Research Center Bioshelter/House Project

Old Snowmass, Colorado

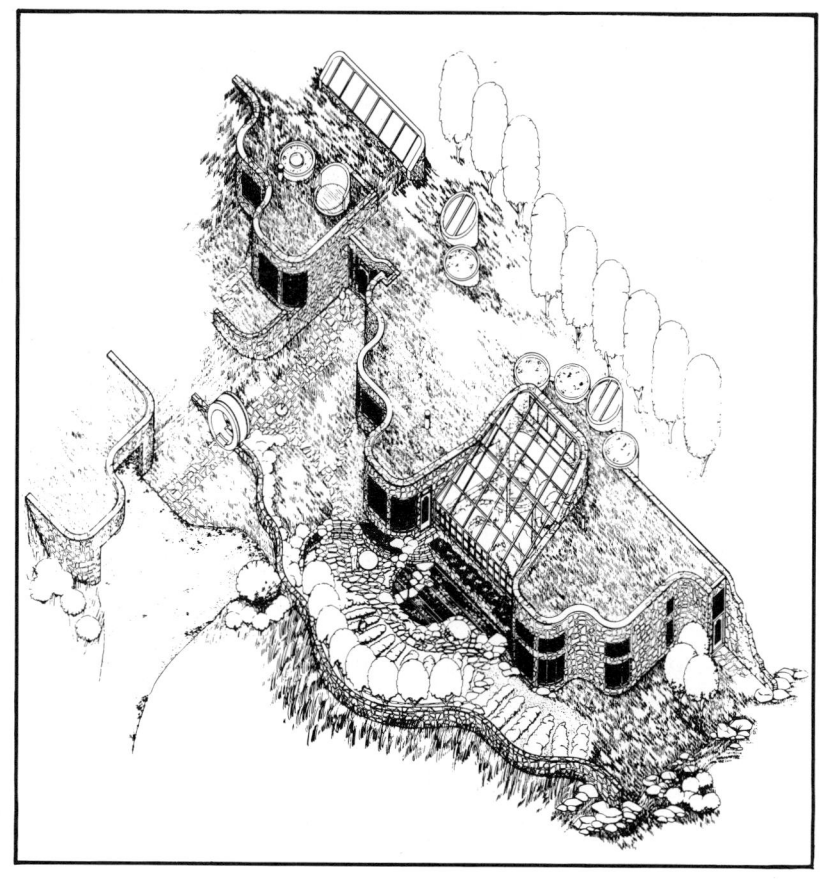

In 1983 an experimental multipurpose structure was completed in Old Snowmass, Colorado, that houses the nonprofit Rocky Mountain Institute and also is the home of Amory and Hunter Lovins. Some of the major concerns of the institute, which include energy, water, and agriculture, are demonstrated in the innovative design of the project. The earth sheltered, passive solar building includes an indoor farm and a number of other experiments related to energy and resource conservation.

Set into a gentle slope in a mountain valley, the 4,100-square foot structure extends along an east-west axis to provide maximum exposure to solar radiation in all spaces. With the entire north wall below grade and the roof covered with earth, the building appears to blend into the natural landscape. A large greenhouse structure extends above the flat roof in the center of the exposed south wall. Curved windows set into the undulating south wall permit sunlight from a variety of angles to penetrate more deeply into the rooms. The linear plan is divided into four major segments—a bedroom area on the east end, a living area, the greenhouse growing area, and a library/research center on the west end with a sleeping loft above for visitors.

The earth-covered roof structure consists of cedar decking supported by 6- by 12-inch joists and 12- by 16-inch oak beams. This is supported on the interior by one-foot-diameter red spruce columns still covered with bark. The exposed south wall, which was slipformed, consists of 4 inches of insulation sandwiched between two 6-inch concrete walls faced with lichened Dakota sandstone from a nearby hillside. The massive concrete walls, adobe floor, and water columns serve as storage for direct passive solar gain while the effective R-value of the roof is 60 and the walls is 40. Windows are made with argon-filled Heat Mirror, which has an R-value

of 5.3. It is anticipated that this tight, well-insulated, earth sheltered structure will require no heating energy in this 8,500-heating-degree-day climate and that interior temperatures will remain in the 70°F to 75°F range. Two wood-burning stoves are included only for aesthetic reasons.

In addition to reducing or eliminating the need for space heating and cooling, this structure is intended to demonstrate reduced energy use in other areas as well as water and land resource conservation. Electrical requirements for the building are 80 to 90 percent below normal because of efficient lighting and appliances as well as a number of innovative devices. An icebox is cooled year-round by a passive night radiator, solar heat is used in a clothes-drying closet, and cooking will eventually be done with biogas or solar-generated steam. Domestic hot water is supplied by an active solar system, and no backup is required because of efficient water use and graywater heat recovery. The greenhouse, which is one of the major aesthetic amenities of the building, will provide occupants with fruit, vegetables, and fish year-round. A waterfall in the greenhouse serves to aerate water from the fishtank and also provides a noise buffer between working and living spaces.

Project Data

Project: Lovins Research Center/Bioshelter/House Project

Location: Old Snowmass, Colorado

Date of Completion: 1983

Architect: The Aspen Design Group, Aspen, Colorado

Structural Engineer: Nicol and Giltner, Boulder, Colorado

Contractor: Built by owner with professional and volunteer assistance

Foremen and Design Consultants: Jock de Swart; Larry Doble, P.E.; Jim Logan; Christopher Cappy; and Charles Manlove

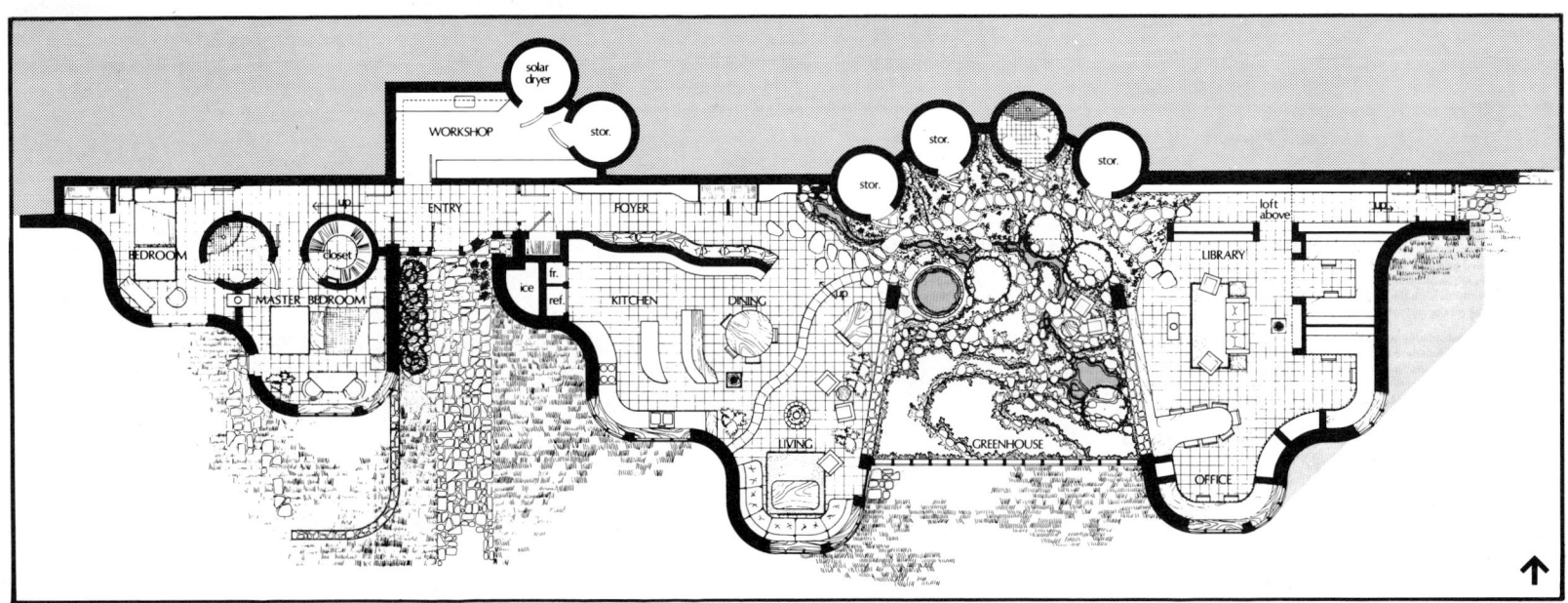

Floor Plan

Photographs: Doug Lee

Gross Floor Area: 4,100 square feet total, including 900-square foot greenhouse, 900-square foot office, and 200-square foot loft area

Structure: Cedar decking on 6- x 12-inch joists and 12- x 16-inch oak beams form roof structure supported by 1 foot-diameter red spruce posts; reinforced concrete walls; adobe floor

Earth Cover: Entire roof except for greenhouse and skylights is covered with 8 inches of topsoil over 6 to 8 inches of gravel, approximately 50 percent of walls are earth bermed

Insulation: 4⅜ to 8⅜ inches of freon-filled polyurethane on roof (R-8.33 per inch), 4 inches of freon-filled polyurethane on below-grade and exposed south walls, 4 inches of polystyrene extending around perimeter of floor

Waterproofing: 40-mil EPDM membrane over roof insulation, tar and 6-mil polyethylene over below-grade wall insulation

Heating System: Direct solar gain stored in masonry walls and floor, no auxiliary heat required; five heat exchangers are used for ventilation

Cooling System: No mechanical cooling required

Heating Degree Days: 8,500-8,900

Cooling Degree Days: 200-400

Energy Use: No heating or cooling required, electrical use for all other purposes is 0.2 Watt per square foot

Construction Cost: $523,000 excluding land and financing

Patterson Residence

Tempe, Arizona

The many benefits associated with earth sheltered housing are sometimes offset by increased construction costs. Costs tend to be higher for two reasons; additional structure required to support heavy earth loads, and the extra costs incurred on unique, custom-built projects, especially when contractors have little experience. In 1979 Earth Systems was formed with the idea of creating a prefabricated building system that would address these problems.

The basic structure devised by the company is a two-story reinforced concrete dome covered with earth. The dome shape is extremely efficient in supporting several feet of earth with a minimum of material. The structure itself is built using a prefabricated kit consisting of arched I-beams, a compression ring, wire and fabric forming panels, and steel reinforcing rods. Four inches of shotcrete are then sprayed over the reinforcing to form the thin shell. Since building their first house in 1980, Earth Systems has developed a number of variations on the basic dome structure, including an elongated dome and a combination dome/barrel vault that is open on one end.

An excellent example of the Earth Systems dome constructed in a hot climate is the Patterson Residence in Tempe, Arizona. Ten steel arches form the 40-foot-diameter, two-story dome structure. The lower floor is completely below grade, while the excavated earth is placed around and over the upper half of the dome. A cupola in the center of the roof and two entrance/light wells provide natural light and ventilation to both levels.

A number of energy-related benefits can be derived from the earth-covered dome structure in this hot climate. The spherical shape is very compact, exposing a minimum amount of surface area to the outside. To reduce heat gain, openings are limited and glazing is shaded by overhangs and trellises. The earth cover has two beneficial effects. Because the earth is covered with grass, solar radiation reaching the building envelope is reduced considerably. Also, some direct cooling from the earth is likely to be available in the deeper portions of the building. Warm air rises along the curved walls and is directed to the central cupola where it can escape. According to Earth Systems, the total electric bills in this house, which range from $40 to

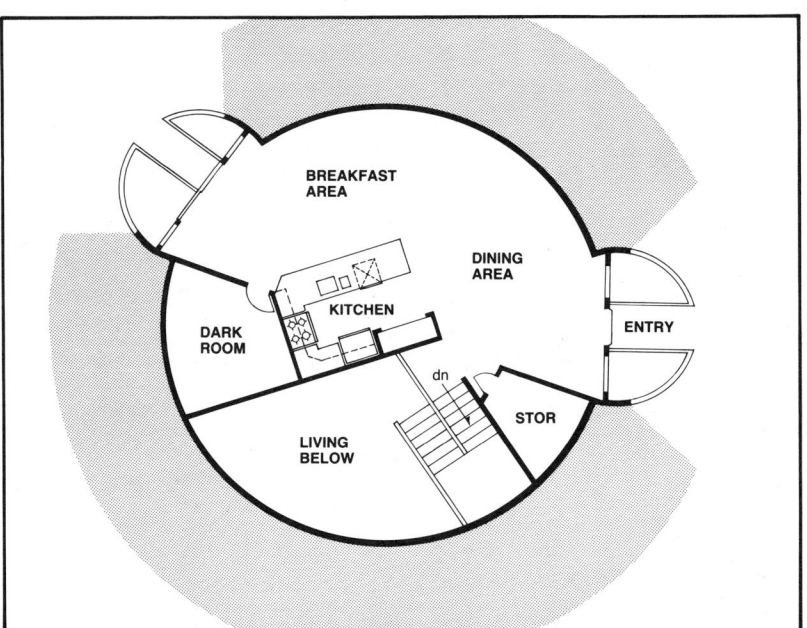

Upper Level Floor Plan

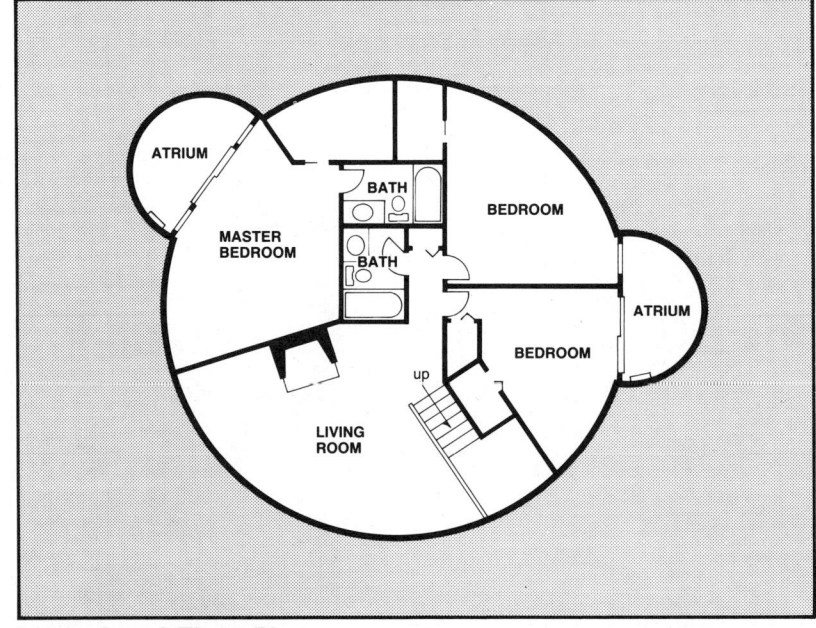

Lower Level Floor Plan

312

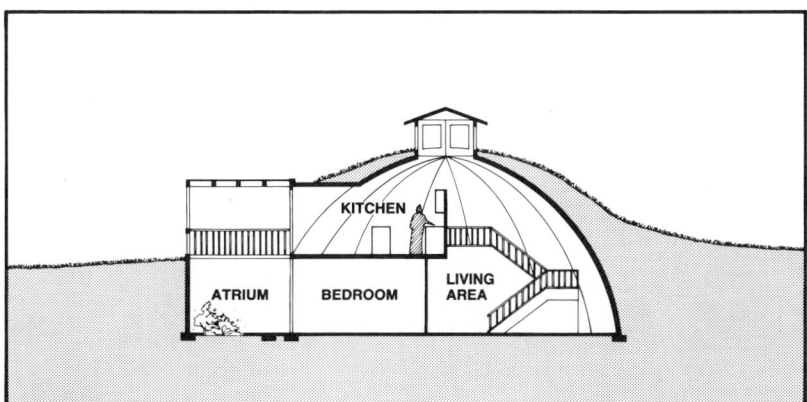

Section

$80 per month, are significantly lower than electric bills for conventional housing in the same area.

Houses utilizing this prefabricated structural system have been built in most regions of the United States. Earth Systems indicates that costs usually range from $28 to $35 per square foot for owner-built homes and $35 to $50 for contractor-built homes. The Patterson residence—including a two-car garage of conventional construction—cost $115,000.

Project Data

Project: Patterson Residence

Location: Tempe, Arizona

Architect: Earth Systems, Durango, Colorado

Structural Engineer: Don Aadland

Contractor: Jim Hold Construction

Photographs: James Brett

Gross Floor Area: 1,900 square feet

Structure: 40-foot-diameter reinforced concrete dome, 4 inches thick

Earth Cover: 90 percent of total roof and wall area is earth covered, average depth on the roof is 6 feet

Insulation: 1 inch of polystyrene on below-grade dome surfaces

Waterproofing: Bentonite-based mixture (Bentonize) sprayed onto below-grade concrete surfaces

Heating/Cooling System: Heat pump

Heating Degree Days: 1,552

Cooling Degree Days: 3,508

Construction Cost: $115,000, including a conventionally constructed two-car garage

Banen Residence

Fountain Hills, Arizona

The Banen Residence in Fountain Hills, Arizona illustrates the climate control advantages and aesthetic potential of earth-integrated design in a hot, arid climate. Faced with a steeply sloping site and community design restrictions requiring new buildings to retain existing vegetation and earth-tone colors, architect James Scalise felt an earth sheltered house was an appropriate solution. In addition, the design met the owner's desire to control summer heat gain and integrate the building with the land.

In this extremely hot southwestern climate, the major design considerations are almost the opposite of those for a cold northern region. The steep, north-facing slope (25-percent grade) selected for the Banen Residence is ideally suited to minimizing solar exposure. Windows and outdoor living areas are placed on the north side where magnificent views of the valley and mountains beyond are available. Earth covers the roof; the southeast and southwest walls of the wedge-shaped house are below grade. Because the house is set into the existing land contours, it is mostly hidden from the road on the south, and thus provides views from the road over the house and privacy for the occupants.

The two-story greenhouse space at the entrance is an important element of the total design. It is a plant-filled, naturally lighted entrance area in which the transition to the below-grade house is made from the surface. The greenhouse also provides natural light to bedroom and living spaces on the south side of the house. Two glass-covered sun wells perform a similar function, and like the greenhouse, help to cool the house in summer and warm it in winter. Vents can be opened in the greenhouse and sun wells to exhaust hot air and induce ventilation when desirable in summer. Since they provide the only direct exposure to the sun in winter, the glass-covered greenhouse and sun wells are sources of passive solar heat, which is distributed by fans into the house.

On the building perimeter, 12-inch-thick reinforced concrete block walls resist earth pressures while a system of flat wood trusses, glue-laminated wood beams, and a plywood roof deck support the weight of 12 inches of earth on the roof. A seamless waterproof membrane was sprayed over the entire wood roof and masonry wall structure.

Compared to conventional housing in the region, the Banen House is very well insulated. The total effective R-value of the earth-covered roof is 40; for the upper part of the below-grade walls, the R-value is 20. Below a depth of 5 feet, the walls are uninsulated to provide direct contact with the moderate earth temperature at that level. As a result of the passive methods of reducing heat gain and benefitting from earth contact cooling, the maximum heat gain was reduced by 55 percent from that of a conventional house of similar size. This permitted the installation of a 3-ton—rather than 7-ton—cooling system. The primary cooling system in the house, however, is an evaporative cooler; the conventional air-conditioning system is only used during humid periods in August. Solar panels mounted on the garage roof provide domestic hot water and heat for the swimming pool if needed [Scalise, 1983].

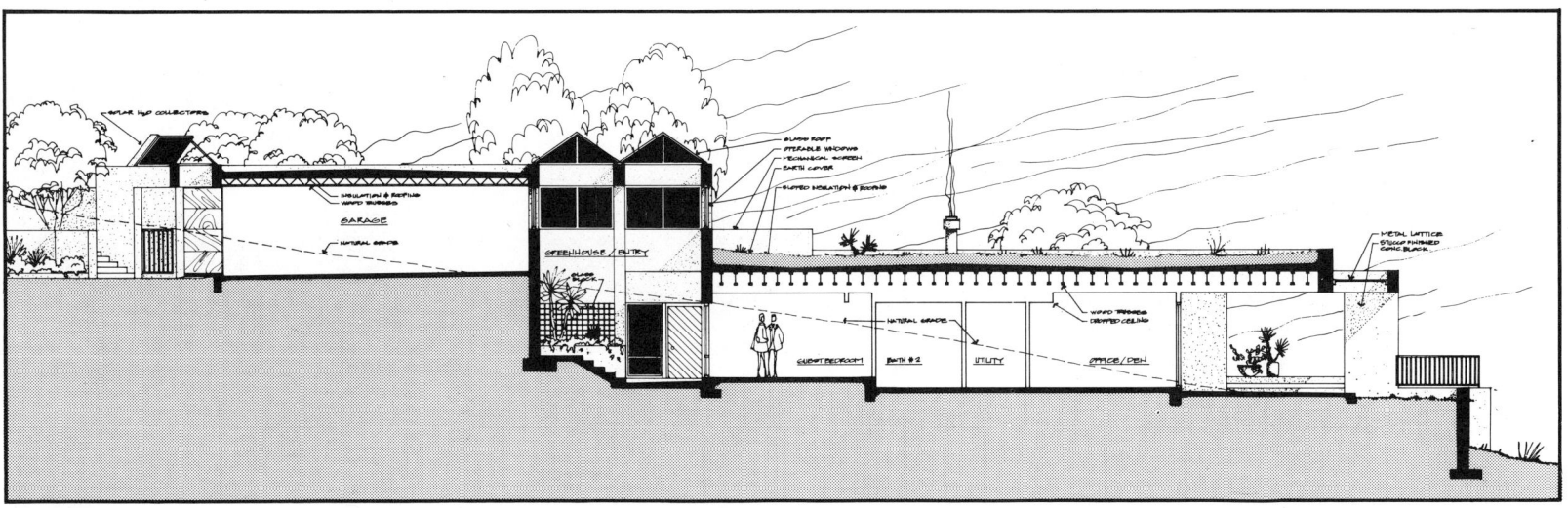

Section

Project Data

Project: Banen Residence

Location: Fountain Hills, Arizona

Date of Completion: 1983

Architect: James Scalise Associates, Phoenix, Arizona

Contractor: Built by owner

Photographs: James Scalise

Gross Floor Area: 3,590 square feet total including 885 square foot garage/shop and 355 square foot greenhouse and sun wells

Structure: 12 inches reinforced concrete block walls, flat wood trusses, and glue-laminated beams support plywood roof deck

Waterproofing: 40-mil GACOFLEX elastomeric membrane (liquid urethane rubber) sprayed on roof and below-grade walls to the footing

Earth Cover: 90 percent of house roof is covered with 12 inches of soil (garage/shop, greenhouse and sun wells are not earth covered); approximately 60 percent of walls are below grade

Insulation: 2 inches of high density polyurethane (R-7.35/inch) on below-grade walls to a depth of 5 feet, 5½ inches fiberglass (R-19) plus 2 inches of high-density polyurethane (R-14.7) on roof

Heating System: Wood-burning fireplaces and electric forced-air backup supplement passive solar heating

Cooling System: Evaporative cooling with electric heat pump backup supplement earth-contact cooling.

Heating Degree Days: 1,552 (Phoenix)

Cooling Degree Days: 3,508 (Phoenix)

Construction Cost: $46 per square foot

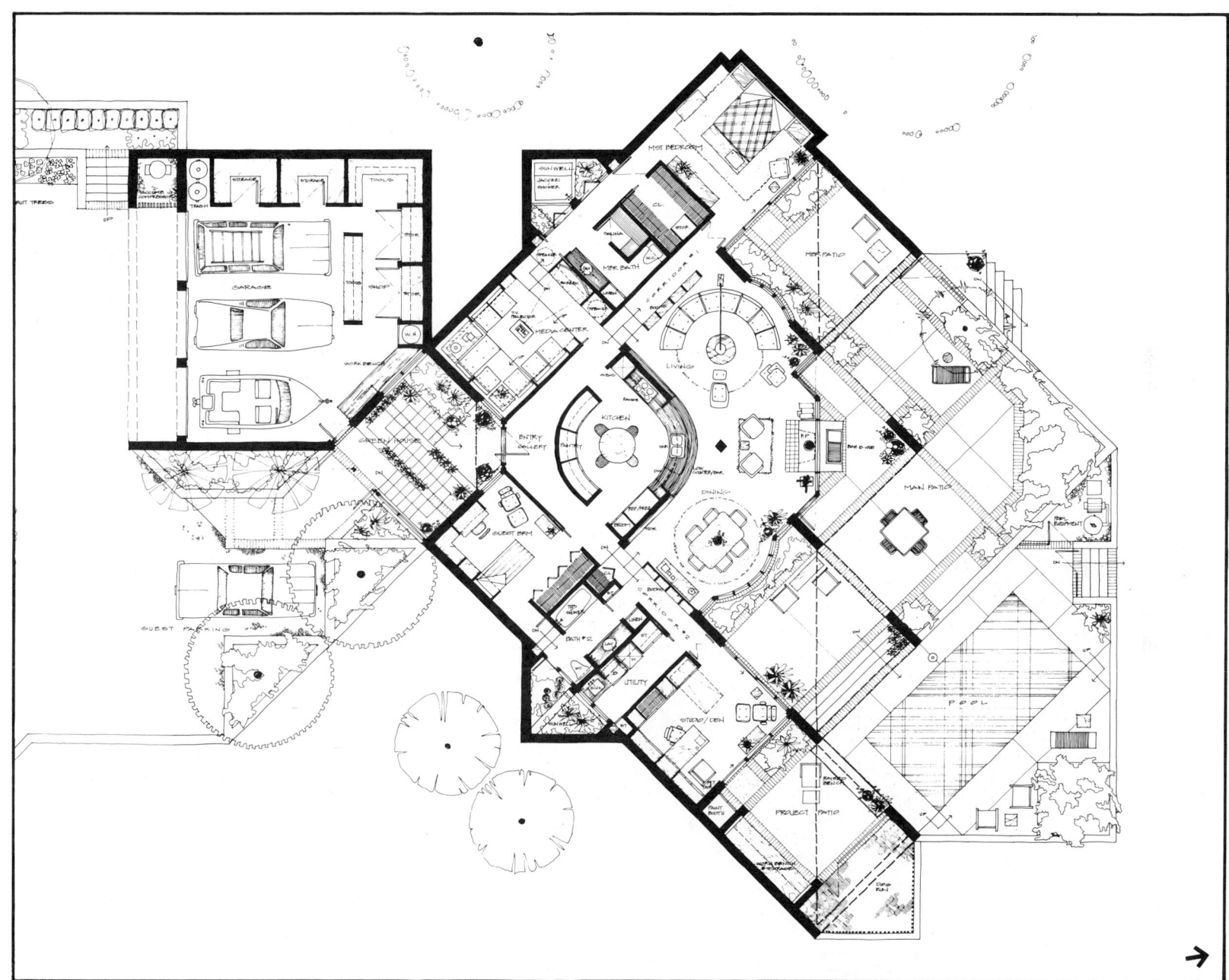

Floor Plan

Bordie Residence

Austin, Texas

A number of conditions imposed by both the climate and the owner were satisfied by this subsurface design. In the face of increasing fuel and energy costs, the client wished to build a house that would be comfortable, yet cost little to maintain and operate. The recent history of two tornadoes passing through this property presented another very real concern to the owner, who expressed a personal desire for an atrium-type plan. The resulting design, in which all rooms surround a central courtyard, is well protected from both tornadoes and the hot climate. Surrounding earth berms divert winds over the structure and the earth-covered roof helps to reduce heat gain in the house. To some degree, the house is passively cooled through the exterior walls in contact with the earth. Cool night air will settle into the courtyard, forcing warmer air to rise out of the spaces. This arrangement also protects the house from any cold winds in winter.

Viewed from the exterior, the Bordie residence is barely noticeable in its rural setting. A patio covered with a trellis and two retaining walls that direct one to the entrance are the most visible elements. The house is not fully subgrade, in fact, the structure has been only halfway recessed into the top of a low knoll and mounded over with 14 to 18 inches of earth. The slope of the underground concrete plank roof gives height to the rooms below and accentuates the mounded form above. Solar collector panels are mounted on a similarly mounded form independent of the house, and all earth cover on and around the building has been replanted with native grasses and wildflowers.

The approximately 20- by 30-foot courtyard is an integral part of the plan in many ways. In addition to admitting daylight and air into surrounding rooms and serving as an outdoor room in itself, the recessed atrium is actually the central circulation space, connecting the children's bedrooms to the main living areas of the house. This exterior detachment is purposeful in ensuring privacy between the different "wings" of the house and will serve this same function when the children have left and their rooms are converted into studies or offices. Although this exterior circulation arrangement may be satisfactory only in southern climates, such a plan could possibly be roofed with a demountable cover

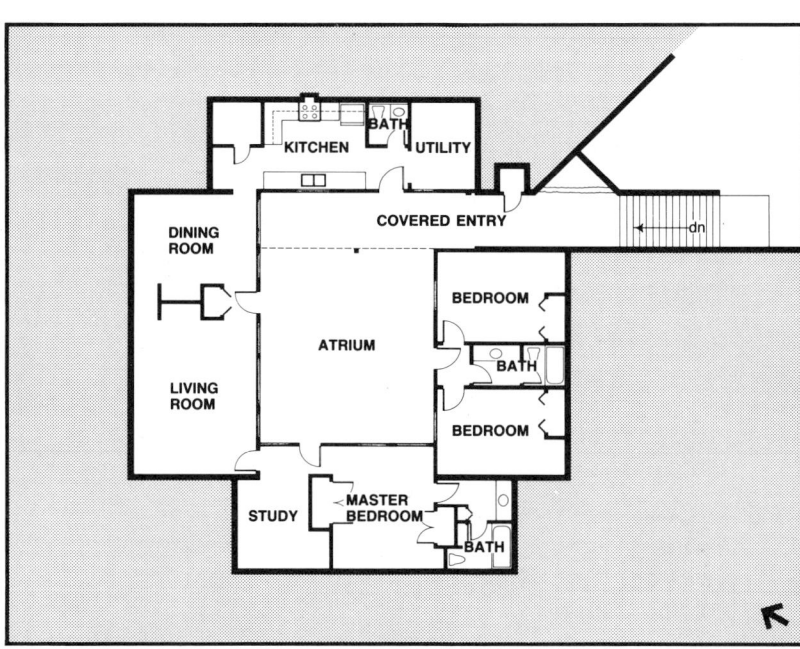

Floor Plan

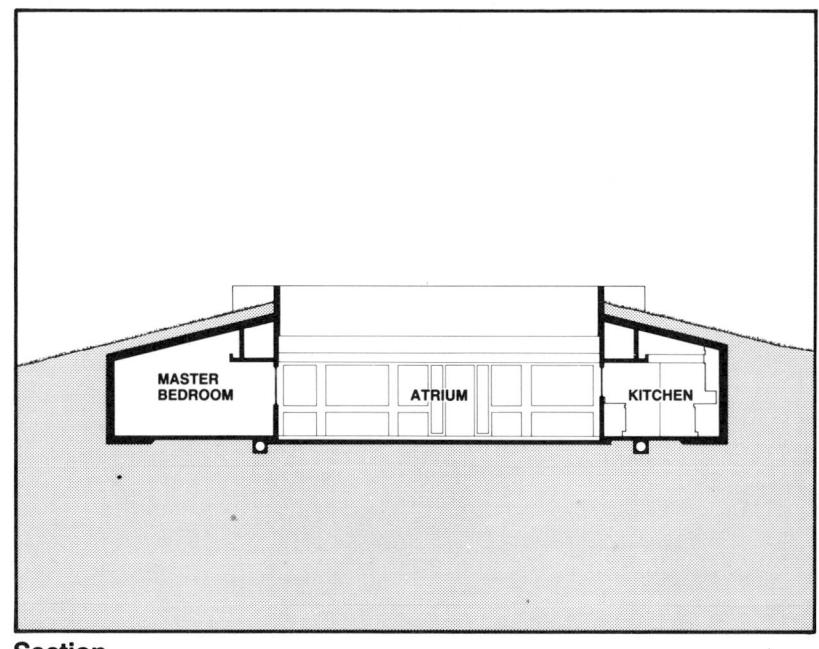

Section

or inflatable dome for protection from northern winters.

In 1975, when the house was constructed, solar collection panels for space heating were considered a very attractive alternative. Placing the structure underground to reduce loads results in a more efficient application of the solar system. Utility bills for this house were estimated to be half those of a comparable conventional structure.

Project Data

Project: Bordie Residence

Location: Austin, Texas

Date of Completion: 1975

Architect: Coffee and Crier, Austin, Texas

Engineer: George Maxwell

Photographs: Coffee and Crier

Gross Floor Area: 2,000 square feet

Structure: Precast concrete plank roof, 8-inch-thick reinforced concrete walls

Earth Cover: Entire roof is covered with 14 to 18 inches of soil, 62 percent of exterior wall area is earth bermed while remaining 38 percent faces interior atrium

Insulation: Polyurethane foam, 3 inches on roof

Waterproofing: Synthetic rubber membrane on roof, mastic and fiberglass mopped on below-grade walls

Heating System: Solar hot water system using electric furnace as a backup source with forced-air distribution

Cooling system: 2-ton direct expansion split system

Heating Degree Days: 1,737

Cooling Degree Days: 2,908

Dune Houses

Atlantic Beach, Florida

Architect William Morgan has been designing earth-integrated structures for many years, including a number of houses that are bermed around the exterior walls but roofed with conventional materials. The Dune Houses are Morgan's first earth-roofed dwellings and are owned and maintained by Morgan Properties as rental units. They are unique in many respects, including the fact that they are the first (modern) underground multifamily units to be built in this country. The Dune Houses are also among the first subsurface dwellings to exploit fully a structural system designed expressly in response to the peculiarities of earth pressure loading.

The main objective in building below grade was to preserve the low profile of the beachfront property from the street side. Approaching from this side, one can see the ocean over the dunelike forms of the house. A small penetration in the center for the entrance is the only indication of a structure below. Viewed from the beach side, the dune forms appear larger but still blend unobtrusively with the landscape of the coast. Two oval-shaped openings are the only man-made forms visible from this side.

The shape of the plan is two ovals connected by a common bearing wall in the center. One living unit

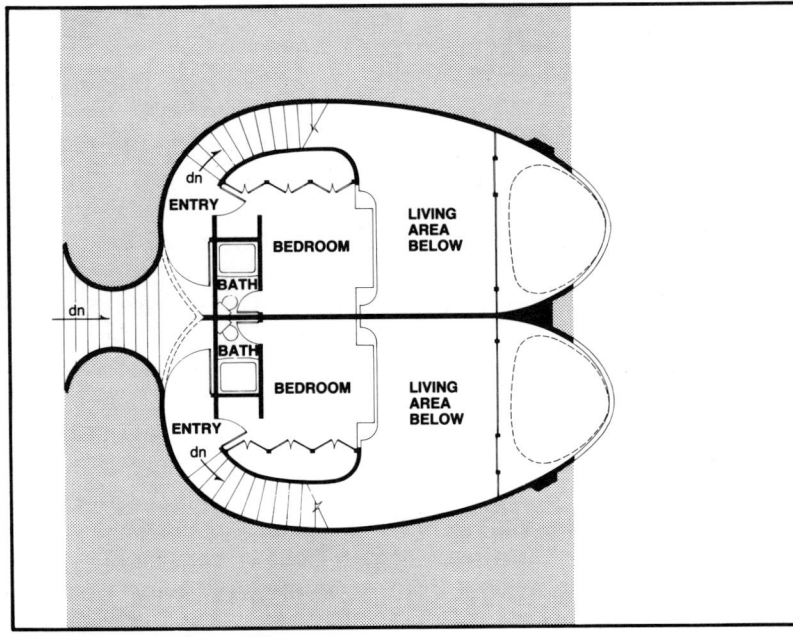

Upper Level Floor Plan

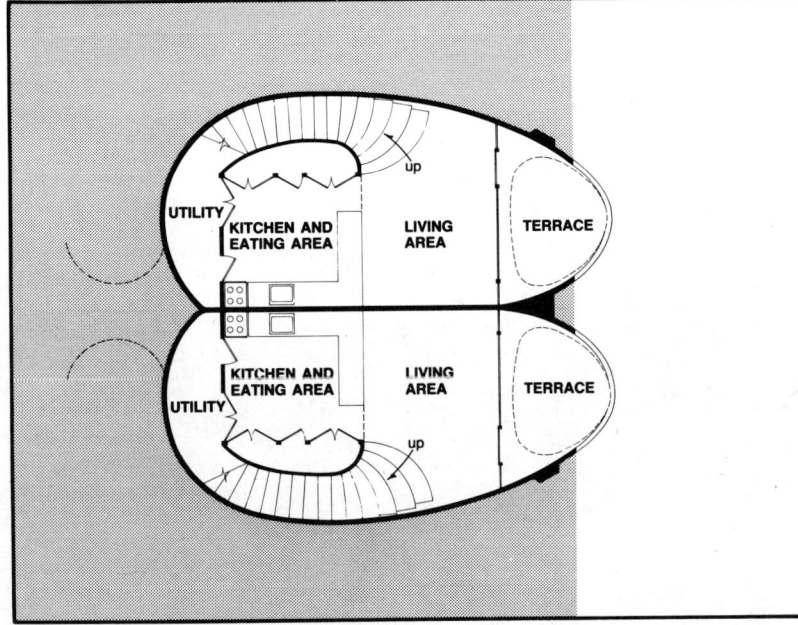

Lower Level Floor Plan

is the mirror image of the other. The units are entered on the upper level, which contains a bedroom loft that overlooks the living space below. One descends a curving staircase, which follows the form of the shell structure to the lower floor. The ocean view can be seen through a single window opening from the kitchen, dining, and living spaces on the lower level. The open plan arrangement and two-story space in the living room permit the curved form of the shell structure to be visible, resulting in a dynamic, sculptural interior design.

Energy conservation was not a prime consideration in the design of these units, since the Jacksonville area benefits from a mild climate all year long. Still, the subsurface design maintains a constant 70°F indoor temperature, although this is affected by the residents' habits regarding cooking, lighting, washing, drying, and leaving doors open.

Morgan stated that "one of the main ideas behind this design has been designing a building that is of the earth, not just in the earth—i.e., an above-grade design uncomfortably overstressed when below grade. We designed the shells in careful balance with the surrounding earth so that the inward pressure of the earth presses uniformly on the shell, locking or post-tensioning the Gunite shell in place. The structure actually is stronger because of the earth pressing on it." Because of the efficient use of materials and potential cost reduction represented by this type of design, shell structures may prove to be one important future direction in the evolution of earth sheltered housing.

Project Data

Project: Dune Houses

Location: Atlantic Beach, Florida

Date of Completion: 1974

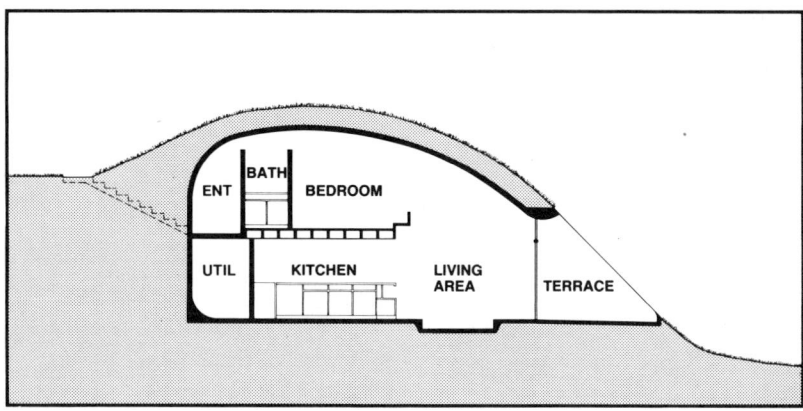

Section

Architect: William Morgan Architects, Jacksonville, Florida

Structural Engineer: Geiger Berger Associates

Mechanical Engineer: Roy Turknett Engineers

Photographs: Alexandre Georges, Creative Photographic Services

Gross Floor Area: 1,500 square feet total building area, each unit is 750 square feet

Structure: Reinforced concrete shell forms walls and roof

Earth Cover: Entire roof is earth covered, minimum soil thickness is 22 inches; approximately 80 percent exterior wall area is in contact with earth

Insulation: None required

Waterproofing: Liquid bituminous, brushed on

Heating and Cooling System: 1-ton water-cooled reverse-cycle heat pump

Heating Degree Days: 1,327 (Jacksonville)

Cooling Degree Days: 2,596 (Jacksonville)

References

Included in this list of general references are the specific references cited throughout the text.

Ahrens, D., T. Ellison, and R. Sterling, 1981. *Earth Sheltered Homes: Plans and Designs.* Underground Space Center, Universty of Minnesota. NY: Van Nostrand Reinhold Company, Inc., 126 pp.

Alternatives in Energy Conservation: The Use of Earth Covered Buildings, 1975. Moreland, F., ed. Proceedings and Notes of conference held in Forth Worth, TX, July 9-12, 1975. Stock No. 038.000.00286-4, 362 pp.

American Institute of Architects Research Corporation, 1980. *Regional Guidelines for Building Passive Energy Conserving Homes,* for U.S. Department of Housing and Urban Development, Contract H-2384. HUD-PDR-355(2).

American Iron and Steel Institute, 1971. *Handbook of Steel Drainage and Highway Construction Products.* American Iron and Steel Institute, New York.

Anderson, B., 1981. *Earth Sheltered Plans for Better Living.* MN: WEBCO Publishing, Inc.

Anderson, B., 1983. *Underground Waterproofing.* MN: WEBCO Publishing, Inc.

Anderson, B., 1984. *Earth Integrated Residential Designs.* National Plan Service, Elmhurst, IL.

Aughenbaugh, N.B., and J. D. Rockaway, 1976. "Go Underground for Low Cost Housing." *Proceedings,* International Symposium on Housing Problems, Atlanta, GA.

Baggs, S.A., 1978. "Underground Architecture," *Architecture Australia,* Vol. 66, pp. 62-69.

Barker, M., 1978. *Building Underground for People: Eleven Selected Projects in the U.S.* AIA Research Corporation, Washington, D.C.

Balcomb, J.D., et al., 1983. *Passive Solar Design Handbook, Volume III.* American Solar Energy Society, New York, 668 pp.

Barnard, J.E., 1974. "Saving by Going Underground," *AIA Journal,* Vol. 61, pp. 48-49.

Basic Building Code, (BOCA). Building Officials and Code Administrations International, Inc., 1313 East 60th Street, Chicago, IL.

Baum, G.T., A.J. Boer, and J.C. Macintosh, Jr., 1980. *The Earth Shelter Handbook.* WI: Tech/Data Publications.

Behr, R.A., 1981. "Life Cycle Cost Performance of Flat Site Earth Shelter Design," *Earth Shelter Performance and Evaluation.* Proceedings of the Second National Technical Conference, Tulsa, OK, (available from Architectural Extension, Oklahoma State University, Stillwater, OK).

Behr, R.A., and E.W. Keisling, 1981. *Design Program: Improved Structural Systems for Earth Sheltered Housing,* Civil Engineering Department, Texas Tech University.

Behr, R.A., E.W. Keisling, and G. Boubel, 1980. "Thin Shell Roof Systems and Construction Techniques for Earth Sheltered Housing," *Earth Sheltered Building Design Innovations.* Proceedings, conference, Oklahoma City (available from Architectural Extension, Oklahoma State University, Stillwater, OK).

Bibliography on Natural Ventilation and Passive Cooling Techniques, 1982. Oklahoma State University, Architectural Extension, 120 Architecture Building, Oklahoma State University, Stillwater, OK 74078.

Bligh, T.P., 1976. "Energy Conservation by Building Underground," *Underground Space,* Vol. 1, No. 1, Mayune, 1976, pp. 19-33.

Boyer, L.L., and W.T. Grondzik, 1983. "Energy Performance of Earth Covered Dwellings in the U.S.," *Energy Efficient Buildings with Earth Shelter Protection.* Proceedings, conference, Sydney, Australia, pp. 295-298, (available from Architectural Extension, Oklahoma State University, Stillwater, OK).

Busch, J.F., A.K. Meier, and T.S. Nagpal, 1984. "Measured Heating Performance of New, Low-Energy Homes: Updated Results from the BECA-A Database," ACEEE 1984 Summer Study on Energy Efficiency in Buildings. Santa Cruz, CA.

Campbell, S., 1980. *The Underground House Book.* VT: Garden Way Publishing.

Carmody, J.C., G.D. Meixel, and L. Shen, 1983. *Preliminary Design Guidelines for Earth Contact Buildings.* A report for the U.S. DOE Passive Cooling Program, Contract No. DE-AC03-80SF11508. Underground Space Center, University of Minnesota.

Carmody, J., and R. Sterling, 1983. *Underground Building Design: Commercial and Institutional Structures.* Underground Space Center, University of Minnesota. NY: Van Nostrand Reinhold Company Inc.

Carter, D., 1982. *Build It Underground.* NY: Sterling Publishing Co., Inc.

Chalmers, L.S., and J.A. Jones, 1980. *Homes in the Earth.* CA: Chronicle Books.

Claesson, J., and B. Eftring, 1979. *Optimal Thermal Insulation and Ground Heat Losses.* A report by Lund Institute of Technology, Department of Mathematical Physics, Lund, Sweden.

Council of Planning Libraries, 1974. "Occupance and Use of Underground Mined Out Space in Urban Areas: An Annotated Bibliography." Exchange Bibliography #602.

Dean, A.D., 1978. "Underground Architecture...," *AIA Journal,* 67(4):34-51.

Dechow, F.J., and K.A. Epstein, 1977. "Laboratory and Field Investigations of Moisture Absorption and Its Effects on Thermal Performance for Various Insulations." Prepared for ASTM Symposium on Advances in Heat Transmission Measurements, Philadelphia.

Dempewolff, R.F., 1977. "Your Next House Could Have a Grass Roof," *Popular Mechanics,* 147(3):78-81.

Desert Housing, 1980. Clark, K.N. and P. Paylore, eds. University of Arizona, Office of Arid Lands Studies, Tucson, Arizona.

Donovan, Hamester, and Rattien, Inc., 1979. *The Earth Sheltered/Underground Buildings Market: A Policy Analysis.* Prepared for the U.S. Department of Energy.

Earth Covered Buildings and Settlements, 1979. F. Moreland, ed. Proceedings of a conference titled Alternatives in Habitat: the Use of Earth-Covered Buildings and Settlements. Available from GPO #CONF-7805139-P2. Also available from NTIS.

Earth Covered Buildings: Technical Notes, 1979. F. Moreland, Higgs, and Shih, eds. Proceedings of a conference titled Alternatives in Habitat: the Use of Earth Covered Buildings and Settlements." Available from GPO CONF-7805139-P1. Also available from NTIS.

Earth Shelter Performance & Evaluation, 1981. L.L. Boyer, ed. Proceedings of the Second National Technical Conference, October 16-17, 1981. Sponsored by Architectural Extension, Oklahoma State University.

Earth Sheltered Building Design Innovations, 1980. L.L. Boyer, ed. Proceedings from a National Technical Conference, April 18-19, 1980. Sponsored by Architectural Extension, Oklahoma State University.

Earth Sheltered Structures in Alternative Energy Sources, III, 1980. T.N. Veziroglu, ed. Vol. 7, Conservation, pp 3-87. Proceedings of the 3rd Miami International Conference on Alternative Energy Sources. Dec. 15-17, 1980.

Earth Systems, Inc., 1984. Product Literature, P.O. Box 3270, Durango, CO 81301.

Eggert, J., 1982. *Low Cost Earth Shelters.* PA: Stackpole Books.

Edelhart, M., 1982. *The Handbook of Earth Shelter Design.* NY: Doubleday and Company, Inc.

Energy Efficient Buildings with Earth Shelter Protection, 1983. S.A. Baggs, ed. Proceedings of Australasian Papers presented at the First International Conference, Sydney, Australia, August 1-6, 1983. Unisearch Limited, P.O. Box 1, Kensington, New South Wales, 2033, Australia.

Energy Efficient Buildings With Earth Shelter Protection, 1983. L.L. Boyer, ed. Proceedings of the First International Earth Sheltered Buildings Conference, August 1-6, 1983, Sydney, Australia. Architectural Extension and University Center for Energy Research, Oklahoma State University.

Fairhurst, C., 1976. "Going Under to Stay on Top," *Underground Space,* Vol. 1, No. 2, pp. 71-86.

Federal Program Presentations and National Solar Data Program: Volume One, 1979. Proceedings of the U.S. Department of Energy's Regional Solar Updates, CONF-790758-Vol I. NTIS, Springfield, VA 22161.

Frenette, E.R., 1981. *Earth Sheltering: The Form of Energy and The Energy Form.* T.L. Holthusen, ed. NY: Pergamon Press.

Fuller, W., 1981. "What's in the Air for Tightly Built Houses?" *Solar Age.* June 1981, pp. 30-32.

Givoni, B., 1979. "Modifying the Ambient Temperature of Underground Buildings," *Earth Covered Buildings: Technical Notes,* Vol. 1. Proceedings of the conference, The Use of Earth Covered Settlements, U.S. DOE CONF-78-05138-P1, pp. 123-138, (available from NTIS, Springfield, VA 22161).

Goldberg, L.F., 1984. Unpublished report submitted to Minnesota Department of Energy and Economic Development under Contract #22100/02540-0265/01.

Goldberg, L.F., R.L. Sterling, and J.C. Carmody, 1984. *MHFA Solar/Earth Sheltered Housing Demonstration Project,* Final Report. Underground Space Center, University of Minnesota.

Grondzik, W.T., L.L. Boyer, and J.W. Zang, 1981. "Analysis of Utility Billings for 55 Earth Sheltered Projects," *Earth Shelter Performance and Evaluation.* Proceedings of the Second National Technical Conference, Tulsa, OK, (available from Architectural Extension, Oklahoma State University, Stillwater, OK).

Hait, J.N., 1983. *Passive Annual Heat Storage.* Rocky Mountain Reserch Center, P.O. Box 4694, Missoula, MT 59806. 152 pp.

Hanzal-Kashi, A., and E.R. Combs, 1984. "Loan Officers Perceptions Concerning Earth-Sheltered Housing: Risk, Complexity, and Advantage," *Underground Space,* Vol. 8, pp. 191-195. NY: Pergamon Press.

Hastings, S.R., and R.W. Crenshaw, 1977. *Window Design Strategies to Conserve Energy.* U.S. Government Printing Office, Washington, D.C.

Houghten, F.C., D.I. Taimuty, C. Gutberlet, and C.J. Brown, 1942. "Heat Loss Through Basement Walls and Floors," *Transactions.* American Society of Heating and Ventilating Engineers, No. 1213, pp. 369-384.

Housing in Arid Lands, 1980. G. Golany, ed. NY: John Wiley & Sons.

International Passive and Hybrid Cooling Conference, 1981. A. Bowen, ed. Proceedings of the International Passive and Hybrid Cooling Conference held Nov. 6-16, 1981, in Miami Beach, FL.

Invited Papers and Appendices: Volume Two, 1979. Proceedings of the U.S. Department of Energy's Regional Solar Updates, CONF-790758-Vol II. NTIS, Springfield, VA 22161.

Jones, L., 1977. "Non Traditional Military Uses of Underground Space," *Underground Space,* Vol. 2, No. 3. NY: Pergamon Press.

Jones, L., 1978. "Underground Construction." Council of Planning Libraries, 1313 E. 60th Street, Chicago, IL 60637.

Keehn, P.A., 1981. *Earth Sheltered Housing: An Annotated Bibliography and Directory.* Bibliography No. 43. Council of Planning Libraries, 1313 E. 60th Street Chicago, IL 60637.

Kern, B., K. Kern, J. Mullan, and O. Mullan, 1982. *The Earth Sheltered Owner-Built Home.* CA: Owner-Builder Publications, PO Box 817, North Fork, CA 93643.

Kim, H.G., and R.L. Sterling, 1983. "A Study of House Design Combining Earth Sheltering and Traditional Korean Architecture," *Energy Efficient Buildings with Earth Shelter Protection.* Proceedings, conference, Sydney, Australia, pp. 231-236, (available from Architectural Extension, Oklahoma State University, Stillwater, OK).

Korell, M.L., 1979. "Financing Earth Sheltered Housing: Issues and Opportunities," a paper presented at a seminar, Financing Earth Sheltered Homes, Minneapolis, MN.

Kusuda, T., 1971. *Earth Temperatures Beneath Five Different Surfaces.* NBS Report 10373, National Bureau of Standards, Washington, D.C., 148 pp.

Labs, K. 1976. "The Architectural Underground," *Underground Space* (Pergamon Press), Vol. 1, No. 1, May-June 1976, pp. 1-8; Vol. 1, No. 2, July-August 1976, pp. 135-156.

Labs, K., 1979. "Land Use Regulation of Underground Housing," PAS Memo, American Planning Association, 1313 East 60th Street, Chicago, IL.

Labs, K., 1981a. *Regional Analysis of Ground and Above-Ground Climate.* Oak Ridge National Laboratory, ORNL/Sub-81/40451/1, 192 pp., plus microfiche, (available from NTIS, Springfield, VA 22161).

Labs, K., 1981b. "Direct-Coupled Ground Cooling: Issues and Opportunities," *Passive Cooling '81.* International Technical Conference (Miami Beach), AS/ISES, University of Delaware, Newark, pp. 131-135.

Labs, K., 1982. "Living Up to Underground Design," *Solar Age,* Vol. 7, No. 8, August 1982, pp. 34-38.

Landa, E.R., 1984. "Radon in Earth-Sheltered Structures," *Underground Space,* Vol. 8, No. 4. NY: Pergamon Press, pp. 264-269.

Lane, C., 1979. "An Essay: Frequently Asked Questions on Earth-Sheltered Housing," *Underground Space,* Vol. 4, No. 3. NY: Pergamon Press, pp. 143-152.

Langley, J.B., and J.L. Gay, 1980. *Sun Belt Earth Sheltered Architecture: Part One.* FL: Sun Belt Earth Sheltered Research, P.O. Drawer 729, Winter Park, FL 32790.

LaNier, R., 1970. *Geotecture.* Library of Congress, Catalogue No. 76-139958, 72 pp.

Lord, D., 1981. "Interior Environment Quality in Earth Shelters," *Earth Shelter Performance and Evaluation.* Proceedings of the Second National Technical Conference, Tulsa, Oklahoma, (available from Architectural Extension, Oklahoma State University, Stillwater, OK).

Martindale, D., 1979. "New Houses Revive the Ancient Art of Living Underground," Smithsonian, 9(11):96-104.

Martindale, D., 1981. *Earth Shelters.* NY: E.P. Dutton.

Mason, R., 1976. "Underground Architecture," *The Futurist,* 10(1), pp. 16-20.

Maxwell, R.K., 1964. "Temperature Measurements and the Calculated Heat Flux in the Soil," Master of Science Thesis, University of Minnesota, 132 pp.

Mazria, E., 1979. *The Passive Solar Energy Book.* PA: Rodale Press, 436 pp.

Meixel, Jr., G.D., and T.P. Bligh, 1983. *Earth Contact Systems Final Report.* Prepared for the U.S. Department of Energy, Contact DE-AC03-80SF11508. Underground Space Center, University of Minnesota and Massachusetts Institute of Technology, Department of Mechanical Engineering, 397 pp.

Metz, D., 1979. "Underground House Design," *Solar Age.*

Metz, D., 1981. *Superhouse.* VT: Garden Way Publishing.

Minnesota Department of Energy and Economic Development, 1983. *Zoning for Earth Sheltered Buildings, A Guide for Minnesota Communities.* Energy Division, DEED, 150 East Kellogg Blvd., St. Paul, MN 55101.

Moreland, F.L., 1979. "Notes on Earth Covered Settlements," *Earth Covered Buildings and Settlements,* Vol. 2. Proceedings of the conference, The Use of Earth Covered Settlements, U.S. DOE CONF-7805138-P2, pp. 278-355, (available from NTIS, Springfield, VA 22161).

Moreland, F.L., et al., 1981. *Earth-Covered Buildings: An Exploratory Analysis for Hazard and Energy Performance.* Prepared for the Federal Emergency Management Agency, Washington, D.C., Contract #81-600091.

Morgan, W., 1972. "Buildings as Landscape: Five Current Projects by William Morgan," *Architectural Record.*

Moschandress, D.J., et al., 1978. *Indoor Air Pollution in the Residential Environment, Volume I, Data Collection, Analysis and Interpretation.* Environmental Protection Agency and U.S. Department of Housing and Urban Development, Gaithersburg, MD.

Muller, C.A., and R.A. Taylor, 1980. "No Cause for Apprehension about Costs of Insuring Earth-Sheltered Homes," *Underground Space,* Vol. 5. NY: Pergamon Press, pp. 28-30.

NAHB Research Foundation, Inc., 1979. *Insulation Manual,* Second Edition. National Association of Home Builders, Rockville, MD.

National Building Code (NBC). American Insurance Association, 85 John Street, NY, NY.

National Concrete Masonry Association (NCMA), 1982. *A Manual of Facts on Concrete Masonry,* NCMA, P.O. Box 781, Herndon, VA 22070.

Oehler, M., 1978. *The $50 and Up Underground House Book.* Mole Publishing Co., Bonners Ferry, ID, 113 pp.

Olgyay, V., 1963. *Design with Climate: A Bioclimatic Approach to Architectural Regionalism.* NJ: Princeton University Press.

Passive and Low Energy Alternatives I, 1982. A. Bowen, ed. First International PLEA Conference, Bermuda Islands. NY: Pergamon Press.

Passive Cooling Handbook, 1980. H. Miller, ed. Passive Cooling Workshop, Amherst, Massachusetts, October 20, 1980. Prepared for the U.S. Department of Energy, Contract W-7405-ENG-48. PUB-375. Lawrence Berkeley Laboratory, University of California, Berkeley, CA.

Passive Solar: Subdivisions, Windows, Underground, 1983. H. Wade, J. Cook, K. Labs and S. Selkowitz, eds. NY: American solar Energy Society, Publications Office.

Potential of Earth Sheltered and Underground Space, 1981. T.L. Holthusen, ed. NY: Pergamon Press.

Regional and Urban Planning Implementation, Inc., 1976. *Home Mortgage Lending and Solar Energy.* Information booklet prepared for US HUD and ERDA. 28 pp.

Rickman, G.A., and L.E. Bennett, 1979. *Go Underground and Save.* Gary Rickman, Route 1, box 160D, Wellsville, KS 66092.

Rollwagen, M., 1983. *The Consumer's Guide to Earth Sheltered Housing.* NY: Van Nostrand Reinhold Company, Inc.

Roy, R.L., 1979. *Underground Houses: How to Build a Low-Cost Home.* NY: Sterling Publishing Co., Inc.

Roy, R.L., 1984. *Earthwood: Building Low-Cost Alternative Houses.* NY: Sterling Publishing Co., Inc.

Rudofsky, B., 1964. *Architecture Without Architects.* NY: Doubleday & Company, Inc.

Rudofsky, B., 1977. *The Prodigious Builders.* NY: Harcourt Brace Jovanovich.

Scalise, J., ed., 1974. *Terratecture: The Environmental Benefits of Earth Integrating Architectural Design Techniques.* College Architecture, Arizona State University.

Scalise, J.W., ed., 1975. *Earth Integrated Architecture.* Architecture Foundation, College of Architecture, Arizona State University, Tempe, Arizona, 286 pp.

Scalise, J.W., 1983. "The Banen Desert Hillside House in Arizona," *Energy Efficient Buildings with Earth Shelter Protection.* Proceedings, conference, Sydney, Australia, pp. 69-74, (available from Architectural Extension, Oklahoma State University, Stillwater, OK).

Scott, R.G., 1979. *How to Build Your Own Underground Home.* PA: Tab Books, Inc., 256 pp.

Severson, J.L., 1981. "Thermal Performance of Various Insulations in Below-Earth-Grade Perimeter Application," presented at DOE-ORNSTM Conference in Clearwater Beach, Florida.

Shapira, H.B., G.A. Cristy, S.E. Brite, and M.B. Yost, 1983. *Cost and Energy Comparison Study of Above- and Belowground Dwellings.* ORNL/Con-91, Contract No. W-7405-ENG-26. NTIS, Springfield, VA.

Smay, E.V., 1977. "Underground Houses: Low Fuel Bills, Low Maintenance, Privacy, Security...," *Popular Science,* 210(4):83-89.

Standard Building Code (SBC). Southern Building Code Conference International, 3617 Eighth Avenue South, Birmingham, Alabama.

Sterling, R., R. Aiken, and J. Carmody, 1981. *Earth Sheltered Housing: Code, Zoning, and Financing Issues.* Revised Edition. Underground Space Center, University of Minnesota. NY: Van Nostrand Reinhold Company, Inc.

Sterling, R.L., J.C. Carmody, and G. Elnicky, 1981. *Earth Sheltered Community Design.* Underground Space Center, University of Minnesota. NY: Van Nostrand Reinhold Company, Inc. 272 pp.

Sterling, R., W.T. Farnan, and J. Carmody, 1982. *Earth Sheltered Residential Design Manual.* Underground Space Center, University of Minnesota. NY: Van Nostrand Reinhold Company, Inc.

Subsurface Space Environmental Protection, Low-Cost Storage, Energy Savings, 1981. S.M. Bergman, ed. Proceedings of the International Symposium, Rockstore # '80, Stockholm, Sweden, June 23-27, 1980. Oxford, UK: Pergamon Press. 1500 pp. in 3 volumes.

Swayze, J., 1980. *Underground Gardens & Homes.* Hereford, TX: Geobuilding Systems, Inc.

Swenson, G.S., 1979. "Zoning Ordinances as Obstacles to Earth Sheltered Housing: A Minnesota Perspective," *Underground Space,* Vol. 3, No. 4. NY: Pergamon Press.

System 7, 1984. *Bentonize Waterproofing Specification Manual.* Division of Effective Building Products, Inc.

Techman, Constructions Inc., 1981. Product Brochure, 19 West Fourth Street, Spencer, IA 51301.

Texas: Earth Sheltered, 1982. C. McKown, ed. Texas Tech Press, Texas Tech University, Lubbock, TX.

Tobiasson, W., and J. Richard, 1979. "Moisture Grain and Its Thermal Consequence for Common Roof Insulation," Proceedings, 5th Conference on Roofing Technology.

Tye, R.P., and C.F. Baker, 1983. "Development of Experimental Data on Expanded Polystyrene Roofing Insulation under Simulated Winter Exposure Conditions," Report SPI-6443 by Energy Materials Testing Laboratory for the Society of the Plastics Industry, 3150 Des Plaines Ave., Des Plaines, IL 60018.

Underground Utilization: A Reference Manual of Selected Works, 1978. T. Stauffer, Sr., ed. Department of Geosciences, University of Missouri, Kansas City, MO.

Uniform Building Code (UBC). International Conference of Building Officials, 5360 South Workman Mill Road, Whittier, CA.

U.S. Department of Housing and Urban Development and U.S. Department of Energy, 1979. *Underground Houses*. A Bibliography available from the Conservation and Renewable Energy Inquiry and Referral Service, Box 8900, Silver Spring, MD 20907.

Vander Meer, W.J., 1976. "Down to Earth Housing," *Solar Age*, September 1976, pp. 8-13.

Wade, H., 1983. *Building Underground*. PA: Rodale Press. 289 pp.

Wampler, L., 1978. *Underground Homes*. LA: Pelican Publishing Company, Inc.

Watson, D., and K. Labs, 1983. *Climatic Design*. NY: McGraw Hill. 280 pp.

Wells, M., 1965. "Nowhere To Go But Down," *Progressive Architecture*, Feb. 1965, pp. 174-179.

Wells, M., 1968. "Down Under, Down Under, ... or How Not to Build Underground," *Progressive Architecture*, March, 1968.

Wells, M., 1971. "The Absolutely Constant Incontestably Stable Architectural Value Scale," *Progressive Architecture*, Vol. 52 No. 3, pp. 92-97.

Wells, M., 1973. "Confessions of a Gentle Architect," *Environmental Quality*, July 1973.

Wells, M., 1977. *Underground Designs*. MS: Brick House Publishing. 88 pp.

Wells, M., and S.G. Wells, 1980. *Underground Plans Book-1*. Available from Malcolm Wells, Box 1149, Brewster, MA 02631. 44 pp.

Wells, M., 1981. *Gentle Architecture*. NY: McGraw Hill.

Wendt, R.L., 1982. *Earth-Sheltered Housing, An Evaluation of Energy-Conservation Potential*. ORNL/CON-86. Oak Ridge National Laboratory, Contract No. W-7405-eng-26.

Weston, M.W., 1979. "Results of Thermal Performance Analysis of Passive Solar Space Heating Systems in the National Solar Data Network," *Volume One: Federal Program Presentations and National Solar Data Program*. Proceedings of the U.S. Department of Energy's Regional Solar Updates, CONF-790758, UC-59a, (available from NTIS, Springfield, VA).

Woods, C.G., 1984. *Natural Architecture*. NY: Van Nostrand Reinhold Company, Inc.

Wright, D., 1981. "A Fiberglass Domed Earth Integrated Farmhouse," *Earth Shelter Performance and Evaluation*. Proceedings of the Second National Technical Conference, Tulsa, OK (available from Architectural Extension, Oklahoma State University, Stillwater, OK).

Bibliography on Earth Contact Heat Transfer

This bibliography was compiled jointly by Kenneth Labs of Undercurrent Design and the Underground Space Center staff.

Abdel-Wahed, R.M., T.P. Bligh and E.R.G. Eckert, 1978. "An Instrument for Measuring the Thermal Penetration Property," *International I. Heat Transfer,* vol. 21, pp. 967-973.

Abrams, D.W., C.C. Benton, and J.M. Akridge, 1980. "Simulated and Measured Performance of Earth Cooling Tubes," *5th NPSC* (Amherst), AS/ISES, Univ. of Delaware, Newark, pp. 737-741.

Abrams, D.W., C.C. Benton, and J.M. Akridge, 1980a. "Simulated and Measured Performance of Earth Cooling Tubes: TI-59 Calculator Program Listing," Step-by-step 380 line listing for programmable calculator developed by Prof. J.M. Akridge, Georgia Tech. College of Architecture.

Ackerman, M.Y., et al., 1982. Alberta Home Heating Research Facility-update III, 1981-82 heating season. Energex '82 Conference Proc., Vol. II/II, Solar Energy Society of Canada.

Ahrens, D., T. Ellison, and R. Sterling, 1981. *Earth Sheltered Homes Plans and Designs,* Underground Space Center, University of Minnesota, Van Nostrand Reinhold Company, 1981, 125 pp.

AIA Research Corporation, 1978. *Regional Guidelines for Building Passive Energy Conserving Homes,* prepared for the Dept. of Housing and Urban Development, HUD-PDR-355, Govt. Printing Office, Washington, D.C. 20402, 312 pp.

Akasaka, H., 1978. "Calculation Methods of the Heat Loss Through a Floor and Basement Walls," *Transactions* of the Society of Heating, Air-Conditioning, and Sanitary Engineers of Japan, No. 7, June 1978, pp. 21-35.

Akridge, J.M., 1981. "A Decremented Average Ground Temperature Method for Estimating the Thermal Performance of Underground Houses." *Passive Cooling '81* International Technical Conference (Miami Beach), AS/ISES, Univ. of Delaware, Newark, pp. 141-145.

Akridge, J.M., 1982. *Investigation of Passive Cooling Techniques for Hot-Humid Climates Final Report,* U.S. DOE Contract DE-AC02-79CS30238, College of Architecture, Georgia Inst. of Technology, Atlanta, GA 30332, 118 pp. + Appendices.

Akridge, J.M. and C.C. Benton, 1981. "Passive Cooling for Hot, Humid Climates," *Passive Cooling '81* International Technical Conference, AS/ISES, Univ. of Delaware, Newark, pp. 66-70.

Akridge, J.M. and J.F.J. Poulos, 1983. "The Decremented Average Ground Temperature Method for Predicting the Thermal Performance of Underground Walls," ASHRAE *Transactions,* vol. 89, part 2A, pp. 49-59.

Algren, A.B. 1949. "Ground Temperature as Affected by Weather Conditions," *Heating Piping and Air Conditioning,* pp. 111-116.

Ambrose, C.W., 1981. "Modeling Losses from Slab Floors," *Building and Environment* (Pergamon), vol. 16, no. 4, pp. 251-258.

American Plywood Association, 1977. "Advantages and Considerations of Insulating Foundation Walls," Technical Notes 2410, APA, Tacoma, Washington.

Anderson, D.B., and G.A. Erickson, 1961. "Field Laboratory for Heating Studies," *ASHRAE Semi Annual Meeting,* Chicago.

Andrews, J.W. and P.D. Mets, 1979. "Computer Simulation of Ground Coupled Storage in a Series Heat Pump System." In Proc. of Int. Solar Energy Society International Congress, Atlanta, GA, May 28-June 1, 1979.

ANSI. *Mathematical Signs and Symbols for Use in Physical Science and Technology,* ANSI Standard Y10.20-1975, 1430 Broadway, New York, NY 10018.

ASHRAE 1981 Fundamentals Handbook, American Society of Heating, Refrigerating, and Air-Conditioning Engineers, Inc., Atlanta, 1982.

Baggs, S.A., 1980. "A Taxonomy of Underground Space," *Collected Papers of the Earth Sheltered Housing Conference and Exhibition-I,* Underground Space Center, Univ. of Minnesota, Minneapolis, MN 55455, pp. 189-197.

Baggs, S.A., 1981. "Effects of Vegetation Upon Earth Cooling Potential," *Earth Shelter Performance and Evaluation,* Technical Conference Proceedings, Architectural Extension, Oklahoma State Univ., Stillwater 74078, pp. 81-90.

Baker, M. and J.M. O'Byrne, A.M. Levy, 1952."Estimating the Heat Loss from Slab Floors and Basements," *Heating, Piping, and Air Conditioning,* November 1952, p. 95.

Baladi, J.Y., R.J. Schoenhals and D.L. Ayers, 1979. "Transient Heat and Mass Transfer in Soils," paper presented at the AIAA-ASME Thermophysics and Heat Transfer Conference, Palo Alto, CA., May 24-26, 1978.

Balcomb, J.D., et al., 1983. *Passive Solar Design Handbook, vol. 3,* (including vol. 2 supplement), American Solar Energy Society, New York.

Balcomb, J.D. and J.C. Hedstrom, 1980. "Determining Heat Fluxes from Temperature Measurements Made in Massive Walls," *Proceedings of the 5th National Passive Solar Conference,* ed., J. Hayes and R. Snyder, Amherst, Massachusetts, October 19-26, 1980.

Bareither, H.O., A.N. Fleming, and B.E. Abernathy, 1948. *Temperature and Heat Loss Characteristics of Concrete Floors Laid on the Ground,* Small Homes Council Technical Report PB 93920, Univ. of Illinois, Champaign.

BASECLAD Exterior Basement Wall Insulation, product brochure. March 1983, Fiberglas Canada, Inc., General Office 3080 Yonge Street, Toronto, Ontario M4N 3N1, 12 pp.

Bathe, K.J., 1978. "ADINAT-A Finite Element Program for Automatic Dynamic Incremental Nonlinear Analysis of Temperatures," Massachusetts Institute of Technology Report No. 82448-5, Acoustic and Vibration Laboratory.

Bathe, K.J., 1981. "ADINAT—A Finite Element Program for Automatic Dynamic Incremental Nonlinear Analysis of Temperatures," Report AE 81-2, ADINA Engineering, Inc., Watertown, MA.

Baver, L.D. 1940/1946. *Soil Physics,* John Wiley and Sons, New York.

Beard, J.T., F.A. Iachtta, M.D. Duvall, J.W. Dickey, L.U. Lillelht, L.A. Dirhan and M.F. Coyle, 1977. "Heat Transfer Analysis of a System for Annual Collection and Storage of Solar Energy." Paper presented at the Heat Transfer in Solar Energy Systems Winter Meeting, ASME, Atlanta, GA., Nov. 27-Dec. 2, 1977.

Bechtel, R.B., 1979. "Psychological Aspects of Earth Covered Buildings," *Earth Covered Buildings and Settlements,* vol. 2 Proceedings of the Conference, The Use of Earth Covered Settlements, U.S. DOE CONF-7805138-P2, pp. 71-77, (available from NTIS, Springfield, VA 22161).

Beyea, J., G. Dutt and T. Woteki, 1978. "Critical Significance of Attics and Basements in the Energy Balance of Twin Rivers Townhouses." *Energy in Buildings.* (Switzerland) 1:3, pp. 261-269, April 1978.

Billington, N.S., 1951. "Heat Loss through Solid Ground Floors," *Journal of the Institution of Heating and Ventilating Engineers,* vol. 19, pp. 351-372.

Billington, N.S., 1952. "Heat Loss through Solid Ground Floors-II," *Journal of the Institution of Heating and Ventilating Engineers,* vol. 20 pp. 325-328.

Billington, N.S. and P. Becher, 1950. "Some Two-Dimensional Heat Flow Problems," *Journal* of the Institute Heating and Ventilating Engineering, 18:183, pp. 297-312.

Bircher, T.L., 1980. "The Thermal Performance of Earth Covered Buildings in Hot, Arid Regions," *5th NPSC* (Amherst), AS/ISES, Univ. of Delaware, Newark, pp. 332-336.

Bircher, T.L., 1981. "Ground-Coupled Cooling in Hot, Arid Regions," *Passive Cooling '81* International Technical Conference (Miami Beach), AS/ISES, Univ. of Delaware, Newark, pp. 136-140.

Black, W.Z. and J.G. Hartley, J.M. Manson, 1981. *Energy Conservation in Underground Buildings by Means of Exterior Insulation,* Paper 81-WA/HT-29, presented at the 1981 Winter Annual Meeting, American Society of Mechanical Engineers, 345 East 47th Street, New York, NY 10017, 8 pp.

Blick, E.F., 1980. "A Simple Method for Determining Heat Flow through Earth Covered Roofs," *Earth Sheltered Building Design Innovations* technical conference proceedings, Architectural Extension/Oklahoma State Univ., Stillwater, OK 74078, pp. III.17-III.22.

Bligh, T., 1975. "A Comparison of Energy Consumption in Earth Covered vs. Non-Earth Covered Buildings." *Alternatives in Energy Conservation: The Use of Earth Covered Buildings.* Proc. Conf., Ft. Worth, TX, NSF-RA-760006, pp. 85-105.

Bligh, T., 1976. "Energy Conservation by Building Underground." *Underground Space.* vol. 1, no. 1, pp. 19-33.

Bligh. T.P., 1980. "Energy Comparisons and Where to Insulate Earth-Sheltered Buildings and Basements," *Energy* (Pergamon), vol. 5, pp. 451-465.

Bligh, T.P., 1983. *Thermal Properties of Dry and Wet Soils: Theory and Measurements Techniques for Laboratory and In-Situ,* Energy Efficient Buildings and Systems Report, Mass. Inst. of Technology, Room 4-209, 77 Massachusetts Ave., Cambridge, MA 02139, 75 pp.

Bligh, T.P. and D.M. Apthorp, 1983. *Heat Flux Meters: Calibration, Heat Flux Distortion, and Installation,* Energy Efficient Buildings and Systems Report No. 22, Mass. Inst. of Technology, Room 4-209, 77 Massachusetts Ave., Cambridge, MA 02139, 268 pp.

Bligh, T.P. and E.W. Grald, 1983. *A Quantitative Energy Study of an Earth Sheltered House,* Energy Efficient Buildings and Systems Report No. 21, Mass. Inst. of Technology, Room 4-209, 77 Massachusetts Ave., Cambridge, MA 02139, 73 pp.

Bligh, T.P. and R. Hamburger, 1974. "Conservation of Energy by Use of Underground Space," *Legal, Economic and Energy Considerations in the Use of Underground Space,* RANN Report NSF/RA/S-74-002, National Academy of Sciences, Washington, DC, pp. 103-118.

Bligh, T.P. and B.H. Knoth, 1982. *A Thermal Study of an Earth-Sheltered Residence: Instrumentation, Data Processing Techniques, Soil Temperature and Heat Flux Data,* Energy Efficient Buildings and Systems Report No. 17, Mass. Inst. of Technology, Room 4-209, 77 Massachusetts Ave., Cambridge, MA 02139, 395 pp.

Bligh, T.P. and B.H. Knoth, E.A. Smith, S.P. Cole, G.D. Meixel, 1982. *An Experimental Plan for an Earth Contact System: Techniques for Monitoring Soil Temperature, Building Heat Flux, Soil Thermal Properties and Soil Moisture Content,* Energy Efficient Buildings and Systems Report No. 18, Mass. Inst. of Technology, Room 4-209, 77 Massachusetts Ave., Cambridge, MA 02139, 109 pp.

Bligh, T.P. and J.H. Magnusson, 1982. *Some Errors in Heat Flux Meter Measurements,* Energy Efficient Buildings and Systems Report No. 14, Mass. Inst. of Technology, Room 4-209, 77 Massachusetts Ave., Cambridge, MA 02139, 52 pp.

Bligh, T.P. and K.K. Replogle, 1982. *A Method for Performing an Energy Balance on a Building Applied to an Earth Sheltered House in Massachusetts,* Energy Efficient Buildings and Systems Report No. 10, Mass. Inst. of Technology, Room 4-209, 77 Massachusetts Ave., Cambridge, MA 02139, 88 pp.

Bligh, T.P. and W.F. Roslansky, 1982. *Building Heat Gain Reduction from Plants such as Sod Cover and Ivy,* Energy Efficient Buildings and Systems Report No. 11, Mass. Institute of Technology, Room 4-209, 77 Massachusetts Ave., Cambridge, MA 02139, 48 pp.

Bligh, T.P., P. Shipp and G. Meixel, 1980. "Where to Insulate Earth Protected Buildings and Existing Basements," Earth Covered Buildings: Technical Notes, 1980, NTIS Publication #CONF-7805138-P1, pp. 251-272.

Bligh, T.P., P.H. Shipp, and G.D. Meixel, 1980. "Energy Comparisons and Where to Insulate Earth Sheltered Buildings and Basements," *Energy,* vol. 5, pp. 451-465.

Bligh, T.P. and E.A. Smith, 1983. *Thermal Conductivity Measurements of Soils in the Field and Laboratory Using a Thermal Conductivity Probe,* Energy Efficient Buildings and Systems Report No. 25, Mass. Inst. of Technology, Room 4-209, 77 Massachusetts Ave., Cambridge, MA 02139, 275 pp.

Boileau, G.G. and J.K. Latta, 1968. *Calculation of Basement Heat Loss,* Technical Paper No. 292 of the Div. of Building Research, NRCC 10477, National Research Council Canada, Ottawa K1A OR6, 19 pp.

Bomberg, M., 1980. "Some Performance Aspects of Glass Fiber Insulation on the Outside of Basement Walls," *Thermal Insulation Performance,* Special Technical Publication STP 718, American Society for Testing Materials, Philadelphia, pp. 77-91. (Also DBR Paper No. 965, NRCC 19272, National Research Council Canada, Ottawa, K1A OR6).

Bowen, A., 1981. "Energy Design of Vernacular Earth Shelters Throughout the World," *Earth Shelter Performance and Evaluation,* Technical Conference Proceedings, Architectural Extension/Oklahoma State Univ., Stillwater 74078, pp. 19-33.

Bowen, A., G. Clark, and K. Labs, 1981. *Passive Cooling '81,* International Technical Conference (Miami Beach), AS/ISES, Univ. of Delaware, Newark, 1052 pp.

Boyer, L.L. and W.T. Grondzik, 1983. "Habitabilty and Energy Performance of Earth Sheltered Dwellings," *Alternative Energy Sources III,* Proceedings of the 3rd Miami International Conference on Alternative Energy Sources (1980), Hemisphere Publishing Corp., Washington, D.C., vol. 7, pp. 39-64.

Boyer, L.L., W.T. Grondzik, and T.N. Bice, 1981. "Energy Usage in Earth-Covered Dwellings in Oklahoma," *Underground Space,* vol. 5, pp. 227-236.

Boyer, L.L., W.T. Grondzik, and M.J. Weber, 1979. "Passive Energy Design and Habitability Aspects of Earth Sheltered Housing" in Oklahoma Proc. 2nd Annual Operational Results Conference on Solar Heating and Cooling Systems. Solar Energy Research Institute, Colorado Springs. Also, *Underground Space* (1980) 4(6):333-340.

Boyer, L.L. and T.L. Johnston, 1981. "Organization of Interior Spaces for Earth Cooling," *Passive Cooling '81,* International Technical Conference (Miami Beach), ASSES, Univ. of Delaware, Newark, pp. 111-125.

Brown, G.Z. and B.J. Novitski, 1981. "Climate Responsive Earth Sheltered Buildings," *Underground Space* (Pergamon), vol. 5, no. 5, March/April 1981, pp. 299-305.

Brown, W.G., 1980. *Mark XI Energy Research Project: Comparison of Standard and Upgraded Houses,* Building Research Note 160, Division of Building Research, National Research Council Canada, Ottawa K1A OR6, 18 pp.

Brown, W.G., 1958. "Ground Heat Exchange Problems," *Journal* of the Institute of Heating and Ventilating Engineering, vol. 25, February 1958.

Brown, W.G., 1963. "Thermal Model Tests for Probe Conduction Errors in Ground-Temperature Measurement," *Geotechnique,* vol. 13, no. 3, September 1963, pp. 241-249, (DBR Research Paper 194, NRCC 7570, DBR/NRCC, Ottawa K1A OR6).

Brown, W.G., 1963a. *Graphical Determination of Temperature Under Heated or Cooled Areas on the Ground Surface,* Technical Paper No. 163, NRC 7660, Division of Building Research, National Research Council Canada, Ottawa K1A OR6, 36 pp. + figures.

Buchan, G.D., 1982. "Predicting Bare Soil Temperature. I. Theory and Models for the Multiple-day Mean Duirnal Variation." Journal *Soil Science,* 33:185-197.

Bull, J., Z. Cumali, S. Nosaki, R. Sullivan, G.D. Meixel, and L. Shen, 1981. *Earth Contact Subroutine Development,* U.S. DOE Contract DE-AC03-80SF11508, Underground Space Center, Univ. of Minnesota, 500 Pillsbury Drive, S.E., Minneapolis, MN 55455, 116 pp.

Burch, P.M., et al. "A Field Study of the Effect of Wall Mass on the Heating and Cooling of Residential Buildings." National Bureau of Standards draft, May 1982.

Burnette, C.H., 1979. *The Architect's Access to Information,* prepared for the National Engineering Laboratory, PB-294-855, 91 pp. (Available from NTIS, Springfield, VA 22161).

Calthorpe, P., B. Wilcox and D. Stauffer, 1978."Preliminary Comparison Study of Four Solar Space Heating Systems." California Energy Resources Conservation and Development Commission, Sacramento, CA. p. 86.

Camillo, P.J., Gurney, R.J. and Schmugge, 1983."A Soil and Atmosphere Boundary Layer Model for Evapotranspiration and Soil Moisture Studies." *Water Resource Research* 19:371-380.

Carlson, A.R., 1977. "Efficient Energy Design Considerations for Artic Residences," *Energy Use Management,* Vol. 1, R.A. Fazzolare (ed.) pp. 343-397, Pergamon Press, Elmsford, N.Y.

Carmody, J.C., G.D. Meixel, and K. Labs, 1983. "Earth Contact Buildings: Applications, Thermal Analysis and Energy Benefits," *Advances in Solar Energy,* vol. 2, American Solar Energy Society, New York (in press).

Carmody, J.C., G.D. Meixel, and L. Shen, 1983. *Preliminary Design Guidelines for Earth Contact Buildings,* U.S. DOE Contract DE-AC03-80SF11508, Underground Space Center, Univ. of Minnesota, 500 Pillsbury Drive, S.E., Minneapolis, MN 55455, 101 pp.

Carmody, J. and R. Sterling, 1983. *Underground Building Design,* Underground Space Center, University of Minnesota, Van Nostrand Reinhold Company, 254 pp.

Carroll, C., H. Schenck, and W. Williams, 1966. "Digital Simulation of Heat Flow in Soils," *Journal of the Soil Mechanics and Foundation Division,* vol. SM 4, American Society of Civil Engineers, pp. 31-49, July 1966.

Carson, J.E., 1963. "Analysis of Soil and Air Temperature by Fourier Technique," *Journal of Geophysical Research,* vol. 68, no. 8, April 1963, pp. 2217-2232.

Carson, W.M., K.C. Watts, and F. Desir, 1980. "Design Data for Air Flow in Plastic Corrugated Drainage Pipes," *Transactions* of the Amer. Society of Agricultural Engineers, vol. 23, no. 2, pp. 409-413, 418.

Center for Natural Energy Design, 1981. *Earth Coupled Cooling Techniques,* DOE Earth Sheltered Structures Fact Sheet 09, Oklahoma State Univ., Stillwater 74078, 6 pp. (republished by W.T. Grondzik, L.L. Boyer and T.L. Johnston in the proceedings of the *6th NPSC* (Portland), AS/ISES, Univ. of Delaware, Newark, pp. 837-841.)

Centre Scientifique et Technique du Batiment, 1975. *Unified Code of Practice, Rules for Calculating Practical Thermal Properties of Structural Components,* Paris, France Rules Th-K77, pp. 34-42.

Ceylan, H.T. and Myers, G.E., 1980. "Long-Time Solutions to Heat Conduction Transients with Time-Dependent Inputs," *Journal of Heat Transfer*, Vol. 102, p 115.

Chang, J. 1958. *Ground Temperature, vol. 1,* Blue Hill Meteorological Observatory, (Harvard Univ.), Milton, MA.

Chang J. 1958a. *Ground Temperature, vol. 2,* Blue Hill Meteorological Observatory, (Harvard Univ.), Milton, MA.

Chen, B. et al., 1983. "Measured Cooling Performance of Earth Contact Cooling Tubes," *1983 Annual Meeting* (Minneapolis), American Solar Energy Society, Univ. of Delaware, Newark.

Chen, B. and T.C. Wang, J. Maloney, S. Chutintaranond, 1982. "The Effect of Deep Earth Heat Migration to the Performance of Continuous Thermal Envelope Structures," *1982 Annual Meeting* (Houston), ASES, Univ. of Delaware, Newark, pp. 697-702.

Chester, C.V., H.B. Shapira, P.R. Barnes, and G.A. Cristy, 1979. "An Earth-Covered Residential Concept for the Humid Continental Region," *Earth Covered Buildings: Technical Notes,* vol. 1, proceedings of the conference The Use of Earth Covered Settlements, U.S. DOE CONF-7805138-P1, pp. 171-194 (available from NTIS, Springfield, VA 22161).

Christian, J.E., 1984. *Cooling Season Performance of an Earth Sheltered Office/Dormitory Building in Oak Ridge, Tennessee.* Oak Ridge National Lab, July 1984.

Christian, J.E., 1983. *Thermal Envelope Field Measurements in an Energy-Efficient Office and Dormitory,* Oak Ridge National Laboratory ORNL/TM-8571, 62 pp., (available from NTIS, Springfield, VA 22161).

Claesson, J. and B. Eftring, 1980. *Optimal Distribution of Thermal Insulation and Ground Heat Loss,* Document D33:1980, Swedish Council for Building Research (Svensk Byggtjanst), Box 7853, S-103 99 Stockholm, 103 pp.

Cochran, P.H., (n.d.). *Thermal Properties and Surface Temperatures of Seedbeds,* Pacific Northwest Forest and Range Experiment Station, U.S. Department of Agriculture Forest Service, Portland, OR, 19 pp.

Cole, S.W., 1980. "Insulating Basement Walls," *The Informant,* vol. 1, no. 5, March 1980, Maine American Society of Civil Engineers, 80 Sunset Avenue, Auburn, ME 04210.

Control Data Corporation, MITAS, CYBERNET Publications Department, Publication No. 86615000.

Crawford, C.B., 1952. "Soil Temperatures, A Review of Published Records," in *Frost Action in Soils,* Highway Research Board Special Report No. 2, NASRC publication No. 213, National Research Council, Washington, D.C.

Cristy, G.A. "Computer Simulation of Heating and Cooling of Ventilation Air for a Passive Solar House." Research Sponsored by the U.S. Department of Energy under contract W-7405-eng-26 with the Union Carbide Corporation.

Crocker, C.R., 1974. *Moisture and Thermal Considerations in Basement Walls,* Canadian Building Digest 161, Division of Building Research, National Research Council Canada, Ottawa K1A OR6, 4 pp.

Cumali, Z., P. Davis, G. Courville and E. Baleo, 1982. "Analysis of the Thermal Mass Effect of Ground Using Multidimensional Response Factors." Proc. of the Building Thermal Mass Seminar. NTIS PC A21/MF A01;1, CONF-8206130.

Davies, G.R., 1979. "Thermal Analysis of Earth Covered Buildings," *Proceedings of the 4th National Passive Solar Conference.* Kansas City, 1979 p. 744-748.

Davis, W.B., 1980. "Earth Temperature: Its Effect on Underground Residences." *Earth Covered Buildings: Technical Notes,* 1980, NTIS Pub# CONF-7805138-P1, pp. 205-209.

Deacon, P.C., 1983. "Glass Fibre as a Draining Insulation System for the Exterior of Basement Walls," *Thermal Insulation Materials and Systems for Energy Conservation in the '80s,* Special Technical Publication STP 789, Amer. Society for Testing Materials, Philadelphia, pp. 413-434.

Dechow, J., and K.A. Epstein, 1977. "Laboratory and Field Investigations of Moisture Absorption and its Effects on Thermal Performance for Various Insulations," Prepared for A.S.T.M. Symposium on Advances in Heat Transulsion Measurements, Philadelphia.

Delsante, A.E., A.N. Stokes, and P.J. Walsh, 1983. "Application of Fourier Transforms to Periodic Heat Flow into the Ground Under a Building," *International Journal of Heat and Mass Transfer,* vol. 26, no. 1, January 1983, pp. 121-132.

deVries, D.A., 1958. "Simultaneous Transfer of Heat and Moisture in Porous Media," *Transactions,* American Geophysical Union, vol. 39, pp. 909-916.

deVries, 1963. W.R. van Wijk (ed.), *Physics of Plant Environment,* North Holland Publishing Co., Amsterdam.

deVries, D.A., 1975. "Heat Transfer in Soils," Chapter 1 in D.A. deVries and N.H. Afgan (eds.), *Heat and Mass Transfer in the Biosphere, Vol. 1: Transfer Processes in Plant Environment,* Scripta Book Co., Washington, DC, pp. 5-28.

Dhaliwal, A.S. and D.Y. Goswami, 1984. "Heat Transfer Analysis in Environmental Control Using an Underground Air Tunnel," Manuscript submitted for presentation at ASME Solar Energy Division 6th Annual Conference, April 1984 (Las Vegas).

Dike, G.A. and L.F. Kinney, 1982. "Superior Energy Performance at Very Low Construction Costs: Design Principles of Six Super-Insulated, Earth-Coupled Houses that Really Work," *7th NPSC* (Knoxville), ASES, Univ. of Delaware, Newark, pp. 865-870.

Dill, R.S., W.C. Robinson, and H.D. Robinson, 1945. *Measurements of Heat Losses from Slab Floors,* Building Materials and Structures Report BMS103, National Bureau of Standards, Washington, DC, 21 pp.

Dirr, T., 1981. *Typical Building Loads: Earth Contact Systems,* U.S. DOE Contract DE-AC03-80SF11508, prepared by The Architectural Alliance (Minneapolis) for the Underground Space Center, Univ. of Minnesota, 500 Pillsbury Drive S.E., Minneapolis, MN 55455, 170 pp.

Druker, E.F. and J.T. Haines, 1964. "A Study of the Thermal Environment in Underground Survival Shelters Using and Electronic Analog Computer," *ASHRAE Transactions* 70:7-20.

Dumont, R.S., M.E. Lux and H.W. Orr, 1982. Hotcan: A Computer Program for Estimating the Space Heating Requirement of Residences. National Research Council of Canada, DBR Computer Program No. 49, Sept. 1982.

EarthTech Research Corporation, 1981. *Thermal Properties of Soils and Soils Testing, Task 1 Report,* prepared for U.S. Dept. of Energy, Contract DE-AC03-80SF11509, EarthTech Research Corp., 6655 Amberton Drive, Baltimore, MD 21227.

Eckert, E.R.G., T.P. Bligh, and E. Pfender, 1976. *Energy Conservation by Subsurface Construction: Heat Transfer Studies in a Large Underground Building, First Annual Report,* Dept. of Mechanical Engineering, Univ. of Minnesota, Underground Space Center, Minneapolis, July 1976.

Eckert, E., T.P. Bligh, and E. Pfender, 1976-1978. *Energy Conservation by Subsurface Construction Heat Transfer Studies in a Large Underground Building, Second Annual Report.* NSF/RA-760431 Dept. of Mech. Engineering, University of Minnesota, Progress Reports 1, 2 and 3, 1976-1978.

Eckert, E.R.G., T.P. Bligh and E. Pfender, 1980. *Energy Conservation by Subsurface Construction: Heat Transfer Studies in a Large Underground Building, Final Report,* Dept. of Mechanical Engineering, Univ. of Minnesota, Underground Space Center, Minneapolis, July 1980, 133 pp.

Eckert, E.R.G., T.P. Bligh and E. Pfender, 1980."Energy Exchange Between Earth-Sheltered Structures and the Surrounding Ground." *Earth Covered Buildings: Technical Notes,* NTIS Pub. No. CONF-7805138-P1, pp. 226-250.

Eckert, E.R.G. and Faghri, M. "A Parametric Analysis of Moisture Migration in an Unsaturated Porous Slab Caused by Convective Heat and Mass Transfer." To be published in Warme-und Stoffubertragung.

Evardsen, K.I., 1970 (1972 translation by D.A. Sinclair). *New Method of Drainage of Basement Walls,* Technical Translation 1603 (NRC TT-1603), National Research Council Canada, Ottawa K1A OR6, 15 pp.

Elliot, J.M. and M. Baker, 1960. "Heat Loss from a Heated Basement," Paper No. 1724, ASHRAE *Transactions,* vol. 66, pp. 400-413.

Elmer, D. and G. Schiller, 1981. "A Preliminary Examination of the Dehumidification Potential of Earthir Heat Exchangers," *Passive Cooling '81* (Miami Beach), ASSES, Univ. of Delaware, Newark, pp. 161-165.

Elmroth, A. and I. Hoglund, 1971 (1975 translation by H.R. Hayes). *New Basement Wall Designs for Below-Grade Living Space,* Technical Translation 1801 (NRC/CNR TT-1801), National Research Council Canada, Ottawa K1A OR6, 44 pp.

Emery, A.F., D.R. Heerwagen, C.J. Kippenhan and G.B. Varey, 1980. "Numerical Procedures for the Simulation of Thermal Environments in Earth Covered Structures," Earth Covered Building: Technical Notes, 1980, NTIS Pub #CONF-7805138-P1, pp. 139-170.

EPRI Final Report No. EL-2128, 1981. "Soil Thermal Resistivity and Thermal Stability Measuring Instrument, Vol. 2: Manual for Operation and Use of the Thermal Property Analyzer and Statistical Weather Analysis Program to Determine Thermal Design Parameters," Ontario Hydro Research Laboratory for the Electric Power Research Institute, 1981.

Evans, R.S. "A Thermal Model of an Underground House," *MSEE Thesis*. South Dakota School of Mines and Technology, Rapid City, S.D., 1980.

Evans, R.S., R.D. McNeill, and L.D. Feisel, 1981. "Validation of a Lumped Parameter Thermal Model for Earth Shelters," *Proc. Earth Shelter Performance and Evaluation Conference*, October 1981, Tulsa, Oklahoma; Arch. Extension, Oklahoma State University, Stillwater, Oklahoma pp. 193-202.

Faust, Mercer, 1979. "Mathematical Models for Liquid- and Vapor-Dominatic Hydrothermal Systems," Geothermal Reservoir Simulation, Water Resource Research.

Feisel, L.D., 1982. "Economic Design Considerations for an Underground House," *Passive Solar: Subdivisions, Windows, Underground*, expanded papers of the 4th National Passive Solar Conference plenary sessions (Kansas City), American Solar Energy Society, New York, pp. 231-244.

Fink, L.H, 1960. "Soil Moisture Characteristics," *Transactions*, Am. Inst. of Electrical Engineers, vol. 79, part 3, pp. 803-819.

Fitton, E.M., and C.F. Brooks, 1931. "Soil Temperatures in the United States," *Monthly Weather Review*, vol. 59, no. 1, January 1931, pp. 6-16.

Fluker, B.J. 1958. "Soil Temperatures," *Soil Science*, vol. 86, July 1958, pp. 35-46.

Forest Service, U.S. Department of Agriculture, "Thermal Properties and Surface Temperatures of Seedbeds."

Francis, C.E., 1981. "Earth Cooling Tubes: Case Studies of Three Midwest Installations," *Passive Cooling '81* (Miami Beach), AS/ISES, Univ. of Delaware, Newark, pp. 171-175.

Francis, E., 1984. "Cooling with Earth Tubes," *Solar Age*, vol. 9, no. 1, January 1984, pp. 30-33.

Frerking, Michael. "The Hull Residence: A Passive Solar Hybrid System," Proceedings 2nd National Passive Solar Conference, Philadephia, PA, March 16-18, 1978.

Garrison, M., 1981. "Thermal Mass in a Hot-Humid Climate," *6th NPSC* (Portland), AS/ISES, Univ. of Delaware, Newark, pp. 817-821.

Geiger, R., 1965. *The Climate Near the Ground*, Harvard Univ. Press, Cambridge, MA, 611 pp.

Gilpin, R.R., 1972. "Study of Some Factors that Influence Ground Temperature." *Can. Congr. of Appl. Mech.*, 4th Proc. Pap, Ec Polytech, Montreal, Que, May 28-June 1, 1972, pp. 771-772. (Available from Ec. Polytech).

Gilpin, R.R., 1976. "The Ground Temperature Boundary Condition Provided by a Moss Covered Surface," *ASME Pub. 76-WA/HT-61*, Aug. 1976, 8 pp.

Gilpin, R.R., and B.K. Wong, 1973. "A Study of Some Factors that Influence Ground Temperature." *Proc. of the Fourth Canadian Congress of Applied Mechanics*, Montreal, May 28-June 1, 1973, pp. 771-772.

Gilpin, R.R., and B.K. Wong, 1975. "The Ground Temperature Regime and its Relationship to Soil Properties and Ground Surface Cover," ASME Paper No. 75-WA/HT-98, American Society of Mechanical Engineers, New York, 12 pp.

Gilpin, R.R., and B.K. Wong, 1976. "Heat-valve Effect in the Ground Thermal Regime," *Journal of Heat Transfer* (ASME), vol. 98, no. 4, November 1976, pp. 537-542.

Givoni, B., 1979. "Modifying the Ambient Temperature of Underground Buildings," *Earth Covered Buildings: Technical Notes*, vol. 1 proceedings of the conference, The Use of Earth Covered Settlements, U.S. DOE CONF-7805138-P1, pp. 123-138, (available from NTIS, Springfield, VA 22161.)

Givoni, B., 1981. "Earth Integrated Buildings-An Overview," *Architectural Science Review*, vol. 24, no. 2, June 1981, pp. 42-53.

Givoni, B., 1981a. "Experimental Studies on Radiant and Evaporative Cooling of Roofs," *Passive Cooling '81,* International Technical Conference (Miami Beach) ASSES, Univ. of Delaware, Newark, pp. 279-283.

Givoni, B., 1981b. "Underground Earth Temperature and its Possible Modification" Proceedings of sym. *Earth Integrated Building and Earth Covered Buildings for Australian Conditions.* University of Sydney. November 1981.

Givoni, B. and L. Katz, (n.d.). *Earth Temperatures and Underground Buildings,* Blaustein Inst. for Desert Research, Ben-Gurion Univ. of the Negev, Kiryat Sede Boqer, Israel, 30 pp.

Gold, L.W., 1963. "Influence of the Snow Cover on the Average Annual Ground Temperature at Otta, Canada," NRCC 7505, National Research Council Canada, Ottawa K1A OR6, 10 pp.

Gold, L.W., 1967. "Influence of Surface Conditions on Ground Temperature," *Canadian Journal of Earth Sciences,* vol. 4, April 1967, pp. 199-208.

Gold, L.W. and A.H. Lachenbruch, 1973. "Thermal Conditions in Permafrost—A Review of North American Literature," *North American Contribution to the Second International Conference on Permafrost* (Yakutsk, Siberia), National Academy of Sciences, Washington, D.C., pp. 3-23.

Goldberg, L.F., 1984. "A Comparative Experimental Evaluation of Five Earth Sheltered Houses," *Underground Space* (Pergamon), vol. 8, no. 1, pp. 36-43.

Goldberg, L.F. and C.A. Lane, 1981. "A Preliminary, Experimental, Energy Performance Assessment of Five Houses in the MHFA Earth Sheltered Housing Demonstration Program." *The Potential of Earth-Sheltered and Underground Space,* (Pergamon) 1981, pp. 321-350.

Goldberg, L.F., and R.L. Sterling, 1982. "Energy Performance Aspects of Five Homes in the Minnesota Housing Finance Agency's Earth-Sheltered Housing Demonstration Program." *Proc. Am. Soc. of Civil Engineers. Conference Energy Conservation in Building Design and Construction,* Sept. 1982.

Goldberg, L.F., R. Sterling and J. Carmody, 1984. *MHFA Solar/Earth-Sheltered Housing Demonstration Project.* Final Report, Underground Space Center, University of Minnesota.

Goodrich, L.E., 1978. "Efficient Numerical Technique for One-dimensional Thermal Problems with Phase Change," *Int'l. Journal of Heat and Mass Transfer,* vol. 21, pp. 615-621 (DBR Paper 791, DBRRCC, Ottawa K1A OR6).

Goodrich, L.E., 1979. "Transient Probe Apparatus for Soil Thermal Conductivity Measurements," *Symposium on Permafrost Field Methods and Permafrost Geophysics,* W.J. Scott and R.J.E. Brown, eds., National Research Council of Canada, Technical Memo 124, pp. 44-55.

Goodrich, L.E., 1982. "The Influence of Snow Cover on the Ground Thermal Regime," (DBR Paper 1050, NRCC), *Canadian Geotechnical Journal,* vol. 19, pp. 421-432.

Goodrich, L.E., 1982a. *An Introductory Review of Numerical Methods for Ground Thermal Regime Calculations,* DBR Paper 1061, NRCC 20742, National Research Council Canada, Ottawa K1A OR6, 32 pp.

Grondzik, W.T., L.L. Boyer, and J.W. Zang, 1981. "Analysis of Utility Billings for 55 Earth Sheltered Projects," *Earth Shelter Performance and Evaluation,* technical conference proceedings, Architectural Extension, Oklahoma Sate Univ., Stillwater 74078, pp. 177-184.

Grondzik, W.T., L.L. Boyer, and T.L. Johnston, 1981. "Variations in Earth Covered Roof Temperature Profiles," *Passive Cooling '81* International Technical Conference (Miami Beach), ASSES, Univ. of Delaware, Newark, pp. 146-150.

Gupta, S.C., Rodke, J.K. and Larson, W.E., 1981. "Predicting Temperatures of Bare and Residue Covered Soil With and Without a Corn Crop." *Soil Sci. Soc. Amer. Jl.:* 45-405-412.

Gustafson, A.W. and C. McKown, 1983. "An Exploratory Study of the Relationship between Owner Attitudes and Characteristics of Earth-Sheltered Housing," *8th NPSC* (Santa Fe), ASES, Univ. of Delaware, Newark, pp. 475-478.

Gustinis, J. and Robertson, D.K., 1982. "Southwest Thermal Mass Study Phase I." New Mexicao Energy Research and Development Institute, Information Center, University of New Mexico. Draft, September 1982.

Hadas, A., 1977. "Heat Transfer in Dry Aggregated Soil: I. Heat Conduction." *Soil Science Society of America Journal,* Vol. 41, No. 6, 1977, pp. 1055-1059.

Hagan, D.A. and Jones, R.F., 1983. *Case Study of the Blouin Superinsulated House.* Brookhaven National Laboratory, BNL 51732, September 1983, pp. 109.

Hamilton, J.J. and S.S. Tao, 1973. "Performance of the Mark IX Steel Basement to 31 March, 1973" Technical Note No. 579 Division of Building Research, National Research Council of Canada, Ottawa, Ontario, Canada.

Hartley, J.G. and W.Z. Black, 1981. "Transient Simulataneous Heat and Mass Transfer in Moist, Unsaturated Soils," *Journal of Heat Transfer* (ASME), vol. 103, no. 2, May 1981, pp. 376-382.

Hartley, J.G. and W.Z. Black, R.A. Bush, M.A. Martin, 1982. "Measurements, Correlations, and Limitations of Soil Thermal Stability," in S.A. Baggs *et al.* (eds.), *Underground Cable Thermal Backfill,* Pergamon Press, Toronto, pp. 121-133.

Hasfurther, V.R. and R.D. Burman, 1974. "Soil Temperature Modeling using Air Temperature as a Driving Mechanism," *Trans. ASAE,* vol. 17, no. 1, Jan-Feb 1974, pp. 78-81.

Hauk, R.W., and R.J. Cooke, 1973. "A Mathematical Analysis of Coupled Soil Heat and Moisture Transfer." *Transactions* of the ASAE, October 1973.

Hayeem, E., 1984. "An Experimental Study of Earth Temperature Modification to Provide Cooling for Earth Contact Buildings in the Desert Regions of Israel," M.S. thesis, Trinity Univ., San Antonio, TX.

Hazer, F., 1975."Cultural-Ecological Interpretation of the Historic Underground Cities of Goreme, Turkey," in F.L. Moreland (ed.), *Alternatives in Energy Conservation: The Use of Earth Covered Buildings* (National Science Foundation), Govt. Printing Office No. 038-000-00286-4, pp. 21-36.

Hedlin, C.P., H.W. Orr and S.S. Tao, 1981. *Thermal Insulation Performance* Special Technical Publication STP718, American Society for Testing Materials, Philadelphia pp. 307-321.

Hendrick, P.L., 1980. "Performance Evaluation of a Terrestial Heat Exchanger," *5th NPSC* (Amherst), AS/ISES, Univ. of Delaware, Newark, pp. 732-736.

Hilleary, J.D., 1975. "Thermal Response and Energy Requirements of a 2-Story Residence." MSc Thesis, Ohio State University, Columbus, OH. 1975.

Hillel, D., 1971. *Soil and Water—Physical Principles and Processes,* Academic Press, New York, pp. 49-77.

History of Soil Temperature Stations in the United States, Key to Meteorological Records Documentation No. 1.4, Department of Commerce Weather Bureau, 1961.

Hollon, S.D. and P.C. Kendall, S. Norsted, and D. Watson, 1980. "Psychological Responses to Earth Sheltered, Multi-level, and Above Ground Structures With and Without Windows," *Underground Space* (Pergamon), vol. 5, no. 3, November/December 1980, pp. 171-178.

Holman, W.P., 1979. Geothermal Home Construction. Patent No. US 4,176,788, filed 12 April 1978.

Holmes, W.W., 1981. "Sub-calc: An Automated Earth Cooling Design Procedure for Passive Solar Earth-Sheltered Structures," *Passive Cooling Proc. Int. Passive and Hybrid Cooling Conference*, Miami Beach, 1981, AS/ISES, pp. 151-155.

Hooper, F.C. and C.R. Attwater, 1977. "A Design Method for Heat Loss Calculation for In-ground Heat Storage Tanks." Paper presented at the Heat Transfer in Solar Energy Systems Winter Meeting, ASME, Atlanta, GA Nov 27-Dec. 2, 1977.

Houghten, F.C., S.I. Taimuty, C. Gutberlet, and C.J. Brown, 1942. "Heat Loss through Basement Walls and Floors," Paper No. 1213, ASHVE *Transactions*, vol. 48, pp. 369-384.

Huang, C.L.D., 1979. "Heat and Moisture Transfer in Concrete Slabs." *Int. J. Heat Mass Transfer*, Vol. 22, No. 2. Feb. 1979, pp. 257-266.

HUDAC, 1982. *External Insulation of Basements,* Housing and Urban Development Assocation of Canada, 15 Toronto Street, Toronto, Ontario M5C 2E3, 10 pp.

HUDAC, date unknown. *External Insulation of Basement Walls*—Report on Phase 2 Program, Task Force on External Insulation of Basement Walls Subcommittee on Foundations and Drainage of the HUDAC Technical Research Committee.

Ingersoll, L.K. and O.J. Zobel, A.C. Ingersoll, 1954. *Heat Conduction with Engineering, Geological and Other Applications,* Revised Edition, Univ. of Wisconsin Press, Madison.

Jackson, K.W. and W.Z. Black, 1983. "A Unit Cell Model for Predicting the Thermal Conductivity of a Granular Medium Containing an Adhesive Binder," *International Journal of Heat and Mass Transfer* (Pergamon), vol. 26, no. 1, pp. 87-99.

Jakob, M., 1949. *Heat Transfer,* vol. I, John Wiley and Sons, Inc., New York.

Johansen, O., October 1975. "Thermal Conductivity of Soil and Rock" in *Frost I Jord,* The Royal Norwegian Council for Scientific and Industrial Research and the Public Roads Administration's Committee on Frost Action in Soils, Oslo, Norway.

Johnston, G.H., 1963. *Instructions for the Fabrication of Thermocouple Cables for Measuring Ground Temperatures,* DBR Technical Paper 157, NRCC 7561, Div. of Bldg. Research, National Research Council Canada, K1A OR6, 11 pp.

Johnston, G.H., 1966. "A Compact, Self-Contained Ground Temperature Recorder," *Canadian Geotechnical Journal,* vol. 3, no. 4, pp. 246-260, (DBR Technical Paper 238, NRCC 9316, DBR/NRCC, Ottawa K1A OR6).

Judkoff, R., D.N. Wortman and J. Burch, 1983. "Empirical Validation Using Data from the SERI Class-A Validation House," Progress in Solar Energy, vol. 6, Passive Systems Division, American Solar Energy Society, p. 705.

Jumikis, A.R., 1966. *Thermal Soil Mechanics,* Rutgers Univ. Press, New Brunswick, NJ.

Jumikis, A.R., 1977. *Thermal Geotechnics,* Rutgers Univ. Press, New Brunswick, NJ, 375 pp.

Kaushik, N.D. and Srivastava, 1980. "Temperature Distribution in Ground: Response Function Technique," *International Journal of Heat and Mass Transfer* (Pergamon), vol. 23, no. 6, pp. 903-906.

Keen, B.A., 1931. *The Physical Properties of Soils.* London, Longmans, Green & Co.

Kersten, M.S., 1948. "The Thermal Conductivity of Soils," *28th Annual Meeting Proceedings* (vol. 28), Highway Research Board, National Research Council, Division of Engineering and Industrial Research, Washington, DC, pp. 391-409.

Kersten, M.S., 1949. *Thermal Properties of Soils,* Inst. of Technology Bulletin No. 28, Univ. of Minnesota, Eng. Experiment Station, Minneapolis, 221 pp.

Kersten, M.S., 1952. "Thermal Properties of Soil," in *Frost Action in Soils,* Special Report No. 2 of the Highway Research Board, NASRC Publication No. 213, National Research Council, Washington, DC, pp. 161-166.

Kessler, H.J., 1982. "Passive Cooling for Hot Arid Regions," *Proceedings of the Passive and Hybrid Solar Energy Update,* Conf. B-20940 U.S. Dept. of Energy) NTIS, Springfield, VA 22161, pp. 302-310.

Khatry, A.K., J.S. Sodha, and M.A.S. Malik, 1978. "Periodic Variation of Ground Temperature with Depth," *Solar Energy,* vol. 20, pp. 425-427.

Kimber, L.K., 1976. "A Thermal Model for the Surface Temperature of Materials on the Earth's Surface." *Iowa Geologic Survey Technical Information Series,* July, 1976, No. 1.

Kirkham, D,. 1972. *Advanced Soil Physics,* Wiley Interscience/J. Wiley and Sons, Inc., New York.

Kristensen, K.J., 1959. "Temperature and Heat Balance of Soil." *Oikos,* vol. 10, no. 1, 1959 (Copennhagen), pp. 104-120.

Kuehn, T.H., 1982. "Temperature and Heat Flow Measurements from an Insulated Concrete Bermed Wall and Adjacent Floor," *Journal of Solar Energy Engineering,* Vol. 104, pp. 15-22.

Kukula, K., 1983. "Place to Insulate," *New Shelter,* 4:7, 66-69, September 1983, Rodale Press.

Kusuda, T., 1967. "Least Squares Technique for the Analysis of Periodic Temperatures of the Earth's Surface Region," *Journal of Research of the National Bureau of Standards,* 71C No. 1-442, January/March 1967, pp. 43-50.

Kusuda, T., 1968. *Least Squares Analysis of Annual Earth Temperature Cycles for Selected Stations in the United States,* Report No. 9493, National Bureau of Standards, Washington, D.C., 167 pp.

Kusuda, T., 1975. "The Effect of Ground Cover on Earth Temperature," *Alternatives in Energy Conservation: The Use of Earth Covered Buildings,* Proc. Conf., Fort Worth, TX, July 1975, NSF-RA-760006, pp. 279-303.

Kusuda, T., 1971. *Earth Temperatures Beneath Five Different Surfaces,* NBS Report 10 373, National Bureau of Standards, Washington, D.C. 148 pp.

Kusuda, T. and P.R. Achenbach, 1963. "Numerical Analysis of the Thermal Environment of Occupied Underground Spaces with Finite Cover Using a Digital Computer," *ASHRAE Transactions,* 69:439-452.

Kusuda, T. and P.R. Achenbach, 1965. "Earth Temperature and Thermal Diffusivity at Selected Stations in the United States," NBS Report 8972, National Bureau of Standards, Washington, DC.

Kusuda, T. and P.R. Achenbach, 1965a. "Earth Temperature and Thermal Diffusivity at Selected Stations in the United States," Article No. 1914, *ASHRAE Transactions,* vol. 71, part 1, pp. 61-75.

Kusuda, T. and P.R. Achenbach, 1963. "Numerical Analyses of the Thermal Environment of Occupied Underground Spaces with Finite Cover Using a Digital Computer," *ASHRAE Trans.,* 69: 439-452.

Kusuda, T. and F.J. Powell, 1970. *An Automated Earth Temperature Station* (Instrumentation), NBS Report 10223, National Bureau of Standards, Washington, D.C.

Kusuda, T. and O. Piet, J.W. Bean, 1983. *Annual Variation of Temperature Field and Heat Transfer Under Heated Ground Surfaces (Slab-on-grade Floor Heat Loss Calculation),* Building Science Services 156, National Bureau of Standards, 61 pp.

Labs, K., 1975. "The Architectural Use of Underground Space: Issues and Applications," Master of Architecture Thesis, Washington University, St. Louis, 170 pp.

Labs, K., 1976. "The Use of Earth Covered Buildings through History," in F.L. Moreland (ed.), *Alternatives in Energy Conservation: The Use of Earth Covered Buildings,* (National Science Foundation) (Govt. Printing Office No. 038-000-00286-4, pp. 7-19.

Labs, K., 1976a. "The Architectural Underground, Part 1: Historical Themes of Development," *Underground Space* (Pergamon), vol. 1, no. 1, May/June 1976, pp. 1-8.

Labs, K., 1976b. "The Architectural Underground, Part 2: Forms and Functions in the Modern World," *Underground Space,* (Pergamon), vol. 1, no. 2, July/August 1976, pp. 135-156.

Labs, K., 1979. *Land-Use Regulation of Underground Housing,* Planning Advisory Service Memo 79-5, May 1979, American Planning Association, 1313 East 60th Street, Chicago, IL 60637, 8 pp.

Labs, K., 1979a. "Underground Building Climate," *Solar Age,* vol. 4, no. 10, October 1979, pp. 44-50.

Labs, K., 1980. "Earth Tempering as a Passive Design Strategy," *Proc. Earth Sheltered Building Design Innovations Conf.,* April 1980, Oklahoma City, Arch. Extension, Oklahoma State University, pp. 111-3 to 111-10.

Labs, K., 1980. "Terratypes: Underground Housing for Arid Zones," G.S. Golany, ed., *Housing in Arid Lands: Design and Planning,* Halsted Press/John Wiley & Sons, Inc., New York, pp. 123-139.

Labs, K., 1981. *Regional Analysis of Ground and Above-Ground Climate,* Oak Ridge National Laboratory, ORNL/Sub-81/40451/1, 192 pp. + microfiche, (available from NTIS, Springfield, VA 22161), Republished (w/o ground temperature tables) in *Underground Space,* vol. 6, no. 6, and vol. 7, no. 1, 1982.

Labs, K., 1981a. "Direct-Coupled Ground Cooling: Issues and Opportunities," *Passive Cooling '81,* International Technical Conference (Miami Beach), ASSES, Univ. of Delaware, Newark, pp. 131-135.

Labs, K., 1982. "The Underground Advantage: Climate of Soils," in Wade, Cook, Labs and Selkowitz (eds.), *Passive Solar: Subdivisions, Windows, Underground,* expanded papers of the 4th National Passive Solar Conference plenary sessions (Kansas City), American Solar Energy Society, New York, pp. 171-199.

Labs, K., 1982a. "Living Up to Underground Design," *Solar Age,* vol. 7, no. 8, August 1982, pp. 34-38.

Labs, K., 1984. "Passive Earth Coupling - State-of-the-art," Prepared for Solar Thermal Energy Conversion Technology and Assessment Project. Rockwell International/SERI, 1984.

Labs, K. and K. Harrington, 1982. "A Comparison of Ground and Above-Ground Climates for Identifying Appropriate Cooling Strategies," *Passive Solar Journal* (AS/ISES), vol. 1, no. 1, January 1982, pp. 4-11.

Labs, K. and D. Watson, 1981. "Regional Suitability of Earth Tempering," *Earth Shelter Performance and Evaluation,* technical conference proceedings, Architectural Extension/Oklahoma State Univ., Stillwater 74078, pp. 41-51.

Lachenbruch, A.H., 1957. "Three Dimensional Heat Conduction in Permafrost Beneath Heated Buildings," *U.S. Geological Survey Bulletin* 1052-B, pp. 51-69.

Lachenbruch, A., 1959."Periodic Heat Flow in a Stratified Medium with Applications to Permafrost Problems" Geological Survey Bulletin 1083-A, U.S. Government Printing Office, Washington, D.C.

Land, W.R., 1981. "Radiant Panel Cooling System for Residential Applications," *Passive Cooling '81* International Technical Conference (Miami Beach), AS/ISES, Univ. of Delaware, Newark, pp. 274-278.

Langbein, W.B. 1949. "Computing Soil Temperatures." *Trans. Am. Geophysical Union,* vol. 30, no. 4, August 1949, pp. 543-547.

Langewiesche, W., 1950. "There's a Gold Mine Under your House," *House Beautiful,* vol. 92, no. 8, August 1950, pp. 92-94, 133-135.

LaNier, R., 1970. "Geotecture," Master of Science Thesis, Univ. of Notre Dame, South Bend, IN, 72 pp.

Larsen, B.T. and R.G. Courtney (ed), 1976. *Digital Simulation of Energy Consumption in Residential Buildings.* Symposium of the International Council for Building Research Studies & Documentation, Garston, Herts, United Kindom, April 1976. Construction Press Ltd., Lancaster, England.

Latta, J.K. and G.G. Boileau, 1969. "Heat Losses from House Basements," *Canadian Building,* vol. 19, no. 10, October 1969, pp. 39-42.

LaVigne, A.B. and M.A. Schuldt, 1981. "Thermal Performance of an Earth-Sheltered Passive Solar Residence," *6th NPSC* (Portland), AS/ISES, Univ. of Delaware, Newark, pp. 54-58.

Lee, W.H.K., 1965. "Review of Heat Flow Data," W.H.K. Lee, ed. *Terrestial Heat Flow,* Geophysical Monograph Series No. 8, Publication No. 1288, National Academy of Sciences (Am. Geophysical Union), Washington, D.C.

Lemelson, J.H., 1978. Building Insulation Systems and Method. Patent No. US 4,075,799 filed August 30, 1975, 6 pp.

Lettau, H., 1954,"Improved Models of Thermal Diffusion in the Soil." *Trans. Am. Geophysical Union,* vol. 35, no. 1, February 1954, pp. 121-132.

Lettau, H., 1951,"Theory of Surface Temperature and Heat Transfer Osillations Near a Level Ground Surface." *Trans. American Geophysical Union,* vol. 32, no. 2, April, 1951, pp. 189-200.

Lettau, H.H. and B. Davidson (eds.) 1957. *Exploring the Atmosphere's First Mile,* vol. 1, Pergamon Press, New York.

Loxley, T.E., 1982. "Inverted Cave Construction System Explores Solar-Geothermal Interface," *1982 Annual Meeting,* ASES, Univ. of Delaware, Newark, pp. 139-144.

Lutz, F.W., 1976. "Studies of Children in an Underground School," *Underground Space* (Pergamon), vol. 1, no. 2, July/August 1976, pp. 131-134.

Lux, M., 1982. *Hotcan Program Manual for Apple II Plus Computer.* National Research Council Canada, DBR and Computer Program No. 48, September 1982.

MacArthur, J.W., 1981. *Analytical Methods for Predicting Heat Flow in Earth Contact Systems,* prepared by Honeywell, Inc. (Minneapolis) for the Underground Space Center, Univ. of Minnesota, 500 Pillsbury Drive, S.E., Minneapolis, MN 55455, 130 pp.

MacArthur, J.W., G.D. Meixel, and L.S. Shen, 1983. "Application of Numerical Methods for Predicting Energy Transport in Earth Contact Systems," *Applied Energy,* vol. 13, pp. 121-156.

Macey, H.H., 1949. "Heat Loss Through a Solid Floor," *Journal of the Institute of Fuel,* 22:128, p. 369.

Mahajan, Bal M., 1984. *National Bureau of Standards Passive Solar Test Facility-Instrumentation and Test Site Handbook.* Prepared for D.O.E. Office of Solar Heat Technologies, NBSIR 84-2911. NTIS Springfield, VA 22161, 1981. pp. 88.

Martin, H.R., P.R. Achenbach and R.S. Dill, 1953."Effect of Edge Insulation Upon Temperature and Condensation on Concrete Slab Floors," MBS Building Materials and Structures Report 138.

Maxwell, R.K., 1964. "Temperature Measurements and the Calculated Heat Flux in the Soil," Master of Science Thesis, Univ. of Minnesota, Minneapolis, 132 pp.

McBridge, M.F., 1983."Development of a Simplified and Manual Energy Calculation Procedure for Residences," Proceedings of the ASHRAE/DOE Conference Thermal Performance of the Exterior Envelopes of Buildings II, New York, ASHRAE.

McBride, M.F. and R.S. Blancett, C.F. Sepsy, C.D. Jones, 1979. "Measurement of Subgrade Temperatures for Prediction of Heat Loss in Basements," Paper PH 79-7, ASHRAE *Transactions,* vol. 85, part 1, pp. 642-655.

Meixel, G.D., 1981. "Energy Use of Non-Residential Earth Sheltered Buildings in Five Different Climates," *The Potential of Earth Sheltered and Underground Space,* proceedings of the 1981 conference of the American Underground-Space Association (Kansas City), Pergamon Press, New York, pp. 227-258.

Meixel, G.D., 1983. "Computer Simulation of Heat Transfer from Earth Sheltered Structures: A Comparison of Varying Levels of Earth Sheltering in Five Different Climates," *Alternative Energy Source III,* proceedings of the 3rd Miami International Conference on Alternative Energy Sources (1980), Hemisphere Publishing Corp., Washington, DC, vol. 7, pp. 65-87.

Meixel, G.D. and T.P. Bligh, 1983. *Earth Contact Systems Final Report,* prepared for the U.S. Department of Energy, Contract DE-AC03-80SF11508, Underground Space Center, Univ. of Minnesota and Massachusetts Inst. of Technology, Dept. of Mechanical Engineering, November 1983, 397 pp.

Meixel, G.D., P.H. Shipp, and T.P. Bligh, 1981. "The Impact of Insulation Placement on the Seasonal Heat Loss through Basement and Earth Sheltered Walls," *Thermal Performance of the Exterior Envelope of Buildings,* Special Publication No. 28, ASHRAE, New York, pp. 987-1001, Also in: *Underground Space,* (Pergamon), vol. 5, no. 1, July/August 1980, pp. 41-47.

Metz, P.D., 1979. "Design, Construction and Operation of the Solar Assisted Heat Pump Ground Coupled Storage Experiments of Brookhaven National Laboratory." Presented at the 4th Annual Heat Pump Technology Conference, Stillwater, OK. April 9-10, 1979.

Middleton Associates, 1982. *Energy Conservation and House Basements.* SRC Pub. E-825-46-C-02. Saskatchewan Research Council, Saskatoon, Saskatchewan. 143 pp.

Milly, P.C.D., 1984. "A Simulation Analysis of Thermal Effects on Evaporation from Soil." *Water Resource Research,* 20:1087-1098.

Mitalas, G.P., 1982. *Basement Heat Loss Studies at DBR/NRC,* DBR Paper No. 1045, NRCC 20416, National Research Council Canada, Ottawa K1A OR6, 58 pp.

Mitalas, G.P., 1983."Calculation of Basement Heat Loss," ASHRAE *Transactions,* Vol. 89, part 1.

Mitchell, J.K., 1976. *Fundamentals of Soil Behavior,* John Wiley and Sons, inc., N.Y.

Mitchell, J.K., and T.C. Kao, 1978. "Measurement of Soil Thermal Resistivity," Paper 14080, *Journal of the Geotechnical Engineering Division* (ASCE), vol. 104, no. GT10, October 1978, pp. 1307-1320.

Moreland, F.L. (ed.), 1976. *Alternatives in Energy Conservation: The Use of Earth Covered Buildings,* RANN Report NSF/RA/760006, (National Science Foundation) 353 pp., (Govt. Printing Office No. 038-000-00286-4).

Moreland, F.L. (ed.), 1979. *Earth Covered Buildings and Settlements,* vol. 2 proceedings of the conference, The Use of Earth Covered Settlements, U.S. DOE CONF-7805138-PZ, 355 pp. (available from NTIS, Springfield, VA 22161).

Muncey, R.W.R. and J.W. Spencer, 1978. "Heat Flow into the Ground Under a House," in C.J. Hoogendoorn and N.H. Afgan (eds.), *Energy Conservation in Heating, Cooling, and Ventilating Buildings,* Hemisphere Publishing Corp., Washington, D.C., vol. 2, pp. 649-660.

Nakshabandi, G.A. and H. Kohnke, 1965. "Thermal Conductivity and Diffusivity of Soils as Related to Moisture Tension and Other Physical Properties," *Agricultural Meteorology,* vol. 2, pp. 271-279.

National Bureau of Standards, 1973. "Dynamic Thermal Performance of An Experimental Masonry Building," Building Science Series 45, National Bureau of Standards, July 1973.

NAVFAC DM 1.4., 1983. *Earth Sheltered Buildings Design Manual 1.4,* Naval Facilities Engineering Command, Dept. of the Navy, (available from Superintendent of Documents, U.S. GPO, Washington, DC 20402), 187 pp. + Appendices.

Newman, J.O., 1979."Seasonal Variation in Heat Transfer through Earth Embanked Wall," *Fourth National Passive Solar Conference* (Kansas City), AS/ISES, Univ. of Delaware, Newark, pp. 739-743.

Newman, J. and Godbey, L.C., 1979. "Soil Temperatures Adjacent to Earth Shelters." Reprint 79-4558 from the 1979 winter meeting of ASAE. New Orleans, LA, December 11-14, 1979. 20 pp.

Newman, J. and Godbey, L.C., 1984. "Soil Temperatures Adjacent to Earth Sheltered Residence." Transactions ASAE meeting Fall, 1984.

Newman, J.O. and L.C. Godbey, 1979. "Solar Heating and Earth Insulation—Keys to Energy Independence," Preprint 3709 from the ASCE Convention and ASCE Exposition held in Atlanta, October 23-25, 1979, American Society of Civil Engineers, New York, 12 pp.

Nickerson, R.J. and H.Y. Choi, S. Markus (1959). *Methods and Equipment for Measuring Soil Temperature and Heat Flow through the Soil: A Literature Survey* prepared for the U.S. Army Signal Research and Development Laboratories, Massachusetts Inst. of Technology, Cambridge, MA, 15 pp.

Ohio State University, 1977. "Residential Fuel Utilization Efficiencies." Ohio State University Engineering Experimentation Station. *Final Report on Project 460X.* Colombus, OH. 1977.

Ontario Hydro Research Division, 1982. *Thermal Properties of Soils Research at Ontario Hydro: A Collection of Papers,* Ontario Hydro, Research Division, 800 Kipling Ave., Toronto M8Z 5S4, 416/231-4111 (20 papers by various authors).

Oswald, R., 1979. *Thermal Insulation of Earth-Covered Building Surfaces.* Progress Report. Final Report. Schriftenreihe Bau-und Wohnforschung des Burdesministers fuer Raumondnung Bauwesen und Staedtebau. V.P. Aug 1979. Availability 03/MF A01. Report No. NP-2901093 in German.

Ovstaas, G. and S. Smith, W. Strzepek, G. Titley, 1983. "Thermal Performance of Various Insulations in Below-Earth-Grade Perimeter Applications," *Thermal Insulation Materials and Systems for Energy Conservation in the '80s,* Special Technical Publication STP 789, American Society for Testing Materials, Philadelphia, pp. 435-454.

Patankar, S.V., 1980. *Numerical Heat Transfer and Fluid Flow,* McGraw-Hill, New York.

Penner, E., 1959.a *The Mechanism of Frost Heaving in Soils.* DBR Research Paper No. 87. NRCC 5451. From *Highway Research Board Bulletin,* No. 225. pp. 1-22.

Penner, E., 1968. "Particle Size as a Basis for Predicting Frost Action in Soils." *Soil and Foundations,* Vol. 8, No. 4. DBR Research Paper No. 406. NRCC 10848. pp. 21-29.

Penner, E., 1970. "Thermal Conductivity of Frozen Soils." *Canadian Journal of Earth Science,* vol. 7, no. 3, 1970, 982-987.

Penner, E., 1974. "Uplift Forces on Foundations in Frost Heaving Soils." *Canadian Geotechnical Journal,* Vol. 11, No. 3, August 1974. Research Paper No. 606, National Research Council Canada, Ottawa, CAN. pp. 323-338.

Penner, E., and C.B. Crawford, 1983. *Frost Action and Foundations.* DBR No. 1090, NRCC 21089. National Reserch Council of Canada, Ottawa. 53 pp.

Penner, E., and L.W. Gold, 1971. "Transfer of Heaving Forces by Adfreezing to Columns and Foundation Walls in Frost-Susceptible Soils." *Canadian Geotechnical Journal,* Vol. 8, No. 4, November 1971. DBR Reserch Paper No. 496, NRC 12177. pp. 592-596.

Penrod, E.B. and W.W. Walton, D.V. Terrell, 1958. "A Method to Describe Soil Temperature Variation," Paper 1537, *Journal of the Soil Mechanics and Foundations Division* (ASCE), vol. 84, no. SMI, February 1958, pp. 1537-1537.21.

Perry, E.H. and G.T. Cunningham, 1982. "A Finite Element Analysis of Heat Losses through Insulated Floor Slabs," *7th NPSC* (Knoxville), ASES, Univ. of Delaware, Newark, pp. 115-118.

Peterson, David K., 1984. "Observation and Prediction of the Heating Season Thermal Mass Effect for Eight Test Buildings With and Without Windows." Report for DOE, Office of Building Energy Research and Development. Contract DE-AC05-840R21400.

Phillip, J.R., 1961. "The Theory of Heat Flux Meters," *Journal of Geophysical Research.* vol. 56, pp. 571-579.

Phillip, J.R., and D.A. deVries, April 1957. "Moisture Movement in Porous Materials Under Temperature Gradients," American Geophysical Union Transactions 38:2 p. 222.

Phillips, D.W. and D. Aston, 1979. *Soil Temperature Averages 1958-1978,* CL 13-79, Atmospheric Engineering Service (Canada), Downsview, Ontario.

Potter, L.D., 1956. "Yearly Soil Temperatures in Eastern North Dakota," *Ecology,* vol. 37, no. 1, 1956, pp. 62-70.

Poulos, J.F.J., 1982. "Thermal Performance of Underground Structures: The Development of the Decremented Average Ground Temperature Method for Estimating the Thermal Performance of Underground Walls," Master of Architecture Thesis, Georgia Inst. of Technology, Atlanta, 112 pp.

Poulos, J.F.J., and J.M. Akridge, 1984. "A New Method to Calculate Heat Losses from Underground Spaces," *Solar Age,* vol. 9, no. 3, March 1984, pp. 20-22.

Raff, J.J., 1978. "Ground Temperature Control," *Underground Space* (Pergamon), vol. 3, no. 1, July/August 1978, pp. 35-44.

Ribot, J.C., J.C. Ingersoll, and A.H. Rosenfeld, 1982. "Monitored Superinsulated and Solar Houses in North America" in *A Compilation and Economic Analysis,* Lawrence Berkeley Lab, Univ. of California presented at the 7th National Passive Solar Conference ASES, Knoxville, TN. August 30-September 1, 1982.

Ribot, J.C., A.H. Rosenfeld, F. Flouquet, and W. Luhrsen, 1982. "Monitored Low Energy Houses in North America and Europe: A Compilation and Economic Analysis." Lawrence Berkeley Laboratory Report, LBL 14576, June 1982. Proceedings of *Passive'82,* the National Passive Solar Conference at Knoxville, TN. August 29-September 3, 1982.

Richmond, W.R., R.W. Besant, and L.G. Watson, 1984. "Temperatures and Heat Losses in Basement Floors With and Without Subfloor Insulation." Dept. of Mechanical Engineering, University of Saskatchewan, Saskatoon, Saskatchewan, Canada.

Riverts, W.J. and W.D. Warde, R. Helm, 1981. "A Comparison of Assessments by Above Ground and Earth Shelter Occupants," *Earth Shelter Performance and Evaluation* technical conference proceedings, Architectural Extension/Oklahoma State Univ., Stillwater, 74078, pp. 245-257.

Robinsky, E.I. and K.E. Bespflug, 1975. "Design of Insulated Foundations," Paper 10009, *Journal of the Soil Mechanics and Foundations Division* (ASCE), vol. 99, no. SM9, September 1973, pp. 649-667.

Romanko, K.J. and W. Rudoy, 1981. "Some Effects of Thermal Mass in Multifamily Dwellings-2. Effects on Heating and Cooling Loads." ASHRAE *Trans.* 87:161-171.

Rosenberg, N.J., 1967. "The Influence and Implications of Windbreaks on Agriculture in Dry Regions," *Symposium on Ground Level Climatology,* Berkeley, CA, Dec. 1965, AAS Publication No. 86, 1967.

Rosenfeld, A.H., W.G. Colborne, et al., 1980. "Building Energy Use Compilation and Analysis (BECA), an International Comparison and Critical Review," *Part A: New Residential Buildings, LBL report no. LBL-8912,* University of California, 1980.

Rubers, K., J.M. Akridge, C.C. Benton, and M.M. Houston, 1981. "Detached Earth Cooling with Radiant Interior Building Elements," *6th NPSC* (PORTLAND), AS/ISES, Univ. of Delaware, Newark, pp. 827-831.

Salomone, L.A., 1983. "Procedures Used to Predict the Thermal Behavior of Soils," *Energy Efficient Buildings with Earth Shelter Protection* conference proceedings (Sydney), Architectural Extension/Oklahoma State University, Stillwater 74078.

Salomone, L.A. and W.D. Kovacs, 1982. "The Determination of Thermal Soil Properties for Energy Transfer Modeling of Buildings," *Energy Conservation in Building Design, Construction, and Management* conference proceedings, Univ. of Minnesota Dept. of Conferences, 315 Pillsbury Drive S.E., Minneapoils 55455, pp. 137-161.

Salomone, L.A. and W.D. Kovacs, H. Wechsler, 1982. *Thermal Behavior of Fine-Grained Soils,* Building Science Series BSS 149, National Bureau of Standards, Washington, D.C., 102 pp.

Salomone, L.A. and W.D. Kovacs, 1984. "The Use of Index Property Tests to Determine the Thermal Properties of Soils," *Geotechnical Testing Journal,* American Society for Testing Materials, Arizona State Univ., Tempe.

Salvadore, J.M., 1974. "A Thermal Response and Environmental Control Equipment Simulation of a Control Residence." MSc Thesis. Ohio State University, Columbus, OH.

Sarkisyan, R.M. and Nersesova, Vyalov, S.S., Zatsarnaya, A.G., 1973. *Handbook on the Determination of the Physical Thermal and Mechanical Properties of Frozen Soiils.* Technical Translation, TT 2064. National Reserech Council of Canada, Ottawa. 202 pp.

Saxhof, B., K.E. Poulsen and F.A. Curtis, 1982. "Foundations for Energy Conservation Houses—A Thermal Analysis Based on Examples from Five Low-Energy Houses at Hjortekaer, Denmark." *Energex '82* Conference Proceedings Vol III, Solar Energy Society of Canada.

Scalise, J.W. (ed.), 1974. *Terratecture: The Environmental Benefits of Earth Integrating Architectural Design Techniques.* 1974 College of Architecture, Arizona State University, Tempe, Arizona.

Scalise, J.W. (ed.), 1975. *Earth Integrated Architecture,* The Architecture Foundation, College of Architecture, Arizona State Univ., Tempe.

Scanada Consultants, 1975. *Design Criteria for Basement Foundation Systems in Canadian Housing.* Housing and Urban Development Association of Canada (HUDAC), Toronto, Ontario.

Scanada Consultants, Ltd., 1979. *'Mimic Box' Monitoring of Heat Losses of Basements in a Range of Climates,* Report prepared by Scanada Consultants (Ottawa) for the National Research Council of Canada.

Scanada Consultants Ltd., 1984. *Simplified Method for Calculation of Below-Grade Heat Loss for Small Residential Buildings.* Report for Div. of Building Research, NRC Canada, May 25, 1984, Scanada Consultants Ltd., 436 MacLaren St., Ottawa, Ont K2POM8.

Schild, E. *et al.,* 1980. *Structural Failure in Residential Buildings: Vol. 3, Basements and Adjoining Land Drainage,* Halsted Press/J. Wiley and Sons, New York-Toronto, 154 pp.

Schwerdtfeger, P., 1970. *The Measurement of Heat Flow in the Ground and the Theory of Heat Flux Meters,* Technical Report 232, (U.S. Army) Cold Regions Research and Engineering Laboratory, Hanover, NH.

Scott, N.R., J.R. Cooke, R.H. Rand, T.A. Koehler, R.A. Parsons, and K.D. Mahan, 1982. *Analysis of Earth-Air-Heat Exchange,* Dept. of Agricultural Engineering, Cornell Univ., Ithaca, NY 14853, 72 pp.

Scott, N.R. and R.A. Parsons, T.A. Koehler, 1965. "Analysis and Performance of and Earth-Air Heat Exchanger," Paper No. 65-840, presented at the *1965 Winter Meeting* (Chicago) of the American Society of Agricultural Engineers, ASAE, Box 229, St. Joseph, MI 46 pp.

Scott, R.F., 1964. "Heat Exchange at the Ground Surface," *U.S. Army Cold Regions Research and Engineering Laboratory Monograph,* M II-A1, July 1964.

Selinfreund, M., Farrer, R., and Munding, P., 1983. "Monitoring An Earth-Sheltered Solar Assisted House." *Energy Efficient Buildings with Earth Shelter Protection.* Proceedings 1st International Earth Sheltered Buildings Conference, Sidney, Australia. August 1-6, 1983. pp 345-351.

Sellers, *Physical Climatology,* Chapter 8,"The Energy Balance".

Shanks, R.E., 1956. "Altitudinal and Microclimatic Relationship of Soil Temperature Under Natural Vegetation," *Ecology,* vol. 37, no. 1, Jan. 1956, pp. 1-17.

Shapira, H.B. and P.R. Barnes, 1980. "Assessing the Performance of an Energy-Saving Design," (at Oak Ridge National Laboratory), *Underground Space,* vol. 5, no. 3, pp. 152-157.

Shapira, H.B., G.A. Cristy, S.E. Brite, and M.B. Yost, 1983. *Cost and Energy Comparison Study of Above and Below Ground Dwellings,* Oak Ridge National Laboratory ORNL/CON-91, 117 pp. (available from NTIS, Springfield, VA 22161).

Shelton, Jay, 1975. "Underground Storage of Heat in Solar Heating Systems." *Solar Energy,* Vol. 17, pp. 137-143.

Shen, L.S.W. and Ramsey, J.W., 1981. *Energy Conservation by Subsurface Construction, Final Report, Part I, Temperature, Heat Flux and Moisture Measurements at Williamson Hall.* Prepared for Inovative Structures Program, Oak Ridge National Laboratory, Contract No. 96X-42533, Dept. of Mechanical Engineering, University of Minnesota. 28 pp.

Shipp, P.H., 1979. "The Thermal Characteristics of Large Earth Sheltered Structures," Ph.D. thesis, Dept. of Mechanical Engineering, University of Minnesota, Minneapolis, MN, 450 pp.

Shipp, P.H. 1980. "The Mechanics of Heat Transfer in Underground Buildings: Research Results from Studies at Williamson Hall," *Going Under to Stay on Top: Nonresidential Applications* conference proceedings (Minneapolis), Undergound Space Center, Univ. of Minnesota, Minneapolis 55455, pp. 15-48.

Shipp, P.H., 1983. "Basement, Crawlspace, and Slab-on-Grade Thermal Performance," *Thermal Performance of the Exterior Envelope of Buildings II* (Las Vegas), Special Publication No. 38, ASHRAE, Atlanta, pp. 160-179.

Shipp, P.H., 1983a. "Natural Convection within Masonry Block Basement Walls," AC-83-09, No. 2, ASHRAE *Transactions,* vol. 89, part 1.

Shipp, P.H. and T.B. Broderick, 1983. "Comparison of Annual Heating Loads for Various Basement Wall Insulation Strategies by Using Transient and Steady-State Models," *Thermal Insulation, Materials and Systems for Energy Conservation in the '80s,* Special Technical Publication STP 789, American Society for Testing Materials, Philadelphia, pp. 455-473.

Shipp, P.H., G.D. Meixel, and J.W. Ramsey, 1980. "Analysis and Measurement of the Thermal Behavior of the Walls and Surrounding Soil for a Large Underground Building," *Underground Space* (Pergamon), vol. 5, no. 2, September/October 1980, pp. 121-125.

Shipp, P.H., E. Pfender, and T.P. Bligh, 1981. "Thermal Characteristics of a Large Earth Sheltered Building (Parts I and II)," *Underground Space* (Pergamon), vol. 6, no. 1, July/August 1981, pp. 53-64.

Singer, I.A., and R.M. Brown, 1956. "The Annual Variations of Sub-soil Temperatures About a 600-Foot Circle," *Trans. Am. Geophysical Union,* vol. 37, no. 6, 1956, pp. 743-748.

Slusarchuk, W.A., 1967. "Frost Heave Protection for Shallow Foundations Using Artificial Perimeter Insulation," M.Sci. Thesis, Univ. of Guelph, Ontario.

Slusarchuk, W.A. and P.H. Foulder, 1973. *Development and Calibration of Thermal Conductivity Probe Apparatus for Use in the Field and Laboratory,* DBR Paper No. 388, NRCC 13267, National Research Council Canada, Ottawa K1A OR6.

Smith, G.S. and T. Yamanchi, 1950. "Thermal Conductivities of Soils for Design of Heat Pump Installation," *ASHVE Transactions* 56:No. 1398.

Smith, W.J., 1976. "A Study of Insulated Shallow Foundations, Timmons, Ontario, 1974-1976," M.Sci. Thesis, Univ. of Toronto, Ontario.

Socolow, R.H. et al., 1979. "Style and Vintage as Determinants of Energy-Costly Faults in U.S. Residential Housing," Princeton, New Jersey.

Speltz, J.J., 1980. "A Numerical Simulation of Transient Heat Flow in Earth Sheltered Building for Seven Selected U.S. Cities," M.S. Thesis, Trinity University, San Antonio, TX.

Speltz, J.J. and P. Haves, 1980. "The Thermal Benefits and Cost Effectiveness of Earth Berming," *5th NPSC* (Amherst), AS/ISES, Univ. of Delaware, Newark, pp. 337-341.

Speltz, J.J. and G.D. Meixel, 1981. "A Computer Simulation of the Thermal Performance of Earth Covered Roofs," *The Potential of Earth Sheltered and Underground Space,* proceedings of the 1981 conference of the American Underground Space Association (Kansas City), Pergamon Press, New York.

Spooner, D.C. "Heat Losses from an Unoccupied House." Cement and Concrete Association, Slough, United Kingdom, 26 pages. NTIS PC E03/MF EO3.

Steinmanis, J.E., 1982. "Thermal Property Measurements Using a Thermal Probe," *Underground Cable Thermal Backfill,* S.A. Baggs, et al., eds., Pergamon Press, Inc., Toronto, Canada, 1982, pp. 72-85.

Sterling, R.L. (ed.), 1981. *Annotated Bibliography on Earth Contact Systems,* for Passive Cooling Division, U.S. Department of Energy, Contract #DE-AC03-80SF11508, December 1981.

Sterling, R., et al., 1978. *Earth Sheltered Housing Design: Guidelines, Examples and References,* Underground Space Center, University of Minnesota, Van Nostrand Reinhold Company, 1978, 318 pp.

Sterling, R.L., J. Carmody, and G. Elnicky, 1981. *Earth Sheltered Community Design: Energy-Efficient Residental Development,* Underground Space Center, University of Minnesota, Van Nostrand Reinhold Company, 1981.

Sterling, R., W. Farnan and J. Carmody, 1983. *Earth Sheltered Residential Design Manual,* Underground Space Center, University of Minnesota, Van Nostrand Reinhold Company, 1983.

Sterling, R.L., and G.D. Meixel, 1981. "Review of Underground Heat Transfer Research," *Proc. Earth Shelter Performance and Evaluation Conference,* Oct. 1981, Tulsa, Oklahoma, Arch. Extension, Oklahoma State University, Stillwater, OK, pp. 67-80.

Stephenson, D.G., 1977. *Insulation to Prevent Ground Freezing,* Building Research Note No. 119, Division of Building Research, National Research Council Canada, Ottawa K1A OR6, 6 pp.

Stephenson, D.G. and G.P. Mitalas, 1963. "The Calculation of Surface Temperature and Heat Flux from Subsurface Temperature Measurements," *Transactions* of the Engineering Inst. of Canada, vol. 6, no. B-4, Paper EIC-63-MECH 4. (DBR Research Paper No. 209, NRCC 7415, DBR/NRCC, Ottawa).

Swinton, M.C. and R.E. Platts, 1981. "Engineering Method for Estimating Annual Basement Heat Loss and Insulation Performance," Paper No. 2656, ASHRAE *Transactions,* vol. 87, part 2, pp. 343-359.

Szydlowski, R.F. 1980. "Analysis of Transient Heat Loss in Earth Sheltered Structures," Master of Science Thesis, Iowa State Univ., Ames, 196 pp.

Szydlowski, R.F., 1981. "An Earth Sheltered Building Research Facility," *Earth Shelter Performance and Evaluation,* technical conference proceedings, Architectural Extension/Oklahoma State Univ., Stillwater, 74078, pp. 185-192.

Szydlowski, R.F. and T.H. Kuehn, 1980. "Analysis of Transient Heat Loss in Earth Sheltered Structures," *Earth Sheltered Building Design Innovations* technical conference proceedings, Architectural Extension/Oklahoma State Univ., Stillwater 74078, pp. III.25-III.37. Also in: *Underground Space* (Pergamon), vol. 5 no. 4, January/February 1981, pp. 237-246.

Szydlowski, R.F. and T.H. Kuehn, 1980a. "Transient Analysis of Heat Loss in Earth Bermed Structures," *5th NPSC* (Amherst), AS/ISES, Univ. of Delaware, Newark, pp. 409-413.

Tao, S.S., M. Bomberg, and J.J. Hamilton, 1980. "Glass Fiber as Insulation and Drainage Layer on Exterior of Basement Walls," in D.L. McElroy and R.P. Tye (eds.), *Thermal Insulation Performance,* Special Technical Publication STP 718, American Society for Testing Materials, Philadelphia, pp. 57-76. (also DBR Paper No. 970, NRCC 19317, Div. of Building Research, National Research Council Canada, Ottawa, K1A OK6).

Tao, S.S. and J.J. Hamilton, 1975. "Performance of the Mark IX Steel Basement to 31 January, 1975," Technical Note No. 595 Division of Building Research, National Research Council of Canada, Ottawa, Ontario, Canada.

Taylor, R.L., 1975. "*HEAT*, A Finite Element Computer Program for Heat Conduction Analysis," Report 75-1, Civil Engineering Laboratory, Naval Construction Battalion Center, Port Hueneme, California, May 1975.

Thayer, M., 1981. "Heat Loss Factors for Single-Family Homes," Los Alamos National Lab. 36 pp., May 1981. Availability NTIS PC A03/MF A01. Report No.: LA-8837-MS.

Timmons, M.B. and L.D. Albright, 1978. "Finite Element Analysis of Floor Heat Loss," Paper No.77-4521, presented to the 1977 *Winter Meeting* (Chicago), American Society of Agricultural Engineers, St. Joseph, MI 49085, 14 pp.

Timusk, J., 1980. *Study of Scandanavian Foundation Insulation Practice.* Prepared for Subcommittee on Foundations and Drainage of the HUDAC Technical Research Comm. HUDAC National Office, Toronto, Ontario. 52 pp.

Timusk, J. 1981. *Insulation Retrofit of Masonry Basements.* 10-80/PW-115. Ontario Ministry of Housing Communications Branch. 125 pp. + 5 App.

Timusk, J. and HUDAC Technical Research Committee, 1981. *External Insulation of Basement Walls: Phase II Report.* (Project No. T79-44). Communications Department, Housing and Urban Development Association of Canada, Toronto, Ontario. 62 pp.

Timusk, J., 1982. "Control of Decay and Heat Losses in Basement Walls." *Design and Rehabilitation of Building Envelopes,* conference proceedings (London, Ontario). Canadian Society of Civil Engineering, Ontario Region. pp. 18-27.

Timusk, J., 1984. The Canadian Basement, How to Minimize Heat Losses and Control Moisture, Prepublication manuscript, Dept. of Civil Engineering, University of Toronto.

Tobiasson, Wayne, John Ricard, 1979. "Moisture Gain and its Thermal Consequence for Common Roof Insulations," *U.S. Army Cold Regions Research and Engineering Laboratory, Proceedings 5th Conference on Roofing Technology,* April 19-20, 1979.

Tymura, E.J., H. Miller, M. Riordan and D. Richards (eds.), 1979. "Solutions to Energy Conservation in Northern Climates." *Proceedings of 3rd National Passive Solar Conference,* Vol 3, p. 708-712. San Jose, CA, USA, January 11, 1979.

Underground Space Center, 1981. *Insulation Principles,* DOE Earth Sheltered Structures Fact Sheet 05, Univ. of Minnesota, Minneapolis 55455, 8 pp.

Underground Space Center, 1981a. *Insulation Materials and Placement,* DOE Earth Sheltered Structures Fact Sheet 06, Univ. of Minnesota, Minneapolis, 55455, 5 pp.

van der Meer, W.J. 1980."Possibilities for Subterranean Housing in Arid Zones," G.S. Golany, ed., *Housing in Arid Lands: Design and Planning,* Halsted Press/John Wiley & Sons, Inc., New York, pp. 141-150.

Vansteenkiste, G.S. and F. de Schutter, 1975. "Comments on Computer Modeling of a Moist Soil," Chapter 7, in deVries and Afgan (eds.), *Heat and Mass Transfer in the Biosphere, vol, 1: Transfer Processes in Plant Environment,* Scripta Book Co., Washington, D.C., pp. 97-108.

van Wijk, W.R. and W.J. Derksen, 1966. "Sinusoidal Temperature Variation in a Layered Soil," Chapter 6, W.R. van Wijk, ed., *Physics of Plant Environment,* North Holland Publishing Co., Amsterdam, pp. 171-209.

van Wijk, W.R. and D.A. deVries, 1966. "Periodic Temperature Variation in a Homogeneous Soil," Chapter 4, W.R. van Wiji, ed., *Physics of Plant Environment,* North Holland Publishing Co., Amsterdam, pp. 102-143.

Voss, C., 1980. TEMPFEM-Manual, Finit element program for trandimensionella varmeledringsberakningar, Data Grundv., W001-0134, November 8, 1980.

Vuorelainen, O., 1960. *The Temperature Field Produced in the Ground by a Heated Slab Laid Direct on the Ground, and the Heat Flow from Slab to Ground,* Publication No. 52, The State Institute for Technical Research, Finland.

Vuorelainen, O., 1963. *A Practical Method for Calculation of the Heat Losses into the Ground,* Publication No. 76, The State Institute for Technical Research, Finland.

Waller, M.J., 1984. *Thermal Properties of Soils Final Report,* U.S. Department of Energy, San Francisco-Operations Office.

Wang, F.S., 1981. "Mathematical Modelling and Computer Simulation of Insulation Systems in Below Grade Applications," *Thermal Performance of the Exterior Envelope of Buildings* (Orlando), Special Publication No. 28, ASHRAE, Atlanta, pp. 456-471.

Watson, D. and K. Labs, 1983. *Climatic Design,* McGraw Hill Book Co., New York, 280 pp.

Wechsler, A.E., 1966. *Development of Thermal Conductivity Probes for Soils and Insulations,* Technical Report 192, U.S. Army Cold Regions Research and Engineering Laboratory, Hanover, NH, 91 pp.

Weisbecker, T.L. and L.D. Jacobsson, 1980. "Analysis of Cooling Air in a Buried Pipe," ASAE Paper No. 80-4555, presented at the 1980 *Winter Meeting* (Chicago), Am. Society of Agricultural Engineers, St. Joseph, MI 49085, 26 pp.

Wielhouwer, A.E. and E.F.P. Burnett, 1984. *A Subgrade Heat Loss Model and Its Application to Warehousing and Light Industrial Buildings.* Department of Energy, Mines and Resources, Canada, by Building Energy Group, Waterloo, Ontario, Feb. 1984.

Williams, G.T., C.R. Attwater and F.C. Hooper, 1979. "A Design Method to Determine the Optimal Distribution and Amount of Insulation for In-Ground Heat Storage Tanks." *Proceedings of International Solar Energy Society Congress,* May 28-June 1, 1979.

Wilson, E.L., and Nickell, R.E., 1966. "Application of the Finite Element Method to Heat Conduction Analysis," *Nuclear Engineering and Design,* 4:276-286.

Yard, D.C., M. Morton-Gibson, and J. Mitchell, 1983. "Simplified Dimensionless Relations for Heat Loss from Basements," unpublished manuscript, Solar Energy Laboratory and Dept. of Mechanical Engineering, Univ. of Wisconsin, Madison, 23 pp.

Yea, P.L., 1976. "Effect of Moisture Migration on the Temperature of a Direct Buried Cylindrical Heat Source." *ASME Paper No. 76-WA/HT-50,* December 1976, 7 pp.

Yoshino, M.M., 1975. *Climate in a Small Area: An Introduction to Local Meteorology,* Univ. of Tokyo Press, Tokyo, 549 pp.

Zoellick, W., 1981. "Predicted and Observed Performance of a Buried Earth-Air Heat Exchanger Cooling System," *6th NPSC* (Portland), AS/ISES, Univ. of Delaware, Newark, pp. 822-826.

Information Sources

Conservation, Solar Design and Renewable Energy Sources

Conservation and Renewable Energy Inquiry Service
Box 8900, Silver Spring, MD 20907
or call toll-free:
800-523-2929 U.S., including Virgin Islands and Puerto Rico
800-462-4983 Pennsylvania
800-233-3071 Alaska and Hawaii

Underground Space Use and Earth Sheltered Buildings

Underground Space Center
University of Minnesota
790 Civil and Mineral Engineering Building
500 Pillsbury Drive Southeast
Minneapolis, MN 55455
Phone: (612) 376-5341

American Underground Space Association
Room 122
500 Pillsbury Drive Southeast
Minneapolis, MN 55455
Phone: (612) 376-5580

Architectural Extension
120 Architecture Building
Oklahoma State University
Stillwater, OK 74078

Geotecture International Association
c/o Dr. S. Baggs
School of Landscape Architecture
The University of New South Wales
PO Box 1
Kensington 2033 NSW Australia

Product Information

There are two major sources for locating building product manufacturers and suppliers which should be available in major libraries. These are:

Sweet's Architectural Catalog File
McGraw-Hill Information Systems Company
Sweet's Division
1221 Avenue of the Americas
New York, NY 10020

Thomas Register of American Manufacturers
Thomas Register Catalog File
Thomas Publishing Company
One Penn Plaza
New York, NY 10001

Some special products and sources of information are listed below:

Wood Foundations: National Forest Products Association
1619 Massachusetts Avenue N.W.
Washington, D.C. 20036

American Wood Preservers Institute
1651 Old Meadow Road
McLean, Virginia 22101

Concrete: Portland Cement Association (PCA)
Old Orchard Road
Skokie, Illinois 60076

Concrete Block: National Concrete Masonry Association
PO Box 781
Herndon, Virginia 22070

Steel: American Institute of Steel Construction, Inc.
101 Park Avenue
New York, New York 10017

National Building Code Organizations

1. Basic Building Code
   Building Officials and Code Administrators
   International, Inc.
   17926 S. Halsted Street
   Homewood, Illinois 60430

2. National Building Code
   American Insurance Association
   85 John Street
   New York, New York 10038

3. Standard Building Code
   Southern Building Code Congress International
   900 Montclair Road
   Birmingham, Alabama 35213-1206

4. Uniform Building Code
   International Conference of Building Officials
   5360 South Workman Mill Road
   Whittier, California 90601

Periodicals

Listed below are some of the periodicals that regularly carry features on earth sheltered construction or energy conservation.

Underground Space
Official journal of the American Underground-Space Association
Department of Civil and Mineral Engineering
500 Pillsbury Drive Southeast
University of Minnesota
Minneapolis, MN 55455

Popular Science
PO Box 2871
Boulder, Colorado 80302

Popular Mechanics
PO Box 10064
Des Moines, Iowa 50350

The Mother Earth News
PO Box 70
Hendersonville, North Carolina 28739

Earth Shelter Living
110 South Greeley
Stillwater, Minnesota 55082

Underline
Quarterly newsletter of the Underground Space Center
University of Minnesota
790 Civil and Mineral Engineering Building
500 Pillsbury Drive Southeast
Minneapolis, Minnesota 55455

Solar Age
Harrisville, New Hampshire 03450

New Shelter
Rodale Press
33 East Minor Street
Emmaurs, Pennsylvania 18049

Geotecture
Journal of the Geotecture International Association
4 de Villiers Avenue
Chatswood, NSW 2067 Australia

Index

A

Access, site, 40, 41, 44, 57, 250, 251
Active solar features, 75, 146, 147, 264, 315, 320
Adobe, 183-84
Air-conditioning systems, 81-82, 83
Air infiltration, 73-74, 76, 77, 79, 80, 81, 84, 88, 107, 127, 131
Air purity, see Indoor air quality
Atrium house designs, 10, 34, 38, 47-52, 57-58, 80, 90, 116, 239-40, 274-79, 318-20
Australia, underground development in, 14-15

B

Banen residence, 314-17
Barnard, John, 11, 17, 149, 278
Basement houses, 15-16, 248
Basements, 35, 103, 124, 151, 211, 217, 248, 251
Bentonite-based waterproofing, 214, 222-23
Bitumen sheets, see Sheet membrane waterproofing materials
Bordie residence, 48, 50, 52, 318-20
Boyer, Lester, 139
Building codes, 37, 48-49, 234, 235-46

C

Cementitious waterproofing materials, 218
China, underground development in, 11-12, 18
Clark house, 52
Clark-Nelson house, 285-87
Clerestory windows, 44, 240
Climatic variations, regional, 87-92
Concrete, 36, 60, 61, 62, 77, 80, 103, 104, 113, 114, 117, 124, 128, 131, 149, 160, 161, 167, 168, 170, 171-74, 176, 177, 178, 179, 181-83, 184-85, 187, 188, 189, 190, 191, 192, 193, 194, 196, 197, 200, 201, 210, 211, 213, 214, 216, 217, 226, 227, 240

Condensation, 85, 88, 90, 91, 97, 99-100, 200
Conduction, 72, 73-74, 76-77, 82, 84-85, 88, 104
Convection, 72, 74, 85
Cooling degree days, 135
Costs, construction, 148-52, 154, 156-57, 229, 230, 238, 278, 280, 294, 310, 313, 322
Costs, life-cycle, 147, 152-57
Courtyard house designs, see Atrium house designs
Courtyards, 27, 34, 40, 41, 42, 47-49, 51, 52, 58, 116, 239, 241, 243, 274, 278, 303, 312, 318
Cut-and-cover construction, 10

D

Dampproofing, 186, 211, 217, 220
Densities, 25, 53, 54, 55, 57, 58-59
Design considerations, 32-62
Details, design, 60-62
Disaster protection, 18, 22, 252, 296
Dome structures, see Shell structures
Drainage, 39, 40, 41, 43, 49, 50, 51, 53, 54, 55, 60-61, 62, 130, 162, 168-69, 175, 177, 186, 191, 200, 203-09, 228, 230, 248
Dune houses, 321-23

E

Earth tubes, 70-71, 79, 132
Ecology Houses, 17, 47, 49, 51, 149, 278-81
Egress, emergency, 235, 236, 237-41
Ehrenkrantz Group Study, 154-55
Elevational house designs, 10, 38-46, 55-57, 58, 117, 264-73, 280-81, 288-91, 296-302
Ellison residence, 288-91
Energy conservation, 18, 22, 30, 32-34, 53, 66, 67-71, 79-80, 82-83, 88, 89, 90, 91, 133, 134, 135, 137, 139-40, 147, 156, 238, 264, 278
Energy performance, monitored, 133-47
Entry, house, 44-46, 49, 50, 51-52
Evaporation, 72, 82, 83, 86, 90

F

Fiberglass insulation, 201, 229, 230-31
Financing, home, 234, 254-61
Finishing materials, 81, 100, 107, 117, 148, 151, 152, 157, 240

Fire resistance, 161, 230, 237
Fire safety, 235, 237-41, 244
Flashing, 213
Floors, 95-96, 98, 99, 103-104, 105, 106, 112, 113-16, 119, 122-27, 164, 181, 185, 191-92, 193, 208-09, 211, 212, 251
Footings, 190, 192-93
Foundations, 164, 181, 182, 192-93, 217
France, underground development in, 13-14, 18-19

G

Garages, 44-46, 51-52, 57-58, 151-52
Greece, underground development in, 13
Greenhouses, 239-40, 241, 243, 282, 300, 306, 315
Grondzik, Walter, 139
Groundwater, 25-26, 41, 49, 70, 174, 192
Guardrails, 244-46

H

Heat exchangers, 132, 201
Heat gain, 26, 82-83, 84, 85, 86, 88, 89, 93, 96, 97, 105, 108, 113, 114, 116, 117, 119, 126, 310, 314
Heat loss, 33, 60, 61, 62, 67, 73, 74, 75, 76, 77-78, 80, 82, 86, 88, 93, 95-96, 97-98, 100, 105, 108, 113, 114, 116, 117, 119, 124, 126, 127, 276, 288, 292
Heat pumps, 70-71
Heat transfer, 67, 72, 93-94, 95, 96, 102-03, 104-27
Heating degree days, 108, 117, 135
Humidity, 81, 82, 87, 89, 91, 100, 129, 131, 144, 145, 146, 200

I

Indoor air quality, 128, 129-32
Insulation, 60, 61, 62, 79, 86, 88, 89, 90, 93-101, 102, 128, 134, 136, 137, 138, 148, 185, 200, 201, 211, 213, 226-31, 293
Insurance, 234, 252-53

J

Japan, underground development in, 18
Johnson, Philip, 16

K

Kansas City, underground development in, 11

L

Landscaping, 29-31, 40, 44, 45, 60-61, 62, 82-83, 148, 162, 191, 264, 296
Lawrence Berkeley Laboratory, 147
Lighting, natural, 43, 235, 236, 241-43, 244, 249, 250
Liquid-applied waterproofing products, 214, 221
Loads, design, 166-70
Loads, floor, 169-70, 192
Loads, foundation, 170, 192
Loads, roof, 35-36, 43, 160, 162, 166-67, 170, 176
Loads, wall, 43, 166, 167-69, 170, 181, 182, 183, 187-88, 189, 190-91, 192, 193
Lovins Research Center/Bioshelter/House Project, 306-09

M

Masonry, 80, 130, 131, 174, 188, 189, 211, 214, 217, 226, 227, 252
Mechanical systems, 71, 74, 76, 77, 85, 89, 105, 107, 128-29, 133-34, 136, 148, 157, 241, 242-43
Mercy residence, 300-02
Metz, Don, 17, 271, 274
Mined space construction, 10-11
Minnesota Housing Finance Agency program, 141-46, 149
Moreland, Frank, 135, 149
Morgan, William, 17, 322
Multiunit developments, 8, 19, 25, 53-59, 150, 157, 250

N

Nuclear fallout shelters, 15, 16

O

Oak Ridge National Laboratory, 150-51, 154, 155
Occupant lifestyle, 74, 76, 82, 131, 133, 134-35, 144, 146
Oklahoma State University, 139, 140

P

Parametric studies, 102-127
Parapet walls, 60-61, 188-89, 205, 206-07
Park Ranger residence, 296-98
Passive cooling, 42, 48, 73, 89, 102, 117, 127, 146, 318
Passive design features, 34, 69, 75-76, 77, 87, 88, 91, 93, 98-99, 127, 134, 136, 137, 146, 147, 276, 280, 282, 288
Passive solar house designs, 15, 18, 34, 133, 135, 185, 274-77, 282-84, 288-91, 300-02, 303-05, 306-09
Patterson residence, 310-13
Penetrational designs, 10, 38
Polyethylene, 205, 206, 208, 211, 217, 225, 226, 228
Polystyrene insulation, 77, 229, 230-31

R

Radiation, 72, 82, 83, 84, 85, 90, 93, 138
Radon, 130-31, 132
Retaining walls, 60, 62, 169, 182, 189-91, 244, 245, 246
Roofs, 35-36, 50, 60-61, 75, 77, 88, 90, 91, 96, 103-04, 105, 106, 108, 109, 113-16, 117-19, 124-27, 138, 152, 157, 160, 162, 166-67, 170, 176-80, 181, 182, 185, 186, 187, 188, 189, 205-07, 211, 212, 213, 226, 244, 245-46, 248-49
Rubberized asphalt waterproofing, 220
R-value (of insulation), 228-31

S

St. John's University, 292-95
Scalise, James, 17, 314
Schwartz residence, 136-37, 282-84
Scott, David, 17
Setbacks, 25, 49, 249-50
Seward town houses, 54
Sheet membrane waterproofing, 214, 215, 219, 220, 225
Shell structures, 36-37, 157, 194-97, 285-87, 321-23
Shippee, Paul, 137
Site considerations, 22-31, 54, 203
Skylights, 43-44, 62, 96, 205, 240, 241
Slopes, *see* Topography
Smoke detectors, 240, 241
Sod houses, 14
Soils, 25-26, 162-65, 204, 206, 207, 228
Solar access, 57
Solar heat gain, 26, 30, 34, 41, 42, 44, 48, 73, 75, 89, 90, 98-99, 134, 135, 136, 226, 274, 276, 282, 283, 292, 306
Solar orientation, 26-27, 39, 41, 42, 47, 58, 134, 314

Solar radiation, 26, 29-30, 39, 47, 48, 51, 67, 81, 82, 84, 86, 89, 98, 99, 104, 116, 303, 310
Solaria, 17, 264-67
South Korea, research in, 18
Spain, underground development in, 13
Sprinkler systems, 240, 241
Steel, 36, 174-75, 176, 178-79, 180, 184, 185-86, 187, 191, 194, 195, 196, 211
Structural materials, 171-97, 210, 211
Structural systems, 35-37, 103-104, 107, 148, 157, 160-97, 226-27
Sun Earth House, 137-39
Sundown House, 303-05
Superinsulation, 75, 91, 135, 146, 147, 288-89
Swayze, Jay, 16

T

Temperatures, air, 67, 73, 76, 78, 84, 89, 90, 138
Temperatures, ground, 69, 70, 71, 76, 77, 79, 84, 85, 86, 87, 88, 89, 90, 93, 98
Thermal breaks, 100-01, 213, 298
Thermal Integrity Factor (TIF), 135, 145-46
Topography, site, 28-29, 42-43, 50-51, 54, 55-57, 135, 203, 209
Tunisia, underground development in, 12-13
Turkey, underground development in, 13

U

Urethane foam insulation, 229, 230-31

V

Vapor barriers, 201, 208, 217, 230
Vault structures, *see* Shell structures
Vegetation, site, 29-31, 44, 74, 86, 89
Ventilation, 28, 34, 37, 39, 43, 44, 47, 62, 70, 73, 79, 83, 85, 86, 89, 90, 91, 129, 131, 132, 134, 136, 201, 235, 236, 241-43, 244, 249, 250

W

Walls, 61-62, 96, 99, 103-04, 105, 106, 108, 110-11, 113-17, 118, 120-21, 124-27, 152, 160, 162, 181-91, 204, 207-08, 211, 212, 226

Waterproofing, 60, 79, 98, 126, 130, 148, 186, 200-25, 226-27, 228, 230
Wells, Malcolm, 16-17, 61, 149, 264
Windows, 28, 34, 36-37, 39, 40, 42, 43, 44, 47, 74, 80, 86, 127, 143, 237-39, 240-43, 249, 250
Winds, 27-28, 29, 31, 42, 44, 45, 46, 73, 76, 80, 127
Winston House, 45, 271-73
Wood, 36, 61, 103, 131, 156, 160, 175, 177, 179-80, 186-87, 188, 189, 190, 192, 193, 194, 196, 211, 226, 227-28, 252
Woods, Charles, 268
Woods/Gundlach residence, 268-70
Wright, David, 136, 282, 303
Wright, Frank Lloyd, 15

Z

Zoning ordinances, 234, 247-51